Hotel, Restaurant, and Travel Law

Hotel, Restaurant, and Travel Law

Second Edition

Norman G. Cournoyer
University of Massachusetts

Anthony G. Marshall
Florida International University

Breton Publishers
A Division of Wadsworth, Inc.
North Scituate, Massachusetts

Breton Publishers
A Division of Wadsworth, Inc.

Library of Congress Cataloging in Publication Data

Cournoyer, Norman G.
  Hotel, restaurant, and travel law.

  Includes index.
  1. Hotels, taverns, etc.—Law and legislation—
United States. 2. Travel agents—Legal status,
laws, etc.—United States. I. Marshall, Anthony G.
II. Title.
KF951.C6   1983   343.73'0786479   83–3718
ISBN 0–534–01273–6   347.303786479

Printed in the United States of America
1 2 3 4 5 6 7 8 9—87 86 85 84 83

Contents

12 Rights of the Hotelkeeper and Restaurateur—459

Preface

Georges Clemenceau, premier of France during World War I, stated that war was too important to entrust only to generals. For a hotel administrator to leave any aspects of running a hotel exclusively to specialists would be equally unwise. Whether a hotel is large or small, its owner has to deal with a proliferation of problems. In a large hotel a staff of cooks, accountants, engineers, lawyers, and personnel managers deal with the diverse aspects of running the hotel. In a small hotel or motel the manager has to rely on ingenuity and skill.

Hotel managers must understand their rights and those of others. They should be aware of laws and regulations pertaining to contracts and labor relations, safety rules and product liability, so that they can limit their exposure to lawsuits of all kinds. They must also know how to fulfill their obligations to the federal, state, and local authorities that regulate the industry.

The intent of this book is not to train lawyers but to inform and educate future hoteliers, restaurateurs, travel personnel, and others in the accommodation industry. With equal skill hotel managers must be able to plan menus with the chef or discuss a troublesome boiler with the engineer, as well as be aware of the legal aspects of running a hotel. Therefore, this book not only provides the essential information that managers need to comply with the law that is applicable to their operations, but it also provides a grounding in preventive tactics by telling them what they must do to avoid lawsuits. And it helps them to identify areas of potential trouble.

If they know where the dangers lie, competent hotel managers can train their personnel to look for trouble. Furthermore, they can knowledgeably deal with hotel guests in case of accidents or differences of opinion. Ignorance of the law is no excuse; the law presumes persons to be aware of their obligations and rights. Preventive law is the solution, and it lies well within the scope of even a modest establishment.

Although some lawsuits result from criminal intent, a great many result from ignorance and neglect. Like many other laypersons, hotelkeepers often have a guarded attitude toward the law. The highly technical methodology of court proceedings, the specialized legal vocabulary, and the ever-present participation of lawyers may encourage this unfor-

tunate attitude. But when a lawyer takes a case, it is already too late—
only preventive measures could have altered the facts of the situation.

In the *New York Times* of March 20, 1977, Russell Baker stated that
only a lawyer has a chance of waking up in the morning and getting to
the bathtub without breaking half a dozen laws for which he can be fined
or jailed, or possibly both, by a prosecutor of middling competence.
Baker's solution is to make law part of the basic school curriculum. In
line with this view, this book seeks to train students to consider the legal
aspects of all management decisions by examining actual cases.

The case method of teaching management principles is superior to
simply citing general rules that are not always easy to illustrate. In the
case method factual situations are described along with the resulting
court decisions. Through the study of actual cases students can learn
decision making, as well as benefit from the unfortunate results of poor
decision making by others. Managers often have very little time to react
to situations, so their knowledge of similar cases must be the basis for
any decisions.

Where possible, the most recent cases have been used. However, an
1850 case dealing with a specific point of law may still be valid today
if it has not been overturned by courts or legislatures. In the older cases
the language tends to be somewhat formal, whereas cases written in
recent decades generally will be more understandable and relevant to
students. The new cases cited also tend to deal more with contemporary
situations.

Hotels, restaurants, and the travel industry have changed enor-
mously since the last century. People today have more leisure time and
travel more than ever before. The hotels and motels of today are larger—
some are virtually small cities—and fast food establishments and condominiums have recently come into their own. Such changes mean that
certain legal situations could not have occurred before the 1950s. The
1964 Civil Rights Act, for instance, completely did away with some principles once held to be sacrosanct to hotelkeepers and restaurateurs.

Obviously, more areas of law are now necessary to cover new areas
in the hospitality field. Therefore, we have included discussions on
camping, mobile homes, and the considerable role and responsibility of
the travel agent. The many changes that have taken place in food and
alcoholic beverage establishment law during the last decade are also
included in the text. A series of problems are included at the end of each
chapter that test the skill and proficiency of future hotelkeepers and
restaurateurs in solving the kinds of problems they may encounter in
real life.

This writing culminates the research of the second edition. One can
rightly ask if there is a difference between the first and second edition.
The answer, of course, is a resounding yes. Law is not a static body of
decisions and statutes but an ever changing body of law that reflects the
changing lifestyles of its citizens. Today's hotel is a many-faceted, com-

plex institution. Within its walls it can be a hotel, apartment house, lodging house, rooming house, and condominium. Now it can even accommodate time sharing.

This edition updates all areas discussed in the first edition and adds new areas that have become relevant in the last few years. We explore the delicate problems of sexual harassment, increasing problems of antitrust action against hotels and restaurants, significant court actions in the area of travel and travel agents, and concerted state action against drunken driving. In fact, we include a list of states that have adopted the Dram Shop Act, which allows innocent persons to sue the establishments serving the liquor. A new chapter also deals with such issues as truth in menu and situations in which the IRS may consider tips a part of income.

In closing, we must admit that all names and places referred to in this text are only too real, as were the situations that brought them to court.

NORMAN G. COURNOYER
University of Massachusetts

ANTHONY G. MARSHALL
Florida International University

Introduction

Why Study Hotel, Restaurant, and Travel Law?

Without a doubt, preventing potential problems is the most important reason for studying hotel, restaurant, and travel law. In addition to satisfying guests, good management prevents accidents, robberies, or incidents that could lead to lawsuits.

Generally, attorneys deal with the facts of a case only after an incident has taken place; whatever evidence is saved is the material the attorney has to work with. With an awareness of legal implications, the owner or manager can save time, aggravation, and money. Knowing one's own rights is also to know one's guests' rights. Many hotels and restaurants employ consulting attorneys who help clarify any questionable points.

Two recent cases illustrate the need for preventive law. In Anzaldo v. Groes, 478 F.2d 466 (S.D., 1973), a five-year-old child fell from a balcony outside her motel room. The court said there was sufficient evidence that the motelkeeper was negligent in not maintaining the balcony and stairway in conformance with community safety standards and that such negligence was a substantial factor in causing the child's injury. The motel manager had a duty to know what was in need of repair and to maintain a checklist of all hazardous places on the property.

In the second case, Aldrich v. Waldorf Astoria Hotel, Inc., 343 N.Y.S. 2d 830 (1973), the hotel leased its checkroom to a concessionaire. The plaintiff deposited her mink jacket in the checkroom while she attended a ball at the hotel. When she returned to claim the coat, it had disappeared. Although the limiting liability statute (a statute that limited the hotel's loss to $500) may have been operative for the hotel under certain conditions, this statute could not be used by the concessionaire. The court found that the plaintiff could reasonably assume that the hotel operated the checkroom; that a tip constituted payment,[1] and that two garments on one check were not uncommon. The hotel was assessed

---

1 In a 1981 New York case, D–M Restaurant Corp. v. Weinberg, 442 N.Y.S. 2d 965 (1981), the court of appeals held that unless a restaurant formally exacted a fee—not simply accepted a voluntary tip for checking service—the restaurateur could not be forced to pay more than $75 for a lost coat or other item. This limit was set by law in 1924.

$1,400. The hotel did file a cross claim against the concessionaire based on an indemnity agreement, but all this took place at the cost of two court actions and a great deal of bad publicity.

Laws of Hotelkeeping Are Unique

Many of the laws dealing with hotels are exceptions to the rule as found in general business law. Even before the 1964 Civil Rights Act, innkeepers were compelled to receive and entertain strangers, and if they did not do so, they could be found guilty of a crime. Restaurateurs, on the other hand, were not legally required to accept all strangers (absent a state statute) until the Civil Rights Act of 1964. Additionally, hotelkeepers are held to an absolute liability for their guests' goods in the absence of a limiting liability statute. And adequate protection must be provided the guest. The Connie Francis rape case, Garzelli v. Howard Johnson's Motor Lodge, Inc., 419 F.Supp. 1210 (N.Y. 1976), in which Francis was awarded $2.4 million for inadequate protection, is a forceful reminder of this common law requirement.

The Dram Shop Act, a statute that holds purveyors of alcoholic beverages liable for the actions of their patrons outside their establishment, is rather unique. In the *Stacy* case, in which the promising young actor James Stacy and his motorcycle companion were hit by a drunk driver, costing Stacy his arm and leg and killing his companion, Stacy received $1.9 million from the bar owner who served liquor to the driver. Over $300,000 was collected by the family of Stacy's companion. Thus, the responsibility attaching to the hotel, restaurant, and travel industry is severe and may be likened to that of common carriers, which must exert greater than ordinary care for their customers. (California has since done away with the Dram Shop Act by legislation because of the lobbying of the hoteliers and restaurateurs.)

Familiarization with Legal Procedure and Research

An exposure to hotel, restaurant, and travel law will not only familiarize students with this area of law but also with how the laws can be researched. Although each state has its own unique statutory and common laws, this book deals with the law followed by the majority of the states and also gives, where possible, the minority view if it helps to illustrate a management principle.

A section on legal research is included in chapter 2 to help students familiarize themselves with the laws and court decisions of any state. Also covered is shepardization, the method by which statutes or legal cases are updated—whether modified or overruled by court decisions or legislation. Although this book is not intended to train lawyers, it will enable managers to speak more intelligently to their attorneys and to understand how a law case proceeds in the courts.

Development of Sound Management Techniques

By learning from the mistakes of others, managers can try to prevent recurrences of certain common legal cases. Probably 20 to 30 percent of common legal cases could be avoided if well-trained managers and personnel were to use a simple but effective creed—graciousness. Carefully trained service personnel are aware of potential problems and how they should be handled; they are gracious in their comments and actions. Often very busy or successful hoteliers and restaurateurs may become somewhat arrogant in their management techniques. They may become imbued with a sense of their own importance; they may lack competitors; or they may lose sight of their own true function—service. The participation of university- and trade school-trained personnel should help increase the number of competent personnel in the service industry.

Vocabulary Enrichment

Unfortunately, the law has long been the exclusive domain of lawyers, and the lay public has been discouraged from mastering its intricacies by the legal jargon encountered. However, investigating an area as important as the law need no longer be denied the layperson. Granted, a vocabulary of the most important words is necessary, and learning 200 to 300 new words can make one quite responsive to the cases and the logic of the law. The glossary at the end of this book contains legal words explained in lay terms.

Familiarity with the Court System

People going into business, as well as today's increasingly active consumers, must understand how they can use the courts. The court systems on state, federal, and constitutional questions are illustrated in chapter 2. To help students understand how a case is brought to trial, a hypothetical situation has been created from the beginning of the action through all of the various appeals open to each of the involved parties.

Knowledge of Federal and State Constitutions and Statutes

Infractions of the federal and state constitutions occur daily. Illegal search and seizure, false imprisonment, and the problems inherent in overbooking make a knowledge of the law essential to all members of this society.

In this book, concrete examples in the form of cases illustrate the correct way to proceed in problem situations that may arise in the hotel, restaurant, and travel industry. For instance, a desk clerk should know that the police must have a warrant before a guest's room may be legally searched; that false imprisonment can mean detaining a person against his will simply by saying, "Wait here;" and that overbooking is actually a breach of contract in which damages may be recovered. This last practice is so prevalent that it could lead to government intervention to protect travelers' rights.

Bringing about Change

To lobby for a change, people must know what they are trying to change and the reasons for the change. A familiarity with hotel, restaurant, and travel law will aid students in recognizing the problems involved. The travel industry, made up of such diverse businesses as hotels, motels, and tourist courts; eating and drinking establishments; gasoline service stations; rooming and boarding houses; trailer parks and campgrounds; retail stores; cleaning and laundry establishments; movie theaters; theatrical and entertainment establishments; sports and other recreational facilities; and transportation carriers such as airlines, buses, railroads, and taxis, has the potential to form one of the more influential lobbies in the United States.

It is possible to lobby for change as demonstrated by the passage of a 1976 Massachusetts statute dealing with how guests may register. Prior to this statute, at least one guest had to sign personally per room. The not infrequent situation of a hundred or so guests arriving at one time led to the need for a change. Now any group larger than five persons may be preassigned rooms, and the guests may go directly to their rooms, with the assignment constituting adequate notice of registration.

Changing Lifestyles and the Law

The law is constantly changing so those in the travel industry must be alert and try to anticipate which changes in mores and life-styles can affect their business operations. In the past *psychographics*, the study of changing lifestyles, was of interest only to sociologists, psychologists, and perhaps statisticians. Today, however, it can help those in the hospitality and travel industry. Psychographics can be used as an indicator of the morality of the times, which in turn reflects upon what customers will expect of a facility insofar as their personal use is concerned. Psychographics can also help delineate to what degree hoteliers can deviate from the rules of accommodation set down during a different time when different codes of conduct prevailed.

A well-known example of changing mores and the changing law is the so-called Lee Marvin case. A woman who had cohabited with actor Lee Marvin for a period of years sought to be compensated for what she had given up while she was Marvin's live-in friend, as well as some form of payment or share of the possessions Marvin had accumulated during this period of cohabitation. Although they were not married, the court awarded Marvin's friend $104,000 for what it labeled "rehabilitation purposes." In August 1981, the court of appeals reversed the award but not the principle on which the case is based. In effect, the state of California gave legal recognition to cohabitation, a form of relationship considered illegal in the past.

Although some twenty-eight states now sanction this sort of relationship, others do not. Assume you are the hotelier in a state that prohibits fornication, lewd cohabitation, and a multitude of other so-called immoral acts and a couple who has been openly living together for years, despite the fact that they are not legally married, wants a room to share in your hotel. Not only have they been accepted by society as not being immoral, but the courts, by permitting cohabitors and former cohabitors access to the courts, are in effect judicially sanctioning the relationship. If the courts viewed the relationship as illegal, those so situated would not be permitted to litigate their disputes in court, for the courts cannot and will not be permitted to be used to enforce or determine rights under an illegal agreement.

Not too many years ago the solution would have been simple: either refuse them accommodations or require them to take two separate rooms. But according to today's code of social conduct, the couple is not being immoral; rather for personal reasons they prefer not to marry. If you refuse them a room, are you violating the duty to accommodate? By making an issue of the fact that they are not married, are you subjecting them to public humiliation by refusing them a room for that reason? If the answer to either of these last two questions is in the affirmative, then you may have just opened yourself to a possible lawsuit.

The law is different in most states so this book cannot supply an answer that would be uniformly applicable to such a case. Rather, the purpose is to admonish students to stay abreast of changes in social attitudes and determine how these changes may affect business. Hoteliers in such situations should present the problem to counsel for their guidance and advice on what legal exposure they would be incurring on behalf of themselves and the house. In short, hoteliers who anticipate and are prepared should find that their legal problems are minimized.

Training in Legal Thinking

Legal study is not the mere communication of facts. What every student should gain from studying the legalities of hotel, restaurant, and travel management is a command, even if only a limited one, of the legal thought process.

Hotels are controlled by both statutory and common law, as are all other business endeavors. Most of the fundamental principles of the American legal system have ancient roots. Interpretations of the law, however, change with the times. And there is sometimes wide diversity between the laws of various states on any one given point. Only the majority view is fully discussed in this book, but the minority view is often given to show differing opinions.

An Outline of This Book

Hotel, restaurant, or travel management students need a firm grasp of both legal and management principles that will govern their future relationships and responsibilities to their guests and employees. English common law is the basis for most American laws and statutes covering hotels and restaurants. The brief survey in chapter 1 introduces students to the traditions and customs that have helped to shape contemporary U.S. laws. In addition, the civil law system—particularly as it pertains to hospitality law—is briefly discussed.

Chapter 2 is an introduction to legal research for future managers. In it are outlined the kinds of legal materials, including official sources, such as constitutions and statutes, and unofficial sources, such as legal encyclopedias and law reviews, that will aid nonlawyers wishing to do legal research.

Throughout this book, cases—court decisions—are used to illustrate general hospitality management principles. The discussion in chapter 2 illustrates the components of cases and traces step by step the journey of a case through the U.S. court system.

Chapters 3 and 4 list some of the principles that govern the legal definitions of types of accommodations, as well as the distinctive responsibilities the managers of each have to their guests. The guest-innkeeper relationship is outlined in chapter 4 and illustrated by several recent important legal decisions. Chapter 4 also includes an important discussion of part of the guest's responsibility to the innkeeper—forms of payment, including money, credit cards, and personal and traveler's checks—as well as a comprehensive section on financial protection for hotel operators.

Chapter 5 discusses licenses—which are special privileges—required by operators of public accommodations, as well as statutory regulations such as zoning that affect such businesses.

The relationships between various patrons and the hotelkeeper are considered in chapter 6, including definitions of when such relationships begin and end and how they are modified by acts of the guest.

One of the most important pieces of legislation ever affecting the hospitality industry is the Civil Rights Act of 1964. The limits that it and other state antidiscrimination statutes put on hotel and restaurant operators are discussed in chapter 7, as well as throughout other chapters.

Chapter 8 outlines important safety principles for hotel and restaurant operators. It defines negligence and the doctrine of torts (personal wrongs). The cases in chapter 8 provide invaluable examples of the need for preventive management.

It is essential for hotelkeepers to recognize the extent of guests' rights. In chapter 9 these rights are outlined in terms of contract law, security and safety, and protection from false arrest or lockout. It also considers the rights of other hotel visitors, such as guests of guests.

Guests' rights are also established by the duties owed them by management. These duties are outlined in chapter 10, which includes cases and discussions of the condition of rooms, public areas, restaurants and bars within the hotel, and outside and special areas. An important duty is owed in a special area—swimming pools, waterfronts, and lake areas.

Not only guests but their property as well are protected by the hotelkeeper's liabilities to guests. Chaper 11 discusses both common law and statutory liabilities to guests' property and where the liability starts and ends. This chapter also extends illustrations and cases to one of the traveler's most significant properties—the automobile.

All this is not to say that hotelkeepers have no protection from negligent or fraudulent guests, however. As chapter 13 shows in cases and illustrations, there are important safeguards in setting reasonable rules for guests, evicting nonpaying or undesirable guests, and in using force and care to deal with unruly patrons. The hotel lien (attachment of the nonpaying guest's property) is an important statutory safeguard for the hotelkeeper. Where this lien right was formerly granted without exception to hotelkeepers, today it is under serious attack from guests in many states. Several states have already outlawed the hotel lien. If goods are kept in these states, the hotelkeeper can be guilty of larceny.

Laws governing the restaurant or tavern operator's relationship with guests often differ from the legal principles governing the rest of the hospitality industry. Chapter 13 discusses both the rights and the liabilities of restaurateurs and tavern operators in two major areas: food service and alcoholic beverages.

As affluence and leisure increase in American society, so does the mobility of its citizens. Chapter 14 is a unique discussion of a new area of the hospitality industry: campgrounds, mobile homes, and tourist courts. It presents cases illustrating the rights and liabilities of managers in this new and growing area.

Mobility also is responsible for the increased use of travel agents, as is shown in chapter 15. Special legal principles govern the agent's relationships with clients as well as with suppliers of such services as transportation and hotel accommodations. While travelers are protected against baggage loss, cancellations, and overbooking, travel agents also have important legal safeguards, as the discussion of disclaimers and insurance illustrates.

Chapter 16 brings new material to the book but not new material to the industry. Sexual harrassment has been with us for many years and is examined with the hope that we can do something about it. How to attack the problem of over 13,000 fires in the hotel industry is faced in this chapter, as well as becoming knowledgeable in the areas of bomb threats, first aid, security, and elevator malfunctions. Truth in menu and how the IRS looks at tips in the industry are also explored.

Finally, the appendixes provide limiting liability statutes by states, states' positions on third party liability for sales to intoxicated persons, statutes dealing with defrauding an innkeeper, and guidelines on sex discrimination.

Hotel, Restaurant, and Travel Law

1 Contents

1   The History of Contemporary Hotel Law

"Litigation is the pursuit of practical ends, not a game of chess."

FELIX FRANKFURTER

S ome laws still on the books seem unnecessarily severe to hotelkeepers and restaurateurs. Laws are easier to get on the books than they are to get off. However, this does not account for the harshness of the laws in the first place. History and custom must supply the cause. In this chapter we consider the major influences on contemporary hotel law.

In fourteenth- and fifteenth-century England, laws pertaining to inns and taverns were of necessity stringent and usually favored the guests of the inn. The obvious and most cited reason was that innkeepers colluded with robbers and in many instances helped to rob their guests.

A quotation from W. C. Firebaugh's *The Inns of the Middle Ages* illustrates that laws were necessary to protect inn guests:

> . . . in the eyes of the law, the innkeeper, the pander, and others of like standing were on the same footing. . . . Innkeepers were not admitted to military service, nor did they form a guild, as did other tradesmen. In past ages, the tavern and innkeeper have been guide, philosopher, and friend to all the evil reprobates in his neighborhood. His establishment was a sanctuary and base of operation for every cut-purse who stalked his quarry along the trade routes or in the rear guard of marching legions. He was their fence, and his commission was always paid.[1]

Obviously, today's innkeepers, hotelkeepers, or restaurateurs are in a different league from their fifteenth-century counterparts. But as late as the eighteenth and nineteenth centuries, innkeepers were still held in low regard by both the law and the public.

The common law rules that protected the fourteenth- to nineteenth-century guest from unscrupulous innkeepers are still part of the current legal system. The rationale of legislators in allowing these archaic rules

---

1   W. C. Firebaugh, *The Inns of the Middle Ages* (Chicago: P. Covici, 1924), p. 12.

to remain on the books must be that if modern hotelkeepers are honest and conduct their business properly, such old laws will not affect them. But if a hotelkeeper deviates from accepted practice, the ancient law will be there to protect the injured guest.

Common Law

Common law is the legal system that evolved in England and that now applies to other legal systems throughout the world, including American laws that are modeled after it. Derived primarily from cases brought to trial by the people of the realm, English common law was not the result of royal decree but rather evolved from ordinary business.

The common law protected travelers in several ways. One of the most important ways was to impose on innkeepers absolute liability for all goods of the guests. If a person lost any bags while a guest, the innkeeper was liable, with certain limited exceptions. This was the law until 1850, when Massachusetts allowed innkeepers to limit their liability by statute. New York followed in 1853, and all states now have such a law with certain variations.

Contemporary Features of Common Law

When the United States adopted much of the English common law in 1776, it modified the English system by statute or altered it through judicial interpretation. Statutory law is law created by legislative enactment, or law created administratively by governmental officials when sanctioned by the executive branch of government. Judicial interpretation refers to any law, either common or statutory, that is interpreted by the judiciary in a case decision. Common law is generally described as law that is applied on a common, unified basis throughout a country. Thus, common law means simply the commonly applied law.

The distinguishing feature of the common law system is the reliance on case decisions that have "the force and effect of law" when applied to future disputes concerning the same or substantially the same issues of law. This concept is expressed by the Latin term *stare decisis*, which means "the matter stands decided." Or it can be stated as the concept of precedence—that an earlier decided case establishes a concept that precedes future cases and can be used as a basis for deciding future cases.

A case decision is the interpretation of a set of facts by the judiciary, and hence the case decision itself becomes part of the law of the state or, if it is a Supreme Court decision, the law of the land. An example is the case of Brown v. Board of Education, 347 U.S. 483 (1954), in which the Supreme Court by judicial interpretation did away with the practice of racial segregation in public facilities such as schools.

In the United States today the precedence principle is enforced whether the area of law has grown solely out of previous case decisions or whether it has been enacted by a legislative body. Put another way, the courts in a common law setting either "make" the law from the beginning through case decisions alone, or they "interpret" the laws passed by legislative bodies, thereby giving them actual content and meaning.

In a common law system, a statute may cover a particular area in question; the statute alone does not decide an individual case. Judicial interpretation of that statute is equally relevant. Or if the area is not covered by statute, then the influential law is that found in case decisions. Both statutory and common law require careful research before information can be gathered and an attempt made to determine the law. And even after information is gathered, it may be vague or the case decisions may conflict, so that an attorney cannot answer with any certainty what the law is; she can only answer in terms of probabilities—even guesses—about how a court would apply the precedents to the particular facts of present issues.

Also, in a common law jurisdiction where a jury is empaneled, questions of fact as distinguished from law questions are decided by the jury. Juries have been known to decide in totally different ways on similar facts, leading one to question whether a case is actually precedent setting. Thus the law is not always interpreted consistently; its execution depends on the vagaries of juries.

History of Common Law

The common law, as we know it, originated in England. Essentially it consisted of those maxims of freedom, order, enterprise, and thrift that had prevailed in the conduct of public affairs, the management of private business, the regulation of domestic institutions, and the acquisition, control, and transfer of property from time immemorial. It was the outgrowth of the habits of thought and action of the people and was modified gradually from time to time as habits were modified, as civilization advanced, and as new inventions introduced new wants and conveniences and new modes of business. Springing from the very nature of the people themselves and developed according to their own experience, it was the body of laws best adapted to their needs. As these people left England for other countries, they took with them their social institutions—among them, this body of laws.

This brief history should not be interpreted as praise of the common law. On the contrary, many of its features were exceedingly harsh; they originated in times of superstition and barbarism. The feudal system, essentially one of violence and disorder, gave birth to many of the maxims of the common law; and some of these, long after that system had passed away, are still present in our law, especially in the rules that govern the acquisition, control, and enjoyment of real estate and in those dealing with innkeeping.

On the whole, the common law system was the best foundation on which to erect the most enduring structure of civil liberty the world has ever known. The peculiar excellence of the common law of England was that it recognized the worth of the individual person and sought to protect individual rights and privileges. The English settlers in America brought with them these principles embodied in the common law, along with the means of modifying it by statutory enactment.

This delving into legal history shows what conditions were like when many of our present laws came into being. Few will deny that the rules that were promulgated were needed at the time, and that the common law framework was vital to the American nation's inception. But how relevant is the common law in contemporary times? Should there only be statutory law or a code that is similar to the civil law?

Hotel Rules and the Common Law

In Briggs v. Todd, 59 N.Y.S. 23 (1889), the court, commenting on the common law, recognized that although many of the conditions that gave rise to the innkeeper's rules have changed or ceased to exist, current conditions have infused the laws with fresh vitality. Inns are no longer few and far apart, and open violence has been greatly curbed. We now seldom hear of incidents where solitary travelers who, seeking refuge at an inn, are murdered for their belongings.

Just as infrequent is the host who betrays the confidence of a guest. The innkeeper's calling is as honorable as any in our modern commercial community. Though owners and managers of modern hotels are people of character and integrity whose skill and business resources have made travel convenient and pleasant, it must be remembered that the unprincipled compete with the honest and that the vocation is open to all. But protection against fraud and depredation still underlies the public policy that will not permit innkeepers to avoid their extraordinary responsibility except by the public enemy, an act of God, or the contributory negligence of their guests. (These concepts will be discussed in detail throughout this book.)

Violence has given place to stealth, the armed robber to the sneak thief. The organization of today's hotels affords easy access to the dishonest and exposes guests to risks that discourage any modification of the law. In a large hotel, with its innumerable rooms, its army of employees, and its incessant stream of arriving and departing transients, the guest's property is at the mercy of many. His room is necessarily accessible to a number of hotel employees who, if dishonest, may cost him great loss. A guest who suffers loss or injury is often frustrated in attempting to prove the loss sustained. The stranger disappears, and the employees protest ignorance and innocence.

It may seem harsh to hold hotelkeepers responsible. Yet they select employees; they should be answerable for the honesty and vigilance of the employees in guarding against the dishonesty of others. Hotelkeepers dictate fees and by means of the hotel lien have a right to confiscate a guest's goods without court procedure to secure those fees.[2] Innkeepers enjoy special privileges and thus should be held to special duties. Even were this not so, considerations of economic prosperity and social welfare require that commerce in and between cities be free and secure, thus reaffirming the wisdom of the ancient rule.

The common law has survived as a way of judicial procedure because its foundations are not so rigid as to deny it the necessary elasticity to develop and adapt itself to the times and encompass social and technological advances. The concepts and objectives remain the same, so the same principles can be applied. The only change is that the wording and subject matters of litigation have been updated.

Civil Law

Not all countries employ a common law system. Two-thirds of the world, including most European countries, are under a type of civil law. The civil law system implies a codification of written law rather than a large body of judicial decisions, as well as written laws, as in the common law system.

The first serious attempt to establish a legal system in Europe was undertaken in 528 by Emperor Justinian, who ordered a compilation and logical ordering of all known law of the time—the *Corpus Juris Civilis*. From 544 to 1804 little was added to European civil law because of disunity and persistent local inhibitions that prevented establishing a unified legal system. Even after the emergence of the modern nation-states, European legal systems remained disorganized. It was not until the *Code Napoleon* in 1804 and the codification of German law under Bismarck in 1900 that the civil law system as we know it today developed.

There are two major points of difference between the civil law system and the common law system. First, in both systems the criminal law—that branch of law dealing with crimes and their punishment enforced by the state or federal government—is codified, as in the United States, but only in a civil law system is the area of civil law codified.

Second, the civil law emphasizes investigation and consequently deemphasizes the courtroom trial; in other words, it emphasizes the codified law and its interpretation for each case, rather than using previous judicial decisions to establish interpretations of law that have some binding, precedential force.

2 At present the question of an innkeepers' lien is in a state of flux because of recent court pronouncements.

Notwithstanding these differences, the common and civil law systems have a great deal in common; both are products of Western European culture. Results in like cases will probably be the same, or nearly so, but may be arrived at by different means. And, in contrast to legal developments of Scandinavian, Oriental, and Pacific tribal cultures, the common law and civil law—culture and ethics—are more allied than separate.

Hospitality Law and Civil Law

Still, some of the differences between the common law and civil law are interesting and important to the travel industry. In common law countries decisions by courts have the force and effect of law. Prior case decisions set precedents for future decisions. In civil law countries, however, decisions in particular cases possess only persuasive authority and do not necessarily require consistency. Thus they do not set a precedent for future decisions because civil law countries rely mainly on the provisions of written law as the primary basis for decision. Each particular case in the civil law countries is decided by a fresh look at the provisions of law and the code (group of laws covering a particular subject) pertaining to the area of interest and by a fresh interpretation of those provisions as they apply to the facts in each case at hand.

A further difference is found in the criminal proceedings of the civil law system. Here such proceedings are said to be inquisitorial, and officers of the court are empowered to inquire into the facts of the case. In the Anglo-American common law system they are said to be adversarial; two parties oppose one another in a law action. A common maxim makes the distinction that in civil law the accused is considered guilty until proved innocent, whereas in the Anglo-American system the accused is presumed innocent until proved guilty. Although civil law may have been based on such a theory in the past, over the years it has become increasingly concerned with the rights of the accused.

The significant distinction, therefore, between the two systems of law now lies in the different roles of the participants, notably the lawyers and the judges. The judge, not the prosecuting and defense attorneys, plays the dominant role in the civil law trial. The judge alone is responsible for bringing forth the evidence in questioning the witnesses. And usually the judge, or a lower functionary in the judiciary, conducts the very thorough pretrial investigation designed to gather all the relevant facts and reduce the issues to only those in contention. The role of the civil lawyer in the judicial process, then, is a much smaller one than in the Anglo-American system.

Foreign Travelers and American Law

Some 25 million foreign travelers come to the United States each year. If we assume each visitor stays a modest eight days, the number of guest days per year comes to two hundred million. These travelers, like American residents, are presumed to know all the laws enforced in every state of the union. By and large, however, they are acquainted with neither our laws nor many of our customs. And despite essential similarities between civil and common law, differences do exist that could complicate the visitor's stay.

Summary

This chapter has discussed the English common law system, the basic influence on the American legal system. Early English laws protected guests against often dishonest, thieving, or murderous innkeepers. These laws, which often dealt harshly and severely with criminals, were adopted by the American legal system. In contrast to the common law system, which is based on previous case decisions and legislated statutes, the civil law system is based on codes of comprehensive written laws. Under civil law, each case is decided separately, without the precedents set by previous decisions in common law.

QUESTIONS FOR DISCUSSION

1 What reasons can be stated to show that early common law was quite stringent on innkeepers?

2 In what ways do the common law and the civil law differ?

3 How does precedent in the common law affect our system of law?

4 Why is the history of innkeeping important to future hoteliers?

5 When an attorney is consulted on a particular problem, why is the advice given usually couched in probabilities?

2 Contents

2 Legal Research and the Trial Procedure

"The patient search and vigil long of him who treasures up a wrong."

LORD BYRON
Mazeppa, Stanza 10

An exposure to law books and their use can be exciting and bewildering. A person entering a law library is often confused by row after row of heavy volumes. The first section of this chapter, therefore, outlines the two major sources of legal material available to students in hotel, restaurant, and travel management. Official sources, such as state and federal constitutions and statutes, regulations, and reported cases, are all available in legal libraries. Unofficial sources, like legal encyclopedias, law reviews, and digests, discuss cases and case commentaries.

The second section of this chapter outlines ways to begin legal research, including five separate methods of finding cases or statutes appropriate for a given problem. Next, it traces the step-by-step process that occurs when a case reaches the courts—from filing suits to pretrial procedures to the trial itself, as well as any appeal step. This short introduction to legal research shows hotel, restaurant, and travel students ways to make legal material readily accessible. The research information in this chapter is typical of that supplied by most state university legal studies departments.

Legal Materials

Two kinds of patience are required for legal research. First, the initial use of legal materials is bound to involve much trial and error. Yet after a short but concentrated period of practice, many early difficulties can be overcome. Second, most novice researchers expect to find a definitive answer to a legal problem. Often, however, as research progresses the water grows muddier rather than clearer, and the best results sometimes resemble a sketch rather than a precise drawing. All researchers try to find definitive answers, but this goal cannot always be attained; the *best* statement rather than *the* statement is the end of legal research.

Lawyers do far more than read law books, however, and this suggests some important limitations of library research. Book knowledge, though admittedly a start, must invariably be supplemented by judgment, common sense, and imagination. But the complete lawyer, as well as the complete hotel, restaurant, and travel student, sees the interrelationship of law on the books and law in practice and realizes that both are necessary for understanding. The laws pertaining to the hotel, restaurant, and travel industry are written for the industry and not for lawyers. Therefore, a knowledge of these statutes and laws is essential to manage any part of this vast industry.

There are a number of official and unofficial sources of legal material. In general, official sources consist of the national and state constitutions, the national and state statutes, and the national and state reported cases. On the local level, charters and ordinances are pertinent official sources. Unofficial sources include legal encyclopedias, law reviews, digests, textbooks, and looseleaf services.

Law lends itself to abbreviations, and they are used extensively by the profession. Nearly every publication has its own system of abbreviations, which are listed either at the beginning or end of the particular publication. It is advisable to look for such a list in whatever publication is being used. A brief discussion of some of the major official and unofficial sources follows in the next few sections.

Official Sources

Constitutions

In the United States, both the national and state constitutions are regarded as fundamental law. These are published in annotated form so that researchers can become familiar with the language of the constitution and, at the same time, can become informed by references to instances in which the constitution has been applied. The U.S. Constitution with annotations can be found in the *United States Code Annotated* (U.S.C.A.). State constitutions are also annotated. For example, the Massachusetts Constitution with annotations can be found in *Massachusetts General Laws Annotated* (M.G.L.A.). In both instances, volumes containing constitutional provisions are updated each year by supplements placed at the back of each volume (pocket parts).

Statutes

National and state statutory materials are also printed with annotations and are periodically supplemented. Statutes pertinent to states are also found in *United States Code Annotated* (for federal legislation) and in, for example, *Massachusetts General Laws Annotated* (for state legislation). The same is true for all other states. The legislative history of federal laws can be found in the *United States Code Congressional and Administrative News* and in the transcript of committee hearings.

Regulations

Often the national and state legislatures enact general provisions that allow administrative agencies to issue regulations. Most regulations of the federal administrative agencies are published in the *Code of Federal Regulations* and *The Federal Register*. In other instances regulations such as the state building code or the rules governing alcoholic beverages must be secured from the agencies themselves.

Reported Cases

Not all cases that are decided find their way into published reports. In the federal system reports are generated by three levels of courts: the U.S. Supreme Court, the U.S. Court of Appeals, and the U.S. District Court. U.S. Supreme Court case reports are published in three places: *United States Reports* (U.S. Reports), *Supreme Court Reporter* (Sup. Ct.), and *Lawyers Edition* (L. Ed. and L. Ed. 2d). U.S. Court of Appeals reports are published in *Federal Reporter* (F. and F. 2d), and U.S. District Court reports in *Federal Supplement* (F. Supp.). Three sample citations for federal cases follow:

1   Brown v. Board of Education, 347 U.S. 483. The reference here is by volume and page number; that is, the *Brown* case is found in volume 347, on page 483, of the *United States Reports*.
2   Tennessee Consolidated Coal Co. v. United Mine Workers, 416 F.2d 1192. The reference here is to volume 416 of the *Federal Reporter*, Second Series, page 1192.
3   Time, Inc. v. Pape, 394 F. Supp. 1087. This is a district court case reported in the *Federal Supplement*, volume 394, page 1087.

Appellate Courts

Most states usually have one set of reporting or appellate courts, but populous states like New York, California, and Illinois may have several levels of reporting courts. In Massachusetts, supreme judicial court decisions are reported in *Massachusetts Reports*. These decisions also appear in the *Northeastern Reporter*, along with cases from other northeastern states. Appellate court decisions of other states are found in state reporters and regional reporters. A sample citation of a Massachusetts case would be *McClean v. University Club*, 327 Mass. 68, 97

N.E.2d 174. The *McClean* case may be found in either volume 327 of *Massachusetts Reports* or in volume 97 of *Northeastern Reporter, Second Series.*

Unofficial Sources

Legal Encyclopedias

Such multivolume treatises as *Corpus Juris Secundum* and *American Jurisprudence* purport to cover, at least generally, all areas of law. The material is arranged in alphabetical order by subject matter and contains general statements concerning principles of law, supported by footnote citations to cases. But unlike general encyclopedias, legal encyclopedias comprehensively cover the subject matter in detail. If a researcher needs information on innkeeping (most legal books still reference "hotels" under "innkeeping"), the appropriate volume is selected; all relevant discussions are listed under this subject title. Researchers should always update the material by consulting supplementary material in the pocket parts.

Law Reviews

Law schools usually prepare these periodicals, which include articles, book reviews, and other commentaries. Law reviews are indexed by topic and author in the *Index to Legal Periodicals.*

Digests

Each reported case is classified in legal digests according to subject matter. Digests most pertinent for use in Massachusetts, for example, include the *United States Supreme Court Digest, Federal Digest,* as supplemented by the *Modern Federal Practice Digest,* the *Massachusetts Digest,* and the *Northeastern Digest. The Descriptive Word Index* to digests refers researchers to sections that contain references to cases.

Each section in the digest represents a particular point of law and is given a "key number." Under each key number in the digest is a listing and brief summary of all cases decided in the jurisdiction that involve that point of law. At the beginning of cases reported in reporters, "headnotes" also list the key numbers and describe the points of law discussed in the opinion.

Textbooks

Books written for law students in various fields are available. They are indexed, as are other volumes in the library, by title and author in the card catalog.

Looseleaf Services

These notebooks generally provide relevant statutes, administrative agency rulings, and case law. They have become popular in recent years and are organized by topic. Commerce Clearing House (CCH) has several looseleaf services dealing with such fields as poverty law, products liability, consumerism, trade regulation, and taxation. Among other looseleaf services are the Selective Service Reporter, the Environment Reporter, and several published by the Bureau of National Affairs (BNA). To locate material in a looseleaf service, researchers should do the following:

1 Consult the directions for the use of the particular service—usually found at the beginning of the publication.

2 Consult the topical indexes, which refer to specific paragraphs of the publication.

3 If the case is known, consult the table of cases; then consult other cases in the same paragraph or subdivision.

4 Update the research by consulting any supplementary material in the volume.

Shepard's Citations

This reference set records the judicial history of a case or statute. Each time a case is cited in a subsequent opinion, that citation is recorded in the *Shepard's Citator*. ("Shepardizing" is discovering the present status or value of a statutory law, court decision, or administrative decision.) Similarly, when a statute has been interpreted in a case, an entry in *Shepard's* will show that reference. *Shepard's* classifies material by volume and page number. For example, to find all the instances in which the case of *Brown* v. *Board of Education* has been cited, students can consult a *Shepard's Citator* for the *United States Reports* and look under 347 U.S. 483. *Shepard's* has both bound volumes and paperback supplements that contain all citations to date. Because the *Brown* decision was reached in 1954, the pertinent period for *Shepard's* would be from 1954 to date.

Similarly, to know the judicial history of the *McClean* case from Massachusetts, students can consult *Shepard's* for Massachusetts under 327 Mass. 68 or *Shepard's* for *Northeastern Reporter* under 97 N.E.2d 174. Statutory provisions may be shepardized in the same way by chapter and section numbers.

American Law Reports (A.L.R.)

This source covers cases, case commentaries, and articles on various topics such as illegal search and seizure, civil rights, voting, and slanders. Descriptive word indexes for the three series of A.L.R. provide access by topic to these articles. Once a highly pertinent article is found, cases occurring after the article's publication can be found by consulting the Later Case Service of A.L.R.

Beginning Legal Research

All legal researchers eventually develop their own styles. They discover the strengths of the various reference materials and use different approaches for different problems. Basically, there are two methods of approach for research in law books: (1) consulting the subject index, generally called the "fact" method, or (2) consulting the table of contents, generally called the "law" or "topic" method. Two additional methods are also peculiar to legal research: the case method, which can only be used when a specific case in point is known; and the word or phrase method, which is used to locate words or phrases that have been defined by the courts in their opinions.

Descriptive Word Method

Factual situations that give rise to legal questions are explored for leads to legal classification. For example, to find out who is involved, the researcher looks up parties—innkeeper, restaurateur, drunk, child, buyer, seller. To find out where it happened, he consults places—highway, barroom, club, auction, and, for events—collision, fistfight, expulsion, defective goods, and so forth. From this distillation and translation of events the researcher moves to descriptive word indexes in encyclopedias, digests, statutes, or the A.L.R. These leads are followed until the desired cases or statutes are found. Known cases and statutes are then shepardized to round out the research.

Topic Method

This method requires thinking more generally about the parties, places, and events presented in the legal problem. If Jane Doe has been injured by a shock caused by a short circuit in a lamp at the Peter Hotel, Peter Hotel becomes "licensee," Jane Doe becomes "invitee," lamp becomes "product," short circuit becomes "defect," and shock becomes "injury." These topics lead to the question, What is the liability of a seller to a buyer when a defect in a product causes injury? It is necessary then to proceed to the overall classifications in the encyclopedias and digests that may include persons, property, contracts, torts, crimes, and remedies. The foregoing question turns out to be best answerable by referring to either contracts (because the injury resulted from the use of a defective product) or torts (private wrongs).

Case Method

When researchers know the name of a case that involves a matter they would like to consider in detail, they can read the case and then follow the way in which the case has been digested. This is found at the beginning of the case in the reports. Researchers will find both prior and subsequent cases on the point. Alternatively they can shepardize the case to learn of instances in which the case has been considered by other courts or in law reviews.

Statutory Method

Some areas of law are primarily statutory, such as taxation, criminal law, and corporation law. A survey of the statute and its annotations will be most helpful in these fields. The statutes and cases in the annotations can be shepardized to uncover additional pertinent material.

Law Review Method

When the researcher believes that a problem is likely to have received law review coverage, the *Index to Legal Periodicals* is a good starting place. Most U.S. Supreme Court cases and many questions in constitutional law, for example, are discussed in law reviews. Law review articles contain numerous footnotes that lead to case law and statutory law and otherwise provide references.

Case Law

Case law, the study of a factual situation and its results, is a way to study law as a tool for management to prevent similar or related occurrences. For the uninitiated, law may be a body of rules fraught with technicalities, loopholes, and other traps. Like any system of government or theory of economics, a legal system contains rules; that is, how the system functions. Law is important, however, not because of its rules but because it serves an end; it is both the result of and an influence on social behavior. Rules are merely the tools with which law operates.

Perhaps the most important components of legal reasoning are doctrine, consistency, and social relevancy. A study of law should help hospitality management students, owners, managers, and employees to consider the many facets of any situation. Seldom is only one point of law involved. In this study of case law, the purely procedural or pleading aspects have been omitted. The points of law presented in this book should help the reader develop *lateral* thinking—to consider the possible ramifications of similar cases—and develop sound management techniques.

The study of case law has a number of important components:

1   The *citation* tells the kind of case we are dealing with, on what level (federal or state), and, of course, where the case can be found in the literature. The date indicates when the case was decided.

2   The type of *action* that brings a case to trial could be a trespass to property or person, a conversion of one's goods, assault and battery, breach of contract, any of a multitude of torts, injunctive relief (preventing someone from doing something), or mandamus (forcing a public official to do something).

3   The *parties involved*, that is, the identity of the plaintiff, the defendant, the appellant, the respondent, and the respondee, must be determined, and the principals and those who are just conduits for the case should be differentiated.

4   Heavy emphasis should be placed on the *facts* of the case. After all, a judicial decision is an official response to a set of facts considered within the broad social milieu. Because general principles are only guides, it must be demonstrated that the facts and the law are compatible—that is, that the principle used is realistically applied to the facts.

5   The *court decision* may occur at more than one level. Often cases that are first tried at the trial level go through one or two appeals, depending on the state. Often cases also deal with more than just one point of law.

6   The *rationale* provides useful background information. Why did the court hold as it did? What general rules and principles did it follow in reaching its decision?

7   What implications does the particular case hold for *management techniques*, especially in the area of prevention?

It is useful for students to trace the abstract terms discussed in a legal decision through the actual process of a legal case. The next section outlines the step-by-step procedure of a lawsuit through pretrial, trial, and appeal procedures.

Journey of a Case through the Courts

Not all conflicts that could be the subject of a lawsuit find their way into the courtroom; normally, what happens in the court is only a small portion of the entire legal process. In fact, a trial may be that part of an iceberg that appears above the water. We are concerned here primarily with the pleadings and the trial itself, not with such aspects of the case as the interview with the client and other witnesses; gathering, analyzing, and organizing the evidence; legal research; planning trial tactics; and other pretrial actions. This study is designed to acquaint students with fundamental legal procedure to provide a better understanding of what takes place in the courtroom. The following list traces the journey of a case through the courts.

1 Filing suit: the complaint
   a Identification of parties
   b Statement of jurisdiction
   c The cause of action
   d The claim for relief
2 Responses to the complaint
   a Preliminary motions
   b Answer
     (1) Admissions and denials
     (2) Defenses
     (3) Counterclaim
   c Motions on the answer
     (1) General
     (2) Motion for judgment on the pleadings
3 Pretrial procedure
   a Discovery
   b Motion for summary judgment
4 The trial
   a Selection of the jury
   b Opening statements
   c The case-in-chief
   d The plaintiff's rebuttal case
   e Summation
   f Charging the jury
   g Jury deliberations
   h The verdict
   i The judgment
5 Appeal

Although the patterns of procedure vary from state to state, certain generalizations can be made. Our model will be the procedures employed in the U.S. district courts. These courts bear a large percentage of the trial-level litigation that takes place in this country. In addition, many state courts have patterned their own rules of procedure after federal rules; some have adopted the federal rules almost verbatim. A study of federal procedure will be a survey of the practice most widely followed throughout the country.

Filing Suit: The Complaint

Suppose that P and his wife are paying guests at D's hotel. After registering and eating in the restaurant, P goes out to his parked car for a map. As he exits the hotel, he leaves the sliding glass doors open. His wife subsequently closes the doors. The lights inside the hotel lobby are on. When P attempts to reenter the lobby, he walks into the glass door, shattering the glass and sustaining injuries to his leg. There are no push bars or other markings on the glass door, and the glass itself is clear and highly polished. P's injuries result in a two-week hospital stay and over one month's recuperation at home.

Through his attorney, P demands compensation for his injuries. P claims that D's failure to mark the door in a conspicuous way constitutes negligence on D's part. Through his attorney, D refuses to pay and in turn claims damages from P for breaking the glass door, stating that P was contributorily negligent in not being more careful in entering the hotel and P's wife was contributorily negligent in closing the door. Unable to reach any compromise settlement, each side decides that the only alternative is to commence suit. *Lawsuits* (civil actions) are commenced by filing a complaint with the appropriate court.

A *complaint* is a request to a court to take some kind of *action* (a claim for relief) for a certain reason (the *cause of action*) and demonstrates to the court that it has the power to do what is requested *(jurisdiction)*. The complaint consists of three parts: (1) a statement showing the jurisdiction of the court, (2) a statement setting forth a "cause of action," and (3) a claim for relief.

Identification of Parties

The first requirement of a complaint is to identify the parties to the action. In the case presented here, the complainant is a resident of the Commonwealth of Massachusetts, with his usual place of dwelling at 1010 Campus Drive, Amherst, Massachusetts 01002. The respondent is a duly organized Massachusetts corporation having its usual place of business at 35 Route Avenue, Greenfield, Massachusetts 01301.

Statement of Jurisdiction

It is necessary to show that the court in which the complaint has been filed has the power to decide the dispute. The statement of jurisdiction sets forth facts that demonstrate a given court has the power to decide a question. No single court has the power to decide all questions. For example, a domestic relations court has the power to decide questions that arise out of the marital status; a probate court has the power to decide questions that arise out of the wills of deceased persons. Neither court, however, has the power to hear cases concerning hotel accidents. Such jurisdiction must be left to a court that has jurisdiction over the subject matter of the suit.

In our example, it is necessary to show that the court in which the complaint is filed has the power to decide questions arising out of a hotel accident. In addition to jurisdiction over the subject matter, it is also necessary to show that the court has, or can establish, personal jurisdiction over parties to the suit.

The Cause of Action

The complaint must set forth a cause of action; it must explain to the court the problem that the court is called on to decide. Basically, the purpose of the trial is to decide the existence or nonexistence of certain facts. In addition, the court must decide whether the presence or absence of these facts entitles either party (plaintiff or defendant) to "relief" as a matter of law. The purpose of the complaint is to inform the court about the nature of the disputed facts and the disputed claim for relief. It also notifies the defendant of the reason for the plaintiff's demand against him—the facts on which the plaintiff's claim is based.

The Claim for Relief

The complaint must set forth a claim for relief. In it, the plaintiff must tell the court what he or she wants the court to do—for example, award damages. Once the complaint has been prepared, it must be *filed* by recording it with the clerk of the court that has jurisdiction over the subject matter. In this way, the court receives notice that a dispute between two or more persons exists and that at least one desires that the court decide the matter. Until the complaint has been filed, no suit has been started.

The system of justice employed in the United States is an *adversary system*. It rests on the premise that when a lawsuit develops between two persons, that suit will best be resolved if the parties to the dispute vigorously present their own side of the case. Thus, once the complaint has been filed with the court, the adverse party must be notified that a suit has been filed against him so that he may prepare his side of the case.

Notifying the defendant is known as *service of process*; usually a specially appointed agent of the court serves the defendant with a *summons* and a copy of the complaint. A summons is issued by the court ordering the defendant to appear and defend the allegations made against him. Among other things, it informs the defendant of the time within which he must appear and the consequences of his failure to do so.

Responses to the Complaint

After the defendant has been served, he may, through his attorney, do several things. He may, for example, file motions addressed to some defect in the complaint or in the service of process. If he concludes that no such defects exist, he will file an answer to the complaint.

Preliminary Motions

Any request to a court in regard to the complaint will be in the form of a motion and must be made in writing if not made during a hearing or the trial. Motions may consist of requests for an extension of time, requests to clarify the complaint, demands that parties make available certain information to other parties, or a request that the suit be dismissed because the court lacks jurisdiction over the parties or the subject matter of the suit.

After any motion has been filed with the court, both attorneys appear at a hearing and argue their respective views, which the judge then either grants or denies. If the judge grants the motion, the case proceeds in accordance with the request. If, for example, the defendant makes a successful motion to dismiss for failure to state a claim on which relief can be granted, the case ends unless the defect in the plaintiff's complaint is subsequently corrected.

The Answer

While the complaint informs the court of facts known to the plaintiff, the answer states the defendant's position and presents facts that he wishes to bring to the court's attention. Thus the answer serves to (1) admit or deny various facts alleged by the plaintiff, (2) set forth any defenses the defendant may have against the plaintiff's claim, and/or (3) state a claim the defendant has against the plaintiff.

Motions on the Answer

Once the defendant has filed his answer, the plaintiff is then entitled to make motions. Plaintiff may, for instance, move for a more definite statement if the answer is vague, or move to strike all or parts of defendant's answer, for instance, because the material is redundant, immaterial, or scandalous. The plaintiff may also move to dismiss any counterclaim alleged by the defendant in his answer.

The complaint and the answer are known as *pleadings*. Once both the complaint and answer have been filed and all motions relating to the pleadings have been made and ruled on, either party may make a motion for judgment on the pleadings. Its purpose is to avoid full trials on issues that are not relevant to the dispute.

The preliminary stages of complaint, answer, and motions addressed to the various pleadings are often conducted with one or both sides having only a vague idea of exactly what the facts are or having little or no evidence of these facts that can be presented to a court. This stage enables each side to investigate the facts, to obtain evidence with which to prove these facts, and, eventually, to make additional motions to further clarify the suit or to end it short of trial.

Pretrial Procedure

Once the complaint and answer have been filed and perhaps clarified through use of the various motions, the basic dimensions of the legal dispute begin to become apparent. But a party cannot win a lawsuit unless he can convince a jury that his version of the facts is the more probable one. So, while the initial stages of a suit are devoted to determining the legal effect of the facts alleged by each side, this second stage is devoted to the collection of facts and evidence with which to convince the jury.

Discovery

A civil case (a wrong against an individual) is based on the presumption that justice will be done only if each side is aware of all the facts. If justice is to be done, all facts and evidence must be equally obtainable by both parties. This is done through discovery—the process by which one side finds out facts and evidence known to the other side.

Discovery may take place at any stage of the proceedings, or even before the filing of the complaint. It is usually accomplished, however, after the filing of the complaint and answer and the decision on any motions addressed to the pleadings. When done at this time, the intervention of a court is usually unnecessary.

Discovery may take any or more of several forms, such as written or oral questions (*interrogatories* and *depositions*, respectively) to the other party or to a witness, inspection of physical evidence, demands to produce documents or other evidence held by the adverse party or by a potential witness, or, if a question of the mental or physical condition of one of the parties is at issue, a physical or mental examination of the party concerned. A trial without the use of discovery would be like playing chess without knowing what pieces your opponent has and without knowing where they are on the board until you run into them.

Motion for Summary Judgment

A motion for summary judgment puts a case to a test of law and not facts. In effect it tells judges that there are no issues of fact for them to determine but rather questions of law. It requires a judge for the purpose of deciding the motion to accept the facts pleaded in the complaint as true and interpret them in the light most favorable to the party against whom the judgment is sought. After doing this, the judge rules whether, as a matter of law, the pleadings show on the part of the complainant (plaintiff) that an actionable cause of action has been pleaded or whether, on behalf of the respondent (defendant), an absolute defense has been established.

If the motion for summary judgment is granted, that ends the case.

The judge has decided that, as a matter of law, judgment should be given to one of the parties.

If the judge denies the motion, he is saying that if the facts are true, the complaint is legitimate, and the matter will be presented to a jury, which will determine which facts are true and which are not. In that way, the jury, under the instructions of the court as to what the law is on the subject matter, can decide whether the case has been proved so as to entitle the plaintiff to receive money damages and also to determine how much the plaintiff has been damaged.

A motion for summary judgment may be granted in part and denied in part. This means, in effect, that some factual issues that are not the subject of bona fide disagreement will not be litigated but that other relevant issues remain over which there is a real dispute.

The Trial

After the preliminaries of filing suit, narrowing the issues, and gathering evidence, the attorney then presents the evidence to an impartial tribunal. This tribunal must decide and weigh the evidence before it and render a verdict as required by the evidence and the law.

Just as there are rules regulating the starting of lawsuits, there are rules that regulate the trial's progress. Again, the rules are designed to develop the resolution of the conflict in an orderly fashion through the orderly presentation of the evidence.

The following trial procedure is generally followed in the states, although there may be some variations in some states:

1　Selection of the jury
2　Opening statements
 a　Plaintiff
 b　Defendant
3　Plaintiff's case-in-chief
 a　Direct examination
 b　Cross-examination
 c　Redirect
 d　Recross
4　Defendant's case-in-chief
 a　Direct examination
 b　Cross-examination
 c　Redirect
 d　Recross
 e　Rebuttal witnesses
5　Plaintiff's case in rebuttal
 a　Direct examination
 b　Cross-examination
6　Summation

      a Plaintiff's summation
      b Defendant's summation
      c Plaintiff's closing summation
  7 Judge's charge to the jury
  8 Jury's deliberations
  9 The verdict
10 The judgment

Selection of the Jury

If the case is to be tried before a jury, the trial begins with the selection of the jury. Prior to the day set for trial, persons selected from the jury lists are notified that they are to appear at the courthouse on a given day.

Once the preliminary selection is over, the problem of selecting an impartial jury gets underway. Most judges will ask jurors very general questions, such as whether they know or are related to either the plaintiff or defendant or their respective attorneys or if they have pending business with them. Jurors who answer affirmatively are dismissed.

When the judge has concluded her general questioning, she turns the jury over to the attorneys for more detailed questioning to ensure an impartial jury.

Individual jurors may be challenged by the respective attorneys for cause when, among other reasons, a juror expresses an inability to render an impartial verdict because of prior knowledge of the facts in the case. Counsel also can make a limited number of peremptory challenges, which will result in the dismissal of the juror without cause.

Opening Statements

Our legal system places the burden of establishing the right to recover on the person who alleges injury. Thus, the plaintiff bears the burden of proving his case *by the preponderance of the evidence.* The plaintiff makes the first opening statement, presents his evidence first, and has the opportunity to make the first and last closing arguments.

The opening statement is the first exposure the jury has to the specific facts of the case. It is not designed for argument but permits the attorneys to place the allegations and the evidence before the jury. Both the plaintiff and the defendant may waive an opening statement.

The Case-in-Chief

After the opening statements, the evidence for the plaintiff is presented. Evidence presented by witnesses is obtained through a process of examination and cross-examination. The party who calls the witnesses questions them to elicit the pertinent information. Each witness is then turned over to the opposing counsel for cross-examination with the purpose of eliciting additional information or discrediting information the witness has already given. Once cross-examination has been concluded, the calling party may ask questions on redirect examination, after which the opposing party will have an opportunity for re-cross-examination.

The defendant presents his case-in-chief in the same manner as the plaintiff, except that the roles of the direct examiner and the cross-examiner are reversed.

The Plaintiff's Rebuttal Case

When the defendant has concluded his case, the plaintiff can present evidence in rebuttal. Suppose, for example, that the plaintiff has sued the defendant for breach of contract, and the defendant contends that at the time he entered into the contract he was insane. In support of this argument the defense has elicited evidence from a psychiatrist. The plaintiff, in his rebuttal case, may then place his own psychiatrist on the stand and present evidence as to the defendant's sanity. The plaintiff's rebuttal case is confined to presenting evidence that refutes the evidence presented by the defendant. He may not place before the court any new evidence unless it contradicts the evidence presented by the defendant.

Summation

After the case-in-chief and the plaintiff's rebuttal case, the attorneys may then summarize the case. The plaintiff proceeds first, followed by the defendant and concluded by the plaintiff. Closing arguments allow the attorneys to review the contentions of their respective sides and to demonstrate how the evidenct supports these contentions.

Charging the Jury

The task of the attorneys is to present the evidence to the jury; the task of the judge is to present the law to the jury. The judge, through a series of instructions, informs the jury of the law that is applicable to the case. For example, in a case that involves a question of negligence, the judge will instruct the jury on the meaning of negligence and that, unless they find from the evidence presented in court that the defendant was negligent within the legal meaning of the word *negligence*, they cannot return a verdict for the plaintiff.

Jury Deliberations

Once the jury has heard the evidence and the law applicable to that evidence, it retires to consider the evidence in the light of the applicable law. The jury must first make findings of fact. Despite contradictory evidence, the jury must determine, for example in our hypothetical case, whether P was contributorily negligent in the way he entered the hotel and whether the hotelkeeper violated any duty owed P. When they have decided what actually happened, they then consider whether, based on the law of negligence told to them by the judge, not marking the door constituted negligence within the meaning of the law. In its deliberations the jury may ask for additional instructions from the judge or to view a particular piece of evidence. It is their duty to consider all the evidence presented in reaching a verdict.

The Verdict

Normally, the jury must reach a unanimous verdict. All members of the jury must agree that the defendant is either liable or not liable. If the jury is divided or "hung," the judge will call a mistrial, and the trial must begin again with a new jury.

Civil action cases such as this one, which concerns a wrong against an individual, normally require the jury to agree upon two questions. First, they must decide if the defendant did or did not do what the plaintiff alleges. If the jury decides that the defendant did damage the rights of the plaintiff, it must decide the extent of that damage in monetary terms. When the jury has reached its decision on all questions, it returns to the courtroom and announces the verdict in open court.

The Judgment

Once a verdict is returned, it is not binding on the losing party until the court has entered judgment on the verdict. Basically, this means that the attorney for the losing party will have a chance to attack the verdict. The attorney may pursue any one or more of the following tactics:

1   Ask that the jury be polled to ensure that the verdict was unanimous.

2   Ask for *judgment notwithstanding the verdict*. This is a claim that no reasonable person, on the evidence, could possibly have come to the conclusion reached by the jury.

3   Ask for a new trial on the grounds that either an erroneous ruling of the judge or a comment made in the presence of the jury that did not fall within the rules of evidence was prejudicial to the client.

4   Ask for a *remittitur*—a claim that the damages found were unreasonable—if he is the attorney for the losing defendant.

If the trial judge denies these motions, a *judgment* (the official decision of a court about the rights and claims of each side in a lawsuit) on the verdict is entered. For example, to collect this judgment, an *execution* (the official carrying out of a court's order or judgment) is issued by the clerk of the court to the sheriff. The latter demands payment and, if payment is not made, may attach, seize, or levy property belonging to the debtor and have it sold to satisfy the judgment.

Appeal

Many events at a trial occur rapidly. The decision that a judge must make with respect to an objection must be made virtually on the spur of the moment. For this reason mistakes will be made from time to time on which each party has a right to an appeal. In such cases either party may be entitled to have an appellate court review the proceedings of a trial in a calm and reflective environment removed from the passions and argumentative nature of the trial itself. The appellate court has the authority to review the handling and decision of a case tried in a lower court.

The right to an appeal, however, is not the right to appeal everything that happened in the trial court. The parties may not appeal questions of fact, only errors of law. For example, if there is conflicting evidence on a point, the losing party cannot appeal the finding of a jury resolving that conflicting point against him. It is not the task of either the trial or the appellate court to rule on questions of fact; that is the duty of the jury.

The Trial Processes

The facts of a case are almost exclusively the province of the jury. But, although law is built on fact, certain facts do not themselves result in liability or nonliability; they do so only if a legal principle states that certain legal results shall come from the establishment of facts of that type. Thus we may identify three separate processes that take place at a trial:

1   What are the facts? Was P contributorily negligent in the way he entered the hotel? Did his wife cause the accident by closing the door?

2   What is the law? The question remains whether the nature of the danger and P's knowledge of it, in view of the surrounding circumstances, was such that a person in his position exercising reasonable care for his own safety would not have been injured. Was P guilty of contributory negligence as a matter of law? What does this principle of law state? These are *questions of law.*

3   How is the general principle of law applied to the particular facts in this case—that is, given this general principle of law and these particular facts, who wins, plaintiff or defendant? These are *questions of law application* or "mixed" questions of law and fact.

Questions of fact are decided by the jury. The jury must listen to the conflicting versions of plaintiff and defendant and decide what probably happened. The judge has the initial function of deciding whether a given item of information (evidence) is sufficiently trustworthy and help-ful for the jury to hear it. Thus the judge decides on the admissibility of evidence.

The judge also decides questions of law. She decides the relevant principle of law for cases of this type and what this principle says by instructing the jury—in effect, giving the jury a short course on one particular principle of law as it applies to the case.

The judge instructs the jury so that it may determine how the general legal principle establishes liability (or nonliability) under the facts. But here the function of the jury is usually far different from its function as fact finder. As fact finder the jury has a large degree of discretion in deciding, for instance, what evidence to believe and what evidence not to believe. In applying the law to the facts, however, the jury only has the discretion the judge wishes to give it in her instructions.

In the case where P sustained injuries upon entering D's hotel, the jury, in deciding whether P was acting in a prudent manner when entering the hotel, is relatively uncontrolled as long as some evidence has been presented to the jury that supports its conclusion. But in deciding whether P or D or no one at all should be held liable, the jury is bound by the judge's instructions. For instance, the judge in instructing may merely define negligence and state that if the jury believes that the actions of D in not marking the glass door meet this definition, then D is liable. Here the jury has unlimited discretion. But if the judge, after defining negli-gence, goes on to state that if P's carelessness in entering the hotel makes him contributorily negligent and therefore liable, the jury has little dis-cretion. In effect the judge is deciding the question of "mixed" law and fact.

Parties may appeal only from things done by the judge—not from things done by the jury. It is not the task of either the trial or the appellate court to rule on questions of fact; that is the duty of the jury.

The one exception is the situation in which the trial judge should have granted a *judgment notwithstanding the verdict,* because, on the evidence, no jury could have returned the verdict this jury did. The parties, however, do have a right to appeal erroneous resolutions of ques-tions of law.

The parties may also appeal the judge's instructions to the jury on the law—the judge's answers to the questions, What is the law? What does it say? And the losing party may also appeal from the resolution of the "mixed" question—the application of the law to fact—to the extent that the judge decides it through limiting the discretion of the jury.

Appellate Court

An appellate court is far different from a trial court. Since the ap-pellate court is not concerned directly with what happened, there are no juries. The court consists of not one judge but anywhere from three to nine judges. A majority is necessary for a reversal of the results of trial. The attorneys on the appeal first submit briefs (written arguments), often quite lengthy, attempting to convince the court that the trial judge was right or wrong. Some time after filing the briefs, the case is set for oral argument, at which time the attorneys argue their views in person before the court and the court members ask questions. The court will then hand down its decision in an opinion justifying its conclusions. All the cases given in this book are appellate decisions.

The court may either reverse the decision of the lower court and order a new trial or order the case to be dismissed altogether. The court may also, of course, affirm the decision of the lower court, in which case the judgment stands. The fact that an error has been made by the lower court does not necessarily mean that a case will be reversed. In addition to demonstrating the error, the appealing party must also show that such

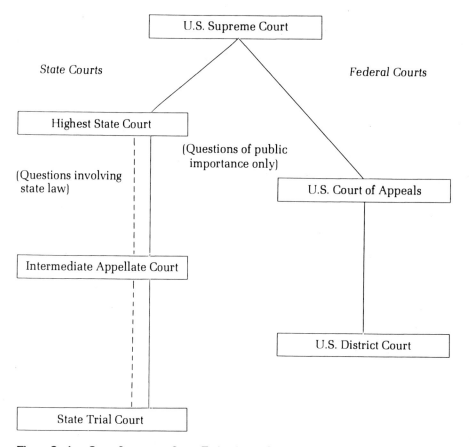

Figure 2–1. Court Systems—State, Federal, and Constitutional Questions. Only questions of public importance are appealed to the Supreme Court (see solid lines). Questions involving state laws reach their final level of appeal at the state supreme court (see broken lines).

an error was a prejudicial one that substantially affected his rights. If he cannot demonstrate prejudice to his rights, the court will hold that the error was harmless and will affirm the previous ruling. Whether an error is prejudicial or harmless depends upon the particular facts of each case.

Normally, each party has a right to appeal to an intermediate appellate court. However, there is not always a right to an appeal to the highest appellate court—the state supreme court (if in a state court system) or the U.S. Supreme Court (if in the federal court system). Appeal to the Supreme Court is governed by the Constitution and statute. The party must demonstrate that his case falls into one of the categories for which appeal to the highest appellate court is permitted by law. Even if this can be demonstrated, the highest appellate court may still, in many cases, refuse review in its own discretion. Figure 2–1 illustrates the appeals process for state, federal, and constitutional questions.

A knowledge of the journey of a case through the courts is essential for understanding the cases in this book. Also, some of the distinctions made will become clearer as you begin to read cases. This chapter should be referred to at frequent intervals as you progress through the book.

QUESTIONS FOR DISCUSSION

1 If one were to shepardize McClean v. University Club, 97 N.E.2d 174 (Mass., 1951), would the first citation be (327 Mass 68) or 141 N.E.2d 513?

2 What "key number" under the descriptive word *innkeepers* in the digest would be used to locate the effect of negligence on the part of the innkeeper?

3 What value can shepardization be to future hoteliers or restaurateurs? Is it difficult to use *Shepard's Citator?*

4 The section called "The Journey of a Case through the Courts" is based on Liebman v. Scott, 391 S.W.2d 540 (Texas, 1965). Has this case been modified by the courts? Is this case used as precedent for other states?

5 In the journey of a case through the courts the discovery process can be very helpful to your case. How?

6 Explain a summary judgment. What is the rationale of this motion?

7 Discuss why you believe or do not believe attorneys should couch their advice in probabilities when a question is asked of them on any particular question dealing with hotel, restaurant, and travel law. List the reasons.

3 Contents

3 Types of Accommodations

"No rule is so general, which admits not some exception."

ROBERT BURTON

Because of the varied types of accommodations available to travelers, tourists, contract tenants, licensees, and the like, it is essential that hoteliers and other accommodations managers be acquainted with pertinent legal definitions that affect management problems. This chapter provides such definitions, as well as some possible implications for management preventive law.

Today the range of available accommodations extends from a conventional hotel room to a penthouse suite of rooms with special services costing over $1,500 per day to a piece of land for a tent. As well as motels, tourist courts, lodging houses, boarding houses, and rooming houses, the accommodation industry also includes condominiums, officers' quarters, enlisted barracks, army base guest houses, luxury ships, Pullman coaches, college dormitories, fraternity and sorority houses, clubs, apartment hotels, summer cottages, and hostels.

A hotel can function as a different kind of accommodation to several types of guests at one time. It may be an apartment hotel to some, a boarding or lodging house to others, and a regular hotel to still others. In addition, a hotel may be part of a condominium—that is, some floors or rooms are sold to individuals who may in turn rent to other tenants themselves or through the regular hotel office. Therefore, it is not surprising that precisely defining an inn, the first form of accommodation known, has been difficult since the earliest times.

The common law doctrine enunciated in Cayle's Case of 1585, 8 Co. Rep. 32 (1585), provoked much discussion and resulted in many divergent decisions on hotelkeeping. This case set forth the duties of innkeepers toward their guests, as well as the rights of the guests. Many states have either reenacted this old common law definition of an inn or have modified the definition to reflect the intent of the legislature.

Inns or Hotels

In legal terminology there is no difference between the terms *hotel* and *inn*. The word *hotel* came into use with the eighteenth-century introduction in London of the "hotel garni," a large house in which furnished apartments were rented by the day, week, or month. The word *hotel* is of French origin, derived from *hostel*, and more remotely from the Latin word *hospes* (Cromwell v. Stephens, 2 Daly 15 [1867]), and was first introduced into this country around 1797. Before that time, houses for the entertainment of travelers were called "inns."

The definition of inns and hotels goes back to the same legal sources: *Cayle's Case*, 1585; Cross v. Andrews, 1598 (Cro. Eliz. 622); Thompson v. Lacy, 1820 (3 B. & Ald. 283); and Cromwell v. Stephens, 1867 (2 Daly 15). The definitions vary to such a degree that it is difficult to find a proper technical meaning that could be all-inclusive (Ambassador East v. City of Chicago, 77 N.E.2d 803 [Ill., 1948]).

In Juengel v. City of Glendale, 164 S.W.2d 610 (Mo., 1942), the court reviewed various definitions, some of which are listed here:

> A hotel is defined as a house which is held out to the public as a place where all transient persons who come will be received and entertained as guests for compensation; or a house where travelers are furnished as a regular matter of business, with food and lodging while on their journey; or a house where travelers are furnished with everything which they have occasion for while upon their way; or a place where transient guests are admitted to lodge, as well as one where they are fed and lodged; or a place where every well-behaved stranger or traveler, who is willing to pay reasonable rates for accommodation, is entitled to receive food, drink, and lodging; or a place kept for the entertainment of travelers and casual or transient guests; or a place where the proprietor makes it his business to furnish food or lodging, or both, to travelers. It is not now essential to constitute a hotel that there should be provision for furnishing food or drink as well as lodging for the guests. Distinctive features of a hotel are that it receives transient guests and furnishes them with lodging. An essential characteristic of the business or occupation of keeping a hotel is that it shall be the regular business of the person so engaged.

This description makes it apparent that there is an irregularity in the definition—that is, whether food must be served to fulfill the common law requirement. Although serving food was a requirement of the old common law, whether this requirement still exists is discussed in the section "Need to Serve Food" in chapter 4.

The terms *innkeeper* and *hotelkeeper* may be used interchangeably since they have the same legal status (Wellsboro Hotel Company's Appeal, 7 A.2d 334 [Pa., 1939]). The word *inn* still has contemporary applicability. The advent of increased automobile traffic has led to the development of tourist camps, motor courts, motor hotels, and the more prevalent motel. Motels resemble the old inns more than hotels do because motels also furnish accommodations for travelers' automobiles (Langford v. Vandaveer, 254 S.W.2d 498 [Ky., 1953]).

The word *inn* now describes a small hotel, and also suggests a country or rural accommodation. However, the largest innkeeper in the world uses the word as part of its trademark—"Holiday Inn, Inc." In early times, to be defined as an inn or hotel, an establishment had to provide transients with lodging, food, drink, and accommodations for stabling their horses. Obviously, these requirements have changed over the years.

Of course, the building itself is a necessary part of a hotel, but now the word *hotel* also includes all personal property that must be used in its operation, including its bedding and heating facilities (Commercial Casualty Ins. Co. v. Adkisson, 4 P.2d 50 [Okla., 1931]; Bisno v. Herzberg, 170 P.2d 973 [Cal., 1946]). A tourist camp is no less a hotel because the business is conducted in a group of buildings rather than in just one building. As the court in Juengel v. City of Glendale, 164 S.W.2d 610 (Mo., 1942), said about tourist camps: "It would be strange indeed if the business or occupation [of keeping a hotel conducted through the use of a single building should be subject to regulation while the same business or occupation] conducted through the use of a group of buildings, such as a tourist camp, should be exempt from regulations." In a case with similar facts, the court in Berall v. Squaw Valley Lodge of Tahoe, 11 Cal. Rptr. 316 (Cal., 1961), said, in a case involving a guest who was injured in a fall in a corridor of one of the buildings, that where the lodge consisted of three buildings, two for guest rooms and a main building housing the public rooms, it was necessarily a hotel.

The legal definition of a hotel is important because the type of accommodation may affect the outcome of a case. In Metzler v. Terminal Hotel Company, 115 S.W. 1037 (Mo., 1909), the plaintiff registered as a transient guest at the defendant hotel, was assigned a room, and afterward checked his valise at the office. When he presented the check for the return of his valise, it could not be found.

The plaintiff instituted an action for the conversion of the lost property and to recover its value and contents from the defendant in his capacity as innkeeper. The defendant argued that he was not technically an innkeeper because he did not furnish meals to guests, and he was therefore not subject to an innkeeper's extraordinary liability for a guest's goods. Nevertheless, the plaintiff ate in a restaurant in the same building, unaware that the restaurant was not part of the hotel and was owned by someone else.

The court held that although the common law liability of innkeepers originated in an era when English travelers were at the mercy of innkeepers and highwaymen, this liability was still applicable. The fact that many modern hotels do not furnish food does not exempt them from this unusual liability. The plaintiff won the case.

Types of Accommodations

Three plans of service are generally accepted in hotels: the European method, the American method, and a modified plan. In a hotel on the European plan, guests must buy meals at an attached restaurant or wherever else they please. The fact that a hotel is conducted on the European plan does not alter its legal character as an inn.

Under the American plan, the room cost includes service and food. Generally, the fact that a guest does not partake of one or more meals under the plan does not entitle one to a rebate. In the modified plan, the cost of the room includes one or more meals. Where a contract is made and has special provisions, it supersedes the general rule and the parties are bound by the provisions of the contract.

Parking

In the last century, an inn provided for both people and beasts. Now stables have disappeared and are no longer required as part of a hotel. In Armwood v. Francis, 390 P.2d 88 (Utah, 1959), the court noted that the world had come a long way since necessity created, with its own distinct liability, the innkeeper-guest relationship as known at common law. (Because of these changes, the court would have to take a second look at the hostelries of the modern era. In some states, for example, if the laws were left as written, travelers aboard covered wagons might arrive at a skyscraper hotel and could demand not only food and refreshment but an attendant to tether, groom, and hay their horses, and barn their wagons.) A hotel need not provide parking for a guest's car, but once it does, liabilities bind it and its guests. This aspect of the innkeeper-guest relationship is covered in chapter 11.

Motels

For all practical purposes the word *motel* is interchangeable with *hotel* and *inn*. Controversies about the status of such terms as *hotel*, *motel*, and *boarding house* often arise in the context of applying health, safety, and welfare codes, zoning restrictions, liquor licensing quotas, statutory limitations and definitions, and rent controls.

In the early 1940s, the motel emerged as a new form of accommodation, and within a short period of time it far surpassed hotels and inns in the total number of rooms and buildings. Motel accommodations may be for overnight or, especially in resorts, for longer periods. Residences occupied for longer periods are quite frequently constructed with cooking facilities.

Where the courts have not followed the rule that a motel is equal to a hotel or inn, incongruous decisions have been reached. The innkeeper—one who manages a public house of entertainment—cannot avoid being an innkeeper simply by denial. Whether a person is an innkeeper depends on her acts, not on her word or wishes. If a person carries on the business of an innkeeper and at the same time avoids being one simply by saying that she does not call herself an innkeeper or that she does not intend to be classed as one, all innkeepers could carry on business free from the duty to serve the public and from the liability of an insurer, which would hold them responsible for any loss sustained by a guest. Such an interpretation would be far from what was originally intended by the common law.

Innkeepers are entitled to determine the scope of their undertaking and are obliged to serve the public only within that scope. For instance, they can decide that they will keep "a public house of entertainment" and can reasonably charge one hundred dollars a day. If they undertake to keep such a house, they are obliged, of course, to receive all proper persons willing to pay that amount. Proper persons are ones who are not drunk, are dressed appropriately, deport themselves in an acceptable manner, and are able to pay the charges levied for services (see chapter 12). Innkeepers are not obliged to receive those who refuse to pay that sum for a room. Yet their status as an innkeeper does not change.

Some courts use the argument that no food is furnished to guests as an indication that a motel or similar establishment is not a hotel (see "Need to Serve Food" in chapter 4). This argument is based on a false assumption that the scope of one's business of entertaining determines whether one is or is not an innkeeper. Every innkeeper or hotelkeeper may serve guests with lodging, board, and a place to park; or may serve them with lodging and board without a place to park; or may undertake to serve them only with lodging. Such a person is still an innkeeper or hotelkeeper in each case, although innkeeping is practiced in varying degrees.

The case that argues against food as a requisite of a hotel is best brought out in the case of Nelson v. Johnson, 116 N.W. 828 (Minn., 1908), in which Justice Start said, "There is no reason why liability should not be imposed on the keeper of a place where the public is offered accommodations whether or not food is served. The need for protection to the traveler's property is incident to his lodging, and not to his eating." This ruling is a most convincing argument for reappraising the requirements of the inn or hotel.

Boarding and Lodging Houses

In a boarding house, a guest is under an express contract for food and lodging at a certain rate for a given time. A boarding house is characteristically less public than an inn or hotel and is often maintained by a private family in the house. The proprietor of a private lodging house is not bound to receive all who apply, but may select guests and contract with each. In contrast, a hotelkeeper must receive everyone who requests lodgings. (Exceptions to this rule are discussed in chapter 12.)

A distinction can be made between tenants and lodgers. Tenants have the exclusive legal possession of the premises; they (and not the landlord) are in control and are responsible for the care and condition of the premises. Lodgers, however, have merely a right to use the premises; the landlord retains control and is responsible for the care and attention necessary. Therefore, owners or landlords who retain general control and supervision over the entire premises and furnish and care for the rooms of necessity retain the right of access for that purpose. They rent to lodgers, as distinguished from tenants.

A register in a lodging house does not make it an inn or hotel, nor does keeping a bar and billiard room, serving liquor, or the occasional entertainment of travelers necessarily change the status of a boarding house, lodging house, or rooming house to a hotel or inn.

The term *boarding house* allows boarders to come and go as they please, providing they use discretion, because the landlord has no control over the private life of the guest.

Under common law the boarding or lodging house had few of the rights or privileges and few of the handicaps of an inn or hotel. A boarding house was not obliged to accept all persons who sought accommodations, nor did the 1964 Civil Rights Act require a boarding house to accept all people who applied for a room. However, statutes give boarding houses the same privileges that were once the sole domain of the inn or hotel.

The case of Brams v. Briggs, 260 N.W. 785 (Mich., 1935), deals with the right of a boarding house to a lien against a tenant's property. Here the defendant (a permanent residence hotel) locked the plaintiff's room and seized his goods when the plaintiff fell behind in his rental payments. The plaintiff had installed his own furniture in the room, and the hotel supplied beds, maid service, and bellboys. The defendant claimed the innkeeper's common law right of a lien.

On appeal, the plaintiff raised the question of whether there, in fact, did exist an innkeeper-guest relationship. An essential element of such a relationship is that the guest be a transient, not a boarder. However, state legislation had extended the right of a lien, already available to boarding or lodging houses, to keepers of furnished apartments. In any case, the court considered the plaintiff a lodger, if not a guest, and a keeper of a lodging house could validly exercise a lien. The plaintiff lost his *replevin action* (a lawsuit to get back personal property in the hands of another person), along with a count for *conversion* (an unauthorized act which deprives an owner of his property permanently or for an indefinite time) against the hotel.

Rooming Houses

Rooming houses are merely houses or buildings with one or more bedrooms that the proprietors rent to such persons as they choose to receive. They are not public places to which any well-behaved persons with money can go and demand lodgings as a matter of right as they can at a hotel. Keepers of rooming houses may receive or turn away whomever they wish. Individual contracts or arrangements between each of the guests and the proprietor about payment and length of stay are unique, an arrangement that only recently evolved from the boarding house. The single material difference between a boarding house and a rooming house is that a boarding house furnishes meals. In a rooming house, it is generally understood that there will be no housekeeping, no full meals will be consumed there, and the room will not be used to any great extent as a sitting room. The room in a rooming house is usually in the immediate possession of (when the occupant is not present) and dependent on the proprietor.

The court has said that a "tenant" is a purchaser of an estate, entitled to exclusive legal possession, and a "roomer" has merely a right to use the premises. In determining whether a person is a roomer or a tenant the legal criterion is the right of exclusive possession (Taylor v. Dean, 78 A.2d 382 [D.C., 1951]).

Taverns and Ordinaries

Formerly, the tavern was a public place where food and alcohol were furnished to guests. Usually the liquors were sold to be consumed on the premises. Now the term *tavern* might be applied to an inn, hotel, saloon, or any restaurant.

An ordinary was a public house where food and lodging were furnished to travelers and their horses at fixed rates and was open to anyone who requested accommodations. Alcoholic beverages were usually sold as in the tavern; therefore, the terms *ordinary* and *tavern* were often interchangeable.

Clubs

The word *club* has no definite meaning. Some clubs severely limit the number of members and select them with great care. (Members of the club usually own considerable property in common.) Furnishing food and drink for money is but one of many conveniences that club members enjoy. Often it is questionable whether a club is a valid one with limited membership, into which admission cannot be obtained by any person at his pleasure, or whether "club" is an assumed name without any real organization behind it. The word has been defined by statutes, although it has been more frequently referred to in statutes and then explained later by court decisions dealing with clubs of various structures and diverse purposes (Commissioner of Corps. and Taxation v. Chilton Club, 61 N.E.2d 335 [Mass., 1945]).

The renting of rooms by clubs concerns us here. Little information is available about the status of a club member who stays at a private club. What is the relationship between the club and its members? The two cases that have come up over the years place the club in a category other than a guest-innkeeper relationship, but still hold the club to the same responsibility.

The first case, McClean v. University Club, 97 N.E.2d 174 (Mass., 1951), deals with important aspects of the club-member relationship. The plaintiff had been a member in good standing of the defendant private club for years. Members paid dues as well as charges for liquor and special services; the club maintained bedrooms for registered, paying members and guests.

As was well known to the club, the plaintiff was accustomed to occupying a room during frequent drinking bouts, and at times he became quite ill. On the morning in question he felt very ill, although he was sober. The club manager refused the plaintiff's request for a doctor, and he was ordered to vacate his room. A few hours later he was led from his room by the manager and another man, who had to support him. His request for a doctor was again refused. As he left the club alone, he collapsed and sustained serious injuries.

The plaintiff initiated a *tort action* (an action to redress a wrong done by another person) for the injuries resulting from his unlawful eviction, as well as a second count for breach of contract between the defendant club and its guest. The defendant was bound by contract to accord guests decent and humane treatment—that is, to see that employees did not abuse or insult guests or unnecessarily subject them to any conduct that would cause them physical discomfort, humiliation, or distress of mind or that would imperil their safety. If the plaintiff became ill while a guest, and the defendant decided to remove him from the premises, the defendant was bound to pay proper attention to the plaintiff's condition and not evict him in such a manner as would impair his health or endanger his safety. However, the defendant was under no obligation to procure a doctor for the guest.

On the count of breach of contract, the jury found for the plaintiff, concluding the manager acted unreasonably. The court also noted that Boyce v. Greeley Square Hotel Company, 168 N.Y. Supp. 191 (1917), had established that mental suffering caused by an innkeeper-guest breach of contract could result in compensatory damages.

The second club case was Dewar v. Minneapolis Lodge, 192 N.W. 358 (Minn., 1923). The plaintiff, an Elk member, rented and occupied a room in the club for a monthly rental. When asked to leave he failed to vacate the room, whereupon his effects were removed and the room locked. The court said that the plaintiff was a lodger because the room was under the general control and supervision of the defendant club.

Ships

A ship that provides cabins or staterooms in which passengers deposit their baggage and rest during the voyage has an innkeeper's responsibilities to occupants and baggage. In Clark v. Burns, 118 Mass. 275 (1875), Chief Justice Gray expressed a minority view, saying that the liabilities of common carriers and innkeepers, although outwardly similar, are actually distinct. No one, he said, is subject to both liabilities at the same time with regard to the same property. The liability of an innkeeper extends only to goods put in his charge as keeper of a public house and does not compare to a carrier that is engaged only in the business of transportation. The ship could only be liable for negligence in breaching its duty to the passenger.

The majority view is given in Adams v. New Jersey, 45 N.E. 369, 151 N.Y. 163 (1896):

> The relations that exist between a steamboat company and its passengers, who have procured staterooms for their comfort during the journey, differ in no essential respect from those that exist between the innkeeper and his guests. . . . No good reason is apparent for relaxing the rigid rule of the common law which applied as between innkeeper and guest, since the same considerations of public policy apply to both relations.

Other Establishments

The question of whether a hospital may be considered an inn or hotel was answered in the negative in Hull Hospital v. Wheeler, 250 N.W. 637 (Iowa, 1933). In this case the hospital made claim to a ring when the patient died, on the assumption that they had a hotel lien on the goods of the deceased for services rendered. The court found that from very early times there has been a marked distinction between a hotel or inn and a hospital that cares for the sick and injured: A guest journeys to the hotel for entertainment, while the patient goes, or is carried, to the hospital for necessary treatment and nursing.

Another type of accommodation that has not always fallen under the laws of innkeeping is the health or pleasure resort. When they were solely for the purpose of health and pleasure and not for entertainment to punctuate a journey, resorts were not inns or hotels; therefore, they could reject guests at will. However, a house of public entertainment that is a hotel or inn does not lose its character merely because it happens to be located at a summer resort or watering place. Today, of course, the seasonal resort is as much a hotel as the year-round hotel and must adhere to the same laws except where ruled by a different set of regulations.

Apartment Hotels

An apartment hotel is a hotel that rents either furnished or unfurnished apartments for fixed periods. The manager of the hotel may or may not supply food and room service to occupants. However, the fact that a particular establishment is called and operated as an apartment hotel does not necessarily bring it within the definition of an inn or hotel. The facts of each case determine this. Nor is an apartment building that rents to more or less permanent occupants but also has rooms for transients necessarily classified as a hotel or inn. In such cases the building might be a hotel to transient occupants and a lodging house or an apartment house to its regular or permanent occupants.

Condominium Hotels

In the 1960s, a new form of accommodation came into vogue—the condominium. The condominium can assume many guises, depending on the desires of its investors. It can be a vacation apartment, an industrial park, a medical center, a second home, or a resort and hotel condominium.

What is different about a condominium when compared to a regular hotel or motel? First, of course, ownership differs from the general concept of land and apartment ownership. A condominium owner not only has exclusive ownership of a particular unit but also joint ownership with other unit owners of common elements, such as hallways, roadways, swimming pools, and golf greens.

There are many forms of condominium, collective, or cooperative ownership. In a collective form of condominium a plurality must vote on the disposition of a piece of property; a cooperative condominium to be sold or leased must be done with the approval of the other owners; a cooperative is owned and operated as an entity.

A condominium hotel, regardless of its location or name, is a hotel. Accordingly, all laws applicable to hotels mentioned here apply to condominium hotels, unless a statement is made to the contrary.

For a land developer (when acting only as a builder or real estate agency) and a condominium owner, the hotelier is the most acceptable party to manage the apartments, rooms, and complexes when the owners are not using them. The owners of condominiums, for the most part, do not want to be involved in the rather complicated business of running a resort hotel, which may include operating food and beverage services, pools, and golf courses. The condominium owners are willing to pay handsomely for this service.

Some of the larger hotel corporations have already employed condominium expansion to increase their holdings and to offer their management expertise to developers and condominium owners. Two factors have helped to bring about this kind of business enterprise. First is a desire on the part of many well-to-do persons to own a second home. Second, condominiums are an attractive investment in rental property (when not in use by the owner).

Today, most successful condominium hotel projects operate on some variation of the rental pool concept, a new management technique introduced in the early 1960s. Under the rental pool, the unit owners pledge their units for a set length of time to the development corporation or management company, which acts as a rental and management agent for a percentage of the gross or net receipts, or net profit. All income and expenses for the units are pooled, and the profits are prorated among the unit owners according to the size of the unit and availability for rental.

Condominium properties are generally protected by fences, guards who check all guests coming onto the property, alarm systems, and more security guards. It is not surprising, then, that few legal cases have come up related to this form of accommodation.

Time Sharing

The quest by entrepreneurs to find different methods of accommodating the vacationing public is limited only by the capabilities of the times and restrictions imposed by law. Since 1972, the concept of time sharing has grown in popularity in the United States. Time sharing is a method of owning another home but sharing that ownership with others. Today, time shares are offered as a means of purchasing houseboats, recreational vehicle campgrounds, yachts, sailboats, cruise ships, hotels and motels, as well as condominium vacation homes and apartments.

Most experts in the field agree that the primary reason that developers resorted to the sale of time shares instead of outright sales of their properties was the real estate recession in the early 1970s. People felt a general lack of confidence in the economy, inflation seemed rampant, interest rates had risen precipitously, and money was tight. Condominiums, especially those marketed as second homes, were not selling because of the cost factors. The advent of time sharing, however, opened the market to tens of thousands of people who could afford such ownership. From 1972 when the new concept was implemented until 1975, sales went from zero to $50 million. In 1980 sales of time shares surpassed $700 million.

In order to meet one of the major objections to the purchase of time shares—that is, that owners are tying themselves to the same vacation place for the same time period every year for an extended number of years—a new adjunct business was spawned. Firms in this business assist time-share owners in exchanging the time period they have at their location for an equal period of time belonging to another time sharer at another location and perhaps even for different times.

The concept of time sharing has ready application to hotels and resorts. For example, owners could easily adapt a certain number of rooms in their facility to the time-share concept and thereby improve their operating profits. The owners of an oceanfront motel at Laguna Shores in California converted thirty-four units into time shares in 1970. Within ten weeks they had sold 1,250 time shares, grossing over $10 million. Programs like this enable many people who could not afford a condominium or room or suite at a hotel to purchase instead a share of the total accommodation and thus obtain a vacation home.

Laws regarding time sharing are constantly changing and vary from state to state. In addition, certain laws are applicable depending upon the purchaser's form of time-sharing ownership.

Time-Share Ownership

The two basic forms of time sharing are ownership and nonownership. Time-share ownership provides purchasers with a fee simple conveyance—that is, a share of total ownership of the land and building with the right to sell or will such property to heirs upon the death of the owner. In addition, this method gives the purchaser an exclusive right of occupancy during designated time periods.

The ownership method of time sharing offers buyers the incentive of building equity or appreciation in the value of the unit. Consequently, a purchaser can generally obtain a mortgage to finance the time-share property. In addition to paying the initial purchase price, the buyer is also responsible for paying specified annual maintenance fees.

In law, this form of ownership is referred to as tenancy in common. Buyers have the right to sell and convey their rights in the property. Title, security, and other problems of ownership may occur, however. For example, the developer or original purchaser may first sell to people who have the same reasons for purchasing as all the others. Subsequent buyers, however, may lead different lifestyles or have very different ideas for the property's use.

When buyers purchase their share of a condominium complex or hotel-motel, with it is conveyed a percentage interest in the commonly owned property by executing an agreement known as the supplemental declaration of covenants, conditions, and restrictions. This agreement sets out the rights and duties of each individual tenant in common, the most important of which is the delineation of defined periods of exclusive occupancy. Through the use of the conveyance in tenancy in common and the supplemental declaration, the time-share developer creates a dual interest: an element of common ownership (the unit) and an element of individual ownership (the period of exclusive possession). The supplemental declaration is vital to the existence of this form of time sharing.

Time-Share Nonownership

Under the nonownership concept, the buyer purchases a right to occupy a specific accommodation for a specific time period over a specified number of years, usually ten to forty. The developer or building owner, not the purchaser, holds the title to the property. Because purchasers do not hold the title, they are unable to obtain mortgages to finance the "right to use."

Although the "right to use" or nonownership form of time sharing can be sold, willed, or given away, it is less valuable than actual ownership. Accordingly, it is less expensive to purchase. In addition, annual maintenance fees are usually less costly than with the ownership method of time sharing. To prevent potential problems with securities laws with the nonownership method, most developers stipulate that a purchaser's right to use may not be sold at a profit. Rentals are also usually forbidden.

Management Principles

In this chapter it becomes evident that legal definitions are important and in many instances crucial to the outcome of a case. A layperson may tend to think of a building in a preconceived way, but the legal definition of a building can have a vastly different effect on the outcome of a lawsuit.

Metzler v. Terminal Hotel Company

Should guests entering a hotel, motel, or restaurant ask, "Who owns this establishment?" Indeed, it would become ludicrous if customers had to pose this query each and every time they walked into a place of business. Although the *Metzler* case took place in 1909, the principles of law involved apply equally today:

1   A guest has the right to assume that all integral parts of a place of business belong to the named company. Without such a rule, it would be most difficult to carry on commerce.

2   The proposition that a hotel need not have a place where food is served is not in question. Only the question of real or apparent ownership is resolved, and the hotel is not allowed to argue that it does not own the restaurant.

3   Generally guests need not determine ownership of a hotel, motel, or tavern. That which is obvious or apparent will be assumed in the absence of strong evidence to the contrary. Therefore, when guests are entertained in a hotel, there is a presumption that the person or persons doing the entertaining are acting as hotelkeepers. The hotel in turn must provide sufficient proof to show that the place in question is not part of the hotel. The hotel can *implead* (bring someone else into lawsuit) the real owner of the place in question and, upon proof, be dropped as a party to the legal action.

4   All parts of an establishment, even though legitimately rented out to someone else, can be the hotelkeeper's responsibility. In the *Metzler* case, the establishment was in fact a hotel. Many cases discussed in this book will show the seriousness of this doctrine. An attorney should be consulted on any rental or use of the premises by an outside group. Insurance and a hold-blameless clause should, of course, be part and parcel of the contract that is signed by both the hotel and the outside group.

Brams v. Briggs

In the *Metzler* case, common law was the basis of the legal principle used to settle the case. *Brams* v. *Briggs*, however, adds a new dimension: the statute that defines the rights of hotelkeepers. In boarding houses and similar places, one contracts for accommodations, and generally the people using the facilities come from the neighborhood.

In *Brams* v. *Briggs*, the legislature has made a boarding house, lodging house, and rooming house equal to a hotel or inn for the purpose of the lien law. Without this statutory enactment, the boarding house keeper would have been at fault. No lien is available to a boarding house at common law.

The law of liens is now under serious attack because of the summary process that allows hotelkeepers to attach the property of guests without going through a legal process. (The law of liens is discussed in chapter 11.) In this and similar cases some legislatures have enacted laws that enlarge the old common law of inns. Boarding houses, lodging houses, and other named accommodations can and do have the right of summary process and a lien.

A lien, of course, is a very powerful weapon to be used against guests who do not pay. Persons acting in the capacity of a boarding house keeper or rooming house keeper should find out whether there is such a law in the state in which they are doing business; otherwise, they may find themselves guilty of larceny and other illegal acts.

McClean v. University Club

A private club is, by definition, a place that makes and abides by its own rules. As shown in *McClean* v. *University Club*, however, a club that has accommodations must be governed by the laws of hotelkeeping.

The *McClean* case is more pronounced evidence for the rule of law that any accommodation with the usual trappings of a hotel is for certain purposes a hotel, no matter what its name. As such, guests have certain rights, even though the club members must adhere to club rules.

Rights of a Guest

What is a hotel guest or a member guest entitled to when a valid guest relationship exists? Most of these rights are implied by law. These laws are not written down, but are part of the common law based on custom and usage.

1 Decent and humane treatment. In the event of illness, a hotel-keeper can remove a guest, but the removal is subject to proper precautions as to the guest's impaired health.

2 No abusive or insulting treatment by employees. The hotel is also responsible for the conduct of its manager within the scope of his employment.

3 Exclusive use of the room, subject to the hotelkeeper's right to enter to take care of the room, with due care taken by the hotelkeeper upon entering.

4 The right to expect the hotelkeeper to foresee potential injuries to a guest under certain conditions (see chapter 7).

5 The right to be protected from personal injuries, even though the guest's faculties might be impaired. Even though the exact form which the injury takes cannot be foreseen, as long as the injury sustained is natural and the probable consequence of an employee's action, the place of accommodation is held liable. This concept deals with the causal connection between the injury and the association that the employees have with the accident or injury.

6 The right to use mental suffering—a difficult concept to disprove—as grounds for recovery in a breach of contract case against a hotelkeeper. This has been accepted as precedent in most states, although it will be shown later that more state courts are allowing mental suffering as grounds for recovery in other areas of concern.

While guests are entitled to a certain degree of care during their stay at a hotel, the hotelkeeper, too, has certain rights. For example, hotelkeepers may remove guests who disturb the peace or conduct themselves in a manner that is offensive to other guests or that brings disrespect to the hotel. Hotelkeepers also have the right to make reasonable rules and to eject any guests who violate those rules. And although hotelkeepers are expected to protect guests from injury, they are under no legal obligation to secure a physician for a guest.

Condominiums

Condominiums are usually owned by people of wealth, whose jewelry, money, bonds, and other valuable items require safekeeping. For this purpose, safety deposit boxes are often provided for guests and condominium owners. Many such dwelling complexes also have guards and security checks of all incoming guests.

In April 1976, the safety deposit boxes of the Palm Beach Towers condominium were robbed of valuables worth between $3 million and $4 million. According to the police, the robbers were professionals who, familiar with the layout of the building, gained entrance by posing as food deliverymen. The condominium guards were easily overpowered by the threat of a gun.

If an apartment condominium has safety deposit boxes, the owners may not come under innkeepers' limiting liability statutes that usually apply to hotels. The relevant law should be researched to determine a condominium owner's responsibility.

As demonstrated in the Palm Beach Towers case, the delivery of food or parcels should be checked with the ordering party. The telephone operator should have checked with the apartment occupant to make sure that the food had actually been ordered. A standard operating procedure for such deliveries should be implemented and techniques developed to prevent similar robberies.

QUESTIONS FOR DISCUSSION

    1 What are the differences between a hotel and a boarding house? Is this difference important? Why?

    2 How does one legally become a guest of a hotel? A boarding house? A condominium?

    3 Is a private club with rooms for accommodating its members considered a hotel?

    4 What distinguishes a hotel guest from a tenant at a hotel that accepts both types of accommodation?

    5 Many condominiums operate under a rental pool system. Explain.

    6 What rights do guests have when they check into a hotel, motel, motor inn, or inn?

4 Contents

4 Requisites of a Hotel

*"It would be better to have no laws at all
than it is to have so many as we have."*

MONTAIGNE

The guest-innkeeper relationship is as hard to define as the words *inn* and *hotel*. It may mean one thing in remote and sparsely settled regions, another in a rural roadside tavern, and something else in the modern urban hotel. Many gradations of service, attention, convenience, and luxury make the relationship between innkeeper and guest one that must adapt to varying conditions and circumstances. But underneath all these differing conditions, a basic legal principle governs the general relationship of innkeeper and guest. Innkeepers are responsible for entertaining and maintaining the comfort of their guests. In the absence of a specific contract, the law implies that they will furnish entertainment according to the character of their inns and reasonable attention to the convenience and comfort of their guests (Odom v. East Avenue Corporation, 34 N.Y.S.2d 312 [1942]).

The courts recognize certain distinctive features of an inn or hotel. However, the status of such a place of public entertainment frequently must be determined from the circumstances of the case.

This chapter outlines the relationship between the innkeeper and the guest, focusing on the innkeeper's obligations. We discuss several facets of this responsibility, including the innkeeper's duty to accept all people, the quality of the accommodation provided, the length of the guest's stay, the need to serve food, and methods of payment.

Name and Physical Structure

Innkeepers cannot evade their responsibility by giving some name other than *inn* or *hotel* to their business. Consequently, neither the building nor the name by which the establishment is known controls its status as a hotel (Edward v. City of Los Angeles, 119 P.2d 370 [Cal., 1941]; Friedman v. Shindler's Prairie House, 230 N.Y.S. 44 [1928]; Weiser v. Albuquerque Oil and Gasoline Company, 325 P.2d 720 [N.M., 1958]; Woods v. Western Holding Corporation, 77 F. Supp. 90 [Mo., 1948]). In Edwards v. City of Los Angeles, 119 P.2d 370 (Cal., 1941), the court gave a broad interpretation of what constitutes an inn or hotel: "Structures placed side by side, or one in the rear of another, or in a circle or semi-circle, and frequently called inns or courts, do not lose their identity as hotels, rooming houses, or apartments merely by bestowing upon them a different appellation, if in fact they are used for lodging purposes if built of stone or steel, brick or wood, or of a framework of cloth, or whether mother earth constitutes the floor and the high heavens the ceiling, if in fact it is a place sufficiently defined in area, the letting or renting of which to guests, roomers, or lodgers is engaged in as a business."

Usually innkeepers use advertising to display the public character of their establishment. A sign is common evidence of the house's character, but it is not essential as an invitation to the public. In some form, no matter how quietly or unostentatiously, the owner of the house must hold himself out as being a public entertainer.

Duty to Accept All People

Early English common law recognized the duty to serve the public without discrimination in many areas. Today, the common law confines this duty to specific callings. Innkeepers, both under early principles set forth by the common law and by the Civil Rights Act of 1964 (Public Law 88, 88th Cong., HR 7152), are obliged to serve the public without discrimination.

Justice Depue in Delaware, Lackawanna, and Western Railroad Company v. Trautwein, 19 A. 178 (N.J., 1890), aptly described this obligation as "a duty imposed by law from considerations of public policy." Professor Wyman of Harvard University also stated that

> . . . the distinction between the private callings—the rule—and the public callings—the exception—is the most consequential division in the law governing our business relations. In private businesses, one may sell or not as one pleases, manufacture what qualities one chooses, demand any price that can be gotten, and give any rebates that are advantageous. . . . All this time in public businesses, one must serve all who apply without exclusive conditions, provide adequate facilities to meet all the demands of the consumer, exact only reasonable charges for the services that are rendered, and between customers under similar circumstances make no discriminations.[1]

1 Wyman, The Law of the Public Callings as a Solution of the Trust Problem, 17 H.L.R. 156 (1903).

Over the years the English inn was regarded as a quasi-public business. English judges interpreted the law in the interest of the general public, laying down the principle that an innkeeper could not refuse a weary traveler a room, except for very definite reasons. The problem of discrimination is further discussed in chapter 7, which also considers interstate commerce regulations and the duty to serve all persons in inns or hotels.

Conditions on Becoming a Hotel Guest

Minimum Stay

A well-established legal maxim that states one cannot do indirectly what one cannot do directly is relevant to the question whether a hotelkeeper can impose a minimum stay on prospective guests before accepting them as guests. In the previous section it was stated that hotelkeepers must accept all persons who come for accommodation because they conduct a quasi-public business. Granted, this duty is not without certain exceptions. No one would expect a hotelier to accept a guest who arrives with a dangerous animal, or someone with a contagious disease, or a person who wants to use the premises for illegal purposes. These examples and others are discussed more fully in chapter 11 under "Rights of the Hotelkeeper."

Before discussing whether a hotel can impose a minimum stay on a guest, it is conceded that a hotel can and does conduct more than one type of accommodation under one roof. For example, a resort hotel probably has the right to contract for a given period of time before accepting a guest. However, can a transient guest who is traveling—be it one mile or one thousand miles away from home—seeking accommodation for one night be refused?

Assuming that the place of accommodation is, in fact, a hotel as well as a boarding or lodging house, and a valid guest willing to pay the price wants to stay only for the night, he cannot be refused accommodation, even though a one-night stay could be less profitable for the hotel. Resort hoteliers and others argue that because the season is so short, they must accept only persons coming for a minimum stay of days to reduce the costs of operation and increase occupancy. This situation is precisely what the common law is intended to prevent—the refusal of a place to stay for the night to a weary traveler. If this requirement were not mandatory, various economic conditions might be imposed on the prospective guest by hoteliers bent on satisfying their financial status.

A published policy, such as advertising a minimum stay, is not controlling, and the hotelkeeper has to accept a valid traveler. Granted, a hotelkeeper and guest can bargain and contract as to the length of stay, especially for a vacation period. On the other hand, the hotelier can refuse transients if the hotel is filled. However, the refusal is a positive defense, and the defendant hotel must prove that it was full. In addition, states like Massachusetts provide by Article 104:7 of the General Law that "an innholder who, upon request, refuses to receive and make suitable provision for a stranger or traveler should be punished by a fine of not more than fifty dollars." Under the Civil Rights Act of 1964, the refusal of accommodation may be equated to a discriminatory practice (see chapter 7).

In summary, hotels and similar places may have a dual function as to accommodation possibilities when they act as hotels, motels, inns, or other places of accommodation. However, they do come under the common law prohibition against refusing valid travelers a one-night stay.

Legal Hotel Night

Because state hotel laws are inconsistent, the duration of the hotel night varies among establishments. Checkout times are usually clearly posted, but check-ins are often at the judgment of the desk clerk. Some hotels may charge part of an extra day's rent if the room is occupied several hours beyond the checkout time. There is, therefore, a need to establish the length of a legal night in a hotel. Possibly the hotel industry should consider the adoption of an agreement on whether the guest can be charged an extra day's occupancy if, through no fault of his own, he has only limited use of the facilities.

The right of hotelkeepers to set reasonable rules for guests' arrival or departure times seems well established. The problem is to determine what is reasonable. Is 8 AM a reasonable time to require guests to leave a hotel? Possibly not; however, it might not be too unreasonable to set an earlier departure hour in a motel than a hotel. This kind of ambiguity, if not settled by the industry itself, could be challenged by a guest and, unfortunately, settled by the courts. Yet, establishing an industry-wide checkout time is difficult because of such variations as location, season, quality of the hotel, and type of accommodation.

Time was central to an English case that could become significant to the American accommodations industry. In a recent ruling a crown court awarded nearly $5,000 in penalties against Clarkson's Holidays, a British tour firm, for advertising a fourteen-night package which, in fact, gave the client only thirteen full nights in the resort hotel (Ford v. Clarkson's Holidays, Ltd., 3 All. E.R. 454 [1971]). This case deals with the thorny problem of what constitutes a legal "bed night." The complainant checked in at the resort at 6 AM, although the normal night's occupancy for a hotel room started sometime in the afternoon. On the night of departure, the complainant had to give up his room after 6 PM, even though the tour's airport coach did not depart until 1 AM the following morning.

The verdict in this case holds wide implications for all industries advertising goods or services in brochures or catalogs. The complainant claimed that the day beginning with his 6 AM arrival constituted the first night of the holiday and that details on this matter were clearly stated elsewhere in the brochure, of which roughly 3 million copies were issued annually.

The airlines have established some ground rules on this troublesome question, and the International Air Traffic Association's Breaches Commission once fined an international carrier for advertising a twenty-one day tour as twenty-two days by claiming the day of departure as the extra day.

Quality of Accommodations

Are all places of accommodation the same? Obviously there are basic differences between the Plaza or the Pierre in New York City and a small hotel in a New England town. Should the type or quality of accommodation affect the type of care guests may expect and receive? The general rule that most states apply obliges innkeepers to use reasonable care, commensurate with the quality of the accommodations offered, to see that guests are not abused, injured, or insulted by hotel employees.

In the case of Tobin v. Slutsky, 506 F.2d 1097 (New York, 1974), Mr. Tobin and his family paid approximately $500 for a week at what was advertised as a "family resort" with supervised activities for children and teenagers, and where his fifteen-year-old daughter was assaulted by a hotel employee. In this case the court construed reasonable care in a first-class family resort to mean a high degree of care. Indeed, the court in applying New York law to this diversity of action suit interpreted this care to be exceptionally great. (A diversity of action or a diversity of jurisdiction suit takes place in a federal rather than a state court when the plaintiff is a resident of one state and the defendant a resident of another. The federal court applies the substantive law of the state in which the case takes place.)

In summary, then, it becomes obvious that a hotel is held to varying degrees of care, depending on the quality of accommodations offered. Consequently, the higher the quality, the greater the care required.

Hotel with a Double Character

A hotel may conduct several businesses under the same roof. The legal relationship between the parties involved will vary on the nature of the business. Consequently, everyone patronizing hotel facilities does not necessarily become a "guest" of the establishment within the technical meaning of that term. (A guest is a transient person who obtains accommodations at a hotel, motel, inn, or similar establishment.) A casual patron of a hotel barbershop, a purchaser of a newspaper from a hotel newsstand, or a person who uses the pay telephone in the hotel lobby by virtue of such patronage is not a hotel guest in a technical sense.

A hotel proprietor may be a technical "innkeeper" with relation to certain patrons and a "boarding house keeper" to others (Albaugh v. Wolverton, 36 S.E.2d 906 [Va., 1946]; see 28 Am. Jur., Innkeepers #20, p. 21; 14 Ruling Case Law 495 and cases cited therein; Walling v. Potter, 35 Conn. 183 [1868]). Thus, when a hotelier operates a restaurant for the accommodation of his guests and the general public, he may be an innkeeper to some of his patrons and a restaurateur to others. Clearly, a patron of a restaurant open to the general public should not be entitled to greater privileges or subject to greater liabilities merely because the establishment is operated by one who also operates a hotel, rather than one who furnishes only food to his customers. In either case the customer seeks only restaurant service.

However, the rule that many businesses may be conducted on hotel premises is not without exception, especially as it pertains to hotel safety deposit boxes. Although a guest may use a hotel safety deposit box in a similar fashion as a bank vault, the hotel or inn is not a substitute for a bank (Oxford Hotel Co. v. Lind, 107 P. 222 [Colo., 1910]). Guests may deposit valuables, including money, in a hotel safe, and it is considered incidental to their stay at the inn.

If we assume that a hotel can be many things to different people, what happens when a valid guest comes into the hotel and then the relationship changes? Are there criteria by which this change can be determined? The case of Asseltyne v. Fay Hotel, 23 N.W.2d 782 (Ohio, 1946), deals with this situation. In this case the plaintiff lost her belongings in a hotel fire and contended that she was a transient guest entitled to recovery. However, she had contracted with the hotel for special, long-term rates, she paid her bill monthly, and she was a permanent resident of the city. Therefore, she was considered to be a lodger, not a guest.

According to the court, the business of a hotel and a boarding house can be carried on in the same building. The legal hotelkeeper-guest relationship consequently depended on the specific arrangement between the hotel and guest. Because the plaintiff was first a hotel guest and then later a lodger, the burden of proof was on her to prove the defendant was negligent. On appeal, the judgment was affirmed for the defendant.

Distance Traveled, Length of Stay, and Transiency

Although some early cases restricted the innkeeper-guest relationship to persons coming from a distance and excluded residents of the town in which the hotel or inn was situated, modern cases place no such limitation on guests. Hence, local residents may be guests at an inn, however slight the distance from home, and receive transient entertainment.

The court in New Southern Hotel Company v. Kingston, 72 N.E.2d 782 (Ohio, 1936), said that the courts "must take cognizance of the changed relation between the inn as known at common law and its successor, the modern hotel. At the inn there would be accommodated those who traveled and remained there but a few nights. The modern hotel has as its guests those who are accommodated overnight and those who may prolong their stay for months. The business of guests who register at a hotel may require that they remain in the city where it is located for considerable periods of time. They may be nonresidents and their business such that they move about from one city to another, remaining in each place for varying times."

When does a guest who comes as a transient change status from guest to lodger, boarder, or roomer? A transient person is one who has come to the inn or hotel for a more or less temporary stay. This person is free to come and go at will. If he is transient, he may become a guest in a legal sense even if there is an express monetary contract between him and the innkeeper, though one of the distinctive features of the relationship is that a guest is received under an implied contract.

A criterion used by the courts to determine the intention of the guest to change his status to boarder or tenant is the amount of furniture that he keeps in his room. For example, moving in a piano indicates an intention to make more than a temporary stay at a hotel. A piano, the court has said, is usually not taken to a hotel by transient guests (Hart v. Mills Hotel Trust, 258 N.Y.S. 417 [1932]). Generally, the length of time that a person stays at an inn makes no difference. But a residence of seventeen months in a hotel could change the relationship between the innkeeper and guest, according to the court, although no definite time was fixed (Hancock v. Rand, 94 N.Y. 1 [1883]; Davidson v. Madison Corporation, 247 N.Y.S. 789 [1931]).

In the following case, *Chawla v. Horch*, an individual renting a room for an extended period of time with a lease attempted to prove he was a hotel guest. The court held he was not entitled to this ruling because of the method used in engaging the room. However, in the *Levesque* case discussed later, which had similar facts, the effect of being a guest brought the limiting liability statutes into play. Although the guest won her case she received only a fraction of her total loss.

Case	Chawla v. Horch
Example	*333 N.Y.S.2d 531 (1972)*
	(BENTLEY KASSAL, Judge)

Plaintiff was a resident at the Master Hotel, located on Riverside Drive in Manhattan and had resided there since September 22, 1971, under a written lease. His Small Claims action was against the hotel for the loss of personal property presumably stolen from his room.

The lease, which was a standard printed form, referred to the lease of "Apartment #615" for an eleven month period commencing September 22, 1971, at a monthly rental of $150. Among the clauses in this lease was the standard paragraph providing that the landlord was only liable for damage or injury resulting from the negligence of the landlord or its employees (par. 15th).

Although not specified in the lease, the landlord provided some "hotel" services, such as maid service and telephone switchboard, both included in the rental. The maid, who cleaned daily, had access to this apartment through a key retained by the housekeeper.

On March 6, 1972, after the tenant had been there for about six months, he returned to his room to discover that numerous items of personal property were missing, including a radio, camera, clock, a number of coins and a fur cap.

At common law, the liability of an insurer was imposed on an innkeeper to protect travelers who, while on their journey, had stopped in transit for food and lodging.

This protection was no longer afforded a guest if he entered into a special contract with the innkeeper which changed his status from that of a hotel "guest" to a boarder or lodger.

A key case concerning the applicability of the innkeeper's liability rule to those residing in hotels is Hackett v. Bell Operating Co., Inc., 169 N.Y.S. 114. Plaintiff in that case occupied a suite of rooms in the Hotel Netherland in Manhattan under a written lease for six months. Some tennis trophies were stolen from his suite while he was absent and he sought to invoke the innkeeper's liability rule, maintaining that he was a guest entitled to such protection. The court disagreed and ruled that he was a roomer or lodger to whom the landlord only owed the duty to exercise reasonable care. It was held . . . that the innkeeper's liability "exists only in the case of one who is a *traveler* and seeks the hospitality of the inn as a transient guest" (emphasis added).

A review of the numerous decisions in this field demonstrates that there are many factors to be considered in making the distinction between a guest and a tenant or lodger. Among these are how long the occupant is residing there and for what purpose, whether there is a written or oral lease, what rights and duties are set forth therein, what services are provided by the hotel management, whether rent is paid daily, weekly or monthly, what kind of furnishings are in the premises and to whom they belong, whether possessions of the occupant indicate an intention on his part to be there for a temporary or more lasting period.

Viewing the case at bar in the light of these criteria, I conclude that the plaintiff is not a guest, to be treated like a transient or traveler at an inn, but rather is a tenant on a regular and permanent basis.

The effect of this rule is that the management of a hotel, probably even this one, will have different responsibilities to occupants, depending upon their status, even where such persons occupy identical accommodations. Nevertheless, this is completely consistent with the rationale behind the common law rule imposing liability.

Therefore, since there was no negligence on the part of the defendant and since plaintiff was not a "guest" in defendant's hotel, judgment will be entered for the defendant dismissing the complaint herein.

Ruling of the Court: For defendant Horch, d/b/a Master Hotel.

In Levesque v. Columbia Hotel, 44 A.2d 728 (Me., 1945), the plaintiff, a long-term resident, had deposited $4,850 in the hotel safe. The safe was subsequently robbed, and the plaintiff lost her money. The jury affirmed her action to recover the sum; however, even though the defendant may have been negligent in his care of the money, a hotel-guest relationship existed and thus the hotel's liability was limited to $300.

The defendant brought the motion for a new trial on the grounds of improper instructions to the jury. The earlier court had defined the word *guest* too narrowly. The appeals court held that a guest was not only a transient, but anyone (even a long-term resident) who occupied a room in a hotel registered as others did, received maid service, and had the benefit of the other incidental hotel services. The defendant's case was affirmed on a motion for a new trial.

Food Service

Originally, an inn or a hotel was required to provide transients with lodging, food, drink, and accommodations for stabling their horses. Now it is no longer necessary that food, drink, and garage accommodations be furnished (Shermer v. Fremar Corp., 114 A.2d 757 [N.J., 1955]). A hotel is essentially an establishment that provides lodging for transients. However, there are a few jurisdictions where the decisions are to the contrary (Dixon v. Robbins, 246 N.Y. 169, 158 N.E. 63 [1927]; Appeal of Wellsboro Hotel Co., 2 A.2d 334 [Pa., 1939]; however, in Armwood v. Francis, 340 P.2d 88 [Utah, 1959] it is dictum). There are also jurisdictions where statutes expressly state that food must be a requirement for an inn or hotel (Atwater v. Sawyer, 76 Me. 538, Am.Rep. 634 [1884]).

Several types of problems come up under the requirement of serving food. The first problem, of course, is whether this requirement is a condition precedent—that is, whether a hotel can be considered a hotel if it does not serve food. In the absence of a statute requiring absolutely that food be served, Kraus v. Birns, 241 N.Y.S.2d 189 (N.Y., 1963), holds that changing times no longer require such services.

A second problem deals with the statutory requirement of serving food as a condition of obtaining a license for the hotel to contract out its food and liquor operation. The next case, *Thacher Hotel, Inc., v. Economos,* addresses this problem. A hotel can use this method of providing food and alcoholic beverages to its guests and still be considered a hotel under the statute requiring food to be served. This case has a double significance to management in that it reviews the type of contract that should be used and the provisions that should be included to avoid a possible lawsuit by the contractee. (See original case for these provisions.)

Case	**Thacher Hotel, Inc., v. Economos**
Example	*197 A.2d 59 (Me., 1964)*
	(WILLIAMSON, Chief Justice)

On appeal. This is an action on a "management contract" between the plaintiff corporation and the defendant relating to the operation of dining rooms in the plaintiff's hotel. The defense is that the contract was illegal in light of the liquor licensing statute, and hence the plaintiff may not recover thereon.

The case was heard in the Superior Court upon an agreed statement of facts. The defendant admits (assuming the legality of the contract) the claims of the plaintiff for minimum payments and expenses incurred for sales, social security, state and federal unemployment and withholding taxes for which judgment was entered for $1267.77 with interest and costs.

For the period in question in 1958, and indeed from the commencement of the "management contract" in 1955, the plaintiff held and exercised a hotel license as a bona fide hotel for the sale of liquor for consumption on the premises. The pertinent provisions of R.S. c. 61, entitled "Laws Relating to Liquor" are:

"§ 1. Definitions. . . . 'Hotel' shall mean any reputable place operated by responsible persons of good reputation, where the public, for a consideration, obtains sleeping accommodations and meals under one roof and which has a public dining room or rooms operated by the same management open and serving food during the morning, afternoon and evening, and a kitchen, apart from the public dining room or rooms, in which food is regularly prepared for the public on the same premises."

"§ 42. Licenses for consumption sale. Licenses for the sale of spirituous and vinous liquor to be consumed on the premises where sold may be issued to clubs and to bona fide hotels. . . ."

The argument of the defendant in substance is: (1) that the plaintiff under the "management contract" with the defendant did not have "a public dining room or rooms *operated by the same management*" (emphasis supplied); (2) that the plaintiff, for this reason alone, was not a bona fide hotel and so was not entitled to a liquor license; (3) that the "management contract" thus dealt with an unlawful enterprise; and (4) that public policy denies recovery thereon.

The key words in the controversy are "operated by the same management." The decision turns upon the meaning of these words in the statute, and their application to the "management contract" as we construe its terms.

Before discussing the facts and the contract in detail we may eliminate certain questions from consideration.

First—As we shall see, there is nothing whatsoever inherently wrongful or unlawful about the "management contract." If it were not for the applicability of the liquor law, liability of the defendant would not be questioned. In such case it would be immaterial whether management of the dining room was in the plaintiff corporation or the defendant.

Second—The "management contract" was unquestionably entered into with the operation of dining rooms to meet the requirement of the liquor laws in the minds of the parties. In short, the contract was in furtherance of the operation of the hotel with a liquor license.

Third—If the contract was in furtherance of an unlawful purpose, that is, to obtain a liquor license by subterfuge with management of the dining rooms *not* in the plaintiff, it would be an illegal contract on which plaintiff could not recover. . . .

A contract in furtherance of obtaining a hotel liquor license unlawfully is plainly against our public policy. That such a contract may not be in direct contravention of a statute does not lessen the force of the public policy against its enforcement.

Fourth—"The law leaves the parties to an illegal contract 'where it finds them.' " Jolovitz v. Redington & Co., Inc., 148 Me. p. 29, 88 A.2d p. 592. The public policy, expressed in law, is designed not to protect the defendant as here from an apparently improvident bargain, but to deter others from entering into like illegal contracts.

We are not concerned with our conception of fairness between the parties. The defendant does not deny that she owes the plaintiff what it claims under the contract. She does no more than say that the power of the State is not available to the plaintiff to establish its claim and to enforce judgment thereon.

Fifth—To invalidate a contract on the ground of public policy, the "impropriety of a transaction," to use Professor Williston's words, must be clearly established. 5 Williston, supra, § 1629A. Our Court in Bell v. Packard, 69 Me. 105, in which the issue was whether Maine or Massachusetts law controlled, said, 69 Me. at p. 111: ". . . no contract must be held as intended to be made in violation of the law, whenever by any reasonable construction it can be made consistent with the law. . . ."

"In general and unless restrained by valid statutes, competent persons have the utmost liberty of making contracts. Agreements voluntarily made between such persons are to be held sacred and enforced by the courts, and are not to be lightly set aside on the ground of public policy or because as events have turned it may be unfortunate for one party. . . ."

From our study of the contract we are satisfied that within the meaning of Section 1 of the statute the plaintiff, that is to say "the same management," operated the dining rooms in the Thacher Hotel and was a "hotel" for licensing purposes.

In so construing the contract, we give effect to the intentions of the parties, which surely were to enter into an arrangement permissible under the licensing laws. The defendant has failed at the least to establish clearly any impropriety compelling the invalidation of the contract on grounds of public policy.

There are in the contract certain provisions often found in employment contracts and others often found in lessee or independent contractor transactions. Taken as a whole, having in mind the purpose of the contract we conclude that the plaintiff retained effective management of the dining rooms. *Webster's New International Dictionary* (second edition) defines "management" as "The collective body of those who manage or direct any enterprise or interest; the board of managers." The defendant in his capacity as "food manager" was not unlike a department or store manager, or the manager of a baseball club. His power and authority, unquestionably broad, do not deny an employer-employee relationship with the plaintiff.

It is significant that the dining rooms were conducted in the name of and as an integral part of the plaintiff's hotel, and that the plaintiff recognized its full and complete responsibility for their operation. The present action was brought in part to recover for taxes paid on goods purchased and employees' wages arising from the "food operation."

The provisions for compensation by which the plaintiff received a percentage of gross income with a minimum guarantee and the defendant received the balance, and bore the losses, if any, do not compel the conclusion that the defendant was not under the direction, control or management of the plaintiff. The minimum guarantee and loss provisions would no doubt more likely arise in a lease or independent contractor situation. It does not follow, however, that if the parties otherwise intend, we may give effect to their contract. We must not lose sight of the provisions for employment of the defendant with the careful restrictions in the use of the "food income," and the full and complete responsibility of the plaintiff for the operation of the hotel in its several departments.

The Thacher Hotel, that is the plaintiff corporation, met without challenge on this record the strict requirement that it is a "reputable place operated by responsible persons of good reputation." It chose to give broad authority to a "food manager." It did not, however, give up or transfer, or lose its "management" of the dining rooms and thereby fail to qualify for the license so obviously a vital part of the business enterprise.

The plaintiff did not inform the Commission of the contract with the defendant in making its application for a hotel license. The defendant urges that it therefore failed to disclose "the complete and entire ownership or any interest in the establishment." . . . Whether the plaintiff failed in this respect is a matter for the determination of the State Liquor Commission and not of the courts in a collateral proceeding.

We do not attempt to establish or to indicate the precise meaning of "operated by the same management" in Section 1 of the statute. We limit our opinion to the facts before us. Public policy does not here require that the defendant escape responsibility for carrying out the terms of her contract.

Ruling of the Court: For plaintiff Thacher Hotel in that the management contract abided by the Maine definition of a hotel. The court did not take up the second point of the liquor license.

This section has shown that hotelkeepers must meet certain requisites in hotel-guest relationships. The next section is a discussion of another important part of that relationship—the various types of payment for services.

Methods of Payment

As a condition of accepting a guest, a hotel may require prepayment. This requisite can be important. A significant problem for hotels, restaurants, and other service establishments is how guests pay for goods and services. Legal tender—so-called fiat money, hard cash, or greenbacks— appears to be the most reliable form of payment and must be accepted by the merchant for payment of charges accrued during the patron's stay. If counterfeit money is passed, the merchant must reimburse the bank at full value, if discovered. Any action by the merchant to recover for the counterfeit money is against the guest who passed the bills.

What is money? Or, put another way, what should businesses accept for payment of goods and services? This section shows that basically there are three kinds of money: commodity money, fiat money, and credit money.

The monetary value of *commodity money* approximates the value of the material it contains. The best example is a gold coin, which, when cashed, can bring its value in the market. Guests seldom, if ever, pay bills in gold or any other precious metal.

Money by government command is designated *fiat money*—for example, paper money and coins. The value of all fiat money is independent of the material from which it is made, as well as independent of any promise of redemption in other money. Paper money is merely the form in which most of the other kinds of money circulate.

All credit instruments, such as checks, credit cards, money orders, and traveler's checks, accepted in payment for goods, services, and debts *without reference to the standing of the person tendering them* are called *credit money*. It is a promise to pay money and therefore presupposes another kind of money that may be redeemed. Quick and easy redemption is the key to its general acceptability. If no barriers are placed in the way of its redemption, it has the same value as fiat money. The three most widely used types of credit monies in paying for goods and services in a hotel, restaurant, or service establishment are personal checks, traveler's checks, and credit cards.

Personal Checks

The personal check is probably the most common and most extensively used form of all negotiable instruments. A check is an order on a bank to pay a sum of fiat money to the holder of the check. The signer or drawer of a check must have enough money in the bank to equal or exceed the face value of the check. Here lies the problem. In view of the possibility that deposited funds may be insufficient to cover a personal check, must a hotel or restaurant accept personal checks for payment of goods and services? Since it is recognized that some hotel customers do pass or "utter" checks with insufficient bank funds, a hotel or restaurant need not accept personal checks for goods and services rendered. However, when an establishment has this policy, it must give notice of its intent not to accept personal checks so that its guests may make other arrangements to pay their account.

Notice can be given when the desk clerk asks how the guest intends to pay for the charges. At that time the guest may be told that personal checks are not acceptable, if that is the policy of the company, or on what terms the hotel will accept a personal check.

Traveler's Checks

A traveler's check is sold by certain banks and corporations specializing in this type of business. Once a traveler's check is sold by a bank or express company, payment is guaranteed. The traveler's check business is a very large industry. In 1980 total sales were over 35 billion a year and growing 13 to 15 percent annually. With this exposure there are bound to be thefts. American Express has said it pays tens of millions of dollars a year in refunds for lost checks and that as high as 50 percent is due to theft. Added to this problem is the widespread counterfeiting of traveler's checks.

What requirements exist for use of traveler's checks? Traveler's checks must be endorsed by the holder in the presence of the cashier. If this signature matches that already on the check, the merchant will accept it and will not be held responsible if the second signature is a forgery, providing it is a good one. Cashiers should follow simple precautions for cashing traveler's checks:

1   The traveler's check should be countersigned in the cashier's presence, preferably with the cashier's pen (invisible ink that lasts only a few hours has been used).

2   The traveler's check holder should fill in the date and the party to whom the check is assigned (in the place marked "pay to order of").

3   A reasonable attempt should be made to compare signatures.

4   If in doubt, the cashier should ask for a driver's license or other identification.

5   If information is available on stolen traveler's checks, the cashier should see if the check can be identified as stolen.

6   The cashier should check the list of lost or stolen traveler's checks.

Credit Cards

One of the most significant recent commercial developments has been the use of the credit card as a substitute for money. In 1977 an estimated 712 million credit-debit-check guarantee cards were used worldwide. The United States accounted for over 586 million cards and Canada for over 34 million. The average American carries 5.2 plastic cards for credit or check cashing, and this statistic is expected to increase to 8.4 within seven years. With such a vast number of credit cards in circulation, honoring cards without requiring additional identification makes credit card fraud a relatively easy form of larceny.

Credit cards are offered by American Express, the Diners Club, Carte

Blanche, and other companies, as well as by all the major oil companies. In what is generally referred to as the three-party credit card system, a contract exists between the issuer of the card and the holder. The holder of the card agrees to pay the issuer for all credit purchases (in one lump sum at the next billing date, or on a time payment basis). In addition, a series of contracts are made between the issuer of the card and numerous retail merchants, motels, restaurants, and other business establishments, agreeing to purchase the amount of their credit card sales—or "charges"— on a weekly or monthly basis. If the issuer is an independent credit card company, it may purchase these charges at discounts ranging from 3 percent to as high as 10 percent.

Almost all the bank credit card systems currently in operation in this country rely on a three-way transaction between the card issuer, the cardholder, and a subscribing retailer. This arrangement basically entails three separate contractual agreements: (1) one between the bank issuing the credit card and the individual cardholder; (2) one between one of the banks in the system and a local merchant; and (3) one between the merchant and the cardholder. In a two-party credit card arrangement in which only the merchant extends credit, the system is basically an accounts receivable system. However, the large oil companies that allow their cards to be used by many types of merchants basically employ a tripartite credit card system similar to a bank's.

Because the legal relationship between the parties is dictated by the terms of their respective agreements, the contract governs the distribution of risk for credit card frauds between the merchant and the issuer. Under most systems, with certain exceptions for negligence on the part of merchants—for example, if they honor an expired card or one appearing on the current "stop list," or if they make a sale for an amount in excess of the cardholder's credit line—the issuer assumes all risks for frauds. Merchants are in the same financial and legal position as if they were receiving certified checks on a bank that does not clear at par, with no risk that checks will be returned or payment stopped, or as if they were receiving checks at a small discount for the bank's services. Under these arrangements, the card-issuing bank takes all the credit risk, which is appropriate to the banking function it performs; the cardholder selects the merchant with whom to deal; and the bank and the cardholder-purchaser expect the merchant to assume the merchandise risk.

The merchant or hotel, restaurant, or motel operator can, under certain conditions, be held responsible for specific types of inappropriate decisions about the use of traveler's checks and credit cards. In the case of Wood v. Holiday Inns, Inc., 508 F.2d 167 (Ala., 1975), a desk clerk acted improperly by investigating the credit rating of the guest when there was no reason to do so. (Gulf allows a $150 credit without contacting higher authority.) What might have prompted this unnecessary investigation by the night auditor? Possibly it was the customary granting of a reward by the credit card company to a person reporting a credit card that was found to be no longer valid, forged, or counterfeit. In any event, the *Wood* case was very costly for all parties. Parts of the case have been rewritten for student clarity.

Case	**Wood v. Holiday Inns, Inc.**
Example	*508 F.2d 167 (Ala., 1975)*
	(LEWIS R. MORGAN, Circuit Judge)

The plaintiff, Glen L. Wood, was a traveler and guest of a Holiday Inn situated in Phenix City, Alabama. The defendants were Jessie Goynes, night clerk at Holiday Inn; Interstate Inns, Inc., franchisee of Holiday Inns, Inc., Tennessee, operating in Phenix City, Alabama, but incorporated in South Carolina; Holiday Inns, Inc., Tennessee, franchisor of Holiday Inns; and Gulf Oil Corporation, a Pennsylvania corporation authorized to handle credit transactions of all Holiday Inns. Innocent participants in this case were National Data Processing, Inc., the company Gulf used to take care of its billing service and the credit manager of Gulf Oil who reviewed the standing of Wood and ordered his credit terminated.

This case arose from circumstances surrounding denial of credit to the plaintiff, Glen L. Wood, a guest of a franchised Holiday Inn in Phenix City, Alabama. The defendant, Goynes, was the night clerk on duty at the local Holiday Inn and was a resident of the State of Alabama. The local Holiday Inn was not owned or operated by the defendant, Holiday Inns, Inc., but was franchised to and owned and operated by the defendant, Interstate Inns, Inc., a South Carolina corporation. Interstate Inns held a franchise agreement from the defendant, Holiday Inns, Inc., a Tennessee corporation, to operate the local Holiday Inn in Phenix City and to use the name, Holiday Inn, and policies of Holiday Inns, Inc., in such operation for a small percentage of the profits.

The Gulf Oil Corporation, a Pennsylvania corporation, by virtue of a contract with Holiday Inns, Inc., was authorized to handle all credit transactions of all Holiday Inns, whether owned by Holiday Inns, Inc., or by some franchise, all credit being established with Gulf Oil, the bills being charged to and paid to Gulf Oil, and Gulf Oil paying the various inns the amounts due them in consideration of an assignment of said credit and a small percentage of the credited items. This court has jurisdiction by virtue of diversity of citizenship and the requisite jurisdictional amount.

On the evening before the morning in question, the plaintiff checked into the defendant Inn at Phenix City and submitted his Gulf credit card for the purpose of having it imprinted on a credit memorandum of the motel. After the imprint was taken, the card was returned to him, and he retired. While the evidence was in conflict as to the transactions between the plaintiff and the defendant Goynes on the following morning, there was evidence from which the jury might have found, and apparently they did find, the following: That, at 5:00 AM the following morning the defendant Goynes called the plaintiff's room, awakened the plaintiff from his repose, and informed him that he would like to obtain the plaintiff's credit card for the purpose of making an imprint on a credit memorandum of the motel as the imprint made the night before was indistinct, and another imprint was needed; that after some conversation it was agreed that Goynes take the card, secure the imprint, and return it within a few minutes to the plaintiff; that some thirty minutes later, the plaintiff, not having resecured his card and feeling that for some purpose someone had fraudulently secured his card, the plaintiff dressed and went to the front desk and was informed by the defendant Goynes that his credit had been revoked and that Goynes had telegraphic authority from National Data Processing, Inc., a computerizing service for defendant Gulf Oil, to pick up the plaintiff's card and terminate his credit. It was conceded that Goynes obtained the credit card and asked the plaintiff to arrange to pay his bill in cash.

The credit manager of Gulf Oil testified that, on the previous day, he had reviewed the credit file of the plaintiff; had found that the plaintiff had been charging in ever-increasing amounts on his Gulf credit card; that he had during the current month paid to Gulf a substantial bill and charged to Gulf another bill which charges almost equaled the plaintiff's total monthly income; that in the last three months the plaintiff had paid his bill more than thirty days after the time the bill was sent to him; and that these facts caused him to suspect that the plaintiff would soon be unable to pay his Gulf account. He, therefore, ordered the credit terminated and the card revoked or picked up.

The method for terminating the credit and picking up the card was that, on order of Gulf, National Data Processing sent out a communication to all Gulf agents and all desk clerks of Holiday Inns, in short, those most likely to come into contact with such credit cards, a list of all credit cards revoked and asked them to secure possession thereof for Gulf for a reward to be paid by Gulf. Suggestions as to how such cards might tactfully be repossessed had been sent out by Gulf, and there was no evidence that Gulf authorized use of rudeness or false pretenses in securing the credit cards.

After repossession of the card, the defendant Goynes was paid by Gulf a reward for the same.

There was evidence that the credit file of Gulf included information received from a credit bureau in Tupelo, Mississippi, showing that the plaintiff had a good credit rating and no derogatory matter showed in the report from Tupelo. Other information contained in the Gulf credit file included information given Gulf by the plaintiff when he made application for credit and times, amounts, and dates of charges and credits to said account received from Gulf's own credit records.

The plaintiff brought suit against Goynes, Interstate Inns, Inc., Holiday Inns, Inc., and Gulf Oil Corporation and recovered judgments of $25,000.00 actual damages against Gulf, $25,000.00 punitive damages against Interstate Inns, Inc., and Jessie Goynes, and $10,000.00 punitive damages against Holiday Inns, Inc. The jury further found that defendants Goynes and Interstate Inns should have judgment over against Gulf Oil for the $25,000.00 punitive damages, the liability which they incurred in executing the alleged agency of Gulf in revoking the credit card.

All defendants made motions for judgments notwithstanding the verdict. Defendants Goynes and Interstate made a motion for new trial, and the plaintiff made a motion for a judgment in conformance with the verdict.

At any rate, Wood's anger and frustration continued to build. Three days later, while he was relating the incident to a friend, he had a heart attack, precipitated apparently by the stress of the incidents surrounding the revocation of credit.

Naturally in such a case, with as many defendants all having formidable general counsels, there were appeals, all types of motions, as well as a judgment notwithstanding the verdict allowed by the district judge who heard the case. Although Wood won on certain parts of his case, a part was supposed to go back for retrial. That part was never retried, probably because of the cost of a retrial. But more important, the appeals court already had laid down what the law would be. In any case, if the case had been retried, the lower court would have had the appeals court decisions to abide by: remanded for proceedings not inconsistent with this opinion.

The first point of law that came up during the trial was: Were Wood's rights violated under the Fair Credit Reporting Act, 15 U.S.C. #1681–1681t (1974)? This act charges consumer reporting agencies with certain responsibilities especially when credit is denied, stating that the person must be notified and supplied with the name and address of the consumer reporting agency making the report. If violated, charges could be brought against Gulf in a civil suit. The section involved, 15 U.S.C. 1681m(a), reads as follows:

"Whenever credit or insurance for personal, family, or household purposes, or employment involving a consumer is denied or the charge for such credit or insurance is increased either wholly or partly because of information contained in a consumer report from a consumer reporting agency, the user of the consumer report shall so advise the consumer against whom such adverse action has been taken and supply the name and address of the consumer reporting agency making the report."

The district court held that there was no evidence that Wood was damaged by Gulf's failure to report the name and address of the reporting agency. Wood renews his argument on appeal, contending that if Gulf had informed him promptly of its decision to terminate his credit, the incident at the Holiday Inn would have been avoided.

Apparently, the only requirement placed upon a "user" of a credit report is the duty to disclose the name and address of the reporting agency when credit is denied (15 U.S.C. § 1681m). There is no evidence that the actions of Goynes or the reaction of Wood would have been any different if Wood had been told at the time his credit card was withdrawn that Gulf held a favorable credit report from the Tupelo reporting agency.

We need not base our decision upon the timing of the notification, however, for there is no indication that Gulf relied upon this report in making its decision to revoke Wood's credit. Gulf certainly had a credit report in its possession, but there is uncontradicted testimony that this report played no part in Gulf's decision. Of course, the jury would normally be free to disregard the denials of a company holding a credit report that it used the report in evaluating a consumer.

Here, however, there was simply nothing in the consumer report which could have caused Gulf to terminate Wood's credit. Not only was all of the information contained in the report already in Gulf's possession, but the only inference that one could draw from the report was favorable to Wood. Indeed the condition which caused the termination of credit— Wood's monthly income in relation to the charges on his account—was in no way conveyed by the report. Hence, we feel that the district judge properly dismissed the cause of action based upon the "user" provision of the Fair Credit Reporting Act.

The second point of law is more involved and asks a serious question as to liability. Was Goynes the agent of Gulf when he seized the credit card or was there just a guest-innkeeper relationship? The court characterized Wood's complaint as an allegation that his injury had been caused by a breach of the common law duty of the innkeeper to his guests. Since there was no evidence that Gulf had acted as an innkeeper in this case, the lower court absolved Gulf of any liability. Alternatively, the judge held that there was no substantial evidence that Goynes acted as the agent of Gulf when he seized the card.

In any case the jury is the final arbiter in most of these points. Note, as you read, the relationship of Goynes with Gulf, with Interstate, and of course with Holiday Inns, Inc., Tennessee. Also note the mistake Wood made in suing both in torts and the common law guest-innkeeper relationship. Only one of these could be used.

Wood stipulated at the pre-trial hearing of October 4, 1973, that one of his allegations was based upon the breach of the innkeeper's duty. However, the pre-trial order indicates Wood also averred that he was subjected to "offensive, abusive and insulting conduct, action and language" by Goynes and that Gulf's liability is predicated "upon the actions of Jessie Goynes, if Goynes is determined to be the agent of Gulf Oil." Therefore, we do not believe that Wood's allegation against Gulf was based upon breach of the innkeeper's duty. Rather, we believe that Wood's alleged cause of action sounds in tort, at least as against Gulf, and it is therefore appropriate to consider the question of the agency relationship between Goynes and Gulf. . . .

The existence and scope of a principal-agent relationship is generally for the jury to determine and the burden of proving agency rests upon the party asserting its existence. . . .

The relationship between Interstate and Goynes is a source of confusion in this case. Not only are both of these parties represented by the same attorney, but the other litigants in the case have consistently treated Interstate and Goynes as a single party, combined, for purposes of reference, under the rubric "innkeeper." It is conceded by all parties that Goynes acted as the agent and servant of Interstate, Gulf and Holiday Inns, Inc. deny a principal-agent relationship with Interstate. However, the culpability of Gulf and that of Holiday Inns, Inc., as principals is based upon the relationship between Goynes and each of the companies as well as the companies' positions vis-a-vis Interstate.

Gulf has argued throughout this appeal that when a local Holiday Inn extends credit on Gulf's credit card, it is extending Gulf's credit rather than its own. Indeed, the Gulf credit system allows the local Holiday Inn to extend up to $150 of Gulf's credit without even contacting a "higher authority" for certification. Moreover, Gulf's agreement with National Data provided that the latter was to supply credit information upon request to "dealers, employees, and agents" of Gulf. At trial Gulf acknowledged that these categories included the Phenix City Holiday Inn. In light of these facts, it would not seem unreasonable for a jury to conclude that the Phenix City Inn was Gulf's agent for the extension of Gulf's credit and the revocation of Gulf credit cards.

Indeed, we believe a jury could have reasonably concluded that Interstate was Gulf's servant in that Gulf controlled the manner in which Interstate rendered the service of extending credit or revoking credit cards. . . . Although Gulf would have us believe that its vast credit network operated virtually without supervision, the record indicates that Gulf, in fact, exercised a great deal of control over its credit operations. By virtue of their respective agreements with Holiday Inns, Inc., all Holiday Inns were required to accept the Gulf credit card and to contract with Gulf for this purpose. Gulf sent out detailed instructions on the use of the credit system and cancellation bulletins three times a month, both of which contained instructions as to the authority and procedure for obtaining dishonored credit cards. Finally, Gulf representatives monitor the Holiday Inns in their respective areas by actually visiting the facilities and providing them with instructions and information as to the use and acceptance of the Gulf card. In light of these facts, we believe the jury could fairly conclude that Gulf, and not Interstate, determined the manner in which Gulf's credit would be extended or refused. Hence, the status of Interstate vis-a-vis Gulf is a matter for the jury.

If Gulf is to be held liable for the actions of Goynes, he must be found to have acted as its sub-agent or perhaps, sub-servant. Gulf certainly did not hire Goynes directly, nor did it control the hours of his employment. But Gulf's agreement with Interstate implicitly assumed that the latter, as a corporate identity, would hire servants to perform the day-to-day details required in extending Gulf's credit or revoking credit cards. As described by the Restatement of Agency, a sub-servant is one who is appointed by the servant to perform functions undertaken by the servant for the master and subject to control as to his physical conduct. . . . In such a situation, the sub-servant would have to be subject to control by the master as to his physical activities before the master would be liable for the sub-servant's tortious conduct.

The district court focused almost entirely upon Goynes' seizure of Wood's credit card in evaluating the extent of Gulf's supervision and control over Goynes. But in the overall context of Gulf's credit network, Gulf's supervision over Goynes appears to be more detailed. By virtue of his employment, as a servant of Interstate, Goynes' duties included the general supervision and management of the Phenix City facility at night. In this capacity, he presumably had authority to extend up to $150 of Gulf's credit, without even contacting anyone.

Goynes' activities in extending credit and obtaining dishonored credit cards obviously inured to Gulf's benefit. In fact, Goynes had obtained dishonored credit cards for Gulf in the past. When he seized Wood's card he acted on the information conveyed to him by Gulf through National Data and pursuant to the authority vested in him by Gulf. The record clearly reveals that Gulf provided Goynes, through Interstate, with instructions on the process for obtaining dishonored cards. Indeed, they specifically cautioned that force, intimidation, or process of law was not to be used in order to obtain a Gulf card. The law is clear that if an agent's act was incident to carrying out the duties assigned to him by his master, the master may be held liable, even though he did not authorize the agent's means, and also though the agent may have sought to accomplish the master's business in a manner contrary to the master's expressed instructions. . . . That Gulf controlled Goynes' activities to some degree is obvious. Whether there was sufficient control of his physical activities by Gulf to render the company liable is a jury question.

"[A] judgment notwithstanding the verdict should not be granted unless under the evidence, together with all inferences that can be reasonably drawn therefrom, there can be but one reasonable conclusion as to the proper judgment. . . ." We believe that the existence of contradictory yet reasonable inferences in the case before us renders the district court's judgment notwithstanding the verdict as to Gulf improper. However, only one of Wood's theories could properly result in Gulf's liability. Since the jury's verdict could have been based on any of the theories we remand this aspect of the case for a new trial on the question of Goynes' status as a servant of Gulf.

A third point of law, which was grounds for the court to grant a new trial, was the awarding by the jury of differing amounts of damages against Holiday Inns and Interstate even though the liability of both parties resulted proximately from the single act of Goynes. The general rule is that both tortfeasors must pay the same amount.

A fourth and perhaps most significant question of law has to do with Goynes and his relationship with Holiday Inns, Inc., Tennessee, the parent company. In other words, must a guest determine ahead of time who owns the hotel—that is, is it a franchised inn or owned by the corporation?

In the original case, the lower court based its decision on the facts that Holiday Inns, Inc., owned no interest in the Phenix City facility, that Holiday Inns, Inc., maintained only a franchise agreement with Interstate, and that Holiday Inns, Inc., had no right of control over Goynes when he obtained the credit card. As one can readily see, with the giants owning 45,000 rooms the problem of who to sue becomes very important. Whom should a guest hold liable in this type of case?

In reaching its determination that Goynes was not the agent of Holiday Inns, Inc., the district court focused almost exclusively on the relationship between Interstate and Holiday Inns, Inc. In assessing the extent of Holiday Inns, Inc.'s, liability for Goynes' actions, it is again appropriate to analyze Goynes' position in "sub-agency" terms. There is considerable evidence in the record indicating a high degree of control over Interstate by Holiday Inns, Inc. The license agreement between the two parties required Interstate to build and maintain the facility as specified by the parent company, and to observe strictly the "Rules of Operation" as promulgated by the Holiday Inns, Inc., board of directors. Interstate was also required to permit regular inspection of the Phenix City facility by Holiday Inn inspectors in order to insure compliance with the Rules of Operation. The agreement further provided that any substantial violation of its terms would give Holiday Inns, Inc., the right to cancel Interstate's license. It was implicit in the agreement that Interstate as a corporate entity would not maintain the Phenix City Inn, but would hire servants for this purpose.

We believe that this was sufficient evidence from which a jury could reasonably conclude that Holiday Inns, Inc., should be liable for Goynes' actions. However, we do not base our holding on the degree of control that Holiday Inns, Inc., maintained over Goynes. Rather we believe that Wood presented more than insubstantial evidence as to the liability of Holiday Inns, Inc., on a theory of apparent authority.

An agency relationship may arise from acts and appearances which lead others to believe that such a relationship has been created. . . . This concept of apparent authority is based upon manifestations by the alleged principal to third persons, and reasonable belief by those persons that the alleged agent is authorized to bind the principal. . . . "The manifestations of the principal may be made directly to the third person, or may be made to the community, by signs or advertising. . . ."

Questions of apparent authority are questions of fact, and are therefore for the jury to determine. The license agreement between Holiday Inns, Inc., and Interstate provided that the Phenix City facility should be constructed and operated so that it would be "readily recognizable by the public as part of the national system of 'Holiday Inns.' " Indeed, the Phenix City facility was required to use the same service marks and trademarks, and exterior and interior decor as the Holiday Inns owned by the parent company. A jury could therefore reasonably conclude that the license agreement required the Phenix City facility to be of such an appearance that travelers would believe it was owned by Holiday Inns, Inc.

The gravamen of Wood's complaint against Holiday Inns, Inc., is based upon the breach of the innkeeper's common law duty to his guests. Although the innkeeper's duty was apparently delictual in origin, . . . breach of this duty in Alabama appears to sound in contract. When Wood contracted with the Phenix City Holiday Inn for lodging he contracted for proper treatment by the servants of the innkeeper. . . . However, there is virtually no way Wood could have known that the servants in the Phenix City facility were servants of Interstate, not of Holiday Inns, Inc. Indeed, the manifestations that Holiday Inns, Inc., required Interstate to make could only have served to convince Wood that Jessie Goynes was a servant of the parent company.

We believe that reasonable men could differ regarding Wood's evidence of apparent authority and that the issue should therefore be determined by the jury. . . . The district court charged the jury below that the relationship of agency between Goynes and Holiday Inns, Inc., could be implied if the jury found that Holiday Inns, Inc., through its advertising and control, held out to the general public that Interstate Inns in Phenix City, Alabama, was its agent. On the basis of these instructions, the jury held Holiday Inns, Inc., liable for Goynes' actions. However, the jury manifested its confusion as to the proper application of law to the facts by holding Holiday Inns, Inc., liable in an amount different from that of Interstate Inns, although the liability of both alleged principals was based upon the same act. Rather than merely reinstating the jury's verdict, then, we believe the interests of justice would be better served by remanding Wood's action against Holiday Inns, Inc., to the district court for retrial.

Cross-appellants Interstate and Goynes appeal the lower court's decision denying indemnification. We believe the district court was correct.

A final point, and a most important one for a hotelier-franchisee, is whether as defendants, Goynes and Interstate should be indemnified by Gulf for the amounts they must pay to Wood. The general rule is that an agent is entitled to indemnification for any amounts they are required to pay for their principal in the performance of their agency. However, the principal is not required to indemnify the agent for harm resulting from the agent's negligence.

Hence, in the absence of agreements to the contrary, an agent has no right to indemnity for damages suffered by reason of his own fraud, misconduct or other tort, even if the wrong was committed within the scope of the agent's employment. . . .

Goynes and Interstate have introduced no substantial evidence upon which a reasonable jury could conclude that Gulf was negligent. The only relevant action undertaken by Gulf was its directive to pick up Wood's credit card. However, by virtue of a statement contained on the card, and in the credit card application signed by Wood, Gulf retained the contractual right to revoke the credit card without notice. Hence, Gulf's decision to terminate Wood's credit was not tortious, and Goynes and Interstate have shown no duty which Gulf is alleged to have breached.

The theory of Wood's case is based upon the harm he is alleged to have suffered because of the manner in which his card was revoked. Any harm to Wood must have resulted solely from the actions of Goynes, since Gulf has not been shown to have been negligent. We therefore believe no substantial evidence has been presented which would justify the indemnification of Goynes and Interstate.

For the reasons set forth above, we affirm in part, reverse in part, and remand for proceedings not inconsistent with this opinion.

The decision in the *Wood* case was as follows:

1 Liability of Gulf as to the Fair Credit Reporting Act: The district court properly dismissed the action based on the "user" provision of the Fair Credit Reporting Act. Gulf therefore was not liable on that point.

2 Indemnity of Gulf to Interstate Inns and Goynes: Interstate Inns and Goynes would not be indemnified by Gulf because Gulf did not act negligently in the case.

3 Gulf Oil Corporation was liable, but because the jury's verdict could have been based on any of the theories, the court remanded this aspect of the case for a new trial on the question of Goynes' status as a servant of Gulf.

4 Holiday Inns, Inc., was liable for Goynes' actions as an agent; therefore, Wood could recover from Holiday Inns, Inc. But the question remains which theory should apply to Goynes and Interstate as to who was the agent of Gulf. As a further complication, the jury allocated different amounts in its verdict.

The *Wood* v. *Holiday Inn* case holds as a principal of law that franchisors can be held liable for the actions of its franchisees where there is adequate control over the franchisees. The question then arises of how much control must be exerted by franchisors or licensors in order to render them liable for the acts of franchisees or licensees.

The case of Bank v. Rebold, 419 N.Y.S.2d 135 (1979), at first looked as though it would sustain a finding of the lower court for the plaintiff, but the Court of Appeals did not. The facts are simple: the plaintiff wanted to travel in Belgium with a friend. She made a reservation in New York for the rental of a vehicle from Avis Rent a Car. The signed agreement was on an Avis form with words Avis in gold print and Locadif (the Belgian company that rented and owned the automobile) in small print. Avis made the international reservation, received confirmation of the reservation from Belgium, and in turn confirmed it with the plaintiff. While her friend was driving the vehicle in Belgium with the plaintiff as a passenger, an accident occurred whereby the plaintiff was injured. She sued her friend and Avis.

The facts indicate that the motor vehicle was being operated at a high rate of speed, and it was alleged that the car had been improperly maintained in that the brakes, signaling devices, and steering mechanism were not functioning properly and that such failure caused the accident and the injuries to the plaintiff. The plaintiff argued in her brief that Avis was liable under either of two theories. The first theory involved the doctrine of apparent authority or agency by estoppel, and the second theory involved the alter ego doctrine.

The court reasoned that in this case neither of the two principles applied. The reasons were woven around the question of control. Avis, it was shown, had only a minority interest in Locadif. Only one of Locadif's five directors and no officers were from Avis. Locadif owned the vehicles, insured them, and fixed the rental charges.

Because of these facts the court said that Locadif could not be considered the alter ego of Avis because liability cannot be sustained on a theory of alter ego where each corporation has separate assets, employees, and business. The connection of Avis and Locadif lay in the fact that Avis in 1970 invested $500,000 in Locadif and became a minority stockholder. Locadif, because of its license with Avis in 1973, had to pay and report to Avis according to their contract. All other business functions were carried out by Locadif.

The court also ruled that the other theory advanced by the plaintiff— that is, the doctrine of apparent authority or agency by estoppel—was similarly without merit. Here the court used the *Wood* v. *Holiday Inn* case as supportive of its positions. It was submitted that because Holiday Inns, Inc., required all franchisees to construct and operate such as to be readily recognizable by the public as part of the national system of "Holiday Inns" that Holiday Inns, Inc., was the true owner of the inn. Furthermore, the hotel franchisees had to use the same service and trademarks as well as exterior and interior decor that was similar to the parent company.

None of this was required by Avis of Locadif nor was it like Avis in the United States. Perhaps the most important factor not present in the *Bank* v. *Rebold* case to take it within the doctrine of apparent authority was that the harm incurred by the injured party had to be caused by the one appearing to be a servant or agent of the franchisor. Furthermore, nowhere did the plaintiff allege that Locadif was in any way responsible for the accident. The summary judgment of the plaintiff was denied and the cross motion for summary judgment dismissing the complaint of plaintiff was granted for Avis.

Accessory Use

A hotel includes furniture, equipment, and many other facilities for guests (Commercial Casualty Ins. Co. v. Adkisson, 4 P.2d 50 [Okl., 1931]; Bisno v. Herzberg, 170 P.2d 973 [Cal., 1946]). Therefore, the maintenance of a candy, tobacco, and newspaper counter by a hotel for the convenience of its guests is an integral part of the business. These facilities distinguish a hotel from a rooming, lodging, or apartment house. Though such services in themselves may be considered separate businesses, they lose their identity as independent ventures when maintained as part of the hotel operation. Consequently, when hotels were allowed in a residential district, the court said that it was necessarily intended that hotels be permitted to operate in the accepted and customary manner (140 Riverside Drive v. Murdock, 95 N.Y.S.2d 860 [1950]). Whenever such accessory uses are part of a hotel, a casual patron does not attain the guest-innkeeper relationship by using the facilities.

The question of what is considered customary in a hotel is of great concern to any hotel operator, and especially to the guest. Mr. Justice Barnes in Wellsboro Hotel Company's Appeal, 7 A.2d 334 (Pa., 1939), spoke on this problem: "It is part of the time-honored business of a hotel or inn to provide those who seek lodging with food and refreshment."

In the case of the Appeal of Sawdey, 85 A.2d 28 (Pa., 1951), it was said that the serving of alcoholic refreshment is regarded to be largely inseparable from a modern hotel (except in prohibition states or areas). This is indicated by the Pennsylvania Liquor Law itself, which makes it mandatory upon the Board to grant a license if the hotel conforms to physical requirements established by the act and the applicant complies with the regulations and is of good repute.

But the real question is not, according to the *Appeal of Sawdey*, whether a liquor license is indispensable, but rather whether it may be regarded as a customary accommodation to the guests as well as a substantial source of revenue to the proprietors of the hotel. Neither furnishing of food nor a cigar or magazine counter are strictly indispensable, but they are primarily regarded as incidental accommodations that serve, enhance, and even finance a hotel. Therefore, where custom is well defined, a license must be issued.

Registration and False Registration

A guest may be accepted at a hotel without registering by the mere presentation of a room key by the clerk, providing that no statute requires a guest to sign a hotel register as evidence of a contract. The fact that a person fails to register or is not required to register is immaterial. The registration of guests at a hotel is not part of the contract between the hotel proprietor and the guest but is solely for the benefit and convenience of the hotel proprietor. Under these conditions a registered occupant of a room, with the knowledge and consent of the hotel management, may turn the room over to another person. When the hotel clerk delivers the key of the room to that person, the second person becomes an accepted guest of the hotel rather than a mere licensee. A licensee is a person who is on the property with permission, but without any enticement by the owner and with no financial advantage to the owner (see chapter 10 for a complete description and example).

However, a guest of the registered occupant of a hotel room who shares the room without the knowledge or consent of the hotel management is not a guest of the hotel because there is no contractual relationship between the third person and the hotel proprietor. The rights of a guest are neither assignable nor transferable. The reasoning in such cases is that a hotel which knowingly permits couples of different sexes to occupy the same room without registering them as husband and wife is regarded as a disorderly house and is liable to prosecution. Hence a hotel must be careful to protect its guests and to maintain its own legality.

Hotelkeepers must give consideration to statutory provisions that are enacted to preserve moral standards. But as mores and life-styles change, should a hotelkeeper or any accommodation establishment attempt to impose its own values on its guests? A hotelkeeper can be prosecuted under the provisions of an immorality statute, but the state must prove that the hotel *knowingly* permitted promiscuity. Normally, it is difficult to determine with certainty that guests are in the hotel to commit immoral acts. Although known pimps and prostitutes can be barred from a hotel, the hotelkeeper's agent in the following case was too anxious to preserve morality.

The facts of Warren v. Penn-Harris Hotel Company, 91 Pa.Sup.Ct. 195 (1927), are as follows. Mrs. Warren, not knowing when her husband would arrive, registered for a single room at the defendant hotel. She informed the clerk she was expecting her husband but did not register for him. When Dr. Warren arrived, he went up to her room without registering. Mrs. Warren was unaware of the fact that he had not registered. Making his rounds, the hotel detective heard a man's voice in a room assigned to a single woman guest. He knocked on the door and, receiving no response, opened it. Although he was informed that the couple were husband and wife, he behaved in front of witnesses in an insulting and abusive manner, making his employer liable for damages.

On appeal, the defendant was upheld against Dr. Warren because he was not an officially registered guest and therefore was owed no duty by the hotel. However, Mrs. Warren's case was upheld against the hotel because she was a guest entitled to the protection and treatment due a guest. The detective had exceeded his authority; he should simply have requested Dr. Warren to register (the rates for single and double occupancy were different), rather than resorting to abuse and name calling.

Management Principles

This chapter has dealt with basic requisites of a hotel and the inherent problems in each type of hotelkeeper-guest relationship. Questions dealing with the kind of physical structure, the establishment name and appearance, length of stay, the serving of food, and the method of payment have been examined to determine the status of the place of accommodation. It has been shown that the quality of accommodations also influences the hotelkeeper-guest relationship as to the degree of care required.

Tobin v. *Slutsky* showed that a hotel that offers or advertises a high-quality level will correspondingly have to present a higher degree of care to its guests. To achieve this, a hotel must select its employees with greater care, as well as hire an adequate number of workers to deal with any foreseeable situation.

The *Asseltyne* case and the *Chawla* case demonstrated the dual nature of a hotel and that it is incumbent on the guest to show clearly what kind of relationship exists. The hotelkeeper should also be able to show by lease or contract that the relationship is a tenancy in order to avoid costly litigation. The existence of a hotelkeeper-guest relationship in the *Levesque* case, however, proved to be beneficial for the hotel because only $300 instead of $4,580 could be assessed against the hotelkeeper.

The *Thacher* case demonstrated that a contract to lease a hotel food concession takes care of the statutory provision that a hotel must serve food to qualify as a hotel. Care in drawing up such a contract could have prevented the *Thacher* case. This case also lists some fifteen provisions that could be helpful for anyone writing a lease.

The *Wood* case demonstrated the pitfalls facing establishments that accept credit cards as payment for services rendered. Managers should instruct desk clerks not to be overeager by trying to catch users of invalid credit cards for the reward money. Such zeal could lead to legal complications for the hotel. Of course, this should not be construed as a rebuke to those employees who check credit cards as a matter of course to see whether they are stolen, canceled, or have limits imposed on their use.

Clerks and other hotel employees should be made aware that if credit is refused by a telecredit system or similar insuring service, they must inform the customer of such refusal as set forth in the Fair Credit Reporting Act of 1974, 15 U.S.C. § 1681. The clerk must disclose the name and address of the reporting agency when credit is denied.

It is recommended that a standard operating procedure (SOP) be adopted for each form of payment—whether it be by check, credit card, traveler's check, or cash. Even payment by cash could prove embarrassing if a guest submitted a $100 bill for a $2.00 telephone charge. Can clerks accept such a large bill, or must they obtain the permission of the hotel executive? Such possibilities should be mapped out.

The following sample SOP for cashing checks assumes the use of a telecredit insuring company:

1   All checks honored should be telecredited for insurance. This service is not free—it costs 4 percent of the amount of the check. To insure a check, dial 1-800-123-4567. (This number is confidential and is not to be given out to customers.)

The operator will ask:	*The hotel clerk replies:*
a Station number	Hotel telephone number
b Type of check	Personal
c Amount of check	To nearest dollar
d Driver's license	Give state, license number, month, date, and year (all on license)

The operator will then provide an insurance number. The hotel clerk should place it next to the maker's name on the front of the check.

2   Telecredit firms require that certain policies must be followed:

a   No two-party checks; all checks must be made out to the hotel.

b   No counter checks; all checks must have the name imprinted on the face.

c   No post or predated checks; all checks must bear the date on which the check is called in.

d   No checks made out to cash.

e   No checks for amounts over $500.

3   If the telecredit company refuses to insure a check, the Fair Credit Reporting Act requires the clerk to inform the customer of the use of telecredit and to give the customer the company's name and address. Generally the company will give the hotel a special "800" phone number for the customer to call.

4   The above procedure does not apply if the customer has a certain kind of credit card, such as Diners Club or American Express, and the amount of the check is under $50.00. Specific credit card companies guarantee checks (free of charge) up to and including $50.

Hotel and restaurant operators should be aware of the varying costs involved when determining which credit card company they want to use. In 1980, for example, a restaurant charge of $25 or more was charged 2.75 percent by Master Card and 3 percent by Visa. When charges were less than $25, Master Card charged 3.25 percent and Visa charged 3.50 percent. In addition, hotel and restaurant operators should be concerned with credit card fraud—that is, the use of stolen, forged, or altered cards to obtain services. Even though both federal and state governments have imposed severe penalties on the fraudulent use of credit cards, such fraud is widespread nonetheless.

QUESTIONS FOR DISCUSSION

1 What requirements must a hotel meet in order to be considered a hotel?

2 Can a hotel refuse lodging to a guest?

3 How many hours must a guest occupy a room in order to constitute a night's stay?

4 If an accommodations establishment is a hotel, must all its guests be treated the same?

5 A guest may change a hotelkeeper-guest relationship to some other form of tenancy. What constitutes such a change?

6 Must a hotel serve food and liquor and offer accommodations to be defined as a hotel?

7 Can a hotel or restaurant refuse to accept a $100 bill from a guest or a nonguest?

8 Though checks are the most common form of payment, is a hotel or restaurant required to accept a personal check? Why or why not?

9 Why must traveler's checks be accepted in payment of a bill?

10 If a credit service reports a customer's account as inadequate to cover a check, what action must be taken by the hotel desk clerk?

5 Contents

5 Licensing and Regulating Houses of Public Accommodation

*"When I hear any man talk of an
unalterable law, the only effect it
produces upon me is to convince me
that he is an unalterable fool."*

SIDNEY SMITH

The state or municipality may license and regulate the operation of an inn, apartment house, rooming house, restaurant, or similar establishment. The authority to regulate and license is based upon the police power of the state in the interest of public health, safety, and welfare. The fixed rule by which the validity of all exercises of police power is measured is that it extends only to reasonable restraints. Populous municipalities must assume more extensive power to cope with situations that endanger the common welfare and safety. Such power must regulate, prohibit, or license certain businesses within the municipal limits.

In common law, persons engaged in a public service, such as innkeepers or common carriers, were held to be under duty to the general public. This duty brought them into the purview of a business affecting the public interest and brought about a grant of legislative authority for its regulation and licensing. Such houses then would not become places for the practice of vice or crime or a menace to the public welfare.

Licenses

To license is to confer the right to do something that would otherwise be prohibited. A license is a special privilege rather than a right common to all. Licenses are required in several general situations. The situation most relevant to hospitality management students is when a public interest affects the right to license a business. It has never been challenged successfully that the operation of inns, lodging houses, or rooming houses does not affect public interest. Therefore, such places are subject to legislative authority to regulate or license them so that they do not become places for the practice of vice or crime or menaces to public welfare.

This chapter describes the procedures necessary to obtain a license and the conditions for keeping a hotel license, including rate ceilings, advertising, state laws, and fees. In addition, it discusses registration and false registration. The final section is a consideration of the legal principles and management implications of statutes governing zoning, competition, rates, trademarks, and taxation.

Obtaining a License for a Hotel

A license to operate a hotel is not always easy to obtain. The case of *Hertenberger v. City of Texarkana* demonstrates the administrative clout a city has in supervising public morals. The reason cited for not giving Evelyn Hertenberger a license was the possibility of the hotel's being used as a house of prostitution. The plaintiff attempted to show that the city council had deprived her of due process of law under the Fourteenth Amendment.

Case Example   **Hertenberger v. City of Texarkana**
272 S.W.2d 435 (Arkansas, 1954)
(ROBINSON, Justice)

The appellant, Evelyn Hertenberger, applied to the City of Texarkana for a license to operate a hotel. The council, after considering the application, refused to issue the license. By certiorari appellant took the matter to the circuit court and has appealed from a judgment of the court approving the action of the city council.

Ordinance B–439 of the City of Texarkana pertains to the licensing of rooming houses and hotels, and provides: "such license shall not be granted unless it shall appear probable to the Council that such applicant will not rent rooms for immoral purposes, or allow prostitutes or pimps to remain on such premises or permit gambling or the sale, storage or keeping of intoxicating liquor on such premises." The city council of Texarkana has the power and authority to enact such an ordinance (Ark. Stats. 19–2304). The ordinance is constitutional (City of Texarkana v. Brachfield, 207 Ark. 774, 183 S.W.2d 304).

One of the principal contentions of appellant is that the right to operate a hotel is a property right and that for the council to fail to authorize the issuance of the license is depriving the appellant of such a right without due process of law . . . (Carr v. City of El Dorado, 230 S.W.2d 485).

Without going into detail as to the evidence, suffice it to say that the council was justified in reaching the conclusion that if Mrs. Hertenberger was granted a license, in all probability the hotel rooms would be rented for immoral purposes; and Ordinance B–439 specifically provides that the license shall not be granted in such circumstances. It is true that the evidence before the council as to Mrs. Hertenberger's record was not the kind of evidence that would be admissible in a court of law. However, the administrative bodies such as the city council, in arriving at facts, are not confined to the rules of evidence prevailing in the courts. . . .

Although the right to operate a hotel is a property right, this fact does not preclude the city council from refusing to issue a license where the issuance of such license would be in violation of a valid ordinance. In the Carr case it was further said: "The legal character of official action by city councils is diverse. The concept of complete separation of powers, however it may exist in other areas of government, does not abide in the city council chamber. Primarily legislative in their functionings, city councils yet perform many acts, pass many ordinances and resolutions, that are administrative or judicial in their nature. . . . It is not impossible that a single aldermanic action may possess characteristics of all three of the classic departments of government—legislative, executive, and judicial."

Appellant complains that she was not given opportunity to be heard; however, it appears that she was present when the council voted on her application; and although she said nothing in her behalf prior to the time of taking the vote, she was given an opportunity to speak when she requested to do so; and after hearing her, the mayor asked if any member of the council desired to change his vote. Thus it appears that she had full opportunity to present her case.

We have reached the conclusion that the ordinance is valid and none of the applicant's constitutional rights were violated in refusing her a license to operate a hotel in Texarkana.

Ruling of the Court: Appeal of plaintiff denied and affirmed for defendant, City of Texarkana.

Failure to Obtain a License

Certain types of businesses must obtain licenses before they may operate, and a hotel, motel, or similar place of accommodation is certainly a business imbued with a public interest. The public, therefore, is owed governmental protection to the extent made possible by inspection of the premises for safety and health standards and an assurance that the owner has certain qualifications to operate such an establishment. When a license is granted, it is said to be for the protection of the public and not for revenue purposes. When the state requires such a license for the protection of the public, most contracts made by an unlicensed person in violation of the act are void.

A hotelkeeper who does not have a license, such as in the case of Randall v. Tuell, 36 A. 910 (Me., 1897), is not able to recover from a guest who does not pay for the lodgings. More recently, the 1975 case of Hiram Ricker & Sons v. Students International Meditation Society evoked a similar problem, but here the stakes were higher. In the Randall case, the amount in question was $28, but the Ricker case involved $77,508.36— a substantial sum. Should the plaintiff (a nonlicensed hotel) be allowed to collect for the goods and services rendered to the defendant when the amount is extraordinarily high? The *Ricker* case indicates that hoteliers, restaurateurs, and others who, for some reason, do not have licenses can recover on such contracts. But legislatures could pass laws that would prevent hotelkeepers from recovering, as they have done for attorneys, teachers, and unlicensed real estate brokers.

Case	**Hiram Ricker & Sons v. Students Int. Meditation Soc.**
Example	*342 A.2d 262 (Me., 1975)*
	(POMEROY, Justice)

. . . The plaintiff-appellee, Hiram Ricker & Sons, a Maine corporation, brought an action for breach of contract in the District Court of Massachusetts, claiming $77,508.36 due from the defendant-appellant, SIMS, a California charitable corporation. Jurisdiction is based on diversity of citizenship.

Ricker and SIMS had entered into an agreement wherein Ricker agreed to furnish lodging and food to approximately 1,000 SIMS students at a one-month teacher training course to be held at Ricker's premises in Poland Spring, Maine, from June 26 to July 28, 1970.

The Poland Spring's complex, once a fashionable spa for those with the leisure and means to enjoy its amenities, was sold in 1962 to Hiram Ricker & Sons. Ricker subsequently leased the premises to the federal government for a Job Corps residential installation.

In December 1969, the installation was closed. Not long thereafter Ricker agreed with SIMS to reopen the buildings vacated by the Job Corps and to furnish both lodging and food to SIMS' students. The one-month course was held at the Poland Spring complex as scheduled, and at the conclusion of the course, SIMS had paid Ricker $185,000.00. A dispute arose between the parties as to the amount of the outstanding balance due Ricker on the contract, and this action followed.

Ricker premised its right to recover on alternative theories; that the money was due either on the contract or in quantum meruit. SIMS responded with a counterclaim for the $185,000.00 it had paid Ricker.

A jury trial resulted in a verdict for Ricker in the amount of $65,780.00 and against SIMS on its counterclaim.

At trial, the evidence conclusively established that Ricker's victualer's license (30 M.R.S.A. § 2751), issued in December 1969, had expired in May 1970. Similarly, the record established that Ricker did not have sanitation licenses for all its premises during the entire period (22 M.R.S.A. § 2482). On appeal the First Circuit Court recognized that the last time the Maine court had had occasion to decide whether failure to comply with licensing statutes precluded recovery on a contract was over three-quarters of a century ago in a case involving $28.00 due an innkeeper (Randall v. Tuell, 89 Me. 443, 36 A. 910 [1897]). The court was understandably in doubt as to the continuing vitality of the rule enunciated in *Randall,*

". . . that where a license is required for the protection of the public, and to prevent improper persons from engaging in a particular business, and the license is not for revenue merely, a contract made by an unlicensed person in violation of the act is void. . . ."

We note at the outset the claim advanced by the appellee that this case is not yet in such posture that it may properly be considered by this court. Specifically, it is appellee's position that a threshold issue as to whether or not compliance with the licensing statutes was required must be addressed by us before consideration of the questions certified. This is so appellee says, because the federal court never resolved that issue.

Questions #1 and #2 of the instant certification ask us to decide whether appellee's "non-compliance with the victualer's license requirement" and "partial non-compliance with the sanitation license requirement" preclude its recovery either on the contract or in quantum meruit.

Question #3 asks whether the substantial performance exception to the requirement of complete performance would apply "If Ricker is permitted to recover despite its lack of licenses;" and if so, whether the jury should be instructed to consider "the degree of the plaintiff's compliance with the license laws."

We consider it to be "apparent from the certification itself" that the question whether the licenses involved were required by Ricker must necessarily have been decided in the affirmative by the federal court prefatory to its reaching the issue of whether non-compliance or partial compliance would preclude recovery for services rendered.

Thus, the issue squarely presented by this certification is whether or not this court's decision in *Randall v. Tuell, supra,* is still viable, thus barring the right of appellee to recover the value of the services and lodging it supplied the appellant.

The licensing statute construed in *Randall* was identical to the one now in force save for omission of the words "or tavernkeeper."

The present statute provides that

"No person shall be a common innkeeper, victualer or tavernkeeper without a license, under a penalty of not more than $50" (30 M.R.S.A. § 2751).

The *Randall* court construed the language of the statute as demonstrating a legislative intent "to prevent improper persons from engaging in a particular business" in the interest of public protection. Had the statute been enacted for revenue purposes only instead of being prohibitory, the court concluded, the innkeeper could properly recover on his contract even though he was in violation of the licensing requirement. . . .

The statute which occasioned both *Randall* and the case now before us imposes a specific penalty upon a "common innkeeper or victualer," who fails to secure an annual license to engage in his occupation. . . .

We note at the outset there is no provision in the innkeeper licensing statute which imposes any penalties or forfeitures in addition to the fifty dollars prescribed in Section 2751 for failure to secure a license. We also note there is no express provision authorizing injunctive relief. This is in contradistinction to Section 2504, for example, which provides for the licensing of persons conducting closing-out sales. That statute expressly provides for injunctive relief and purports to confer jurisdiction in the Superior Court.

The court in *Randall v. Tuell* rested its decision to bar recovery on the contract by a non-complying innkeeper on its conclusion that the statute was intended to prohibit the exercise of the business, and by inference, recovery on any contract entered into in contravention of such prohibition.

"If the statute in question was enacted for revenue purposes only, instead of being prohibitory, the plaintiff might properly recover. But we are satisfied that such was not the intention of the legislature. The statute being by implication prohibitory by reason of the penalty attached, the plaintiff is precluded from recovering. Basing his action upon a clear violation of the statute, he cannot successfully invoke the aid of the court."

We do not so construe the licensing provision. In the absence of any express legislative intention to declare contracts made and performed by unlicensed innkeepers void, we will not infer such intention.

The statute fixes its own penalties. The additional penalty of nonenforceability of agreements is a judicial engraftment we now expressly reject as unduly harsh and unsound.

"Why should one party to a contract be allowed to avoid the payment of debts he has contracted to pay and thus gain an unconscionable advantage because the other party deliberately, or through inability or mere oversight, has failed to discharge an obligation to the city when there is available to the city . . . a . . . remedy for the wrong. . . . As the law has been construed for a long time by this and most other courts of last resort, it appears to furnish an inducement to evil-disposed persons to watch opportunities to contract with any one upon whom a license tax has been imposed at a time when, for perhaps only a day, he has neglected to pay his tax, and thus acquire merchandise or service without payment therefor."

Cases in other jurisdictions which have discussed the question of enforceability of contracts under similar licensing statutes demonstrate a reluctance to apply *Randall*-type rules where such application would produce an unduly harsh result. In some cases, the decision turns on the same distinction made in *Randall*, viz., whether the purpose of the statute is the collection of revenue (in which case the express statutory penalties are held to be exclusive), or the protection of public health and safety (in which case non-enforceability of the bargain may be inferred as an additional penalty). . . . Other courts have eschewed such distinctions, but have allowed recovery under circumstances where equitable considerations weighed heavily against the imposition of a forfeiture. . . .

In some instances, the courts have circumvented rigid application of the rule by determining that a license was not required because the transaction was an isolated one and the plaintiff not really practicing the profession or engaged in the business described in the licensing statute. . . .

Finally, a few unlicensed plaintiffs have been allowed to recover, on a theory of quantum meruit, for the fair value of their work where such recovery would avoid inequities and unjust enrichment. . . .

We are satisfied it would be unjust and inequitable for us to rule that Ricker's noncompliance with the licensing statute makes its contract with SIMS void. We will not so hold in any case unless the legislature has mandated such result by specific terms in the statute. To the extent *Randall v. Tuell* . . . held, otherwise, it is overruled. . . .

Revocation or Suspension of a License

The actual operation of hotels or motels may be undertaken only after a license has been granted by the proper authorities. That right is not inalienable; it may be granted or withdrawn under due process of law.

The legislature empowers a licensing board to revoke a license when it is "satisfied that the licensee is unfit to hold a license" (Hertenberger v. City of Texarkana, 272 S.W.2d 435 [Ark., 1954]). Innkeepers who allow illicit gambling and drinking by minors on their premises can be found unfit to hold a license. In the case of Manchester v. Selectmen of Nantucket, 138 N.E.2d 766 (Mass., 1956), the licensee's right to conduct a summer hotel in Nantucket was suspended for one week because the board received a petition signed by twelve residents and property owners of Nantucket complaining of the manner in which the hotel was conducted. In another case in which a nightclub and motel had been actively used for bootlegging activities (Bailey v. Runyon, 293 S.W.2d 631 [Ky., 1956]), the Commonwealth of Kentucky had the right to bring forfeiture proceedings against the property and to withdraw the license.

Is topless dancing a form of expression allowed licensed bars of New York and protected by the First Amendment of the U.S. Constitution? The U.S. Supreme Court judged no (N.Y. State Liquor Authority v. Bellanca, 101 S. Ct. 2599 [1981]). The rationale is quite simple. The states have absolute power under the Twenty-first Amendment to totally prohibit the sale of liquor within their boundaries. They can regulate the times, places, and circumstances under which liquor may be sold. The Supreme Court upheld the constitutionality of a statute prohibiting acts of gross sexuality, including the display of the genitals as well as live or filmed performances of sexual acts in establishments licensed by the state to serve liquor.

The essence of the *Bellanca* case is that the states' power to ban the sale of alcoholic beverages applies to the sale of liquor on premises where topless dancing occurs too. According to the court's opinion, New York has chosen to avoid disturbances associated with mixing alcohol and nude dancing by means of a reasonable restriction upon establishments that sell liquor for consumption on the premises. Nudity coupled with alcohol in public places begets undesirable behavior. Hence, states can control liquor establishments by removing their licenses.

If the law is definite that a license can be revoked for cause, it is also definite that there must be due process of law to revoke or suspend a license. How does due process of law affect the revocation of a license? It may require adequate notice, a hearing, or a notice that defines the charges the innkeeper will be called upon to answer.

In *Manchester v. Selectmen of Nantucket* in which the licensee was charged with operating a hotel improperly, the court said that the following notice was not adequate under the statute: "You are herewith advised that under Chapter 140, Section 30, of the General Laws of Massachusetts, a hearing will be held at 10 AM Wednesday, August 24, 1955, at the Selectmen's Rooms, 17 Federal Street, on complaints received by the board as regards your operation of the premises known as 'Nantucket

New Ocean House'." This notice was not adequate because it failed to inform the license holder of the general charges he faced.

An appearance in person or by an attorney at the hearing amounts to a waiver of any irregularity in the service of notices. In addition, persons who appear in an administrative proceeding without the notice to which they are entitled by law have no grounds to complain of lack of notice. A licensee who receives a notice to appear before the licensing board and believes the notice is inadequate should request additional information concerning the charges. Such a person can also ask for post-ponement if further time is needed in which to prepare the case.

Reasonable Class Legislation

The regulation and licensing of hotels, apartment houses, rooming houses, and motels based on the "number of rooms" has long been es-tablished as a reasonable exercise of police power as well as reasonable class legislation (legislation that operates on a portion of a particular class of persons or things). Thus, classifications for the purpose of in-spection, sanitary measures, and protection from fire that are based upon the number of rooms, the number of guests, the locality of the establish-ment, and the capacity for service accommodation in restaurants have been held to be reasonable.

However, the classification must be natural and not arbitrary. It must bear a reasonable relation to the subject matter under legislation and must furnish some legitimate ground of differentiation. Therefore, in Geele v. State, 43 S.E.2d 254 (Ga., 1947), a statute requiring hotels to be "three stories in height," to charge guests "$2 per day and more" and to provide fire escapes was held unconstitutional, because the classification based upon the amount charged the guests "had no conceivable relation to the purpose of the law."

But statutes that provide for the inspection of hotels containing "ten or more sleeping rooms" (Hubbell v. Higgins, 126 N.W. 914 [Iowa, 1910]) and requiring hotels "more than two stories high" to have fire escapes and certain modes of egress (State v. McFarland, 110 P. 792 [Wash., 1910]) have been held valid as being reasonable in their classification (Miller v. Strahl, 239 U.S. 426 [1915]). Thus, to prevent fire, a hotel of "more than fifty rooms and being four or more stories high" has to adhere, according to statute, to certain rules regulating the hotelkeeper's duty toward guests.

Unreasonable class legislation is generally not a problem to hotel or motel operators until it affects them personally. Contesting the con-stitutionality of a statute is expensive, time-consuming, and often dis-appointing, because the courts generally favor legislative intent. Classification is permissible when it is based upon some distinction reasonably justifying differentiation in treatment. A classification is not void because it does not embrace within it every other class that might be included. And a statutory discrimination will not be set aside if any state of facts may be reasonably conceived to justify it.

A person or group, however, can change a statutory enactment, as a 1975 case indicates. In 1953 the California legislature had enacted Sections 17564–17567, "Motel and Motor Court Rate Signs," as part of the Business and Professions Code. This statute was first contested in 1971 in Gawzner Corporation v. Minier, 120 Cal.Rptr. 344 (1975).

In essence, this statute prohibited outdoor rate signs unless such signs showed the rates charged for all rooms, the number of rooms offered for rent at each rate, and the number of persons accommodated at the posted rate. Also, the posted rates had to conform to a certain size and had to be displayed prominently. The section that was considered unreasonable class legislation read as follows: "[This] shall apply to operators and owners of *motels, motor courts, and like establishments*" (emphasis added).

As to whether the legislators had intended that hotels were to be included in "and like establishments," the court stated that the omission of express reference to hotels compelled the conclusion that the legislative intent was to regulate establishments that, at the time of enactment of the legislation, were commonly known as motels and motor courts, as distinguished from hotels. In its opinion, the court questioned whether there was a reasonable distinction between hotels and motels with respect to the purpose of Section 17564, justifying the legislative control specifically of motel rate advertising.

The defendant (the district attorney of the County of Santa Barbara, who attempted to dissolve the permanent injunction from enforcing the rate sign) contended that the California legislation was designed to protect the motoring public from deceptive advertising and thus the "legislature in distinguishing motels, motor courts and other like establishments from hotels created a valid legislative classification." This reasoning assumes that hotels do not seek the business of the motoring public. This is obviously untrue in present-day California and other parts of the nation. As noted in People v. Sprengel, 490 P.2d 65 (Colo., 1971), the automobile is the usual means of transportation. Just as motels have expanded their services to compete with hotels, hotels have added parking facilities to compete with motels.

According to the avowed purpose of Section 17564, hotels and motels are similar. To discriminate between them as to outdoor rate advertising denies motels the equal protection of the law. It thus appears that Business and Professions Code, Section 17564 is unconstitutional in its application to owners or operators of motels in the *Gawzner* case. The order denying the defendant's motion to dissolve the permanent injunction was affirmed.

In Carlin v. City of Palm Springs, 92 Cal.Rptr. 535 (1971), the court held unconstitutional an ordinance that prohibited the use of outside rate signs. However, the court also stated that the reasonable regulation of signs and billboards constituted a valid exercise of the state's police power. The size, location, and other physical attributes of signs may also be regulated in the interest of public safety. The number of signs that may be posted or installed may also be limited. Signs that overhang or encroach upon a public highway or public property may be restricted or prohibited. And signs advertising prices that may be deceptive are subject to the police power.

License Fees

Municipal corporations have no right to use the power to license as a means of increasing their revenues. However, a municipality can require a reasonable fee to be paid for a license. In the decision in City of Fayetteville v. Carter, 12 S.W. 573 (Ark., 1889), the court said,

> The amount the municipality has a right to demand for such fee depends upon the extent and expense of the municipal supervision made necessary by the business in the city or town where it is licensed. A fee sufficient to cover the expense of issuing the license, and to pay the expenses which may be incurred in the enforcement of such police inspection or super-intendence as may be lawfully exercised over the business, may be required. It is obvious that the actual amount necessary to meet such expenses cannot, in all cases, be ascertained in advance, and that it would be futile to require anything of the kind. The result is, if the fee required is not plainly un-reasonable, the courts ought not to interfere with the discretion exercised by the council in fixing it; and, unless the contrary appears on the face of the ordinance requiring it, or is established by proper evidence, they should presume it to be reasonable.

Registration

A city's right to pass ordinances that require motels, tourist courts, and similar businesses to maintain a register of guests' names and addresses has been held valid in Allinder v. City of Homewood, 49 So.2d 108 (Ala., 1960). However, this authority must be governed by the police power granted by legislative enactment. A municipality may also pass laws that are more restrictive than state laws if such restrictions do not conflict with state law and are not unreasonable.

In C. L. Maier Company v. City of Canton, 201 N.E.2d 609 (Ohio, 1964), the problem of state supremacy came up. A city ordinance required a hotel, rooming house, or lodging house to procure a license to operate within the city. The court ruled this ordinance unconstitutional to the extent that it pertained to hotels and motels, because it conflicted with state statutes that provided for hotel permits.

A registration statute requiring motelkeepers or tourist court operators to enter the license number and make of guests' automobiles, the date and hour of arrival, and the number of the room rented on the hotel register was held to be valid by the court because it could aid authorities in locating lost or stolen automobiles and finding wanted persons. Also, this ordinance could serve other useful purposes by providing for the safety, good order, comfort, and convenience of the citizens of the municipality.

The claim that motor courts, motels, and tourist courts have been discriminated against because hotels do not have to keep such registers cannot be sustained. The equal protection clause of the Fourteenth Amendment permits classification when dealing with regulatory measures under police power, provided such classification rests upon some rational basis. Hotels, on the other hand, are not required to make note of such details as there is a difference between these types of accommodation, and legislatures have not found it useful or necessary to apply these requirements to hotels.

In Silver v. Silver, 280 U.S. 117, 50 S. Ct. 74 (1929), the Supreme Court said, "There is no constitutional requirement that a regulation, in other respects permissible, must reach every class to which it might be applied—that the Legislature must be rigidly held to the choice of regulating all or none." Furthermore, "it is free to recognize degrees of harm, and it may confine its restrictions to those classes of cases where the need is deemed to be clearest." And again in United States v. Carolene Products Company, 304 U.S. 144 (1938), the Supreme Court said, "A legislature may hit at an abuse which it has found, even though it has failed to strike at another."

Another aspect of such regulations makes it unlawful for a hotelkeeper knowingly to accept as a guest a person who has registered under a pseudonym. The statutes are levied against the so-called victimless crimes leading to immoral acts in hotels. What type of evidence is required to convict a hotelkeeper or motelkeeper of permitting immoral conduct in the hotel? A great deal depends on the state statute, but in the main the state must prove that the hotel knowingly permitted such infractions. Certainly, the next case reads as if the defendants knew what was going on, but as the results indicate, the state did not prove absolutely that the hotelkeeper knowingly permitted the individuals to use the hotel for illegal purposes.

Case Example	Commonwealth v. Altenhaus
	57 N.E.2d 921 (Mass., 1944)
	(SPALDING, Justice)

The defendant, a hotel proprietor, was found guilty by a jury on two complaints. In one he was charged with having knowingly permitted, as a licensed innholder, the premises under his control to be used for immoral conduct, in violation of G. L. (Ter. Ed.) c. 140 § 26. The other complaint alleged that while in charge of a hotel register he knowingly permitted "to be written in said register another or different name . . . than the true name or name in ordinary use of the persons registering," in violation of G. L. (Ter. Ed.) c. 140 § 29.

At the close of the evidence, the defendant moved for a directed verdict on each complaint and excepted to the judge's denial of the motion. Exceptions were also saved to the denial of a motion to quash the complaints, to the denial of a motion for a new trial . . . .

The following is a summary of the pertinent evidence. The defendant and his brother as partners own and operate a hotel of twenty-six rooms in the city of Taunton. Sometimes the defendant works at the desk where guests are registered and at other times his brother performs this duty. On July 8, 1943, at about 10 PM a police officer observed two girls at the window of a room on the second floor of the defendant's hotel. One of the girls was whistling to attract the attention of some soldiers who were passing. There was no evidence tending to show that the defendant had knowledge of this. Later that evening, the officer observed some soldiers in the room, one of whom was "kissing and hugging" one of the girls. On the following night, July 9, at midnight the officer (accompanied by his captain) called at the hotel and told the defendant what he had observed. The defendant and the two officers then proceeded to the room which was occupied by the two women. Upon questioning by the police officers, the women admitted that since registering on July 8, they had engaged another room and that each had entertained a soldier in her room the night before. Both denied having participated in any immoral conduct although their explanation was such that it might well have been disbelieved. They accompanied the officers to the police station where, after further questioning, they were placed under arrest. It does not appear that the soldiers had registered or that the defendant knew of their presence in the rooms.

Five days later on July 14 around 2 AM, a sailor and a girl (each without baggage) were seen by a police officer to enter the hotel. Later, after ascertaining that the couple had registered as "Mr. and Mrs. Ray Conway, U.S.N." and had been assigned to a room, the officer, together with his captain, entered the hotel with a search warrant and, accompanied by the defendant, went to the room. After some delay, they were admitted and discovered that the occupants were not husband and wife and had registered under fictitious names. Both were arrested and charged with being lewd and lascivious persons.

On July 24, an officer observed a soldier and a woman enter the hotel around 1:30 AM and later learned that they had engaged a room and had registered as "Private William Petiauage and wife, Camp Myles Standish, serial number 3748123." On the following day, July 25, a police officer accompanied by the defendant went to the room and found it occupied by a woman who admitted that she had occupied it the night before with a soldier (whose full name she did not know) from Camp Myles Standish, who was not her husband.

In the early morning of August 4, two sailors entered the hotel with two women and each couple registered as husband and wife and were assigned to rooms for the night. It later developed from investigation by the police that neither couple were husband and wife and all had registered under fictitious names. One of the men stated that at the time he registered he was "pretty drunk."

The defendant took the stand and admitted that he was present or in charge when the various persons on the occasions in question registered.

He further testified, in substance, that he had no reason to believe that any of the couples were not married or were engaging the rooms for improper purposes.

The evidence clearly warranted findings that the rooms of the defendant's hotel were used for immoral conduct and that guests on several occasions registered under false names. But more than this must be proved in order to convict the defendant. Under both statutes there must be evidence that the defendant "knowingly" permitted these things to be done. There are, to be sure, many instances in the law where the legislature has made the mere doing of an act an offense without proof or scienter. . . .

When, as here, knowledge is an essential element of an offense, it may be and generally is, proved by circumstantial evidence; and it may be inferred from a great variety of circumstances. No useful purpose would be served in analyzing in detail the evidence in the present cases. Probably in no two cases under these statutes would the evidence ever be the same, and to a large extent, each case must be decided on its peculiar facts. We are of the opinion that the evidence in the cases at bar, on decisive issue of knowledge, is as consistent with the defendant's innocence as with his guilt.

"When the evidence tends equally to sustain either of two inconsistent propositions, neither of them can be said to have been established by legitimate proof."

The refusal to order a verdict of not guilty on each complaint was error.

Ruling of the Court: For the defendant, Altenhaus, on both counts. In view of this conclusion, it is unnecessary to consider the defendant's other exceptions.

All courts do not hold as the *Altenhaus* case did. In Killeen v. United States, 224 A.2d 302 (D.C., 1966), where there was evidence of homosexuality taking place in the restaurant, the court said that it was not necessary to prove that the defendants had actual knowledge of acts done on the premises if it could be shown that they reasonably should have known what was happening. Keeping a disorderly house could be proved inferentially, since proprietors are presumed to have knowledge of that which goes on in their business.

Right of Inspection

A municipality has the right to pass laws, such as the right of inspection, that have as their basic purpose the public health, safety, and welfare of the community. Most "right of entry statutes" or "inspection statutes" state that the inspection must be at a reasonable time. If entry is refused, they set forth the procedure that must be followed by the inspector to gain admittance.

The question of whether a warrant is needed for an inspection was answered in the negative in Frank v. State of Maryland, 79 S. Ct. 804 (1959). Here the court said that inspection without a warrant was permissible where need required it.

Soliciting Patrons

A statute or ordinance regulating the solicitation of patronage has been judged as a reasonable exercise of the police powers of a state or municipality. Such a statute is not considered an unreasonable restriction upon the privilege of a business.

Unquestionably, ordinances that regulate or require licensing as a condition for soliciting patronage for a hotel are valid. Furthermore, prohibiting such action is legal. The court in Emerson v. McNeil, 106 S.W. 497 (Ark., 1907), went a little further and said that soliciting of hotel patronage need merely be a "serious annoyance" and not necessarily flagrant in order to be regulated.

Subordinate municipal administrative officers, such as police commissioners, cannot make regulatory rules unless such power and authority is specifically delegated by statute. The New York legislature had passed laws on the licensing and regulation of trades affecting the public, but the police commissioner, lacking statutory provision authorizing him to make rules and regulations, was powerless to act. The court in Levy v. Valentine, 17 N.Y.S.2d 768 (1940), said, "If the Commissioner believes that the business of hotel runners is no longer desirable in this city [New York], he should request the proper legislative body to outlaw the business and to abrogate the statute under which runners are licensed. He cannot take unto himself the authority specifically authorized by law."

In Board v. O'Brien, 98 N.Y.S.2d 1 (1950), affirmed 100 N.E. 177, in which the New York City police commissioner tried to limit a chauffeur (taxicab driver) by denying him a license as a hotel runner, the court said that a major field of business opportunity was thus entirely closed to the runner by the regulation; consequently, "We find that the regulation in question so curtailed the licensed business as to defeat the legislative policy of continuing it. These regulations cannot be justified as an administrative execution of the law. They are in effect a formulation of law and a nullification rather than an implementation of the law. Being in excess of legal authority, the regulations must be invalidated."

Advertising

Counterbalancing the government's right to regulate signs and advertising is the right of property owners to make reasonable use of their land, or the right of business persons to conduct businesses. The right to advertise is a property right. A business sign is a part of the business itself just as the structure housing the business is part of it, and the authority to conduct a business carries with it the right to maintain a business sign on the premises, subject to reasonable regulation by the government. The right to advertise parallels the right to free speech; free speech necessarily embodies the means used for its dissemination.

In Eskind v. City of Vero Beach, 159 So.2d 209 (Fla., 1963), the Florida Supreme Court reviewed a city ordinance that prohibited "the use of outdoor signs to advertise for accommodations in motels, hotels, tourist homes and other types of lodging houses." In holding the ordinance unconstitutional, the court stated that it could find no justification from an aesthetic viewpoint to prohibit motel signs advertising rates and permitting any other type of motel advertising sign. Motels, which offered attractive rates, were prohibited from announcing their rate advantage, while more luxurious establishments were permitted to advertise air conditioning, televisions, swimming pools, bars and grills, and other tourist attractions.

Similarly, motels were prohibited from advertising their rates on signs, while other businesses, including restaurants, bars, and filling stations, could attract passing motorists with signs announcing fees for their goods or services. According to the court, a sign in front of a motel was no more offensive to aesthetic sensibilities than a rate sign in the same immediate area advertising the fees of the other business activities. Furthermore, a sign advertising rates was not aesthetically distinguishable from a sign advertising various other aspects of a motel's services. The court concluded that the ordinance could not be upheld as beneficial to the general economic welfare of the community because it tended to favor the economic welfare of luxury motels and hotels that could not compete on a price basis with more modest establishments. The court stated: "We have the view that the subject ordinance is nothing less than an attempted exercise of the police power to restrict competition between favored and unfavored segments of the same business activity."

The state legislature of Florida passed a statute requiring hotels, motels, and rooming houses to advertise full details of room charges if they advertise their rates. This statute, the court said, was within the prerogative of the legislature to enact social legislation and does not deprive advertisers of equal protection of the law.

Consequently, in City Center Motel, Inc., v. Florida Hotel and Restaurant Commission, a sign was placed on the highway with a price quoted in four-foot high figures and letters of seven or nine inches. The sign was misleading and had to be changed. The statute was considered constitutional even though it interfered with business and possibly violated certain rights guaranteed under the Constitution.

Case Example	City Center Motel, Inc., v. Florida Hotel and Restaurant Commission *134 So.2d 856 (Fla., 1961)* *(WIGGINTON, Judge)*

Petitioner seeks review by certiorari of an order entered by the State Hotel and Restaurant Commissioner finding it guilty of displaying a sign in front of its motel relating to rates charged for accommodations furnished therein contrary to the provisions of the statute applicable to matters of this kind.

The statute in question provides: "No person shall display or cause to be displayed any sign or signs which may be seen from a public highway or street, which sign or signs include in dollars and cents a statement relating to the rates charged at a public lodging establishment unless such sign or signs include in letters and figures of similar size and prominence the following additional information: the number of apartments or rooms in the establishment and the rates charged for each; whether the rates quoted are for single or multiple occupancy where such fact affects the rate charged; and the dates during which such rates are in effect. The said rates shall in each instance coincide with the rates posted in each room of the establishment and with those filed with the hotel and restaurant commissioner as required by subsection (1)" (F.S. § 509.201(2) (a), F.S.A.).

One of the requirements set forth in the foregoing statute provides that signs displayed by operators of public lodging establishments which include in dollars and cents a statement relating to rates charged must also include other required information in letters and figures of similar size and prominence. An interpretation of the words "of similar size and prominence" is the crux of this review.

The evidence taken before the commissioner discloses without conflict that the sign forming the subject of the alleged violation contains the following words and figures "$6 Couple." The figure "$6" measures four feet in height and is located forty-three feet from the ground. The letters in the word "Couple" are two feet nine inches in height. The sign also contains the words and figures "Single $5," which are nineteen inches in height and located thirty-five and one-half feet from the ground. That portion of the sign which reads "32 units. Rates same at all times—extra person $1." is composed of letters and figures either seven or nine inches in height and located twenty-six feet from the ground. A motorist approaching the motel could read a portion but not all of the sign when he reaches a point 1600 feet away. Another portion of the sign may be read by an approaching motorist only when he reaches a distance of not more than 600 feet away. The remainder of the sign is readable only when the motorist reaches a distance not more than 200 feet away.

Based upon the foregoing evidence the Commissioner found that the words and figures appearing on the rate sign displayed by petitioner were in violation of the statute which requires that the rates and other information be in words and figures of similar size and prominence.

It is petitioner's contention that since the sign complained of contains all the information required by the statute, that it fully complies with the spirit and intent thereof and cannot be held to constitute a violation. It bases this position upon the decision of the Supreme Court rendered in Adams v. Miami Beach Hotel Association, 77 So.2d 465 (Fla., 1955). The *Adams* decision construed the statute as it then existed and prior to the time it was amended in its present form. In all material respects as concerns the question now under consideration, the provisions of the two statutes are the same. The *Adams* decision merely held that the statute was not violative of any constitutional provision, and was a legitimate exercise of the police power by the State.

Appellant's contention ignores the fact that the violation of which it is found guilty does not concern a failure to include on the sign all the information required by the statute. The essence of the violation is the failure to so construct the sign as to make all figures and letters appearing thereon of similar size and prominence. It indeed taxes the credulity of this court to urge the contention that letters or figures four feet in height and erected forty-three feet from the ground are of similar size and prominence to other figures and letters seven or nine inches in height and erected twenty-six feet from the ground. This is especially so when the larger figures and letters are readable as far away as 1600 feet, while the small letters and figures are readable at a distance of not more than 200 feet from the sign.

To support petitioner's contention would require that the court ignore and read out of the statute the salutary provision which requires that all figures and letters appearing on rate signs in front of public lodging establishments shall be of similar size and prominence. It was the prerogative of the legislature to make such requirement, and the court would be guilty of invading the province of the legislature if it attempted to ignore it. In the performance of his duty to enforce the provisions of the statute now under consideration, the Commissioner acts in a quasi-judicial capacity. His findings of fact are entitled to great weight and should not be reversed unless clearly erroneous, or unless there is no competent substantial evidence to support them.

Petitioner further contends that to interpret and enforce the statute in the manner attempted by the Commissioner would stifle free competition, invade the free enterprise system and violate the rights guaranteed under the Constitution. We are of the view that the constitutionality of a statute such as the one now under consideration has been laid to rest by the Supreme Court in the *Adams* case mentioned above.

We have carefully considered the remaining assignments of error, but find them to be without merit.

Ruling of the Court: Certiorari denied.

Statutes Affecting Hotels

Undeniably, a legislature may pass laws that apply differently to hotels and motels as long as the statutes constitute reasonable class legislation. For example, the State of Florida promulgation of a statute that authorized certain facilities to be located in hotels having one hundred or more rooms was held to be not unreasonable in view of the special needs of larger hotels that are not present in smaller hotels (City of Miami Beach v. Eason, 194 So.2d 652 [Fla., 1967]). Similarly, statutes requiring the presence of lifeguards and lifesaving equipment at hotel or motel pools were ruled a proper subject matter for regulation for health and safety purposes under the police power of the county (Henry Grady Hotel Corp. v. Watts, 167 S.E.2d 205 [Ga., 1969]).

The problem, of course, is with the statutes already on the books—especially those from before 1940, when there were few motels. All accommodations managers should familiarize themselves with this area of the law, as it is increasingly coming under scrutiny. Zoning laws in particular are frequently being utilized by environmentalists.

Currently, a twofold problem exists. First, it is difficult to write legislation that will meet all the requirements of an industry undergoing radical changes and a populace becoming increasingly aware of environmental problems. Second, the laws passed before the motel era are now being interpreted by a new generation of judges and juries with contemporary values. In many cases, consumer causes are championed by idealistically motivated groups that seriously question any deviation from the statutes. Granted, once laws are passed, it is left to the courts to interpret their meaning, often by referring back to the legislative intent or to the generally accepted rules of statutory construction.

Laws are not inflexible, but must yield to social trends and evolving value systems. Their purpose is not to create doubt but to remove it. A statute, therefore, is subject to construction and interpretation only when its meaning is unclear. If the wording of the statute is lucid and unambiguous, however, the statute must be literally enforced.

Another important point is that when the word *hotel* or *motel* is defined by statute, it should be judged in the community of its location and be given the plain, usual, and ordinary implication of the word as used in the statute, for the object of all interpretation and construction is to ascertain and apprehend the intention of the legislature.

There is one final point. Statutes, being in derogation of (abolishing or limiting) the common law, are to be strictly construed or interpreted and cannot be extended in their operation or affected by doubtful implication. Innkeepers, therefore, cannot avail themselves of a statute unless they comply strictly with each provision. This point is emphasized throughout this book—a person must abide by the provisions of a statute before using it in defense. For example, before hotelkeepers can limit their liability for the goods of their guests, they must first prove that they have complied strictly with the statute passed to benefit them. Any deviation may remove them from its protection.

A California court held that, where a motel manager had reason to suspect the guests who had registered were engaged in prostitution or in selling narcotics and this awareness might have ripened into a guilty knowledge subjecting the motel owner to prosecution, the manager had the right to listen in on a guest's telephone conversation. The court ruled that the telephone conversation was not "confidential communication" within the meaning of a statute prohibiting electronic eavesdropping.

The court arrived at this conclusion because the manager had the right to guard against the misuse of her property for reasons of prostitution or drug trafficking. The guests were therefore excluded from entertaining a reasonable expectation of privacy as against the manager if the property were to be misused. The court said that this rule was congruent with the rule that when there is reason to believe that a hotel room is being used for an illicit purpose, the management may reassert control to the extent necessary to carry out a protective search to determine whether it is or is not. The court further stated that where a telephone extension is not equipped with features for recording or amplifying, it is not considered an "electronic amplifying or recording device" to eavesdrop or record confidential communications, and for that reason also was not violative of California's anti-eavesdropping statute (People v. Soles, 136 Cal.Rptr. 328 [1977]).

The right to eavesdrop, however, does not permit the police to obtain without legal process a list of telephone calls made from a guest's room while that person is a guest of the hotel. In People v. McKunes, 124 Cal.Rptr. 126 (1975), a Hyatt House employee gave a list of the telephone calls made by the defendant guest to the police without legal process. The court said that guests have the same rights as if the calls were made from their homes. In a hotel, calls are recorded for billing purposes only. Again the court reiterated the fact that a hotel room is in reality a residence, however temporary. As such, a guest has a right to expect that any encounter, however brief, between the persons who impart and receive information will be held confidential.

Rates

A municipality may pass an ordinance whereby hotels or motels must make known the price charged for each room. Generally, the hotel itself sets the prices and files them with the appropriate bureau. The legislature does not attempt to fix the price of any room in a hotel, nor does it require that the hotel furnish its accommodations or services at any particular rate. But when a law has been duly passed and the hotel company has fixed its rate, the hotel must abide by the stated price. With this statute the hotel has the privilege of raising the rate, but it must file the new schedule within the time stipulated by the statute.

The court in State v. Norval Hotel Company, 133 N.E. 75 (Ohio, 1921), said, "It is a matter of common knowledge that at times when large numbers of the public meet in cities or towns for conventions, or similar gatherings, the capacity of hotels and places for public accommodation is overtaxed and opportunity is thereby given for the exaction of exorbitant or unfair charges." This is an important case on the question of the constitutionality of statutes governing hotel rates and charges.

The case of Archibald v. Cinerama Hotels clearly answers the question of what rates can be charged for a hotel room. However, the concurring opinion by Justice Friedman sets forth a real question on rates that embodies one of the perplexing problems in the hotel, motel industry: the antitrust problem. Justice Friedman stated that the conspiracy charged against defendants in the second count of the complaint is nothing other than concerted price rigging, a contract in restraint of competition. In this case, the plaintiffs did not view the case as an antitrust violation, but again Judge Friedman stated that in view of the heavy accretion of federal and state antitrust laws, the viability of a common law tort action is dubious. This particular tort is within the flow of interstate commerce, within the ambit of federal antitrust legislation, and within the domain of the federal courts.

Case Example	**Archibald v. Cinerama Hotels**
	140 Cal.Rptr. 599 (1977)
	(REGAN, Associate Justice)

This is a plaintiff's appeal from a judgment of dismissal entered upon an order sustaining demurrers without leave to amend. The first amended complaint, to which the demurrers were sustained, is for breach of an innkeeper's duty. It contains three causes of action. It asserts a class action by plaintiff as a member of a class of persons who are citizens and residents of California and who have been guests of hotels and motels in Hawaii which are owned or operated by a multitude of named defendants who do business in California. Also included is a named travel agency and several other fictitiously named travel agencies who make reservations for California visitors at such hotels.

The first cause of action alleges that the rate charged to plaintiff for rooms in the hotels is higher than a so-called "Kamaaina" (local resident) rate, which is offered or available to residents of Hawaii. It is alleged that this is "unlawfully discriminatory." The second cause of action alleges a conspiracy among defendants in furtherance of the discriminatory acts described in the first cause of action. The third cause of action alleges that defendants "violated certain laws, statutes, rules and regulations and the policies of the State of California and engaged in unfair and deceptive acts and practices and principals [sic] contrary to the public policies of the State of California." Plaintiff seeks general damages in each of the three causes of action totalling $300,000,000 and punitive damages totalling another $300,000,000.

The demurrers to all the causes of action were sustained on the ground that none set forth facts sufficient to constitute a cause of action.

Plaintiff contends the first cause of action is good since it alleges a breach of the common law duties of an innkeeper not to discriminate; and also, impliedly if not directly, by alleging "unlawful discrimination" it has alleged violations of constitutional rights under equal protection, privileges and immunities, and commerce clauses of the United States Constitution. To bolster these contentions, plaintiff has prepared a selective dissertation on the common law duties of an innkeeper, a short treatise on the economic doctrine of laissez-faire as it relates to the modern emphasis on equality of contract between providers and consumers, a discussion of certain state equal rights legislation pertaining to places of accommodation of travelers, a discussion of certain constitutional rights as they may pertain to residents versus travelers or nonresidents, and an exposition of the assertedly illusory distinction between "discount" and "overcharges" pertaining to hotels. Plaintiff's efforts have left us unpersuaded that the trial court erred.

It is alleged in the first cause of action that the rates charged plaintiff and members of her class are higher than those charged to residents of the State of Hawaii. It is not alleged that the rates charged Californians are different than the rates charged any person or class of persons from any-

Even if the legal barriers to application of Civil Code Sections 51 and 52 are put aside, statutory construction indicates they are not applicable here. The language in the Cox case does not make them applicable. Plaintiff was not arbitrarily excluded from any business premise, nor was she arbitrarily discriminated against in any way. Plaintiff has alleged no tort, breach of contract or other actionable wrong. The trial court therefore did not err in sustaining the demurrers to the first cause of action.

Our research has disclosed no California statute, rule or policy which requires a hotel to charge a uniform rate to all its guests. The only statute remotely pertinent is of no aid to plaintiff. This is Civil Code Section 1863 which requires posting of the range of rates and prohibits charging more than the posted rate. Insofar as policy or rules are concerned, an innkeeper has a duty to receive and accommodate all persons at a reasonable charge. This rule or policy is based upon the common law doctrine referred to above as well as Civil Code Sections 51 and 52 and is reiterated in certain court decisions. In fact, an innkeeper who refuses accommodations without just cause (such as inability to pay, infectious disease, or the like) is not only civilly liable but is guilty of a misdemeanor (Pen. Code, § 365).

Ruling of the Court: The judgment is affirmed.

(FRIEDMAN, Acting Presiding Justice)

I concur, but have a somewhat divergent view touching the second count of the complaint. That count alleges a conspiracy to charge a higher level of hotel rates to mainland tourists than to "kamaainas." The negation of civil conspiracy as an independent tort does not quite obliterate the complaint's second count. Conspiracy is nothing but a pejorative term for a contract or agreement. The conspiracy charged against defendants in the second count of the complaint is nothing other than concerted price-rigging, a contract in restraint of competition.

Persons injured by such a contract might conceivably pursue a common law tort action on a theory of intentional deprivation of prospective economic advantage. In view of the heavy accretion of federal and state antitrust laws, the viability of a common law tort action is dubious. This particular tort lies within the flow of interstate commerce, within the ambit of federal antitrust legislation and within the domain of the federal courts.

This is the second appeal in this class action. The first (which turned on a forum non conveniens issue) was fully and fairly presented as a battle over venue (Archibald v. Cinerama Hotels, 126 Cal.Rptr. 811, 544 P.2d 947). The present appeal "on the merits" of the pleading is a scarcely concealed battle over venue, an attempt by the class plaintiffs to keep the lawsuit in the California state courts and an attempt by defendants to move it anywhere but California. Some enigmatic tactical purpose has motivated the defense to debate the pleading in terms of the common law "innkeeper" verbiage selected by plaintiffs rather than to unmask it as a charge of violating the federal antitrust laws by restraint of competition in interstate commerce.

Plaintiffs, at any rate, must lose this disguised battle over venue. A class of plaintiffs may maintain a civil damage action for violation of the federal antitrust statutes. As a civil damage action alleging restraint of competition in interstate commerce, the second count lies within the exclusive subject-matter jurisdiction of the federal courts. It is outside the subject-matter jurisdiction of the California courts. Although defendants have not challenged state court jurisdiction, they may not consent to it.

Violations

Most states have passed ordinances that regulate how innkeepers or hotelkeepers must use their establishments. Barring specific requirements, all regulations designed to promote the public health and safety can be said to be no more than a reiteration of the common law duty of innkeepers with respect to guests.

In the significant case of Miller v. Strahl, 239 U.S. 426 (1915), in which the plaintiff-guest was injured as a result of the defendant's violation of a Nebraska state law, the hotel was held liable for the guest's injuries. The court expressed the general rule:

> It is quite certain that he who assumes duties may be required to perform them. When the defendant engaged in the business of hotelkeeper he undertook its obligations, and we need not consider whether the statute exacts from him and his employees heroic conduct. The command of the statute is that in case of a fire the keepers of hotels must give notice of the same to all guests and inmates thereof at once, and to do all in their power to save such guests and inmates. Could the statute exact less? It is the dictate of humanity, and gets nothing from its expression as a legal obligation except a penalty for its violation, and the facts of the case reject any charge that it was enforced to the extent of risk of the life of anybody or to the injury of anybody.

Antitrust Problems

Federal antitrust laws affect practically every facet of modern corporate life. Both giant corporations and small hotels may find themselves accused of participating in agreements in violation of the federal antitrust laws. The penalties for such violation have recently been increased. Violators of the Sherman Act are now charged with a felony. They can be sentenced to up to three years in prison and fined up to $100,000 for individuals or up to $1 million for corporations.

In 1977, four hotel firms and the Hawaii Hotel Association pleaded no contest to federal criminal antitrust charges of price fixing. Sheraton Hawaii Corp. and Hilton Hotels were fined $50,000 each, and Cinerama Hawaii Hotels and Flagship International were each ordered to pay $25,000, while the trade group was fined $10,000 by the U.S. Justice Department.

The Sherman Act of 1890 says: "Every contract, combination in the form of trust or otherwise, or conspiracy, in restraint of trade or commerce among the several States, or with foreign nations, is hereby declared to be illegal." What constitutes a violation of this act? The agreement between competing hoteliers on prices or services. The agreement need not be implemented; conspiracy alone is a violation of the antitrust laws. Seldom will there be a written contract as a result of such agreements. As the court said in Esco Corp. v. United States, 340 F.2d 1000 (1965), a "knowing wink can mean more than words." For example, business persons who simply stand up in a room may be indicating their mutual pledge to the nonreduction of prices. More obvious violations include price-fixing agreements; boycotts by a group against a competitor, supplier, or customer; the division by a group of competitors of their territory among themselves so as to eliminate competition; and tying contracts, whereby a franchisee owner agrees to license or furnish the franchise the tying product on condition that the franchisee agrees to buy other products of the franchisor.

In *United States v. Hilton Hotel Corporation*, the court had little trouble in finding that the actions of a group of hoteliers amounted to restraint of trade when they agreed to coerce suppliers with loss of hotel business unless the supplier paid the trade association's assessment, which it planned to use in promoting convention business in Portland.

What is perhaps most disturbing about the *Hilton* case as far as hoteliers and restaurateurs are concerned is that high officials of the corporation can be held liable for the actions of their employees when being tried under the antitrust statutes. The results can be quite serious. Certain large hotel chains have taken elaborate steps to avoid the consequences of being tried under the antitrust statutes by giving detailed instruction on what an employee can and must do. Additionally, officials are now following through on checking whether employees are carrying out their instructions.

Case Example   **United States v. Hilton Hotels Corporation**
467 F.2d 1000 (Oregon, 1972)
(BROWNING, Circuit Judge)

This is an appeal from a conviction under an indictment charging a violation of section 1 of the Sherman Act, 15 U.S.C. § 1.

Operators of hotels, restaurants, hotel and restaurant supply companies, and other businesses in Portland, Oregon, organized an association to attract conventions to their city. To finance the association, members were asked to make contributions in predetermined amounts. Companies selling supplies to hotels were asked to contribute an amount equal to one per cent of their sales to hotel members. To aid collections, hotel members, including appellant, agreed to give preferential treatment to suppliers who paid their assessments, and to curtail purchases from those who did not.

The jury was instructed that such an agreement by the hotel members, if proven, would be a per se violation of the Sherman Act. Appellant argues that this was error.

We need not explore the outer limits of the doctrine that joint refusals to deal constitute per se violations of the Act, for the conduct involved here was of the kind long held to be forbidden without more. "Throughout the history of the Sherman Act, the courts have had little difficulty in finding unreasonable restraints of trade in agreements among competitors, at any level of distribution, designed to coerce those subject to a boycott to accede to the action or inaction desired by the group or to exclude them from competition."

Appellant argues that in cases in which the per se rule has been applied to refusals to deal, the defendants intended "to destroy a competitor or a line of competition," while the purpose of the defendants in the present case "was solely to bring convention dollars into Portland." But the necessary and direct consequence of defendants' scheme was to deprive uncooperative suppliers of the opportunity to sell to defendant hotels in free and open competition with other suppliers, and to deprive defendant hotels of the opportunity to buy supplies from such suppliers in accordance with the individual judgment of each hotel, at prices and on terms and conditions of sale determined by free competition. Defendants, therefore, "intended" to impose these restraints upon competition in the only sense relevant here. The ultimate objective defendants sought to achieve is immaterial.

Running through appellant's argument is the theme that the suppliers complied with the urgings of the hotels to contribute because they wished to maintain friendly business relations with these important customers; that this sort of "coercion," and submission to it, is common in American business life, and should not be subject to the Sherman Act unless it is shown that in the particular case it was intended to have, or had, an unreasonable impact upon price, quality, or service.

If the argument is that the evidence did not show an agreement on the part of the hotels to prefer suppliers who paid their contribution over those who did not, we reject it on the ground that the evidence was clearly sufficient to establish such an agreement. If the argument is that such use by the defendant hotels of their combined economic power to coerce suppliers violates the Sherman Act only if price, service, or quality is adversely affected, we reject it on the authority of Klor's Inc., v. Broadway-Hale Stores, 359 U.S. at 212, 79 S.Ct. 705.

Appellant argues that since the suppliers were also members of the association, the per se rule is inapplicable because "the request for contribution and the alleged coercive action was among members of the same association" and the "implied threat of coercion or preference can be said simply to be an incidental effect of regulations within the group inter se."

The circumstance that both the boycotters and their victims were members of the same trade association would not diminish the impact of the boycott on competition, and appellant does not explain why it should affect the legality of the boycott. This same factual circumstance appears to have been present, for example, in Fashion Originators' Guild v. FTC, 312 U.S. at 461, 61 S.Ct. 703.

The evidence does not show that the suppliers joined in the agreement that the hotels would cease dealing with those that failed to pay, but the result would not be changed if it had. It is not the primary purpose of the Sherman Act to protect deserving private persons, but to vindicate the public interest in a free market.

This is not a case in which joint activity having a primary purpose and direct effect of accomplishing a legitimate business objective is also alleged to have had an incidental and indirect adverse effect upon the business of some competitors. The primary purpose and direct effect of defendants' agreement was to bring the combined economic power of the hotels to bear upon those suppliers who failed to pay. The exclusion of uncooperative suppliers from the portion of the market represented by the supply requirements of the defendant hotels was the object of the agreement, not merely its incidental consequence.

Appellant's president testified that it would be contrary to the policy of the corporation for the manager of one of its hotels to condition purchases upon payment of a contribution to a local association by the supplier. The manager of appellant's Portland hotel and his assistant testified that it was the hotel's policy to purchase supplies solely on the basis of price, quality, and service. They also testified that on two occasions they told the hotel's purchasing agent that he was to take no part in the boycott. The purchasing agent confirmed the receipt of these instructions, but admitted that, despite them, he had threatened a supplier with loss of the hotel's business unless the supplier paid the association assessment. He testified that he violated his instructions because of anger and personal pique toward the individual representing the supplier.

Based upon this testimony, appellant requested certain instructions bearing upon the criminal liability of a corporation for the unauthorized acts of its agents. These requests were rejected by the trial court. The court instructed the jury that a corporation is liable for the acts and statements of its agents "within the scope of their employment," defined to mean "in the corporation's behalf in performance of the agent's general line of work," including "not only that which has been authorized by the corporation, but also that which outsiders could reasonably assume the agent would have authority to do." The court added:

"A corporation is responsible for acts and statements of its agents, done or made within the scope of their employment, even though their conduct may be contrary to their actual instructions or contrary to the corporation's stated policies."

Appellant objects only to the court's concluding statement.

Congress may constitutionally impose criminal liability upon a business entity for acts or omissions of its agents within the scope of their employment. Such liability may attach without proof that the conduct was within the agent's actual authority, and even though it may have been contrary to express instructions.

The intention to impose such liability is sometimes express, but it may also be implied. The text of the Sherman Act does not expressly resolve the issue. For the reasons that follow, however, we think the construction of the Act that best achieves its purpose is that a corporation is liable for acts of its agents within the scope of their authority even when done against company orders.

It is obvious from the Sherman Act's language and subject matter that the Act is primarily concerned with the activities of business entities. The statute is directed against "restraint upon commercial competition in the marketing of goods or services." In 1890, as now, the most significant commercial activity was conducted by corporate enterprises.

Despite the fact that "the doctrine of corporate criminal responsibility for the acts of the officers was not well established in 1890", the Act expressly applies to corporate entities. The preoccupation of Congress with corporate liability was only emphasized by the adoption in 1914 of section 14 of the Clayton Act to reaffirm and emphasize that such liability was not exclusive, and that corporate agents also were subject to punishment if they authorized, ordered, or participated in the acts constituting the violation.

Criminal liability for the acts of agents is more readily imposed under a statute directed at the prohibited act itself, one that does not make specific

intent an element of the offense. The Sherman Act is aimed at consequences. Specific intent is not an element of any offense under the Act
except attempt to monopolize under section 2, and conscious wrongdoing
is not an element of that offense. The Sherman Act is violated if "a restraint
of trade or monopoly results as the consequence of a defendant's conduct
or business arrangements."

The breadth and critical character of the public interests protected
by the Sherman Act, and the gravity of the threat to those interests that led
to the enactment of the statute, support a construction holding business
organizations accountable, as a general rule, for violations of the Act by
their employees in the course of their businesses. In enacting the Sherman
Act, "Congress was passing drastic legislation to remedy a threatening
danger to the public welfare. . . ." The statute "was designed to be a
comprehensive charter of economic liberty aimed at preserving free and
unfettered competition as the rule of trade. It rests on the premise that the
unrestrained interaction of competitive forces will yield the best allocation
of our economic resources, the lowest prices, the highest quality and the
greatest material progress, while at the same time providing an environment
conducive to the preservation of our democratic political and social institutions."

With such important public interests at stake, it is reasonable to assume that Congress intended to impose liability upon business entities for
the acts of those to whom they choose to delegate the conduct of their
affairs, thus stimulating a maximum effort by owners and managers to
assure adherence by such agents to the requirements of the Act.

Sherman Act violations are commercial offenses. They are usually
motivated by a desire to enhance profits. (A purpose to benefit the corporation is necessary to bring the agent's acts within the scope of his
employment.) They commonly involve large, complex, and highly decen-
tralized corporate business enterprises, and intricate business processes,
practices, and arrangements. More often than not they also involve basic
policy decisions, and must be implemented over an extended period of
time.

Complex business structures, characterized by decentralization and
delegation of authority, commonly adopted by corporations for business
purposes, make it difficult to identify the particular corporate agents responsible for Sherman Act violations. At the same time, it is generally true
that high management officials, for whose conduct the corporate directors
and stockholders are the most clearly responsible, are likely to have participated in the policy decisions underlying Sherman Act violations, or at
least to have become aware of them.

Violations of the Sherman Act are a likely consequence of the pressure
to maximize profits that is commonly imposed by corporate owners upon
managing agents and, in turn, upon lesser employees. In the face of that
pressure, generalized directions to obey the Sherman Act, with the probable
effect of foregoing profits, are the least likely to be taken seriously. And if
a violation of the Sherman Act occurs, the corporation, and not the individual agents, will have realized the profits from the illegal activity.

In sum, identification of the particular agents responsible for a Sherman Act violation is especially difficult, and their conviction and punishment is peculiarly ineffective as a deterrent. At the same time, conviction
and punishment of the business entity itself is likely to be both appropriate
and effective.

For these reasons we conclude that as a general rule a corporation is liable under the Sherman Act for the acts of its agents in the scope of their employment, even though contrary to general corporate policy and express instructions to the agent.

Thus the general policy statements of appellant's president were no defense. Nor was it enough that appellant's manager told the purchasing agent that he was not to participate in the boycott. The purchasing agent was authorized to buy all of appellant's supplies. Purchases were made on the basis of specifications, but the purchasing agent exercised complete authority as to source. He was in a unique position to add the corporation's buying power to the force of the boycott. Appellant could not gain exculpation by issuing general instructions without undertaking to enforce those instructions by means commensurate with the obvious risks.

We have examined the government's evidence in light of this standard and conclude that it is sufficient.

Ruling of the Court: Affirmed.

Zoning

Three states—Massachusetts, New Hampshire, and New York—have interpreted the applicable statutes as not encompassing the construction and operation of a motel within the meaning of the word *hotel*. Von der Heide v. Zoning Board of Appeals, 123 N.Y.S.2d 726 (1953), deals with the question of whether a motel is to be considered a hotel, at least in conjunction with zoning. In this case, the plaintiff filed an application with the building inspector of Somers in Westchester County, New York, to erect a motel. The building inspector decided that the town ordinance did not permit motels in the business district. Justice Eager said, "The court generally has no right to enlarge upon the commonly accepted definition of a word used in a zoning ordinance, for to do so would be to legislate rather than to construe. Of course, if a particular word is expressly defined in the ordinance, the court would be bound by the specified definition, but the word *inn* is not defined in this particular ordinance."

The ordinance in question was passed around 1923 when the motel as a place of accommodation was unknown to legislatures. Using this rationale to determine the legislative intent of the statute, the court construed the statute according to its meaning at the time of this enactment (1923), and concluded that a new meaning should not be given to the words of the statute, even though conditions of living and travel had changed.

In the Von der Heide appeal, 126 N.Y.S.2d 852 (1953), the court did not decide the case on its own merits but decided rather on a recent amendment. The amendment clearly differentiated between a hotel and a motel, stating that the terms *boarding house* and *inn* as used in the statute should not include motels or tourist camps. The court concluded by stating that the amendment resolved all doubt on the question and was the determinant.

In a later decision in the same New York county (Maturi v. Balint, 130 N.Y.S.2d 122 [1953]), the court, with similar facts before it, did not follow the *Von der Heide* case. This later decision stated, "If the municipality seeks to differentiate between different types of hotels, it must do so specially by ordinance." A departure from the *Von der Heide* case is also found in Lindner v. Frisina, 194 N.Y.S.2d 843 (1959), in which the statute did not define a motel as such. Justice Meyer said, "Clearly, the building which petitioner seeks to erect is a hotel as that word is defined in this ordinance. This is so despite the fact that a motel has been held not to be an inn as defined in a zoning ordinance, and despite the fact that, as a matter of unfair competition (Hotel Syracuse v. Motel Syracuse, 127 N.Y.S.2d 485, affirmed, 130 N.E.2d 620) and of trademark registration (Thruway Motel of Ardsley v. Hellman Motel Corp., 170 N.Y.S.2d 552), hotels and motels are to be distinguished."

Even when the use of a building sought by a petitioner clearly falls within the definition of *hotel* and the court and the parties are bound by such a definition, the petitioner is required to exhaust all administrative remedies before resorting to the court. Mandamus, therefore, will not be issued where another solution is available or provided by law.

In *Spicer v. City of Claremont*, "motel" and "hotel" were not held as synonymous. In most jurisdictions, they are considered the same, but as in the *Spicer* case the legislature may differentiate between the two for certain purposes.

Case Example **Spicer v. City of Claremont**
189 A.2d 496 (N.H., 1963)

This is a zoning appeal to the Superior Court by the plaintiffs from a decision of the board of adjustment of the city of Claremont, sustaining the decision of its building inspector in issuing two building permits to the defendants Charles Hardy and Barbara Hardy, for the development of a motel on the premises owned by them. The facts are not in dispute and the parties have agreed that for the purposes of this case the zoning ordinance of the city of Claremont is valid and that the proceedings and decisions of the board of adjustment in this case are procedurally correct and are supported by the evidence. The dispute is limited to a question of the interpretation of the zoning ordinance. The defendants' property is located in a residence zone adjacent to that of the plaintiffs and it is agreed that the defendants' premises are insufficient in size to meet the requirement of a minimum of twenty rooms specified for a hotel as defined in the zoning ordinance.

Although three questions have been transferred without ruling to this court, counsel have treated the second question as the "primary and main issue in this case." In other words, the question is whether, under the zoning ordinance of the city of Claremont, the term "motel" is synonymous with the term "hotel" and is subject to the same limitations as imposed on hotels as defined in Article 1, Section 1 of Ordinance 27 as amended. This ordinance defines a hotel as "a building in which twenty rooms or more are available for hire and incidental hotel services are provided." We conclude that the answer to this question is "no" for the reasons hereinafter stated.

The plaintiffs argue that motels are a modern development of hotels, have many similarities thereto and have been classed as synonymous in certain zoning cases (Maturi v. Balint, 204 Misc. 1011, 130 N.Y.S.2d 122; Schermer v. Fremar Corp., 36 N.J.Super. 46, 114 A.2d 757; Purdy v. Moise, 223 S.C. 298, 75 S.E.2d 605). Additionally it is pointed out that hotels and motels have been classified together for purposes other than zoning (Weiser v. Albuquerque Oil & Gasoline Co., 64 N.M. 137, 325 P.2d 720; Davis v. State, Fla., 87 So.2d 416; Parrish v. Newbury [Ky.Ct. of App.], 279 S.W.2d 299).

On the other hand the defendants rely on cases which have reached a contrary conclusion or have emphasized the differences between motels and hotels (Von der Heide v. Zoning Board, 282 App.Div. 1076, 126 N.Y.S.2d 852; Hotel Syracuse, Inc., v. Motel Syracuse, Inc., 283 App.Div. 182, 127 N.Y.S.2d 485, aff'd 309 N.Y. 831, 130 N.E.2d 620; see Costa v. Board of Appeals of Watertown, 340 Mass. 380, 381, 164 N.E.2d 149). In each case, however, the court seeks to ascertain the meaning and intent of the specific municipal zoning ordinance or the governing legislative act . . . which frequently carries more weight than generalized statements from conflicting cases.

In the present case, the zoning ordinance of the city of Claremont has placed a restrictive definition and a limitation on what constitutes a hotel by requiring a minimum of twenty rooms. It has not defined motels, restrictively or otherwise, but has indicated an intention to treat motels as distinct from hotels. . . . The following stipulation in the reserved case is significant: "10. The Claremont ordinance has not previously been construed to impose a twenty-room minimum size requirement upon motels, but on the other hand, the only motels for which permits have been issued under the ordinance have been upon the basis of permits for less than twenty rooms and such permits have been issued without variance proceedings." While the administrative construction of the ordinance by the zoning authorities is neither conclusive nor binding on this court in its construction of the ordinance, it is entitled to consideration.

The cases that have held motels and hotels to be synonymous are generally those in which motels are not mentioned in the zoning ordinance. This is not true of the zoning ordinance involved in this litigation. In this state, motels have been separately classified for various purposes. . . . There is no legislation which prohibits such separate classification for the purpose of zoning.

While motels may also be subject to the same limitations as hotels for zoning purposes, in this case, however, the limitations with respect to hotels contained in Article 1, Section 1 of the Claremont zoning ordinance were not made applicable to motels. The permit for a motel issued to the defendants under the zoning ordinance of the city of Claremont was proper and is not subject to the limitations imposed on hotels for a minimum of twenty rooms.

Ruling of the Court: For defendant to build a motel. Plaintiff's appeal dismissed.

Trademark Registration and Unfair Competition

Many successful service corporations are emulated by other companies desiring to trade on their name, style, and the image they portray to the public. In 1963 a federal court in Raleigh, North Carolina, enjoined a restaurant company, which was imitating Howard Johnson's trade name, color combination, and architecture, from using the name "Henry Johnson's" (Howard Johnson Co. v. Henry Johnson's Restaurant, Civil Case 1258 U.S.D.C. [No. Carolina, 1964]). Judge Bell, who heard the case, found that Howard Johnson's had established for its name "a secondary meaning separate and distinct from the personal name of Howard Johnson."

What happens when a company is adjudged to have used the name of a previously registered corporation? In the case of *Gas Town*, a Massachusetts corporation of 200 service stations doing business in New England, New York, and Louisiana, a federal court in Hartford, Connecticut, ordered the company to take down all its signs (Gas Town, Inc., of Delaware v. Gas Town, Inc., 341 F.Supp. 626 [Conn., 1971]). The reason cited was that the Marathon Oil Company of Ohio had registered the name about eighteen months before the owner of the Massachusetts company.

The critical law on trademarks is found in Section 43(a) of the Lanham Act (15 U.S.C. 1125 [a]), which prohibits the passing off of services by one person under the guise that they are the services of another. It states that "any person who shall affix, apply, or annex, or use in connection with any . . . services . . . a false designation of origin, or any false description or representation, including words or other symbols tending falsely to describe or represent the same . . . shall be liable to a civil action by any person . . . who believes that he is or is likely to be damaged by the use of any such false description or representation."

In Steak & Brew, Inc., v. Beef & Brew Restaurant, Inc., 370 F.Supp. 1030 (Ill., 1974), the plaintiff, Delaware Corporation of Peoria, Illinois, attempted to prevent the defendant, Beef & Brew, operating in Rock Island, Illinois, from using the word *Brew* in its name. Peoria and Rock Island are approximately 100 miles apart. The court commented that ordinarily the prior appropriation of the name settles the question. But when two parties independently are employing the same mark upon goods of the same class, but operate in remote and separate markets, the question of prior appropriation is legally insignificant unless it appears that the second adopter has selected the mark to benefit from the reputation of the first user's goods or to forestall the extension of the first user's trade. The descriptive word *Brew* could not be considered a word subject to exclusive appropriation. Such a word would be subject to protection only upon proof that it attained a secondary meaning identified with the plaintiff in the market area involved.

In this case, the court ruled there was no factual basis for a finding that the defendant's use of the name "Beef & Brew" violated the Lanham Act. The defendant had innocently adopted the name for use in a market area in which the plaintiff was unknown; therefore, he was allowed to continue using the name in that region.

However, where prior knowledge of a trademark is a factor, the courts will stop its use. In the case of Tisch Hotels, Inc., v. Americana Inn, Inc., 350 F.2d 609 (1965), the court ruled that the use of the word *Americana*, the name of a luxury hotel in Florida that was adopted by a Chicago hotel company, was illegal. "Not only did the defendant pirate the name, but it also adopted the plaintiff's fanciful name in all details, namely, 'americana' all in lowercase with a white line extending through the first *a* and a five-pointed star as the dot over the *i*."

In protecting a business name, the mere spelling of that word may be important. Indeed, American business firms spend millions of dollars each year just to remind the public to begin trademarks with a capital letter. According to the trademark law, a valuable brand name may be lost through becoming a part of the language—that is, just another word that anyone may use. Over the years this has happened to such notable trademarks as Aspirin, Mimeograph, Linoleum, Dry Ice, Escalator, and Kerosene. In each instance, what began as an initial capital-letter private name ended as an initial small-letter public word. Doubtless the English language has been enriched, but the manufacturer is the poorer—penalized, ironically, because its product became too popular.

How does the law determine that a trademark has gone into the public domain? Mainly, the prerequisite is that the public has come to consider the word as the generic name of the thing itself, rather than as an indication of the specific product and its manufacturer. For example, a court held that "Cellophane" was no longer a trademark, largely because so many consumers found no other way to describe that kind of product.

Ordinarily, a company cannot gain trademark rights in a word that was part of the language to begin with. For this reason a manufacturer of aluminum-covered washboards was denied trademark rights in the word *aluminum*.

One case that encompasses many trademark and unfair competition laws is *Holiday Inns, Inc., v. Holiday Inn*. The case also presents historical background on a giant of the hotel industry, explains how to register a trademark, submits a test of what constitutes trademark infringement, illustrates the effect of delay in bringing action against an infringer of a trademark, discusses the rights of the traveling public not to be deceived, and affords an insight into federal versus state registration. The case reveals much valuable information about the largest hotel and restaurant chain in the world, and shows how a goliath of the industry can be fought by a relatively small company.

Case Example	Holiday Inns, Inc., v. Holiday Inn
	364 F.Supp. 775 (S.C., 1973)
	(CHAPMAN, District Judge)

This action is brought by the plaintiff, Holiday Inns, Inc., a Tennessee corporation, and the largest company in the restaurant and lodging business in the United States, hereinafter referred to as "the Chain." The suit is for alleged unfair competition and service mark infringement against the defendant Holiday Inn, a South Carolina corporation that operates a motel and restaurant at Myrtle Beach, South Carolina, under the name of Holiday Inn. This defendant has counterclaimed, alleging infringement and unfair competition under the common law of South Carolina and false representation and designation of origin by plaintiff under 15 U.S.C. § 1125(a), and seeks cancellation of certain of plaintiff's registrations under 15 U.S.C. § 1119.

The defendant, Holiday Inn, brought in as additional defendants on the counterclaim Fleming Jensen and Strand Development Corporation (hereinafter referred to as Strand), which is a South Carolina corporation and a franchisee of the Chain. Strand operates motel facilities at Myrtle Beach, South Carolina under the name of HOLIDAY LODGE and HOLIDAY DOWNTOWN. Strand also operates a facility under the name of HOLIDAY INN in the town of North Myrtle Beach, South Carolina. Fleming Jensen is an officer of Strand Corporation.

The plaintiff's basic charges against defendant are:

a   That defendant intentionally adopted and used a sign designed substantially identical to the registered "great sign" used by the plaintiff.

b   That defendant adopted and used a mark YOUR HOST ON THE COAST and YOUR HOST WHILE IN MYRTLE BEACH, which are claimed to be substantially identical to the mark registered by the plaintiff: YOUR HOST FROM COAST TO COAST.

c   That the usage set forth in items **(a)** and **(b)** above are likely to cause confusion, mistake and deception among customers of hotel services in Myrtle Beach, South Carolina area.

d   That the usages set forth in items **(a)** and **(b)** above constitute infringement and acts of unfair competition under the Trademark Act, 15 U.S.C. § 1051 et seq., and the common law of South Carolina.

In reply to defendant's counterclaim, the plaintiff raised additional charges of infringement and unfair competition against defendant stemming from defendant's alleged use of signs and other materials which present the name HOLIDAY INN in a script form identical to that used by plaintiff and registered by plaintiff.

The issues raised by defendant Holiday Inn charge the plaintiff and Strand Corporation with trademark and service mark infringement, unfair competition under the South Carolina common law, false representation and false designation of origin under 15 U.S.C. § 1125. These charges are based upon plaintiff and Strand's use of the names and marks HOLIDAY LODGE and HOLIDAY DOWNTOWN in Myrtle Beach, South Carolina, and HOLIDAY INN in North Myrtle Beach. Defendant also seeks to cancel plaintiff's registration Nos. 592,539 and 592,540 because of alleged false statements made in connection with affidavits filed by the Chain pursuant to 15 U.S.C. § 1065.

This matter was heard before the court without a jury and the court has given considerable time to reading the voluminous depositions, considering and examining numerous exhibits, listening to argument of counsel, and reviewing briefs and memoranda of law submitted. Now in accordance with Rule 52, Federal Rules of Civil Procedure, the court makes the following finding of facts.

Findings Of Fact

1 The plaintiff Holiday Inns, Inc., hereinafter referred to as the "Chain," is a corporation organized and existing under the laws of the State of Tennessee, having its principal place of business in Memphis, Tennessee. It was founded in 1952 and since that time has grown to the point that it is now the largest factor in the restaurant and lodging business in the United States, and also does a considerable volume of business outside the United States. The plaintiff's principal business is providing restaurant and lodging services operating under the name Holiday Inn. These services are provided either through company owned facilities or facilities franchised by the Chain. At present the Chain has a facility in almost every major city in the United States, including 33 in the State of South Carolina. The Chain presently owns or franchises approximately 1,300 facilities in the United States.

2 The Chain's original concept was to establish a network of motels and restaurants spanning the entire country upon which the traveling public could rely in obtaining satisfactory services. The facilities affiliated with the Chain are readily recognizable, with quality controls exercised by the Chain and many similar services available at all facilities, such as free use of baby cribs, no charge for children under 12 when sleeping in the room with the parent, kennels for pets, acceptance of Gulf Oil credit cards, etc.

3 The Chain had developed and prominently displays on each facility a large sign, generally referred to as the "great sign." This sign is one of the major features by which travelers generally identify a motel as belonging to or affiliated with the Chain. This sign is quite large, but in some cities smaller versions are used in order to comply with local zoning restrictions. The sign has a green background with the name HOLIDAY INN in large distinctive script lettering, a large star at the top and smaller stars by the name HOLIDAY INN, a large orange arrow starting at the bottom of the sign and running in a sort of semicircle with the point indicating the location of the facility. There is always an attraction panel near the bottom of the sign.

4 In addition to the "great sign" most of the Chain facilities prominently display the words HOLIDAY INN in very large lettering in the distinctive script form directly on the side or face of the building.

5 In the promotion of its services, the plaintiff also uses certain slogans, one of which is YOUR HOST FROM COAST TO COAST. . . .

6 Each of the above registrations was lawfully issued, is valid and currently subsisting. The requisite affidavits having been filed and accepted, these registrations have been accorded an incontestable status pursuant to 15 U.S.C. § 1065.

7 The above registered service marks of plaintiff are well known to the American traveling public. They have been extensively used and advertised in promoting plaintiff's services and the services of its franchisees. Numerous advertisements have appeared in magazines, newspapers, on radio and television and billboards, as well as a house magazine and a directory of member facilities of which more than ten million are printed and distributed each year. To indicate that its service marks are registered, the plaintiff has consistently used the ® or "Reg. U.S. Pat. Office" designations in association with its marks.

8 The defendant Holiday Inn was incorporated in 1960. Prior to that time the business had been operated as a partnership or a proprietorship by Mr. and Mrs. George Hendrix. Mr. Hendrix died in 1959 and the following year Mrs. Hendrix incorporated the business and is the major stockholder and the president of the corporation. In 1966 she married William A. Smith, who since 1966 has held the office of vice-president and general manager of the motel known as Holiday Inn located at 1200 North Ocean Boulevard in Myrtle Beach, South Carolina.

9 When Mr. and Mrs. Hendrix began business in 1948 their resort consisted of an eight-unit frame structure operating under the name Ocean Front Lodge. This facility was expanded to 20 units in 1949 and the name was changed to Holiday Inn having been derived from the popular movie "White Christmas." This name was presented in block letters until defendant's facility was expanded by the addition of approximately 15 units, which construction was completed in August 1955. At this time a new sign was erected and comprised the words HOLIDAY INN and applied directly to the newly constructed building. The lettering on this sign was in script form substantially identical to the distinctive script which plaintiff had adopted in 1952 and registered in 1954.

10 The defendant's facility grew over the years to its present 87 units.

11 In the beginning of defendant's business it did very little advertising. It operated a small facility offering rooms and apartments on a European plan without a restaurant. As the additions were made to defendant's facility it began to advertise on two or three billboards in the Myrtle Beach area using the script lettering of Holiday Inn. It also advertised on a limited scale in newspapers in South Carolina, North Carolina, and occasionally in other states and certain parts of Canada. Many Canadians vacation at Myrtle Beach in the spring.

12 The plaintiff first learned of defendant's facility in 1956 when a franchisee of plaintiff, who was constructing a motel facility in Myrtle Beach received a letter from defendant's lawyer objecting to the proposed usage of HOLIDAY INN within the Myrtle Beach area. Plaintiff's franchisee obtained permission from plaintiff to operate the facility within the plaintiff's system under the name HOLIDAY LODGE. This facility has been operated continuously since 1956 as a typical member of the plaintiff's system and has been advertised as such. A great sign was erected in front of the facility presenting the words HOLIDAY LODGE in large script lettering above the words HOLIDAY INNS OF AMERICA SYSTEM. In all other respects the great sign was the same as used by the Chain throughout the system. Holiday Lodge is now operated by Strand and still uses the name Holiday Lodge and has been identified as such from its inception in 1956. Defendant has known of this facility since prior to its opening.

13 In 1956 a complaint was filed by Mrs. Hendrix (now Mrs. Smith) and her husband in the Court of Common Pleas for Horry County seeking to restrain plaintiff's franchisee from using the name Holiday Inn, Holiday Lodge, or anything including the name Holiday in the Myrtle Beach area. This complaint was not answered and the action never pursued. It was eventually stricken from the court's records for lack of prosecution. This removal from the court docket did not occur until 1969, but no action was taken after the original filing of the complaint.

14 In recent years the defendant has placed stars near the words Holiday Inn in script and on one occasion has used a slogan YOUR HOST ON THE COAST on postcards distributed to its guests and prospective customers and has also used the slogan YOUR HOST WHILE IN MYRTLE BEACH on highway signs that present the words Holiday Inn in plaintiff's script form. The defendant has also used towels, parking lot identification stickers, and notices to guests that have the words HOLIDAY INN®.

15 In 1968 the defendant's general manager ordered a sign constructed and placed in its parking lot immediately across the street from its facility. He requested the sign maker to design a sign which would resemble, but not exactly duplicate, the plaintiff's "great sign" and delivered to the sign maker one of plaintiff's brochures to use as a guide. This sign is so similar to the "great sign" of plaintiff that Mr. Smith in his testimony could not explain any differences without being furnished with photographs of each sign. When comparing the two photographs, the court can distinguish one from the other, but the signs are so similar that the traveling public would be easily confused and upon seeing defendant's sign would conclude that it was a franchisee of plaintiff or affiliated with it. The colors of the two signs are almost identical. The use of stars, the big arrow, the attraction panel, and the script of Holiday Inn are so similar that the court can only conclude that defendant erected this sign with the intent and purpose of infringing the rights of the plaintiff and unfairly competing with it.

16 Mr. Smith testified that he showed the plans of the sign to his attorney before it was constructed and that it received the attorney's approval. This attorney is now deceased and the court can only conclude that he did not receive all of the facts in the matter or else he was not overly familiar with trademark law. Regardless of the advice given by the attorney, such an obvious act of infringement by the defendant could not be justified or excused by a statement that it was made upon advice of counsel.

17 In 1969 Strand began construction of a motel facility franchised by the Chain in Myrtle Beach and another in North Myrtle Beach, which is a separate community located approximately 15 miles north of Myrtle Beach, South Carolina. The facility in Myrtle Beach is now open and operates under the name of HOLIDAY DOWNTOWN and the facility in North Myrtle Beach under the name HOLIDAY INN NORTH MYRTLE BEACH. The "great sign" was erected on the premises of both of these facilities and the facility in Myrtle Beach does not use the word "Inn" but instead used the words HOLIDAY DOWNTOWN in large script on the "great sign." These facilities have been in operation since 1970 and make use of numerous items inside the premises such as towels, brochures, wastebaskets, stationery, shoeshine cloths, bags, etc., which have imprinted thereon the various marks of plaintiff, including HOLIDAY INN®.

18 Within the city limits of Myrtle Beach only defendant's resort facility is advertised by means of road signs and billboards under the name Holiday Inn. In the telephone directory, the various Strand facilities are listed by their respective names and are indented under the name Holiday Inns of America. The defendant facility is listed under the name Holiday Inn.

19   The plaintiff maintains a nationwide registration system known as Holidex, which is connected with a computer and a significant portion of the reservations at the Strand facilities are made through this system. Other reservations are made by direct telephone contact with the individual motel and other travelers know of the existence of the Strand facilities through plaintiff's directory.

20   Since the two new Strand facilities began operations the defendant has experienced no significant loss of business. During the summer season, it is always full and enjoys approximately 80 percent repeat business. In the off season, a substantial portion of its business is also repeat.

21   There was no evidence that advertising by radio, television, national directory, national magazines, and billboards on the part of the plaintiff or Strand had caused any customer confusion between the facilities of Strand and defendant.

22   There was no evidence that usage on the inside of Strand facilities of materials bearing the marks of plaintiff had caused customer confusion between the facilities of Strand and the defendant, and there was no evidence that usage of the "great sign" by Strand facilities has caused customer confusion.

23   Confusion has developed as a result of the similarity of names and there have been mix-ups in bills, letters, reservations, deliveries, etc. Some of this confusion was natural in view of the similarity of names, but the considerable part of it can be charged to the defendant's erection of a sign quite similar to the plaintiff's "great sign."

24   It is clear from the evidence that Strand made every effort to indicate that its facilities were a part of plaintiff's system and there was no evidence to show that the plaintiff or Strand ever attempted to indicate any connection beween them and the defendant.

25   In the immediate Myrtle Beach area, there are six other lodging facilities using the name Holiday in addition to Holiday Lodge, Holiday Downtown, and Holiday Inn. None of these are connected with the plaintiff except the Strand facilities. It is not uncommon for a town much smaller than Myrtle Beach in season to have more than one Holiday Inn facility. The town of Florence, South Carolina, at the time this action was commenced had three Holiday Inns and it is much smaller than Myrtle Beach in the summer season. Some confusion may result in the future because of the similarity of names in the Myrtle Beach area, but this can be kept to a minimum if the defendant will discontinue its efforts to identify itself in the public eye with the plaintiff.

26   The defendant contends that it has exclusive use to the name Holiday Inn in the Myrtle Beach area which it states includes approximately 75 miles of beach running from Georgetown, South Carolina north to Little River. Although Myrtle Beach is the largest city along this "Grand Strand," defendant has introduced no evidence to establish that the words "Holiday Inn" have been associated with its services by any segment of the general public outside the city of Myrtle Beach. North Myrtle Beach is an independent city having its own government, businesses, recreation areas, golf clubs and large expanse of beach. It is separated from Myrtle Beach by a span of unincorporated areas and the motels in Myrtle Beach do not compete directly with those in North Myrtle Beach. While the court finds that there has been some confusion on the part of travelers in Myrtle Beach, such confusion has not been fostered, intentionally or otherwise, by the plaintiff or Strand. In the past confusion has been deliberately and systematically nurtured by the defendant in an effort to profit from the national recognition and goodwill of the plaintiff.

In addition to constructing a sign similar to the "great sign" and adopting large script lettering substantially identical to that of the plaintiff, the defendant has used the ® designation in association with its name on towels, parking stickers, notices to guests, and occasionally in advertisements. Defendant contends that due to the tremendous size of the plaintiff and the name of the defendant many suppliers ship supplies to defendant in response to its orders which have the ® designation thereon, since such suppliers assume that the defendant is affiliated with the Chain. Defendant also contends that it has previously received towels from the local laundry belonging to one of the Strand facilities and containing the ® designation, but that these are infrequent occasions and rarely used by defendant. The court finds this position of the defendant in conflict with the testimony of plaintiff reply witness Wyatt Thompson, sales manager of a Myrtle Beach radio station, who registered at defendant's facility several days before this case was tried and made photographs of items in his room containing the ® designation. These items included two towels, a sign to guests on the mirror, and a parking lot sticker. Although Mr. Smith testified that he had never ordered any supplies with the ®, he had not returned such items to the supplier when received with such designation. The court cannot accept Mr. Smith's explanation that Mr. Thompson by chance was assigned to the only room of the 85 operated by the defendant where items containing the ® were in use.

27   As previously stated, the Strand facilities in Myrtle Beach and North Myrtle Beach use many items inside the facilities containing the name Holiday Inn. These include blankets, sheets, pillowcases, towels, washcloths, wastebaskets, ashtrays, fly swatters, disposable bags, stationeries, etc. Travelers staying at the Strand facilities know that they are dealing with affiliates or franchisees of the Chain, and the use of these various articles inside the facilities do not in any way confuse the traveling public or damage the defendant.

28   The defendant has counterclaimed to cancel plaintiff's registration Nos. 592,539; 592,540; and 592,541, all issued July 13, 1954. These registrations present the words Holiday Inn in script form. The defendant has recently sought to obtain federal registration of its name Holiday Inn and alleges that the plaintiff filed affidavits with the Patent Office which were fraudulent in obtaining incontestable status of the above registrations. Defendant alleges that there was litigation pending in Horry County, South Carolina, regarding the use of the name Holiday Inn at the time plaintiff filed its affidavits pursuant to 15 U.S.C. § 1065 of the Lanham Act for the purpose of gaining the incontestable status for the various Holiday Inn registrations. It is the defendant's position that because of the 1956 lawsuit brought by Mr. and Mrs. George Hendrix against the plaintiff's then Myrtle Beach franchisee, which action was still pending in 1960 when plaintiff filed its affidavits, that such incontestable status was improperly and fraudulently obtained.

Title 15 U.S.C. § 1065 provides, subject to certain exceptions, that the right of a registrant to use its registered mark in commerce for goods or services on or in connection with such registered mark has been in continuous use for five consecutive years subsequent to the date of such registration, shall be incontestable upon filing an affidavit with the Commissioner of Patents, stating:

"(1) There has been no final decision adverse to the registrant's claim of ownership of such mark for such goods or services or to registrant's right to register the same or to keep the same on the register; and (2) there is no proceeding involving said rights pending in the Patent Office or in a court and not finally disposed of. . . ."

The suit in Horry County did not involve the "registrant" and only involved the right of plaintiff's franchisee to use the name Holiday Inn in the Myrtle Beach area. It did not involve plaintiff's right to register its marks or plaintiff's right to maintain the same on the register. This suit had never been defended or pursued by the parties and in 1960 was subject to being stricken from the docket for lack of prosecution under the court rules, although this action was not taken for a number of years thereafter. No evidence was presented by the defendant amounting to any fraud on behalf of the plaintiff in filing the affidavits in connection with the incontestable status and plaintiff's registration Nos. 592,539; 592,540; and 592,541 are properly entitled to the incontestable status.

29   The court finds that there is no confusion between the name, the facilities and services offered by defendant and by Strand's HOLIDAY INN TRAV-L-PARK trailer camp facility. Defendant offers motel and restaurant facilities, while the trailer park caters to the traveling public transporting its own sleeping facilities.

30   The sign constructed by the defendant similar to the "great sign" has now been taken down and the use of the slogan YOUR HOST ON THE COAST has not been used by defendant for a number of years.

31   Prior to the taking of testimony in this action all parties advised the court that they were waiving monetary damages upon their various claims.

Conclusions of Law

1   This court has jurisdiction over the parties and the subject matter of this civil action, and venue is properly laid in this district, pursuant to Title 28, U.S.C. § 1338, 15 U.S.C. § 1121, and 28 U.S.C. § 1391(c).

2   Upon review of the evidence the court is compelled to conclude that the defendant's course of conduct proves it guilty of both unfair competition and service mark infringement against the plaintiff. The elements of these actions are set forth in John Walker & Son, Ltd., v. Bethea, 305 F.Supp. 1302, 1309 (D.C.S.C.1969):

"The elements of both actions are decidedly similar and the courts often lump them together and discuss them as one cause of action. However, there is a distinction between the two forms of action. It is often said that the law of trademark infringement is part of and included in the broader law of unfair competition. However, the law of trademarks is governed by federal statutes, while the related law of unfair competition is of common law origins. . . . It is clear that the action for unfair competition does embrace the law of trademark infringement and extend beyond it. Trademark infringement is a statutory action provided for under the Lanham Act (or Trademark Act, 15 U.S.C. § 1051 et seq.), while unfair competition is a somewhat more comprehensive field, developed under the common law. Being an equitable action developed by case law the court has a great deal more flexibility and may consider a wider number of factors in an unfair competition controversy. Possible confusion in the minds of the buying public is at the core of the law of trademark infringement. Likewise the hallmark of that portion of the law of unfair competition which deals with trademarks is possible confusion as to the source of goods. . . . Additionally, factors bearing on unjust enrichment are frequently considered by the courts in unfair competition controversies."

3   The test for trademark infringement, set forth in 15 U.S.C. § 1114(1), is whether the use of the accused copy or colorable imitation of the registered mark is "likely to cause confusion, or to cause mistake, or to deceive." The test is to be applied with regard to the effect of the marks on an ordinary purchaser having an indefinite recollection of the mark to which he has been exposed on a previous occasion.

As found above, the sign erected by the defendant in 1968 is substantially identical to the plaintiff's "great sign" and although differences are obvious when pictures of the two signs are compared side by side, the effect of the defendant's sign was obvious and was likely to cause confusion, mistake or to deceive the public. Not even the general manager of the defendant could explain differences in the two signs without having pictures of them before him.

4   The script form in which defendant presents its name Holiday Inn is substantially identical to the distinctive script used by plaintiff and shown in its various registrations for Holiday Inn. Although there may be slight differences in the location of the stars, the overall effect is such as is likely to cause confusion, mistake and to deceive the public.

5   Defendant's slogan, YOUR HOST ON THE COAST and YOUR HOST WHILE AT MYRTLE BEACH, differs from the plaintiff's slogan, YOUR HOST FROM COAST TO COAST, and if these slogans alone were the basis of the plaintiff's complaint, this court would not find them to be an infringement. However, when considered with the other acts of the defendant, beginning with the adoption of the script in 1956 and progressively continuing through the erection of the substantially identical sign in 1968, the court must conclude that the use of these slogans by the defendant was an effort to trade upon the goodwill of the plaintiff and represent an infringement of its protected mark, YOUR HOST FROM COAST TO COAST.

6   Although intent is not a necessary element of trademark infringement, there can be no question of defendant's intent to infringe upon the plaintiff's marks. The defendant's president admitted that defendant did not begin to use the distinctive script in writing its name until after she knew of the plaintiff and after the record shows that the plaintiff had registered this script. The court cannot believe that the defendant accidentally or innocently chanced upon the same style script as that used by the plaintiff or that it adopted its slogan without hoping to benefit from the recognition factor already developed by the plaintiff in a similar slogan. The burden of a proper explanation of defendant's action is on the defendant and no suitable explanation was given at the trial. The defendant's contention that the imitation of the plaintiff's "great sign" was intended only as a directional sign and was located across the street from the defendant's motel and restaurant carries no weight and represents no excuse or explanation. The defendant's actions speak so loudly that the court must strain to hear the feeble explanations.

7   The plaintiff's marks are famous throughout the United States and are becoming well known in many other countries. Great effort and expenditure of funds by the plaintiff have not only built up its successful business but have created in the mind of the public strong recognition of its name and service marks. The script, the name, the "great sign" and the slogans of plaintiff have individually and in combination acquired a strong secondary meaning and suggest the plaintiff's services to the general public. These property rights of the plaintiff are entitled to broad protection. . . .

8 The infringements of the defendant have been willful and deliberate and represent unfair competition and an effort on the part of the defendant to identify with and trade upon the plaintiff's goodwill.

9 The defendant contends that the plaintiff has known of defendant's use of the script since it was first used by defendant more than 15 years ago, and that the plaintiff through its delay in moving to protect the script style of its name is barred from asserting an infringement. Under different circumstances the court might follow defendant's argument on this point, but the infringing by the defendant upon the plaintiff began with the use of the script and increased and expanded over the years until the erection of its sign in 1968, which apparently brought about this lawsuit. The elements of estoppel are not present in this case and simple laches or delay is not a sufficient defense. . . . "The intentional use of another's trademark is a fraud; and when the excuse is that the owner permitted such use, that excuse is disposed of by affirmative action to put a stop to it. Persistence, then, in the use is not innocent; and the wrong is a continuing one, demanding restraint by judicial interposition when properly invoked. . . . Where consent by the owner to the use of his trademark by another is to be inferred from his knowledge and silence merely, 'it lasts no longer than the silence from which it springs; it is, in reality, no more than a revocable license'. . . ."

10 The defendant has asserted and this court finds that it is the prior user of the name Holiday Inn in Myrtle Beach, South Carolina. This fact does not excuse the defendant from its course of conduct in infringing upon the plaintiff's trademarks. The acts of infringement and unfair competition by the defendant constitute unclean hands which cause a court of equity to hesitate in rushing to its relief from alleged acts of infringement and unfair competition on the part of the plaintiff and/or Strand. The defendant is entitled to continue the use of the name Holiday Inn within the city limits of Myrtle Beach, South Carolina, but this court will not prevent the plaintiff and/or Strand from operating its facilities now known as Holiday Lodge and Holiday Downtown in Myrtle Beach or Holiday Inn North Myrtle Beach or Holiday Inn Trav-L-Park under the names they are presently using, and it will not prevent Strand from continuing to use the normal articles of personal property, such as: sheets, towels, pillowcases, blankets, etc., bearing the name Holiday Inn, since these articles, which are used inside facilities and not seen by the traveling public, prior to deciding to register at such facilities, do not add to the existing confusion.

11 In the present case, the plaintiff's wrong, if any, is delay, while the defendant's wrong is intentional deception and use of plaintiff's marks to the detriment of the plaintiff and the confusion of the public. The court has the responsibility of protecting the public from such confusion, mistake or deception. . . .

12 While the court might be justified in leaving the parties to their competitive struggle in the town of Myrtle Beach with each using the name Holiday Inn, the rights of the traveling public require the court to resist the temptation and alleviate some of the confusion by requiring the Strand facilities to continue operating under their present names and allowing the defendant to continue using its name, but restraining it from using the distinctive script writing of Holiday Inn on the outside of its building or on billboards or other advertising. The defendant's rights to use the name Holiday Inn are limited to such rights established prior to the date of publication of plaintiff's registered mark, namely August 20, 1954. The defendant made no showing that its name had obtained secondary meaning outside the City of Myrtle Beach prior to August 20, 1954. In Burger King of Florida, Inc., v. Hoots, 403 F.2d 904, 908 (7th Cir. 1968), the court stated:

". . . Congress intended the Lanham Act to afford nationwide protection to federally registered marks, and that once the certificate has issued, no person can acquire any additional rights superior to those obtained by the federal registrant. . . ."

Now, Therefore, It Is Ordered, Adjudged and Decreed:

1 The defendant, its officers, agents, servants, employees and attorneys and all those persons in active concert or participation therewith, who receive actual notice hereof, are hereby perpetually enjoined and restrained from:

a Using either directly or indirectly a script identical to or any colorable imitation of plaintiff's script Holiday Inn on the outside of its building, on any billboards or on any advertising material.

b Using directly or indirectly its version of plaintiff's "great sign" or any colorable limitation thereof.

c Using directly or indirectly the slogan YOUR HOST WHILE AT MYRTLE BEACH or YOUR HOST ON THE COAST or any colorable imitation thereof.

d Using directly or indirectly any sign, script, slogan or star design, color combination or other indicia of plaintiff that suggests or tends to suggest a connection with the plaintiff.

e Using directly or indirectly any indication that the defendant name is registered in the U.S. Patent Office. . . .

2 The defendant shall have ninety (90) days from the date of this order to comply with this injunction as set forth above and defendant's attorney within such time shall submit to the court evidence of compliance.

3 Since plaintiff's registrations were properly filed and issued and the plaintiff has filed the required affidavit under 15 U.S.C. § 1065, defendant's third counterclaim seeking to cancel plaintiff's registration Nos. 592,539; 592,540; and 592,541 is dismissed.

4 The defendant has the right to continue using the name Holiday Inn within the town of Myrtle Beach, South Carolina, and in order to protect the public from unnecessary confusion the court finds that the defendant Strand must continue to operate its Myrtle Beach, South Carolina, facilities under the name of Holiday Lodge and Holiday Downtown; however, it may continue to operate its North Myrtle Beach, South Carolina, facility under the name of Holiday Inn and plaintiff may continue to operate Holiday Inn Trav-L-Park under its existing name. Strand may continue to use Holiday Inn and Holiday Inn® on towels, sheets, blankets, etc., and other items used inside the Myrtle Beach, South Carolina, facilities.

5 The defendant's counterclaim No. 3 for infringement and unfair competition under the common law of South Carolina and for false representation and false designation of origin under 15 U.S.C. § 1125 is dismissed.

6 Plaintiff's motion for attorney's fees and costs because of defendant's dismissal of its antitrust claims, allegedly brought without merit, is dismissed.

7 Each party shall bear its attorney's fees and plaintiff is awarded the cost of this action.

And it is so ordered.

Taxation of Hotels

Taxation is a state prerogative. However, where a license tax is involved, a county or municipality may also levy a tax or increase the tax on hotels and motels. In County Board of Arlington County v. Foglio, 205 S.E.2d 390 (Va., 1974), the trial court reduced the license tax rate set by the County Board of Arlington County. The Supreme Court of Virginia reversed the judgment on the ground that the legislature's act was not subject to judicial review unless the rate it imposed was confiscatory or prohibitive. The power of taxation under our system of government rests with the legislative and not with the judicial branch, and the amount of tax is at the discretion of the legislative body. If this power is exercised in a discriminatory, unjust, or oppressive manner, the constitutional remedy is by an appeal, not to the courts, but to the legislators' sense of justice.

Two cases—People v. Reilly, 198 N.Y.S.2d 654 (1959), a criminal case, and William Reilly Construction Corp. v. City of New York, 334 N.Y.S.2d 459 (1964), a civil case—should be noted here because of the length of time that elapsed between them. In the first case a motel company officer was charged with failure to file a tax return pursuant to the provisions of the New York administrative code. The code imposed a tax on the occupancy of rooms in hotels, apartment hotels, and lodging houses, but it did not mention motels. Here the court said there was a distinction between a motel, hotel, and lodging house that was firmly established in the mind of a reasonable person and if the municipality sought to differentiate between different types of hotels in local law by imposing a tax on occupancy of hotel rooms, the municipality had to do so specifically. The defendant Reilly won his case.

Later, the court in *William Reilly Construction Corp.* reversed itself and held that if on premises dominated by either a hotel or motel, rooms are used for lodging, then the rents derived from letting the premises are subject to the tax imposed on rent for every occupant of the room or rooms in the hotel, apartment, or lodging house. The court further stated that the name *motel* or a similar word was immaterial, and the name did not create separate and distinct grounds for an exemption from tax.

On the question of whether the first case was *res judicata* ("a thing decided"), the court said, "That acquittal on a criminal charge is not a bar to a civil action by the Government, remedial in its nature, arising out of the same facts on which the criminal proceedings were based, has long been settled."

Clubs, however, are not always treated like hotels. In Ambassador Athletic Club v. Utah State Tax Commission, 496 P.2d 883 (1972), the Utah Supreme Court held that an athletic club that was not open to the general public for the purpose of renting rooms or for any other services and that was restricted to a limited and clearly defined group of persons, such as members, guests, or members of clubs in other cities with which there were reciprocal agreements, did not fall within the definition of "hotel" and was not required to pay taxes on the amounts received from room rentals.

In 1981 the U.S. Supreme Court resolved whether the Internal Revenue Service can collect social security and federal unemployment taxes from the employer based upon the value of meals and lodgings furnished to the employee by the employer for the employer's convenience and benefit. It had long been established that such meals and lodgings did not constitute income or wages subject to income taxes, but the IRS continued to assess and collect taxes for social security and federal unemployment taxes on them. In the case of Rowan Companies v. United States, No. 80–780, the court, holding that such meals and lodgings were not wages for the purpose of these taxes either, concluded that Congress intended "wages" to "mean the same thing" under social security, unemployment, and income taxes. Because the IRS established a different interpretation, the regulations were "invalid" and the IRS "erred in relying on them."

Management Principles

A hotel is private property devoted to public use and is subject to public regulation. This chapter has discussed the relationship of hotels to government and its administrative agencies. As a quasi-public business, the hotel industry is licensed with certain rights, duties, and privileges. To conduct business properly, hotelkeepers must have some knowledge of bureaucratic controls. All laws passed have as their primary objective the safeguarding and good of the public, and most people recognize that some governmental control is necessary.

But how much control should be exercised, should the industry help to formulate the laws governing it, and should consumers be protected by a lobbying group? Are all the laws passed beneficial to the industry and to the public? What can be done about unreasonable and arbitrary laws? This book attempts to answer such questions.

The case of Hertenberger v. City of Texarkana dealt with the principle that a hotel must be licensed. It is usually a local decision as to which businesses will be licensed, and since a city council is not a court of law, it need not follow the same rules governing the acceptance of evidence. Therefore, when a case of importance comes up, hotel operators should attend such a meeting only in the company of their attorneys, who will protect their rights. Another general rule of good management is to never accept or act on the "legal advice" of a person who is not a lawyer, particularly if the question is a legal one.

The fairly recent *Hiram Ricker and Sons* case added a new dimension to management rights. Prior to this decision, there was some ambiguity as to whether an unlicensed business had any standing in law. In reality, statutes implicitly stating that recovery cannot be had unless a business is licensed are the exception, not the rule. Granted, one may be fined for not having a license but will not lose over $77,000 as the Rickers almost did. The Rickers won the case but only at a tremendous cost in attorney's fees and time.

Such situations can be avoided by maintaining a due-date calendar that indicates when a license must be renewed. Usually one month's prior warning is adequate. In addition, all reports, inspections, and forms that must be posted should be included on this calendar.

The *Altenhaus* case, which favors hotelkeepers, found that the management must knowingly be aware that guests are using the hotel for immoral or illegal purposes before it can be criminally convicted of maintaining a bawdy house. To practice good management is to be aware of what is going on in one's hotel. However, there are limits to how far hotelkeepers may go in determining the nature and intent of their guests. For example, a hotel may ask for credit references, such as credit cards, or may insist that the guest pay in advance. There is a presumption (in the absence of a statute) that when persons represent themselves as husband and wife that this is indeed their status. Of course, the hotelier may want to discretely ask for proof—but what constitutes proof? Few people carry marriage certificates with them. And the questioning of someone's marital status may result in slander or defamation of character charges. Since women increasingly are retaining their birth names after marriage, a Mr. Smith and Ms. Martindale may actually be married.

Rates

In the absence of a statute, a hotel or restaurant may charge whatever it wishes for its accommodations and products. Nevertheless, an increase in fee to certain people and not to others could be construed as a discriminatory action under the 1964 Civil Rights Act or state law. For example, if all white guests were charged $50 for a double room and all minorities $85 for the same room, the hotelkeeper is doing indirectly what he cannot do directly—that is, practicing discrimination. Granted, certain rooms command higher prices than others, and different rates can certainly be charged for the same room depending on the time of year. But the courts would regard most unfavorably the use of one price for one group and another price for others. (Of course, conventioneers or airline tour groups may be allowed a special price, which does not constitute unlawful discrimination as to race, color, or creed.)

Trademarks

If a trade name is a valuable asset to a business, it must be registered in the office of the secretary of the state (or states) or the federal government for all states. Although unregistered trademark rights are protected under common law, registration constitutes notice of the registrant's claim of ownership and creates certain presumptions of ownership, validity, and exclusive right to use the mark.

Zoning

Many owners of hotel, motel, and restaurant property will face a zoning board or some other governmental agency during the conduct of their business. The operator may want to obtain a variance for such needs as an enlarged parking lot or swimming pool, or a new sign. A good manager will stay well informed on community policy and problems. Zoning should not be construed as a rigid and inflexible set of rules; many communities modify their zoning statutes to keep pace with changing life-styles.

A request for a zoning change or, for that matter, any new plan a manager might want to incorporate in an establishment must be well planned and expressed. The following points may be useful for managers:

1   Seek the services of a local attorney well-versed in local zoning problems.

2   Talk to a local planner who is familiar with the planning board members and their personality traits.

3   Seek out appraisers, market researchers, and public relations people who can prove the need for the proposal and determine its value to the community.

4   Get the aid of traffic experts to prove that the project will not snarl traffic in the area or increase residential traffic.

5   Hire a landscape architect to develop a site plan. Don't present ideas on "the back of an envelope."

6   Employ an engineer to solve sewage disposal, storm water run-off, and water supply problems.

7   Make sure the development looks attractive from all angles. Don't present a sea of parked cars to the general public.

8   Determine the benefit the local community will receive from tax revenues resulting from the development.

9   Convince nearby homeowners that the plans will not be detrimental to their environment. Make a special effort to inform neighboring and abutting property owners of the plans. Inform them by mail, or if the time allows, talk to each neighbor individually. Opposition often melts away on a face-to-face basis. Remember, public opposition always reaches a maximum when a small notice of the request for a variance or zone change appears in the local newspaper.

    10 Present a good, colored rendering of the site. Most people, including many board members, do not fully understand a plan.

    11 Show pictures of similar eye-appealing developments that may have been completed, or a change in a similar property.

    12 Show up personally at zoning hearings. Don't depend on consulting professionals to answer all the questions.

    13 Keep temper under control. Act respectful of other people's ideas.

    14 Never ask for a variance or zone change just before elections.

Antitrust

The following should help to ward off antitrust legal action:

    1 Before attending a meeting with competing hotels, have your lawyer review the agenda. If there is a last-minute change in the agenda, be sure to leave the meeting. A good idea is to have a lawyer present at such meetings.

    2 Do not exchange data on prices or service to guests with other hoteliers, especially at meetings.

    3 Marketing strategy should not be discussed as it pertains to market allocations or customers, reciprocal buying, or the boycott of suppliers or customers.

    4 At a meeting of competing hotels, be careful when persons use the words "I recommend" or "I think we should agree" on any matter regarding pricing or services furnished a guest. At such a meeting, never say, "Let's do it together" or "We're all in it together." Any of these words used while discussing prices or service could be interpreted as a possible violation of the antitrust laws.

    5 Don't take the antitrust law lightly by making fun of it, especially if minutes are kept of the meeting.

    6 Don't exchange menus or price lists.

    7 Be sure an attorney checks your bylaws and certificate of incorporations to see if they comply with antitrust laws.

In view of the severe penalties and the jail sentences for antitrust violations, one should be most careful in this area of concern.

QUESTIONS FOR DISCUSSION

    1 Can a state or city refuse a restaurant a victualer's (food) license? Why or why not?

2 A license to operate a hotel is mandatory. Comment on this statement.

3 A hotel may raise its rates whenever it so desires, even to keep out undesirable customers. Comment on this statement.

4 The police powers of a state are designed to protect the public from abuse, and any law supporting this purpose is allowable. Comment on this.

5 Can a state prohibit a private business from advertising?

6 May fees to obtain a license for a hotel, restaurant or bar be to raise revenues as well as to protect the public?

7 Is a hotel responsible for what its guests do in the privacy of their rooms?

8 Can any hotel, restaurant, or club be inspected at any time by the state inspector?

9 Zoning merely protects the rights of the public. Comment on this statement.

10 To protect one's business, an owner should register (trademark) the business name as well as his or her own name. Comment on this. How can a name be registered? Must a trademark be registered in both state and federal governments?

11 A hotel can easily be found to have breached the provisions of the antitrust laws. List all the possibilities that exist along with an example of each.

6 Contents

6 Relationship between Hotel Patron and Hotelkeeper

"Laws can never be enforced unless fear supports them."

SOPHOCLES

Not everyone patronizing or seeking to patronize the facilities of a hotel or inn becomes a "guest" in the technical sense of that term. A hotel proprietor may be technically an "innkeeper" to some patrons and a "boarding house keeper," restaurateur, or landlord to others.

This chapter outlines the relationship between the guest and the hotelkeeper, including the legal principles of such a relationship, its limits, the status of a guest, and illegal acts of guests. It also considers the beginning and end of such a relationship, as well as other types of relationships that may exist in a hotel.

Guest-Innkeeper Relationship in Law

Most of the duties and obligations of innkeepers to their guests are imposed by law, and there is no need for a special contract between the parties. Once the relationship has been established, the rights and duties of both are at once fixed by law and remain fixed as long as the relationship continues. Since the obligation of the public hotel or innkeeper to the guest is created by and depends upon the law and not the will of the parties, the nature of the obligation must depend upon the law that creates it. Hence the law may and does vary greatly from one state to the other.

The common law has held the business of an innkeeper to be of quasi-public character with many privileges and great responsibilities.

In areas where the general rule of the common law has not been modified by statutory enactment, innkeepers have the undisputed right to conduct their hotels as they deem best, as long as they do not violate the law.

In the absence of a specific contract, the law implies that innkeepers will furnish such entertainment as the character of their inns will afford and give reasonable attention to the convenience and comfort of their guests. The fact that a hotel supplies unpretentious accommodations and simple comforts should not increase the risk to the guest or lessen the responsibility of the proprietor.

Since common law days this rule has aimed at the protection of the public, and no modern change has resulted in its restriction or abatement. Certain changes in the basic guest-innkeeper relationship have been made by some state legislatures, but none as yet have significantly modified the old common law. This and other aspects of the guest-innkeeper relationship are discussed in greater detail in subsequent chapters.

Presumption of Guest-Innkeeper Relationship

In a place of public accommodation, a person is presumed to be a guest if there is no evidence to support this person's status as a boarder or some other type of tenancy. The question of whether a person is a hotel guest is generally one of fact to be determined by a jury on either definite or circumstantial evidence.

In the *Langford* v. *Vandaveer* case, the court ruled that a jury must decide whether the two minor girls were guests of the motor court when one was hurt in a gas heater explosion. Though the girls had not registered, evidence was presented that they were in the car and the operator could have seen them when he passed the car twice. The male guests had registered for four persons without identifying the two minor girls. Generally, when a person alleges that a guest-innkeeper relationship exists, it is incumbent upon that person to prove it. If in this case the guest-innkeeper relationship did not exist, the minors would be considered trespassers who were owed little duty.

Case Example	Langford v. Vandaveer
	254 S.W.2d 498 (Ky., 1953)
	(STANLEY, Commissioner)

The judgment for $4,644.68 is for reimbursement of expenses incurred by the appellees in the hospital care and medical treatment of their minor daughter who was severely burned in the explosion of a butane or propane gas heater in a cabin of a motor court operated by the appellant, Clyde B. Langford. The case was tried with that of the daughter for damages for personal injuries in which a verdict of only $900 was returned. We are not here concerned with her case other than to say that both causes of action were based on the allegation that she was occupying the room as a "lawful guest for pay."

The instructions, obviously, predicated liability to the parents upon liability to the daughter. It was thus defined:

"It was the duty of the defendant, Clyde B. Langford, on the occasion spoken of in the evidence to exercise ordinary care to maintain the heating unit, its pipes and equipment in his tourist cabin No. 4 in a reasonably safe condition for use as such. If you shall believe from the evidence that he negligently failed to so maintain them, or any part of them, and that by reason of such failure on his part, if any there was, gas was permitted to and did escape from such unit, pipes or equipment into cabin No. 4, in such quantities as to ignite or explode, and that the defendant knew of this condition or in the exercise of ordinary care should have known of it, and shall further believe from the evidence that such accumulated gas, if any there was in said cabin, did explode or ignite and burn and do bodily hurt and injury to the plaintiff, Ruth Vandaveer, while in said cabin No. 4, then the law is for the plaintiff and you should so find. But unless you believe as above required, you should find your verdict for the defendant."

It is to be noted that the instruction, in effect, holds as a matter of law that the relationship was that of innkeeper and guest. The appellant insists that the relationship did not exist and that his legal responsibility should have been measured by the duty to a trespasser, or, alternatively, that her status should have been submitted to the jury.

The term "innkeeper" has become obsolete except in legal terminology. Originally, to constitute an inn it was necessary that there should be a stable provided for the accommodation of the horses of the travelers. . . . In process of time "inn" and "hotel" became synonymous. With the advent of automobile traffic came similar facilities called tourist camps, motor courts or the coined word "motels." These really come closer to the old inn than ordinary hotels for they furnish accommodations for the motor cars of the travelers. Of such was the defendant's place, which consisted of several cabins or rooms with spaces between for the shelter of automobiles. It is clear the character of the place as respects the relationship of guest and the legal responsibility of the operator as an innkeeper is not lost because of the type of structure or facility being called by a different name. The same rules of law have been applied in cases of injuries to occupants of motor courts. Our present inquiry is whether the court properly held as a matter of law the young lady was a guest.

On Sunday afternoon of January 22, 1950, four young people, C. P. Howe, Bill Nash, Ruth Vandaveer, and Myna Walker, drove to Henderson, Kentucky, from Albion, Illinois, a distance of sixty miles or more. Miss Vandaveer, the daughter of the appellees, 17 years old, and Miss Walker, about 15, were students in the high school at Albion and the young men worked in the oil fields near Henderson. The men went into a hotel where Howe's brother was staying but could not procure accommodations. The party then drove to Langford's Motor Court, a short distance from the city. This was about 8:30 o'clock. The car was stopped in a well lighted place near the entrance of the office and restaurant. Howe met Langford at the door and asked for rooms for four oil men, saying that one of them was then at work but would return early enough to get some rest before checking out time. Langford and two other witnesses testified to this. Langford showed the cabins to the two men, lighted the heaters and explained to them how the valves worked. He and Howe returned to the office and Howe filled out a registration card, giving his address and an automobile license number and signed it, "C. P. Howe and party." He filled in the figure "4," showing the number of people in the party and paid $6 for the two rooms. Neither Howe nor Miss Walker testified. Miss Vandaveer and Nash testified he stood by the side of the automobile at all times. It is undisputed that Langford passed twice within ten or fifteen feet of the parked automobile. He says he looked at the car and could have seen anyone in it but saw no one. As the car started over to the cabins he noted that the license number was not the same as that registered and he entered the correct number on the card. (It appears that Howe had given the number of his own car instead of Nash's which he was driving.) Miss Vandaveer testified that when Langford passed the automobile she was sitting on the edge of the back seat looking into the small mirror in front, combing her hair, and Miss Walker was on the front seat doing the same thing. Both were erect and could be easily seen. Ewing Lowry testified that on leaving the office to go home he passed close to the automobile parked near the door and looked into it. He saw no one but if one had been hiding on the floor, she could not be seen.

According to Miss Vandaveer and Nash, the party entered one of the cabins and then the other where they spent some time together. Then the boys left about ten o'clock to go to work. They planned to return early enough to drive the girls back to Albion in time for school. After they had gone, she and Myna concluded to occupy separate cabins. She took No. 4 and retired about eleven o'clock. Neither had any baggage. On the contrary, Langford and his sister testified that about 11:15 Howe came to the restaurant, ate a sandwich, drank a cup of coffee and then left with three colas. Nash testified he and Howe left the motor court about ten o'clock and worked until seven the next morning. However, there is evidence that immediately following the explosion Howe was there. A man in or about the cabin was heard to say, "I told you not to do that." One of these witnesses, according to Langford, first told him of the presence of the girls on the premises.

The relation of innkeeper and guest is a mutual contractual one, and the existence of intention by both parties is an essential element. It is an exceptional case where that requisite is not clearly established, usually by implication. Ordinarily, where one holds himself out to the public as an innkeeper, and is accustomed to receive all who apply and a transient goes to the house to procure accommodation and receives entertainment, the relationship is created. But it is not necessarily the result. . . . It may require circumstances of more evidentiary value where the matter of mutual rights and obligations concerns the occupancy of a room and personal injuries are sustained than where, for example, it is a matter of bailment or the loss of baggage. All authorities agree that it is not essential that the guest shall have registered, for that is merely evidence, though it may be an important circumstance in determining the status.

In the case at bar, the intention of the young lady to become a guest in the legal sense is apparent. The question is whether or not she was intentionally or knowingly received as such by the proprietor of the motor court. Generally, an innkeeper, though the conductor of a semi-public institution, is not under obligation to receive as a guest everyone who applies. He has the right to reject or expel persons whom he reasonably deems objectionable.

Under this rule of law a person may not impose himself upon the proprietor and become a guest without his knowledge or intention to receive him. One becomes a guest only if he is received to be treated as a guest and the intention to become such must be communicated to the innkeeper or his agent. This is a fact to be proved by evidence, definite or circumstantial. . . . As is well said in Moody v. Kenny, 153 La. 1007, 97 So. 21, 22, 29 A.L.R. 474, "a mere guest of the registered occupant of a room at a hotel, who shares such room with its occupant without the knowledge or consent of the hotel management, would not be a guest of the hotel, as there would be no contractual relations in such case between such third person and the hotel proprietor."

The appellees submit that irrespective of knowledge of the appellant, their daughter should be deemed a guest of a hotel guest. There is no doubt that an innkeeper owes to persons invited to the premises the duty of ordinary or reasonable care to protect them from injury and that usually that duty applies to a guest of a guest, he being deemed an invitee or licensee.

The case at bar is distinguished from the Moody case where, with the assistance of a hotel clerk, a man and wife were assigned a room of a registered guest at his suggestion because there was no available room for the couple, and he consented to occupy another room with a friend. Here we have the acceptance of four men as guests when there were in fact two men and two women. Under the appellant's evidence, the young lady slipped into the cabin and occupied the room for the night without the proprietor's knowledge or consent. This places her in a different category from an invitee of a bona fide guest. It has been held by a court of original jurisdiction that the rights of hotel guests are not assignable or transferable, so where a registered guest, without permission from anyone representing the hotel, transferred a room to a woman, she had no right to its possession . . . .

It seems to us that it was error to hold as a matter of law that the appellees' daughter was a guest of the motor court and not to have submitted the question of fact to the jury. There is no dispute in the evidence that Howe procured the two rooms for four men. But if the proprietor of the motor court saw the young women in the car under the circumstances described and could reasonably have anticipated or understood that they, or at least the plaintiffs' daughter, would occupy the cabin, then the jury could find he accepted her as a guest and assumed the legal responsibility owing in such relationship. The given instruction defining the duties of the defendant as an innkeeper is not criticized and seems to be correct.

Ruth testified that the heating stove was burning low when she went to bed. She awakened and "smelled something funny—some funny odor, I didn't know what it was." She sat on the edge of the bed and lighted a match so she could see her way to turn on the electric light switch near the door in order to see what was causing the odor. Immediately there was a violent explosion. She denied going about the stove. The explosion occurred about four o'clock in the morning. The plaintiffs' evidence is that the heater was not properly ventilated to carry off the fumes and unburned gases and did not have proper safety devices.

The defendant's proof is to the effect that the heater and appliances were properly installed and ventilated. They had been regularly inspected and found in good order. After the explosion, the pipes were checked and no leaks found. The stove valve had been partially opened and the gas was not burning. There were a number of burnt matches beneath the door of the heater and scattered about the floor. They were not there when the room was turned over to Howe and Nash.

The evidence authorized the submission of the issue of the defendant's negligence toward a guest. It is not sufficient if the young lady be regarded as a trespasser.

The court refused an offered instruction on contributory negligence. In addition to the foregoing evidence of the conditions which may afford an inference that an attempt had been made to light the heater, the young lady was a high school senior studying chemistry in which she used a Bunsen burner. She lived in the midst of the Illinois oil fields and was familiar with the odor of natural gas. The jury may well have believed that lighting the match under the conditions was contributory negligence. We are of opinion that the evidence required an instruction on that defense.

Ruling of the Court: The judgment is reversed for defendant hotel-keepers.

In *Adler* v. *Savoy Plaza* the court took an entirely different approach to the question of the guest-innkeeper relationship. It ruled as a matter of law that the woman was a guest of the hotel even though she did not spend the night there. Though both the *Langford* and *Adler* cases hinge on the existence of the guest-innkeeper relationship, certain basic differences distinguish them. The *Adler* v. *Savoy Plaza* case dealt with personal property, whereas the *Langford* case dealt with personal injuries. Although the guest won in the *Adler* case, her recovery was only $100 of the $23,300 she lost because the hotel met the provisions of the limiting liability statute.

Case	**Adler v. Savoy Plaza**
Example	*108 N.Y.S.2d 80 (1951)*
	(PECK, Presiding Judge)

This is an action for the loss of jewelry and personal effects contained in a suitcase which was delivered by plaintiff to defendant for safekeeping. The claimed value of the jewelry was something over $20,000 and the claimed value of the personal effects about $3,300.

The jury returned a verdict in plaintiff's favor for $2,000, which the trial court on plaintiff's motion set aside as a compromise. A new trial was ordered. Defendant appeals from the order setting aside the verdict and ordering a new trial and also from the denial of its motion to reduce the verdict to the sum of $100.

The facts are as follows: The plaintiff was accustomed to staying at the defendant's hotel whenever she visited New York and had been a guest of the hotel many times. She and her husband had requested reservations for May 15, 1946. Upon their arrival at 10 o'clock that morning, they were advised that their reservation was for the following day, but that the hotel would try to accommodate them, so they registered, hoping that a room might be assigned during the day. At the same time, they delivered their luggage to the bell captain, and it was deposited in a section of the lobby set aside for the luggage of arriving and departing guests. Plaintiff's husband attended to business during the day while plaintiff was in and out of the hotel. When both returned to the hotel in the afternoon, they found that a room was still not available, so they whiled away some time in the lounge bar and had dinner in the room of a friend who was a guest of the hotel.

All during the day defendant's manager was seeking accommodations for the couple but was unable to locate them in the hotel. He finally secured accommodations for them for the night at the Sherry Netherlands Hotel where they registered at about 8:00 PM, taking with them two suitcases and a cosmetic case, and leaving the suitcase with the valuables and two matching cases at defendant's hotel.

Plaintiff testified that before leaving defendant's hotel for the night she told the bellman that she had better do something about her jewelry which was in the large suitcase, suggesting that it would be necessary to take the jewelry out of its leather box and put into envelopes which the hotel provided for deposit in its safe. Whereupon, according to plaintiff, the bellman replied: "It won't be necessary, we will put the whole suitcase in the vault." The bellman charged with this assurance testified that he had no such conversation with plaintiff.

When plaintiff returned to defendant's hotel the next morning to take up a residence for two or three weeks and requested delivery of her luggage, the large suitcase was missing. During the night the suitcase had been delivered by the night manager of the hotel to an imposter. The circumstances of this delivery are not altogether clear as the night manager was deceased at the time of the trial. Whether there was some complicity on the part of one or more of the hotel employees, as plaintiff suggests, we are not called upon to surmise. It is quite apparent that defendant was negligent, probably grossly negligent, and if the case would be determined simply on a question of negligence plaintiff would be entitled to recover the amount of her loss.

Unquestionably defendant had given due notice to its guests of the availability of a safe for the deposit of their valuables. If plaintiff was a guest of the hotel, she was bound by the notice so given and obliged to deliver her jewelry to the office for deposit in the safe, or suffer the peril of its loss. That is, unless defendant waived compliance with the statute. The questions as to the jewelry, therefore, were whether plaintiff was a guest of the hotel and whether defendant had waived compliance with the statute.

Any issue as to whether plaintiff was a guest (and it may be noted that in her first cause of action plaintiff alleges that she was a guest and in her second cause of action for the same recovery omits that allegation) was not submitted to the jury in such a way that it is possible to determine whether the jury passed upon or even considered the question. We are prepared to rule, however, as matter of law on the admitted facts, that plaintiff was a guest.

It was, therefore, required of plaintiff, if she wished to give her jewelry hotel protection, to deliver it or at least tender it to the defendant for deposit in its safe. Both as a matter of experience and sense, plaintiff knew that this should be done, according to her testimony she had the foresight to suggest that such a deposit be made. It was only upon the alleged assurance of the bellman that the entire suitcase would be placed in the vault that she was satisfied.

There may be a question of the bellman's authority or apparent authority under the circumstances, which we do not consider on this appeal.

That question will remain for the court or jury on the next trial. Assuming, however, that plaintiff would be justified in relying on the bellman's assurance, the factual question is whether such assurance was given with a consequent waiver of the provisions of Section 200 of the General Business Law.

While it is defendant's contention that the jury could have found, and that the verdict should be interpreted as a finding, that defendant was entitled to the protection of Section 200, we are utterly unable to say or guess whether that was the jury's view or whether the question even entered into their consideration. There was no clear submission of the question to the jury and their attention certainly was not focused on the question. Nor were they told what facts or considerations would bear upon their decision of such a question.

One factual issue which would have to be put to the jury before the court would know their finding, or either could pass on the applicability of Section 200, is whether or not plaintiff had the conversation she testified to having with the bellman. If she did not have such conversation, there would be no purported compliance on her part with Section 200 or waiver of its protection by defendant. Without that issue being submitted to the jury, we are unable to parse the verdict or give it the interpretation which defendant contends for. The verdict was, therefore, properly set aside.

We will make only one further observation for the guidance of the court on the next trial, and that is in connection with the applicability of Section 201 of the General Business Law to the lost property other than jewelry. Plaintiff being a guest, Section 201 applies. No value in excess of $100 having been stated or written receipt secured, defendant's liability for the value of the suitcase and its contents, other than the jewelry, was limited to $100. Negligence or even gross negligence on the part of defendant is no consideration in this connection. . . .

Ruling of the Court: The order appealed from setting the verdict aside and ordering a new trial should be affirmed, with costs. Order affirmed with costs to respondent.

Limited Guest-Innkeeper Relationship

It is not always essential that the requirements that constitute a guest-innkeeper relationship be in effect. Some cases hold that a person who intends to become a guest at a hotel, by delivering baggage or other property to the proprietor (either actually or constructively), becomes a guest. The responsibility of the proprietor as innkeeper starts at the moment of the delivery of the goods, and that person is answerable for the loss of the goods prior to the guest's formalized registration. People become guests with relation to their delivered property, but they do not become guests as to their actual person (29 Am. Jur., 106, p. 88).

The theory behind this limited guest-innkeeper relationship rests upon the fact that the acquiring of a prospective guest's baggage is incident to the guest-innkeeper relationship. The rules of law applicable to that relationship determine the rights and liabilities of the parties. But if, when a person delivers her baggage to the innkeeper or his employee, she indicates her intention of not becoming a guest of the hotel, the guest-innkeeper relationship does not exist, and the innkeeper's liability is merely that of a bailee of the delivered property—that is, someone to whom property is delivered in trust for another.

Intent of Parties

The guest-innkeeper relationship is a mutually contractual one, and the existence of intention by both parties is an essential element. A transient usually becomes a guest when he enters a hotel to procure accommodations, provided that the innkeeper has a room available and that other conditions that will be discussed later exist (see chapter 12). If, for instance, personal injuries are sustained, it might well be necessary to present more evidence than is required in a bailment involving personal property—that is, the giving of personal property by one person to another in trust. For that reason, "all authorities agree that it is not essential that the guest shall have registered, for that is merely evidence, though it may be an important circumstance in determining the status" (Langford v. Vandaveer, 254 S.W.2d 498 [Ky., 1953]).

What is considered an intent by the parties? For one thing, an application to the innkeeper for entertainment is sufficient notice of the traveler's intention to become a guest. Also, if the traveler visits the inn to receive entertainment and is entertained by the hotelkeeper, this constitutes intent. Another view is that the assignment of a room (Ross v. Kirkeby Hotels, 160 N.Y.S.2d 978 [1957]) or the definite contemplation of occupancy (Adler v. Savoy Plaza, 108 N.Y.S.2d 80 [1951]; Dilkes v. Hotel Sheraton, 125 N.Y.S.2d 38 [1953]) is an essential element. According to the interpretation of the New York courts (Adler v. Savoy Plaza), these are the valid criteria that should be used in determining what relationship exists between a guest and a hotelkeeper. Intent is the one factor that distinguishes hotels and similar establishments from other types of businesses.

In determining whether a person is or is not a hotel guest, the following factors have been considered by the courts and given varying degrees of weight: registration, contemplated length of stay, existence of a special contract, agreement upon a certain rate, method of payment, permanent residence status of a guest, the incidental services offered by the building in a guest-innkeeper relationship (lobby, bar, dining room, laundry service, etc.), whether the rooms are provided with cooking facilities, and the existence of hotel maid service. Although none of these factors alone is necessarily controlling, unless legislation permits them to be, they can often be highly persuasive in showing the intent of the parties.

Under certain conditions the intent of the parties may be inferred by what formerly occurred, as in the case of *Freudenheim v. Eppley.*

Case Example

Freudenheim v. Eppley
88 F.2d 280 (Pa., 1937)
(BUFFINGTON, Circuit Judge)

In the court below, the partnership J. Freudenheim & Sons brought suit against the receivers of the Pittsburgh Hotels Corporation to recover damages suffered by the alleged negligence of the defendant in failing to safely keep some $40,000 worth of its diamonds deposited with defendant by Sol. J. Freudenheim, one of the partners, who was an alleged guest of the hotel. On trial, a verdict was had for the plaintiff for $41,893.13. The court below entered judgment in favor of the defendant n.o.v. on the ground that plaintiff was not a guest of the defendant's hotel at the time of the deposit; that the deposit was a gratuitous bailment and that there was no proof of gross negligence on the part of the defendant. This is an appeal by plaintiff from said judgment.

After a study of the proofs, we are of opinion that the court could not as a matter of law have decided Freudenheim was not a guest at the hotel, but that the determination of that fact, was, in view of the proofs, a question to be decided by a jury.

Now the uncontradicted facts in the case are that Freudenheim was the traveling salesman of his diamond firm, and that, as shown by defendants' cross-examination, he was accustomed to visiting Buffalo, Detroit, Cleveland, Toledo, Chicago, Indianapolis, Cincinnati, and Pittsburgh. That if trade justified, he stayed at hotels which had vaults for the deposit of valuables and he left his bag containing diamonds in their vaults. Prior to 1922–23, he had stopped at other hotels in Pittsburgh, but since then had stopped at the William Penn. Prior to 1930 he came to Pittsburgh eight or nine times a year and stayed at the William Penn two, three, or four days at a time, depending on trade conditions. In 1933 he was twice in Pittsburgh, received his mail at the hotel, but did not stay overnight. On every one of his trips to Pittsburgh he used the vault at the William Penn. On the morning of December 5, 1933, after visiting other cities, he arrived in Pittsburgh from Cincinnati before 7 AM. After checking his personal bag at the railroad station, he went to the hotel. His proof was: "I intended to stay here as long as I could do business here." He arrived at the hotel around 7 o'clock, but the cashier's office, where the hotel had vaults, was not open, and the cashier, Schaller, had not arrived. His testimony was: "I waited around the lobby until about seven-thirty and around seven-thirty I went back to the cashier's office and I saw Mr. Schaller there and he greeted me. I told him I wanted a box, or he said, 'I suppose you want a box . . . .' Whether he knew me by name, I don't know, but he knew me quite well." Continuing, the witness said: "Mr. Schaller came out of the cage, which is controlled by a wire door—grill—there, and he brought out a couple of keys and a tag. He tore off part of the tag and gave me the bottom of it, and asked me to sign the upper part, which I did and returned it to him, and he gave me this stub bearing the same number as appears on the part bearing my signature which I gave to him. He then gave me two keys, which were attached to this little ring bearing a metal disc on which is noted the letter

'C.' He then inserted the key which was attached to this ring and opened the box—opened the door—and I put my brief case in which my merchandise had been placed right inside that box. I closed the door and I went downstairs."

The testimony of Schaller, a witness of defendants, was virtually to the same effect.

It will be noted that the hotel had provided interlocking printed checks for its hotel vault service. One was the stub check given to Freudenheim, in form following:

WILLIAM PENN HOTEL
VAULT CHECK
C 6306

Checked by _____
Room _____

The other was a corresponding numeral, 6306, signed by Freudenheim and retained by the hotel. From these facts, could an inference be reasonably drawn that Freudenheim was a guest of the hotel?

In the first place, we have the fact that Freudenheim was known to the hotel as a past guest and that there was the possibility of his lodging at the hotel if trade warranted such stay. There was, therefore, in the mind of both parties that the hotel would have Freudenheim as a guest. He was recognized by the cashier; inquiry was made whether he wanted a box; he was given the box; his merchandise was deposited; and the operation recognized by both parties by the corresponding vault checks with similar numbers. This was a service or accommodation which the hotel had extended before and Freudenheim had enjoyed before.

Now it is clear that vault service for valuables is a customary hotel accommodation, and that it was the intention of both parties that Freudenheim should have that accommodation, and the relation of guest and hotel being once established, the doctrine in Wright v. Anderson, 1 K.B. 209, applies viz.: "The responsibility of an innkeeper for the safety of a traveler's property begins at the moment when the relation of guest and host arises, and that relation arises as soon as the traveler enters the inn with the intention of using it as an inn, and is so received by the host. It does not matter that no food or lodging has been supplied or found up to this time of the loss. It is sufficient if the circumstances show an intention on the one hand to provide and on the other hand to accept such accommodation."

Moreover, later on, and before he left, Freudenheim, who was busy with his customers all morning and into the afternoon and took no lunch, did take his dinner in the general dining room of the hotel. It is true he did not take a room and register, but his omission to do so does not put him out of guest protection. . . . "It is not necessary that a traveler shall register at an inn as a guest in order to become such, but it is sufficient if he visits the inn for the purpose of receiving entertainment and is entertained accordingly."

The jury having found a verdict in favor of the plaintiff, and the court having erred in holding as a matter of law that Freudenheim was not a guest, the judgment below is vacated, and the record is remanded, with instruction to the court to enter judgment on the verdict in favor of the plaintiffs.

Determining a Guest's Status

In Arcade Hotel Company v. Wiatt, 4 N.E. 398 (Ohio, 1886), the plaintiff sought to recover $2,195 that he claimed he had deposited with the Arcade Hotel Company while a guest of the hotel. Upon formal request for the return of the money, he was refused and was told that the clerk had stolen the money. The vital issue was whether Wiatt was a guest when he deposited the money with the clerk. Wiatt testified that he entered the hotel shortly after 2 AM, accompanied by a friend, and applied to the clerk for accommodations.

At the time the clerk took charge of his money, Wiatt had not registered his name; it was not entered upon any of the books of the hotel and no room had been assigned him. While none of these facts were necessary to constitute him a guest of the hotel, they would have been valuable aids in determining whether that relation in fact existed.

To entitle a person visiting an inn to be treated as a guest and to hold innkeepers responsible for money deposited with them for safekeeping, the visit must be for the purposes for which inns are kept. Under common law if a person registers only to secure a safe depository for money, that is not sufficient. Unless the person requires the entertainment or accommodations of the inn, the clerk has no authority to bind his principal by receiving the money. In this case the judgment was reversed and the defendant won because the plaintiff was not a guest of the hotel.

It would seem that the question of who is a guest and who is not should be easily resolved, but many times it is quite difficult to determine. The case of Rocoff v. Lancella, 251 N.E.2d 582 (Ind., 1969), provides a good example. The plaintiff had lived in the same room in the defendant's building and had paid thirty dollars per month for rent for a period of two years prior to the time he fell on the stairs. The court ruled that since the building displayed an exterior sign bearing the inscription "hotel" and the defendant maintained a guest register book, determination that Rocoff was a guest rather than a tenant was authorized.

In an Oklahoma case, Buck v. Del City Apartments, Inc., 431 P.2d 360 (Okl., 1967), the court said the chief distinction between a tenant and an innkeeper's guest lies in the element of possession. A tenant is deemed to have exclusive legal possession of the premises and stands responsible for their care and condition, whereas a guest merely has a right to the use of the premises. In this situation the innkeeper retains control over the premises—including responsibility for supplying the necessary daily care of and attention to the premises—and retains the right of access for such purpose. A guest is anyone who is a patron of an inn and as such receives the same treatment as that accorded to short-term guests.

The status of the patron on the premises as a tenant or as a guest is to be determined from the terms of the contract between the parties, the character of the premises, the nature of business operated upon them, the extent of control or supervision maintained by the proprietor or possessor over the premises, the manner in which the premises are operated, the character of the part occupied by the patron, and the character of the use to which the premises are generally adapted and devoted. The fact that the property was operated and managed as a motel under license from the state and that it advertised itself as a motel on a highway sign afforded a proper basis for inference that the patron of the establishment was a guest. Neither length of stay nor the fact that payment for the accommodation was made at a fixed rate per week rather than per day and that for a time the hotel was the patron's only home precluded the patron from being considered a guest. The court thus ruled that the motelkeepers who granted the plaintiff the right to use a motel cabin but not the right to exclusive possession of the cabin stood in relation of innkeeper and guest and had an innkeeper's duty toward her at the time that she slipped on the icy steps in front of her motel cabin.

Illegal Acts Affecting Guest-Innkeeper Relationship

Many states have passed statutes that require a prospective guest to register. A question arises concerning the relationship of the patron who registers falsely or after registering commits an illegal act.

Cramer v. Tarr, 165 F.Supp. 130 (Me., 1958), was an action to recover damages for personal injuries allegedly sustained by the plaintiffs when they attempted to escape a fire in the lodging house where they were staying. The plaintiffs admitted they were not husband and wife and had illegally signed the register as such. The defendant claimed that by reason of their unlawful purpose they were trespassers, and he owed them no duty to exercise reasonable care.

The court, however, stated that without any demonstration of a causal connection between the plaintiffs' alleged statutory violations and their injuries that neither false registration nor an illegal or immoral purpose in occupying a room in the defendant's boarding house would affect their status as guests to whom the defendant owed the duty of reasonable care. Therefore, the plaintiffs could pursue the case, even though false registration for an illicit purpose could be inferred.

Beginning and Duration of
Guest-Innkeeper Relationship

The relation of guest and innkeeper begins as soon as a traveler enters an inn with the intent of using the establishment as an inn and is received by the innkeeper acting in that capacity. Generally, the relationship starts when the guest registers and engages accommodations, but it may also begin sooner. For example, it may begin when baggage is entrusted to innkeepers or their employees, assuming that the accommodations will be engaged within a reasonable time. But simply handing a bag to the hotel porter does not make the bag's owner a guest if he intends neither to eat nor sleep at the hotel but only to utilize the hotel facilities without expense. Nor does a person become a hotel guest merely by sending his goods to be taken care of by the hotelkeeper without some other intention of becoming a guest (Grinnell v. Cook, 3 Hill 485 [N.Y., 1842]).

Once the intent of the parties has been manifested and a guest-innkeeper relationship brought about, the rights and duties of both parties are fixed. These rights and duties remain set until they are intentionally terminated by a positive act on the part of either or both of the parties. The intent of the guest is usually shown in payment of the bill and will be discussed in the next section.

Hotel guests do not lose their status because of a temporary absence. They retain the status of a traveler, and their liability to pay for accommodations continues. The paying of a bill does not end the guest-innkeeper relationship, however, if there is an agreement that the guest will return later and does so. But when a guest pays the bill to avoid liability for the day, while intending to return that night, the innkeeper-guest relationship is ended by that act. He has paid his bill, and his name has been stricken from the register of guests. Any subsequent loss of luggage is not recoverable under the guest-innkeeper relationship. The theory is that as long as innkeepers rent or hire for profit, they are liable and should pay for the losses. The right to charge is the criterion of the innkeeper's liability (Miller v. Peeples, 60 Miss. 819, 45 Am. Rep. 423 [1883]).

In Korr v. Thomas Emery's Sons, Inc., 93 N.E.2d 781 (Ohio, 1949), the plaintiff sought to recover damages alleged to have resulted from the loss of luggage received by the Netherland-Plaza Hotel doorman when the plaintiff arrived by taxi. Was the plaintiff a guest of the hotel? The answer was yes.

The taking in custody by a hotel employee, pending registration and the assignment to a room, of a guest's bags is incident to the innkeeper-guest relationship, and the applicable rules of law determine the respective rights and liabilities of the parties. The recovery of this case was limited by statute to $50.

Termination of Guest-Innkeeper Relationship

Ordinarily, the guest-innkeeper relationship is terminated when the guest pays the bill and departs. Yet the strict liability does not cease at the moment of paying the bill; it continues for a reasonable time to allow the guests to remove their luggage. The case of *Spiller v. Barclay Hotel* deals with this problem, which can be very costly for the hotel. It is customary when a guest checks out of a hotel for the bellhop to put the luggage in a prearranged place to await further instructions from the guests after they pay their account. In this case the bellhop agreed, or at least did not disagree, that he would watch the bags during the checkout time. The plaintiff recovered both for personal items and jewelry in the stolen bags. Why?

Case	**Spiller v. Barclay Hotel**
Example	*327 N.Y.S.2d 426 (1972)*
	(LEONARD H. SANDLER, Judge)

Plaintiff, a guest of the Barclay Hotel, sued for the value of property, primarily wearing apparel and jewelry, lost on the steps of the hotel while she was in the process of leaving.

Plaintiff testified that after her two bags were brought to the lobby floor, she asked a bellboy to take them to the cab area and to watch them while she checked out. When she came to the cab area, only one of her bags was there and the bellboy was not present. A search failed to disclose the missing bag or its contents.

No directly contradictory testimony was presented. A representative of the hotel did testify to a telephone conversation in which the plaintiff allegedly gave a different version of the event and described the personal property as business samples. However, I accept as substantially accurate the plaintiff's trial testimony as to the property that was lost and the manner in which it was lost.

Accordingly, I find that the property was lost through the actual negligence of the defendant. No doubt the bellboy was under no inherent duty to watch the bags, and it may well be that his implicit undertaking to do so violated his instructions. Nonetheless, when he accepted the bags with the accompanying request to watch them, without explicitly declining the latter request, an obligation of care was assumed, which quite clearly was not fulfilled.

As to the claim for lost property other than jewelry, it is clear that the limitations of value set forth in Section 201 of the General Business Law, are not applicable because of the actual negligence of the defendant. That section, relating to loss of clothing and other personal property, explicitly exempts from its coverage losses due to "fault or negligence". . . .

The claim for the items of lost jewelry presents a more troublesome problem. Section 200 of the General Business Law excludes recovery by a hotel guest for loss of, among other categories enumerated, jewels, ornaments and precious stones where the hotel provides a safe for such items, gives appropriate notice of that fact, and the guest does not use that facility. It was conceded that the hotel maintained such a safe and had posted the required notice.

Preliminarily, I find that the items of jewelry here involved, which included a necklace, a pendant, earrings, and the like, come within the definition of "jewels" and "ornaments," as those terms are used in Section 200. The distinction drawn in the leading case of Ramaley v. Leland, 43

N.Y. 539, 542 (1871), which has been consistently followed, is between articles "carried for use and convenience" and articles worn as an "ornament."

Moreover, although the question is less clearly settled than one would have supposed, it now appears to be the law that a guest who has failed to deposit property for safekeeping in accordance with the requirement of Section 200 may not recover for the loss even if the hotel was actually negligent.

What seems to me decisive here is that Section 200 was not designed to apply to a loss occurring under the circumstances of this case. Section 200 clearly contemplates a procedure for safeguarding the specified categories of property during a guest's stay at a hotel. Its provisions do not seem to me to be reasonably applied to a loss that takes place when a guest is about to leave, has gathered together her property preparatory to an imminent departure, and is arranging for the transfer of luggage to a vehicle for transportation.

Although that situation presents some conceptual difficulties, I am satisfied that the sensible and fair approach is to consider a loss occurring at that point in time neither in terms of the provisions of Section 200, nor in terms of the traditional common law liability of innkeepers, but rather on the basis of the presence or absence of actual negligence. . . .

Having found that the loss here resulted from the negligence of a hotel employee, acting within the scope of his employment, I hold that the plaintiff is entitled to recover the value of the lost jewelry.

In fixing the value of the lost jewelry, I have concluded that their cost to the plaintiff fairly represents their value at the time of loss. As to the other items of property I have considered, among other factors, their cost to the plaintiff, the nature of the articles, the time of purchase, and the amount of use.

Accordingly, I fix the value of the jewelry at $592.05, and the value of the other items of personal property at $1,125.00.

Judgment may be entered for the plaintiff in the total amount of $1,717.05.

Another case, *Salisbury v. St. Regis–Sheraton Hotel*, had similar facts but a totally different ending. The court said the guest-innkeeper relationship had not ceased and that Section 200 of the General Business Law did apply. In this case, the guest recovered only $100 for her personal property, which was worth $60,000. The *Spiller* case took place in 1972, whereas the *Salisbury* case took place (as to judgment) in 1980. No mention was made of the *Spiller* case in the *Salisbury* case.

A different type of question arises when a guest plans to return to the hotel at a later date and wants to leave luggage with the hotel in the meantime. Does the guest-innkeeper relationship end when the guest leaves and a new relationship, such as bailment (the delivery of property by the owner to another person for temporary care), come about? Or does the guest-innkeeper relationship continue during the absence? The answer to both questions is yes—it all depends in which state the guest leaves the luggage (see chapter 11). In Ohio, for example, in Hotel Statler Company, Inc., v. Safier, 134 N.E. 460 (Ohio, 1921), the court held that the guest-innkeeper relationship ended when the guest checked out of the hotel and that the new agreement became a bailment. However, in Dilkes v. Hotel Sheraton, 482 App. Div. 488, 125 N.Y.S.2d 38 (1953), the decision was that the relationship of guest-innkeeper carried through the interim period, and therefore the limiting liability statute was in effect. The *Statler* case resulted in the plaintiff's recovering the amount of his luggage, whereas in the *Dilkes* case, the guest won only a fraction of the amount lost because of the limiting liability statute.

Other Relationships

Depending on the circumstances, innkeepers may have guest-innkeeper relationships with some patrons and may act as private business persons with certain privileges toward others. When they act as innkeepers, the inn is a public place, and they surrender some of the rights they would otherwise have. For example, an innkeeper cannot arbitrarily turn away persons who come as guests in a proper manner and at suitable times as long as accommodations are available for them; neither can an innkeeper arbitrarily refuse to continue furnishing a guest with proper accommodations (Alpaugh v. Wolverton, 36 S.E.2d 906 [Va., 1946]).

A large hotel has many types of functions going on within its doors. Each day great numbers of people enter to conduct private business, to visit, or just to use its facilities as a public building. One criterion determines the character of the relationship and the consequent liability of the hotelkeeper: whether the innkeeper is acting in the character of an innkeeper or that of a private business person. The liabilities of the innkeeper differ in each case.

A large hotel could not hope to exist on only its room sales. Modern hotels and motels have had to expand and diversify to make money. The types of businesses that one can find in a large hotel include professional offices, beauty salons, tailors, masseurs, transportation services, such as airlines or buses, and business shops, such as jewelers, florists, and drugstores. The convention business and the facilities to cater large banquets have also become an important aspect of the hotel business.

Banquets and Other Functions

A hotelkeeper's liability for a banquet guest is no greater than that of a nonhotelkeeper who may execute the contract either in a hotel or elsewhere. The banquet guest need not be registered at the hotel, but if the banquet is furnished to a hotel guest as one of the provided meals, it would be controlled by the guest-innkeeper relationship.

In the leading case of Carter v. Hobbs, 12 Mich. 52, 83 Am. Dec. 762 (1863), the plaintiff was attending a fireman's ball at the defendant's hotel when his gloves and coat were found missing. Carter sued Hobbs, the innkeeper, for their return. The court said that because arrangements had been made with the innkeeper to furnish only a room for dancing and supper and a cloakroom, the relation of guest and innkeeper did not exist. The innkeeper did not receive the clothing in his capacity of innkeeper but merely as an ordinary bailee. According to the court, "The common law liability of an innkeeper, for the loss of the goods of his guest, is special and peculiar, depending upon peculiar grounds of public policy; and while ordinary bailees are held responsible only on proof of loss arising from some fault on their part, such as negligence or want of diligence, the innkeeper is held liable without proof of any negligence or fault; and except in special cases, cannot discharge himself by showing that the loss occurred without his fault, or that of those in his employ." The court concluded by saying that if the plaintiff were a guest at all, he was the guest of the fire company. On this particular occasion the defendant was not acting as an innkeeper and the plaintiff did not come to the hotel for any purpose that would bring him within the common law definition of a hotel guest.

The same type of ruling was found in another case in which a hotel guest acted under two identities at the same hotel; however, being a guest of the hotel and being a guest at a dance given at the hotel by another group were considered two separate matters. Consequently, when the guest was hurt at the dance, the injuries were not related to the guest-innkeeper relationship and he could not recover.

Another method by which courts determine whether a person is in a hotel for a purpose other than travel is to pose the following question: Is the hotelkeeper "acting in the character of an innkeeper," or is the guest in the hotel for a "special purpose"?

The final type of problem here unfortunately often occurs in a place of business. In the Shoreham Hotel case, a dining room "guest" claimed he was shortchanged by the waiter, and then insulted, humiliated, and embarrassed. As a "hotel guest," he would have been able to recover under the exception that mental suffering and embarrassment are actionable. The court, however, clearly showed that a guest in the hotel dining room was not a "hotel guest" as such and hence could not recover. (It is not clear why the plaintiff did not use slander [the speaking of false and malicious words that injure another's reputation, business, or property rights] as his cause of action, which would possibly have allowed him to recover damages.)

The Shoreham Hotel decision is undoubtedly based on a sound basis of logic and law. However, in Summer v. Hyatt Corporation, infra, 266 S.E.2d 333 (Ga., 1980), a guest of the hotel, while dining in the hotel's rotating restaurant, lost her valuables in her purse, and the court decided as a matter of law that she was a hotel guest and as such had to comply with the limiting liability statute requiring that jewelry and valuables had to be in the safe. Applying this rule to the *Wallace* case, and adding the fact that the insulted patron was also a guest of the hotel, such a person could then recover for mental suffering and embarrassment. This situation could prove to be a very worrysome problem for the hotelier. The hotelier should remember that all guests must show—that is, if they are guests—is that they were embarrassed and humiliated, and it's up to a jury to decide if so and to what extent.

Case	**Wallace v. Shoreham Hotel Corporation**
Example	*49 A.2d 81 (D.C., 1946)*
	(HOOD, Associated Judge)

       This appeal is from an order dismissing a complaint for failure to state a cause of action. The substance of the complaint is that plaintiff, in company with his wife and four friends, was a guest at the cocktail lounge of defendant's hotel; that, in payment of the check rendered, plaintiff gave the waiter a $20 bill but received change for only $10; that the waiter insisted he had received from plaintiff a $10 bill and stated publicly for all in the lounge to hear: "We have had people try this before"; that in fact plaintiff had tendered a $20 bill, which fact was later admitted by representatives of the hotel and proper change given plaintiff; that the language of the waiter indicated to those present in the lounge that plaintiff was underhanded and of low character and that his demand for change was illegal and comparable to that of a cheat or other person whose reputation for honesty is open to question; that by reason thereof plaintiff was "insulted, humiliated, and otherwise embarrassed." The plaintiff sought judgment "for exemplary or punitive damages" of $3,000.

       Both here and in the trial court the plaintiff expressly disavowed any claim to an action for slander, and asserted that his claim is one for damages for humiliation, insult and embarrassment. Since plaintiff declined to amend his complaint, it is assumed that he has stated his case in its strongest and most favorable light. The question thus presented is whether a patron of a cocktail lounge has a cause of action for humiliation and embarrassment resulting from insulting words of a waiter.

       It has been held that an innkeeper owes a duty of extending to a guest respectful and decent treatment, and that the innkeeper is liable to a guest for insulting words or conduct; and a similar duty is placed on common carriers with respect to their passengers. Such duty, however, rests on the peculiar relationship between innkeeper and guest or carrier and passenger. In the instant case the defendant is an innkeeper. The complaint alleges plaintiff was a "guest" at the cocktail lounge and not a registered guest of the hotel. One was a casual patron of the lounge and not a registered guest of the hotel. One who is merely a customer at a bar, a restaurant, a barber shop or newsstand operated by a hotel does not thereby establish the relationship of innkeeper and guest. . . . The situation, as we see it, is the same as if the plaintiff had been the customer of any restaurant or tavern where drinks are served.

       We have found no rule of law imposing on the keeper of a drinking establishment, whether called cocktail lounge, bar, saloon or some other name, a higher degree of civility toward its patrons than is imposed on the operator of a store, a barber shop, a filling station or any other mercantile activity. This dispute over the proper change could have arisen just as easily in any place where one pays for goods or services. Our question, therefore, is whether the customer of a business establishment has a cause of action for humiliation and embarrassment resulting from insulting words or conduct of an employee of the establishment. As far as the complaint discloses, the remark of the waiter was undoubtedly made in the course of his employment.

Ordinarily the gravity of a defendant's conduct and the amount of injury caused are factors in arriving at the amount of recovery, and are not determinative of the right to recover. Under the rule proposed, however, it would be necessary to hold that not only the extent of recovery, but the existence of the cause of action is dependent on the amount of damage sustained. If one has a cause of action for an insult only when that insult exceeds the trivial and goes beyond all bounds of decency, and only when such insult produces suffering of a genuine, serious and acute nature, then there must be some rules or standards by which a jury before reaching the realm of amount of recovery may first determine the right of recovery. The jury would have to have some instructions to guide them in determining the bounds of decency and some test to apply in distinguishing between trivial and serious. We know of no workable rule and the authorities furnish us none.

In determining the right of recovery, would the bounds of decency and the seriousness of the insult be the same in the cocktail room of "an internationally known hostel" as the plaintiff asserts the defendant's hotel to be, and a "beer joint" in an unsavory section of the city? Will the seriousness of the insult, and therefore the existence of the cause of action, depend on the social or business standing of either the one giving or receiving the insult? Will the acuteness of plaintiff's suffering, and therefore defendant's liability, depend on the sensitivity of the particular individual? Are all these matters to be left to the "common sense" of the jury, with no rules for their guidance? . . .

Again we are brought back to placing liability on the seriousness of the mental disturbance suffered by the defendant, but with no rule for distinguishing between serious and nonserious distress. If insults beyond the bounds of decency, causing serious mental disturbance, give rise to legal liability, and if there are no rules or standards by which courts may be guided in determining whether the evidence warrants submitting the case to the jury, and no rules or standards for the jury in determining whether the evidence sustains the charge, then every case of fancied insult and hurt feelings must be submitted to the jury and its verdict must stand. This, as Professor Bohlen says, would make life intolerable. Without rules and standards there is no way to avoid getting into the realm of the trivial . . .(50 H.L.R. 725 [1937]).

The law does not, and doubtless should not, impose a general duty of care to avoid causing mental distress. For the sake of reasonable freedom of action, in our own interest and that of society, we need the privilege of being careless whether we inflict mental distress on our neighbors. It is perhaps less clear that we need the privilege of distressing them intentionally and without excuse. Yet there is, and probably should be, no general principle that mental distress purposely caused is actionable unless justified. Such a principle would raise awkward questions of de minimis and of excuse. "He intentionally hurt my feelings" does not yet sound in tort, though it may in a more civilized time.

As we read the complaint in the case before us, plaintiff's charge in substance amounts to nothing more than that his feelings were hurt by the waiter's remarks. This, the U.S. Court of Appeals has said, does not state a cause of action. The complaint was properly dismissed.

Ruling of the Court: Affirmed.

Ross v. Kirkeby Hotels, 160 N.Y.S.2d 978 (1957), is also relevant. A couple attending a wedding reception at the hotel with no intention of occupying a room there were not "guests" of the hotel within the New York statute limiting liability. The court said that when those who come to a hotel solely to attend a marriage function and do not request a room to be assigned to them, they are not guests within the language or intent of the statute. Here the court had two possible courses of action. It could have found that the patrons were there for purposes not related to the main purpose of the hotel or that the hotelkeeper was not acting in the character of an innkeeper but as a business person catering to a special function or banquet. Therefore, a bailment was constituted when the patron delivered his automobile (containing luggage) to the doorman with the specific instruction to place it in a garage. Leaving the automobile on the street constituted a violation of the terms of the bailment and warranted a finding of negligence, rendering the hotelkeeper liable for the full value of the stolen property.

Other Facilities

What are the rights of travelers to such facilities as lobbies, telephones, and newsstands? The general rule is that the innkeeper usually extends the general public an invitation to enter the lobby and lounging rooms without charge, but those who utilize these facilities are not guests, nor does the innkeeper's absolute liability extend to articles of property they may bring with them. On the other hand, when owners or occupiers of land, by express or implied invitation, induce or lead others to come upon the premises for any lawful purpose, they are liable for damages or injuries occasioned by any failure to exercise ordinary care in keeping the premises and approaches safe. This applies to hotel areas to which the public is generally given access. The theory in this case is that the use of the premises and facilities by an invitee is no more than might be assumed within the scope of the invitation, and the visit is for the ultimate mutual advantage of the parties (Coston v. Skyland Hotel, 57 S.E.2d 793 [N.C., 1950]).

In the law of torts there are three possible categories under which a person entering a hotel might be classified: trespasser, licensee, or invitee. One who enters without permission or other right is a trespasser; one who enters with permission but solely for his own purpose is a licensee; and one who enters by invitation, express or implied, is an invitee.

Management Principles

The type of relationship that exists between a guest and host in a place of accommodation will greatly influence the results in a lawsuit. The relationship is unique because it is imposed by law based on custom and usage. As seen in the *Langford* case, motels often have the problem of determining precisely who their guests are. They are not always able to screen people who may be waiting in the car. Some questioning is in order; otherwise a serious legal problem may arise.

The New York *Adler* case also hinged on the existence of a guest-innkeeper relationship. Here the guest had not even stayed in the hotel, but the court ruled as a matter of law that there was such a relationship. Granted, the more logical legal view would have been that there was a bailment of goods. Under such an interpretation the guest would have won, but, in this case, the New York law clearly favored the hotelkeeper. In defense of the outcome, however, it must be admitted that the hotelkeeper had no way of ascertaining that the plaintiff's bags contained $23,000 worth of jewelry.

The *Freudenheim* case also dealt with the guest-innkeeper relationship. On appeal, the plaintiff was considered a guest even though he had not registered. A bailment would also have resulted in a decision in his favor. Here it was incumbent on the hotelkeeper to prove that he came under the limiting liability statute so he would not be required to pay the total loss of over $40,000.

The 1886 *Arcade* case ruled against the guest, holding that he used the hotel solely as a bank and not as a registered guest. It is questionable, though, whether the results would be the same today. Registration is not generally necessary absent a statute for a person to be treated as a guest; what is important is the person's intention of becoming a guest.

Generally injuries or other incidents occurring in a hotel that are not directly connected to a statutory violation (such as false registration, trespass, or possible cases of adultery, fornication, or immoral acts) would be judged solely on the status of the guest-innkeeper relationship. Several states, however, have rendered opposite interpretations, holding that the guest-innkeeper relationship does not exist if the guest registers falsely. Hence, there is no mutuality of acceptance (both parties, knowing all the facts, agree), and any subsequent injury is not the hotelkeeper's responsibility.

The case of Curtis v. Murphy, 22 N.W. 825 (Wisc., 1885), holds that persons are *ab initio* (from the beginning) not guests if their acceptance is based on trickery or on an illegal act to be committed later. But it is questionable whether similar cases would be upheld today. One view is that hoteliers would not have accepted such a person as a guest if they knew what the person was there for. This view is in the minority, however. The majority view maintains that the fact that a guest is there for a purpose other than what one expects is of no consequence—that is, unless the illegal act or actions had something directly to do with the accident in question. In any case, such violations are criminal and must be prosecuted by the state.

Beginning and Duration of a Guest-Innkeeper Relationship

Generally, the relationship between a guest and an innkeeper begins when there is a mutual agreement that a guest will become a guest and the hotel has an available room. It could also start at the airport when the traveler steps into a hotel car or bus, alights from a taxi, or comes into the lobby to register—assuming a room is available and the customer is not one who may be refused legally.

The relationship ends either when the contracted time for the room has elapsed, the bill is not paid when due, due notice is given to vacate the hotel, or when the bill has been paid. In any case, the guest is allowed a reasonable time after vacating the room to leave the hotel; the length of this period (a half hour, one hour, or longer) depends on the facts of the case.

Hotel managers should keep in mind the *Korr, Spiller,* and similar cases on the custody of a guest's baggage when arriving at or leaving the premises. Reasonable rules should delineate hotel employees' duties concerning the baggage while the guest is paying the bill or arranging to leave the hotel. Careful training of employees to familiarize them with the rules will help prevent legal cases.

If a hotel engages a concessionaire to manage its checkroom, a specific contract agreement should be made about the concessionaire's responsibilities—that is, the concessionaire must conform to all state laws and must carry adequate insurance to cover all claims against the hotel, and if possible, checkroom personnel should be bonded with an adequate escrow account to take care of all petty loses. In case of loss, a customer will usually sue the hotel, and the hotel will implead—that is, sue—the concessionaire. But if the concessionaire is not able to pay for the loss, the hotel must pay.

The *Wallace* case indicates the importance of training hotel personnel in graciousness and instituting a procedure that will circumvent possible claims of shortchanging. A standard procedure should be set for all personnel who handle money.

The case of *Ross* v. *Kirkeby* illustrates another serious problem. When guests arrive for a hotel function and leave their car with the doorman, the doorman often leaves the car on the street, where he can retrieve it quickly. Most locked cars can be opened by professional criminals in seconds. The hotel is liable if a car entrusted to its care is burglarized, even if the car is parked on the street.

This chapter has considered various relationships between the guest and the hotelkeeper that are governed by statutes and common law. In the next chapter the hotelkeeper's responsibilities to guests under the Federal Civil Rights Act of 1964 are discussed.

QUESTIONS FOR DISCUSSION

1   How is a guest-innkeeper relationship formed?

2   If a hotelkeeper knows or should have known that a person is in the hotel illegally, can that person still be considered a guest requiring the protection due a bona fide guest?

3   In what ways may a customer manifest an intention of becoming a hotel guest without registering?

4   What are the rights of hotel guests who use a hotel for illegal purposes?

5   How and when may a guest-innkeeper relationship be terminated? Give the various views on this subject.

6   Is a hotelkeeper liable for torts committed by a concessionaire or other business in the hotel?

7   If a person uses a hotel in any way, is a guest-innkeeper relationship always formed?

7 Contents

7 Civil Rights and Hotels, Restaurants, and Other Service Industries

"If you do not think about the future, you cannot have one."

JOHN GALSWORTHY
Swan Song, Part II,
Chapter 6

Many hoteliers, restaurateurs, and managers of other service industries have been affected by the federal Civil Rights Act of 1964 and by state civil rights statutes, as well as by the courts' interpretative analyses of these statutes. Primarily, this chapter is designed to acquaint readers with the provisions and limitations of such civil rights acts.

Under common law, no guest desiring to stay in a hotel or inn can be refused accommodations—except under certain conditions. In actuality, the common law has had little influence in southern hotels, where it had been either ignored or bypassed. Even if a guest brought a cause of action against the hotel, a court trial was expensive and often futile.

In the case of restaurants and other food establishments, the common law applied the private property concept and, with no state statute to the contrary, an owner could refuse any person without fear of legal action. Furthermore, trespass, disturbing-the-peace, and similar statutes gave the restaurant owner legal standing in the removal of unwanted guests by the police.

Discrimination can take many forms, some of them quite subtle. Prior to 1964, at least eighteen states practiced discrimination in one form or another. The other thirty-two states that had legislated against discrimination in places of public accommodations differed so much in their approach as to render any synthesis practically impossible. But since the historic 1964 Civil Rights Act, the road has been clear.

The federal civil rights statutes encompassing hotels, motels, inns, restaurants, eating places, and similar establishments specifically forbid these places from discriminating on account of race or color. These statutes set the stage for an eventual complete desegregation and a new social order. The Civil Rights Act of 1964 generally outlawed discrimination because of "race, color, religion, or national origin" in transient lodgings, dining facilities, and entertainment affecting interstate commerce. Its general intent and overriding purpose was to end discrimination in certain facilities open to the general public, thereby eliminating the inconvenience, unfairness, and humiliation of racial discrimination.

This chapter considers the implications of the Civil Rights Act for service industry managers. It also discusses other forms of discrimination relevant to hotelkeepers or restaurant owners, such as sex and language discrimination, state antidiscrimination laws, and discriminatory advertising. Although federal and state laws generally forbid discrimination, there are some important exceptions. These are discussed in a section on reasonable rules establishment owners may impose.

Constitutional Tests

Accommodations

The constitutionality of the 1964 Civil Rights Act was immediately tested in two landmark cases. The first involved accommodations and the second the serving of food in a restaurant. In the first case, Heart of Atlanta Motel, Inc., v. United States, 379 U.S. 241, 13 L.Ed.2d 258, 85 S.Ct. 348 (1964), the plaintiff owned and operated a motel with 216 rooms. The plaintiff solicited patronage from outside the state of Georgia through various national advertising media and also maintained over fifty billboards and highway signs within the state. He accepted convention trade from outside Georgia, and approximately 75 percent of his registered guests were from out of state. Before passage of the Civil Rights Act, the motel did not rent rooms to blacks. This suit was filed in an effort to perpetuate that policy.

In holding the Civil Rights Act constitutional, the Supreme Court stated that "the action of the Congress in the adoption of the Act was applied here to a motel which concededly served interstate travelers is within the power granted it by the Commerce Clause of the Constitution, as interpreted by this court for 140 years."

Today, all places of public accommodation named in the Civil Rights Act that serve transient guests are uniformly subject to the act. Still, there are a few exceptions. The most notable is the tourist home, covered in what is appropriately referred to as Mrs. Murphy's boarding house clause. The act stipulates that an establishment with five or fewer rooms for rent or hire that is actually occupied by the proprietor is excluded.

Also, although sex discrimination as such is not covered under the Civil Rights Act, many states have enacted laws barring such discrimination. (Sex discrimination, as covered under the Fourteenth Amendment, is discussed in a later section of this chapter.) The relevant cases show that accommodations not directly mentioned do come under the act. In the case of United States v. Beach Associates, Inc., 286 F.Supp. 801 (Md., 1968), a beach apartment that was offered for rent by the week to persons wishing to utilize the beach provided "lodging for transient guests and therefore came under the Act."

In Stout v. Young Men's Christian Association of Bessemer, Alabama, 404 F.2d 687 (Ala., 1968), the YMCA was considered a place of public accommodation. A dormitory facility offering rentals by the week, even though it was a charitable corporation, also came under the act. The court said that "the facility did not meet the criteria of a 'private club' which is exempt from the Act" (Mitchell v. Young Men's Christian Association of Columbia, 310 F.Supp. 13 [R.I., 1970]). A trailer park was also ruled an "other establishment which provides lodging to transient guests" and subject to the act when it offers to serve transient guests (Dean v. Ashling, 409 F.2d 754 [Fla., 1969]; Ohio Civil Rights Commission v. Lysyj, 313 N.E.2d 3 [Ohio, 1974]). In addition, any health clubs, swimming pools, or gymnasiums that are operated by a hotel or motel are considered a part of the facility and as such come under the act.

Not all refusals to accommodate transients are considered discriminatory. In United States v. Gray, 315 F.Supp. 13 (R.I., 1970), the plaintiff testified that he had telephoned the defendant motel owner, who told him there was a room available. He then drove to the motel and told the defendant that he had just called for a room. The defendant denied talking with him, whereas the plaintiff insisted that he had talked to the defendant. An argument ensued, and the defendant told the plaintiff to remove his automobile from the motel premises. In this case, the court ruled that the refusal was justified because of the contentious conduct and argumentative nature of the plaintiff.

Restaurants

In the second constitutional test case of the Civil Rights Act, Katzenbach v. McClung, 379 U.S. 294, 13 L.Ed. 290, 85 S.Ct. 377 (1964), the family-owned restaurant, Ollie's Barbecue, in Birmingham, Alabama, catered to a family and white-collar trade, with only take-out service for blacks. In the twelve months before the passage of the act, the restaurant had purchased approximately $150,000 of food, almost half of which was meat that had moved in interstate commerce.

The Supreme Court said the major question in the *Katzenbach* case was whether Congress could validly impose Title II restrictions on restaurants that serve food that has moved in interstate commerce. (Title II of the Civil Rights Act is a valid exercise of the power to regulate interstate commerce insofar as it requires hotels and motels to serve transients without regard to their race or color.)

The court concluded that racial discrimination in restaurants has a direct and adverse effect on the free flow of interstate commerce. It ruled that Congress acted well within its power to protect and foster commerce in extending the coverage of Title II only to those restaurants offering to serve interstate travelers or serving food that has moved in interstate commerce. As the court said: "The Civil Rights Act of 1964, as here applied, we find to be plainly appropriate in the resolution of what the Congress found to be a national commercial problem of the first magnitude. We find it in no violation of any express limitations of the Constitution and we therefore declare it valid. The Judgment is therefore reversed."

Before 1964, a restaurant or other place that served food was considered private property and, unless a statute prohibited discrimination, the proprietors of such places could legally refuse service to any person. The private property concept could not be applied to hotels and inns because the common law always held accommodations to be quasi-public and, as such, a hotel had a duty to accept all transients who came seeking accommodations. Whenever blacks or other minority groups came into a restaurant for sit-down service, the owner could have them evicted by the police, using the trespass or disturbing-the-peace statute. Many such confrontations occurred in the 1950s and 1960s, and restaurants had more problems desegregating than any other type of establishment.

Tests for Food Service Establishments

If *Katzenbach v. McClung* was meant to resolve the discrimination question in all restaurants, it was not totally successful. Restaurants or food service establishments come under the act only if the following conditions are met.

1   Is the establishment principally engaged in the selling of food?
2   Is the food it sells in a form fit for consumption on the premises?
3   Does it serve or offer to serve interstate travelers?
4   Does a substantial portion of the food it serves move in interstate commerce?
5   Does the discrimination or segregation come about because of state action?

These criteria are met by such facilities as drive-in restaurants (Newman v. Piggie Park Enterprises, Inc., 88 S.Ct. 974, 390 U.S. 400, 19 L.Ed. 1263 [S.C., 1968]), retail store lunch counters (Hamm v. City of Rock Hill, Ark., 1 S.C., 85 S.Ct. 384, 379 U.S. 306, 13 L.Ed.2d 300 [1964]), and sandwich shops and snack bars in privately owned recreational facilities that serve travelers (Codogan v. Fox, 266 F.Supp. 866 [Fla., 1967]). A hospital cafeteria serving interstate travelers food renders the hospital a place of "public accommodation" within the act (U.S. v. Medical Society of South Carolina, 298 F.Supp. 145 [1969]). Certain establishments such as golf courses that do not come under the Civil Rights Act change their status when a lunch counter serving interstate travelers is part of the golf course (Evans v. Laurel Links, Inc., 261 F.Supp. 474 [Va., 1967]).

A Louisiana restaurant that refused to serve a white woman because she was in the company of blacks was found in violation of the Civil Rights Act (Robertson v. Johnston, 376 F.2d 43 [La., 1971]). In Black v. Bonds, 308 F.Supp. 774 (Ala., 1969), the actions of the restaurant's waitresses in refusing black customers service also constituted discrimination in violation of the Civil Rights Act. In both cases an unsuccessful attempt was made to distinguish these food service establishments from regular restaurants.

Exempt Establishments

In general, bars, lounges, nightclubs, bowling alleys, and golf courses do not come under the Civil Rights Act if they do not serve food, offer entertainment, or affect interstate commerce (Selden v. Topaz 1-2-3 Lounge, Inc., 447 F.2d 165 [La., 1971]). Unless there is a state statute, such an establishment may refuse service to any person.

When the Plaquemines Parish Commission Council (Louisiana) adopted an ordinance prohibiting all persons operating bars and cocktail lounges from admitting or selling beverages to "any military personnel in the uniform of the military services," the court, in United States v. Cantrell, 307 F.Supp. 259 (La., 1969), declared the ordinance unconstitutional, noting that the "invidious character" of the ordinance was to be contrasted with the "spectacle" of political leaders attempting to submit young men in uniform to indignities and discrimination at home, while urging "support for our boys" facing hostile fire abroad.

The argument by the defendant that bars without food service were not covered by the act was held to be inoperative because a state ordinance violated the act. Although a class action (a lawsuit brought for many in the same situation) could not be conducted, injunctive relief was granted because the Civil Rights Act of 1964 was not designed to permit a bar owner to exclude uniformed military personnel pursuant to a "perfidious as well as prejudiced" ordinance.

In an interesting case of a tavern owner who wanted to desegregate his establishment but was prevented from doing so by a city ordinance, the court, in Pania v. New Orleans, 262 F.Supp. 651 (La., 1967), concluded that the federal government had no legal right to force the tavern owner to integrate his business if that business did not fall within the purview of the Civil Rights Act of 1964; and it also concluded that the owner of the bar could integrate his establishment if he wished to do so.

However, if such establishments serve food or present entertainment to the viewing public, the Civil Rights Act applies.

The law stipulates that a restaurant comes under the Civil Rights Act of 1964 *only* when it offers to serve interstate travelers or when a substantial portion of the food or beverage that it serves moves in interstate commerce. Can one imagine either of the two situations not existing? Can a restaurant serve food or liquor without a portion coming from out of state or without its customers being travelers? Also, the court has said that any advertising would bring the place under the interstate commerce umbrella.

Additionally, two catchalls certainly bring any food place under the act. First, the offer to serve everybody, and second, the offer to serve white strangers. These offers have been interpreted by the court as tantamount to an offer to serve interstate travelers. Therefore, the save clause in fact has no foundation that allows a restaurant to discriminate (Gregory v. Meyer, 376 F.2d 509 [1967] and Wooten v. Moore, 400 F.2d 239 [1968]).

In Fazzio Real Estate Company v. Adams, 396 F.2d 146 (La., 1968), the court held that a bowling alley was covered by the Civil Rights Act because a refreshment counter was physically located within the premises. The court said that "it is clear that the Act, for purposes of coverage, contemplates that there may be an 'establishment' within an 'establishment.' " The court also said that the act must extend coverage to all major and minor aspects of any business enterprise that serve separately identifiable functions—for example, a barbershop within a hotel. Because the hotel is covered, so is the barbershop. This principle is known as the *unitary rule.*

A bar or lounge is governed by the act if it provides entertainment. A Florida bar that provided alcoholic beverages originating from outside the state and provided its customers with the use of a piano, juke box, and television set manufactured outside the state was "a place of entertainment within the meaning of the Act" (U.S. v. Deetjen, 356 F.Supp. 688 [Fla., 1973]).

Private Establishments with State Involvement—Right of Refusal

An interesting kind of discrimination was at issue in a case concerning Kenneth S. Uston, a gambler who utilizes his memory to assist him in playing blackjack. Uston is a counter. He uses his good memory and a system when playing blackjack to determine what the odds are in favor of his getting a winning hand. If certain cards remain to be played after a given percentage of the cards have already been played, the odds that the house had enjoyed at the beginning of the game would be severely diminished and might even favor the better. Thus, when the odds favor them, counters increase their bets to the house limits, and because the odds are now in their favor, they inevitably win. Almost all casinos in the United States bar counters from their tables and eject from the casino those they suspect of counting cards.

Uston was ejected from casinos in Nevada and brought suit against three of them in the U.S. Federal District Court for the Northern District of California. In his suits, he alleged that the casinos had violated his federal civil rights by denying him the opportunity to play blackjack because he was a "competent blackjack player," and therefore, the prohibition was discriminatory. Furthermore, he alleged in one case that the casino had violated his rights under the common law duty of an innkeeper to accept all who apply for a room and specifically his rights to the casino as part of the hotel.

In two of the cases, Uston v. Grand Resorts, Inc., 564 F.2d 1217 (Cal., 1977), and Uston v. Hilton Casinos, Inc., 564 F.2d 1218 (Cal., 1977), the court declined to decide the cases because it did not have jurisdiction over the defendants. The court did, however, find that it could take jurisdiction over the remaining case, Uston v. Airport Casino, Inc., 564 F.2d 1216 (Cal., 1977), but made short shrift to Uston's claims for money damages.

As to the allegation that he had been denied his federal civil rights, the court said that the complaint did not involve discrimination on the basis of race, color, creed, religion, national origin, or sex, and therefore, there was no discrimination recognizable under the federal law. Furthermore, inasmuch as there was no state action alleged, the provisions of the Fourteenth Amendment as to discriminatory denial of due process of law or equal protection of the laws were not invoked. In view of this situation, Uston's claim based upon violation of federal civil rights was unfounded. As to his claim that the casino violated the common law duties of an innkeeper by its actions, the court found that even though the casino may have been an innkeeper in the common law sense, it was not acting as an innkeeper in its dealings with Uston. The court said, "The relationship was not one of innkeeper and patron, but rather one of casino owner and prospective gambler. The policies upon which the innkeeper's special common-law duties rested are not present in such a relationship."

Although this ruling would be enough to stop the average person, Uston, however, persisted in bringing actions against casinos. He changed his tactics in that, instead of relying on violation of civil rights or violation of innkeeper's duties, he claimed that the casinos had usurped a function reserved to a state administrative agency when they ejected him from their casino. In Uston v. Resorts Int'l Hotel, Inc., 431 A.2d 173 (N.J., 1981), Uston claimed that Resorts International was a state-regulated facility that catered to the public under legislation that called for maximum public participation in gaming and, therefore, only the New Jersey Casino Control Commission and not the individual casinos could bar him from casinos in New Jersey. He stated that when he brought his eviction before the commission, they told him that a casino had a common-law right to evict him as a trespasser. The three judges sitting on the Appellate Division of State Superior Court that heard the case unanimously held that the plaintiff was correct. They stated, "It is plainly implicit that a casino itself is not empowered to blacklist and exclude a person despite the apparent failure of the commission as yet to execute this delegation of authority." The court went on to say that the common law right to bar people from public places applied to "undesirables" and that the plaintiff was not an undesirable.

Resorts International and the commission filed an immediate appeal from the courts finding and were also granted a stay of the courts ruling pending the appeal.

The outcome of the case is as yet undecided. If, however, the ruling of the appellate court is upheld, and the commission delegates authority to casinos to evict counters or passes a regulation permitting the eviction of counters, what then? Such a ruling could give Uston the "state action" necessary to get him before a federal court to determine whether or not the eviction of counters by the commission constitutes a type of discrimination protected by the due process and equal protection of the law clauses contained in the Fourteenth Amendment. Uston may also seek to establish an illegal delegation of legislative authority to determine who they will evict or will not evict.

Private Clubs

The ban on discrimination in the Civil Rights Act of 1964 does not apply to "private clubs or other establishments not in fact open to the public." The act, however, does not give a test of what constitutes a "private club." During the legislative debates on the act, Senator Hubert Humphrey said, "The test as to whether a private club is really a private club or whether it is an establishment not open to the public is a factual one" (110 Cong. Rec. 13697 [1964]). The courts do not agree whether the test is a factual question or a question of law (Katzenbach v. Jordan, 302 F.Supp. 370 [La., 1969]; United States v. Richberg, 398 F.2d 523 [Miss., 1968]).

In attempting to bypass the Civil Rights Act, many individuals and groups formed "quickie" private clubs to circumvent serving blacks and other minority groups. The case of Daniel v. Paul details some of these techniques. What constitutes a valid private club? No definition can give the precise requirements, as exempted by Section 201(e) of the act. The act merely states that a private club is exempt and, therefore, the courts must interpret the legislative intent that prevailed at its inception. It should be noted that nonprivate establishments, such as the Stork Club or the Twenty-one Club, can call themselves clubs, even though they are not private (Walton Playboy Clubs, Inc., v. City of Chicago, 185 N.E.2d 719 [Ill., 1962]). In considering whether a club is private, one or more of the following tests have been applied by the courts, but not in a consistent way:

1 Is the membership genuinely selective? (The more selective, the more chance it is a private club.)

2 Do the members of the club have any control over its operations? (The more control they have, the greater the chance of its being ruled a private club.) Who can change the bylaws? Who owns the club property? How is the club funded?

3 How was the membership corporation created? Was advertising conducted to solicit members? Is there a reasonable limit to the membership?

4 Does the club observe certain formalities, such as a procedure for becoming a guest?

5 How does the club compare to similar clubs in such activities as dues and initiation fees?

The opinion of the court may be helpful in analyzing the status of a club, although its comments are not inclusive or exclusive:

I.　A private club is an organization if it has officers, bylaws, rules, and regulations. The club must conform to all laws of incorporation (*Katzenbach* v. *Jordan*).

II.　It may be organized as a social, fraternal, civic, and/or other organization, which *selects* its own members. To meet this test, the club membership must be genuinely selective on some reasonable basis and have control over its operation (*United States* v. *Richberg*). The court said a club is a pluralistic enterprise. It cannot be one man's principality or domain. It cannot be his alter ego. A club must have substance, and it is up to the claimants to prove it is genuine and not a sham establishment.

III.　Furthermore, a club must not have been established as a way of bypassing or avoiding the effect of the Civil Rights Act—if it was not really a club (Katzenbach v. Jack Sabin's Private Club, 265 F.Supp. 90 [La., 1967]). The word *club* has no very definite meaning. Clubs are formed for all sorts of purposes, and there is no uniformity in their constitutions and rules. A "club" is generally an association or a corporation comprised of individuals joining together for social intercourse or some other common object. A club need not have a misanthropic membership committee which peppers the candidates list with blackballs, but there should be a mutual relationship of some contemplated permanence . . . that would be entered into (Carpenter v. Zoning Board of Appeals of Framingham, 223 N.E.2d 679 [Mass., 1967]). In Wright v. Cork Club, 315 F.Supp. 1143 (Texas, 1969), the claimants attempted to use the fact that they qualified as a "private club" under the Texas Liquor Control Act. This was not persuasive as to whether the organization was a private club exempted from the Civil Rights Act.

When a so-called private club becomes a "place of public accommodation," it loses its purely private character and subjects itself to legislative mandate, as the following case shows.

Daniel v. Paul
       89 S.Ct. 1697 (1969)
       (BRENNAN, Justice)

Petitioners, Negro residents of Little Rock, Arkansas, brought this class action in the District Court for the Eastern District of Arkansas to enjoin respondent from denying them admission to a recreational facility called Lake Nixon Club owned and operated by respondent, Euell Paul, and his wife. The complaint alleged that Lake Nixon Club was a "public accommodation" subject to the provisions of Title II of the Civil Rights Act of 1964, 78 Stat. 243, 42 U.S.C. § 2000a et seq., and that respondent violated the act in refusing petitioners admission solely on racial grounds. After trial, the District Court, although finding that respondent had refused petitioners admission solely because they were Negroes, dismissed the complaint on the ground that Lake Nixon Club was not within any of the categories of "public accommodations" covered by the 1964 Act. . . .

Lake Nixon Club, located 12 miles west of Little Rock, is a 232-acre amusement area with swimming, boating, sun bathing, picnicking, miniature golf, dancing facilities, and a snack bar. The Pauls purchased the Lake Nixon site in 1962 and subsequently operated this amusement business there in a racially segregated manner.

Title II of the Civil Rights Act of 1964 enacted a sweeping prohibition of discrimination or segregation on the ground of race, color, religion, or national origin at places of public accommodation whose operations affect commerce. This prohibition does not extend to discrimination or segregation at private clubs. But, as both courts below properly found, Lake Nixon is not a private club. It is simply a business operated for a profit with none of the attributes of self-government and member-ownership traditionally associated with private clubs. It is true that following enactment of the Civil Rights Act of 1964, the Pauls began to refer to the establishment as a private club. They even began to require patrons to pay a 25-cent "membership" fee, which gains a purchaser a "membership" card entitling him to enter the Club's premises for an entire season and, on payment of specified additional fees, to use the swimming, boating, and miniature golf facilities. But this "membership" device seems no more than a subterfuge designed to avoid coverage of the 1964 Act. White persons are routinely provided "membership" cards, and some 100,000 whites visit the establishment each season. As the District Court found, Lake Nixon is "open in general to all of the public who are members of the white race" (263 F.Supp., at 418). Negroes, on the other hand, are uniformly denied "membership" cards, and thus admission, because of the Pauls' fear that integration would "ruin" the "business." The conclusion of the courts below that Lake Nixon is not a private club is plainly correct—indeed, respondent does not challenge that conclusion here.

We, therefore, turn to the question whether Lake Nixon Club is "a place of public accommodation" as defined by Section 201(b) of the 1964 Act, and, if so, whether its operations "affect commerce" within the meaning of Section 201(c) of that Act.

Petitioners argue first that Lake Nixon's snack bar is a covered public accommodation under Sections 201(a) (2) and 201(c) (2), and that as such it brings the entire establishment within the coverage of Title II under Sections 201(b) (4) and 201(c) (4). Clearly, the snack bar is "principally engaged in selling food for consumption on the premises." Thus, it is a covered public accommodation if "it serves or offers to serve interstate travelers or a substantial portion of the food which it serves . . . has moved in commerce." We find that the snack bar is a covered public accommodation under either of these standards.

The Pauls advertise the Lake Nixon Club in a monthly magazine called "Little Rock Today," which is distributed to guests at Little Rock hotels, motels, and restaurants, to acquaint them with available tourist attractions in the area. Regular advertisements for Lake Nixon were also broadcast over two area radio stations. In addition, Lake Nixon has advertised in the "Little Rock Air Force Base," a monthly newspaper published at the Little Rock Air Force Base in Jacksonville, Arkansas. This choice of advertising media leaves no doubt that the Pauls were seeking broad-based patronage from an audience which they knew to include interstate travelers. Thus, the Lake Nixon Club unquestionably offered to serve out-of-state visitors to the Little Rock area. And it would be unrealistic to assume that none of the 100,000 patrons actually served by the Club each season was an interstate traveler. Since the Lake Nixon Club offered to serve and served out-of-state persons, and since the Club's snack bar was established to serve all patrons of the entire facility, we must conclude that the snack bar offered to serve and served out-of-state persons.

The record, although not as complete on this point as might be desired, also demonstrates that a "substantial portion of the food" served by the Lake Nixon Club snack bar has moved in interstate commerce. The snack bar serves a limited fare—hot dogs and hamburgers on buns, soft drinks, and milk. The District Court took judicial notice of the fact that the "principal ingredients going into the bread were produced and processed in other States" and that "certain ingredients [of the soft drinks] were probably obtained . . . from out-of-State sources." . . . Thus, at the very least, three of the four food items sold at the snack bar contain ingredients originating outside of the State. There can be no serious doubt that a "substantial portion of the food" served at the snack bar has moved in interstate commerce.

The snack bar's status as a covered establishment automatically brings the entire Lake Nixon facility within the ambit of Title II. Civil Rights Act of 1964, §§ 201(b) (4) and 201(c) (4).

Petitioners also argue that the Lake Nixon Club is a covered public accommodation under Sections 201(b) (3) and 201(c) (3) of the 1964 Act. These sections proscribe discrimination by "any motion picture house, theater, concert hall, sports arena, stadium or other place of exhibition or entertainment" which "customarily presents films, performances, athletic teams, exhibitions, or other sources of entertainment which move in commerce." Under any accepted definition of "entertainment," the Lake Nixon Club would surely qualify as a "place of entertainment." And indeed it advertises itself as such. Respondent argues, however, that in the context of Section 201(b) (3) "place of entertainment" refers only to establishments where patrons are entertained as spectators or listeners rather than those where entertainment takes the form of direct participation in some sport or activity. We find no support in the legislative history for respondent's reading of the statute. The few indications of legislative intent are to the contrary. . . .

The remaining question is whether the operations of the Lake Nixon Club "affect commerce" within the meaning of Section 201(c) (3). We conclude that they do. Lake Nixon's customary "sources of entertainment . . .

move in commerce." The Club leases 15 paddle boats on a royalty basis from an Oklahoma company. Another boat was purchased from the same company. The Club's juke box was manufactured outside Arkansas and plays records manufactured outside the State. The legislative history indicates that mechanical sources of entertainment such as these were considered by Congress to be "sources of entertainment" within the meaning of Section 201(c) (3).

Ruling of the Court: Reversed.

Sex Discrimination

Sex discrimination is not covered by the Civil Rights Act of 1964 for accommodations and restaurants. However, a person may obtain redress for discrimination in places of public accommodation through the Fourteenth Amendment. Thus, in Seidenberg v. McSorley's Old Ale House, Inc., 308 F.Supp. 1253 (1969), the court pointed out that the Civil Rights Act of 1964 did not forbid discrimination on account of sex in public accommodations. In this case, two female members of the National Organization for Women (NOW) entered the defendant establishment, a bar primarily engaged in serving alcoholic and nonalcoholic beverages. They were told by the bartender that the establishment did not serve women and that it had consistently adhered to this practice throughout its 114 years of existence. Although the court denied the defendant's motion to dismiss the complaint for other reasons, it said that Congress had not included sex as an impermissible basis of discrimination in public accommodations, as it had in employment practices, and that the court should not gratuitously do what Congress had not seen fit to do by superimposing such a condition on the public accommodations law. In a later opinion, the court in Seidenberg v. McSorley's Old Ale House, Inc., adhered to the view that Congress in the Civil Rights Act of 1964 had not forbidden discrimination in public accommodations on account of sex, but it did find that such discrimination, based on the facts of this case, violated the Fourteenth Amendment.

Attention should also be called to De Crow v. Hotel Syracuse Corporation, 288 F.Supp. 530 (N.Y., 1968), in which an unescorted woman brought suit against a hotel for refusing to serve her in the bar operated in one of its restaurants, although, according to her, she was sitting quietly and was in no way disturbing any other patrons. Alleging that she was forced to leave the bar, which caused her severe mental anguish and embarrassment, she maintained that the hotel's action ran contrary to the Fourteenth Amendment, the Civil Rights Act (42 U.S.C. Sections 1983, 1985), and the Civil Rights Act of 1964.

Stating that it did not agree with the plaintiff's analogy (which intimates that because the 1964 Civil Rights Act prohibits discrimination by sex in matters of employment practices, then "any discriminatory practice based solely on sex must be unconstitutional"), the court pointed out that even a "hasty examination" of the 1964 Civil Rights Act made the fallacy of such an analogy apparent. The conduct of hotels and restaurants is governed by 42 U.S.C., Section 2000(a), the court continued, and while the full and equal enjoyment of public accommodations without discrimination on account of "race, color, religion, or national origin" had been guaranteed by Congress, no such guarantee had been made on account of sex. The court said that it should not gratuitously do what Congress had not seen fit to do, and suggested that the woman address her complaint to Congress and not to the court.

If a restaurant has a bar that is covered under the Civil Rights Act's unitary rule, as well as under a state statute barring discrimination, how far can the discrimination go? Does it encompass bars that advertise in such a way as to attract only males? The case of Rosenberg v. State Human Rights Appeal Board, 357 N.Y.S.2d 325 (1974), sheds light on this question. The plaintiff in this case asked that the owners of the Silent Woman Tavern, which had a policy of not serving women at the bar during certain hours, stop discriminating against women, remove all signs restricting the presence of women, and change the name of the restaurant. According to the New York State Human Rights Appeal Board:

> Petitioners argue that since the owner conceded that the sign and name were intended to attract male patrons, they are intrinsically discriminatory and must be changed in order to effectuate the purpose of the Human Rights Law. We cannot agree. The law does not prohibit appealing by signs or trade name to one sex or another. Rather, the prohibition is against displaying notice or advertisement to the effect that any of the facilities or privileges will be refused or withheld from or denied a person on account of sex (Executive Law Section 206 [2]). In this case, signs of this nature were in fact ordered removed by the Commissioner. There is nothing about the name or the exterior sign, in the form used here, that would suggest that women would be refused the use of the facilities. The Commissioner did not abuse his discretion in not ordering that the name and sign be changed. Further, it was not an abuse of discretion not to order the owner to give public notice through the media as requested by petitioners. It appears that this matter has been followed by the local newspaper news media and the interested segment of the public is no doubt aware of the changed rules of the restaurant.
>
> Determination unanimously confirmed without costs.

Age Discrimination

The law does not prohibit all discrimination. Thus the treatment of a certain class of people in a way different from another is not necessarily illegal. Such is the case with discrimination because of age.

Although it has been legislatively proclaimed that someone who is old cannot be discriminated against, what about someone who is young? This question manifests itself in the various laws, rules, and regulations pertaining to minors, especially prohibiting them from drinking alcoholic beverages in an otherwise public place. It has long been established that states or municipalities can constitutionally pass statutes or ordinances prohibiting the sale of alcoholic beverages to people under a certain age. However, can a restaurant or hotel ban a person from a dining room where both food and alcoholic beverages are sold because that person is below the legal drinking age?

A federal court in the District of Columbia faced this question in D.T. Corp. v. District of Columbia, 407 A.2d 707 (D.C., 1979). The D.T. Corporation, which wanted the Alcoholic Beverage Commission of the District of Columbia to approve a transfer of its license, barred those under eighteen from entering its premises. The commission, however, held that the rule violated the District of Columbia human rights law barring discrimination because of age and refused to grant the transfer.

The court held that the commission was wrong and cited as its reasons the fact that the sale and consumption of alcoholic beverages are highly regulated areas of commercial activity and that there was a good deal of public concern about alcohol abuse by teenagers, a concern reflected in the drinking age laws. To undermine these efforts by requiring admission of minors to establishments serving liquor as well as meals would be inconsistent with these policies.

The Supreme Judicial Court of the State of Massachusetts ruled in August 1981 that the discriminatory laws applying to acts of discrimination involving age were against the law only if applied to those in the older age groups and not when applied to younger. If this is the proper thinking, then one need not fear liability for the practice of rules that discriminate against the young rather than the aged.

Discrimination by State Law or Rule

Federal statute 42 U.S.C. § 2000a-1 bars any establishment from discrimination or segregation of any kind on the grounds of race, color, religion, or national origin if such discrimination or segregation is or purports to be required by any law, statute, ordinance, regulation, rule, or order of a state or any agency or political division thereof. However, states often do discriminate against individuals.

In the case of Robertson v. Johnson, 249 F.Supp. 618 (La., 1966), the court held that a white woman arrested for vagrancy had a cause of action under 42 U.S.C. § 2000a-1 when she alleged that the purpose of the arrest was to enforce a custom in New Orleans forbidding or discouraging white women from frequenting predominantly black places. The court observed, "If appellant is able to prove that discrimination or segregation is carried on under color or any custom or usage required or purported to be required by officials of the City of New Orleans, and that her arrest was for the sole purpose of enforcing such custom and usage, she may well be entitled to injunctive relief under Section 2000a-1 of the act. . . ."

Any person denied rights protected by the act because of "race, color, religion, or national origin" can file suit as a plaintiff. This action may be a class action to vindicate protected rights when common questions of law and fact affect so many people in the area that it is impractical to bring them all before the court.

Relief

The Civil Rights Act of 1964 provides several kinds of relief for people who have been discriminated against. *Injunctive relief* requires a party to refrain from doing a particular act or activity. It is a preventive measure, which guards against future injuries rather than affords a remedy for past injuries. *Declaratory relief* is received by requesting a court judgment "to establish the rights of the parties or express the opinion of the court on a question of law without ordering anything to be done." A declaratory judgment stands by itself with no executory process to follow. Actions for damages are not directly authorized by the act (Newman v. Piggie Park Enterprises, Inc., 390 U.S. 400, 19 L.Ed.2d 1263, 88 S.Ct. 964 [dictum] 1968). However, it is possible to sue under either 42 U.S.C. § 1983 or 42 U.S.C. § 1985(3) for damages for the denial of rights covered by the Civil Rights Act of 1964 (Sherrod v. Pink Hat Cafe, 250 F.Supp. 516 [Miss., 1965]).

The act authorizes the allowance of attorney's fees, and courts have indicated the general desirability of this practice. Attorney's fees are the charges made by the attorney for services in representing a client in the course of preparing and trying a case. The Supreme Court has said that one who succeeds in obtaining an injunction under Title II "should ordinarily recover an attorney's fee unless special circumstances would render such an award unjust" (*Newman v. Piggie Park Enterprises*).

The act provides that no civil action is to be begun until the expiration of thirty days after written notice is given to a state or local agency with power to deal with discrimination, where such an agency exists (42 U.S.C. § 2000a-3 [c]). A civil action is any lawsuit other than a criminal proceeding, and it is brought about to enforce a right or gain payment for a wrong. Where there is no such state or local antidiscrimination agency, a federal court can refer the problem to the Federal Community Relations Service for up to 120 days (42 U.S.C. § 2000a-3 [d]). The act is clear on the point that there is no need to exhaust administrative or other remedies before seeking judicial relief in the federal courts (42 U.S.C. § 2000a-6). The statutory language indicates the remedies are exclusive "but nothing in this subchapter shall preclude any individual from asserting any right based on any other federal or state law not inconsistent with this subchapter . . . or from pursuing any remedy, civil or criminal, which may be available for the vindication or enforcement of such right."

Another way the state can become involved in a civil rights complaint is in the leasing of land for a private endeavor. In Golden v. Biscayne Bay Yacht Club, 521 F.2d 344 (Fla., 1975), the City of Miami leased publicly owned land in 1962 to the defendant club so that it could provide dockage for its members. The club had a policy of membership by sponsorship only. There had never been a Jewish or a black member, with the exception of one honorary black member. The plaintiffs were attempting to become members of the club.

Although the parties stipulated that the defendant was a private club, the fact that a club is private does not always mean that it is exempted from the requirements of the Civil Rights Act. Private conduct abridging individual rights does fall within the prohibitions of the Fourteenth Amendment when the state has been found to have become involved in it to some significant degree.

In the *Biscayne Bay Yacht Club* case, the defendant club enjoyed a select privilege—dock space—not available to each citizen but rather one coveted by many citizens in the south Florida area. More critically, the privilege was essential to the club's operation. In this case, the court held that a "symbiotic relationship" between the state and the club existed, thereby making any discriminatory action by the club a violation of the Fourteenth Amendment. By virtue of the lease, the acts of the club became those of the state and any deprivation of an individual's rights by the club became a deprivation by the state.

Language Discrimination

With the influx of Cubans, Mexicans, Puerto Ricans, and South Americans into the United States, Spanish has become a second language in many areas of this country. Can a place of public accommodation preclude Spanish from being spoken in that place of business? *Hernandez v. Erlenbusch* should put to rest many questions on the speaking of a foreign language in a bar or restaurant. In addition, this case discusses the protection that a bartender or owner owes to non-English-speaking patrons.

| Case | Hernandez v. Erlenbusch |
| Example | *368 F.Supp. 752 (Oregon, 1973)* |

The events in August 1972 which produced this case took place in a nondescript little tavern in Forest Grove. They involved nothing more—nor less—lofty than the right of some American citizens to enjoy a bottle of beer at the tavern bar and to speak in Spanish while doing so. . . .

Findings of Fact   Their actions brought pursuant to the provisions of 42 U.S.C. §§ 1981, 1982, and 1985 were consolidated for a court trial. At that trial, a preponderance of the evidence showed the following: The setting for both cases is the same—a community of approximately 8,500 persons in which more than 2,000 Mexican-Americans have been living for at least the last four years. The plaintiffs in these cases are all U.S. citizens, most of them native born. Some two years ago, the defendants Erlenbusch, owners of the Taffrail Tavern ("Tavern"), issued these orders to their bartenders:

"You are instructed to observe the following in addition to the standard OLCC regulation . . . .

"11.   Do not allow a foreign language to be used at the bar, if it interferes with the regular trade. If there should be a chance of a problem, ask the 'Problem' people to move to a table and turn the juke box up. (Use house money)."

The rationale for this policy, as explained by its formulators and enforcers, is that the tavern has many Anglo and Chicano patrons, with attendant friction between the two groups caused by the dislike by some of the local white populace of the "foreigners" in their midst. According to the Erlenbusches, the tavern's owners, the language rule as carried out by them and their employees served everyone's interests by accommodating both Anglo and Chicano customers and ensuring peaceful continuance of the tavern business. The complaints concerning Spanish spoken at the bar allegedly stem from fear on the part of the white clientele that the Chicanos are talking about them. It was in this atmosphere ridden with mistrust and apprehension that the following incidents occurred:

On August 23, 1972, Gilberto Hernandez and Abel and Alfredo Maldonado went to the tavern where defendant Krausnick, the bartender, served them beer. While drinking, the three men began conversing in Spanish, their native tongue. Anglo customers, who were also sitting at the bar, were "irritated" and complained to Krausnick. She advised the Chicanos that if they persisted in speaking Spanish, they would have to go to a booth or leave the premises.

Hernandez and the Maldonados took issue with these orders and an argument ensued. Krausnick poured out their remaining beer and refused to refund any money. The police were called, the plaintiffs left peacefully.

Two days later, the scene was reenacted with different plaintiffs and an additional three antagonists. Krausnick "pulled" the beers of Gonzalez, Perez and Vasquez who were then followed out of the tavern and assaulted by defendants Salisbury, Dunn, and Clary, three Anglo regular customers. Clary was subsequently tried and convicted in state court for battering Gonzalez over the right eye with a fire extinguisher. (Gonzalez was the only plaintiff who was physically struck.)

Defendant Krausnick testified that she agreed with and willingly enforced "Rule 11." Clary, Dunn, and Salisbury concurred, saying they knew of the rule and wholeheartedly endorsed it. John Erlenbusch testified he adopted the policy simply to avoid trouble and to preserve his license.

Conclusions of Law   There is no question but that 42 U.S.C. §§ 1981 and 1982 have been interpreted to ban the discrimination alleged in these cases. . . . Regardless of defendant Erlenbusch's contention that his policy is "in accordance with and because of the rules and regulations" of the Oregon Liquor Control Commission and O.R.S. 471.315(1)(d), this is clearly private discrimination, as differentiated from unequal treatment under color of state law which would be actionable under 42 U.S.C. § 1983. The applicability of 42 U.S.C. § 1985, the conspiracy statute, will be discussed later.

In examining the practical effect of the tavern's policy against the speaking of foreign languages at the bar, it is obvious that it amounts to patent racial discrimination against Mexican-Americans who constitute about one-fourth of the tavern's trade, regardless of an occasional visit by a customer able to speak another language. The rule's results are what count; the intent of the framers in these circumstances is irrelevant. . . . In the instant case, Rule 11, as intended and applied, deprives Spanish-speaking persons of their rights to buy, drink and enjoy what the tavern has to offer on an equal footing with English-speaking consumers.

Plaintiffs' Section 1981 rights "to make and enforce contracts . . . and to the full and equal benefit of all laws and proceedings for the security of person and property as is enjoyed by white citizens" have been violated. Likewise, plaintiffs have been denied their Section 1982 guarantee that "[a]ll citizens of the United States shall have the same right . . . to . . . purchase . . . personal property." The "property" involved in the "contract" here is a bottle of beer instead of a job, a house, or a ticket to a recreational activity, but the principle is the same as that involved in the lunch counter and bus cases of the 1960s. Just as the Constitution forbids banishing blacks to the back of the bus so as not to arouse the racial animosity of the preferred white passengers, it also forbids ordering Spanish-speaking patrons to the "back booth or out" to avoid antagonizing English-speaking beer-drinkers.

The lame justification that a discriminatory policy helps preserve the peace is as unacceptable in barrooms as it was in buses. Catering to prejudice out of fear of provoking greater prejudice only perpetuates racism. Courts faithful to the Fourteenth Amendment will not permit, either by camouflage or cavalier treatment, equal protection so to be profaned.

Although damages are due, I recognize that under the circumstances of this case only a modest amount should be awarded. This award cannot pretend to offset or negate the undercurrents of discrimination. As to those, I also recommend, later in this opinion, other remedial measures. Therefore, for the humiliation and distress resulting from this discriminatory policy damages are awarded against the Erlenbusches and Krausnick as follows:

a In No. 72–811, each Plaintiff shall recover $100;
b In No. 72–812, each Plaintiff shall recover $100.

Despite the common law duty of tavern owners to protect their patrons from injury in or in the reasonable vicinity of their tavern, the evidence does not justify a finding that the owners or the bartender had reason to anticipate that the outside ruckus on August 25, 1972, would occur because of Rule 11. . . .

Ruling of the Court: For the assault and battery in No. 72–812, no damages are awarded as against the tavern owners or bartender. Plaintiffs Vasquez and Perez are each awarded $100 general damages and $100 punitive damages as against the remaining three defendants. Plaintiff Gonzalez is awarded, as against the same three defendants, $200 general, $49.51 special, and $250 punitive damages. . . .

Garcia v. Gloor Lumber and Supply, Inc., 101 U.S. 923 (1981), concerned an employee in Texas who was fired because he violated the company's rules of speaking only English on the job except when dealing with Spanish-speaking customers. The company claimed this policy was necessary to avoid offending customers who speak only English, to maintain the worker's fluency in English, and to enable English-speaking supervisors to monitor employee activities.

Garcia, who spoke both English and Spanish, charged that the rule discriminated against him by forbidding him to use his native language. At the administrative level, the U.S. Equal Employment Opportunity Commission had decided there was reasonable cause to think Garcia was fired because of discrimination in violation of federal law. On appeal, the Texas courts held that such a rule was not discriminatory against Garcia. The U.S. Supreme Court apparently agreed because it failed to grant certiorari, an order that has the effect of affirming the state court decision.

Reasonable Rules of an Establishment

The management of a service establishment, like any other business enterprise, must have rules to maintain order and express the nature of the establishment and the philosophy of its management. This concept is a valid management prerogative. Granted, the instituted rules must be reasonable, not arbitrary or capricious.

In *Feldt* v. *Marriott Corporation*, the management had a rule that excluded any person who was shoeless. Is this a reasonable rule? Can a restaurant require coats for men and some specific attire for women? Can women with shorts be excluded from a dining room? Few such cases have been tried in the appellate division, but many have been tried at the lower court level, and some analogies can be made that pertain to the "reasonable rule doctrine."

Case	**Feldt v. Marriott Corporation**
Example	*322 A.2d 913 (D.C., 1974)*

This appeal is from a directed verdict against appellant at the close of her evidence in an action for false arrest. [Appellant originally sued in the United States District Court for malicious prosecution and false arrest. The District Court granted summary judgment against appellant on her malicious prosecution claim, and certified the false arrest claim to the Superior Court for trial.]

Appellant's evidence showed the following facts without material contradiction. She, a young woman about 26 years of age, and her male escort had attended a dance at a fraternity house and after leaving the dance went to a Junior Hot Shoppe, owned and operated by appellee. They went through a cafeteria line, selected, and paid for some food and then sat at a table and began to eat. The manager of the shop approached the table and told appellant she would have to leave because she was not wearing shoes. [Appellant had worn her sister's shoes at the dance but found they were too small and removed them. When she entered the Hot Shoppe she left her shoes in her escort's automobile parked near the entrance. Her escort described her attire as "a very attractive pants suit . . . floor length." In her testimony, she referred to her "long dress."] No sign to that affect was posted, but the manager said it was the company's policy to serve no one who was not wearing shoes. She replied she would leave as soon as she finished eating. The manager did not offer to refund her money, and she asked for no refund. [There was testimony that the manager offered to get a bag so she could take the food (a hamburger and french fries) with her.] He continued to insist that she leave, and she continued to insist she would leave only when she had finished eating. The argument continued, and she finally said to the manager: "Will you, please, go to hell." He walked outside and returned with a police officer. The manager again asked her to leave, and the officer told her she would be violating the unlawful entry statute if she refused to leave after the manager had asked her to leave. She replied she would leave when she had finished eating. The officer took her arm and said unless she left he would arrest her. She arose and walked to the door and then, observing the officer behind her, began struggling with him and hit him. [Appellant apparently did not think she was under arrest as she walked to the door, but the officer considered her arrested at the table when he placed his hand on her arm.]

Appellant was then placed in a patrol wagon, taken to a precinct station, and later taken to the Women's Detention Center where she was fingerprinted, photographed, and placed in a lineup. Hours later she was released on her personal recognizance and told to appear in court the next day. When she appeared in court, she was told the charge against her would be dropped and she was free to leave.

It is clear that appellant entered the premises lawfully, but it is also clear that under our unlawful entry statute (D.C. Code 1973, § 22–3102) one who lawfully enters may be guilty of a misdemeanor by refusing to leave after being ordered to do so by the person lawfully in charge of the premises. Our question is whether the police officer was justified in arresting appellant when she, in his presence, refused to leave after being ordered to do so by the manager.

At common law, a restaurant owner had the right to arbitrarily refuse service to any guest. Absent constitutional or statutory rights, the common law still controls in this jurisdiction. This is not a case of racial discrimination or violation of civil rights. We do have a statute making it unlawful for a restaurant to refuse service to "any quiet and orderly person" or to exclude anyone on account of race or color; but, as we have said, there was no racial discrimination here and we do not think the requirement to serve any quiet or orderly person prevents a restaurant from having reasonable requirements as to the dress of its customers, such as a requirement that all male customers wear coats and ties or, as here, that all customers wear shoes. Had the restaurant manager observed that appellant was not wearing shoes when she first entered the restaurant, he could have properly and lawfully refused to serve her and requested her to leave. Our question narrows down to whether the fact that the restaurant had served appellant food and received payment for it, prevented the restaurant from ordering appellant to leave when her shoeless condition was observed. [There is no indication in the record that the manager or any employee of the restaurant observed appellant's lack of shoes until after she was served and was seated.

Perhaps her "floor length" clothing made her lack of shoes not readily observable.]

The status of a customer in a restaurant, as far as we can ascertain, has never been precisely declared. It is not the same as a guest at an inn. It resembles but is not the same as a patron in a retail store. With respect to the duty of care owed by the restaurant, the customer is a business invitee. The once debated question of whether there is a sale, in the technical sense, of food to the customer, has been settled, in respect to implied warranty, by the Uniform Commercial Code, which declares that the serving for value of food to be consumed on the premises is a sale.

However, we are not here concerned with a question of negligence or wholesomeness of food, but instead with the right of a customer, having been served with food, to remain on the premises after being ordered by the management to leave.

The nearest analogy we have found in the reported cases to the one here is that of a patron of a theater, racetrack, or other place of public entertainment, who, after having purchased a ticket, is ordered to leave. It has been generally held that such patron has only a personal license, which may be revoked at any time, leaving him only with a breach of contract claim.

We think that is the applicable rule here. When appellant was ordered to leave, her license to be on the premises was revoked, whether legally or illegally, and she had no right to remain. Her remedy, if any, was a civil action for breach of contract. That the purchase of food for consumption on the premises established a type of contract between the restaurant and appellant did not give appellant a right in the premises superior to that of the restaurant. As observed by Justice Holmes in Marrone v. Washington Jockey Club, 227 U.S. 633, 33 S.Ct. 401, 57 L.Ed. 679 (1913), a contract such as this binds the maker but creates no interest in the property, and appellant had no right to enforce specific performance by self-help.

Our conclusion is that when appellant, in the presence of the police officer, refused to leave on the demand of the restaurant manager, the officer was justified in arresting her for violation of the unlawful entry statute.

Ruling of the Court: Affirmed.

In 1924 the question of reasonable rules came up in connection with something we now seriously question: the right of management to set a rule that a male guest must wear a coat and tie in a dining room. In Fred Harvey v. Corporation Commission, 229 P. 428 (Okla., 1924), the Fred Harvey Company refused to admit a coatless male patron into its dining room where table d'hôte meals were served; if he wanted to dine coatless, he could eat at Fred Harvey's lunch counter where only a la carte service could be had at relatively higher prices. The argument was that the guest eating at the lunch counter paid more for his meal; therefore, the coat rule resulted in an unjust discrimination among patrons. In its opinion, the court stated that Fred Harvey furnished jackets to all coatless patrons wishing to eat in the dining room. The coat requirement was applied equally to all, and all persons were equally capable of complying; therefore, the rule was not discriminatory. The court continued, "The obstinate patron, who, by refusing to wear a coat, pays at the lunch counter a higher price for a meal than he would pay in the dining room, must charge his loss to his own stubbornness and bear his self-inflicted injury without complaint of discrimination." The court also remarked that American society had dictated certain regulations of dress for years in first-class dining rooms, and these social conventions could not be entirely ignored.

Laws are not originally created by the legislature; they are first made by the people. Edith Johnson, a noted writer on subjects related to this, testified in the *Fred Harvey* case, "The enforcement of certain social conventions has a tendency to maintain and elevate the tone of society . . . in its general sense." According to her, the rule is a reasonable one.

The fact that a man is required to wear a coat serves notice that decorum is expected and creates a wholesome psychological effect. In the words of the court, Fred Harvey equipped his dining rooms luxuriously, and the surroundings were calculated to stimulate patrons' appetites. Excellent food was served by well-dressed and efficient attendants. Certainly it was not amiss to require the gentlemen dining there to wear coats.

Ejection of Objectionable Persons

Patrons who do not leave the premises after being requested to leave, or those who enter the premises despite a warning not to, may be guilty of criminal trespass (People v. Ulatowski, 368 N.E.2d 174 [Ill., 1977]). In order to be guilty, patrons must know that they are on the premises against the owner's will. Even if the patrons entered the premises lawfully, they could be found guilty of trespass if they remained after being told to leave by the owner (People v. Cheyne, 402 N.Y.S.2d 971 [1978]).

What should hoteliers and restaurateurs do if an individual they have asked to leave the premises refuses to do so? The best response is to call upon the proper authorities to handle the matter.

A perfect example of what can happen to those who try to solve the problem themselves is contained in Moolenaar v. Atlas Motor Inns, Inc., 616 F.2d 87 (V.I., 1980). In this case, the restaurant manager acted properly by calling the police, but unfortunately the officers who responded to the call did not know they could arrest a person without a warrant for a public offense when committed or attempted in their presence (Avants v. State, 544 P.2d 530 [Okla., 1975]). The officers told the manager that they could not arrest Moolenaar because they had not witnessed any crime. This situation would not have occurred if indeed they had witnessed a refusal by Moolenaar to leave after having been asked to. If the dress code was a reasonable rule and if the manager had asked Moolenaar to leave, Moolenaar's refusal would have been a violation of law taking place in the presence of the police officers, and the officers therefore would have had the right to make a warrantless arrest.

In the lower court, the jury awarded Moolenaar both compensatory and punitive damages. The defendants' request to charge the jury, among other things, set forth two Virgin Island statutes as authority for hotelkeepers to evict persons under certain circumstances such as intoxication, disorderly conduct, or violation of the hotel's stated rules and regulations. The trial court's ruling was that the right to evict for a house rule violation was limited to a bona fide guest of the hotel and not to a patron at a public place. Therefore, Moolenaar could be arrested without liability to the hotelkeeper only if he was guilty of disorderly conduct.

The circuit court held that the statutes applied to all persons, but were relevant only on the issue of the jury's finding of punitive damages, not on the issue of the hotel's liability. Furthermore, the court held that the statutes authorized an eviction, but not a citizen's arrest, which requires the commission of a felony or a public offense in the hotel's presence. The trial court did not instruct the jury on this question of whether the patron had committed such a trespass. Therefore, the case was remanded for a new trial.

Discriminatory Advertising

Section 40 of the New York Civil Rights Law is typical of state statutes that prohibit the use of circulars or advertisements that contain statements, express or implied, that any accommodations, facilities, or privileges will be denied because of race, creed, color, or national origin. Violations can result in a penalty of not less than $100 or more than $500, and also give the person who has been discriminated against the right to bring a court action for such amount. In addition, the violation is a misdemeanor punishable by a fine of not less than $100 nor more than $500, or imprisonment of not less than thirty days nor more than ninety days, or both.

In Moon v. Getty Realty Corporation, 118 N.Y.S.2d 784 (1952), the court pointed out that although an individual can bring a cause of action against any agency, bureau, corporation, or association that he has been aggrieved by, the action is strictly personal. The statute will not allow for recovery other than from an individual. A corporation as such is not an individual and therefore cannot sue in the corporate name.

Management Principles

Any attempt to circumvent the 1964 Civil Rights Act invites difficult and costly legal problems. The predictions that the Civil Rights Act would cost the service industry immeasurable economic losses have not come true. In actuality, it has expanded the base of possible customers by some 20 million to 30 million persons.

Minority groups can deal with discriminatory practices in several ways. They can organize a mass attempt to gain entrance to a business; or a case may be brought before the state or federal commission against a hotel or restaurant and, when allowed by statute, a club or bar. The resulting multiple fine and the possible closing of a place of business can be very expensive. And a class action suit is also possible. Managers with doubts about their position should consult an attorney.

Although private clubs, bars, boarding houses, and lodging houses are not covered by the act, owners should check the local state law; they might well be covered there. A bar, bowling alley, or similar place that serves food may come under the "unitary rule" and thus under the Civil Rights Act. The private club exemption is increasingly coming under attack and may soon be covered by the act.

Without a state statute to the contrary, sex discrimination is not covered by the 1964 Civil Rights Act. Again, state statutes should be checked out with an attorney. It may be to the advantage of the service industry voluntarily to eliminate sex discrimination. When such cases do come up in court, they will probably be held unconstitutional under the Fourteenth Amendment as was the *Rosenberg* case discussed in this chapter. The Civil Rights Act does, however, prohibit discrimination against a person speaking a foreign language.

Managers can institute *reasonable* rules governing their place of business, but obviously they must not contravene the law. The following are considered reasonable rules (though some statutes explicitly prohibit certain regulations):

1 A dress code
2 A prohibition of bare feet
3 A prohibition of pets
4 Limited hours of service
5 A required checking of coats
6 A noise prohibition

Discrimination may appear in many guises, such as advertising. A place of business can be prevented from using advertising that implies a restricted clientele. Service industry advertising should portray all possible types of customers.

To avoid discrimination in a place of business, all personnel should read rules that clearly show the establishment policy and should sign the nondiscrimination agreement. This step should eliminate at least management's responsibility for discrimination if it takes place. For example, in Jackson v. Imburgia, 55 N.Y.S.2d 549 (1945), in which employees did discriminate against black customers, the court said, "If the waiter was acting contrary to the defendant's (owner's) orders, without his knowledge or consent, not merely in a colorable way, then the defendant would be entitled to show such disobedience as relevant upon the authority of the servant to refuse the entertainment."

If the owner had in good faith given directions to the bartenders to make no discrimination among patrons on account of color, it would exonerate the owner from liability under the state civil rights law. If it were not shown that the owner gave such directions, it is presumed that the employees were acting in the scope of their employment and therefore the owner would be held liable.

By using good management principles, managers should be able to keep evictions of any type to a minimum. However, if an eviction must be made, the following guidelines should be used:

1 Determine the status of the person. That is, are they hotel guests, invitees, licensees, trespassers, or tenants?

2 In doubtful cases between hotel guest or tenant, institute dispossess proceedings.

3 Use every reasonable means to avoid use of physical force.

4 A hotel or restaurant has the right to evict any guest who violates its rules (naturally the rules must be reasonable). Such eviction must be done in a reasonable manner. If guests refuse to leave after their attention has been called to the violation, have been requested to leave, and given a reasonable opportunity to do so, the hotel or restaurant may forcibly evict them from the premises. In doing so, the hotel or restaurant may use only such force as is reasonably necessary to accomplish this end. (See 40 Am.Jur. 2d Hotels, Motels, etc., 68–80 for a discussion of who can be evicted.)

5 If hotels or restaurants use their own off-duty police or so-called bouncers, these people should be carefully instructed on how to evict, when to call the police, and the amount of force that can be used, including any possibility of using firearms.

6 Instruct all personnel on what constitutes defamation of character—that is, injury to one's reputation. Examples of potential defamatory situations include a clerk's questioning whether the wife of a patron really is his wife; a dispute overheard by others regarding a patron leaving the premises with merchandise possibly belonging to the company but which turns out to belong to the patron; a dispute over a patron's identity when cashing a check; or doubts expressed about the validity of a patron's credit card. If handled in a sufficiently crude manner, any of the above might be defamatory if heard by others.

QUESTIONS FOR DISCUSSION

1 Does the 1964 Civil Rights Act state that no type of discrimination is permitted in any place of public accommodation? Explain.

2   What types of accommodations are covered by the 1964 Civil Rights Act?

3   If a public place is not specifically covered by the 1964 Civil Rights Act, what could bring it under the act?

4   What constitutes a private club? Are the Kiwanis, Rotarian, Elks, YMCA, and similar clubs private? Must they accept all persons who apply for membership?

5   Is sex discrimination covered under the 1964 Civil Rights Act? Does any federal law deal with sex discrimination? Is language discrimination covered by the Civil Rights Act?

6   How may relief be obtained under the 1964 Civil Rights Act?

7   Can a restaurant bar a person with bare feet? Can it set a rule requiring men to wear ties and jackets? Can a hotelkeeper keep out backpackers? Explain.

8 Contents

8 Obligation of Hotelkeepers and Others for Their Guests' Safety

> *"Justice is a machine that, when some one has once given it the starting push, rolls on of itself."*
>
> JOHN GALSWORTHY
> Justice, Act II

Obviously, an obligation or duty is owed to persons using the premises of a hotel, motel, restaurant, bar, club, or similar facility by its owners. More to the point is the question: *How much* duty is owed to each type of guest using the facilities? Closely related are the difficult questions: Under what conditions does this duty (if any) become operative, and under what conditions can owners negate liability for their guests' safety?

This chapter attempts to analyze these questions through cases and rhetoric, allowing management to see what factors might affect the safety of their guests and how to prevent these situations. Conceivable cases range from a guest stepping on a needle in his or her room to a guest jumping off the roof of a high hotel.

No reliable number of the accidents that occur each year in hotels, motels, and restaurants is available, although, as this chapter shows, many do occur. An element of carelessness on the guests' part because they are on vacation, coupled with the feeling that they can depend on the service employees to do their work properly, could lead to conditions wherein accidents can occur.

A recent case is illustrative. A restaurant that was engaged to service a wedding party of about 100 people for cocktails and dinner had a beautiful view of the surrounding mountains and valley from its outside porch. Without notice to the owners or management, fifteen guests went out on the small porch to admire the view and to talk, and the porch gave way under their combined weight. All guests on the porch were injured, some very seriously. Who was responsible for the injuries? It was later learned that the porch had been considered safe for only five or six people.

The owner or manager should have known of this weight limitation, and some precaution should have been taken to warn guests of it. The trial court found it foreseeable that guests would go outside if not prevented, especially when such a beautiful view existed. The multiple suit by the guests forced the owner to close the restaurant permanently.

Although most hotels and restaurants usually have insurance, it may not always be adequate to cover cases brought against the establishment. And even insurance should not be substituted for good management that could prevent such accidents.

An important aspect of a case often overlooked by management is the time spent with one's attorney discussing the case, the time for preliminary hearings, and the time spent in court, all of which must be considered part of the total expense. Any accident involving a guest or employee is therefore expensive, even without a judgment against the owner, because such other factors are also costly, though not in a monetary sense. Seemingly, the answer lies in preventive law, using well-trained employees to prevent accidents from happening. Good managers seldom have cases of this type brought against them.

What type of action can be brought against restaurants or hotels in which such accidents occur? Generally, it will be civil action in the civil courts under the broad category of law called a tort. This chapter examines the nature of a tort, including its definition and the tort of negligence as it applies to hotel and restaurant operators. Various doctrines associated with a tort—including the "prudent man" test, *res ipsa loquitur* ("the thing speaks for itself"), the assumption of risk, as well as several kinds of negligence—are also considered and illustrated with cases relating to the hospitality industry.

Definition of a Tort

The simplest definition of a *tort* is that it is a private or civil wrong caused by the act or failure to act of another person. This wrong is independent of a contract. Most people find it difficult to distinguish torts from contractual law on the one hand and from criminal law on the other. Contractual law covers specific agreements between two or more competent parties, the breach of which can be legally remedied. A *crime* is a wrong against the state; a *tort* is an offense against an individual. Of course, the same act may be both a public and a private wrong. Thieves who take property belonging to someone else commit both a crime and a tort. They have harmed the state in breaking a rule essential to the welfare of society and have harmed the individual by taking away some lawful possession. A tort may involve real or personal property, or it may consist of an injury to a person or the reputation or feelings of a person. Damage to a car is a property tort. Libel—that is, published false and malicious statements that injure a person's reputation—is a personal tort.

Torts are generally divided into two broad categories: involuntary and voluntary. An *involuntary tort* is best described as an accident that is accompanied by an act of negligence. A *voluntary tort*, such as an assault or battery, occurs through a deliberate or intentional act. *Assault* is an intentional show of force or a movement that could reasonably be construed as threatening physical attack or harmful physical contact. *Battery* is any intentional, unwanted, unprovoked, harmful physical contact by one person (or an object controlled by that person) with another person. A tort case can arise where a positive duty is imposed by law, a negative duty is imposed by law, or an obligation is imposed by contract and law as it applies to all occupiers of land. For instance, a negative duty is one in which the law states that a person may not drive while drunk. Examples of positive duties are when the law states that all doors in a public place will open outward, that a sprinkler system will be in place before a building can be used, and that it is an employer's duty to rescue an employee who is injured in the course of employment.

Negligence

Some duty or care is owed to patrons entering hotels, motels, restaurants, and similar places of accommodation. This rule applies equally to other types of businesses, but because a hotel is a quasi-public place, more care is required in some instances.

Most tort cases today arise in the area of *negligence* that exists whenever the defendant has acted with less care than would be exercised by a reasonable person under the same circumstances. The omission of an act on the part of either an individual or corporation, or the failure to act in a wise manner at the proper time, may result in an injury that constitutes a tort. Negligence without resulting injury is not actionable. For example, if a city is aware that a manhole in the sidewalk outside a place of business needs repairing and does nothing about it, no tort is committed unless someone is hurt by such negligence. On the other hand, if someone falls through this manhole and sustains an injury, the city could be liable.

Negligence, according to Prosser's *Law of Torts*,[1] is a matter of risk—that is, of recognizable danger of injury. It is also defined as "conduct that involves an unreasonably great risk of causing damage," or, more fully, conduct "that falls below the standard established by law for the protection of others against unreasonably great risk or harm." According to Professor Prosser, negligence is conduct and not a state of mind. In most instances, it is caused by a heedlessness or carelessness by negligent parties who are unaware of the results that may follow from their acts. But negligence may also exist where parties have considered the possible consequences carefully and have exercised their own best judgment. Using "due care" to describe conduct that is not negligent should not obscure the fact that the real basis of negligence is not carelessness but, rather, behavior that involves unreasonable danger to others.

The standard of conduct that is the basis of the law of negligence is determined by balancing the risk, in the light of the social value of the interest threatened and the probability and extent of the harm, against the value of the interest that is to be protected and the expedience of the course pursued. For this reason it is seldom possible to reduce negligence to any definite rules; it is "relative to the need and the occasion." Conduct that would be proper under some circumstances becomes negligent under others.

Although it is impossible to fix definite rules for all conceivable human conduct, the utmost that can be done is to devise some formula. The standard of conduct that the community demands must be external and objective, rather than an individual judgment. And it must be, as far as possible, the same for all persons since the law can have no favorites. At the same time it must make proper allowance for the risks apparent to people, for their capacity to meet it, and for the circumstances under which they must act.

Elements of the Tort of Negligence

The tort of negligence provides a remedy for injuries resulting from acts that are not intentional, but are within the control of the perpetrator. Therefore, four elements must be present to constitute an actionable case in negligence.

1 *The existence of a duty or care* is required on the part of the defendant. A simple duty owed would be to maintain the elevators in a building in good condition. There are cases, however, where no duty is

1 William L. Prosser, *The Law of Torts* (Minneapolis: West, 1955), p. 42.

owed, even though the results bring great harm to the plaintiff. The case of Maya v. Home Ice & Fuel Company, 29 Cal.2d 295, 379 P.2d 513 (1963), is pertinent. A pregnant mother watched on the sidewalk as a truck negligently ran down her child in the street. She attempted to warn the driver and the child, but to no avail. The shock caused her to miscarry and suffer actual physical and mental harm, and she sued the driver and his employer for harm to herself and the infant child.

The decision was for the defendant truck driver. The court reasoned that the truck driver owed her no duty, although the harm sustained by the mother was the result of the driver's negligence. The court stated that legal responsibility for one's act must stop at some point; otherwise, liability would run into infinity. Hence, the only duty owed by the driver was to the person in the street.

2 A violation or *breach of the above duty* must exist. In the *Maya* case, there was a duty owed the child in the street, and that duty was breached. The mother, of course, could sue for his death or injuries.

3 The breach of duty must have been the *proximate cause* of the injury. In the *Maya* case, the mother's miscarriage and other physical effects were not due primarily to the driver's negligence toward her, but by the intervening cause of fright for her child. However, the injuries of the child in the path of an oncoming truck were directly related to the duty owed; this negligence was the proximate cause of the injuries. (Some exceptions to this concept will be discussed later in this chapter.)

4 Injuries or *damages* must be sustained by the plaintiff. Again, in the *Maya* case, the injuries were substantial; hence, a tort for negligence could be brought in court by the mother for her son's death. Another example will help to distinguish conduct and negligence. A car speeding down a crowded street is unreasonable conduct or negligent driving, but it does not constitute the tort of negligence because there is no injury. The same act, followed by the hitting of a pedestrian, does bring about the tort of negligence. The act and injury are directly connected, and we say that the act was the proximate cause of the injury. As we shall see, the problem of causation sometimes becomes difficult because a number of different factors, some often unknown, frequently work together to produce a result that is difficult to interpret.

The "Prudent Man" Test of Negligence

Everyone or everything is judged by certain criteria. The student is judged by examinations, the politicians by the voters, and a tree by its beauty. In law the courts have agreed on a test that creates a general standard of care in negligence cases. This is the test of the "reasonable man of ordinary prudence." Sometimes the person is described as reasonable or prudent, or as a person of average prudence, or even as a person of ordinary sense using ordinary care and skill. All such phrases mean much the same.

The courts have gone to unusual lengths to emphasize the abstract and hypothetical character of this mythical person. Such a person is not to be identified with an ordinary individual who might occasionally do unreasonable things; he or she is a prudent and careful person who is always up to standard. He or she is a personification of a community ideal of reasonable behavior, determined by the jury's social judgment.

In Darly v. Checker Company, 285 N.E.2d 217 (Ill., 1972), a hotel guest sustained injuries when she fell from a makeshift "rope" made of sheets while climbing out of the window of her fourth floor room in an attempt to escape from a hotel fire. The court stated that in such a situation, a guest need not exercise the same degree of coolness, self-possession, and judgment necessary under ordinary circumstances. A person must be judged by the standard of conduct of a prudent person acting under similar circumstances.

An example may help to clarify the point. If the defendant in a particular case is handicapped—for example, blind—the question is not: Did the defendant act as an ordinary person with sight? but, rather: Did the defendant act as a reasonable, prudent blind person? Persons with special skills, such as doctors, are often required to perform certain acts with a high standard of performance. They are held to the standard of a reasonable, prudent physician, not to the standard of a reasonable, prudent layperson.

Minors and the Prudent Person Test

Public policy extends special protection to minors in almost every area of the law. In the law of negligence, account is taken of a minor's immaturity and lack of judgment. Essentially, a minor is held to the standard of a reasonable, prudent minor with the mental characteristics of the particular subject. Young children are considered incapable of negligence both because they need extra protection and because they cannot appreciate dangers obvious to more mature persons. Nor are they able to weigh cause and effect accurately. In cases involving minors, the question of the standard to be applied to the minor is a jury question.

A further exception that applies to children is the "attractive nuisance doctrine," although this doctrine refers only to the tort of trespass, and not all states adhere to it. The general rule is that an occupier of land is not liable for injuries to trespassers and owes such persons only the duty of refraining from causing intentional harm once the presence of trespassers is known. But he is not under any duty to warn of dangers or to make the premises safe to protect trespassers from harm. The intent of the attractive nuisance doctrine imposes liability upon an occupier of property that may attract young children because of their inability to appreciate peril. The requirement is that some object of exceptional interest to children draws them onto the property, such as machines and swimming pools. There is no set age limit to which the doctrine applies; however, the courts have frequently turned down claims of children over twelve, saying they were old enough to have recognized and avoided the hazard involved.

To what extent should children of tender years be protected from themselves and from dangers they cannot understand? The case of Albanese v. Edwardsville Mobile Home Village, Inc., 529 P.2d 163 (Kan., 1974), is illustrative. Donald, a minor, lived with his family in the Edwardsville Mobile Home Village, a project with an area of 120 acres and containing 146 trailers. The owner of the village had assured residents that playgrounds and play equipment would be provided for the children, but these assurances had not been fulfilled at the time of Donald's accident. Workers employed by the village knew that the children played in the neighboring ditch; therefore, it could be inferred that the defendant permitted the residents to use the area. There was no fence or warning signs, nor did the law require a fence or posting. A ditch caved in while Donald was playing on top of it, and he was killed. The father sued the owner, the defendant, to recover for Donald's wrongful death and the pain and mental anguish the boy suffered.

The trial court instructed the jury on the attractive nuisance doctrine. Was this an error? The higher court said no, pointing out that the attractive nuisance doctrine is based upon negligence. When the condition maintained on the premises constitutes an attractive nuisance, simple negligence on the part of the operator and the owner in failing to maintain an adequate fence, as required by ordinance, is sufficient to impose liability upon both. The lower court's judgment was affirmed for the plaintiff, Donald's father.

The Test of Proximate Cause

One of the more difficult concepts to apply in testing negligence is that of proximate cause or causation, defined as the direct or immediate cause of an event without which an injury would not have occurred. The question that must be answered is: Who really can be blamed for the accident? Was there an intervening cause? Negligence involves unreasonable conduct on the part of the defendant leading to injury to the plaintiff. Therefore, there must be a cause-and-effect sequence between the unreasonable conduct and the injury.

The cause-and-effect concept may be carried to bizarre extremes. Suppose an auto accident victim had left earlier and had not had an argument with a neighbor; then he would not have been at an intersection when the defendant hit him, and the accident would not have occurred. Is the neighbor liable for his accident? Obviously not. Proximate cause is, therefore, an attempt to confine liability only to acts that are "direct" or "immediate" causes of injury.

One of the tests of whether a defendant is liable for injuries or damages sustained by the plaintiff is whether the negligent act was foreseeable. Is it reasonably foreseeable that an argument with a neighbor would set the stage for a motorist being struck by another car some time later? Again, the answer is no. In this case, the proximate cause is lacking, even though a cause-and-effect relationship may exist. Perpetrators are not held for completely unpredictable consequences of their acts. They are held to understand, however, the ordinary dangers, if any, that a reasonable person would associate with an act. Most questions of proximate cause will be decided by applying common sense to the facts of each case.

In *Southern Public Utilities Company v. Thomas*, such a case was presented. The facts questioned whether the defendant's actions were the proximate cause of the child's injuries. However, juries usually favor the plaintiff or injured party in such cases.

Case   **Southern Public Utilities Company v. Thomas**
Example   *78 F.2d 107 (C.C.A., N.C., 1935)*
        (SOPER, Chief Justice)

Melvin Thomas, a child not quite five years of age, was seriously burned in May 1933 when he poured into the fire in his mother's kitchen stove some gasoline that workmen in the employ of the Southern Public Utilities Company, defendant in the court below, had unintentionally left on the porch of the Thomas home after they had repaired a washing machine sold by the Utilities Company to the father of the child. The question in the case is whether the failure of the workmen to take the gasoline away with them when they had finished the job constituted negligence that was the proximate cause of the accident.

The washing machine was on the back porch, and it was there that the work was done. The crankcase of the machine was drained and washed out with gasoline, which the workmen had brought with them in a gallon tin can supplied with a screw cap. After the machine was cleaned, more than a pint of gasoline remained in the can. The cap was replaced and the can set down upon the porch. In gathering up their tools, the men overlooked the can and went away without it.

While the men worked on the porch, three children, including the infant plaintiff, stood by and watched them. One child picked up a knife and was made to put it down. Two of the children went off to school before the work was finished, but Melvin remained. After the men had left, he accompanied his mother when she went to drive the cow into a lot a short distance from the house. Upon their return, he preceded her. He found the gasoline, poured some of it into a fruit jar, and then, entering the kitchen, poured it into the stove because he thought it was lamp oil and "wanted to make mamma's fire burn better." Previously, Mrs. Thomas had used kerosene in building fires.

The verdict below was for the plaintiff, and the defendant complains of the action of the district judge in refusing to direct a verdict in its behalf.

It is said that a person of ordinary prudence in the workmen's place could not have foreseen, as a natural and probable result of their omission to take the gasoline away, that the boy would remove the cap from the can and pour some of the contents into the fire. Hence, it is contended that the proximate cause of the injury was not the negligent act of the defendant, but the child's own conduct.

We agree that, in determining what was the proximate cause of the accident, the test is whether the injury was a reasonably foreseeable event or the natural and probable consequence of the omission of the defendant's workmen. . . . On this point there is no disagreement. The controversy arises in the application of the rule to the facts of the case. In similar situations, it has been deemed pertinent that explosive substances have been left unguarded and accessible to children in a place where they had the right to be, and where they might be expected to come.

Bearing in mind that gasoline is a substance inherently dangerous . . . we are unable to conclude that there was no actionable negligence in the instant case. We cannot say, as the defendant argues, that there was nothing about the gasoline can to attract the child, or that his conduct was so unexpected that it could not have been reasonably foreseen. Quite the contrary seems to us to be the tendency of the evidence. The workmen had come into the child's own home, bringing with them a volatile liquid, highly inflammable when contact with fire is established. It was noticed that the curiosity of the child . . . was provoked by the [washing machine] repairing. Thoughtlessly, the dangerous substance was left behind (where the child was most likely to play). What was more probable than that he should find the can (or more natural than that he should dangerously handle it)? In our opinion, the district judge was right in submitting the question to the jury, and the judgment of the district court is affirmed.

Ruling of the Court: Judgment of the district court affirmed.

Doctrines Associated with a Tort

In the law of torts, it is necessary for the plaintiff to prove each element of the tort. In the case of negligence, the plaintiff must prove that there was a duty owed and that the duty was breached—there was an injury and the cause of it was brought on by the defendant-wrongdoer—that is, he was the proximate cause of the damages the plaintiff sustained.

In many cases, this is an advantage to the defendant because the witnesses are usually in the employment of the defendant; the evidence is difficult for the plaintiff to produce; and, generally, the case is tried in the jurisdiction where the accident happened. In each of the torts, there are requisites that must be proved by the plaintiff before the defendant can come back to disprove any part of the charges. Over the years, certain doctrines have been enunciated by courts or passed by legislatures that give one party or another an advantage in pleading the case.

The Doctrine of *Res Ipsa Loquitur*

The injured plaintiff usually has the sometimes difficult burden of proving how and when the defendant was negligent. It became obvious in the early development of the tort of negligence that certain situations do occur in which all circumstances point to the defendant's negligence, yet no proof of specific acts of negligence is possible on the part of the plaintiff. These situations come under the doctrine of res ipsa loquitur ("the thing speaks for itself").

The classic case for the application of this doctrine has simple facts. The plaintiff is passing a building and is struck by a brick that suddenly falls for some unexplained reason from a cornice of the building. No specific acts of negligence can be established because the owner claims to have no idea what caused the accident, but the result indicates negligence on the part of someone. Under the circumstances, proof of the occurrence of the injury is sufficient evidence for the jury to find the owner of the building negligent. The courts apply the following basic rules to such cases:

1   The injury must have been caused by an accident that does not happen without negligence in the ordinary course of events. Bricks do not just fall without carelessness on the part of the defendant in not maintaining property.

2   The thing causing the injury must have been within the defendant's realm of control. The defendant is in control of the building.

3   The accident producing the injury must have happened without any voluntary action by the plaintiff. The plaintiff must not have been throwing rocks or anything else to make the brick fall.

4   In some jurisdictions, the plaintiff must have no prior knowledge of the cause of the accident.

The *res ipsa loquitur* doctrine has been applied in a hotel case. In McCleod v. Nel-Co Corporation, 112 N.E.2d 501 (Ill., 1953), the plaintiffs were sleeping in a double bed in a room in the defendant's hotel when some plaster from the ceiling fell on them. The court said the *res ipsa loquitur* doctrine applied because ceilings do not normally fall, and the cause of the injury to the plaintiff was under the control and management of the defendant. Proper care and management could have prevented such an occurrence.

The same results were obtained in the following cases: Hotel Dempsey v. Teel, 128 F.2d 673 (1942), in which a guest, while trying to lower a window shade, had the shade and roller fall on her; and Dempsey v. Miller, 58 S.E.2d 475 (Ga., 1950), in which a fan in a meeting room fell on the plaintiff.

But this doctrine is not always available to the plaintiff. A contrary ruling was obtained in Fineberg v. Lincoln Phelps Apartment Company, 9 N.E.2d 1011 (Ga., 1935), in which the plaintiff was injured by falling plaster and pleaded res ipsa loquitur. The court stated the doctrine did not apply since the premises had been inspected regularly, and no visibly precarious condition had existed.

In the case of McKeever v. Phoenix Jewish Community Center, 374 P.2d 875 (Ariz., 1962), the courts refused to instruct the jury on the question of res ipsa loquitur when a ten-year-old girl drowned. An experienced and qualified lifeguard was at his station attending to his responsibilities; he had the necessary equipment to effect a rescue, and he was at the scene of the rescue immediately on being called. The court said that the doctrine of res ipsa loquitur is simply a rule of circumstantial evidence and gives rise to an inference of responsibility for an injury. Furthermore, the court said the plaintiff must still prove proximate cause and show that no injury would have resulted but for some negligence on the part of the defendant. The plaintiff must prove that the instrumentality causing the injury was within the exclusive control of the defendant at the time of the injury.

Simply put, the significance of this doctrine is that if res ipsa loquitur can be used by the plaintiff, it becomes a prima facie case. In most cases, this will win the case for the plaintiff. A prima facie case is one in which all facts are considered true unless disproved by contrary evidence. This doctrine has been used so many times that hoteliers and restaurateurs should be aware of it. If any equipment or area could lead to an accident, the plaintiff could plead res ipsa loquitur.

The Doctrine of Last Clear Chance

The doctrine of last clear chance is a theory of liability that a plaintiff seeks to evoke for the purpose of imposing liability upon a defendant in instances where the plaintiff admittedly may have been guilty of contributory negligence. Under ordinary circumstances, a plaintiff guilty of contributory negligence will be denied recovery against a negligent defendant, but if the factual situation is one where the doctrine can be applied, then it makes no difference if it was the negligent acts of the plaintiff that initially put the person into a position of peril.

Four elements must be established before the doctrine will come into play:

1 The plaintiff has been negligent.
2 As the result of this negligence, he or she is in a position of peril that cannot be escaped by the exercise of ordinary care.
3 The defendant knew or should have known of the plaintiff's peril.
4 The defendant had a clear chance, by the exercise of ordinary care, to avoid the injury to the plaintiff, but he or she failed to do so.

If any one of these four elements is absent, the doctrine of last clear chance will not apply.

Whether the doctrine will apply is a factual matter. As such, it does not have to be pleaded in any way by the plaintiff, but will be applied if the evidence warrants it. The defendant will be trying to use the plaintiff's contributory negligence as a defense to the suit, so it will be up to the plaintiff to bring forth the evidence that would impose the liability upon the defendant despite the plaintiff's contributory negligence.

The doctrine requires exactly what its name implies: that the defendant actually had a last *clear* chance to avoid the infliction of the injury. Defendants cannot be held liable because they failed to respond to an emergency with extraordinary reflexes. If they had only a split second to avoid an injury, typically they would be guilty of no negligence on their part, for they are only required to react with ordinary care as a reasonable person would react, bearing all existing factors in mind.

In the case of *Pence* v. *Ketchum*, the court applied the doctrine of last clear chance and, as you read the case, you will readily observe that the factual situation clearly demonstrated the four criteria necessary for its application. The plaintiff had been negligent in becoming intoxicated; her intoxication placed her in a condition of obvious helplessness; the defendants were aware of her peril; and, although they had a chance to protect her from harm that they could reasonably see could befall her, they failed to use the opportunity to avoid harm to her. All states do not accept the last clear chance doctrines.

Case	**Pence v. Ketchum**
Example	*326 So.2d 811 (La., 1976)*
	(SANDERS, Chief Justice)

Plaintiff, a patron of a bar, brought this action against the owners of the bar and another to recover damages for injuries sustained when she was struck by an automobile after being ejected from the bar in an intoxicated condition. The district court dismissed the suit on an exception of no cause of action filed by the owners of the bar. The court of appeal affirmed the district court, 314 So.2d 550 (1975), relying upon our holding in Lee v. Peerless Insurance Company, 248 La. 982, 183 So.2d 328 (1966). We granted writs, La., 319 So.2d 440 (1975), to reconsider the legal issues raised.

The ultimate question before us is whether the petition states a cause of action for damages against the defendants. We hold that it does.

In the present case, plaintiff seeks damages for personal injuries she suffered when she was struck by an automobile operated by defendant Ketchum as she was attempting to cross U. S. Highway 190 in West Baton Rouge Parish. She alleges that her injuries were caused by the negligence of Ketchum and, alternatively, by the joint and concurrent negligence of Ketchum, Anthony J. Silvio, and Victor J. Silvio. The petition alleges that the Silvio defendants:

". . . at the time of the accident were the owners and operators of a bar located on Highway 190 in West Baton Rouge Parish, known as the Candlelight Inn, in that said defendants and their agents, employees, and representatives forced plaintiff to leave the Candlelight Inn premises when they knew or reasonably should have known that she was in no condition, due to her state of intoxication, to be placed on the busy Highway 190, in disregard of their duties owed to a patron and customer such as plaintiff after the personnel running the Candlelight Inn had served plaintiff an excessive amount of alcoholic beverages, which consumption by plaintiff of an excessive amount of alcoholic drinks was encouraged and coaxed by employees of Candlelight Inn, all resulting in plaintiff being in a helpless state when she was forced to leave the Candlelight Inn and permitted by one or both of the defendant owners or their employees to attempt to cross the highway when she was unable, due to her impaired condition, to do so.''

Plaintiff's action is based upon Articles 2315 and 2316 of the Louisiana Civil Code that provide:

"Article 2315. Every act whatever of man that causes damage to another obliges him by whose fault it happened to repair it. . . .''

"Article 2316. Every person is responsible for the damage he occasions, not merely by his act, but by his negligence, his imprudence, or his want of skill.''

In order to sustain a cause of action under these articles, the petition must adequately allege fault, causation, and damage. Fault is a broad concept and, of course, includes negligence. Negligence is conduct that falls below the standard established by law for the protection of others against unreasonable risk of harm. It is a departure from the conduct expectable of a reasonably prudent man under like circumstances. For analysis, negligence is often divided into *duty* and *breach of duty*.

We find that plaintiff's petition adequately alleges that defendants breached at least two duties they owed to plaintiff: the statutory duty of a retailer of alcoholic beverages not to serve alcoholic beverages to an intoxicated person, and the duty of a business invitor to avoid affirmative acts increasing the peril of his intoxicated patron.

LSA–R.S. 26:88(2), applicable only to retailers of alcoholic beverages, prohibits a retailer from serving or selling such beverages to an intoxicated person. The statute was designed, at least in part, to protect intoxicated persons from their own helplessness and incompetence. It embodies a legislative judgment that an intoxicated person is a menace to himself. Moreover, in our opinion, the statute creates no higher standard of conduct than that generally required of a reasonable man under like circumstances.

Under the allegations of the petition, plaintiff falls within the protected class, and the risk encountered was of the type the duty was designed to prevent. Hence, a court can look to the statute as a standard for determining negligence, or fault, under Articles 2315 and 2316 of the Louisiana Civil Code.

A violation of the statute, causing harm to an intoxicated patron, gives rise to a viable cause of action. In Soronen v. Olde Milford Inn, 202 A.2d 208 (1964), the New Jersey Court held:

"The duty to the visibly intoxicated persons is both common law and statutory. Intoxication is a state of impairment of one's mental and physical faculties, due to overindulgence in alcoholic drink. A person in that condition is unable to exercise normal powers of judgment and prudence. He is a potential menace, not only to himself but to others. Common sense requires that a tavern keeper refuse to serve alcoholic drink to such a person.

This common law principle is carried into our Alcoholic Beverage Control Act that through implementing regulations, specifically prohibits a licensee from serving alcoholic drink to a person actually and apparently intoxicated. We conclude that plaintiff's complaint sets forth a justiciable cause of action."

Some courts, however, have barred a cause of action under these circumstances on the theory that the consumption of the alcoholic beverage, not the act of the retailer in serving it, is the proximate cause of any injuries suffered by the intoxicated patron. In our opinion, this theory is unsound.

The petition adequately alleges factual causation. The usual test is whether but for defendant's conduct the injury to plaintiff would have occurred. For a defendant's conduct to be actionable, it must be a necessary antecedent of plaintiff's harm. It need not, however, be the sole cause contributing to the harm. Hence, factual causation becomes an issue to be resolved at the trial.

Proximate cause, however, is often used in a different sense from factual causation. A consideration of the doctrine often requires a duty analysis. It requires a determination of whether or not the duty, statutory or non-statutory, is designed to protect the plaintiff from the event that did in fact occur. Insofar as the concept is pertinent here, it is satisfied by our legal conclusion that the risk and harm allegedly encountered fall within the scope of protection of the duty.

The second duty allegedly breached by defendants arises from the invitor-invitee relationship. The defendants cater to the public in their business operations. The standard of conduct to which they must conform is that of a reasonable man under like circumstances (LSA–C.C. Arts. 2315, 2316). The patrons are drinking and, in some instances, drunken persons from whom unstable and erratic conduct is to be expected. Intoxication is a status that demands increased care to avoid injury to the inebriate and to satisfy the above standard.

The duty requires that defendant refrain from affirmative acts that increase the peril to his intoxicated patrons. If the defendant ejects an intoxicated patron into an environment made hazardous by known dangers, such as the highway in the present case, and foreseeable injury results, the invitor is guilty of actionable negligence.

Dean William L. Prosser, in his treatise,[2] summarizes the law as follows:

"[T]here is at least a duty to avoid any affirmative acts that make his situation worse. . . . There may be no duty to take care of a man who is ill or intoxicated, and unable to look out for himself; but it is another thing entirely to eject him into the danger of a railroad yard; and if he is injured, there will be liability."

In the present case, the petition alleges that the defendants and their employees knew of plaintiff's helpless condition, but nonetheless ejected her from their place of business into an area adjacent to a busy highway. They then permitted her to attempt to cross the highway, where she was injured. As to this duty also, the petition alleges a cause of action, absent other overriding doctrines.

---

2   William L. Prosser, *The Law of Torts,* § 56 at 343 (4th ed., 1971).

The court of appeal apparently concluded that the petition disclosed contributory negligence barring recovery as a matter of law. We disagree.

To warrant the dismissal of a petition on an exception pleading contributory negligence, the recitals of the petition must be such as to clearly show contributory negligence and to exclude every reasonable hypothesis of liability.

The doctrine of last clear chance is well established in Louisiana and represents an exception to the general rule that contributory negligence bars plaintiff's recovery. Since it is evidentiary in nature, the doctrine need not be specially pleaded.

If a person is in an advanced state of intoxication so as to render him helpless, or incapable of self-protection, the law accords him the benefit of the doctrine of last clear chance.

Plaintiff's negligence in becoming intoxicated had allegedly placed her in a condition of obvious helplessness. Defendants were aware of her peril. Nonetheless, the defendants failed to use an opportunity to avoid harm to the plaintiff. Hence, the petition leaves adequate room for the application of last clear chance.

Plaintiff's final movements into the highway do not defeat the application of last clear chance. Under this doctrine, the law looks to plaintiff's incapacity, rather than to her antecedent conduct. As the court stated in Small v. Boston & M.R.R., 159 A. 298 (1932), "While a sober person cannot have the benefit of the last chance rule that an intoxicated person may by reason of his incapacity, there is no favor to the latter. It is the situation of incapacity, however it arises, that invokes the duty of saving action by the defendant."

We conclude that the petition adequately alleges fault, causation, and damage under Articles 2315 and 2316 of the Louisiana Civil Code. Hence, we hold that the petition states a cause of action in favor of the injured patron. Because of the posture of the case, our decision is limited to this narrow holding.

Admittedly, our holding here conflicts with the decision in Lee v. Peerless Insurance Company. There, with a similar petition, the court held that the petition did not state a cause of action. The rationale was that the intoxicated patron was guilty of contributory negligence as a matter of law and that the proximate cause of the injury was the consumption of the alcoholic beverage and not the sale. The decision has been widely criticized as unsound. The leading decision relied on: Cole v. Rush, 45 Cal.2d 345, 289 P.2d 450, 54 A.L.R.2d 1137 (1955), has since been overruled in Vesely v. Sager, 5 Cal.3d 153, 95 Cal.Rptr. 623, 486 P.2d 151 (1971). As noted in Vesely v. Sager, most of the recent decisions have rejected the no-proximate-cause rubric. Accordingly, Lee v. Peerless Insurance Company is overruled.

Ruling of the Court: For the reasons assigned, the judgment of the court of appeal is reversed, the peremptory exception of no cause of action is overruled, and the case is remanded to the district court for further proceedings consistent with the views herein expressed. The costs of the present appellate proceedings are taxed against the defendants. All other costs are to await the outcome of the suit.

Assumption of Risk

The assumption of risk doctrine is widely accepted in the United States, sometimes with disastrous consequences. It is based on the maxim *volenti non fit injuria* that means that there is an implied, or at least a qualified, consent and an assumption of knowledge of the dangers. Therefore, assumption of risk will not be found unless the danger supposedly assumed is apparent. For example, a baseball fan who is hit by a foul ball in the stands is said to have assumed the risk of the sport. A person skiing also assumes much of the risk of the sport. In a recent court decision, however, James Sunday of Burlington, Vermont, received a $1.5 million award in a skiing accident at Stratton Mountain. The court held that no longer could ski areas automatically be considered free of responsibility because of inherent dangers in the sport. The ruling went against more than twenty years of legal precedent in Vermont (Sunday v. Stratton Corporation, 390 A.2d 398 [Vt., 1978]).

The court in Montes v. Betcher, 480 F.2d 1128 (Minn., 1973), said that to justify any instructions on assumption of risk, there must be evidence to support three jury findings:

1   That the plaintiffs had knowledge of the risk,
2   That they appreciated the risk,
3   That they could either avoid the risk or chance it, and voluntarily chose to chance it.

In the *Montes* case, when the plaintiff dove into a lake and hit a cement block, there was no assumption of risk. The plaintiff took the risk of hitting the lake bottom but not the risk of coming into contact with a cement block that he knew nothing about.

Another example is easily understandable. When a person rides with another driver, the rider is taking the risk of the speed at which the car is being driven; however, this does not mean that the rider assumes another risk of which he is unaware, such as the failure of the driver to watch the road.

In the *Montes* case, there was no evidence that the plaintiff was aware of, appreciated, or voluntarily assumed the risk of hitting the cement block when he dove into the lake. He had often dived from the boat dock and never encountered obstructions. The court ruled that the plaintiff could hardly have assumed a risk of which he was not aware.

What are the requirements for a case to come under the doctrine of assumption of risk? In *Ball v. Hilton Hotels, Inc.*, all the factors were not present to hold the defendant guilty, and the plaintiff had in fact assumed the risk of her actions.

Case	**Ball v. Hilton Hotels, Inc.**
Example	*290 N.E.2d 859 (Ohio, 1972)*
	(HESS, Presiding Judge)

This appeal from a summary judgment was entered by the Court of Common Pleas of Hamilton County, in favor of defendant. · · ·

It appears from the record that the plaintiff, a resident of Michigan, went to Cincinnati, Ohio, on May 27, 1967, with a reservation to stay at the defendant's hostelry, known as the Terrace Hilton Hotel.

Upon arrival at the hotel, she was informed by the defendant's doorman that there was a downtown area electric power failure and there was no lighting or elevator service in the hotel. The hotel lobby and registration desk were on the eighth floor of the hotel building. The plaintiff checked her baggage with the doorman and then inquired about the use of restroom facilities.

In response to her request, the doorman advised plaintiff the restroom was downstairs; that it would be quite dark on the staircase due to the electric power failure; that plaintiff would not be able to see the doors to the restrooms; and that the doors to the restrooms were located to the right of the bottom of the stairway. The doorman gave the plaintiff a small lighted candle, and she proceeded down the darkened stairway, moving slowly and carefully groping along the handrail.

After arriving at the platform portion of the stairway, plaintiff began to grope about for the restroom door and, while so doing, she fell to the bottom of the stair steps and received personal injuries that are the subject of this appeal.

In her complaint against the hotel, plaintiff alleges that her personal injuries and resulting damage were directly and proximately caused by the negligence of the defendant in inducing her to enter a hazardous, darkened area of the hotel facility. . . .

Before the defendant would be entitled to a summary judgment on the theory of assumption of the risk, it must be proven that plaintiff had full knowledge of a condition; that the condition was patently dangerous; and that she voluntarily exposed herself to the hazard created. . . .

The plaintiff's own deposition supports the conclusion that she was told that the electric power in the downtown area had failed and there was no light or electric power in the defendant's hotel; that it was dark in the stairway leading to the hotel restrooms; that plaintiff had full knowledge of the darkness when she walked down the stairway with a small lighted candle; and that she moved slowly and carefully as she descended the stairway.

The plaintiff contends that her action at the hotel did not establish assumption of risk, but presented the question of contributory negligence. It has been recognized that contributory negligence and assumption of risk may coexist. Assumption of risk and contributory negligence are not synonymous, because contributory negligence is based upon carelessness, whereas assumption of risk is based upon venturousness.

Since it appears there is no genuine issue of any material fact, the trial court correctly determined the plaintiff assumed the risk of her injury and damage when she proceeded into the darkened area of the premises in question. It follows that for the reasons presented herein, assignment of error number two is not well taken.

Therefore, it is ordered that the judgment of the Court of Common Pleas of Hamilton County, Ohio, should be, and hereby is, affirmed.

Ruling of the Court: Judgment affirmed for defendant.

In some cases the question of whether the plaintiff voluntarily assumed the risk and whether the guest was contributorily negligent is a jury question. Mizenis v. Sands Motel, Inc., 362 N.E.2d 661 (Ohio, 1975), is a good example.

The plaintiff's acceptance of risk—in this case, going back and forth on an icy stairway to his motel room—cannot be considered voluntary because of the innkeeper's tortious conduct—that is, his negligence in maintaining the common passageway that was the only exit from the premises. Therefore, Charles Mizenis cannot be said to have assumed the risk voluntarily, although he knew of the danger.

Nevertheless, there are some cases where the course of danger may be so extreme as to be out of all proportion to the value of the interest to be protected, and the plaintiff may be charged with contributory negligence in his own unreasonable conduct. Thus, in the *Mizenis* case, there may be an element of contributory conduct in the plaintiff's conduct on which reasonable minds could differ, and thus a jury question of contributory negligence exists. This issue also raises a jury question as to whether the defendant, as an innkeeper, acted in a way a reasonably prudent person would have acted; thus, a jury issue of negligence of the defendant arises.

Contributory Negligence

If the preceding doctrines assist the plaintiff, the doctrine of contributory negligence is very much on the side of the defendant. In essence it says that in a case where any act or omission amounting to a lack of ordinary care on the part of the complaining party that *concurring* with defendant's negligence, is the proximate cause of the injury, the plaintiff cannot recover in the absence of a statute allowing for comparative negligence.

The case of Karna v. Byron Reed Syndicate #4, 374 F.Supp. 687 (Neb., 1974), clearly shows the advantage of the contributory negligence doctrine. The Continental Towers hotel-motel had twin glass entrance doors, one side of which was permanently locked. After several days' use of the doors, the plaintiff-guest walked into the locked door, which caused injury to his nose requiring surgery and resulting in a permanent scar. He also lost a raise and his job as a result of the accident. He sought recovery for those damages, as well as for future embarrassment resulting from having to explain the injury to his nose. The plaintiff contended that the doors were negligently designed, maintained, and installed— the glass should have been thicker, and a metal push bar should have been placed across the doors to warn users. The court admitted that the defendants were, in fact, negligent for their arrangement of the glass door in combination with other factors, but since the plaintiff had used the doors previously, the court decreed that the plaintiff was contributorily negligent. The court maintained that the plaintiff knew or should have known of the dangerous condition as a result of his prior use of the doors.

Does the landowner's duty to keep the premises reasonably safe for invitees give the invitees immunity from the consequences of their own inattention? In the case of Wise v. Roger Givins, Inc., 618 P.2d 951 (Okla., 1980), the court said that the motel was not liable to the plaintiff for injuries he sustained when he stepped over a curb onto a paint can that was in a hole on the sidewalk, but protruded above the ground approximately one-half of its height (three to six inches). It would have been plainly visible if the plaintiff had been watching where he was walking. As a result of stepping into the paint can, the plaintiff fell and suffered injuries. The court granted judgment to the motel and said the guest was an invitee. Thus, the motel owes a duty merely to keep the premises reasonably safe, and the invitee assumes all ordinary and normal risks incident to the use of the premises. The duty to keep the premises in a reasonably safe condition applies only to the defects or conditions that are in the nature of hidden dangers, traps, snares or other pitfalls, and the like—things not readily observable by the invitee in the exercise of ordinary care. This means that a guest cannot be oblivious to all that is around him and expect the hotel or motel to pay if he is injured by something that he could have easily avoided if he had exercised ordinary care. This is not a contributory negligence case barring recovery. Rather, it is a situation where there never was a violation of the innkeeper's duty to begin with because duty does not extend to that which should be obvious to the guest.

In Hunn v. Windsor, 193 S.E. 57 (W. Va., 1937), a hotel guest sustained a broken ankle when she fell on hotel steps covered by a plank that slipped while cement on new threads was drying. The question is whether she assumed the risk so as to preclude recovery from the hotel— she had previously walked on the planks, and there were other exits that she could have taken. The court said that the doctrines of contributory negligence and assumption of risk are not identical. The essence of contributory negligence is carelessness; of assumption of risk, venturousness. Thus, an injured person may not have acted carelessly and, in fact, may have exercised the utmost care, yet may have assumed, voluntarily, a known hazard. If so, she must accept the consequence. The doctrine rests on two premises: that the nature and extent of the risk are fully appreciated and that it is voluntarily incurred.

The court said that where persons have knowledge of and fully appreciate a danger and, under such circumstances, without any special exigency compelling them, they expose themselves to such danger or peril, their acts on the premises may be deemed to have been voluntary. Contributory negligence in such a case cannot properly be said to be an element in the accident, for certainly the voluntary act of a party in exposing himself or herself to a known and appreciated danger is wholly incompatible with an act of negligence or carelessness; for it must be manifest that carelessness in regard to a matter is not the same as the exercise of a deliberate choice in that respect. Freedom of the will, in fact, is what is emphasized by the principle asserted in the maxim *volenti non fit injuria*—that is, he who consents cannot receive an injury.

The Comparative Negligence Doctrine

The comparative negligence doctrine allows both parties, where negligence is concurrent and contributes to injury, to recover damages proportionately. In *Montes* v. *Betcher*, discussed earlier in this chapter, the plaintiff sustained injuries when he took a running dive off a short boat dock and received a severely lacerated scalp and a vertebral fracture on a jagged piece of concrete anchor the owners had constructed. The defendant attempted to show the plaintiff assumed the risk by diving off the boat dock. The jury did not so find, but after receiving instruction by the court, it did apply the doctrine of comparative negligence and adjudged the defendants 90 percent negligent and the plaintiff 10 percent negligent. That is, the plaintiff received 10 percent less than he would have if he had not been adjudged 10 percent negligent.

The old rule of contributory negligence often completely barred recovering damages in many states. Many states now follow some type of comparative negligence rule that can reduce the amount of damages that may be recovered. States that follow some form of the comparative negligence rule are Arkansas, Alaska, California, Colorado, Connecticut, Florida, Georgia, Hawaii, Idaho, Maine, Massachusetts, Minnesota, Mississippi, Nebraska, Nevada, New Hampshire, New Jersey, New York, North Dakota, Oklahoma, Oregon, Rhode Island, South Dakota, Texas, Utah, Vermont, Washington, Wisconsin, and Wyoming. Consequently, it is possible that more suits will be brought against hotels and motels, and that insurance rates will rise to cover the increased number of suits and possible recoveries. Because the laws vary considerably from state to state and may change rapidly, it is wise to consult an attorney.

The Good Samaritan Rule as It Applies to Tort Cases

A tort is a wrong caused by the act or failure to act of another person. Does this mean that a person must assist someone in distress? In some modern minds, the Confucian advice to "see no evil" has been translated into "don't get involved." To a considerable degree, this attitude has been sanctioned by the common law. Traditionally, there has been a reluctance to impose any legal penalty for the mere failure to be helpful. For example, courts have turned down damage claims against the following individuals:

1   A man who watched impassively while a young woman drowned, even though he could easily have gone to her aid;

2   A man who called no warning to a neighbor's child whom he saw hammering on a tube of gunpowder;

3   A man who failed to remove a rock from the road, even though he knew it was a menace to traffic.

In each case, the moral duty was plain enough, but the courts all agreed that moral duties were a matter of conscience, not law. In recent years, however, the law has required people to lend a hand in an increasing number of situations—particularly when there is a special relationship between the parties, such as a host toward his guest, a hotel toward its patron, or a railroad toward its passengers.

Legislators, too, can create a duty to act in specific circumstances. Hit-and-run statutes, for instance, may require motorists to give aid to accident victims, regardless of whether they were legally to blame for the accident. This kind of responsibility is based on the humanitarian feeling that when a moral duty is clear, the law ought to enforce it.

An interesting case took place in Australia where a couple, sitting alone on the edge of a deep swimming pool, quarreled bitterly. In a pique, the wife, who could not swim, jumped into the water, obviously making a bid for attention. Her husband sat there and watched her flounder until she drowned. Apparently he told of this, because he was duly convicted for criminal homicide (Rex v. Russell, 1933 Victoria Law Rep. 59 [1932 Victoria Supreme Court]). The court said that since they were married, the husband was under legal duty to render aid. The clear implication was that if they were not married, he would be under no such duty.

Others also owe some duty to assist, such as the master of a ship to a seaman who is ill or in peril. Public carriers have a similar duty, as do headmasters, teachers, and counselors of schools, camps, and similar establishments. But courts are reluctant to recognize a contractual duty of care in simple business-visitor situations. If a woman shopper faints on the floor in a department store, the writings seem to indicate that she may with impunity be left there by the store management, as long as she is not stepped on. However, if she is removed to the ladies' room, she has been taken in charge and must be given reasonable attention and care (Zelenko v. Gimbel Bros., 287 N.Y. Supp. 134 [1935]).

Obviously, inroads have been made in the once-inviolate principle of do-nothingism. The case of Sneider v. Hyatt Corporation, 390 F.Supp. 976 (Ga., 1975), seriously questions a hotel's nonparticipation in a guest's problems. Although the case did not hold that a hotel's inaction to prevent a guest's suicide can make it liable, it did not say that the contrary is true—that it cannot be held liable. The important point in this case is that a hotel may have a duty to help guests under certain circumstances, because a hotel is a quasi-public place where a special relationship between the parties imposes a duty on the hotelkeeper to keep guests safe.

In Sneider v. Hyatt Corporation, the plaintiffs (the decedent's husband and daughter) sought to recover for the death of Mrs. Sneider, who had registered as a guest at the hotel and committed suicide the next day by jumping from the twenty-first floor. The plaintiffs cited the prior history of suicides and attempted suicides in the same location, as well as the decedent's inebriation and confused actions in support of their case. The hotel should have foreseen the risk of suicide and taken preventive action. The plaintiffs sought to bring their case within the holdings of hospital cases that have imposed liability for patient suicides. The court, however, did not find the standard of care owed by hospitals identical to that owed by hotels. The defendant maintained it had no legal duty to prevent the suicide.

The Good Samaritan rule is not without exception, but the argument is still made that the circumstances and facts are different from those prescribed generally. In the case of Palace Bar, Inc., v. Fearnot, 376 N.E.2d 1159 (Ind., 1978), the customer entered the Palace Bar at the express or implied invitation of the owners to transact business (drinking) to the mutual advantage of both the customer and the owners and operators. The relationship was that of business invitee, and there is no question that the owner owed the invitee the duty of ordinary care under these circumstances. This includes maintaining the premises in a reasonably safe condition, as well as exercising reasonable care to discover possibly dangerous conditions and taking reasonable precautions to protect the invitee.

In this case, the customer fell down an open stairway. His widow alleged that the bar operator or his employees failed to obtain medical assistance for the deceased for over an hour after they became aware of his peril. Furthermore, she argued that this was sufficient grounds to create a jury question as to whether the owner of the bar had an obligation to exercise reasonable care for the safety of the customer and to assist him once he learned of his injury.

The court said that at common law, there is no general duty to aid a person who is in peril (Good Samaritan rule); however, "under some circumstances, moral and humanitarian considerations may require one to render assistance to another who has been injured, even though the injury was not due to negligence on his part and may have been caused by the negligence of the injured person. Failure to render assistance in such a situation may constitute actionable negligence if the injury is aggravated through lack of due care." The court reasoned "that there may be a legal obligation to take positive or affirmative steps to effect the rescue of a person who is helpless and in a situation of peril when the one proceeded against is a master or an invitor, or when the injury resulted from use of an instrumentality under the control of the defendant."

The doctrine of law as set forth in the Restatement (Second) of Torts 322, p. 133, adds credence to this case, as well as to another Indiana case, L.S. Ayres & Co. v. Hicks, 40 N.E.2d 334 (Ind., 1941): "If the actor knows or has reason to know that by his conduct, whether tortious or innocent, he has caused such bodily harm to another as to make him helpless and in danger of future harm, the actor is under a duty to exercise reasonable care to prevent such further harm.''

Statutory Protection for Good Samaritans

If, as the cases seem to indicate, there is a movement underway to transform what was in the past primarily a moral obligation to assist an unfortunate fellow human being into either a legal obligation to act or else into a situation where society would scorn one who failed to act toward a person who was sick, injured, or in grave peril, then the law must afford such actors protection from liability for their acts. The medium through which this is accomplished is the Good Samaritan statutes. In effect, they provide that a person who reacts in an emergency situation by endeavoring to administer to a sick or injured person or help someone in peril, that person will not be liable to the assisted person for any injuries resulting from the efforts to render assistance if the means used were reasonable insofar as they relate to the person who did the assisting and to the emergency conditions in existence at the time that the assistance was rendered. In the absence of such statutes, even medically trained people might avoid giving assistance under emergency conditions outside the sterile confines of their offices, for if anything went wrong, they might find themselves embroiled in a lawsuit.

Hoteliers and restaurateurs might be called upon to act in emergency situations. A classic example occurs with the so-called café coronary. Patrons experiencing this difficulty are not having a heart attack, but because the symptoms are so much like those observed in a heart attack, even the medically trained can be confused between the two. A café coronary occurs when a piece of food gets lodged in a person's airway, thereby blocking off all air to the lungs. Such a situation presents a grave condition because there is very little time to act. A person with a blocked airway will be unconscious in about a minute, will suffer irreversible brain damage in about four to five minutes, and will die usually within the next couple of minutes. These situations occur with significant frequency so as to be recognized as a real problem in the restaurant industry.

At least for the present, it appears as if the law throughout the country is that if a restaurant patron chokes on a piece of food that blocks his or her airway and lapses into unconsciousness, the owner and all of the employees are not obliged to help. They will be free from any liability for their apparent indifference to suffering and death. But if someone— the owner perhaps—had acted and had not been able to save the patron from dying and, perhaps, may have done something improper, then that person may be sued.

In order to encourage people to try to save the afflicted person's life, some states have enacted statutes to protect the actors in such situations. A law that took effect in New York State in September 1980 requires that every restaurant and cafeteria in the state display prominently a poster showing first-aid procedures (termed the *Heimlich maneuver*) to utilize in assisting a person who has a blocked airway and is choking. The legislation, however, does not require anyone to act; there is no duty upon restaurateurs or their employees to render any assistance to the choking victim. Should restaurant owners, or any of their employees, or any other patrons assist the choking party in accordance with the instructions on the poster, they will not be liable to the injured party except for gross negligence according to a built-in Good Samaritan clause contained in the statute. The statute also says that the restaurant cannot be held liable for injuries or death of the choke victim if the poster is not displayed. One question does arise: If a person seeking to help a choking victim deviates slightly from the instructions on the poster, will there be liability then?

It is apparent that all of the states that have enacted legislation on the subject are reluctant to impose any duty on the part of the operator or employees of the restaurant or food-dispensing facility to act in any way to try to help the choking victim, even though they include a Good Samaritan clause that would indemnify the actor from liability.

Strict or Absolute Liability

Negligence is not always the criterion used to hold someone liable for the results of his or her acts. In certain situations, the hotelkeeper becomes an "insurer" (one who assumes absolute liability) of the guest's property or the insurer of those who may be injured by his or her acts. In such cases, the undertaking is generally hazardous and harm is foreseeable, even though the greatest precaution is taken; yet the undertaking is of sufficient social benefit that it will be permitted. The actor is permitted to proceed, but is required to assume all the risks of the undertaking. Examples would be keeping wild or vicious animals, spraying from aircrafts, or using explosives.

One area of importance to hotel and restaurant managers in which the courts have expanded the doctrine of strict absolute liability is product liability, as the case of *Shoshone Coca-Cola Bottling Company v. Dolinski* clearly shows. (Product liability from the guest's point of view is treated in chapter 13.)

Case Example   **Shoshone Coca-Cola Bottling Company v. Dolinski**
420 P.2d 855 (Nev., 1967)
(THOMPSON, Justice)

The important question presented by this appeal is whether Nevada should judicially adopt the doctrine of strict tort liability against a manufacturer and distributor of a bottled beverage. Subordinate questions are also involved and will be discussed.

Leo Dolinski suffered physical and mental distress when he partially consumed the contents of a bottle of "Squirt" containing a decomposed mouse. As a consequence, he filed this action for damages against Shoshone Coca-Cola Bottling Company, the manufacturer and distributor of "Squirt." His complaint alleged alternative theories of liability; breach of the implied warranties of quality, which theory this court has rejected, in the absence of privity of contract, negligence, and strict tort liability. The breach of warranty and negligence claims were subsequently abandoned, and the case was presented to the jury solely upon the doctrine of strict tort liability. The jury favored Dolinski with its verdict and fixed his damages at $2,500. This appeal by Shoshone ensued.

We affirm the verdict and judgment since, in our view, public policy demands that one who places upon the market a bottled beverage in a condition dangerous for use must be held strictly liable to the ultimate user for injuries resulting from such use, although the seller has exercised all reasonable care, and the user has not entered into a contractual relation with him. Perhaps the supporting policy reasons are best expressed by William L. Prosser in his article, "The Fall of the Citadel," 50 Minn. L.Rev. 791, 799 (1966): "The public interest in human safety requires the maximum possible protection for the user of the product, and those best able to afford it are the suppliers of the chattel. By placing their goods upon the market, the suppliers represent to the public that they are suitable and safe for use; and by packaging, advertising, and otherwise, they do everything they can to induce that belief. The middleman is no more than a conduit, a mere mechanical device, through which the thing is to reach the ultimate user. The supplier has invited and solicited the use; and when it leads to disaster, he should not be permitted to avoid the responsibility by saying that he made no contract with the consumer, or that he used all reasonable care."

In Escola v. Coca-Cola Bottling Co., 24 Cal.2d 453, 150 P.2d 436, 440 (1944), Justice Traynor, in a concurring opinion, wrote: "Even if there is no negligence, however, public policy demands that responsibility be fixed wherever it will most effectively reduce the hazards to life and health inherent in defective products that reach the market." That point of view ultimately became the philosophy of the full court in Greenman v. Yuba Power Products, Inc., 27 Cal.Rptr. 697, 377 P.2d 897 (1962). There Justice Traynor wrote: "The purpose of such liability is to insure that the cost of injuries resulting from defective products are borne by the manufacturer that put such products on the market, rather than by the injured persons who are powerless to protect themselves."

We believe that the quoted expressions of policy are sound as applied to the manufacturer and distributor of a bottled beverage. Indeed, eighteen states have judicially accepted strict liability, without negligence and without privity, as to manufacturers of all types of products; and six more have done so by statute. Though the appellant suggests that only the legislature may declare the policy of Nevada on this subject, the weight of case authority is contra. As indicated, most states approving the doctrine of strict liability have done so by court declaration.

Our acceptance of strict tort liability against the manufacturer and distributor of a bottled beverage does not mean that the plaintiff is relieved of the burden of proving a case. He must still establish that his injury was caused by a defect in the product, and that such defect existed when the product left the hands of the defendant. The concept of strict liability does not prove causation, nor does it trace cause to the defendant.

In the case at hand, Shoshone contends that insufficient proof was offered to establish that the mouse was in the bottle of "Squirt" when it left Shoshone's possession. On this point the evidence was in conflict, and the jury was free to choose. The vice-president and general manager of Shoshone testified, in substance, that had the mouse been in the bottle while at his plant, it would have been denuded because of the caustic solution used and extreme heat employed in the bottle washing and brushing process. As the mouse had hair when examined following the plaintiff's encounter, the manager surmises that the rodent must have gotten into the bottle after leaving the defendant's possession. On the other hand, the plaintiff offered the expert testimony of a toxicologist who examined the bottle and contents on the day the plaintiff drank from it. It was his opinion that the mouse "had been dead for a long time" and that the dark stains (mouse feces) that he found on the bottom of the bottle must have been there before the liquid was added. The jury apparently preferred the latter evidence that traced cause to the defendant.

We turn to the question of tampering. Shoshone insists that a burden is cast upon the plaintiff to prove that there was no reasonable opportunity for someone to tamper with the bottle after it left Shoshone's control. Underhill v. Anciaux, 226 P.2d 794 (Nev., 1951), where the claim was based upon negligence, may be read to suggest that such a burden is cast upon the plaintiff. We cannot agree with that suggestion.

The matter of tampering is inextricably tied to the problem of tracing cause to the defendant. This is so whether the claim for relief is based on negligence or strict liability. Whenever evidence is offered by the plaintiff tending to establish the presence of the mouse in the bottle when it left Shoshone's possession, the defense is encouraged to introduce evidence that the mouse must have gotten there after the bottle left Shoshone's control, thus interjecting the possibility that the bottle and its contents were tampered with by someone, perhaps as a practical joke or for some other reason. In this case, as in most cases, positive proof either way is not available. Inferences must be drawn from the best available evidence produced by each side. We have already alluded to that evidence.

It is apparent that the moment plaintiff produces evidence tending to show that the mouse was in the bottle while in the defendant's control, he has, to some degree, negated tampering by others. The converse is likewise true. A fortiori, once it is decided that enough evidence is present to trace cause to the defendant, that same evidence is sufficient to allow the jury to find an absence of tampering. For this reason, any notion that there is a burden of proof as to tampering simply does not make sense. The sole burden is upon the plaintiff to prove that his injury was caused by a defect in the product, and that such defect existed when the product left the hands of the defendant. The defendant, of course, may offer evidence suggesting tampering under a general denial of liability. Therefore, we expressly disapprove any contrary implication in Underhill v. Anciaux.

The jury awarded Dolinski $2,500 as compensatory damages. Shoshone urges that the award is excessive. Upon drinking the "Squirt," Dolinski immediately became ill, visited a doctor, and was given pills to counteract nausea. At the time of trial more than two years later, he still possessed an aversion to soft drinks, described by a psychiatrist to be a "conditioned reflex" that could continue indefinitely. He lost twenty pounds. In these circumstances, we cannot say that the damages must have been given under the influence of passion or prejudice, or that our judicial conscience is shocked.

Ruling of the Court: Judgment affirmed.

The doctrine of strict liability in tort extends to the design and manufacture of all types of products. It follows that in proving a case under the doctrine of strict tort liability, there must be adequate and proper standards to determine who is liable, the type of harm for which liability exists, and, of course, the duration of time over which that liability extends.

In Ginnis v. Mapes Hotel Corporation, 470 P.2d 135 (Nev., 1970), where the following events took place, the question of who was liable was a question for the jury. The plaintiff, Georgia Ginnis, her husband, and a friend, Mrs. Atkinson, were customers in the casino area of the Mapes Hotel when they decided to leave. Mr. Ginnis left first, followed by Mrs. Atkinson. Both negotiated the first of two sets of automatic doors successfully. As Georgia Ginnis, who followed Mrs. Atkinson by a few feet, stepped across the threshold of the inner door, it closed on her, knocking her over the rail alongside the door and pinning her to it. Mr. Ginnis tried to extricate her from the predicament alone, but when he could not force open the door, sought help from a hotel cashier, Fred Brocklehurst. Mr. Ginnis said it took them both to force the door open. Brocklehurst, a 240-pound man, said he opened the door alone with one hand.

In the plaintiff's complaint, she alleged that the door supplied by Dor-O-Matic was "created, designed, manufactured, operated, repaired, inspected, delivered and supplied . . . in a dangerous and defective condition and manner." During the trial, evidence was submitted that the door malfunctioned because a relay in the door mechanism was faulty. The court's opinion was that the most accurate test for a "defect" within strict tort liability was set forth in Dunham v. Vaughan & Bushnell Mfg. Co., 247 N.E.2d 401, 403 (Ill., 1969), where it was held: "Although the definitions of the term 'defect' in the context of products' liability law use varying language, all of them rest upon the common premise that those products are defective that are dangerous because they fail to perform in the manner reasonably to be expected in light of their nature and intended function."

The gist of the plaintiff's appeal is that the court refused instructions that would have permitted the jury to consider the doctrine of strict tort liability against Dor-O-Matic. The appellate court thought that was an error requiring reversal and a new trial. Additionally, the fact that there were similar accidents involving the same door were relevant to causation and a defective and dangerous condition under the strict liability theory. Although such information is not ordinarily pertinent to the issue of notice or knowledge, it may be considered pertinent in determining whether or not the product was hazardous, especially if the accident occurred at the same or in a similar place, under the same or similar conditions. This information, the court maintained, is just as relevant as a prior accident to show that the condition was in fact dangerous or defective, or that the injury was caused by the condition.

The plaintiff's attorney withdrew the res ipsa loquitur instruction against Dor-O-Matic, and therefore it was not considered. The finding of no liability on the part of the Mapes Hotel Corporation was affirmed, but the case was remanded for a new trial as to Dor-O-Matic.

Negligence Per Se Doctrine

The doctrine of negligence per se—or negligence as a matter of law—refers to conduct, whether of action or omission, that may be declared and treated as negligence without any argument or proof as to the particular surrounding circumstances. This is because it is so palpably opposed to the dictates of common prudence that it can be said without hesitation that no careful person would have been guilty of it. For example, assume a statute specifically states that a certain restaurant and night club has to have five exits (based on occupancy) in case of a fire; yet four exits are kept barred to prevent entry by nonpaying guests. Sixty people subsequently die in a fire because the doors cannot be opened from the inside. This is an instance of negligence per se.

Negligence per se differs from res ipsa loquitur in that the latter doctrine cannot be applied when direct evidence of negligence exists. Negligence per se is a violation of a specific requirement, or law, or ordinance; the only fact for jury determination is the omission or commission of the specific act inhibited or required.

The negligence per se doctrine nullifies the common law defense of contributory negligence. This, of course, assumes that the defendant's action in not complying with the statute or ordinance was the proximate cause of the injuries.

Negligence of Employees Imputed to Employer

Hotels, motels, and restaurants employ many people. In general, hotelkeepers are liable not only for their own actions, but also for acts of their servants while on their jobs, acts of other guests or strangers, and, under certain conditions, for injuries sustained by persons other than guests.

Under the broad doctrine of negligence, employers must protect patrons, customers, or other invitees from the negligence of their employees. However, the courts do not uniformly agree under which theory the patron, customer, or other invitee can recover. The guests may bring a cause of action against the proprietor in four broad categories:

1   Under a contractual basis,
2   For negligence in selection of employees,
3   Under the doctrine of respondeat superior,

4 Under a theory that the state, in protecting a certain class of people, imposes by law a minimum duty that the employer must meet.

Contractual Basis

Apparently, a duty owed under a contractual relationship is an extension of the doctrine that makes a carrier liable to a passenger for having failed to protect him against an assault by the carrier's servant. In one of the leading cases, Clancy v. Barker, 103 N.W. 446 (Neb., 1905), the infant son of a hotel guest, having heard the sound of music, entered the room where a porter was playing the harmonica and was shot by the porter. The porter contended that he was only trying to frighten the boy by brandishing the revolver. The court held the proprietor of the hotel liable for the injury on the theory that it constituted a breach of the implied contract that requires a hotelkeeper to treat guests with due consideration for their safety and comfort. The court also stated that this rule was not limited to the master, but applied to the employee as well. The contention that the servant was not in the discharge of his duty when the accident occurred was immaterial, according to the court, because the duty to guests is a continuing one.

In the federal court, Clancy v. Barker, 131 F. 161 (Neb., 1904), ran contrary to the decision reached in the state court. In the federal jurisdiction, the court held that the hotelkeeper was not liable when the porter accidentally shot and injured the infant guest. This result may seem strange—that is, that one can have two diametrically opposed results. It must be remembered, however, that this case was tried in both a state and a federal court, where different results can be obtained. In any action where a case is tried in both courts, the results may be different because, first, the juries are different and, second, although the substantive law of the state is applied in both courts, the procedural law can be different. These two reasons could account for the different verdicts in the *Clancy* case.

In *Tobin* v. *Slutsky*, the court ruled there was a contractual duty on the part of the hotel to maintain its facilities in such a manner that its guests should be safe and afforded treatment commensurate with the quality of the accommodations offered. Hotels, motels, and inns can range from a luxurious $1,500-a-day penthouse to a $1 flophouse. They all have in common the fact that they are places of public accommodation, but the type of care owed may vary greatly, as shown by this case.

**Case
Example**   **Tobin v. Slutsky**
506 F.2d 1097 (1974) N.Y.

This lawsuit grows out of an unfortunate incident at the hotel operated by defendants in Ellenville, New York. Mr. and Mrs. Tobin and their 15-year-old daughter, Donna, were guests in July 1970. Mr. Tobin paid approximately $500 for a week at what was advertised as "a family resort" with supervised activities for children and teenagers. Despite such claims, four days after the Tobins arrived, Donna was assaulted by an employee of the hotel.

Donna had returned from horseback riding at about 3:00 P.M. and was waiting for an elevator to go to her family's room. Robert Stevens, an employee of the hotel who had been sitting in the lobby, came over and stood beside her. When Donna entered the elevator, he followed. Stevens then directed the elevator to the top floor, pulled out a knife seven to eight inches long, and told Donna that if she said anything, he would "slash" her throat. With his knife at her back, Stevens forced Donna down a hallway and toward a door to the roof, which he opened with a key. Once on the roof, Stevens molested Donna, unbuttoning her shirt and unzipping her pants, placing his hands inside her shirt and down into her underwear, and exposed himself. Donna attempted to get away, but Stevens held the knife at her throat and threatened to kill her if she tried to escape. Only after she promised Stevens not to tell anyone about the occurrence did he allow Donna to leave.

Donna testified about the incident, recalling that she cried and shook as it occurred and was so scared that she could not stop, even when Stevens told her he would not let her go until she stopped shaking. Testimony had to be halted as Donna began to cry at the trial while she told of the attack. Mr. and Mrs. Tobin were also trial witnesses, but the judge effectively precluded them from giving much evidence as to the effect of the incident on Donna. There was no medical testimony. Various answers to interrogatories established that Stevens was a service employee at the hotel who had been hired three days before the incident through the Louis Employment Agency and after a brief interview by the hotel's housekeeper.

The jury returned a verdict of $30,000 for plaintiff.

Defendants' principal claim on appeal is that the district judge erred in taking the issue of liability away from the jury and directing a judgment for plaintiff on that question. Defendants also argue that the judge should have directed a verdict for them because there was no showing that the acts of Stevens were within the scope of his employment, or that the hotel was negligent in any way. Finally, defendants claim that the damage award was excessive. . . .

We construe the law of New York to oblige an innkeeper to use reasonable care, commensurate with the quality of the accommodations offered, to see that his guest is not abused, injured, or insulted by his employees. In the case of a first-class family resort, reasonable care would mean a high degree of care. Indeed, examination of the New York cases leads us to believe that this duty of reasonable care has generally been interpreted to be a severe one. We have been able to find only one case where a patron injured by an employee was denied recovery from the establishment. . . . And, in that case, it appears that the plaintiff may have brought the injury upon herself.

No matter how strict the standard, however, the hotel is not an insurer, and proof of injury to a guest caused by a hotel employee should not entitle a plaintiff to a directed verdict. In that respect, we believe that the district judge erred here in taking the issue from the jury. Indeed, we have lingered over defendants' second contention that the verdict should have been directed against, rather than for, plaintiff because there was insufficient proof of lack of reasonable care. But there, too, we conclude that under New York law, a jury issue was created in the circumstances of this case; for example, was it reasonable to have no policing of the lobby or of the elevators to prevent incidents such as this?

Accordingly, we remand for a new trial. For the guidance of the district court and the parties, we note that we agree with the judge's rulings on the record before him that punitive damages could not be removed, and that the compensatory damages awarded by the jury were not excessive.

Ruling of the Court: Judgment reversed and case remanded for further proceedings consistent with this opinion.

Selection of Employees

The second category in which the employer owes a duty to the invitee is in the selection and retention of employees, and it is predicated on the theory that owners should exercise reasonable care in protecting their customers, patrons, or other invitees. Therefore, employers must use due care to avoid the selection or retention of employees whom they know or should know are undesirable because of their habits, temperament, or nature.

In Bradley v. Stevens, 46 N.W.2d 382 (Mich., 1951), in which an employee raped a customer, the court raised the question of whether Stevens, the employer, knew that the employee had been accused of a prior crime of common law rape. The employer indicated that he knew that the employee had been previously in trouble; however, there was no clear evidence whether he was referring to the employee's criminal propensities or to a charge of nonsupport that had been brought by the employee's wife. The court said that if Stevens knew of the employee's propensities and criminal record, he would be guilty of negligence in the selection and retention of this employee. But since the burden of proof is upon the plaintiff to establish such negligence by a fair preponderance of the evidence, Stevens was not held liable for the actions of his employee.

Doctrine of Respondeat Superior

The doctrine of respondeat superior ("let the master answer") recognizes that a master is civilly liable to third persons for the tort of his employees. This doctrine is not confined to directly authorized or ratified acts, but it may also hinge on the question of whether the acts are incidental to the type of work that the employee has been hired to perform. When the assault by an employee is purely personal and has no real connection with the master's business, the doctrine of respondeat superior is inapplicable.

The doctrine appears to be founded on the theory of agency or representation—that the employer is constructively present. This, of course, is fiction. But the law, by implication, makes the act of the employee that of the employer. Qui facit per alium, facit per se ("he who

acts through another acts himself") clearly indicates the responsibility—
the acts of an agent are the acts of the principal.

Employers can be either primarily or secondarily liable for the torts
of their employees. What is the difference? Many reasons can explain
why an employer does not want to be held primarily liable for an assault
by one of his employees on his patrons. Here the question of damages
is important. The broad distinction seems to be that the master who is
primarily liable for an assault of this nature may be assessed punitive
damages in the same manner as any person who commits an assault. A
master convicted under the doctrine of *respondeat superior* is only secondarily liable. (See 372 A.L.R.2d 372.)

An employer who personally participates in a servant's assault on
a customer obviously would be held liable as a joint tortfeasor (wrongdoer) with the servant for injuries inflicted or damage caused. In addition
to personal participation, the employer may become primarily liable for
a personal assault by the servant upon a party when he has ordered such
an assault or has ratified (confirmed or approved) the action.

The case of Buckley v. Edgewater Beach Hotel Company, 247 Ill.
App. 239 (1928), illustrates the ambiguity of what constitutes an authorized act. The plaintiff in this case contended that because the servant
was employed to maintain peace and quiet in the hotel, the employer
was expressly authorizing the servant to assault a patron when an argument arose between the parties. The court rejected this argument and
pointed out that the evidence did not show that he was employed for
the purposes of assaulting the plaintiff, but only for the purposes for
which any officer would ordinarily be employed in discharging the duties
of such an office and with full regard for the rights of those on the
premises.

It is the general rule that when an act cannot be delegated, it cannot
be ratified. Also, when an act is done in violation of the law or contra-
venes public policy, which would be a crime against the state, it cannot
be ratified. Some courts have also held that personal assault—including
an assault that is purely that of the servant against the customer and
arises outside the scope of his employment—is not an act that can be
ratified, as the following two cases illustrate. In Fisher v. Hering, 97
N.E.2d 553 (Ohio, 1948), a waitress struck a restaurant patron in the face
when he accused her of shortchanging another customer. The court held
that the employer had not ratified the act of the employee by continuing
her in his employment, stating that the act must be done within the scope
of the employment before there can be ratification. In the second case,
McChristian v. Popkin, 171 P.2d 85 (Cal., 1946), a special police officer
assaulted a theater patron while collecting ticket stubs and maintaining
order. The court pointed out that failure to discharge the employee was
tantamount to ratifying the illegal act of the employee.

The test under the doctrine of *respondeat superior* is that the act
must have been done within the scope or course of the employment and

must be in furtherance of, or for the protection of, the master's interest. The courts have used the following factors to judge whether the master is responsible for the assault under the doctrine:

1 Mental condition of employee prior to the attack (except for an assault committed in the spirit of horseplay, or where the employee is attempting to gratify some lustful desire);

2 Personal motivation. If the altercation is purely personal, without any thought to furtherance of the master's business, this would be a basis for not holding the master liable;

3 Past disagreements or animosities;

4 Acts of mischief or horseplay indulged in by the employee;

5 Completion of the master's business. If the master's business is completed, the master is no longer liable for the servant's actions;

6 Assault committed off the premises of the employer.

Courts use a number of factors to determine whether the assault by the employee is in the scope of employment or in the master's interest. Many courts recognize yet another principle—the master's responsibility for an assault committed by his servant that may arise solely because the employment may include the use of force—for example, when an employee's duties are to preserve order upon the premises or to protect the employer's property from theft or vandalism. In these cases, an inference arises that force, to a reasonable extent, may be, or is expected to be, used in the fulfillment of the duties of employment.

The case of D.C. Baldwin v. Wiggins, 289 S.W.2d 729 (Ky., 1956), clearly shows the type of situation that a proprietor can become involved in without really anticipating the severe consequences. In this case, the master was held liable under the doctrine of *respondeat superior* when a restaurant employee set fire to Wiggins, a customer who had dozed off at the counter. Wiggins's burn necessitated nine days' hospitalization. He was awarded damages from the restaurant proprietor Baldwin, as well as from the employee. Baldwin appealed the decision as he was not present on the day in question. He admitted, however, that such savage horseplay had gone on for years, and that he himself had participated on other occasions, although this was the first time injury had resulted. The appeals court found Baldwin liable for his employee's actions and affirmed judgment for the plaintiff.

Case	**Baldwin v. Wiggins**
Example	*289 S.W.2d 729 (Ky., 1956)*
	(STANLEY, Commissioner)

George Pope, counterman in a Cynthiana restaurant called "The Lunch Box," owned and operated by D.C. Baldwin, sprayed or poured flammable fluid used in automatic cigarette lighters on the shirt of Nelson Wiggins, a patron, and then set it afire. Wiggins had dozed off asleep while seated at a counter where he had drunk a cup of coffee. Pope testified Wiggins had been drinking intoxicants, but he denied it. Wiggins suffered burns which necessitated hospitalization for nine days. In his action for damages, the jury returned a verdict for the plaintiff for $1,274.50, with the added provision that the defendant, Baldwin, should pay $1,200 and Pope, the counterman, should pay $74.50. The plaintiff had incurred doctor and hospital expenses of $174.50. Baldwin's motion for an appeal under KRS 21.080 is sustained and an opinion delivered because of the novelty and importance of the legal principles involved, particularly pertaining to an instruction on damages.

The proprietor, Baldwin, was not present on this occasion, and Pope was in charge of the restaurant. This sort of vicious and savage horseplay had been going on for about four years. Baldwin admitted he had personally engaged in it. He stated this was the first time any harm had resulted and attributed plaintiff's injury to the fact that he had run in front of a fan.

This case is not within the principle, as the defendant contends it is, that a master is not legally liable for a wrongful act of his servant that was outside of the scope of his employment or not within the contemplation or the service of his employment. The case is under the rule that where an employer leaves one in charge of his business during his absence, and that one wrongfully does something to injure a patron, which the employer has reason to know he may do, the employer is liable therefor. He is deemed to have delegated his obligation to protect and not to harm the patron. The defendant's liability clearly comes within the latter rule. . . . In the present case, the proprietor had set the example for his employees to follow and knew they were doing it. He had thereby countenanced and sanctioned such vicious horseplay as a distorted sense of fun in his restaurant. Its inherent danger presaged injury. . . .

In the case at bar, the sole actor was the employee. The employer's liability is purely derivative and is dependent solely upon the doctrine of *respondeat superior*. There was no independent negligence on his part. His responsibility is imputed as a matter of law. The liability for all damages is inseparable as between the employer and employee.

For the past twenty years, this court, in line with the great majority, has been holding that where an employer and employee are jointly sued for injurious consequences of an indivisible wrongful act of the employee, his exoneration by a jury from personal liability requires that the verdict against the employer be set aside. . . . To avoid such inconsistent and incongruous verdict, the instructions should not permit a separate recovery. . . .

In the present case, the jury did not absolve the employee of liability, but found him guilty of negligence and apportioned the recovery under an erroneous instruction authorizing a separate verdict. However, the appellant is in no position to rely upon the error. The record does not show that the appellant, as defendant, or his co-defendant either, offered any instruction except a peremptory. No objection was made, even in the motion for a new trial, to the instructions that the court gave. It is an imperative rule that: "No party may assign as error the giving or the failure to give an instruction, unless he objects thereto before the court instructs the jury, stating specifically the matter to which he objects and the grounds of his objections" (CR 51). Other than the addition of the provision for stating the ground of objection, the Civil Code of Practice, Section 333, so provided.

Ruling of the Court: The judgment is affirmed for plaintiff.

Quasi-public places are required by law to be operated in such a way that good order prevails. Assaults by employees, found to have been committed for the purpose of maintaining order, although unjustified, are generally held to have been committed in the course and scope of their employment. Because the amount of force required to quell disturbances or eject unruly patrons is subject to discretion, there is no excuse if excessive force has been used, even though, as it sometimes appears, the servant has in part been motivated by personal resentment or malice. An example is Anderson v. Covert, 245 S.W.2d 770 (Tenn., 1952). Here, the disorderly plaintiff Covert was thrown out of Anderson's restaurant by an employee, who gave him a brutal beating in the process. The court held Anderson liable for his employee's actions as they were committed within the scope of his employment.

Although the liability that attaches to a master is severe, the public is owed some protection. The liability also insures that employers will be more careful in the selection of servants to represent them as agents. Also, the question of the "deep-pocket" or "risk-spreading" theory is involved. It has been urged with increasing vigor that loss should be shifted from employee to employer if the latter is more able to sustain the loss. The gist of the argument is that in this way, a loss will be spread more generally in the community among those who benefit from the activity out of which the loss arises.

Can a guest's employer be liable to a hotel for damages caused by the employee as the result of his starting a fire? The answer was yes in the case of Edgewater Motels, Inc., v. Gatzke, 277 N.W.2d 11 (Minn., 1979). The guest, Gatzke, negligently started a fire in the hotel he was staying at when he threw a match in a plastic wastebasket, causing over $330,000 in damages.

Gatzke was opening a new restaurant for his employer, the Walgreen Company, and had been working extremely long hours for three weeks in this endeavor. On the day in question, he had worked seventeen hours and then, with some colleagues, stopped at a bar, where he consumed four brandy manhattans in about an hour while he and his colleagues discussed business.

Between 1:15 and 1:30 A.M., Gatzke walked back to the Edgewater, the motel. Witnesses testified that he acted normal and appeared sober. Gatzke went directly to his motel room and then "probably" sat down at a desk to fill out his expense account because "that was [his] habit from traveling so much."

While Gatzke completed the expense account, he "probably" smoked a cigarette. The record indicates that Gatzke smoked about two packages of cigarettes per day. A maid testified that the ashtrays in Gatzke's room were generally full of cigarette butts and ashes when she cleaned the room. She also noticed at times that the plastic wastebasket next to the desk contained cigarette butts.

After filling out the expense account, Gatzke went to bed, and soon thereafter a fire broke out. Gatzke escaped from the burning room, but the fire spread rapidly and caused extensive damage to the motel.

It is reasonably inferable from the evidence—and not challenged by Walgreen's or Gatzke on appeal—that Gatzke's negligent smoking of a cigarette was a direct cause of the damages sustained by the Edgewater. The question raised here is whether the facts of this case reasonably support the imposition of vicarious liability on Walgreen's for the conceded negligent act of its employee. To support a finding that an employee's negligent act occurred within his scope of employment, it must be shown that his conduct was, to some degree, in furtherance of the interests of his employer. Other factors to be considered in the scope of employment determination are whether the conduct is of the kind that the employee is authorized to perform and whether the act occurs substantially within authorized time and space restrictions.

The jury found that Gatzke was involved in serving his employer's interests at the time he was at the bar; Gatzke was in any case within the scope of his employment when he filled out his travel expense account; and Gatzke's hotel room was his office away from home.

The question of whether smoking can be within an employee's scope of employment is a close one, but after careful consideration of the issue, we are persuaded by the reasoning of the courts that hold that smoking can be an act within an employee's scope of employment. It seems only logical to conclude that employees do not abandon their employment as a matter of law while temporarily acting for their personal comfort when such activities involve only slight deviations from work that are reasonable under the circumstances, such as eating, drinking, or smoking.

A crucial question arises when the hotel leaves a plastic wastebasket in a room that it knows will be used for cigarette butts. In this case, the court held that instead of having Walgreen's liable for the entire amount, it was liable only for 40 percent and the hotel, 60 percent of the damage. The jury believed that a person would presumably dispose of a cigarette in a wastebasket rather than next to it, which provided a reasonable basis from which the jury finding of proximate cause is supported. The trial court's granting of judgment to Walgreen was set aside, and the jury's verdict was reinstated in its entirety.

It can be said that the master (owner or corporation) is in a better position to pay for the injuries inflicted by his servants on the guest. The case of Lehnen v. E.J. Hines & Company, 127 P.612 (Kan., 1912), shows clearly the authority, either actual or constructive, that was given to the employee. Unfortunately, in many cases in which an assault seems clearly out of the scope of the employee's duties, the court invariably comes up with a different answer. In this 1912 case, Lehnen and her female companion were violently ejected in the middle of the night from their hotel room by an intoxicated desk clerk with the aid of a policeman. They were arrested and subsequently held in jail for several days. Lehnen claimed they were asleep at the time of the intrusion, while the hotel claimed they were drinking liquor, smoking cigarettes, and making a disturbing noise. Lehnen recovered for damages. The hotel appealed the decision, claiming the desk clerk was acting outside the scope of his employment. The appeals court did not support this, and the prior judgment was affirmed.

The following case, James v. Governor's House, Inc., 225 So.2d 815 (Ala., 1969), illustrates still another facet of *respondeat superior*. As you read it, keep in mind the cost in time of management, costs of counsel, and the publicity inherent in such a case. Mrs. James, a guest, had just returned to her room from the pool with her eighteen-month-old son, who had to be changed. She left the door open, and the bellboy "knocked" and entered, ostensibly to lock the doors adjoining the next room. He then sexually accosted her. Mrs. James complained to the manager, who said, "Don't come here with your damn lies." When Mrs. James sued for $200,000 in an action for assault and battery and for indignities and humiliation, the trial court found for the defendant hotelkeeper. In the appeal for a new trial, the Supreme Court of Alabama granted Mrs. James a new trial, because the trial court's instructions to the jury that the motel owner was not liable if the assault on the guest was committed by the employee solely to satisfy his sensuous desires and not in furtherance of business of the owner were improper in this case. The Supreme Court held that that law may be correct in a number of cases, but that was not the case in a suit by a guest against an innkeeper. The guest-innkeeper relationship differs from other relationships inasmuch as there exists between the parties an expressed or implied contractual requirement of decent and respectful treatment. This requirement arises as the result of the relationship between the parties. The implication arises whenever one person is placed in control or protection of another. It grows out of peculiar and special relationships. Therefore, the liability of the innkeeper would be imposed not on the basis of whether the bellboy was acting within the scope of his employment when he attacked the plaintiff, but rather, whether the innkeeper's contractual duty of providing the guest with decent and respectful treatment had been violated.

Management Principles

The hotelier or restaurateur is in the best position to prevent accidents and injuries to guests. Of course, managers cannot control all circumstances, such as careless guests, acts of God, or the acts of complete strangers. They must develop preventive strategies by foreseeing all probable and possible mishaps, keeping in mind how a court of law might regard the situation. They should familiarize themselves and their employees with the various doctrines of negligence that affect their legal status. An employee newsletter, for example, might be an effective educational medium.

In *Ball* v. *Hilton*, the court ruled that the woman had assumed the risk of going downstairs during a blackout, and her injuries were caused by her own negligence. But it could have rendered a different decision, holding that a flashlight should have been used, or that the hotel was negligent in allowing a person to go down the stairs into an unfamiliar area without more assistance. The management principle here is to be prepared for fires, elevator malfunctions, blackouts, and bomb threats. Set a firm policy and disseminate such information to employees. Though the hotel won the case, it lost a great deal in attorney's fees, time, and goodwill.

An establishment with a large expanse of plate glass should make guests aware of its existence and location. The *Karna* case was upheld for the defendant hotel, but most of the thousands of glass cases that come up each year go against the defendants. Placing decals or artwork on such glass may help to prevent guests from mistaking glass doors for openings. The thickness of the glass is another factor that should be considered.

Most people wish to help those in trouble; unfortunately, sometimes such action turns out to be costly. The Good Samaritan rule is an anachronism that should be drastically changed. Massachusetts, Florida, and other states have passed statutes allowing certain types of aid to be given to those in need. The case of *Sneider* v. *Hyatt* raises more problems than it solves. When should one attempt to help a person? For instance, is a person choking because of a food particle lodged in his throat, or is he suffering from a heart attack? The decision to help may have far-reaching consequences, sometimes ending in a lawsuit.

Among the most serious responsibilities of hoteliers and restaurateurs are personnel problems. In general, owner-managers are held responsible for the actions of their employees when they are acting within the scope of their employment. The following procedures may help to avert trouble:

1 Check a new employee's history of fighting or other violence.

2 Evaluate new personnel during at least the first month to see if they are unduly aggressive or antisocial toward guests or co-workers.

3 Train personnel to recognize belligerent customers and to call a supervisor in time to avert a disturbance.

4 Train personnel to deal with the following situations—how guests should be asked to leave; what to do if they won't leave; and whom to call if they won't leave.

5 Train personnel to avoid false arrest situations. If employees ask that a person be arrested, and he or she is held without being informed of his or her rights, the hotel will become liable. In *Cicurel* v. *Mollett*,

149 N.Y.S.2d 397 (1956), the plaintiff was held in his room for eight hours by the police, who had been asked to arrest him, and he was later fingerprinted. He won a $3,000 award for false arrest.

  6 Train personnel not to lose their tempers, especially not to defame a person in the presence of others.

  7 In any situation where you believe trouble may arise, take the necessary action ahead of time. For example, if a guest arrives without luggage:

> **a** Request one night's payment in advance.
> **b** Mark "walk-in" on the guest folio.
> **c** Notify all cost centers.
> **d** Alert the night auditor that no charges can be incurred without the manager's permission.
> **e** At an appropriate time the next morning, ask if the guest will be staying longer, and if so, get another night's rent in advance.
> **f** Set a predetermined limit on any such guest's account.

  8 If a state statute permits the use of antichoking techniques, such as the Heimlich maneuver, train personnel in its use. An excellent film explaining the Heimlich maneuver can be obtained from Paramount Oxford Films, 5451 Marathon Street, Hollywood, California 90038.

As shown in the *Baldwin* case, horseplay has no place in a restaurant, or for that matter in any place of business. The owner was held liable even though he was not present, although he had participated in such horseplay at other times.

Certain states follow the attractive nuisance doctrine that is most favorable to minors. If your state follows this doctrine you should inform all of your employees of the consequences. The *Albanese* case may be similar to one type of case you will run into.

Former students who are now hotel managers have found that meetings where tort doctrines are discussed help employees envisage what can and does happen. You should give specific examples to employees to see how they would react given situations similar to those related in this book. You could use the last clear chance doctrine, the doctrine of *res ipsa loquitur*, or the example found in the *Pence* case.

A hotelkeeper generally does not have to have a doorman on duty unless the manager expects a large number of people in the hotel. Forecasting what type of use the hotel will be subjected to at any particular time is very important. Whether you have enough personnel is a jury question, and juries have not been solicitous of hotel problems. Accordingly, every day should be forecasted as to crowd management.

In this chapter we have discussed the obligations of hotelkeepers for guests' safety. The next chapter considers additional hotelkeeper responsibilities in terms of guests' rights.

QUESTIONS FOR DISCUSSION

1 What is a tort? Define libel and slander. What part does negligence play in a tort?

2 If a duty is owed a customer, what are the requisites of this duty? How is this duty measured? Why does the court use the "prudent man" test? Who is a prudent person?

3 Are the rights of a minor greater than those of an adult? Explain. Must a minor who has limited contract rights be accepted in a hotel? Why or why not?

4 What is the theory underlying the proximate cause concept? Why is it important?

5 Many doctrines are associated with negligence in a tort. Why is it important to use doctrines such as *res ipsa loquitur*, attractive nuisance, *prima facie*, last clear chance, assumption of risk, and contributory negligence?

6 What is the doctrine of comparative negligence? How does it affect hotelkeepers?

7 The Good Samaritan rule is an antiquated legal concept. What is this rule? How can it be detrimental to hotelkeepers and restaurateurs?

8 Are hotelkeepers held to an absolute liability with regard to their guests' welfare? Why or why not?

9 If an employee is negligent in his or her care of a guest, will the hotelkeeper or restaurateur be held responsible? Why or why not?

10 What is the doctrine of *respondeat superior*, and what is its significance to a hotelkeeper? What factors make this concept work?

11 Cite instances where the guests assume or do not assume the risk that is found in a hotel, restaurant, or any type of related travel situation.

12 A guest in a gathering of twenty-five of his colleagues from his union has two or three martinis and is eating a steak and lobster dinner when he starts to choke. Within a short time, he is taken to the restroom, where he passes by you as the manager. You do not assist him personally because his friends are helping him, but you do call the police and hospital. They respond in three minutes. He is taken to the hospital, where he dies. His wife is now suing your restaurant for $750,000. What points of law are involved?

9 Contents

9 The Hotelkeeper's Obligation toward Guests and Others

"The first and worst of all frauds is to cheat oneself."

PHILIP JAMES BAILEY

In the next three chapters, we will discuss what hotelkeepers, motelkeepers, and restaurateurs should know about the rights of their guests, as a corollary to their own rights (as discussed in chapter 12). These rights should be examined from the viewpoint of the guest, patron, or customer, and hotelkeepers should conduct their business in conformance with them. We will now examine guests' rights as delineated by the legislature, by common law, or by judicial interpretation of the law.

An important concern of hotel guests is occupying the room or rooms they have contracted for. The hotelkeeper's objective is to fill all rooms with the guests who have contracted for them. Despite these mutual requirements, both parties sometimes breach their contract.

Because guests often make reservations at more than one hotel (similar to multiple airline reservations) or do not arrive (a "no-show"), hotelkeepers feel justified in overbooking. From past experience, hotelkeepers believe they can predict that a certain percentage of guests will not show. Therefore, to achieve as close to a 100 percent occupancy as possible, they will accept reservations in excess (by 5 to 15 percent) of actually available rooms. However, guests often do not act predictably—and the estimated no-shows do in fact come in for accommodations.

Before we proceed with a detailed examination of overbooking, it is wise to consider the law of contracts, as well as the terminology of the industry.

General Contract Law

A contract is a relationship that comes into existence between parties, either as the result of an expressed agreement between them or else one that is implied by law as the result of the actions and conduct of the parties or either of them.

A contract can be written and signed, or it can be oral. For that matter, it can come into existence without a word being written or spoken. Hundreds of contracts involving millions of dollars are made daily on the commodity exchange floors or at auction houses merely by the nod of the head or a wink of the eye. No matter how the contract is expressed or formulated, there are, in all instances, certain basic essentials present.

Lack of Individual Capacity to Contract

Parties to the contract must have the legal capacity to contract. The law has imposed restrictions determining who can enter into a contract. Basically, these restrictions were rooted in the desire to protect certain segments of society from the consequences of their own acts, resulting in the creation of improvident (bad) contracts. Therefore, as a matter of law, minors, intoxicated persons, and insane or otherwise mentally incompetent persons do not have the capacity to contract.

In many states, until more recent times, married women could not contract with their husbands or anyone else. Minors and drunken, insane, or otherwise mentally incompetent persons are denied the capacity to contract because they lack sufficient mental ability to understand and appreciate fully the nature of the commitment that they are undertaking, and thus they could easily be victimized. The restrictions on married women allegedly were based upon the concept in law that a man and wife are one and, as such, it was felt that a person could not contract with himself. More realistically, the motivation behind the rule might be found to be the desire of husbands to retain greater degrees of control over their wives' property.

Lack of Corporate Capacity to Contract

Three separate circumstances deny corporations the capacity to contract. To understand these incapacities, one is required to understand just what a corporation is, how it gets its powers, and how it works.

1 A corporation is an entity created by the state. Its birth is conditioned upon those seeking to bring it into existence, complying with the statutory requirements that must be met for its creation. Failure to meet any one of these requirements would mean that the corporation would never come into existence. If that happened, it is immaterial that those who purported to act in its behalf were of the opinion that it had and also believed that they were acting in its behalf, because inasmuch as there never was a corporation validly formed, there was nothing to contract with.

2   When a corporation is formed, it must inform the state as to its purposes. The corporation charter is granted so that the corporation can perform those purposes for which it was created. Its powers are limited to the purpose of its creation, coupled with the powers granted by the state. The corporation does not have the legal capacity to contract beyond the purposes for which it was created and empowered by law. These are called *ultra vires acts* of the corporation.

3   The remaining area where the corporation lacks the capacity to contract also concerns the nature of a corporation. When we do business with a corporation, we are not doing business with the person with whom we are dealing. In fact, we are not entering into a contractual relationship with people at all. We are entering into a contract with a business entity. The human beings with whom we are negotiating are merely its representatives and are limited in their ability to contract; they must remain within the confines of the authority granted to them by the board of directors and/or stockholders.

Mutuality

Once the capacity to contract is established, we look for what is referred to as *mutuality of the parties*. That is, there must be an "offer" by one party and an "acceptance" by the other. There also must be consideration, which will be discussed later. These requisites are gauged by the objective manifestation of an intention to contract; that is, any subjective mental reservations or modifications will have no effect on the contract. It is what is objectively said and done that counts. The offer basically is a communication extended to those with whom the offeror is seeking to do business, and it also gives the offeree the power to turn the offer into a legally binding contract by accepting it. The acceptance also must be objectively communicated to the offeror. Once that has been done, we have a contract. Thus, when the buyer (offeree) winks at the auctioneer (offeror), he or she communicates his or her acceptance of the offer, and a legally enforceable contract is born.

Expiration or Termination of Offer

Unless a time limit has been imposed and communicated, the offer will remain open for a reasonable period of time. If time is not mentioned, the acceptance of the offer will result in a binding contract if it takes place at any time prior to the revocation of the offer, its expiration, or within a reasonable period of time from the date it was made. The offer will also terminate if it is rejected by the offeree, if the offeree makes a counteroffer, or if the offeror dies or becomes insane prior to its acceptance. One other recognized manner of termination of an offer does not involve the intent of the parties at all; this is a termination by operation of law—for example, in the event that performing the contract would require one of the parties to do something that was legal at the time the offer was made, but was deemed to be illegal before the offer was accepted.

Illegal Contract

There is a limitation on what can be contracted for. No one can contract to do anything that is illegal. For example, if an agreement is entered into between A and B to rob a bank, the agreement would call upon one or more of the parties to do something that would amount to a violation of the law. It would constitute an illegal contract. Not only would either party not have rights against each other by virtue of the agreement, but in certain cases, may well be paving the way for criminal charges to be brought against them for conspiring to commit a crime.

Unenforceable Contract

An illegal contract is not the same as an unenforceable contract. In the former, the parties tried to contract to do something against the law, and that prevented a contract from ever coming into existence. In the latter, the parties contract for something that is not illegal, but because its performance would be against public policy or for some other reason, the courts would refuse to force the parties to honor the contract. Thus, the parties have no place to go to satisfy their contract.

An example of this would be in the area of discrimination. Assume A sold B a house located next door to theirs, and in the contract B agreed to not sell the house to noncaucasians. After two years, B sells his house to C, who is not a caucasian. A sues B and C, seeking to set aside the sale because it violated the original agreement. A also asks that if the court does not set the sale aside, in the alternative, the court should award A a money award against B for breach of contract. The courts would say that the country and states have adopted strong positions against discrimination because of race, color, religion, or place of origin, and any contract that seeks to foster or encourage it in any way is against public policy. Although the court recognizes that A, as an individual, had the constitutional right to enter into such a contract, the court will not lend its good offices to support the contract, but will leave the parties where it found them.

Consideration

Generally, in order for an agreement to be binding and enforceable, there must be a consideration. A consideration can be money, property, or a promise, for example, that one party agrees to give the other party in return for something the other party agrees to do. There is an exception to this requirement in most states, however: if an agreement is under seal—that is, with a particular sign attached that imports consideration as a necessary part of a valid contract. This exception is not applicable in instances where the agreement involves the sale of goods or negotiable instruments. In essence, the presence of the seal conclusively establishes the presence of the consideration.

In the absence of a seal, consideration usually consists of a legal detriment and a bargain or exchange. The persons furnishing the consideration promise to do something or actually do something that they had no prior legal obligation to do, or they do not do or promise not to do something that they had a legal right to do. In all instances, there is something flowing from one who had no prior obligation to supply it. The benefit from the persons supplying the consideration need not flow directly to the person with whom they are contracting. It is enough that the agreement makes them promise to do, or forbear from doing, something that they had a legal right but no legal duty to do. This bargaining, or exchange, makes the contract binding and enforceable.

Statute of Frauds

The statement that contracts may be oral or in writing must be qualified: Some contracts must be in writing to be enforceable. This requirement has been imposed upon contracting parties since the early common law days on what has been labeled the statute of frauds. The restrictions have been either codified or enacted into statute in all states. Failure to comply with the mandate of the statute does not result in preventing a contract from coming into existence; it merely denies one the right to come into court to enforce the contract.

Section 1 of the Massachusetts General Laws Chapter 259 is an example of such a statute:

No action shall be brought:
First, to charge an executor or administrator, or an assignee under the insolvency law of the Commonwealth, upon a special promise to answer damages out of his own estate;

Second, to charge a person upon a special promise to answer for the debt, default or misdoing of another;

Third, upon an agreement made in consideration of marriage;

Fourth, upon a contract for the sale of lands, tenements or herediments or any interest in and/or concerning them; or,

Fifth, upon an agreement that is not to be performed within one year from the making thereof;

Unless the promise, contract, or agreement upon which such action is brought, or some memorandum or note thereof, is in writing and signed by the party to be charged therewith or by some person thereunto by him lawfully authorized.

The writings required need not be formal; notes or letters are sufficient. A memorandum can be on one piece of paper or can be pieced together from several writings. Generally, the writing should specify the essential elements, except for those that can be proved by other legal evidence. This seems to indicate that the memorandum need not set out both sides of the bargain, but it must state clearly the promise of the party sought to be charged. In fact, the statute does not require both parties to sign the writing; only the one who is sought to be charged must sign. If the party doing the suing has not signed the agreement, he or she can sue the other party for a breach of the agreement, but the other party cannot sue him or her. The signing need not be the formal signature of the party being charged; it is sufficient even if his or her name was typed in, or if he or she merely initialed the writing.

The first three items under Section 1 of the statute are self-explanatory. In effect, the fourth item under Section 1 says that in order to have an enforceable lease, easement, mortgage, or to create any equitable restrictions on land, there must be a writing or a memorandum signed by the party against whom one is endeavoring to establish the liability. Although a tenancy-at-will or a tenancy-at-sufferance can be created without a writing, a lease cannot. A license to go upon land—that is, to enter a hotel or restaurant—can be given, but it can be revoked in the absence of a writing of some sort.

One should be careful with the fifth item covered in Section 1. For example, does item 5 conflict with item 4? Item 4 says that you cannot create an interest in land, such as a lease, without a writing of some kind. Item 5 seems to say that you do not need a writing in order to enforce a contract that can be performed fully within one year. Neither item refers to the other as to whether one is excludable from the dictates of the other. A lease is a contract dealing with an interest in real estate, and a six-month lease can be performed in less than a year. The question is: Can an oral six-month lease be enforced, or is its enforcement prohibited by the statute of frauds?

Consider an example. A and B orally agree that A will paint the hotel B owns. A is to start painting it in three months from the date of the agreement, and both parties agree that the job will take ten months. Three months after the date of the agreement, A says that he will not paint the hotel. B hires another person to paint the hotel, but has to pay $350 more for the job than the first agreement called for. Can B sue A for the $350? No. The statute of frauds bars this action because even though the job itself would have been completed in ten months, or within one year from the date it was started, the requirement of the statute is that it be completed within one year from the date that the agreement was made. Inasmuch as the agreement was made three months before the starting date, then the job would not have been completed until thirteen months after the agreement. Therefore, the statute was violated, and in the absence of a writing, B would have no standing in court.

Parole Evidence Rule

Usually in the course of negotiating a contract, many words flow over the lips before the understandings and agreements of the parties are reduced to a final writing signed by the parties. This writing should contain the entire agreement between the parties. If it is intended to be a final expression, then the parole evidence rule would prohibit the hearing of any evidence of statements made by either of the parties prior to, or contemporaneously with, the signing of the contract that would vary with or contradict what is written in the contract.

The parole evidence rule does not apply to statements made after the signing of the contract. Therefore, evidence can be introduced of statements made after the signing that tend to vary or modify the agreement. Parole evidence may also be introduced to clear up any ambiguity that may arise as a result of reading the written contract. This is not violative of the rule stated above because the terms and conditions of the contract are not being varied or altered, they are being explained. The parole evidence would be admitted to explain what the written words were intended to mean.

Custom and Usage

In addition to parole evidence, meaning of words in accordance to "custom and usage" in the industry can be used in order to clear up any ambiguities. Certain words have certain meanings when used in certain ways in certain places, and although their meaning may be different in generally accepted parlance, evidence can be introduced to show that their meaning was different in this instance. The classic example concerns the meaning of ton. Assume that Jolly O freighter lines sends one of its agents to call upon a steel manufacturer in Birmingham, England, and an agreement is made to transport 1,000 tons of steel at a certain price per ton. A question would arise as to what is meant by a ton; for although in the United States, rates are quoted by short tons, which are 2,000 pounds by weight, it is the custom to use long ton weight, 2,240 pounds, when quoting shipping or volume by the ton. Therefore, in such a circumstance, it will be permissible to introduce in evidence that in Great Britain, tonnage is by custom and usage quoted at long ton weight and not short ton.

Anticipatory Breach of Contract

At one time, no cause of action could occur for a breach of a promise prior to the time that that which was promised had arrived. The theory

was that until a party was called upon to perform that which was promised, one could not say that the party had not performed. However, a
doctrine known as *anticipatory breach* or *anticipatory repudiation* has
developed. For example, a party enters into a written lease that calls for
payment of $100 per month for twenty-four months, and after six months
the party moves out, telling the lessor that he will not be back. In the
absence of a contractual agreement accelerating the time, the lessor would
have to wait for each month to pass to sue for $100. The alternative
would be to wait until the entire period had passed, when the lessor
could sue for the aggregate of months. This doctrine hampered commerce
and created a lot of litigation.

In states that adopted the doctrine of anticipatory breach and anticipatory repudiation, once the lessee had moved out and conveyed the
intention to breach or not perform the balance of the contract, the lessor
could bring an immediate action against the lessee for the entire remaining balance due under the lease. However, this action was subject
to one qualification—that is, that the lessor owes the lessee the duty to
mitigate damages. For example, the lessor cannot just sit back and let
the months go by without trying to get someone to lease the space vacated
by the lessee. The lessor must try to get a guest or tenant for the premises,
and if successful, the amount of rent collected from the new guest or
tenant would be deducted from the damages due from the lessee. This
example demonstrates the application of the doctrines to leases. However, the doctrines of anticipatory breach and repudiation, as well as the
duty to mitigate damages, are applicable to all contracts, not just leases.

In order for the repudiation to be effective, it must be clear and
unequivocal. There must be no doubt that the repudiating party does not
intend to perform the agreement when the date for performance arrives.

Penalties for Failure to Perform the Contract

The general rules applied are that the nonbreaching party is entitled
to the benefit of his or her bargain or to compensatory damages—that is,
the damages necessary for reimbursement of losses arising or resulting
from the breach. Many states in the past were reluctant to permit recovery
for any emotional suffering unless there had been impact from an outside
force. There was also reluctance to allow punitive damages as well in
matters involving mere breaches of contract, the theory being that damages of that type were properly assessed only in instances where torts
had been committed. However, many states have moved from this position. These matters are treated in other sections of the book.

Assignment of Contract Rights

Contract rights are assignable from one party to another. The duties
and obligations due under a contract can be delegated as well. However,

the original party to the contract is still liable on the contract, unless the other party to the contract agrees to a release and accepts the delegatee in substitution of the original party. Under those circumstances, the law finds that there is what is called a *novation* that amounts to a release of a party from the obligation to perform, and then entrance into a new contract with the substitute party. Although the duties under the contract can be assigned even if the other party fails to agree to the assignment, it does not prohibit the assignment.

However, the original contracting party cannot be relieved of liability for the acts of the assigned party to the contract in its performance of duties and obligations. The most the delegating party can do is to get an indemnification agreement from the party who will perform the contract instead. An indemnification agreement occurs when the surrogate (substitute) performer enters into a contract with the party delegating the performance of the contract to him or her, whereby he or she agrees that should the delegator be held liable in damages for failures or negligence on the part of the surrogate in the performance of the contract, then said surrogate agrees to pay all resulting damages and costs.

Now that we have covered some of the principles of contract law in a rather general way, let us look at the case of *Cardinal Consulting Company v. Circo Resorts, Inc.* As you read the case, try to pick out those points that you recognize to see how the court applied them.

Contracting for many rooms from a hotel or motel is big business, and its use today represents millions of room nights per year. The type of contract that the hotel makes with the tour operator is an important document, as this case clearly shows. When you read the case, bear these points in mind: What constitutes a breach of contract? How should terms of a contract be resolved? What constitutes a profit, especially for a new company? Were the requisites of a contract met (an offer, acceptance, and consideration)? How can one prove damages suffered? What are the prevailing customs in the hotel field and the travel industry? Be aware also of how to start a business, the legal implications, and why it is important to keep track of all dealings.

Case Example	**Cardinal Consulting Company v. Circo Resorts, Inc.**
	297 N.W.2d 260 (Minn., 1980)
	(SHERAN, Chief Justice)

The plaintiff, Cardinal Consulting Co., was established by William O'Neill and Wayne Haas in August 1974 to operate one-stop charter tours (OTCs) to Las Vegas and other holiday areas. For an OTC program to be approved by the Civil Aeronautics Board (CAB), many stipulations had to be complied with. Cardinal's program had been approved. The defendant was Circo Resorts, Inc., a Nevada corporation that operates the Circus Circus Hotel in Las Vegas. Jay Valentine was the sales manager for Circus Circus Hotel and had made the original contract with Cardinal Consulting Co.

Valentine verbally agreed that Circus Circus would set aside fifty rooms at a price of $16 per night for Cardinal, and if rooms had to be cancelled later, it would pose no problem because that period was traditionally slow in Las Vegas.

In November 1975, the management of Circus Circus was reorganized under the leadership of Mel Larson, who took the position previously held by Valentine's superior. In an attempt to make the operation of the hotel more efficient and to ensure that all rooms were full, Larson decided to draft formal contracts to govern Circus Circus's relations with all tour operators using its facilities. Valentine was not consulted about the contract Cardinal was asked to sign, which was contrary to the agreement they had negotiated and would make Cardinal's performance impossible.

On December 10, 1975, Valentine called Cardinal from Las Vegas to set up a meeting in Minneapolis for December 13. Haas told Valentine then and on December 13 that Cardinal was cancelling the first three tours. Valentine then told him to put it in writing, which he did in his letter of December 16.

At their meeting, Valentine presented Haas with the proposed written contract between Cardinal and Circo, which Haas refused to sign because it did not represent their agreement. Although Valentine agreed to take it back and get it redrafted, Larson refused to alter the contract and took the position that without the signature of O'Neill and Haas, there was no agreement.

On January 5, 1976, Cardinal received a letter from Circus Circus cancelling the rooms that had been reserved by Cardinal for the entire 1976 season. O'Neill and Haas immediately called Las Vegas, and Larson told them that since they had refused to sign the agreement, they had no rooms. After notifying all the agents and participants that Cardinal would have to cancel its program because it had lost its hotel booking, they tried again to work something out with Circus Circus. Larson, however, would only let them have the rooms subject to the terms of the contract letter, an offer they refused.

When Cardinal learned of the cancellation of January 5, 1976, the flights scheduled to leave for Las Vegas were not all full. The first departure from Mason City, for which participants had only two remaining days to subscribe, was about 60 percent full, the next flight from Mankato was 40 percent full, and the third flight from Eau Claire was sold out. O'Neill testified that although most still had space at the time of cancellation, they would all have been full had they been permitted to operate.

After Circo's cancellation, O'Neill and Haas attempted to salvage their tour package. They contacted numerous Las Vegas hotels, and, finally, through their ground operator, they learned that the Marina Hotel, which had just opened, still had rooms available. By the time they got back to their local agents, however, a number of the tours had already been cancelled. Nevertheless, they were able to salvage eight tours that operated at 100 percent capacity, although not back-to-back. Because they had to use the money they would have earned from these tours to cover the charges of bringing back empty planes, Cardinal never made a profit.

The disastrous nature of the 1976 season ruined Cardinal Consulting Company, although in subsequent years the OTC business from the Upper Midwest to Las Vegas flourished. O'Neill and Haas did not sever their relationship with the travel industry, however, and both currently own retail travel agencies.

On appeal from a jury verdict for Cardinal, Circo raises the following issues:

1 Was there a binding contract between Cardinal and Circo that was breached by Circo?

2 Did Cardinal prove lost profits with sufficient certainty to permit recovery?

3 Was the amount of the jury verdict supported by the evidence?

Circo takes the position that it did not breach the contract by cancelling the rooms reserved for Cardinal because the contract expressly and by custom recognized the parties' mutual right of cancellation upon thirty-day written notice. Alternatively, it argues that if the hotel had no right to cancel, the contract would be void as a matter of law because it lacked mutuality of obligation or consideration.

Our perusal of the record convinces us that there was sufficient evidence from which the jury could have found a contract for the reservation of fifty rooms at the Circus Circus Hotel from January 22 to April 29, 1976, that permitted Cardinal to cancel by thirty-day notice, oral or written, without according an equal right to Circo. Haas, O'Neill, and Valentine, Circo's national sales manager at the time the agreement was made, all testified that they had never discussed the hotel's reservation of a right to cancel the entire contract on thirty-day written notice. Although Larson, who replaced Valentine in the Circo hierarchy, claimed that the contract as written merely recited the terms discussed by the parties, the strong, negative response of Haas and O'Neill to the suggestion that they sign it supported a jury finding to the contrary.

Similarly, there was sufficient evidence to permit the jury to find that it was not the usual custom and practice in Las Vegas to allow for mutual rights of cancellation by either party upon thirty-day written notice. Although Circo introduced expert testimony that all Las Vegas contracts had such clauses, Cardinal's experts disagreed. Moreover, both Valentine and the director of travel at Minnesota AAA explained why tour operators need more cancellation flexibility than hotel operators.

Circo's argument that the contract lacked mutuality and, thus, was not binding on the parties has no merit. The concept of mutuality has been widely discredited in contract law, and it is now generally recognized that the obligations of the parties need not be substantially equal for there to be a binding contract. Moreover, "Minnesota has long recognized the principle that where a contract is supported by valuable consideration (such as a detriment incurred in exchange for a promise), . . . then a right of one party to terminate it at will does not render it invalid for lack of mutuality."

Although Circo takes the position that Cardinal's interpretation of the contract permitted it to cancel at will without limitation, Cardinal introduced evidence that it recognized and complied with the thirty-day cancellation period. Haas and O'Neill testified that they advised Valentine in October that the tours in early January might have to be cancelled, and that they in fact orally cancelled on December 10 and December 13, both of which were within the thirty-day cancellation period. Cardinal also maintained that by advertising its relation with Circus Circus, it not only acted to its detriment, but conferred a benefit upon Circo, both of which are sufficient to satisfy the consideration requirement. Thus, it was not improper for the court to reject the mutuality argument.

Circo next contends that Cardinal's claim for lost profits should have been dismissed because Cardinal was not an established business and could not prove its lost profits with the requisite degree of certainty to support recovery. It attacks the damage award on three grounds: (1) that Cardinal did not prove the fact of lost profits because it could show no past or future profitability; (2) that Cardinal did not prove causation because other factors, such as its undercapitalization and lack of advertising, more plausibly explained its failure; and (3) that Cardinal incorrectly calculated and inadequately documented the amount of lost profits.

The general rule in Minnesota is that damages in the form of lost profits may be recovered where they are shown to be the natural and probable consequences of the act or omission complained of and their amount is shown with a reasonable degree of certainty and exactness. This means that the nature of the business or venture upon which the anticipated profits are claimed must be such as to support an inference of definite profits grounded upon a reasonably sure basis of facts. . . . This rule does not call for absolute certainty.

The controlling principle is that speculative, remote, or conjectural damages are not recoverable. Our earlier cases held that lost profits of unestablished businesses were not recoverable because they were speculative, remote, or conjectural, and thus incapable of proof, but this is no longer the law in Minnesota. "Although the law recognizes that it is more difficult to prove loss of prospective profits to a new business than to an established one, the law does not hold that it may not be done."

The Nebraska Supreme Court noted in El Fredo Pizza, Inc., v. Roto-Flex Oven Co., 199 Neb. 697, 705, 706, 261 N.W.2d 358, 363–64 (1978), that the rule that lost profits from a business are too speculative and conjectural to permit the recovery of damages therefore ". . . is not a hard and fast one, and loss of prospective profits may nevertheless be recovered if the evidence shows with reasonable certainty *both* their *occurrence* and the *extent* thereof. . . . Uncertainty as to the *fact* of whether any damages were sustained at all is fatal to recovery, but uncertainty as to the *amount* is not. . . ."

The fact that a business is new is relevant only insofar as that fact affects the certainty of proof of lost profits; it does not establish as a matter of law that damages for lost profits may not be recovered.

While we have not yet addressed the issue of how a new business can prove its lost profits, other courts have suggested substitutes for past profitability that will remove a plaintiff's anticipated profits from the realm of speculation and support such a damage award. These substitutes include past performance as employee plus subsequent success; other examples of that type of business; and plaintiff's skill and expertise together with proven existence of a market for the product. What is important is that the loss be established with reasonable certainty, and this depends upon the circumstances of the particular case.

We agree with Circo that the evidence relating to lost profits that was presented by Cardinal lacks precision. Nevertheless, we cannot say that it was unreasonable for the jury to award lost profits to Cardinal, given the unusual circumstances of this particular enterprise and the devastating effect of Circo's breach.

Although Cardinal was able to demonstrate no past or future profitability, one of several substitutes was available in the evidence presented at trial. Haas and O'Neill were portrayed as persons with extensive experience in arranging tours who were also familiar with Las Vegas. They entered the OTC market early with packages that others, such as retail agencies or social clubs, would be selling for them. Moreover, the market they chose was a fertile one. Las Vegas was very popular with the people from the Upper Midwest, and the small cities on which they were concentrating offered an untapped source of tour participants. Temporally, they were planning to operate their tours during the peak tourist period, when 75 percent of the Midwest's tourists visit Las Vegas. This same market and time period have been extremely profitable for those travel agencies who began OTC packages the following year. Thus, the jury could have reasonably based its decision that Cardinal lost profits either on evidence of the skill and expertise of plaintiff's principals plus the proven existence of a market, or on evidence of profitability of OTC programs operated by other travel agencies in the same general geographic area at the same time of year.

Similarly, the evidence, although weak, supports the inference that were it not for the cancellation by Circo, Cardinal would have been able to fill all its flights except the first three. The jury could reasonably have based such a finding on the fact that Cardinal sold out the eight trips it actually ran, which could not have been accomplished but for the energy and skill of Haas and O'Neill, and the significant unmet demand for a travel service of this kind. That they were able to do so well on such short notice is persuasive to us, particularly because the substituted hotel, being new, lacked the appeal that the better known and advertised Circus Circus Hotel would have had for prospective customers. What is significant is that Cardinal had moved into a travel field that opened up as a result of a change in CAB regulations and had, by virtue of its contracts with North Central Airlines and Circo, placed itself in control of the essential elements of a successful enterprise. Thus, it was reasonable for the jury to determine that what doomed Cardinal's tour program was the change of management at Circus Circus and the cancellation of the fifty rooms. As the wrongdoer, Circo should not be permitted to evade its liability just because its wrongful cancellation involved a new business rather than an established one.

Moreover, Circo's suggestion that the cause of Cardinal's collapse was not its cancellation, but the low capitalization of the enterprise and the lack of advertising, is not compelled by the evidence. Cardinal does not appear to have been an enterprise that was dependent upon extensive personnel, capital, or advertising. Because travel agencies and clubs located in small, Upper Midwest communities comprised the "market" for its tours, and because there was a fairly high demand for economy trips of this kind, after making the initial flight and accommodation arrangements, O'Neill's and Haas's principal task was to contact the agencies that would make the availability of these trips known to their clients.

Moreover, although Cardinal's capital was limited, the business depended more on the character and personality of the entrepreneurs than on the amount available either for investment or advertising. It was their standing in the tour operator community that enabled them to obtain charter planes from North Central Airlines and to persuade Circo to reserve the fifty rooms more than six months in advance. If they were able to conclude these agreements with the principal suppliers of the travel and lodging services needed to make the 1976 season successful, their limited capital is determinative of nothing.

Circo also challenges the manner in which Cardinal attempted to prove its case. It contends that lost profits signify lost net profits that can only be determined if plaintiff introduces evidence of expenses saved as a result of nonperformance, and that the only way of showing expenses saved is through the use of expert financial evidence. These rules, however, have numerous exceptions. Thus, plaintiff may be awarded damages on the basis of its anticipated gross profits if the breach has not significantly reduced overhead, and expert testimony is not always required to prove lost profits, especially when the plaintiff is himself, as here, an expert in his field.

Here, Cardinal really had no saved expenses, because it attempted to mitigate its damages by running as many of its tours as it could using the Marina Hotel. Furthermore, once one accepts that the flights would have been full, it is relatively easy to calculate the profits. As the trial court explained in its memorandum denying defendant's posttrial motions, "although the plaintiff did not present its damages in a classical manner, all of the elements and factors as to the expenses and losses of the plaintiff were in fact submitted to the jury for their consideration."

Finally, Circo contends that the damage award was excessive and seeks either a reduction of the amount or a new trial on the issue of damages. The general rule in Minnesota, however, is that the trial court has broad discretion in determining whether defendant should get a new trial for excessive damages. "[T]he primary responsibility for the reduction of excessive damages lies in the trial court, and . . . a trial court's ruling on this point will only be disturbed where a clear abuse of discretion is demonstrated."

Of the total verdict of $71,500, $69,595 consisted of lost profits. The court was satisfied that this figure represented what Cardinal lost by not being able to run its tour package from January 22, 1976, until April 25, 1976, with its costs fixed as they were on January 5, 1976, when Circo wrongfully breached the contract. We do not believe it abused its discretion in so determining.

Ruling of the Court: Affirmed.

Should a party to a contract who believes the contract is harsh be held to the provisions of that contract? Almost invariably, yes. In some instances, if the obligation that the contract imposes upon a party is illegal or contrary to public policy, the courts will declare that portion of the contract null and void or unenforceable, thereby relieving the oppressed party from performance. However, the principle that agreements contrary to public policy are void will be applied with caution, and only in cases plainly within the reasons upon which that doctrine rests. The general rule is that competent persons shall have the utmost liberty in contracting, and that their voluntarily and fairly made agreements shall, if nor for illegal purposes or contrary to public policy, be held valid and will be enforced in the courts. Therefore, the impropriety injurious to the interests of society that will relieve parties from the obligations they have assumed must be clear and certain before the contract will be found void and unenforceable.

Contract Law in the Hotel Industry

There are two types of promises: social and business. The law does not provide a remedy for the breach of a social promise (for instance, a promise to play tennis) or for some business promises. For example, where coercion, fraud, and the like are employed, the requirement that a promise be made *voluntarily* is not satisfied. Let us examine contracts in the industry.

Contracting for a Room

A guest may contract for a room or rooms at a hotel in several ways. First, of course, one may be a walk-in guest. Such a guest cannot be refused a room unless the hotel is full (this is a positive defense on the part of the hotelkeeper) or for other reasons given in chapter 12. The second method is to call or write for a room. For this contract to be valid, the hotelkeeper must accept the offer. If it is accompanied by a deposit, the keeping of the deposit will constitute an acceptance. Generally, the hotel requires the guest to arrive by a stipulated time. If the guest does not arrive by the stipulated time, the contract ends, unless the room was prepaid or payment guaranteed.

A verbal contract is quite legal, although evidence is necessary to prove or disprove whatever is contended by either side. All the elements of a valid contract are found in a verbal contract: an offer, an acceptance, consideration, and capacity of the parties to contract. If these conditions are met, a verbal contract to rent a room is quite valid.

If at all possible, reservations for hotel and motel rooms should be made in writing, and the terms should be clear and specific to avoid misunderstanding. Most large hotels have specific offices that handle reservations. If a person requests in writing a specific number of days, a specific date, and the kind of accommodation needed, the problem is minimal. But if a guest requests such vague reservations as "one to three days or possibly a week," such ambiguity complicates the operation of a reservation office.

Many types of reservations are currently employed:

1 Guaranteed reservation: Payment for the room is promised even if the guest fails to arrive.

2 Prepaid reservation: Payment of the first day's charge is made by a guest to either a travel agency or through a computer network.

3 Confirmed reservation: The hotel has agreed, usually in writing, to the guest's reservation request.

4 Computerized reservation: Large hotel chains and some independent companies have their own reservation systems using WATS telephone lines and their own computers. Such reservations are immediately confirmed, usually by mail.

5 Blanket reservation: A block of rooms is held for a particular group, with individual members requesting assignments from that block.

6 Company-made reservation: A reservation is guaranteed by the guest's company.

7 Walk-in: A guest without a reservation requests and receives accommodations.

Not all hotels, motels, and inns overbook or cancel reservations. A sound hotel management technique and philosophy can minimize many reservations problems. However, computerized reservation systems that enable reservations to be handled quickly and efficiently are subject to error, sometimes selling rooms that do not exist. Even computer errors are the result of poor management—computers are programmed by people.

When there is a contract for a room, the desk clerk is often faced with a dilemma as to who is entitled to have access to the room in the absence of expressed instructions from the guest or company that contracted for the room. Does any member of the family of the person who rented the room have a right to get a key and enter? Does any employee of a company that contracts for a room have the right to enter it? Does a spouse have the right to enter into a room rented by the other spouse?

The following case deals with just such a situation. Would you have reacted as the desk clerk did in this instance, or would you have let the woman in? Right or wrong, the desk clerk's decision cost the hotel money in legal fees and resultant loss of goodwill. Assume the desk clerk made a different decision. Would there have been legal expenses just the same, and might the hotel have incurred greater loss? In this particular case, was being right the most important thing? Should a desk clerk bend the duty to accommodate someone and maybe save the hotel money for legal fees and embarrassment? After reading the case, try to think of other relationships between a guest and others that could present more compelling reasons to motivate a desk clerk in permitting entry.

Case	Campbell v. Womack
Example	*345 So.2d 96 (La., 1977)*
	(EDWARDS, Judge)

This suit was brought by Elvin Campbell and his wife for damages resulting from breach of contract and embarrassment, humiliation, and mental anguish sustained by Mrs. Campbell as a result of the defendants' refusal to admit Mrs. Campbell to her husband's motel room. The defendants' motion for summary judgment was granted, and the action was dismissed. From this dismissal, plaintiffs have appealed.

Plaintiff, Elvin Campbell, is engaged in the sand and gravel business.

Since the nature of his business often requires his absence from his home in St. Francisville, Mr. Campbell generally obtains temporary accommodations in the area in which he is working. For this purpose, Mr. Campbell rented a double room on a month-to-month basis at the Rodeway Inn in Morgan City, Louisiana. The room was registered in Mr. Campbell's name only.

From time to time, Mr. Campbell would share his room with certain of his employees; in fact, he obtained additional keys for the convenience of these employees. It also appears that Mr. Campbell was joined by his wife on some weekends and holidays, and that they jointly occupied his room on those occasions. However, Mrs. Campbell was not given a key to the motel room. On one such weekend, Mrs. Campbell, arriving while her husband was not at the motel, attempted to obtain the key to her husband's room from the desk clerk, Barbara Womack. This request was denied, since the desk clerk found that Mrs. Campbell was neither a registered guest for that room, nor had the registered guest, her husband, communicated to the motel management his authorization to release his room key to Mrs. Campbell. Plaintiffs allege that this refusal was in a loud, rude, and abusive manner. After a second request and refusal, Mrs. Campbell became distressed, left the Rodeway Inn, and obtained a room at another motel. Mr. Campbell later joined his wife at the other motel and allegedly spent the weekend consoling her. Shortly thereafter, suit was filed against the motel and the desk clerk, Barbara Womack.

Plaintiffs' main contention is that Mrs. Campbell was entitled to a key to her husband's room since she had acquired the status of a guest from her previous stays with her husband in the motel room. The leading pronouncement in Louisiana on the creation of a guest status is found in Moody v. Kenny, 153 La. 1007, 97 So. 21 (1923). There it is stated at page 22:

". . . a mere guest of the registered occupant of a room at a hotel, who shares such room with its occupant without the knowledge or consent of the hotel management, would not be a guest of the hotel, as there would be no contractual relations in such case between such third person and the hotel. . . ."

Plaintiffs would have us conclude from this statement that once the motel management gained knowledge on the previous occasions that Mrs. Campbell was sharing the motel room with the registered occupant, the motel was thereafter estopped to deny Mrs. Campbell the key to that room. The fallacy of this argument is apparent since under it, even a casual visitor to a hotel guest's room would be entitled to return at a later time and demand a key to the guest's room, so long as the hotel management had knowledge of the initial visit.

The motel clerk was under no duty to give Mrs. Campbell, a third party, the key to one of its guest's rooms. In fact, the motel had an affirmative duty, stemming from a guest's rights of privacy and peaceful possession, not to allow unregistered and unauthorized third parties to gain access to the rooms of its guest (LSA–C.C. Art. 2965–67). This duty is the same, regardless of whether we consider the contractual relationship one of lessor-lessee or motel-guest.

The additional fact that Mrs. Campbell offered proof of her identity and her marital relation with the room's registered occupant does not alter her third-party status; nor does it lessen the duty owed by the motel to its guest. The mere fact of marriage does not imply that the wife has full authorization from her husband at all times and as to all matters (LSA– C.C. Art. 2404). Besides, how could Mrs. Campbell prove to the motel's satisfaction that the then present marital situation was amicable? This information is not susceptible of ready proof.

Ruling of the Court: Having found that Mrs. Campbell was not entitled to demand a key to the motel room, and, further, that no authorization to admit her was communicated to the motel by her husband, there was no breach of contract.

The Courts and Overbooking

All tried cases of overbooking have focused on breach of contract. The underlying concept of each case is the confirmation of the guest's reservation. Several examples included here illustrate the problems of overbooking.

In Kellogg v. Commodore Hotel, 64 N.Y.S.2d 131 (1946), the plaintiff had received written confirmation of a room reservation; yet he was informed there were no accommodations available when he arrived in person. The plaintiff sought damages for breach of contract, citing injury to his nerves and depression. The court awarded him $5,000 instead of the requested $10,000, allowing no recovery for mental suffering.

Brown v. Hilton Hotels Corporation, 211 S.E.2d 125 (Ga., 1974), is similar. Again the plaintiff's prepaid, confirmed reservations were not honored. As they could find no other accommodations, they were forced to fly home. The stress and strain involved caused Mrs. Brown's heart condition to deteriorate, requiring hospitalization. The plaintiffs sought and received damages for breach of contract, but not for a tort arising out of a contract (as the tort did not result from negligence in the performance of the contract). The lower court decision was upheld by the appeals court.

There are few excuses for breach of contract between a guest and a hotel. The impossibility of performance—for example, when fire destroys the hotel—usually may be considered an excuse. But the courts are often reluctant to interfere because of the principle of freedom of contract.

The hotel contract, once made, is valid, and the guest may sue the hotelkeeper. *Dold v. Outrigger* is an example of what one hotelier did when travelers had made reservations that he could not fulfill. Not all hoteliers act as the Outrigger did, but one should always review one's reservation system to see if it is accomplishing management objectives and still satisfying the guests. The second case, *Freeman v. Kiamesha Concord, Inc.*, has to do with the reverse of the overbooking concept: The guest does not want to live up to the conditions of the contract or become a no-show.

Dold v. Outrigger Hotel
501 P.2d 368 (Ha., 1972)
(KOBAYASHI, Justice)

This is an appeal by the plaintiffs, Mr. and Mrs. D. F. Dold and Mr. and Mrs. Leo Manthei, from a judgment in their favor. Plaintiffs' amended complaint prayed for actual and punitive damages and alleged three counts for recovery, breach of contract, fraud, and breach of an innkeeper's duty to accommodate guests. (Count II for fraud was voluntarily dismissed at trial.) Though the judgment was favorable to them, the plaintiffs contend that the trial judge erred in not allowing an instruction on the issue of punitive damages. This is the issue before the court.

Facts   The plaintiffs, mainland residents, arranged for hotel accommodations from February 18 to February 23, 1968, through the American Express Company, the agent of the defendant, Outrigger Hotel, hereinafter referred to as "Outrigger." Hawaii Hotels Operating Company, Ltd., managed and operated the Outrigger. Both are Hawaii corporations.

Upon arrival at the Outrigger on February 18, 1968, the plaintiffs were refused accommodations and were transferred by the Outrigger to another hotel of lesser quality because the Outrigger lacked available space. On February 19 and 20, the plaintiffs again demanded that the defendants honor their reservations, but they were again refused.

Though the exact nature of the plaintiffs' reservations is in dispute, the defendants claim that since the plaintiffs made no cash deposit, their reservations were not "confirmed" and, for that reason, the defendants justifiably dishonored the reservations. Plaintiffs contend that the reservations were "confirmed," as the American Express Company had guaranteed to Outrigger a first night's payment in the event that the plaintiffs did not show up. Further, the plaintiffs claim that this guarantee was in fact the same thing as a cash deposit. Thus, plaintiffs argue that the defendants were under a duty to honor the confirmed reservations. Although the jury awarded $600 to the Dolds and $400 to the Mantheis, it is not known upon which count the recovery was based.

An examination of the record in the instant case shows the following:

1   It was the policy of the Outrigger that a reservation was deemed confirmed when either a one night's cash deposit was made, or the reservation was made by a booking agent that had established credit with the Outrigger.

2   The plaintiffs made their reservations through the American Express Company, which had established credit with the Outrigger.

3   In lieu of a cash deposit, the Outrigger accepted American Express Company's guarantee that it would pay the first night's deposit for the plaintiffs.

4   On February 18, 1968, the Outrigger referred twenty-nine parties holding reservations at the Outrigger to the Pagoda Hotel, which deemed these referrals "overflows."

5   On February 18, 1968, the Outrigger had sixteen guests who stayed beyond their scheduled date of departure.

6 From February 15 to 17 and 19 to 22, 1968, the Outrigger also had more reservations than it could accommodate. Plaintiffs' exhibits nos. 23 to 29 indicate the number of overflows and referrals of the above-mentioned reservations made by the Outrigger to the Pagoda Hotel on the following dates:

February 15	20 referrals
" 16	20 "
" 17	32 "
" 19	44 "
" 20	9 "
" 21	9 "
" 22	20 "

7 Evidence was adduced that the Outrigger made a profit from its referrals to the Pagoda Hotel. Upon advance payment for the rooms to American Express, who in turn paid Outrigger, the plaintiffs were issued coupons representing the prepayment for the accommodations at the Outrigger. On referral by the Outrigger, the Pagoda Hotel's practice was to accept the coupons and bill the Outrigger for the actual cost of the rooms provided. The difference between the coupon's value and the actual value of the accommodations was retained by the Outrigger.

The plaintiffs prevented a profit from being made by the Outrigger by refusing to use the coupons and paying in cash for the less expensive accommodations.

May Plaintiffs Recover Punitive Damages for Breach of Contract?   The question of whether punitive damages are properly recoverable in an action for breach of contract has not been resolved in this jurisdiction.

In the instant case, on the evidence adduced, the trial court refused to allow an instruction on the issue of punitive damages, but permitted an instruction on the issue of emotional distress and disappointment.

In a case involving a similar pattern of overbooking of reservations, the court in Wills v. Trans World Airlines, Inc., 200 F.Supp. 360 (S.D. Cal., 1961), stated that the substantial overselling of confirmed reservations for the period in question was a strong indication that the defendant airline had wantonly precipitated the very circumstances that compelled the removal of excess confirmed passengers from its flights.

In Goo v. Continental Casualty Company, 52 Haw. 235, 473 P.2d 563 (1970), we affirmed the public policy considerations behind the doctrine of punitive damages and acknowledged the fact that some jurisdictions allow a recovery of punitive damages where the breach of contract is accompanied by some type of contemporaneous tortious activity. However, the Goo case did not afford the proper factual setting for this court to consider the propriety of an assessment of punitive damages in contract actions.

Various jurisdictions have adopted their own rules regarding the nature of the tortious activity necessary to recover punitive damages in a contract action. Some require that the breach be accompanied by an independent willful tort, or by a fraudulent act, or by a concurrent breach of a common law duty.

We are of the opinion that the facts of this case do not warrant punitive damages. However, the plaintiffs are not limited to the narrow traditional contractual remedy of out-of-pocket losses alone. We have recognized the fact that certain situations are so disposed as to present a fusion of the doctrines of tort and contract (Goo, 52 Haw. at 241, 473 P.2d at 567). Though some courts have strained the traditional concept of compensatory damages in contract to include damages for emotional distress and disappointment (Kellogg v. Commodore Hotel, 187 Misc. 319, 64 N.Y.S.2d 131 [1946]), we are of the opinion that where a contract is breached in a wanton or reckless manner as to result in a tortious injury, the aggrieved person is entitled to recover in tort. Thus, in addition to damages for out-of-pocket losses, the jury was properly instructed on the issue of damages for emotional distress and disappointment.

May Plaintiffs Recover Punitive Damages for Breach of an Innkeeper's Duty to Accommodate?   We now consider count III of plaintiffs' complaint. It has long been recognized that an innkeeper, holding himself out to the public to provide hotel accommodations, is obligated, in the absence of reasonable grounds for refusal, to provide accommodations to all persons upon proper request. This duty traditionally extended to the traveler who presented himself at the inn. However, where the innkeeper's accommodations had been exhausted, the innkeeper could justly refuse to receive an applicant. It is well recognized that punitive damages are recoverable for breach of an innkeeper's duty to his guest where the innkeeper's conduct is deliberate or wanton.

We are not aware of any jurisdiction that renders an innkeeper liable on his common law duty to accommodate under the circumstances of this case. Consequently, plaintiffs are not entitled to an instruction on punitive damages on count III of their complaint.

Ruling of the Court: Judgment affirmed.

Case Example	**Freeman v. Kiamesha Concord, Inc.** *351 N.Y.S.2d 541 (1974)* *(SHANLEY N. EGETH, Judge)*

Determination of the issues in this Small Claims Part case requires a present construction of the meaning of language contained in Section 206 of the General Business Law as it applies to current widespread and commonplace practices and usages in the hotel and resort industry. Although the pertinent statutory provision has essentially been in effect since its original enactment ninety years ago (L.1883, ch. 227 § 3), there appears to be no reported decision that directly construes or interprets its meaning and applicability.

The relevant portion of Section 206 reads as follows:

". . . no charge or sum shall be collected or received by any . . . hotelkeeper or innkeeper for any service not actually rendered or for a longer time than the person so charged actually remained at such hotel or inn . . . provided such guest shall have given such hotelkeeper or innkeeper notice at the office of his departure. For any violation of this section, the offender shall forfeit to the injured party three times the amount so charged and shall not be entitled to receive any money for meals, services, or time charged."

Is a resort hotel that contracts with a guest for a minimum weekend or other fixed minimum period stay in violation of Section 206, General

Business Law, and subject to the liability provided therein, if it insists upon full payment from a guest who checks out prior to the expiration of the contract period?

Plaintiff, a lawyer, has commenced this action against the defendant, the operator of the Concord Hotel (Concord), one of the more opulent of the resort hotels in the Catskill Mountains resort area, to recover the sum of $424.00. Plaintiff seeks the return of charges paid at the rate of $84.80 per day for two days spent at the hotel ($169.60), plus three times said daily rate ($254.40) for a day charged and not refunded after he and his wife checked out before the commencement of the third day of a reserved three-day Memorial Day weekend. Plaintiff asserts that he is entitled to this sum pursuant to the provisions of Section 206, General Business Law.

The testimony adduced at trial reveals that in early May, 1973, after seeing an advertisement in the *New York Times* indicating that Joel Gray would perform at the [Concord] during the forthcoming Memorial Day weekend, plaintiff contacted a travel agent and solicited a reservation for his wife and himself at the hotel. In response, he received an offer of a reservation for a ''three-night minimum stay'' that contained a request for a $20.00 deposit. He forwarded the money confirming the reservation, which was deposited by the defendant.

While driving to the hotel, the plaintiff observed a billboard, located about twenty miles from his destination, that indicated that Joel Gray would perform at the Concord only on the Sunday of the holiday weekend. The plaintiff was disturbed because he had understood the advertisement to mean that the entertainer would be performing on each day of the weekend. He checked into the hotel, notwithstanding this disconcerting information, claiming that he did not wish to turn back and ruin a long-anticipated weekend vacation. The plaintiff later discovered that two subsequent *New York Times* advertisements, not seen by him before checking in, specified that Gray would perform on the Sunday of that weekend.

After staying at the hotel for two days, the plaintiff advised the management that he wished to check out because of his dissatisfaction with the entertainment. He claims to have told them that he had made his reservation in reliance upon what he understood to be a representation in the advertisement to the effect that Joel Gray would perform throughout the holiday weekend. The management suggested that since Gray was to perform that evening, he should remain. The plaintiff refused and again asserted his claim that the advertisement constituted a misrepresentation. The defendant insisted upon full payment for the entire three-day guaranteed weekend in accordance with the reservation. Plaintiff then told the defendant's employees that he was an attorney, and that they had no right to charge him for the third day of the reserved period if he checked out. He referred them to the text of Section 206, General Business Law, which he had obviously read in his room where it was posted on the door, along with certain other statutory provisions and the schedule of rates and charges. The plaintiff was finally offered a one-day credit for a future stay if he made full payment. He refused, paid the full charges under protest, and advised the defendant of his intention to sue them for treble damages. This is that action.

I find that the advertisement relied upon by the plaintiff did not contain a false representation. It announced that Joel Gray would perform at the hotel during the Memorial Day weekend. Gray did actually appear during that weekend. The dubious nature of the plaintiff's claim is demonstrated by the fact that when he checked in at the hotel, he had been made aware of the date of Gray's performance and remained at the hotel for two days and then checked out prior to the performance that he had allegedly travelled to see.

The advertisement contained no false statement. It neither represented nor suggested that Gray would perform throughout the holiday weekend. The defendant cannot be found liable because the plaintiff misunderstood its advertisement.

We now reach plaintiff's primary contention. Simply put, plaintiff asserts that by requiring him to pay the daily rate for the third day of the holiday weekend (even though he had given notice of his intention to leave and did not remain for that day), the defendant violated the provisions of Section 206, General Business Law, and thereby became liable for the moneys recoverable thereunder. Plaintiff contends that the language of the statute is clear, and that under its terms, he is entitled to the relief sought, irrespective of whether he had a fixed weekend, week, or monthly reservation, or even if the hotel services were available to him.

It must be noted at the outset that the plaintiff checked into the defendant's hotel pursuant to a valid, enforceable contract for a three-day stay. The solicitation of a reservation, the making of a reservation by the transmittal of a deposit, and the acceptance of the deposit constituted a binding contract in accordance with traditional contract principles of offer and acceptance. Unquestionably the defendant would have been liable to the plaintiff had it not had an accommodation for plaintiff upon his arrival. The plaintiff is equally bound under the contract for the agreed minimum period.

The testimony reveals that the defendant was ready, willing, and able to provide all of the services contracted for, but that plaintiff refused to accept them for the third day of the three-day contract period. These services included lodging, meals, and the use of the defendant's recreational and entertainment facilities. In essence, plaintiff maintains that under the terms of the statute, his refusal, for any reason, to accept or utilize these facilities for part of the contract period precludes the defendant from charging him the contract price.

Section 206 is silent as to its applicability to circumstances that constitute a breach of contract or a conscious refusal to accept offered services. This is one of those instances in which, upon analysis, a statute that appears to be clear and unambiguous is sought to be applied to a situation not envisioned by its framers. Nothing contained in the statute provides assistance in answering the question presented in this case; that is, may a resort hotel hold a guest to his contract for a stay of fixed duration when that guest has, without cause, breached his contract?

There is no legislative history available to assist in determining the intention of the legislature, nor are there any reported decisions construing the statute that can be of assistance in this regard. Recourse must therefore be had to general principles of statutory construction. . . .

Hotels such as the one operated by the defendant have developed techniques to provide full utilization of their facilities during periods of peak demand. One such method is the guaranteed minimum one week or weekend stay that has gained widespread public acceptance. Almost all of these enterprises have offered their facilities for minimum guaranteed periods during certain times of the year by contracting with willing guests who also seek to fully utilize their available vacation time. These minimum period agreements have become essential to the economic survival and well-being of the recreational hotel industry. The public is generally aware of the necessity for them to do so and accepts the practice. . . .

A hotel such as the defendant's services thousands of guests at a single time. The maintenance of its facilities entails a continuing large overhead expenditure. It must have some means to legitimately ensure itself the income that its guests have contracted to pay for the use of its facilities. The minimum period reservation contract is such a device. The rooms are contracted for in advance and are held available while other potential guests are turned away. A guest who terminates his contractual obligations prior to the expiration of the contract period will usually deprive the hotel of anticipated income if that guest cannot be held financially accountable upon his contract. At that point, replacement income is virtually impossible. Indeed, on occasion, some hotels contract out their entire facilities to members of a single group for a stipulated period many months in advance. No great imagination is required to comprehend the economic catastrophe that would ensue if all such guests were to cancel at the last minute, or to check out prior to the end of their contract period, without continuing contractual liability. I cannot believe that the public policy of the state sanctions such contractual obliteration.

The construction sought by the plaintiff could result in other consequences that are equally bizarre. The defendant has contracted to supply the plaintiff with a room, three meals a day, and access to the use of its varied sports, recreational, or entertainment facilities. As long as these are available to the plaintiff, the defendant has fulfilled its contractual commitment. If the plaintiff's construction of the statute is tenable, he might also argue with equal force that unless a guest receives an appropriate rebate or adjustment of bill, the defendant would incur statutory liability if such guest visited a friend in the vicinity, slept over, and failed to use his room for one or more nights of his contracted stay; became enmeshed in an all-night game of cards and failed to use his room; was dieting and failed to avail himself of all the offered meals; did not play tennis, golf, or swim, or became sick and made no use of the available recreational or entertainment facilities.

I conclude that plaintiff may not recover because he has not proved a cause of action based upon a violation of Section 206 of the General Business Law. The evidence does not prove the existence of the type of wrong for which redress was provided in the 1883 enactment. The statute was not intended to prevent a hotel from insisting that its guests comply with the terms of a contract for a fixed minimum stay. There can be no statutory violation by a hotel that fulfills its part of the contract by making its services and facilities available to a guest who refuses to accept them. Such act of refusal by the guest does not justify imposition of the penalties set forth in the statute.

Ruling of the Court: Judgment is accordingly awarded to the defendant with costs.

Damages to Be Recovered

Most cases of overbooking that deal with breach of a valid contract never go to court because lawsuits are expensive, especially when the damages are not consequential. Generally, the damages the guest may recover for breach of contract have been limited to actual damages or compensatory damages. In essence, this is the actual and real loss, as opposed to nominal damages on the one hand, and "exemplary" or "punitive" damages on the other. Punitive damages redress a wrong committed by the hotelkeeper, either because of intentional infliction of injury to feelings and reputation or because of emotional distress and disappointment.

If an aggrieved person can also sue for torts, the recovery would be for emotional distress and disappointment, as in *Dold* v. *Outrigger Hotel,* described earlier in the chapter. In a few cases, guests have received large settlements for breach of contract by the hotelkeeper. For example, Judge Kadela and his family of Dearborn, Michigan, had confirmed reservations at the Statler Hilton in New York City that were not honored. The Kadelas staged a twenty-four-hour sit-in in the private dining room of the hotel to enforce the "reservation contract." Later Judge Kadela sued the Hilton Hotel Corporation for $3 million, charging that his children were subjected to insecurity and harassment. The case was settled later for a fraction of the demanded damages, probably as a nuisance case. The significance of this case is that adverse publicity may be very costly to the hotel.

Undeniably, overbooking has long been practiced by hotels; perhaps figures closer to the actual occupancy rate should be set by the industry. To continue such mistreatment of the public may be to invite governmental intervention, as in airline overbooking.

Overbooking and Air Travel

In Wills v. Trans World Airlines, Inc., 200 F.Supp. 360 (1961), a federal court awarded $5,000 exemplary damages (when actual damages only amounted to $1.54) to a passenger who was bumped from a flight. The federal court is not bound by state law and thus may award punitive damages under the Civil Aeronautics Act of 1938 and as amended in 1958.

In 1973 Ralph Nader was bumped from an Allegheny Airline flight (Nader v. Allegheny Airlines, Inc., 365 F.Supp. 128 [1973]; reversed 512 F.2d 527; cert. granted 96 S.C. 355). In that case, the airline confirmed reservations for Nader and then overbooked the flight. The court ruled that the airline had deliberately oversold seats, thus causing Nader to miss a scheduled public rally.

As in *Wills,* a federal statute was involved. According to the court, the defendant knowingly and intentionally misrepresented a material fact: that Nader had a guaranteed reservation for a seat on which he and others had relied, and the airline intentionally did not inform the public of its practice of overbooking and the attendant risks. The actions were considered wanton and done with malice.

Nader was awarded $10 compensatory damages and $25,000 punitive damages; in addition, the court awarded the Connecticut Citizens' Action Group (before whom Nader was to speak) $51 in nominal damages and $25,000 in punitive damages. The court stated that it was conceivable the defendant's intentional misrepresentation had damaged the Connecticut plaintiffs' fund-raising efforts because of the absence of Nader.

In March 1977, the Civil Aeronautics Board ordered airlines to post warnings on ticket counters that passengers may be bumped from confirmed reservations as airlines deliberately sell more tickets than there are seats available. The warning must also state that bumped passengers may collect on-the-spot cash compensation for resulting delays. A notice to this effect must also be included in all ticket envelopes sold in the United States. Such warnings have been contained in tariff books for some time; for this reason, some airlines objected to the need for public notices. The CAB, however, deemed it unrealistic to expect passengers to read tariff documents. It also dictated the exact wording of the warning. Depending on the cost of the original ticket, bumped passengers can collect up to $200 and keep and use their ticket if the airline cannot get them to their domestic destination within two hours of their original arrival time, or to their foreign destination within four hours.

Guest Cancellation

When a guest who makes a deposit cancels the reservation in ample time to rerent the room, the deposit may be returned immediately—with or without a deduction to cover the expense of rerenting the room—or the hotel may claim compensation for breach of contract. In that event, the deposit is retained and set off against the total cost of the room. In any case, the guest cannot demand the return of the deposit in full it if is small. The action taken by the hotel depends on the circumstances and its philosophy.

The case *2625 Building Corporation (Marott Hotel) v. Deutsch* shows how the plaintiff Deutsch was able to recover his advance payment because he timely cancelled his contract for rooms, and whereas the defendant hotel could not show that it was financially damaged by the cancellation. The Freeman case is one end of the spectrum and the Marott Hotel case is at the other end.

Case   **2625 Building Corporation (Marott Hotel) v. Deutsch**
Example   *385 N.E.2d 1189 (Ind., 1979)*
              (MILLER, Judge)

This is an appeal by the defendant, 2625 Building Corporation, doing business as The Marott Hotel (Marott), from a judgment for the plaintiff (Deutsch) granting recovery of his advance payment for hotel rooms that were reserved for the 1973 Indianapolis "500" Mile Race weekend, but were not used.

A summary of the facts shows that on December 7, 1972, Deutsch, a resident of Connecticut, made reservations by telephone for six rooms at the Marott for the 1973 "500" Mile Race weekend (May 27, 28, 29). Marott requested advance payment for the rooms. Deutsch complied with Marott's demand and paid by check in the amount of $1,008.00 in full for the reserved rooms. At the end of March, or the beginning of April, 1973, Deutsch, by telephone, cancelled the reservations and requested the return of his advance payment. Marott refused his demand. Deutsch did not use the rooms and later brought action against Marott to recover the $1,008.00 advance payment, alleging the above facts and, in addition, that Marott had relet the rooms and was not harmed by the cancellation.

At trial before the court, after Deutsch presented his evidence and rested, Marott moved for dismissal on the ground that Deutsch had failed to present evidence in support of his allegation that Marott had relet the rooms and was not harmed and, therefore, had failed to establish a *prima facie* case. The judge took the motion under advisement, reserving his ruling until the conclusion of all the evidence. Marott presented no evidence and rested. The judge then took the entire matter under advisement and, about thirty days later, entered the following judgment in favor of Deutsch and against Marott:

"This cause having been taken under advisement at the close of the plaintiff's evidence; the defendant having made a motion for involuntary dismissal, which the court took under advisement; and the defendant then resting its case without the presentation of evidence; and the court, now being duly advised, finds as follows:

"The court deems the plaintiff's complaint amended to conform to the evidence. The contract between the parties was an oral special contract that was cancelled by the plaintiff before the date to be performed by the defendant. Therefore, it is in the nature of an executory contract that was never performed. The plaintiff is, therefore, entitled to the recovery of his deposit less any actual damages suffered by the defendant. (The defendant having failed to show any actual damages, the plaintiff is entitled to recover the entire deposit.) To allow the defendant to retain the entire amount would constitute a penalty that the law abhors and would unjustly enrich the defendant. The plaintiff has failed to prove the date of the original demand for return of the deposit and, therefore, interest will be allowed from the filing of this lawsuit, which also constitutes a demand.

"It is therefore ordered, adjudged, and decreed that the plaintiff recover from the defendant the sum of one thousand and eight dollars ($1,008.00), with interest at 8 percent from January 3, 1974. It is further ordered that the defendant's motion for involuntary dismissal be and is hereby overruled. Costs of this action are assessed against the defendant."

On appeal, Marott argues that the decision of the trial court was not sustained by sufficient evidence, that the decision of the trial court was contrary to law in that the court found the contract between the parties to be an executory contract and to contain a provision for a penalty upon cancellation, and that the trial court abused its discretion in deeming Deutsch's complaint amended to conform to the evidence without a request from Deutsch and without any indication of the court's intention to do so before he entered judgment.

Initially we examine Marott's contention that the court erred in finding the room reservation to be an oral special contract that was executory in nature and that contained a provision for a penalty upon cancellation. In absence, Marott argues that the contract was fully executed at the time Deutsch tendered his advance payment for the reservations, and, thereafter, it was obligated to hold the rooms open and available for Deutsch on the dates reserved. Hence, Marott argues it was not required to refund Deutsch's advance payment when the reservations were cancelled.

An executory contract is defined in 17 Am.Jur.2d, Contracts, Section 6, p. 341, as follows:

"An executory contract is one in which a party binds himself to do or not to do a particular thing, whereas an executed contract is one in which the object of the agreement is performed and everything that was to be done is done. The distinction would seem to relate to the legal effect of a contract at two different stages. An executory contract, it is said, conveys a chose in action, while an executed contract conveys a chose in possession."

Contrary to Marott's contention, the contract was not fully executed at the time the reservations were cancelled. Under the facts of this case, the contract was executory in nature, part of which had been executed when Deutsch cancelled his reservations. That is to say, the portion of the contract pertaining to Deutsch's tender of payment in full and Marott's acceptance of said payment was an executed portion of the contract, and the obligation of Marott to provide its facilities for Deutsch's use remained executory until Deutsch's cancellation. Marott's further contention that it was obligated to keep the rooms available for Deutsch after he cancelled his reservations is also without merit. Deutsch's repudiation of the contract was an anticipatory breach thereof that relieved Marott from its future obligations and enabled it, if it desired, to sue at that time for damages caused by such breach.

We next examine Marott's claim that the evidence did not support the trial court's conclusion that full payment for the rooms constituted a penalty. The general nature of an agreement for hotel reservations was recently defined in Freeman v. Kiamesha Concord, Inc., 76 Misc.2d 915, 351 N.Y.S.2d 541 (1974), as follows:

"The solicitation of a reservation, the making of a reservation by the transmittal of a deposit, and the acceptance of the deposit constituted a binding contract in accordance with traditional contract principles of offer and acceptance."

The Marott cites this decision in support of its proposition that it had a right to refuse to refund $1,008.00 to Deutsch when he cancelled his reservations. However, we find the facts in the case at hand to be clearly distinguishable. In Freeman the guest had checked into the hotel pursuant to the contract, whereas in this case Deutsch had not. Moreover, Freeman involved a "last minute" checkout prior to the end of the contract period, whereas Deutsch gave the Marott approximately two months' advance notice of his cancellation.

We do not disagree with the reasoning in Freeman as applied to the facts therein, and such reasoning is certainly applicable in "last minute" cancellation cases, especially at resort-type hotels. Thus, we recognize there may be instances when a guest's cancellation of reservations would not justify a refund of an advance payment. As noted previously, the making and acceptance of the reservation in this case constituted a binding contract. Upon Deutsch's breach, Marott was entitled to *actual damages* in accordance with traditional contract principles. However, we agree with the trial court that to allow Marott to retain damages representing payment for use of all the rooms, regardless of the fact that damages could be ascertained, would be to enforce a penalty or forfeiture. To hold otherwise under the facts and circumstances of this case would be inconsistent "with the principles of fairness and justice under the law" as set down in Skendzel v. Marshall, 261 Ind. 226, 301 N.E.2d 641 (1973), in which our Supreme Court stated:

"Forfeitures are generally disfavored by the law. In fact, '. . . [e]quity abhors forfeitures and, beyond any question, has jurisdiction that it will exercise in a proper case to grant relief against their enforcement.' This jurisdiction of equity to intercede is predicated upon the fact that 'the loss or injury occasioned by the default must be susceptible of exact compensation.' "

The evidence in the record reveals that Deutsch made reservations, tendered full payment for the use of the rooms in advance, and approximately two months prior to Marott's time for performance, cancelled the reservations and demanded refund, which demand was refused. In addition, we take judicial notice that the Indianapolis "500" Mile Race has the largest attendance of any single, one-day, arena-type sporting event in the world. The influx of dedicated racing fans to the Indianapolis metropolitan area in order to witness this spectacle of racing is legend. Attendant with this influx is the overwhelming demand for, and shortage of, hotel accommodations.

Therefore, we find that the facts of this case justified the trial court's conclusion that assessing Deutsch for the full amount of his room payments would cause him to suffer a loss that was wholly disproportionate to any injury sustained by Marott. Since there was no evidence that Marott sustained any damage, we cannot say, as a matter of law, that the trial court erred in allowing Deutsch full refund of his money.

Ruling of the Court: Judgment affirmed.

Contracts of Spouses and Minors

A question often arises about the validity of contracts entered into by spouses and minors. A spouse can enter into a contract individually (for example, for hotel accommodations) or as an agent for the other spouse. If, for example, a married woman fails to pay the account, she can be sued for the debt and made to pay from her own funds. If her husband is to be sued for the debt, it is necessary to prove that she had his authority to incur the debt, which is difficult in most cases. As a matter of fact, the husband may escape liability by proving that he had forbidden her to pledge his credit or that her funds were inadequate.

In law, minors cannot be held liable on contracts made by them, except for "necessaries" and if the services supplied were for their benefit. Minors may be acting as agent for their parents when furnished these necessaries; in such cases, the parents could be sued as principals for an unpaid account, but parents are not otherwise liable. Under common law, minors must be accepted as guests.

Contract Limitations and Warranties

When guests make a contract with a hotel, the rule of *caveat emptor* ("let the buyer beware") generally applies. However, guests can make certain assumptions. First, they can assume that the room is fit for habitation. Second, in most states there is an implied warranty that the food is fit for human consumption. The hotel must not misrepresent or overstate the nature of what it offers, though some exaggeration in advertisements cannot be considered actionable.

When guests have relied on statements of a hotel that turn out to be incorrect in some important respects, they may be entitled to repudiate the contract (for example, in the location of the room). The size, furnishings, or cleanliness of a room can become valid issues in cancelling a contract. Whatever a guest's complaints may be, their influence on the contract must be determined by the facts of the case.

Criminal Penalties: Misdemeanors

Various states have enacted criminal penalties prohibiting hotelkeepers from breaching their common law duty. If they commit such a breach, they are guilty of a *misdemeanor* and, in theory, criminal penalties can be applied. California and New York have such statutes, and Massachusetts law has a penalty for refusing guests: "An innholder who, upon request, refuses to receive and make suitable provision for a stranger or traveler shall be punished by a fine of not more than fifty dollars," (Chapter 140, § 7 of the General Laws of Massachusetts).

Jurisdiction

The traveling public that encounters a problem on a trip (injury or loss of goods, for example) does not always have to bring suit in the state or country where the problem occurred. It is possible, under certain conditions, to have the cause of action tried in one's home state. If certain conditions are met, a case can be tried in the federal courts of the guest's state. To sue in federal court, certain requisites must be met. One of the parties must come from a different state than the other, and damages must be reasonably accumulated to be over $10,000. The jurisdictional problem is not easy to determine. The question is whether one can get personal service—that is, direct hand-to-hand delivery of a summons—on the other party or his agent for service of process in one's own state.

The case of *Frummer v. Hilton Hotels International, Inc.*, clearly demonstrates a jurisdictional problem. If the plaintiff could not have gotten service in New York on Hilton, his only chance to win would be to have the trial of the case in England. It becomes apparent that jurisdiction is important to the hotel, and particularly to the traveler-guest.

Case Example

FRUMMER v. HILTON HOTELS INTERNATIONAL, INC.
281 N.Y.S.2d 41 (1967)
(FULD, Chief Judge)

This appeal calls upon us to determine whether jurisdiction was validly acquired over one of the defendants, Hilton Hotels (U.K.) Ltd., a British corporation (hereafter referred to as Hilton [U.K.]).

The plaintiff alleges that in 1963, when he was on a visit to England, he fell and was injured in his room at the London Hilton Hotel while attempting to take a shower in an "ovular," modernistic-type bathtub. He seeks $150,000 in damages, not only from the defendant Hilton (U.K.), but also from the defendants Hilton Hotels Corporation and Hilton Hotels International, both of which are Delaware corporations doing business in New York. The defendant Hilton (U.K.), which is the lessee and operator of the London Hilton Hotel, has moved (pursuant to CPLR 3211, subd. [a], par. 8) for an order dismissing the complaint against it on the ground that the court lacks jurisdiction of the defendant's person.

Both parties argue that "the applicable statute" is CPLR 302 (subd. [a], par. 1) that authorizes our courts to exercise personal jurisdiction over a foreign corporation if it "transacts any business within the state" and the cause of action asserted against it is one "arising from" the transaction of such business. However, the plaintiff does not allege that he had any dealings at all with the British corporate defendant or its agents in this state. Therefore, it may not be said that his cause of action *arose* from the British corporation's transaction of any business here, and he is not entitled to avail himself of CPLR 302 (subd. [a], par. 1) in order to bring the defendant within the jurisdiction of our courts.

Jurisdiction was, however, properly acquired over Hilton (U.K.) because the record discloses that it was "doing business" here in the *traditional* sense. As we have frequently observed, a foreign corporation is amenable to suit in our courts if it is "engaged in such a continuous and systematic course of 'doing business' here as to warrant a finding of its 'presence' in this jurisdiction." In International Shoe Co. v. State of Washington, 326 U.S. 310, 315, 66 S.Ct. 154, 158, due process requirements are satisfied if the defendant foreign corporation has "certain minimum contacts with [the state] such that the maintenance of the suit does not offend 'traditional notions of fair play and substantial justice.' "

In Bryant v. Finnish Nat. Airline, 260 N.Y.S.2d 625, the court declared that the "test for 'doing business' . . . should be a simple, pragmatic one," and, applying that test, went on to hold that the requisite minimum contacts with New York were made out when it appears that the defendant foreign corporation, an airline, "has a lease on a New York office, . . . employs several people, and . . . has a bank account here, . . . does public relations and publicity work for defendant here, including maintaining contacts with other airlines and travel agencies, . . . transmits requests for space to defendant in Europe, and helps to generate business."

In the case before us, these same services are provided for the defendant Hilton (U.K.) by the Hilton Reservation Service that has a New York office, as well as a New York bank account and telephone number. The Service advertises that it was "established to provide the closest possible liaison with travel agents across the country," that lodging "rates for certified wholesalers and/or tour operators [could] be obtained [from the service] on request," and that it could "confirm availabilities immediately . . . and without charge" at any Hilton hotel, including the London Hilton. Thus, it does "public relations and publicity work" for the defendant Hilton (U.K.), including "maintaining contacts with . . . travel agents" and tour directors; and it most certainly "helps to generate business" here for the London Hilton—which, indeed, was the very purpose for which it was established.

Moreover, unlike the *Bryant* case, where the defendant's New York office did not make reservations or sell tickets, the Hilton Reservation Service both accepts and confirms room reservations at the London Hilton. In short—and this is the significant and pivotal factor—the Service does all the business that Hilton (U.K.) could do were it here by its own officials.

The defendant's reliance on Miller v. Surf Properties, 176 N.Y.S.2d 318, is misplaced. In that case, we held that the activities of a "travel agency" were not sufficient to give our courts *in personam* jurisdiction over a Florida hotel when the agency's services "amounted to little more than rendering telephone service and mailing brochures" for the hotel and thirty other independent and unassociated Florida establishments. Indeed, in *Bryant*, we found it significant that in the *Miller* case, the New York activities were carried on "not [by] an employee of the defendant [Florida hotel], but [by] an independent travel agency representing defendant in New York City." Although, in the case before us, the Hilton Reservation Service is not the "employee" of Hilton (U.K.), the Service and that defendant are owned in common by the other defendants, and the Service is concededly run on a "nonprofit" basis for the benefit of the London Hilton and other Hilton hotels.

It is to be borne in mind, contrary to certain intimations in the dissenting opinion, that this appeal deals with the jurisdiction of our courts over a foreign corporation, rather than the liability of a parent company for the acts of a wholly owned subsidiary. The "presence" of Hilton (U.K.) in New York, for purposes of jurisdiction, is established by the activities conducted here on its behalf by its agent, the Hilton Reservation Service, and the fact that the two are commonly owned is significant only because it gives rise to a valid inference as to the broad scope of the agency in the absence of an express agency agreement.

We are not unmindful that litigation in a foreign jurisdiction is a burdensome inconvenience for any company. However, it is part of the price that may properly be demanded of those who extensively engage in international trade. When their activities abroad, either directly or through an agent, become as widespread and energetic as the activities in New York conducted by Hilton (U.K.), they receive considerable benefits from such foreign business and may not be heard to complain about the burdens.

Since, then, Hilton (U.K.) was "doing business" in New York in the traditional sense and was validly served with process in London, as provided by statute (CPLR 313), our courts acquired "personal jurisdiction over the corporation for any cause of action asserted against it, no matter where the events occurred that give rise to the cause of action."

Ruling of the Court: The order of the appellate division should be affirmed, with costs, and the certified question answered in the affirmative.

Rights of Guests in the Hotel Industry

Right of Guests to Privacy and Protection against Insults

Though the use of insulting and abusive language has been universally recognized as being morally reprehensible, the courts have been slow to regard it as a basis of civil liability. Law text writers, on the other hand, have consistently advocated the recognition of intentional infliction of mental suffering as an independent tort, whether caused by words or by acts (15 A.L.R.2d 112). Many jurisdictions do not recognize abusive language as amounting to a tort, but the courts have allowed recovery in cases where an innkeeper and guest were involved.

DeWolf v. Ford, 86 N.E. 527 (N.Y., 1908), was one of the earliest cases in point. Here the court said that "one of the things that a guest for hire at a public inn has the right to insist upon is respectful and decent treatment at the hands of the innkeeper and his servant, that it is an essential part of the contract, whether express or implied."

When the hotelkeeper intrudes upon the privacy of a guest, the results can be costly for the hotelkeeper. In the case of Emmke v. DeSilva, 293 F.17 (1923), in which the innkeeper accused a husband and wife of being unmarried and ordered them out of his hotel, he trespassed in entering their room and was liable for the humiliation his conduct caused. Nowhere in its opinion did the court indicate that the results would have been different if the defendant had stood outside the room and shouted his insults through the transom. Indeed, any such distinction would have been quite preposterous.

Furthermore, it is far from clear that the mere entry into a room, apart from the attendant indignities, would have been the basis of an action of trespass for nominal damages. The court based its decision on a much broader ground—that is, that the innkeeper, carrying on a business of a public nature, is by law expected to extend to his guests "respectful and decent treatment," and to refrain from conduct that would interfere with their comfort or humiliate and distress them. In other words, for reasons of policy and because of the relationship of the parties, the law gave the plaintiff redress for mental distress and humiliation caused by the defendant's insulting conduct. In Emmke v. DeSilva, liability was imposed not only upon the hotel corporation, but upon the wrongdoing agent as well. (See also 49 H.L.R. 1051.)

In cases where alleged insulting language arises, and there is a violation by the plaintiff of a reasonable rule of the hotel, recovery is not permitted. In the case of Hurd v. Hotel Astor Company, 169 N.Y.S. 359 (1918), the hotel had a rule forbidding the presence of any man in the bedroom of a woman guest when the room was not registered in the name of husband and wife, unless special permission was first obtained. The husband registered and was assigned a room on the same floor as his wife, who had registered earlier with another woman. The plaintiff was accused of soliciting men for improper purposes when the chambermaid reported a male guest in her room. The court held that there was no basis for substantial damages since the rule was reasonable and had been violated by the plaintiff and her husband. Unlike the *DeWolf* case, there was no intrusion on the privacy of the plaintiff's room. The conversation took place in the hall and was not conducted in an offensive or abusive manner. Also, there was no proof of damage, so that any award would have had to be compensating and not punitive.

A similar result is obtained when a person is not a guest of the inn. In Jenkins v. Kentucky Hotel Co., 87 S.W.2d 951 (Ky., 1935), the plaintiff was waiting in the lobby for someone who was attending a banquet. The hotel detective approached the plaintiff and, in a rude and insulting manner, told her that no such meeting was going on in the hotel, ordering her to leave the premises. Fearing bodily harm, she left. The court held that although the detective's manners were rude and highly objectionable, there was no assault and, consequently, no recovery since "bad manners are not actionable." The plaintiff in this case was not a guest, and so reasonable force could have been used to eject her if she had refused to leave the hotel when asked.

Recovery was allowed in Stevenson v. John J. Grier Hotel Company, 251 S.W. 355 (Ark., 1923), when a husband and wife were insulted by language imputing adultery. Although the court said that it was not necessary for the plaintiff guest to be physically injured before she could recover, in this case the court found there was a constructive physical injury, for there was an actual restraint and coercion of the plaintiff by the defendant, who ejected her from the hotel. The law did not require her to continue her explanations and protestations to the point where the restraint and coercion would become actual, rather than constructive. When she saw the right to remain in the hotel as a guest would not be accorded her, she had the right to minimize her damages by leaving before actual physical injury was inflicted, and the defendant could not argue that the plaintiff obeyed the command of the hotel manager.

Right of Guests to Proper Hotel Management

The hotel and its many employees are under the control of the hotelkeeper and staff. Should a guest expect and even depend on the hotelkeeper to conduct the establishment in a manner befitting a quasi-public place? What can a guest expect from a hotel and its employees with regard to (1) room security, (2) security in the common areas, such as the lobby or hallways, and (3) prevention of assault by hotel employees?

The first question of security in a guest's room is demonstrated in Danile v. Oak Park Arms Hotel, Inc., 203 N.E.2d 706 (Ill., 1964), in which the plaintiff was raped by an intoxicated bellboy who had obtained the passkey to her room. It was shown that the employee could not have procured her room key without lax management control. The hotel appealed the judgment for the plaintiff, but the lower court decision was affirmed as the hotel staff should have been aware of the bellboy's intoxication; nor did the appeals court find the $25,000 in damages excessive.

Second, security in common areas is illustrated in *Jenness v. Sheraton-Cadillac Properties*, in which a prostitute followed a guest from the hotel lobby to his room, propositioned him there, and being refused, hit him with a hard object, resulting in injuries. The ensuing lawsuit cost the hotel $50,000 for the husband and $5,000 for the wife (who was not there but sued for lack of consortium). This case falls in the realm of preventive law; it should alert hotelkeepers to the importance of continually checking people in the hotel lobby.

Case Example
Jenness v. Sheraton-Cadillac Properties, Inc.
211 N.W.2d 106 (Mich., 1973)
(QUINN, Presiding Judge)

This action was for recovery of damages for personal injuries sustained by Fred A. Jenness and arising from a physical assault on him while he was a guest of defendant. The wife, Dorothy Jenness, joined the action on her derivative claim for loss of consortium. Trial resulted in jury verdicts and judgments in favor of the husband for $50,000 and the wife for $5,000. Defendant appeals.

Fred A. Jenness had engaged a hospitality suite of defendant for the entertainment of business clients. He went to the hotel about 2:25 P.M. on November 2, 1967, to set up the suite, obtained the room keys, and took the elevator to the twentieth floor. As he walked from the elevator to the suite, an attractively dressed young lady asked him if he had a cigarette. Jenness told her to wait a moment, and he unlocked the suite, entered it, and removed his coat and gloves. She followed him into the room uninvited; he lit a cigarette for her and she propositioned him. Jenness declined the proposition, but permitted her to use the bathroom. During all of this time, the door to the suite remained open.

After using the bathroom, the young lady inquired the way to the elevator, and Jenness offered to show her the way, as he was returning to the lobby. While walking to the elevator, she fell somewhat behind Jenness, struck him over the head with a hard object, described as a tire iron, and fled. Jenness was not robbed; he did not lose consciousness and was found moments later by a security guard.

Both sides agree that defendant owed plaintiff husband a duty of ordinary care for the latter's safety. The contest is whether or not the record contains sufficient proof of the breach of that duty to create a fact question for jury determination. Defendant moved timely for directed verdict and for judgment notwithstanding the verdict, and it asserts as reversible errors on appeal the denial of these two motions. We review the facts in the light most favorable to plaintiffs, and the facts disclose:

1 The female assailant had been in defendant's lobby long enough prior to the assault for one of defendant's employees, an elevator starter, to become suspicious of her. This employee reported the presence of this female to defendant's front office manager about one and one-half hours prior to the assault. The latter told the employee to advise him if this female entered an elevator. The manager suspected the female was there "to turn a trick."

2 It was the policy of defendant to question suspicious persons in the lobby before permitting them access to the upper floors. Defendant employed a security guard, but he did not report for duty until 3:00 P.M. One of the duties of the guard was to make periodic rounds of the parade area, lobby, and of the floors; he often questioned people in the lobby who were suspicious either to him or to others. No one questioned this suspicious female.

3 This female took an elevator to the twentieth floor, and this fact was reported to the front office manager as soon as the elevator returned to the lobby. Then he and an assistant manager went to the twentieth floor to find the suspicious female, but they were unsuccessful.

On these facts, we are unable to say that all men would agree that defendant exercised ordinary care for the safety of Fred A. Jenness. On the question of defendant's negligence, a fact question for the jury was presented, and it was not error to deny defendant's motion for directed verdict and judgment notwithstanding the verdict because there was no proof of negligence.

In its motions, defendant asserted that Fred A. Jenness was guilty of negligence and/or contributory negligence as a matter of law. While the actions of Jenness with respect to his future assailant were not prudent, they did not amount to negligence or contributory negligence as a matter of law. He had no prior knowledge that defendant's employees were suspicious of this female, and he testified that he believed her to be a guest or an employee coming to work. There is record basis for a jury finding that Jenness was negligent or contributorily negligent, but the record does not support such a finding as a matter of law.

Ruling of the Court: Affirmed, with costs to plaintiffs.

The right of a guest to be free from attack by hotel employees is covered in Crawford v. Hotel Essex Boston Corporation, 143 F.Supp. 172 (Mass., 1956), in which the plaintiff recovered from a hotel for an attack by the house detective. The trial judge found that Massachusetts law created a contract to be free from attacks by hotel employees, in effect making the hotel an insurer against such assaults. All service and accommodation sectors of the industry follow the same rule. This rule (in relation to restaurants and bars) is thoroughly covered in chapter 13.

Right of Guests Falsely Arrested, Imprisoned, or Illegally Locked Out of Their Rooms

A hotelkeeper is not under a duty to prevent the arrest of a guest by officers of the law who are seemingly acting within their authority.

Neither should a hotel company investigate the legality of the officer's arrest. However, if the arrest is due to a false statement by the hotel company or its agents, the hotel company could be liable.

If an employee or employer puts a guest in a compromising position, and because of this action the guest is arrested, the hotelkeeper can be sued for false arrest and imprisonment, as the case of Jensen v. Barnett, 134 N.W.2d 53 (Neb., 1965), depicts. The hotel guest, Jensen, sought and received $2,500 damages for a false arrest and imprisonment instigated by the hotel clerk. On appeal, the judgment was affirmed as the clerk had given the arresting policeman false information, and the amount of damages was upheld as the incident had harmed Jensen's professional reputation.

In *Perrine v. Paulos*, two young women were locked out of their room for no apparent reason. The hotel soon discovered that eviction can be a serious undertaking. The plaintiffs received $500 general damages each, and $500 more each for exemplary damages.

Case Example

Perrine v. Paulos
224 P.2d 41 (Cal., 1950)
(DRAPEAU, Justice)

Two young women were evicted by defendants from a hotel in Los Angeles. Returning from work one evening, they found padlocks on their rooms. They could not get to any of their personal belongings or clothing. They could not find other accommodations and had to sleep in their automobiles for three nights. Then, on demand of their counsel, they were permitted to again occupy their rooms.

The case was tried by the court, with judgment for plaintiffs for $500 each for general damages; and $500 more each, exemplary damages.

Defendants argue that there was no relationship of landlord and tenant between the parties, that plaintiffs were merely lodgers; that the proof fails to establish that the manager of the hotel had authority to evict them; that assuming the agent was so empowered, no exemplary damages can be imposed; that in any event, exemplary damages may not be assessed because the defendants believed they were acting in accordance with their rights; that plaintiffs failed to minimize their damages; that the complaint presented but one issue, breach of duty by a landlord to a tenant, and did not plead breach of duty by an innkeeper to a guest; and that it was error for the court to permit testimony as to statements of the manager of the hotel of her employment by one of the defendants.

While the complaint may not be a model of pleading, it states a cause of action predicated on the duty of an innkeeper to his guest. It alleges that defendants were owners of the hotel; that plaintiffs were tenants on a weekly basis; and that they were unlawfully evicted.

With reference to the question of evidence: Several witnesses testified that one of the defendants stated she owned the hotel, and that title to it was in the other defendant "for convenience." This testimony, together with the presence of the manager in the hotel and the admitted fact that the manager padlocked plaintiffs' rooms, collected the rents, and took care of the place, was sufficient to support the judgment. No prejudice to defendants is apparent from the admission of the questioned testimony.

All the rest of defendants' objections are disposed of by the record. Applying elementary rules on appeal relative to the effect and value of evidence, the evidence supports the findings of the trial court.

The evidence establishes without contradiction that defendants owned the hotel and that plaintiffs were guests.

At common law, innkeepers were under a duty to furnish accommodations to all persons in the absence of some reasonable grounds.

Whether a person is a guest or a boarder at an inn is a question of fact to be determined from the evidence.

An innkeeper who refuses accommodations without just cause is not only liable in damages, but is guilty of a misdemeanor.

In such cases, exemplary damages may be assessed.

In this case, no showing whatever was made by defendants in excuse or in justification of their treatment of plaintiffs. They just locked them out.

Ruling of the Court: The judgment is affirmed, and the appeal from the order denying motion for a new trial is dismissed.

False Imprisonment

The plaintiff in Jacques v. Childs Dining Hall Company, 138 N.E. 843 (Mass., 1923), accompanied by her aunt, entered the defendant's restaurant and proceeded through the crowded restaurant up one flight of stairs to the ladies' room. As the aunt did not desire anything to eat, the plaintiff went downstairs alone and was served. Later the plaintiff and her aunt passed the cashier's desk where she paid the amount of her check. As she started out of the restaurant, she was called back and told that her check paid only for one. She replied that her aunt did not eat and again started away. The cashier commanded her to wait, and the plaintiff and her aunt were detained some twenty-five minutes while an investigation was being made.

The court said that the defendant undoubtedly had the right, if the plaintiff apparently had not paid, to detain her for a reasonable time to investigate the circumstances, but that if she were detained for an unreasonable time, or in an unreasonable way, she was entitled to recover. The court further stated that the question of an individual who is arrested without a warrant is confined to cases of the actual guilt of the party arrested, and the arrest can only be justified by proving such guilt. The defendant restaurateur must also be held to have intended the result of the acts of his servant. The court found for the plaintiff-guest for false imprisonment.

Right of Guests to Be Secure in Their Rooms

When a guest is assigned a room in a hotel, it is either expressly understood or implied that he or she has exclusive rights to this room and has the right to be secure in this room. The hotel management does have the right of access to a guest's room, but only at such times as is necessary in the general conduct of the hotel or in attending to the needs of a particular guest. If the room is to be examined for any other purpose, a search warrant is required.

Rules Governing Hotel Room Searches

Illegal Search and Seizure

In Sumdum v. State, 612 P.2d 1018 (Alaska, 1980), the defendant, Rick Sumdum, contends that the police's entry into his motel room was the product of an illegal search, and that the evidence of stolen goods found on his person pursuant to that entry should be suppressed. The superior court denied the motion to suppress, as did the court of appeals. The facts were as follows: At 5:30 A.M. on May 7, 1978, Pete Heger was awakened by an intruder in his motel room at the Driftwood Lodge in Juneau. Later that morning, Heger's roommate, Roy Claxton, discovered that his watch, cash, and marijuana were missing. The Driftwood's manager, Leona Gran, was notified of the theft, and the police were summoned. In the presence of the police, Heger described the burglar to other lodgers, one of whom pointed to room 38 and said Rick Sumdum was the one they wanted.

The rules governing a search of a hotel room can be at best difficult. In the Sumdum case, the court first cited the general rule that guests in a motel have a constitutionally protected right to privacy in their motel room, and motel personnel cannot consent to a search of the room. But after the rental period has terminated, management has an unrestricted right to enter. In this motel and similar places, guests frequently left without paying their bills, so the manager would attempt to reach them in their rooms by phone and then check the room if there was no answer. In this case, the police were on hand (they were investigating a burglary) when the door was opened, and it was ruled that merely because the police were there did not make the search illegal. It was also decided that the motel manager had the authority to consent to the police entering the motel hallway to investigate the burglary.

The defendant contended that the presence of the police was not inadvertent and, therefore, the search did not come within the "plain view" exception to the requirement that no search and seizure can be made without a warrant. (The mere observation of objects in plain view does not constitute an illegal search.) Inadvertence is a precondition to a valid seizure of evidence under the plain view exception. Judgment was affirmed for the state; the search and seizure was legal.

The Fourth Amendment, illegal search and seizure, does not apply to searches by private individuals "untainted" by "state action." Nor does its progeny, the exclusionary evidence rule, apply. This rule prohibits use at trial of evidence obtained by searches and seizures in violation of a person's Fourth Amendment rights and also forbids use of indirect, as well as direct, products of illegal search or seizure.

If, however, the manager acts solely as the agent of the police, without personal initiative and absent any independent right of access available to him, the exclusionary rule would be applicable. In People v. Minervini, 98 Cal.Rptr. 107 (Cal., 1971), the evidence was clear that the manager went to the rooms of the defendants and opened them on his own initiative, uninfluenced by the police. The manager had information that the defendants were stealing television sets from the motel. The court further stated that if the manager had a right to enter the rooms because of circumstances affecting the relationship between him and the defendants and/or between him and his property, that right would not be diminished if he sought police assistance in exercising it, or even if he was encouraged by the police to so exercise it. In this case, the search was not to examine the effects of the guests, or to observe their activities, but rather to secure the premises themselves and prevent the theft of property belonging to the motel.

The guest then has rights that the innkeeper is not at liberty to willfully ignore or violate. What are these rights? Can they be equated to a home away from home? The Supreme Court in Stoner v. California, 376 U.S. 483 (1964), exemplifies the guest's position vis-à-vis the hotelkeeper and others who would transcend the basic rights of the guest while occupying a hotel room. When a search of a guest's room or a guest's belongings is declared legal, this does away with any possible action against the hotelkeeper. This is not to say that the guest will not attempt a lawsuit against the hotel—on the contrary. However, situations have come up where circumstances have made a search by the police legal.

Search of Items Left by Guests

The presence of lost, mislaid, or forgotten property can create many problems for hoteliers and restaurateurs, problems that can result in serious exposure to liability in a lawsuit if they are not handled properly. Let us examine the case of Berger v. State.

This case involves a criminal prosecution initiated by the state of Georgia and is not a suit against the hotel for civil damages. The issue here is whether the marijuana taken from Berger's briefcase was taken in violation of his constitutional rights and therefore cannot be used as evidence against him. This aspect of the case must be discussed first to set the groundwork for the analysis of its possible civil impact on the hotelkeeper or restaurateur.

Case
Example

Berger v. State
257 S.E.2d 8 (Ga., 1979)
(QUILLIAN, Presiding Judge)

This is an appeal, via the interlocutory route from the denial of a motion to suppress.

The assistant manager of the Hyatt Regency Hotel was given a brief-case that had been found in the main lobby. It was closed but not locked. It was not an unusual occurrence to find several misplaced briefcases each day in the hotel. He opened the briefcase to see if it contained any identification of its owner. It contained a wallet, a large amount of "business papers," and "bundles of money." Two men who inquired about the brief-case were directed to his office. One man, the defendant, stated that it was his briefcase. The manager asked him if he had any personal identification. The defendant told him his identification was in the wallet in the briefcase. The manager stated that it was hotel policy that identification must be made from the person and not from the lost object, and "if the person can't identify themselves, obviously we can't give it out." The manager was particularly concerned about this item because of the large amount of cash it contained. Both men were getting "agitated" and "a bit loud."

Police officers Derrick and Cochran were employed by the hotel as security personnel while they were off duty. Officer Derrick received a call over his "beeper" and was directed to report to the assistant manager's office. Officer Derrick testified that when he arrived, the assistant manager briefed him on the situation, and he identified himself to the defendant and asked him if the briefcase was his. The defendant stated that it was. Officer Derrick asked defendant if he had "any identification, driver's license or anything like that." The defendant "said it was in the briefcase. . . ." According to Officer Derrick, the briefcase was unlocked and "the top was mostly down." He "opened up the case, pulled out the bill-fold" and left the briefcase open. Officer Derrick asked the defendant to write out his signature for comparison purposes. "As I was looking at the signatures on the driver's license and . . . the signature on the piece of paper, the case was right in front of me, and I noticed there was a bag of what I thought was marijuana inside the case in the back of it . . . and [the defendant] saw me see the marijuana . . . that's when he said . . . "I don't want you to search the briefcase." On cross examination, Officer Derrick admitted at the preliminary hearing he had testified that "It was hard to determine exactly when [the defendant] said [he didn't want him to look in the briefcase]. . . . I don't know if he saw me see it, and then said it, or what." He reaffirmed his testimony given at the suppression hearing and, on redirect, acknowledged he had testified at the preliminary hearing: "My best recollection is it was almost at the same time when I saw it. He saw me see it, that's when I said you are under arrest, and he said you cannot search my briefcase." Officer Cochran corroborated portions of Officer Derrick's version of the event.

The defendant testified that when he was asked for identification by the assistant manager, he took his wallet out of the briefcase and told the manager what was in it, and at that time the officers came in. He stated the briefcase was closed and the wallet was in his hand. When asked for identification, he showed Officer Derrick his driver's license, and he signed his name to let the officer make a comparison. He testified that Officer Derrick said: ". . . yeah, that's you all right . . . but that doesn't prove this is your briefcase. . . . I am going to have to look in it. . . . It was closed. . . . I said I would prefer that you do not look in it." Although [the defendant] repeated his request not to look in the briefcase, the officer opened it and searched through the briefcase until he found the marijuana, cocaine, and $7,000 in cash. The court denied the motion to suppress. Defendant brings this appeal.

Held: Defendant argues that warrantless searches and seizures are invalid except under recognized exceptions. They contend that under United States v. Chadwick, 433 U.S. 1, 97 S.Ct. 2476, 53 L.Ed.2d 538, the defendant had a reasonable expectation of privacy in his briefcase that was protected by the Fourth Amendment. Counsel is correct in his interpretation of *Chadwick,* where the U.S. Supreme Court held that federal agents violated the Fourth Amendment by searching a locked footlocker at the police station that was in possession of the defendant when he was arrested.

However, *Chadwick* is inapposite under the facts. Here the defendant was not arrested, nor did he have the briefcase "in his possession." The briefcase had been misplaced. Innkeepers of this state have a statutory liability to guests for property coming into their possession. (See Code Ann. §§ 52–108, 52–109 [Code §§ 52–108, 52–109].) It is not an unauthorized search for hotel management personnel, including security personnel, to open unlocked items found on their premises in an attempt to determine ownership so that the lost or misplaced property can be returned to its proper owner. Nor do we discern any difference in the situation here when the security officer was a police officer employed by the hotel in his "off time." He was acting in his capacity as a hotel security officer and not attempting a search for incriminating evidence.

In Lowe v. State, 230 Ga. 134, 136, 195 S.E.2d 919, a police officer at the scene of a fire had his attention directed to papers and a money bag in an automobile belonging to the defendant that had been pushed away from the burning house. The officer confiscated the articles for "safekeeping [because] he had no idea whose property they were." The court held that the situation was "devoid of any implications of an unconstitutional search and seizure . . . [as] the incriminating evidence came into the possession of the law enforcement authorities inadvertently and unmotivated by any desire to locate incriminating evidence by any unlawful search and seizure" (Lowe v. State at 136, 195 S.E.2d at 921).

In the same manner, in the instant case, the incriminating evidence came into possession of the law enforcement authorities inadvertently and unmotivated by any desire to locate incriminating evidence. Assuming without deciding that Officer Derrick was acting as a police officer, we find nothing unlawful about a police officer opening an unlocked, lost, or misplaced item to determine ownership. The marijuana was then in plain view, and the officer was authorized to confiscate the contraband.

In his finding of fact, the trial court determined: "The briefcase was ajar, but in order to reach in and get the wallet, Officer Derrick lifted the top of the briefcase and retrieved the described wallet. . . . With the briefcase open, some of the contents were in plain view. Officer Derrick noticed a clear plastic bag containing what appeared to him to be marijuana. He then told the defendant he was under arrest. . . ." In a motion to suppress, "[f]actual and credibility determinations of this sort made by a trial judge after a suppression hearing must be accepted by appellate courts, unless such determinations are clearly erroneous."

The trial court chose to believe the police officers' version of the sequence of events, and there is evidence to support his finding. His findings are not "clearly erroneous." This enumeration is without merit.

Ruling of the Court: Judgment affirmed.

The court held that the actions of the assistant manager and the security people did not violate the rights guaranteed to Berger by the Fourth Amendment, so the marijuana could be introduced into evidence against him during a criminal trial prosecuted by the state. But what if there had been an invasion of Berger's rights to privacy in the search conducted by the security officer? In a 1981 case that came down from the state of California, it was held that off-duty police officers employed as security people are functioning as arms of the state when they search someone's belongings. Therefore they do not have the status of a private citizen, and the products of their illegal searches and seizures will be excluded from evidence in a criminal trial.

Our interest in the *Berger* case is whether hotel employees violated any rights of privacy of the individual, and whether any such violation would render the hotel liable in damages. In this case, all parties will admit that Berger had the right to a reasonable expectation of privacy in his briefcase, not only insofar as the Fourth Amendment is concerned, but also as to his civil rights. He has a right to privacy against state and federal government intrusion and also against intrusions by private individuals. The violation of the right by the state or federal government would result in civil liability against the acting authority for damages, as well as the suppression of any evidence seized in violation of these rights. When the invasion of privacy is occasioned by a private citizen, the remedy is a civil suit for damages.

Berger's right to privacy yielded to a reasonable search of the briefcase on the part of the assistant manager in an effort to try to determine the identity of the owner. As the court said, the innkeeper was obliged by statute to his guests for property that came into his possession. Therefore he had to open an unlocked briefcase found on the hotel premises in an effort to determine its owner. It follows that any hotel management personnel who opened the briefcase under these conditions would not be making an unauthorized search.

Hoteliers must be concerned with the civil liability aspect of their actions and not merely with permissible conduct on the criminal side of the courthouse. Civil liability can have heavy financial ramifications. This is a difficult area, so hoteliers must be cautious.

Legal Permission to Search a Hotel or Motel Room

The Fourth Amendment to the Constitution deals with the right of privacy and ensures against illegal searches and seizures of property. It is enforceable against the states.

Apart from a search incident to an arrest or a search with a legal warrant, can a search of a room in a hotel, motel, or rooming house be valid? This section explores this aspect of the law, but does not contravene the situation in the *Stoner* case as the general rule. These cases are more an exception because of extenuating circumstances.

Termination of Guest-Innkeeper Relationship

In Abel v. United States, 362 U.S. 217, 4 L.Ed.2d 668, 80 S.Ct. 683 (1960), a search warrant was not obtained to search the plaintiff's hotel room after it had been vacated by an alien arrested under an administrative warrant issued as a preliminary proceeding to his deportation. This search was valid because the management freely gave its consent to it. Even the contents of the wastepaper basket could be examined because they were abandoned.

In People v. Crayton, 344 P.2d 627 (Cal., 1959), it was held that a manager of a motel, having complete control of the premises, was empowered to remove the defendant-guest's belongings and prepare the room for future guests after the defendant's occupancy of the room ended at noon. He could also permit a search of the room, and it would be legal.

The question of whether a hotel employee or manager should allow a search of a room without a warrant comes up much more often than it should. When a police official asks to search a room, there is no effectual consent to such search and seizure that will be binding on the owner or occupant of the premises. If the officer coerces the employee to permit a search, submission to lawful authority in such a case does not rise to the dignity of a consent by either employee or occupant, even if incriminating data are found. *People v. Raine* shows the narrow line between legal and illegal search by a police officer.

Case   **People v. Raine**
Example   *58 Cal.Rptr. 753 (1967)*
    (AGEE, Associate Justice)

Defendant appeals following jury conviction of second degree burglary (Pen.Code §§ 459, 460) and five counts of forgery (Pen.Code § 470). His main contention is that certain evidence used to convict him was obtained by an illegal search and that without such evidence, the testimony of his accomplice was not sufficiently corroborated as required by Penal Code Section 1111.

Seymore, the accomplice, testified that he and appellant broke into the Dennis Roofing Company in Richmond about midnight on December 22, 1964. They took a television set, some credit cards and identification cards issued to Gilbert or Delphine Dennis, numerous keys and tools, and some blank company bank checks, several of which appellant filled out while still on the burglarized premises.

The next day, appellant and his wife cashed four of these checks at four different stores in Walnut Creek. Seymore used a fifth check to buy a used car. The forgery counts are based on these five transactions.

On the evening of March 10, 1965, appellant's wife requested a room for two persons at the Tahoe Sands Motel. She signed the registration card as "Mrs. D. Dennis" of "Dennis Roofing Co." and gave her residence address as 1378 Thomas Road, Phoenix, Arizona. She was assigned to room 24. Nothing in advance was paid or requested.

By the next evening, the motel manager had become worried about the bill, particularly because of the size of the charges incurred for food and beverages. A phone call to Phoenix disclosed the fact that there was no "Mrs. Dennis" at the address given.

The office of the Sheriff of El Dorado County was then asked to check on the occupants' MG automobile. Investigation disclosed that it was a stolen car.

About 6:30 the next morning, March 12, deputy sheriffs went to room 24 and arrested the occupants, appellant and his wife, for car theft. The arrest was made without a warrant, but there is no contention that it was unlawful.

The motel manager thereafter phoned the sheriff's office and asked the deputy who answered to inquire about payment of the bill, which totaled $78. While holding the phone, he heard appellant's wife say, "We don't have a dime." When the deputy came back on the line, he advised the manager that "they weren't going to be able to pay it [the bill]."

About 9:00 or 9:30 that same morning, the officers returned to the motel and asked to be allowed to search room 24. The manager gave his consent, unlocked the door, and entered with them. Some of the credit cards and identification cards taken in the Dennis burglary were found hidden behind a baseboard that had been pulled slightly away from the wall. These cards are the evidence that appellant contends were obtained by means of an illegal search.

After the search, the manager had the maid remove and store the occupants' belongings. The room was then prepared for the next occupancy. Three months later, the appellant paid the bill and retrieved the belongings.

The search was made without a search warrant and was not incident to the arrest; neither appellant nor his wife expressly or impliedly consented to the search; there is nothing in the record that would justify a belief by the officers that the motel manager was authorized by appellant or his wife to permit such a search. (See Stoner v. State of California, 376 U.S. 483, 84 S.Ct. 889, 11 L.Ed.2d 856 [1964].)

Under such circumstances, the search was lawful only if the right of appellant and his wife to the occupancy of the room had then terminated.

Appellant asserts that the "tenancy did not terminate until 11:00 A.M., on March 12," the day of the arrest and search. Such conclusion is based entirely upon the implication arising from the fact that this was the motel's daily checkout time.

The manager testified that a request for payment could be made at any time and that, if "these people hadn't been arrested that morning," he "would have went in and said, we want our money."

It is our opinion that if the reply to such request had been that "we don't have a dime" and are not "going to be able to pay," the manager would have had the right to require appellant and his wife to give up their occupancy of the room.

The actual situation is parallel. While the request for payment was made by telephone and only appellant's wife was contacted, she was the only person with whom the motel had dealt. In fact, appellant himself was never seen by any of the motel personnel until the time of his arrest. We think that the circumstances sufficiently show that appellant had authorized his wife to act for him in connection with their tenancy of the motel room.

Furthermore, when a day-to-day room guest of a hotel or motel departs without any intention of occupying the room any longer and without making any arrangement for payment of his bill, an inference arises that he has abandoned his tenancy. In such a situation, the management should not be required to wait until checkout time to reoccupy the room to the exclusion of such guest. This is so even though the guest leaves some of his personal belongings behind.

The above generalization is without doubt applicable to a voluntary departure and, while the departure here was involuntary, it was occasioned by a *lawful* arrest. We see no reason to distinguish between these two situations, particularly when appellant and his wife made no effort to arrange to pay the bill even after being contacted by the hotel manager.

Under the circumstances of this case, as detailed above, we hold that the manager regained the right to complete control of room 24 upon the departure of appellant and his wife and, therefore, his consent to the search made it lawful. . . . The evidence obtained thereby is therefore admissible.

In view of this holding, it is unnecessary to detail the additional corroborating evidence. Such evidence includes proof that appellant pawned the television set, hid the keys in a trailer, and wrote out the subject checks on blanks obtained in the burglary.

In addition to accomplice Seymore and the witnesses who testified as to the motel episode, the prosecution called seven factual witnesses and one handwriting expert. Their testimony, standing alone, overwhelmingly proves appellant's guilt of each of the six counts. In our opinion, there is no reasonable possibility of a different result, even if the motel evidence were to be excluded. . . .

Ruling of the Court: Judgment affirmed.

Bypassing a Warrant

In Johnson v. United States, 333 U.S. 10, 68 S.Ct. 367, 92 L.Ed. 436 (1948), a known informer advised the Seattle police that unknown persons were smoking opium in the Europe Hotel. The police then relayed this information to federal narcotics agents who came to the hotel. All were experienced in narcotics work and recognized at once the unmistakable odor of burning opium coming from a room whose occupant was unknown. After knocking and identifying themselves as police, the agents were admitted to the room by the occupant.

The officers then determined the identity of the occupant and discovered opium and incriminating smoking apparatus. A federal district court refused to suppress this evidence, and a circuit court of appeals affirmed the decision. On further review, however, the Supreme Court reversed the decision, holding first, that the circumstances were "certainly . . . not enough to bypass the constitutional requirement" of presenting the evidence to a magistrate and obtaining a search warrant; and second, that the arrest did not justify the search inasmuch as it was based upon observations made after admission to the room had been gained under color of police authority.

In People v. Parren, 182 N.E.2d 662 (Ill., 1962), the court ruled that information provided by an anonymous informer, though relevant to the issue of reasonable cause, was not a sufficient basis to forego the constitutional requirement of obtaining a search warrant. The court did point out, though, that information given by an informer may under some circumstances be a reasonable basis for search or arrest without a warrant—that is, where the identity and reliability of the informer is known and, presumably, where some emergency exists to justify the failure to seek out a warrant.

Disturbing the Peace

Can a hotel room be entered by hotel employees when a disturbance is going on in that room or for other reasons? The hotel has a right to quell a disturbance in a room, but what action should be taken when narcotics or other forbidden substances are noticed by an employee? Does the presence of those illegal goods justify the hotel's reporting them to the police to investigate without a warrant? These questions are explored in People v. Henning.

Case Example	People v. Henning
	96 Cal.Rptr. 294 (1971)

Sometime after ten o'clock P.M. (the curfew hour), on the evening of December 25, 1969, the desk clerk of Hillside Inn called the police department asking assistance concerning a disturbance in one of its rooms. An officer responded. He was told that a guest had complained about a disturbance at room 109, where a group of juveniles and adults were pounding on the door demanding admittance. The officer and a hotel employee went to the room. No one was then present in the outside hall, but inside "a very loud radio" was turned on. The officer knocked on the door repeatedly and called the name of the defendant Henning, to whom the room was registered. There was no response whatever, and there was no diminution of the radio's sound output. At the officer's request, the hotel employee unlocked the door. The officer again knocked on the door, with a similar lack of response within. The door was then pushed slightly ajar. The officer testified, "At that time I could see in, and I could see the lower half of a male's body extended in a prone position over the end of the bed fully clothed." The man was lying face down. Fearful that the man was in trouble, the officer entered to "check on his welfare." Upon the entry, in plain sight on the floor, on a table, and protruding from the prone man's pocket, the officer saw, and recognized the nature of, a portion of the narcotics and dangerous drugs that were later the subject of Henning's motion to suppress. The man partially on the bed was Henning, who appeared to be in a deep sleep.

From this evidence, it could reasonably be concluded that the officer entered Henning's room with consent of the hotel employee; that the initial purpose of the entry was to silence a loud radio that was annoying the hotel's guests; and that upon seeing Henning prone and in an unusual position on the bed, an additional purpose developed—concern for the man's safety. It may clearly be inferred that the officer at no time prior to the entry had a purpose to arrest anyone or to search the room. And he may reasonably be considered as an agent of the hotelman, who understandably did not wish, unattended, to risk a hostile confrontation in silencing a source of annoyance to the hotel's guests.

We have no hesitancy in concluding that a hotelkeeper himself may enter a rented, but presently unoccupied, room when *reasonably necessary* to quiet a "very loud radio" that is presenting a substantial annoyance to other guests. Indeed, it has been held that an innkeeper is under an obligation not to harbor persons "dangerous to the peace and comfort of those for whose comfort he is bound to provide, . . . to protect his patrons from 'annoyance,' . . . and to exercise proper care for the safety and tranquility of the guest."

It seems most reasonable for the hotel people to have called upon a police officer for assistance, rather than risk violence in pursuit of their duty of care for the nighttime comfort, tranquility and quiet of their guests. If so, then it was equally reasonable for the police officer, on request and with their consent and under the facts before us, to assist in such an undertaking.

The additional purpose of the officer, upon observing the condition of Henning within the room, was clearly without Fourth Amendment or other fault. Reason tells us, and valid authority holds, that an entry is proper when a police officer reasonably and in good faith believes such entry to be necessary in order to render aid to a person in distress.

The question presented is whether there was any substantial evidence supporting the superior court's determination of no Fourth Amendment violation. . . . If so, even though contrary inferences might be drawn from the evidence, and we ourselves might draw them, we are nevertheless bound by the findings of the superior court.

It must be conceded that an inference could be drawn that the police officer entered Henning's room either to make an unauthorized arrest or an unauthorized search. But it is contended that another reasonable inference could be, and was, properly drawn by the court that the officer acted only in aid of the hotel management late at night to quell a disturbance— a loud radio—in the room.

We therefore direct our inquiry to that portion of the evidence, and reasonable inferences drawable therefrom, that tend to support the conclusion of the trial judge.

Having entered Henning's room for such purposes, the police officer was not required "to blind [himself] to what was in plain sight simply because it was disconnected with the purpose for which [he] entered."

Ruling of the Court: It is said that: "there is no exact formula for the determination of reasonableness. Each case must be decided on its own facts and circumstances . . . and on the total atmosphere of the case. . . ." Applying this principle, and in the absence of more specific countervailing authority, we must conclude that there was substantial evidence in support of the superior court's order denying Henning's motion to suppress evidence.

Abandoned Luggage

In United States v. Cowan, 396 F.2d 83 (N.Y., 1968), the defendant had registered for one night with luggage that later was proved to be stolen. The manager gave consent to the FBI to examine the contents of the unlocked suitcases. The court stated that because the hotel could sell (after notice, with a brief description of the goods) the luggage in a manner prescribed by law, the hotel had the right, if not the duty, to determine the lawful owners of the luggage and its contents. Under these circumstances the hotel, not the defendant, was entitled to retain possession of the seized baggage. There was no interference with the defendant's property rights, such as they were, in the luggage.

Additionally, the court said that the luggage had been abandoned at the time of the search. The question of whether the luggage was intentionally discarded, which is a requisite of abandonment, was settled by defining abandonment as not requiring the performance of a ritual; rather, it was a question of intent.

The abandonment of property by a guest is the relinquishing of all title, possession, or claim to or of it—a virtually intentional discarding of the goods. It is not presumed; proof supporting it must be direct or affirmative. The defendant's conduct indicated that he intended to relinquish possession of the property. Not paying his bill, not communicating with the hotel, and his statement that he would stay only one night support this view.

When does the possession of a room revert back to the hotel? If a person registers for one day and is not gone by checkout time, the hotel may assume either the guest is staying on for another day, or that the contract is completed and the luggage can be removed. It is critical for hoteliers to know their rights, and each registration card should be marked for the departure date.

Lawful Charges and Customs in the Hotel Industry

In New York, the General Business Law statute calls for a posting of "charges or rate of charges by the day and for meals furnished and for lodging." A further stipulation provides that "no charge or sum shall be collected or received by any hotelkeeper for any service not actually rendered." Therefore, when the Waldorf Astoria charged all guests a 2 percent sundry fee, it was considered illegal in Application of State by Lefkowitz, 323 N.Y.S.2d 917 (1971), and the hotel had to return all monies collected. The court said:

> The business of an innkeeper is of a quasi-public character, invested with many privileges, and burdened with correspondingly great responsibilities. . . . The charge for message services delineated as sundries was fraudulent and unconscionable. Accordingly, petitioner's application is granted to the extent that respondents are permanently enjoined from engaging in the fraudulent and illegal acts and practices complained of herein.

This situation generally comes up when a state has a statute similar to New York's. Otherwise, the question will be raised only under a discriminatory practice situation or a contention that the costs are not reasonable (reasonable rule doctrine), if not in conflict with some other statute.

Telephone Charges

At one time, telephones were considered to be in hotel and motel rooms for the convenience of guests. There was no duty on the part of hoteliers to supply telephone services. Whether the law will continue to look upon them merely as a matter of convenience could be the subject of debate. In a 1981 case, a jury in Texas awarded a woman who was raped while a guest at an economy motel, part of a national chain, $188,275, which included $75,000 in punitive damages. The jury not only found that the lock used in the door was inadequate to protect guests, but they also took the motel to task for having failed to have a telephone in the room, as well as an employee on duty at the desk so that the woman could have summoned help. The jury's conclusion could be interpreted as a warning informing hoteliers that the failure to have a telephone in the room may violate the innkeeper's duty to keep the room safe for guests and to provide them adequate security.

A telephone may be the only source of communication in the event of an emergency situation. Suppose guests are trapped in their rooms during a fire? How could instructions be communicated to them? Or, suppose a guest was suddenly taken ill and was unable to leave the room. How would help be summoned? In numerous situations, telephones are necessities in a hotel room, not a luxury or a convenience item.

In the past, hoteliers avoided installing elaborate telephone systems because they lost money on supplying these services. The charges that they could impose were severely restricted by both state and federal regulation. Local and intrastate calls were regulated by state public utility commissions that allowed only a very small surcharge. Interstate and international calls were regulated by the Federal Communication Commission, which allowed no surcharge at all. In recent years, however, some states (about thirty so far) have done away with regulations limiting the surcharge that hotels may impose on local and intrastate calls, thus providing hotels with a new source of revenue. In states where surcharge regulations still exist, hoteliers are bound to conform to them and may not impose a surcharge greater than that allowed by the state regulatory authority.

Regarding interstate calls, hoteliers purchase such service at the best price possible and then resell the service for whatever price they wish. They may not impose a surcharge.

Forwarding Letters and Packages

Hotel guests (particularly traveling sales representatives) often do not receive letters and packages delivered after their departure. What policy should be followed on guests' letters and packages after they leave? What are the customs of the hotel industry? The case of Baehr v. Downey, 94 N.W. 750 (Mich., 1903), details the problems and possible solutions. In this 1903 case, a fur salesman who was checking out requested the Hotel Downey to forward any mail or packages to his next destination. A package from his company containing furs subsequently arrived, was receipted by a hotel employee, but never reached the forwarding address. The circuit judge held for the defendants, maintaining the plaintiffs parted with their right of possession when they shipped the furs to their salesman. The appeals court found this judgment to be in error. The hotel was under a strict liability to protect the property of guests—particularly in carrying out the contract of forwarding mail. Even when the defendants subsequently became bailees of the plaintiff's goods, their failure to return the goods made them liable. The lower court judgment was reversed in favor of the plaintiff.

Rights of Persons Other Than Guests

This section deals with persons other than conventioneers and party-goers—generally innocent guests or, in the Holly case, an innocent bystander. The Holly case treats the problems that arise when a party gets out of control.

Of necessity, hotelkeepers must have the right to control certain aspects of the hotel operation, including the right to bar any person that they believe undesirable for reasons not related to race, color, or creed. Therefore, a person who is not a guest or patron may not remain on the hotel premises against the will of the operator (see further discussion in chapter 12).

Many different activities go on in a hotel that are often attended by persons other than guests. Parties are not uncommon, especially when a hotel has a convention. The case of Holly v. Meyers Hotel and Tavern is a good example of a party that got out of control. Such occurrences are not the rule in hotels or motels, but they need happen only once to cause great aggravation and trouble for the hotel manager.

Case	Holly v. Meyers Hotel & Tavern
Example	*83 A.2d 460 (N.J., 1961)*
	(JAYNE, J.A.D.)

This is a case of defenestration (the act of throwing something or someone out of a window).

Since the trial judge granted a motion for the involuntary dismissal of the cause of action at the conclusion of the plaintiff's case, our summary of the testimony is stated in its aspect most favorable to the plaintiff's alleged claim.

It is acknowledged that the defendant was in control of the management of the sixty-six-room hotel in Hoboken at the time of the mishap and thus occupied the legal status of an innkeeper.

On the afternoon of March 31, 1949, the captain of a ship engaged three rooms at the hotel for the accommodation of a group of five Canadian sailors. The rooms so assigned were situated on the third floor, and evidently one of the rooms faced on Hudson Street. The chronological sequence of events is significant.

At seven o'clock in the evening, the sailors arrived at the hotel and proceeded to their rooms. Between 9:30 and 10 o'clock, they communicated with the hotel clerk concerning the purchase of a bottle of rum. It was not supplied to them by the hotel.

At about 10:45 P.M., a female guest occupying a room on the third floor telephoned to the hotel clerk and imparted to him the information that the sailors were causing an unusual amount of noise. The clerk notified the sailors by telephone of the complaint, and the sailors assured him that "they would be quiet." About twenty minutes later, the same guest again communicated with the clerk and apprised him that "the noise had not subsided and they (the sailors) were throwing around what sounded like a shoe." Thereupon, at about 11:05 P.M., the hotel clerk personally announced his presence at the entrance of the room occupied by the sailors and again requested them to be quiet, asserting that otherwise they would be ejected from the premises.

Approximately two hours later, the plaintiff was walking with her escort on the sidewalk alongside of the hotel when a Coca-Cola bottle was thrown out of the window above by one of the sailors. The bottle crashed on the pavement beside the plaintiff and a fragment of the broken glass entered the plaintiff's left eye. We may pause to state that the injury to her eye has been relatively serious.

The police were immediately summoned. The lights were still illuminated in the room inhabited by the sailors, and the police officers promptly visited the room, observed its disordered condition, and interrogated the sailors, except one who was on the bed drifting peacefully with the tides of sleep.

Initially there was a denial that any one of the group had thrown a bottle out of the window. The sailors were apprehended, and subsequently one of them supplied the admission that in attempting to throw the bottle from the table into a wastepaper basket beneath the open window, it accidentally passed out the window. The explanatory testimony of the crafty or repentant sailor taken at some proceeding of a criminal nature was incorporated in the transcript of the evidence in the present action.

Inasmuch as the hotel clerk had been previously notified that the sailors were engaged in throwing some object about, the court admitted testimony relating to the condition of the room upon the removal of its occupants. There were broken bottles and broken water glasses on the floor. There were "half-moon-shaped" indentations on the wall with shattered fragments of glass beneath. A plywood movable closet was broken, chairs were overturned, and beds pulled out of position.

It must be immediately recognized that the subject matter of this appeal is confined solely to the consideration of the legal obligations of the defendant hotel company in the circumstances, and more specifically to the determination of whether the evidence adduced by the plaintiff was sufficient to sustain a *prima facie* cause of action against the hotel company for submission to the jury.

Basically, the cause of action must necessarily be erected upon the existence of a duty that the defendant owed to the plaintiff and the failure of the defendant to fulfill that duty to the injury of the plaintiff. Moreover, to sustain a recovery, there must be some causal connection between the fall of the bottle and the omissions of duty of the proprietor of the hotel, his servants, or persons for whose acts he may be held responsible. Obviously there is no proof that the hotelkeeper or any servant of his threw the bottle. The case implicates a consideration of the legal relation existing between those who occupy rooms of a hotel as transient guests and the proprietor's responsibility for their acts.

The rights of the proprietor are not unrestricted. When a guest is given the key to his room, it symbolizes the surrender of the quarters to the guest, subject only to such visitations at reasonable times as the proprietor or his servants may deem necessary properly to maintain the rooms and to supervise their use so that they may not become obnoxious to the proprieties of behavior, morality, and the law of the land. Apart from these privileges accorded the management, the guest is entitled to possess the free and unmolested use and enjoyment of his room or apartment without interference from anyone. Indeed, unwarranted and unjustifiable interference by a proprietor or his servant may occasion consequential liabilities.

On the other side, the hotel proprietor has the undoubted right and, in some circumstances, the duty to evict a disorderly, malevolent, and incorrigible guest.

The responsibility of the hotel proprietor for the injurious consequences of the wrongful acts of his guest to outsiders is recognized in that narrow zone between his inhibitions against unwarranted interference and his duty with respect to the management of his premises exemplified by the maxim *sic utere tuo ut alienum non laedas* (to use one's own property in such a manner as not to injure that of another).

The generally accepted view is that an innkeeper is liable to a stranger for personal injury where the innkeeper or his servants knew, or by the exercise of reasonable care could have known, that the behavior of the guest was such as to indicate to one of average prudence that the guest might commit acts that would naturally result in injury to others.

Contemplating, therefore, the nature of the legal duty that descended upon the defendant, we next encounter the questions whether in the circumstances divulged by the evidence, the defendant, by the course of conduct of its representative, was shown in at least a *prima facie* degree to have been negligent in the observance and fulfillment of its duty, and if so, was the dereliction in that particular made to appear by a similar degree of proof to have been a natural and proximate cause of the injury eventually sustained by the plaintiff?

In approaching the determination of those questions, we are cognizant of the applicable general principles. The law makes no unreasonable demands. It does not require from anyone superhuman wisdom, perspicacity, foresight, and vigilance. It does not convert the innkeeper into a constant watchman and guardian of the conduct of his guests. The dictates of reasonable care do not impose unreasonable burdens.

In the pertinent decision rendered in Bruner v. Seelbach Hotel Co., 117 S.W. 373 (Ky., 1909), the Court of Appeals of Kentucky remarked: "Besides, the fact must be remembered that ordinarily innkeepers have no control over their guests. It is only when they know, or by the exercise of ordinary care could know, that the guest's conduct is such that injury will naturally result to others that they have the right to eject the guest, or take precautions to control his conduct."

The following quotation is taken from the well-considered opinion of the Supreme Court of Pennsylvania in Wolk v. Pittsburgh Hotels Co., 131 A. 537 (Pa., 1925): "Undoubtedly, the proprietor could no more be held responsible for the consequences of his guests' willful acts in throwing articles to the street, unless he could prevent it, than he would be for the wrongful act of his servants outside the scope of employment. Nor would he be liable for the result of articles placed on the window sill falling to the street, unless he knew, or had reason to know, the thing placed there was of a dangerous nature or likely to fall to the street."

If, in the deliberate and impartial consideration of that issue, fair-minded men or women might honestly differ as to the conclusions to be logically drawn from the circumstances, then the issue should have been submitted to the jury for determination.

In these matters, the fair-minded person is no less a theoretical personification than the ordinarily prudent person. To determine whether the fair-minded person could, from the evidence, conclude within the precincts of rationality the existence of a state of facts that in the law established a *prima facie* cause of action is appropriately the prerogative of the judge; to decide whether amid those existing facts, if deemed actionable, the defendant acted or failed to act in conformity with the standard conduct of the ordinarily prudent person is appropriately to be presented to the forum of common knowledge and experience in which the jury functions.

Therefore, in the consideration of the ruling under review, we have endeavored to envision the entire field of the mental reactions that we conceive that a fair and logically minded person might experience in the cogitation of the factual circumstances of the present case.

We apprehend that the fair-minded person might entertain the following convictions: that the hotel clerk knew that there had been admitted to the hotel a group of sailors, off ship and apparently on temporary leave; that he learned from his first message from them that one or more had a propensity to indulge in intoxicating liquor and desired a bottle of rum;

that he later learned that they had become boisterous to a degree annoying to a guest in other quarters; that he evidently regarded the complaint to be credible and sufficiently significant to induce him to admonish them; that it is not evident that the sailors denied the truth of the complaint, but promised to cease; that about twenty minutes later, he learned that the sailors had willfully disregarded his previous request, and that they were engaged in "throwing" some object or objects about the room (we ascribe considerable significance to the information that the sailors were "throwing" objects because that is the type of mischief that ultimately caused the plaintiff injury); that the hotel clerk was then aware that the sailors were unusual guests in that they were uncommonly boisterous, inordinately mischievous, if not quarrelsome, and certainly disobedient; that in this instance, he visited the entrance to the room, conversed with one of the sailors, again giving warning against a further continuance of their misconduct; that the clerk did not enter the rooms to ascertain what objects they had been throwing, and, notwithstanding his knowledge that the sailors had previously ignored his warning from which he might have anticipated the likelihood that they would do so again, he returned to the office, out of the range of hearing them, and gave the matter no further attention because of the absence of a third complaint.

Additionally, perhaps, the fair-minded person might have inferred that the obstreperous "throwing" of bottles and drinking glasses continued spasmodically after the clerk's visit in proportion to the increase of their consumption of liquor; that such should have been reasonably anticipated, and that in view of the knowledge of the extraordinary behavior of these guests, a reasonably prudent and cautious clerk would have followed up his supervisory endeavors and kept those particular guests under some measure of surveillance, in which case the mishap would not have occurred.

Manifestly, the pivotal point relates to the character of the conduct of the clerk following his visit to the rooms.

Reasonable anticipation, spoken of in the law of negligence as foresight for harm, is the expectation generated in the mind of the person of ordinary vigilance and circumspection in consequence of his reaction to a set of circumstances. The element of "foresight for harm" seems to be regarded as a factor of cogent significance in cases of this particular nature. Appreciating the knowledge of the clerk that the window was open and that a public street was beneath it, and his reason to believe that the sailors were in a devil-may-care mood and throwing objects in the room, we are unable to agree that his situation was so clearly beyond the range of the reasonable apprehension of injury to someone as to be excluded from the consideration of the jury and treated as a matter of law rather than as a factual problem. Moreover, in the present case, we apprehend that the factual circumstances in material respects were not entirely free from divergent inferences. Illustrative are the following: Did all of the disorderly conduct of the guests precede in the point of time the clerk's visit and thereupon cease, or did it thereafter persist? Did the sailors heed the clerk's last warning, desist from their offensive behavior, and was it in truth in the endeavor of the sailor to toss the bottle into the wastebasket that it passed out of the window; hence, an intervening act distinctly independent of and disassociated with the exhibitions of previous malfeasance? Unfortunately, the complaining guest did not appear at the trial and impart her information concerning a continuance, if any, of the misbehavior.

Upon mature reflection, we are constrained to conclude that this alleged cause of action in the existing state of evidence and in recognition of the principles of law applicable to the measure of responsibility of the innkeeper ought to have been submitted to the jury. To warrant an involuntary dismissal, it is not enough that the facts are without contradiction; the inference that is drawn from such facts must likewise be, in a legal sense, indubious—that is, one about which reasonable men might not honestly differ.

Ruling of the Court: Judgment reversed and a new trial directed.

Connolly v. Nicollet Hotel, 95 N.W.2d 657 (Minn., 1959), depicts what can happen during a convention. In this case, the plaintiff lost use of her left eye after being struck by an object falling from the Nicollet Hotel as she walked on a public sidewalk. The plaintiff contended the hotel was negligent in maintaining order and controlling its guests (a chamber of commerce convention). The hotel had been forewarned, as much mischief and damage had already occurred as a result of the convention. The appeals court found the hotel negligent.

Interestingly, the fact that a passerby is hit and injured by a chair apparently thrown out of a hotel window does not mean that person can recover damages for the injuries from the hotel. The fact that there is injury does not mean that someone has to pay for the damages, nor does it follow that the hotel must pay, even though the chair came from the hotel. There must be a basis for imposing the liability on the hotel. This was pointed out in the case of Larson v. St. Francis Hotel, 188 P.2d 513 (Cal., 1948), which presented just such a situation. It was V.J. Day, and the plaintiff was walking by the hotel when suddenly a chair came down on her head and rendered her unconscious and otherwise injured her. No one had seen where the chair had come from; in fact, no one had seen it until it was just a few feet above the plaintiff's head. Nevertheless, the court allowed that it was a reasonably permissible inference to deduce that the chair had come from the hotel. The plaintiff sought to recover against the hotel under the doctrine of res ipsa loquitur, the theory being that the hotel had exclusive control over everybody and everything within its confines. The lower court granted the defendant's motion for a nonsuit and the plaintiff appealed. The appellate court stated that in order to proceed under the doctrine, the plaintiff had to prove that there was an accident, and that the thing or instrument that caused the accident was such that it would not have happened in the ordinary course of events if the defendant had used ordinary care. Because the plaintiff could not establish the requisites necessary to permit her the use of the doctrine in establishing her case, she had to introduce evidence to show that the hotel's negligence was the proximate cause of her injury, but this she failed to do.

Guests of Guests

Friends, relatives, and acquaintances may visit guests in a hotel or place of accommodation. Generally, the rights of such people are similar to those of the guest, with some exceptions. For example, the hotelkeeper has the right to institute reasonable rules governing the time they may visit guests or where they may go in the hotel. Any other rule that is not customary to the accommodation industry must be posted or communicated to guests and their visitors.

In the case of *Steinberg v. Irwin Operating Company*, the guests' visitors had the right to go certain places in the hotel, but went beyond the purview of their invitation.

Case Example   **Steinberg v. Irwin Operating Co.**
90 So.2d 460 (Fla., 1956)
(THORNAL, Justice)

We are called upon to determine whether appellant, Essie Steinberg, was an invitee or a licensee on the premises of the appellee, a hotel operator, at the time she was injured.

Appellant, Essie Steinberg, accompanied two friends to the Cadillac Hotel operated by appellee. The purpose of the mission was to enable one of the friends to deliver a message to a registered guest at the hotel. Inquiry at the desk revealed that the registered guest was not in. Thereupon, Mrs. Steinberg and her friends decided to explore various lounges and other rooms adjacent to the lobby. This was done for their own diversion. They first went into a "TV Room." They didn't like the program then showing. They then apparently attempted to enter an adjoining "Movie Room." This room was dark except for the light cast by the movie screen and projector. The floor level of the "Movie Room" was four inches lower than the floor level of the "TV Room." Claiming that she did not see the difference in level, Mrs. Steinberg fell and suffered injuries. She and her husband filed a complaint seeking compensation for damages resulting from the alleged negligence of appellee. The alleged negligence was the difference in the floor level. Appellee moved for summary judgment. The trial judge granted the motion. He stated in his order that it was his opinion that Mrs. Steinberg was a mere licensee and, as a matter of law, was not entitled to recover under the circumstances. Final judgment was entered for appellee. Reversal of this judgment is now sought.

Appellants contend that at the time of the alleged injury, Mrs. Steinberg was an invitee of the hotel. They seek recovery on the theory that the hotel was obligated to furnish its invitees with reasonably safe premises.

Appellee contends that Mrs. Steinberg was merely a licensee. They assert that the only duty owed to her was to refrain from willfully or wantonly injuring her.

There is no doubt that a registered guest of a hotel is a business invitee and is entitled to receive the degree of care applicable to invitees. We are of the view that one entering a hotel to communicate with a registered guest is entitled to receive and enjoy the same degree of care. This rule is subject to the limitations hereafter expressed. A hotel is not to be considered an insurer of the safety of every person who decides to roam around its lobby or other public rooms. On the other hand, by the very nature of the business, the operator of the hotel is bound to anticipate that a registered guest is apt to have business and social callers. The invitation to such callers arises by operation of law out of the relationship between the hotel and its registered guests. The operator of the hotel should provide reasonably safe ways of ingress and egress for those legally entering and leaving the place pursuant to the implied invitation implicit in the relationship between hotel operator and registered guests.

However, this implied invitation is not without its limits. The invitation to enter the hotel to visit a guest is circumscribed by the rule that it extends only to appropriate usage of the means of ingress and egress, such as the lobby, elevator, hallways, and room area rented to the guest.

It would be stretching the doctrine of implied invitation beyond justifiable limits to hold that such invitation extends to all of the private or semipublic rooms of the hotel. When the visitor crosses the boundaries of the invitation, he ceases to be an invitee. His status then changes to that of a licensee or even a trespasser. He is entitled to the status of an invitee only to the extent justified by the implied invitation.

In this case, it is perfectly clear that Mrs. Steinberg enjoyed the status of an implied invitee when she entered the hotel lobby. This status continued so long as she used the facilities of the hotel reasonably included within the invitation. When, for her own pleasure and convenience, she crossed the bounds of the invitation on her own initiative, sought entertainment in the "TV Room," and later in the "Movie Room," she became at most a licensee. While she was in this status, the hotel owed to her only the duty to refrain from willfully or wantonly injuring her. The record is clear that there was no willful or wanton injury.

Ruling of the Court: The judgment is affirmed.

Management Principles

Guests in hotels have important rights. One basic right is to be allowed a room if available. The practice of overbooking, however, has sometimes led to lawsuits.

Harry Millikin, the head of Western International Hotels and president of the American Hotel and Motel Association, said, "Study, discipline, market education, and monitoring will provide the solution to no-shows and overbooking, those chronic ailments of the hotel industry."

This solution can be achieved by analyzing past, present, and future reservations; finding out where guests come from; and determining what problems exist. Monitoring should be undertaken to observe closely reservations and reservation procedures. Such study should result in an industry-wide standard operating procedure for handling reservations. The following suggestions are pertinent to this discussion.

The major chains and large independent companies should work together toward a solution, possibly utilizing the facilities of a large university to study the problems.

Because most business and pleasure travelers (about 85 percent) use confirmed reservations, some type of prepayment plan could be instituted, particularly for resort hotels. Bonded, certified travel agents have a particular advantage in handling such prepayments because they can bring a cause of action against the customer in his state of origin. Although a fee would be involved, no-shows and overbooking are far more expensive. An escrow account could be instituted to alleviate any problems of poor fiscal policy, or a bank or another hotel could be used as a receiver of prepayments.

Commercial hotels generally have solidly booked weekdays and empty weekends. Corporate bookings during the week include conventions, meetings, and transient business guests. Overbooking and no-show control could be handled by the hotel sales department that solicits the business; its estimate should come within one or two rooms of the number of rooms actually occupied.

With corporate transient reservations, the control mechanism could lie with each individual reservation. Millikin suggests that a toll-free 800 number be used solely for this type of customer. The guest can call the hotel directly, at which time certain information should be taken down— arrival time, length of stay, billing procedure, how long to hold the reservation, and whether the company will guarantee payment without a cancellation. Even here, prepayment through a certified travel agent should be considered.

Making reservations is only part of the problem. The reservation system should be segmented into types of guests—corporate, transient, travel agents' clients, or group business—and different phone numbers designated for specific types of reservations. Under this system, Millikin suggests that every reservation accepted by a hotel have a backing—either a travel agent or a corporate, association, or tour group account. Payment stipulations for both parties should be clearly spelled out.

The strength of any system lies in education. The reservations quagmire can be eliminated by educating consumers on how to make a reservation and on the problems caused by double and triple reservations, as well as educating the hotel staff on a standard operating procedure in the area of cancellations. For example, a person who cancels a reservation is given a coded cancellation number. If questioned, the guest must produce this number, preventing the possibility of having a person say he cancelled when he actually did not.

An overbooked hotel should find the guest other accommodations as courteously as possible. Though the settlements in law cases involving overbooking have up to this time been quite low, enormous damages have been awarded in Dram Act cases, cases of negligence in rape, and other types of tort cases. Basically, overbooking reflects sloppy management in a hotel or any other business.

Once a guest makes a reservation, the reservation is an enforceable contract. Most hotels and airlines do not want to enforce this contract, but in *Freeman v. Kiamesha Concord, Inc.*, the resort hotel did in fact collect for the three days contracted for, even though the guest left before the third day.

Hotel managers should train their personnel to recognize the following rights of the guests:

1 The right to the exclusive use of the room exists, as long as the guests do not abuse this right. The room is their home away from home and they have the same right of privacy as in their home. A hotel employee may enter only for maintenance, subject to the guest's privacy;

2 The right to respectful treatment;

3 The right to be free from an illegal search of the room. A warrant is required for any search;

4 The right to be free from humiliation and mental suffering (guests may sue in such cases);

5 The right to security in their room and in common areas such as lobbies and hallways;

6 The right to be free from attack by hotel employees;

7 The right to assume that the hotel is properly managed and that the keys are well secured;

8 The right to assume that only legitimate charges will be made for accommodations;

9 The right to a reasonable time in which to vacate their room;

10 The right not to be falsely arrested or illegally locked out of their room;

11 The right to receive and have telegrams and information delivered;

12 The right by custom and usage to have mail and packages forwarded;

13 The right to receive guests, subject to the reasonable rules of the hotelkeeper;

14 The right of guests, guests of guests, and strangers not to be harmed by unruly hotel guests, drunks, or hangers-on;

15 The right of guests and guests of guests to have exits in proper condition and properly marked.

QUESTIONS FOR DISCUSSION

1 When is a contract for a hotel room deemed final? Explain. What types of contracts for a room are there?

2 If a hotel overbooks, can a guest recover? What is the legal action called? What damages are possible if recovery is allowed?

3 What rights do people have when they become guests of a hotel?

4 What constitutes false imprisonment as it pertains to a guest or a hotel employee?

5 Can a guest's room be searched for narcotics when the hotelkeeper has it from good authority—the chambermaid—that there is a goodly amount in the guest's luggage? Explain.

6 What is the difference between interstate and intrastate telephone charges? Can guests be charged a telephone service charge for local calls, out-of-state calls, and calls out of the country?

7 If a hotel agrees to forward mail and packages and those items are lost, can the hotel be made to pay for such losses? Explain.

8 Conventions are generally very lucrative business for hotels. What are the problems inherent in such business?

10 Contents

10 Duty Owed Guests by Owners and Occupiers of Land

"I am further of opinion that it would be better for us to have [no laws] at all than to have them in so prodigious numbers as we have."

MICHEL DE MONTAIGNE

Accidents can and do happen. The question is *must they happen?* A person can be injured in many ways—away from home and at home. For instance, during World War II there were more casualties among Americans from accidents than there were deaths and wounds inflicted on the battlefield. In World War II, 313,000 soldiers were killed. By comparison, 386,082 persons were killed in accidents during the same period.[1]

The 1979 death and accident figures are staggering: deaths, 103,500; injuries, 68,958,000; disabling injuries, 10,000,000; and an economic cost of $75.7 billion.[2]

Accidents, of course, happen everywhere—including hotels, motels, restaurants, bars, clubs, and every other area in the tourism-travel sector of the economy. For instance, in 1979 there were 11,500 fires in hotels and motels with an economic loss of $100 million. Restaurants and taverns had 30,500 fires with losses of $284 million.[3]

The type of law discussed in this chapter is not unique to the hotel-restaurant industry. Indeed, the law in this chapter applies to all sectors of the economy dealing with owners and occupiers of land; the law is

1 National Safety Council Facts (1980).

2 Ibid.

3 Fire Journal (September 1980).

applicable to one's entry onto someone else's property for any reason whatsoever.

When a person goes on someone's property, the court regards his or her presence on that property in three possible ways: He or she may be a *trespasser*, a *licensee*, or an *invitee*. Because people are in one of these three categories when they come on the property, or can change their status because of what transpires on the property, a definition and explanation of these terms is necessary.

Trespassers

Trespassers enter the land or building without the occupier's permission or any other right to do so. Occupiers owe no duty to a trespasser with reference to the condition of the premises, save this: They must not intentionally arrange the premises in such a way that the plaintiff-trespasser is hurt (for example, by setting a spring gun trap). In 1971 the Iowa Supreme Court ruled that a trespasser could recover $20,000 actual damages and $10,000 punitive damages when the plaintiff Katko was struck in the right leg by a blast of a shotgun set by the defendant Briney in an abandoned farmhouse he owned. Katko admitted he was trespassing and pleaded guilty to a charge of larceny in the nighttime. The court said that the law "has always placed a higher value upon human safety than upon mere rights of property. . . . there is no privilege to use calculated force resulting in death or serious injury to repel trespassers" (Katko v. Briney, 183 N.W.2d 657 [Iowa, 1971]).

This does not imply that owners of land cannot take steps to repel a trespass. If the owners are present, they may use force against trespassers, but only that amount necessary to effect the repulse. Moreover, if the trespasser threatens harm to property only—even a theft of property—the possessor is not privileged to use deadly force, even if there is no other way to prevent the trespass. However, one may use deadly means, either in person or by device, when it is necessary to repel an invasion that either threatens life or serious bodily harm to the possessor or to someone he or she is legally entitled to protect.

Edwards v. *Great American Insurance Company* shows the necessity of reporting attempted burglaries or other trespasses on hotel or restaurant property to be sure that groundwork has been laid for any action taken when a prowler does in fact come on the property.

Case	**Edwards v. Great American Insurance Company**
Example	*146 So.2d 260 (La., 1962)*
	(AYRES, Judge)

This is an action in tort wherein plaintiff, as natural tutrix [guardian] of Andrew Harris Edwards, a fifteen-year-old minor, seeks to recover damages sustained by the minor when struck by a blast from a shotgun. Made defendants are Maurice F. Bullard, who fired the shot, Charles E. Brown, Bullard's employer, and Brown's public liability insurer. Following trial, there was judgment rejecting plaintiff's demands and she has appealed.

The record establishes these pertinent facts. Brown is the owner of the Hollywood Tourist Courts, a motel . . . situated at 4240 Hollywood Avenue in the city of Shreveport. Bullard, who lives in a residence to the rear of the courts, has been manager of the courts for approximately ten years. He is charged with the responsibility of managing and protecting the property.

The incident complained of occurred during the night of August 30, 1961. About 10:25 P.M., Lonnie Meredith and Ida Mae Meredith, who live nearby, observed, from their residence, two men in a vacant lot adjacent to the east side of the tourist courts. From appearances, as the Merediths viewed and appreciated them, the men were engaged in removing a window screen from the rear of one of the cabins. Information that someone was attempting to break into one of the rooms was communicated by telephone by the Merediths to the office of the tourist courts. This information was relayed to Bullard, who then seized a shotgun and repaired to his back yard, where he saw a man attempting to remove a window screen at the rear of one of the cabins. In the darkness of the night, and from a distance of approximately sixty-five feet, Bullard could not tell whether there was one or two of the parties endeavoring to enter the cabins, or what tools, if any, were being used. Bullard fired one shell loaded with no. 6 squirrel shot at the man, after which he saw someone run into the vacant lot, which was overgrown with grass and weeds about knee high. Bullard returned to his residence and phoned the police. A search by him and the police followed, but no one was found.

Andrew Harris Edwards, who at the time of the occurrence was four-teen years of age and, at the time of trial, was five feet, nine inches tall, testified that he and a companion, Larry Young, were walking through a vacant lot near the tourist courts, and, on stopping to light a cigarette, were fired upon and Edwards was shot. Edwards's testimony, corroborated by that of Larry Young, is to the further effect that they were not armed, and that after Edwards was shot, Young ran away, but afterwards returned and dragged Edwards from the scene to a tree, where they hid during the search made by the officers.

After the officers had left the scene, Young carried Edwards on his shoulder to the latter's residence. During this evacuation, the youths avoided being seen or contacted by anyone or by the police. On reaching his home, Edwards's mother telephoned the police and then carried him to the Confederate Memorial Medical Center, where he remained for a period of three days.

The youths were unable to satisfactorily explain their presence on the vacant lot to the rear of the tourist courts, across which there were no paths or walkways.

The record establishes the additional facts that on numerous, recent occasions, window screens of the motel had been torn off and the rooms broken into. Music boxes in the cabins had been torn off the walls and money taken from them. Although the particular room that the youths were attempting to enter was occupied, the record does not disclose Bullard knew that fact.

From a preponderance of the evidence, no conclusion could be reached other than that the youths were attempting to burglarize the tourist courts at the time one of them was shot. Under these circumstances, the defendants admit the shooting, but seek to avoid liability on the grounds that the youths were prowlers or intruders with the intent to harm the guests of the tourist courts, if need be, in their attempt at burglary. In view of the surrounding facts and circumstances, notably apprehension and fear, brought about by the frequent appearances of prowlers and the actual commission of burglary in the immediate past, the conclusion is inescapable that Bullard acted as a reasonable and prudent man in the act taken to repel the invasion of the courts.

The general rule is that innkeepers or keepers of lodging houses or restaurants must protect their guests, while in their places of business, against injury by third persons, whether such third persons are guests or strangers, where it is within their power to do so. Such responsibility may be entrusted to employees or other subordinates. Although the keepers of inns, lodging houses, or restaurants are not the insurers of the safety of their guests, they are under an obligation to exercise at least ordinary or reasonable care to keep them from injury.

In view of the facts and circumstances shown to have existed in this case, may it be said that Bullard's action in shooting Edwards was justified? The question for determination is, therefore, whether Bullard reasonably believed the intruder was likely to cause death or serious bodily harm to his guests unless expelled, and if the intrusion could be prevented only by the use of the force applied. . . .

We recognize the correctness of the rule that resort to the use of a dangerous weapon in order to repel a supposed attack upon a defendant's person or upon persons to whom he owes a duty to protect cannot be countenanced as justifiable save in exceptional cases where the actor's fear of the danger is not only genuine, but is founded upon facts that would be likely to produce similar emotions in men of reasonable prudence.

The trial court, in our opinion, in giving consideration to the hour of the night; the character of the neighborhood; that intruders had broken into the tourist courts on several occasions, both frequently and recently; that Edwards appeared to be attempting to enter a room of the tourist courts through a window; and that the room was occupied at the time, properly and correctly held that Bullard believed, and had good ground and reasons to believe, that Edwards was likely to cause death or serious bodily harm to his guests in the tourist courts. It would also appear reasonable for Bullard to assume, as he did, that the intruders were armed and that the intrusion could be prevented only by the use of the force applied. Such apprehension appears to have been reasonable under the facts and circumstances disclosed by the record. . . .

For the aforesaid reasons, we find no manifest error in the judgment appealed, and, accordingly, it is affirmed at plaintiff-appellant's cost.

Ruling of the Court: Affirmed.

Licensees

Licensees enter land with the occupier's permission, but only for purposes that are not connected with the occupier's interests. The occupiers must warn them of concealed dangers on the premises that they actually know about and must refrain from unreasonably dangerous *active conduct*—that is, they must take reasonable precautions in carrying on activities that might be injurious to licensees. Generally, licensees take the premises as they find them and assume the risk of any dangers arising out of their condition.

Two types of cases come readily to mind. In the first, a person comes on the property as a bona fide invitee but then, because of his or her actions (for example, by going someplace that is not allowed), reverts to becoming a licensee.

Case Example	Ortner v. Linch
	128 So.2d 152 (Fla., 1960)
	(CARROLL, CHAS., Judge)

The facts were few and without material dispute. Mrs. Hansen had rented a room in the hotel on some basis that was not shown. She was in the process of moving in, and the plaintiff was assisting her. They had brought some of Mrs. Hansen's things into the hotel, entering by the front door, and had left them in her room. Both ladies then proceeded to leave the hotel by a rear door, with the plaintiff walking ahead of Mrs. Hansen. Plaintiff explained that they left by the rear door because Mrs. Hansen's room was located near it, and because they were not well dressed. She said they descended several steps to reach the floor level on the inside, and that she fell when she stepped out of the rear door, expecting a step where there was none, between the door sill and the ground. It appeared that the sill of the rear door was high enough from the ground level to have required a step, but that there was no intervening step or platform step. It was eight o'clock at night, and the substance of plaintiff's statements in her deposition, concerning the lighting, was that there was a dim light at the rear door; that she was able to see where she was going, and that she was looking, but expected a step and none was there. Mrs. Hansen, in her affidavit, said they had no reason to anticipate that a step would be missing. There was no showing of any direction against use of the rear door of the hotel, or of any warning respecting the condition of that exit.

The trial court granted the defendant's motion and entered a summary judgment, holding that the plaintiff was a licensee rather than an invitee. In so holding, the learned trial judge was in error because as a guest of a guest in the hotel, that status of the plaintiff was that of an invitee, . . . and when the facts and evidence, which were before the trial court on the motion for summary judgment, are considered in the light of the duty owed by the defendant hotel operator to an invitee, it seems clear that the question of negligence as to whether the condition of the rear exit was unsafe or required a warning and the question of whether the plaintiff was guilty of contributory negligence were questions for jury trial. . . .

Therefore, . . . the plaintiff in the instant case, who was a guest of a guest in the hotel, was an implied invitee of the owner or operator of the hotel. Also, it would seem that because the plaintiff was assisting the hotel guest to move her possessions into the hotel, she should be considered a business invitee of the hotel, to the same extent as would a delivery man or mover engaged to render such assistance.

Appellee pointed out that the complaint referred to the hotel guest as a "tenant," and argued that while a person paying by the day is a guest in a hotel, one paying by the week or longer period is a tenant. It was then contended that while one visiting a hotel "guest" may be an invitee, a person visiting a hotel "tenant" is only a licensee. We cannot agree. The invitee status of a guest in a hotel, or of a guest of such guest, is not dependent on whether the rent is fixed by the day, by the month, or by the year. It is not material, in determining the status of a guest of a hotel guest, whether the latter is referred to as a "guest" or as a "tenant" of the hotel.

It was argued on behalf of the appellee that the plaintiff lost her status as an invitee by seeking to leave the hotel by the rear door, instead of leaving by the front door. Ordinarily, an invitee in a hotel is privileged to use the front door, or a rear door or other door that is available for entrance or exit, in the absence of restrictions or warnings to the contrary. The plaintiff in the instant case was not exploring the hotel—she was departing, using a ready and convenient means. She encountered no warning or prohibition against the use of the exit she chose. If a guest of the hotel would not lose the status of an invitee by using the rear door, then this guest of a guest, while departing by the rear door, would be and remain an invitee.

For the reasons stated the summary judgment appealed from is reversed and the cause is remanded for further proceedings not inconsistent herewith.

Ruling of the Court: Reversed.

The second type of case, although not without some contrary decisions, is in the area of the social guest. In this type of case an invitee is not truly an invitee. Therefore, if the plaintiff is a social guest in the defendant's home, the great weight of Anglo-American authority classifies this person as a bare licensee, even though he or she was expressly invited. For example, in Vogel v. Eckert, 91 A.2d 633 (N.J., 1952), a guest was injured by the collapse of a rotted bench she was sitting on. It was one of several pieces of outdoor furniture that the defendant had made several years before and had left to weather without protective paint or creosote. The plaintiff claimed that the bench was a trap. The court thought it might be, but denied recovery because the defendant did not know of the condition and had no duty to the guest to acquire such knowledge.

Such a limitation of duty probably conforms to people's reasonable expectations in the ordinary host-guest situation. If hosts do not inspect and maintain their property on their own account, the guest can scarcely expect an exception to be made on the occasion of his or her visit. In this country, moreover, where most social contact is among people who are on a similar footing, the host is usually in no better position than the guest to absorb or distribute the loss. As insurance becomes more prevalent, however, it may change the matter of duty owed to social guests.

Invitees

The occupier of land owes invitees the affirmative duty of care to discover conditions on the premises that may be unreasonably dangerous for the invitee, and either to remedy the defect or inform the invitee of the danger. In addition, the occupier must also refrain from conduct that is foreseeably and unreasonably dangerous to his invitee.

Definitions of an invitee are not as clear as one would like. Some believe it lies in conduct by the occupiers—for example, their arrangement of the premises—that encourages people to enter with a sense that it has been prepared for their safety. In some cases, there must be a need for the visit—to serve the business interest and pecuniary gain of the occupier.

The fact that an invitee is difficult to define is made more complicated because there are fifty different jurisdictions as well as certain federal jurisdictions. A few imaginative situations quickly focus on the problem. Suppose a person comes to a hotel: (1) to be a hotel guest, (2) to meet a friend, (3) to use the phone, (4) to use the restroom, (5) to have a meeting in the hotel, (6) to purchase an airline ticket, (7) to take a shortcut through the building, or (8) to rob a guest. The reasons for entering an establishment can be as diverse as the reasons for taking a vacation.

In Chance v. Lawry's, Inc., 24 Cal.Rptr. 209, 374 P.2d 185 (1962), the plaintiff, a patron, was injured when she fell into an open planter box in the foyer of a restaurant. One of the defendants, Shaw, was a contractor who had been remodeling the foyer. His employees had left the planter box unguarded when they quit work for the day. On appeal from a verdict against him, Shaw contended that the plaintiff, though an invitee of the restaurant, was only a licensee to him. The Supreme Court upheld the plaintiff's verdict, reasoning as follows:

> It is clear that where an independent contractor exercises control over the owner's premises, his duty of care towards third persons is commensurate with that of the owner. . . . In other cases, his duty of care is said to be that of a licensor . . . or is "analogous" to that of an invitor. . . . The exact duty of care imposed on an independent contractor varies with the seemingly endless combinations of relationships possible and cannot be defined by any general formula.
>
> The imposition of a legal duty by precisely defining the status of the injured person vis-à-vis the tortfeasor is hard enough and often arbitrary where the defendant is an owner or occupier of real property. . . . But where defendant is not an owner or occupier, the application of these legal distinctions becomes impossible in fact and without reason. These limitations on the duty of care of the owner or occupier "originated in an overzealous desire to safeguard the rights of ownership as it was regarded

under a system of landed estates. . . . For that reason, it can be forcefully argued that this immunity should not be extended to others. . . . [The] duty of care is owed to all those whom the contractor may reasonably expect to be affected by his work; whatever the capacity in which they come, whether as invitees or licensees or as other contractors. . . ."

The problem hotels, restaurants, and other businesses have to contend with is the fact that *they are open to the public* and the public can consist of practically anyone who for whatever reason enters the place of business. The case of Krensky v. Metropolitan Trust Company, 123 N.E.2d 345 (Ill., 1954), shows the problems a hotel has in this type of case when outsiders want to use the property for their own purpose. A group of girls visiting a drugstore decided it would be shorter or probably more exciting to leave by the hotel exit, which was considered a shortcut. The thirteen-year-old girl put her hand through the glass door and was injured. The hotel argued that the girls were merely licensees because they were not invited by the hotel to go through the premises. However, the hotel in this case was considered an invitee of all persons, not only those who were guests, but also drugstore guests and, not unreasonably, the general public.

Could the hotel have restricted the general public from going through its premises? This case seems to say no, but leaves open the question of whether custom and usage puts the premises in the domain of public use. Certainly locked doors (if permitted) and signs (if permitted) would decrease use by the general public.

Case Example	**Krensky v. Metropolitan Trust Company**
	123 N.E.2d 345 (Ill., 1954)
	(ROBSON, Justice)

This was an action brought by Cynthia Krensky to recover damages caused by the negligence of defendants in the operation of the Madison Park Hotel located on Hyde Park boulevard and Madison Park avenue, Chicago, Illinois. The cause was tried before a jury, who rendered a verdict for the plaintiff in the sum of $6,500, upon which the court entered the judgment from which defendants appeal.

Defendants' first contention is that plaintiff failed to prove any negligence on the part of defendants. The record reveals that on August 31, 1948, defendants Edward E. Glatt, Marion F. Green, and Harold J. Green were the beneficiaries under a trust charged with the operation of an apartment hotel in Chicago, Illinois. The hotel rented space on its ground floor to several stores, including a Stineway drugstore, which was located in the southeast corner of the building. Some of the stores had entrances and exits from the lobby only and some from the street and lobby. Stineway enjoyed street and lobby entrance and exit.

On August 31, 1948, plaintiff, who was then thirteen years old, went to a neighborhood movie with two girl friends in the afternoon. Upon leaving the movie at about 4:30, she and her friends went to the drugstore and entered through the street doors. She made a purchase and left the drugstore to go to her home through the lobby to the exit on the Madison

Park avenue side of the hotel, at which are located two French inner swinging doors, each containing three panels of glass in five rows. She and her friends walked abreast up to the doors. Plaintiff placed her right hand on the push plate of the right door. The door was locked, and her hand slipped off the push plate and went through a pane of glass, cutting her wrist. Plaintiff introduced testimony to show that the glass in the door was thinner than ordinary window glass and was defectively mounted; the putty was cracked and missing, and the glass was loose. Tenants of the hotel would bang the door with their baby buggies and would break the glass about once a month and on other occasions would crack it. There was evidence that on windy days, it was customary to latch the door in question to prevent drafts. Plaintiff stated, however, she had never found the door latched. There was no warning sign of any kind that the door was locked.

The law does not charge one with anticipating dangers and negligent conditions, but one may assume that others have done their duty to give proper warning of hidden dangers.

Defendants next contend that the plaintiff as a matter of law did not prove herself free from contributory negligence. She was thirteen years of age when the accident occurred. The law of this state is that as to a child between the ages of seven and fourteen, the question of culpability is one of fact and must be left to the jury to determine, taking into consideration the age, capacity, intelligence, and experience of the child. On this point, the record reveals that Helen Schwartz, a witness for defendants, testified that immediately prior to the accident she was walking behind plaintiff and her two friends as they left the drugstore. As they approached the door the other girls were trying to get something that plaintiff was holding in her hands. The friends were making playful gestures at trying to get it. As plaintiff and her friends reached the door, she had stopped just behind them to open the door to the ladies' room. She saw, first, the plaintiff's hand against the center pane second from the top. She put the key in the door of the ladies' room. She began to turn the key. She even opened the door. Then she heard a crash of glass, and then she looked up and saw plaintiff's arm had gone through the glass. She then went into the restroom. She did nothing about the injury to the plaintiff and made no inquiry about it.

Mr. Firmin R. Therond, manager of the hotel at the time, a witness for defendants, testified that the morning following the accident, he had seen missing from the right-hand door the center pane in the second row from the top. Upon cross-examination he admitted that at the time of a deposition given approximately one year after the accident, he had had no certain recollection which panel he had found missing at the time he had examined the door. He said that a Mr. Valento, who later died, used to be at the hotel, did all the repair work, and replaced the glass in the door. He said that on the average, one pane a month was broken by tenants who pushed the protruding ends of baby buggies or strollers into the doors to open them. He denied that the right-hand door had been revarnished, repainted, or repaired between August 31, 1948, when plaintiff sustained the injury, and March 1949, but admitted that there might have been some very slight repairs that he did not know about.

Henry A. Kuehl, an engineer and contractor, testified for defendants that he had some time in March 1949, at the request of defendants, examined the door and found repairs to the pane located second from the top in the center. The others showed varnish on their edges, whereas that one was perfectly clear. The bottom of that pane is fifty-one inches from the ground. Mr. Kuehl's examination was made almost seven months after the accident. He did not know when the last coat of varnish had been put on, nor when repairs were last made.

The plaintiff, Cynthia Krensky, denied that she had anything in her hand that the other girls were trying to get. She denied she had her hand raised. One of the other girls with her at the time testified that neither she nor the other girl was trying to get anything from the Krensky girl's hand. She denied that Cynthia's hand was raised. They were not frolicking. Nor were they running, jumping, or scuffling. They were walking. They saw no one behind them, no one opening the door to the ladies' room. The Krensky girl, in testifying, pointed to the pane in the row adjacent to the brass push plate, third from the top and bottom, as the pane through which her hand crashed as it moved off the metal plate.

In view of the sharp conflict in the testimony, and considering that plaintiff was thirteen years of age, we are of the opinion that this was a question of fact for the jury.

Defendants contend that plaintiff was not an invitee but a mere licensee, and that they were obligated only to refrain from willfully causing her injury. Coupled with this contention is their objection to plaintiff's instruction given by the court to the effect that if plaintiff immediately prior to the accident was a patron of the drugstore, and she was leaving the drugstore through the lobby of the hotel on her way home at the time of the accident, then she was an invitee on defendants' premises. They contend that the court erred in refusing to give their instruction to the effect that plaintiff must prove by a preponderance of the evidence that she was invited upon the premises of the defendants by one of the tenants occupying quarters in the hotel. If she failed to prove that at the time of the occurrence in question she was so invited into the hotel or the lobby, then the defendants should be found not guilty.

Hotels that invite the public to enter upon their premises for the purpose of gain or profit are under a duty not to permit the existence of a danger that might cause an injury to their invitees.

In the instant case, the rental paid by the several stores in defendants' hotel was of necessity based upon the patronage of the general public, as well as guests of the hotel. There is no evidence in the record that the hotel restricted use of its lobby entrances and exits to its guests, and the general public was invited to use the lobby, as well as the street entrances and exits to its lessees' stores. In the case of *Murphy v. Illinois State Trust Co.*, the plaintiff, after visiting a tavern, was injured while leaving through the back door onto the porch that was under the control of the landlord. The evidence showed that the rear entrance was customarily used by patrons of the tavern with the consent of the landlord. The court held that the landlord, by permitting its use by patrons of the tavern, was liable.

We conclude that plaintiff was an invitee of defendants. It follows that the giving of plaintiff's instruction was proper, and that the refusal of defendants' instruction was not error.

Defendants next contend that the verdict was excessive. They state that there was no formal proof of plaintiffs out-of-pocket expense; that she suffered no permanent damage and has practically the complete function of her hand. Dr. Kobak testified that a reasonable charge for his services would be $1,000; that the reasonable charges of the hospital services would be approximately $400. No objection was raised by defendants to the reasonable value of Dr. Kobak's services at the time. When certain questions pertaining to the hospital bill were corrected, defendants did not object. They, therefore, cannot object now. Defendants say that it may be true that plaintiff sustained a severe injury, but that she recovered completely; that she has complete function. The record reveals that there were severe injuries to her hand. She was in the operating room for over four hours; in the hospital five or six days. Thereafter, for a year or more, she was given physical therapy and rehabilitation treatments to restore and maintain proper nutrition and muscle tone of the hand. There has been only a partial regeneration of the median nerve of her hand. Sensory function has been permanently lost in the area of the injury. Motor function is impaired. Further regeneration is not to be expected. The wound left an ugly livid keloidal scar across the entire surface of her inner wrist. Under the circumstances, we cannot say that the verdict of $6,500 was excessive. . . .

Ruling of the Court: Judgment affirmed.

Another aspect of this relationship is illustrated by Davis v. Garden Services, Inc., 270 S.E.2d 228 (Ga., 1980), which concerns a musician employed by someone who rented a hotel ballroom. While Davis was performing at a party in the ballroom, he sustained injuries when he fell from the stage when the metal stripping that held the carpeting secure gave way.

The court held that Davis was a business invitee on the premises. Therefore, those who come on the premises as guests of the business invitee (tenant) for business purposes beneficial to the guest and those doing business with him stand in the shoes of the tenant insofar as they suffer injury due to the negligence of the owner or occupier of the premises. It was not necessary for there to be a contractual relationship between the hotel and the injured musician. It was sufficient that he had entered into a contract with the hotel's tenant. Because the hotel knew that the tenant was going to have a dance in the rented room and that musicians were going to be hired to play for the dance, it follows that: The musician stood in the shoes of the tenant that hired him; the hotel owed him the same degree of care that it owed the tenant; this was the duty to exercise ordinary care. Whether the hotel had exercised ordinary care insofar as the injured musician was concerned is a jury question. Furthermore, the lower court judge who had directed a verdict for the defendant was in error, and this court reversed his action.

Duty Owed Guests in Room Conditions

Having explained what constitutes negligence, it is appropriate to examine specific cases dealing with hotels, restaurants, bars, and other public places as to the liability of the owner-manager when guests have an accident. A person who becomes a valid guest of an establishment is an invitee and is owed a certain amount of care. This chapter examines various parts of the hotel or restaurant to see what the proprietor must do to protect guests from injury and the degree of care owed guests.

Cleanliness of the Room

The leading case on the cleanliness of a room is Nelson v. Ritz Carlton Restaurant and Hotel Company, 157 A.133 (N.J., 1931). The plaintiff was assigned to a hotel room that had been recently vacated by guests. The room was very messy; wastebaskets were not emptied, and the floor was covered with lint and cigarette ashes. The plaintiff left for a few hours to allow the maid time to clean. When she returned, she found that only the bed had been changed and clean towels put in the bathroom. She retired for the night. In the morning, the plaintiff got up to answer a knock on the door and stepped on a needle that broke after breaking the skin. She received medical attention, but as a result of the accident the foot became infected. The plaintiff was awarded $2,500 compensation because of the accident. The court stated that the proprietor of a hotel is bound to use due care to have a room thoroughly cleaned before reassignment. Because the hotelkeeper failed in the performance of this duty and did not properly explain such neglect, he was held liable.

Beds and Other Furniture

Courts have generally permitted recovery for injuries caused by defective beds and furniture, although the rationale varies from case to case. In Shattuck v. St. Francis Hotel and Apartments, 60 P.2d 855 (Cal., 1936), recovery was made on the implied warranty that the folding bed in one of its rooms was safe; consequently, the court permitted recovery for the plaintiff, who was injured when a headboard fell on her.

In Lyttle v. Denny, 71 A. 841 (Pa., 1909), the plaintiff's room contained a bed that could be folded in an upright position when not in use. When he arose one morning, the top of the extremely heavy folding bed struck him on the head, causing severe injuries. The lower court held that it was up to the plaintiff to prove in detail what was wrong with the bed and the reason it fell. The court of appeals disagreed, stating that such an extraordinary accident cast the burden of explanation on the defendant hotelkeeper. The accident was so unusual that it probably could not have resulted from anything less than negligence by the hotel management. Beds do not usually operate as spring traps to close upon and catch a trusting guest. The facts judicated a lack of reasonable care on the hotelkeeper's part, and it was for him to show why he should be relieved from liability. The judgment for the defendant was reversed and remanded.

Although most cases require a hotel or other public accommodation to prove it was not negligent, a few hold that although the hotel owes a duty to keep its premises and furnishings reasonably safe for use, it is not an insurer of its guests' safety, and its duty is not isolated when the defective condition is latent and not capable of being discovered by frequent inspections.

In Nettles v. Forbes Motel, Inc., 182 So.2d 572 (La., 1966), the hotel manager assumed incorrectly that a stool would not be used by a short person to change the temperature on the air conditioner, located eighty-one inches from the floor. Needless to say, this assumption was erroneous—the plaintiff did use a stool to change the air conditioner setting and was injured when the stool collapsed. Was the plaintiff contributorily negligent in using the stool? The answer in this case was no because the premises were not safe for the guest.

The defendants denied any negligence as the plaintiff had stood on the stool when she knew that it was intended for another purpose, and she had failed to exercise proper care in doing so. The record revealed, however, that a number of the motel's stools had previously come loose as they had been improperly assembled. The court held the motel liable since the stool in question had not been inspected for soundness—an exercise of reasonable care to keep the premises safe for guests. Nettles received over $3,500 for pain and suffering and for special damages.

Brewer v. Roosevelt Motor Lodge, 295 A.2d 647 (Me., 1972), raises a different question about the actions of the plaintiff-guest. In this case, the motor lodge had forty rooms on the ground level. After showering, the plaintiff left the window open, covered only by a screen that had no locking device. An intruder broke into her room, assaulted and raped her, and stole her wrist watch. The defendant motor lodge operator was not found liable for her safety. While in Nettles v. Forbes the court said it was not up to the plaintiff to prove her case, in the Brewer case, the plaintiff had to prove that it was negligence to not provide a locking device on the half screen in the motor court. The court ruled that all necessary protection was incorporated in the room: A chain lock was on the door, the window had a lock on it to keep the window locked, and there was an operating air conditioner to remove postbath vapors. Whether these measures were adequate was a jury question.

Furniture used by guests is sometimes abused or just wears out. To what extent should a hotel be liable when furniture collapses and a guest is hurt? In Gary Hotels Courts, Inc., v. Perry, 251 S.E.2d 37 (Ga., 1978), the webbing for a chair seat was missing. But a cushion was on the seat, and when the guest sat on it and it collapsed, it caused him injury. The court said the hotel owed the guest the duty of ordinary care to afford the guest premises that are reasonably safe for use and occupancy. The same results were obtained in Palagano v. Georgian Terrace Hotel Co., 181 S.E.2d 512 (Ga., 1971), where the injury was sustained as a result of the collapse of a bed in the defendant's hotel. The court said, "There was some evidence from which a jury might find that the bed was defective and that such defect could, or should, have been discovered by a reasonable inspection." A similar result followed where the plaintiff was seated in the defendant's restaurant and the chair collapsed, injuring him. Again a jury would be authorized to conclude that the defendant was in full control of the chair and as such was responsible for its maintenance . . . (and) . . . would be authorized (jury) to infer negligence from the evidence that the chair collapsed during ordinary use by the plaintiff (Gresham v. Stouffer Corp., 241 S.E.2d 451 [Ga., 1978]).

Windows, Window Fixtures, and Screens

In Rue v. Warner Hotel Company, 186 So. 625 (1939), the plaintiff-guest in the defendant hotel was trying to close a window when it shattered, injuring her arm. The court ruled the plaintiff had a cause of action because testimony showed that the putty around the window pane was old and decayed, a defect that could have been ascertained by a reasonable inspection. The same results were obtained in another case in which an invitee of a guest was injured by a transom glass that fell when the plaintiff closed the door to the guest's room. Evidence showed that the glass had been broken some time before the accident (Kramer Service v. Wilkins, 186 So. 625 [Miss., 1939]).

A window shade falling on a guest and injuring her was pleaded properly when the doctrine of res ipsa loquitur ("the thing speaks for itself") was used. The court in Hotel Dempsey Company v. Teel, 128 F.2d 673 (1942), affirmed the verdict, stating that in the absence of an intervening cause, such an occurrence would not ordinarily happen without negligence on the part of the innkeeper.

However, where children are involved, there is no unanimity of decisions. The leading case of Baker v. Dallas Hotel Company, 73 F.2d 825 (1934), held that recovery could be made in the case of a child falling to his death when a screen that was insecurely fastened fell out. But a contrary ruling was held in Schlemmer v. Stokes, cited in Cross White v. Shelby Operating Corp., 30 S.E.2d 673, where the facts differed only in that the child pushed through a screen and fell out of a window. The court held that no liability could be imposed where the evidence showed no visible defect in the screen and where, despite their inspection, neither the plaintiff nor the defendant had found any defects in the screen before the accident.

The case of Messina v. Sheraton Corporation of America, 291 So.2d 829 (La., 1974), had a different twist. The plaintiff was the promoter of a boxing match that was to feature Beau Jaynes. The night before the fight, Jaynes injured his hand in his room at the Sheraton Charles when a venetian blind collapsed as he was adjusting it. The boxing commission cancelled the fight, and the plaintiff sued the defendant hotel to recover his lost revenue. The court said that although Jaynes might have an action against the defendant, the plaintiff could not sue in contract for the alleged negligent injury. It is a basic principle of law that a tortfeasor (wrongdoer) is responsible only for the direct and proximate result of his acts; when a third person suffers damage because of a contractual obligation to the injured party, such damage is too remote and indirect to become the subject of a direct action.

The doctrine of res ipsa loquitur was said to apply in Panepinto v. Morrison Hotel, Inc., 218 N.E.2d 880 (Ill., 1966), when a transom over the door to the plaintiff's room fell and struck her as she was leaving for a convention meeting in the hotel. Her recovery was later reduced from $100,000 to $65,000 for technical reasons.

Lighting and Heating

Injuries resulting from lighting and electrical shocks have not produced many cases. The early case of Reid v. Ehr, 174 N.W. 71 (N.D., 1919), has not been modified through the years. In that case, the plaintiff suffered a shock when she turned on an electric light in her room. The court said that the injury was occasioned by the lack of reasonable care on the part of the defendant in maintaining and inspecting the electrical equipment in the room.

In most cases, the failure to furnish safe heating has resulted in the injured guest's recovering damages. In Wilson v. Benoit, 231 S.W.2d 916 (1950), the court held that the proprietor of tourist cabins was under a duty to provide safe cabins for guests. It further held that when a guest was killed by a gas explosion in his cabin, the decision whether the explosion was caused by a defective hose connection on a gas heater was a jury question. The court said the fact that the plaintiff was drunk had no causal connection with the explosion and ruled out a verdict of contributory negligence.

Animals and Insects

Very few cases in the United States have considered injuries from animals or insects. In one 1940 case, Cunningham v. Neil House Hotel Co., 33 N.E.2d 859 (Ohio, 1940), the plaintiff-guest at the defendant hotel was awakened by a burning and stinging sensation on her right arm caused by an insect bite. The plaintiff pleaded res ipsa loquitur. It was held that the principle of res ipsa loquitur does not apply to every cause of injury or accident, but only to those whose occurrence implies a breach of duty. The insect that stung or bit the plaintiff was not known or identified, nor was it known where it came from, how long it had been in the room, or the conditions under which it had entered the room. In this situation, to permit the jury to draw an inference of lack of due care on the part of the hotel company would have been conjecture not appropriate in the application of the doctrine of res ipsa loquitur.

The plaintiff in Williams v. Milner Hotel Company, 36 A.2d 20 (Conn., 1944), was bitten by a rat while lying in bed at night. Evidence showed that there were numerous rat holes in the baseboard of the room prior to this event. The defendant claimed that he had taken all necessary precautions by employing a cleaning man and a competent exterminator and that the room was routinely inspected. In affirming for the plaintiff, the court said that the question of whether the defendant had exercised reasonable care to keep the hotel in a safe condition was for the jury to decide.

A case that often disturbs students is that of *DeLuce v. Fort Wayne Hotel*. The case attracts sympathy for the plaintiff who, having been bitten by a rat, was depicted running out of the hotel with the rat unwilling to give up the finger it bit. However, as unpleasant as the case may be, it does illustrate what one may expect in certain hotels as to the rodent situation; what is required of hotelkeepers to avoid being sued; whether it is reasonably foreseeable that rats will enter the lobby; and what statutes protect guests from this type of situation. Such information not only pertains to rats and mice, but also to cockroaches and other animals and vermin that may create havoc when they are discovered by a guest.

Case Example	**DeLuce v. Fort Wayne Hotel** *311 F.2d 853 (Mich., 1962)* *(MC ALLISTER, Circuit Judge)*

This is an appeal by the Fort Wayne Hotel from a judgment in the amount of $25,000 awarded to one of its guests, Virginia DeLuce, appellee herein, who claimed to have suffered injury and disability as a result of being bitten by a rat on the hotel premises. Her claim is based on negligence of the hotel in failing to keep its premises free from rats.

According to the evidence introduced on her behalf, Miss DeLuce, after being bitten, was treated by first aid and given an injection of penicillin. Afterward, at a hospital, she was given a tetanus antitoxin injection and a further injection of penicillin. According to appellee's evidence, she later developed postencephalitic Parkinsonism and, two years after the accident, at the time of the trial, she suffered from that disease, being permanently disabled and incapacitated for the work she had previously carried on as an actress, singer, and dancer in films, television, night clubs, and Broadway shows.

The district court charged the jury that the relevant statute of the state of Michigan made it mandatory upon a hotel owner to keep his premises free from rats; that the statute was not only mandatory, but imposed an absolute liability rather than a duty to use due care; that if appellee had been bitten by a rat while on the hotel premises, appellant hotel would be guilty of negligence, and she was entitled to recover. The court properly instructed the jury on the questions of proximate cause and contributory negligence.

Appellant hotel claims that the district court erred in refusing to charge the jury that the hotel was not liable for the injury unless it knew, or, by the exercise of reasonable care, should have known, of the presence of rats on its premises.

The background of the case is as follows: Miss DeLuce was a registered guest at the hotel on the date of the accident. On the day after her arrival, arrangements were made by her producer to present a preview of a show for executives of an automotive company at the home of one of the executives. Miss DeLuce had been informed that there was a swimming pool where the performance was taking place, and that she could go swimming if she so desired. She brought her swim equipment, which consisted of a snorkel, a mask, hand fins, and foot fins. Because of the coolness of the weather, she decided not to go swimming. Following the conclusion of the show at 8:30 P.M., a buffet dinner was served, and she, with other performers, afterward left the executive's home at approximately 10:00 P.M. and was taken back to the appellant hotel. When she got out of the car and entered the hotel, she had with her all her music and swimming paraphernalia. She went through the lobby, put her things on a chair, and went to the desk to ascertain whether she had any messages. She then made a call to see if certain performers in the show had returned to the hotel.

As she went back to the desk, she saw a man in the vestibule, who appeared to be hitting the top of the radiator with one of her swim fins. She ran across the lobby, through the door, and found that the man had thrown her fins down on the floor by the radiator. She reached down to pick them up and felt a sharp bite on her hand. She stood up quickly, and a rat approximately a foot long was hanging from her finger. Calling for help, she opened the door of the hotel with her left hand, rushed out onto the sidewalk, and started to shake the rat, and it fell and ran away.

Charles B. Nunley, an employee of the hotel, was called as an adverse witness by plaintiff's counsel. Mr. Nunley was a night bellman, whose duties required him to be, at times, in front of the hotel to carry guests' baggage to and from their rooms. There was no doorman at the hotel. Mr. Nunley testified that he often saw rats coming out of the alley around the hotel. The alley was seventy feet from the hotel entrance. He had also seen rats on the sidewalk outside of the hotel, and he had actually chased them off the sidewalk. He testified that the hotel doors had been left open that night, prior to the time Miss DeLuce was bitten by the rat. The vestibule, where she had stepped down to pick up her swim fins, and the lobby floor are level with the sidewalk. When Mr. Nunley was asked whether rats could run right into the hotel when the door was open, he said: "If somebody scares a rat, you know, you can't tell which way he will run." When Miss DeLuce was bitten by the rat, Mr. Nunley was serving food in guests' rooms upstairs, and had just come down on the elevator. The Fort Wayne Hotel produced Mr. Bart Edds as a witness. He testified that he was maintenance man for the hotel and had seen, in the alley next to the hotel, numerous rats flattened out where cars had run over them at night. Ivor Bennett, a former pest-control operator, whose company was employed by the hotel for the extermination of vermin, including rats, testified that the location where the Fort Wayne Hotel was situated was one of the worst rat-ridden areas in the city. He called it the "second worst place" in Detroit for rats.

Other witnesses testified as to seeing rats in the adjacent alley, and also as to seeing the rat clinging to the hand of Miss DeLuce before she ran to the street and shook it off. Rats are ferocious and dangerous carriers of disease and, in Michigan, a bounty is paid for killing them.

The issue before us is whether there was an absolute liability on the part of the hotel to keep its premises free from rats, or whether it was subject only to the duty to use due care.

In view of the fact that the Michigan statute, which used mandatory language, has not been held by the Supreme Court of that state to impose an absolute liability, but only liability if the owner knew or should have known of such dangerous condition of his premises, . . . we are of the view that by analogy, the same rule applies to the owner's responsibility for keeping his premises free from rats.

It is further contended by appellee that the evidence of the presence of rats in the alley adjoining the hotel and on the sidewalk in front of the hotel created an affirmative duty on the part of the hotel to protect its paying guests from the foreseeable event that such rats might enter the hotel through its doors, especially in view of the fact that the doors were on a level with the sidewalk, and the hotel took no precautions to keep rats out of its vestibule and lobby. In brief, counsel for appellee submits that under the uncontradicted and uncontested facts of the case, the hotel must have foreseen that a rat might enter the hotel if the doors were left open. Negligence and contributory negligence are ordinarily questions of fact for the jury. It is only where the facts are such that all reasonable men must draw the same conclusion from them that the question of negligence becomes one of law for the court. There is no evidence that any rats had ever been seen in the hotel vestibule or lobby before the night of this accident, or that any guest had ever been bitten by a rat. Although counsel for appellee cogently argues this issue, we are of the view that the question of whether it was reasonably foreseeable that a rat might enter the vestibule or the lobby of the hotel is a question of fact for the jury, and failure of the hotel to use such care as was necessary to avoid a danger, which should and could have been anticipated, would constitute negligence. If, through the hotel's failure to use due care to keep its premises free from rats, the rat in question was on the premises at the time of the accident, the hotel would be guilty of a violation of the statute and, therefore, negligent per se.

Ruling of the Court: In accordance with the foregoing, the judgment is set aside and the case remanded for a new trial.

Bathroom Appliances and Hot Water

Generally, an innkeeper will be held liable for injuries sustained by a guest when the evidence indicates that the innkeeper has breached his or her duty to maintain a safe bathroom. The innkeeper may be absolved in one of three ways: (1) where, as a matter of law, the innkeeper is not negligent; (2) where a defect is latent and cannot be detected by normal inspection; (3) where the guest is contributorily negligent. Two cases clearly show the problems that the hotelkeeper has in bathroom cases. Brown Hotel Company v. Marx, 411 S.W.2d 911 (Ky., 1967), is a "hardware" case, in which the plaintiff, while turning on the water faucet, cut his hand when the porcelain faucet broke into pieces. The plaintiff used the doctrine of res ipsa loquitur, which was upheld by the court. Naturally, when this doctrine is accepted, it is most difficult for the defendant to win, and as expected in this case, he lost. Not all similar cases are permitted to use the doctrine of res ipsa loquitur, but where it is, the plaintiff normally wins.

In the second case, Hull v. Holiday Inns of America, the plaintiff was scalded by excessively hot bath water. What temperature should water be in a hotel? This case gives management insights about hot water temperature and the type of mixing valves needed.

Case	**Hull v. Holiday Inns of America, Inc.**
Example	*478 F.2d 224 (Mich., 1973)*
	(PER CURIAM)

This is an appeal by Charles Hull, plaintiff-appellant, from a judgment of no cause of action by the United States District Court for the Eastern District of Michigan, Southern Division. The plaintiff brought an action against Holiday Inns of America, as defendant, to recover damages for injuries alleged to have been sustained by excessively hot water in the bathtub of a Holiday Inn in Detroit, Michigan. Holiday brought in other parties as third party defendants, but this opinion will involve only the plaintiff and defendant as briefed by the parties.

The plaintiff had been a guest of the inn in question for thirty-five days, and on the morning of September 11, 1967, he undertook to take a bath in the bathtub. He turned on the hot water only, and in attempting to test the temperature of the water while sitting on the edge of the tub, he slipped in the tub and sustained the injuries of which he complains. The plaintiff received severe burns to his right hand and right buttocks.

It is claimed on behalf of the plaintiff that the water in the bathtub was excessively hot, of a temperature in excess of what is regarded as safe for such use, and that the defendant violated its duty to maintain its premises in a reasonably safe condition for plaintiff, as an invitee. The severity of plaintiff's injury is not in question. It was admitted for the purpose of the motion for a directed verdict that if the defendant supplied water in excess of 150°F to plaintiff's room for bath purposes, it would have been in excess of that customarily permitted and regarded as safe.

The district judge, in granting the motion for judgment of no cause of action, held that the plaintiff had failed to offer evidence that the temperature of the water was in excess of 150°F or that the defendant had violated its duty toward plaintiff to maintain its premises in a reasonably safe condition.

In considering a motion for a directed verdict, the judge must consider all of the testimony in the light most favorable to the plaintiff.

Obviously, there is no evidence available of the exact temperature of the water at the time the plaintiff fell into the tub and received his injuries. Mechanically, there was a separate boiler to furnish hot water to the rooms of the motel. The gauge on it was set at 180°F. There is a Holby mixing valve that mixes the hot water as it comes from the boiler with cold water to a proper temperature for the rooms. There is a gauge or thermometer on this mixing valve to regulate the temperature of the water that goes to the rooms. There is no evidence of the temperature at which that gauge or thermometer was set. There was also a limit switch that was supposed to cut off when the water got up to a certain temperature. There is no evidence of the temperature setting of it or whether it was functioning.

Dr. Joseph D. Carlysle, a plastic surgeon who treated the plaintiff, testified that the nature of plaintiff's burns were such as might be received in water of 180°F in thirty seconds. He did not testify whether such burns could be received in water of a temperature of 150°F or less, or how long it would take to get such burns as the plaintiff had in water of 150°F or less.

The plaintiff testified that he turned on the hot water and sat on the side of the tub. When he reached over to test the water with his hand, he slipped and fell into the tub. He caught himself on his right hand and right hip and, as he went down, he bumped his head on something that caused a bump on his head, as reported by the hospital. To extricate himself, he reached for the basin, which was right by the tub, with his left hand and pushed himself out with his hand and hip. In the process, he knocked a glass off of the basin, which broke on the side of the tub and caused some cuts on the left hip and left buttocks.

He testified further that he was in a daze and didn't know exactly how long he was in the water. He said he got up as fast as he could and estimated that he was in the water seven, eight, or ten seconds.

Dr. Carlysle testified: "The infliction of a burn depends on the temperature of the agent, the duration that the patient is in contact with the agent, and also the area of the skin involved, and even the age of the patient. . . . To have these burns inflicted, the water would, in my opinion, would have to be excessively hot—as I said before, in excess of 150, and even approaching ranges of 180 and above."

On cross-examination he testified that at 135°F one might receive burns comparable to the ones the plaintiff had in five minutes.

Thus, a crucial fact in the case is the length of time the plaintiff was in the water. We consider that the jury is entitled to draw inferences from the physical facts, as well as the oral evidence. We conclude from the fact that only the plaintiff's right hand and right buttocks were burned that the jury might well infer that no other part of his body was in the water, and that he could not have remained in that position over a few seconds, which would indicate that the water was excessively hot.

Counsel for the defendant argues that the plaintiff was guilty of contributory negligence as a matter of law. The district judge did not decide this question. We consider, however, that it is a question for the jury to decide under all of the facts of the case.

Ruling of the Court: Judgment reversed and the case is remanded to the district court for trial to a jury.

In Bearse v. Fowler, 196 N.E.2d 910 (Mass., 1969), a guest sustained injuries when she slipped and fell in her bathroom at the defendant's motel. The trial court entered judgment for the defendant, and the plaintiff appealed. The Supreme Court held that even though the guest was injured falling from a tub because she was unable to shut off the hot water on a shower fixture, the motel was not negligent because the fixture was new, the motel owner made a daily inspection of the shower handles, and there was no evidence that any defect in the fixture was known to the owner, or that in the exercise of due care the owner should have known of any defect.

Duty Owed Guests and Others in Public Areas

This section deals with those areas that the hotel considers its public areas, such as its lobby, stairs, elevators, bars, doors, and dining rooms.

Lobby

Because the lobby is the most frequently used area, special precautions should be taken, especially when cleaning the floors and furniture. Where possible, barriers should be set up until the area is again fit for use.

Elevators

The elevator is an indispensable part of a hotel, and since hotels often position restaurants and bars on high floors to take advantage of the view, more elevator accidents are taking place. The type of accidents range from a nonleveling accident to the malfunctioning elevator that plunges down out of control.

In general, a hotelkeeper who operates an elevator for the transportation of guests from one floor to another is bound to use at least ordinary care in the maintenance and operation of the elevator; and in some states, a high or the highest degree of care is required.

Blackhawk Hotels Company v. Bonfoey, 227 F.2d 232 (Minn., 1955), concerns a passenger elevator that fell about forty-five feet, injuring the plaintiff-guest. At the time of the accident, the elevator carried nine persons, which was not an overload. When the operator tried to stop the elevator after leaving the third floor, he exclaimed he could not stop it. The operator had received fifteen minutes of training from another operator and did not have a license as required by law.

The elevator was approximately twenty-five years old, was maintained by a service group, and had not been modernized over the years. It was the hotel's contention that the service group should be held responsible for the accident because of negligently maintaining the elevator. The court said that the hotel had a nondelegable duty as to elevators to see that reasonable care was used in furnishing safe elevator transportation. The general rule on this subject matter is that normally an employer is not liable for the acts of an independent contractor or their servants for work performed on the property. Elevators are, of course, one of the exceptions to this rule.

In elevator cases, the doctrine of res ipsa loquitur can be used, but it can be used only against the hotel because only the hotel has exclusive control of all instrumentalities causing the accident. The independent contractor had no control over the operators nor on modernization; hence the doctrine of *res ipsa loquitur* could not be used against them. Furthermore, unless the hotel could show that the independent contractor was guilty of negligence that proximately caused or contributed to the happening of the accident, the Blackhawk Hotel would not have a claim for indemnity or contribution against them; hence, only Blackhawk was guilty.

Another elevator case deals with an accident caused by nonleveling. In Jenkins v. Missouri State Life Insurance Company, 69 S.W.2d 666 (Mo., 1934), the plaintiff alleged that she was injured by the defendant's failure to bring his hotel elevator level with the third floor so that she might alight with reasonable safety. The plaintiff testified that she got in the elevator to go from the lobby to the third floor. When the operator stopped the elevator at her floor, she glanced down before starting out, but because the elevator and hall were dimly lighted, she did not notice whether the elevator floor was level with the hall floor. When she attempted to step out, she struck her foot against the wall of the elevator shaft, which caused her to plunge "right out through the opening of the elevator door into the hall," breaking her right arm at the elbow. The elevator operator testified that as the plaintiff got off the elevator, "she turned around and started to say something to me, and when she turned back she fell over." The elevator was electric and automatic, but the plaintiff said that she had never operated it. The question of whether the operator brought the elevator to the floor level or whether he was negligent in its operation was held to be a question for the jury.

The reviewing court said, "A carrier of passengers by an elevator has the same liability and duty of care for their safety as a carrier by railroad or a carrier of any other kind. One of these duties is to provide passengers a reasonably safe means of exit. Stopping the elevator at the third floor and opening the doors to the hallway was an invitation to the plaintiff to leave. It amounted to an assurance by the operator that she could do so in safety. Before giving such an invitation and assurance, it was his duty to place the elevator in such a position that plaintiff had a reasonably safe means of leaving it."

When an innkeeper leaves the door to an elevator open or unlocked so that a guest falls into the well and is injured, the innkeeper is ordinarily held liable (Hayward v. Merrill, 94 Ill. 349 [1880]). But in spite of the innkeeper's neglect of duty, guests cannot recover if they themselves were negligent. Thus, in a case where the guest was familiar with the elevator, found the door partly open, pushed it further, and fell in, his recovery was barred by his contributory negligence. If the hallway were not well lighted, however, it would be a jury question as to whether the guest was contributorily negligent (Bremer v. Pleiss, 98 N.W. 945 [1904]).

Automatic or passenger-operated elevators are distinguished from a manually operated elevator in that the latter is the agent of the innkeeper. The automatic elevator, when in serviceable condition, has three distinguishing features: (1) It is operated by push button; (2) its doors interlock so that it cannot be moved while any door is open; (3) it is designed to be operated by any passenger. The conventional or manual elevator lacks one or more of these characteristics. Certain consequences follow from these distinctions, and in the event of an accident, may distinguish the case from one involving a conventional elevator. The manufacturer or contractor installing the automatic elevator, the operating owner or lessee, and those under contract to service or inspect it must act with a higher degree of care because of these features. They know the automatic elevator will usually not be in the hands of a skilled operator, but will be run by passengers of all ages and aptitudes who often have little familiarity with such elevators. For that reason, the doctrines of res ipsa loquitur, "dangerous instrumentality," and "attractive nuisance" are more readily applicable to an accident involving an automatic elevator than to one caused by a conventional elevator. Conversely, passengers using the automatic elevator may rely to a great extent on its automatic features and are seldom held contributorily negligent (6 A.L.R.2d 391).

The cases in point are split as to the degree of care required. Where the courts hold the innkeeper only to reasonable care, however, the results are substantially the same. Therefore, in Parker v. Manchester Hotel Company, 85 P.2d 152 (Cal., 1938), in which the plaintiff tripped and fell to the floor of the lobby while leaving the automatic elevator, thereby sustaining injuries that were the direct result of the defendant's negligence, testimony was introduced to show that the hotel had had previous difficulties with the elevator. The court stated the defendant's liability in the case as follows: "There is no question about the rule in California that the owner of an elevator is responsible for injury occasioned by the slightest neglect that human care and foresight might have guarded, and that, though not insurers of the absolute safety of passengers, they are bound to utmost care and diligence to every cautious person."

In 1977 the Nevada Supreme Court in the case of American Elevator Company v. Briscoe, 572 P.2d 534 (Nev., 1977), held that the doctrine of res ipsa loquitur applied. The case involved a claim against the Holiday Hotel in Reno of negligently maintaining its elevators. On February 22, 1974, Briscoe, an employee of the hotel, entered the elevator at the fifth floor, intending to go to the sixth floor. Although Briscoe pressed the correct button, the elevator suddenly began a descent, ending with a series of jarring stops at or near the first floor and finally settling on the basement level. Other employees observed Briscoe in a somewhat shaken state, suffering apparent back pain.

The elevator company had a contract to service and maintain the elevators in the hotel where Briscoe was employed and the injury took place. The court said that Briscoe had introduced a reasonable amount of evidence showing that the elevator company had deviated from recognized standards of maintenance so as to permit the application of the doctrine of *res ipsa loquitur*. In its opinion, the court said that it was not necessary to establish that the elevator company had total exclusive control over any possible cause of the accident before the doctrine would apply. It was sufficient to introduce evidence from which it could be said that it was more likely than not that the negligence of the defendant in the area where it had exclusive control caused the malfunction.

The court said, "*Res ipsa loquitur* is a balancing doctrine, and while the plaintiff need not show the exact cause of an injury, he must at least show that it is more probable than not that the injury resulted from the defendant's breach of duty. If that is shown, an inference of negligence on the part of the defendant arises, and it is then incumbent on the defendant to come forward with rebuttal evidence." The court held that the plaintiff established a *prima facie* case when it introduced evidence of deviations from standard maintenance practices, and that brought the doctrine into play. But if it is shown, as the defendant alleged, that the rapid descent caused the injury, and this was the result of a manufacturer's design failure rather than negligence in servicing and maintaining the elevator, then the burden was on the defendant to introduce evidence to that effect to rebut the consequences of the doctrine.

Now not all elevator-related injuries are compensable. In Reimer v. Marriott Company, 372 S.2d 738 (La., 1979), the plaintiff and others were delivering flowers to be used as table decorations in conjunction with a luncheon that they were going to be attending. When the plaintiff and her party arrived, they were directed to use the freight elevator. A security officer claims that he told them that they could not use the freight elevator, but the plaintiff persisted, and he told her that she would have to wait for a catering manager to take her up. The elevator had an inside steel mesh door that closed from top to bottom and met at the middle. Approximately ten or twelve seconds before the top steel mesh door starts closing, a bell starts to ring and continues ringing until the door is fully descended. About sixty seconds after the steel mesh door has fully descended, the outside door closes automatically unless held open by pushing an "open" button. The plaintiff claims that as she was approaching the elevator with decorations in each hand, the closing inner steel mesh door struck her on the head, causing her to fall and injure herself. The plaintiff sued both the elevator company and the hotel.

The court held that there was no liability on the part of the elevator company because there was no evidence of faulty installation, defective condition, or failure of maintenance. As to the claim against the hotel, there was evidence that the plaintiff knew that the door was closing and that she tried to "beat" the closing door. As a consequence it struck her head, and she was knocked to the ground outside the elevator. This was carelessness on the part of the plaintiff, the court held, and her actions constituted conduct falling below the standard required for one's protection. Therefore, this amounted to contributory negligence on her part because she was fully aware of the impending danger. As a result, she could not recover from the hotel. (See also Chimeno v. Fontainbleau Hotel Corp., 251 S.2d 351 [Fla., 1971].)

Doors, Glassed-in Areas, and Halls

Innkeepers who have a quasi-public building owe guests and other invitees the duty to exercise reasonable, ordinary, or due care to keep the premises reasonably safe for their use. This duty is not absolute, but is commensurate with the circumstances; innkeepers are not considered insurers of the safety of customers, patrons, and other invitees. What would constitute a situation in which the innkeeper would be liable? In Schubert v. Hotel Astor, 5 N.Y.S.2d 203 (1938), the court stated that under ordinary circumstances, hotel owners need not have a doorman; but if they knew that an extraordinary crowd would be using the revolving doors, they had a duty to employ a doorman to prevent the accident that occurred. This liability is premised on the theory that the innkeeper should have foreseen this situation. Hence, if the situation is not foreseeable, the proprietor cannot be held liable for the unexpected conduct of other customers.

This duty of innkeepers to keep the premises, as far as they are ordinarily used by customers, in a reasonably safe condition includes the construction, maintenance, and proper arrangement of all parts of the premises (Promisel v. Hotel Statler Corp., 189 N.E. 804 [Mass., 1934]). This includes such areas as sidewalks, balconies, stairs, rugs, and swimming pools.

The liability attached to the innkeeper is not completely one-sided. In the case of Clark v. New York Hotel Statler Company, 227 N.Y.S. 671 (1928), a jury question was presented when the plaintiff entered a revolving door while it was in motion. The court stated that it was common knowledge that revolving doors are often in motion when in public use. In cases pertaining to doors, the courts have been reluctant to apply the doctrines of res ipsa loquitur or "attractive nuisance."

Hallways that are being cleaned can be troublesome, especially when being washed or waxed. The case of Bellevue v. Haslup, 150 F.2d 160 (D.C., 1945), is typical of what one can expect in a hotel unless safety precautions are taken. In this case, the plaintiff slipped and fell on a hallway floor that was wet from waxing. The defendant maintained that the hotel employee doing the waxing had verbally warned the plaintiff to walk on the dry side of the hallway—which the plaintiff denied. Indisputably, no warning signs or notices had been placed in the hall. Thus the court found that the defendant had failed in his duty to keep the place in a reasonably safe condition.

Stairways, Steps, and Their Coverings

Because the steps and stairways of a hotel constitute a potential danger to guests, hotelkeepers must provide safe coverings or carpets and adequate lighting for them. However, it has been held that this duty does not extend to stairs or steps that the guest cannot be reasonably expected to use, although innkeepers should refrain in such cases from active negligence that would render the premises unsafe.

Stairs and coverings of stairs must be kept in a good state of repair. Innkeepers will be held liable, in absence of contributory negligence on the part of the guest, if they have knowledge of defects and do not repair them. In Handel v. Rudnich, 78 So.2d 709 (Fla., 1955), the plaintiff, while descending the stairs from the first floor to the lobby, caught her heel on a button protruding from one of the steps and catapulted to the tile floor below, sustaining severe injuries. Evidence introduced indicated a rug had been removed some years ago, leaving a button about the size of a silver dollar protruding. The jury held that the defendant hotel was negligent. The court rejected the contention of the defendant that the size of the button was not dangerous and said that guests are entitled to assume that steps and passageways are clear of dangerous impediments. Also, when guests use stairs instead of the elevator, they are not guilty of negligence unless the steps are barricaded.

Innkeepers must see that the steps are properly constructed. But once the steps meet the standards set by custom and usage and are not inherently dangerous, the courts hold that their construction will not impose liability on the innkeeper. It is up to the guest to use a higher degree of care. But where an offset or step in the corridor leading from the lobby or street is not readily discernible and is not properly illuminated, a verdict for the plaintiff is upheld.

Is a handrail or bannister needed to protect persons on a stairway? This question immediately raises the further question of construction. Is there a time limit to weathering that qualifies a building as sound and well constructed? The case of *Orlick* v. *Granit Hotel & Country Club* cites an instance in which a building was considered safe because no accidents had occurred in twenty-three years, whereas a four-year period did not carry this sanction.

Case	**Orlick v. Granit Hotel & Country Club**
Example	*331 N.Y.S.2d 651 (1972)*
	(BURKE, Judge)

Plaintiffs were paying guests at the Granit Hotel where plaintiff, Sarah Orlick, fell down a flight of four stairs sustaining personal injuries. She fell on the same day that she had registered as a guest. The complaint claimed that defendants had been negligent in the construction and maintenance of the corridor and the stairway in it, alleging that the stairway had been improperly constructed as it had no handrails and no signs or other warnings of the approaching stairway, which had to be descended in order to reach plaintiffs' room, which was off a corridor. Plaintiffs had to pass through a foyer and walk down four steps.

An architect testified in plaintiffs' behalf that the construction of the stairway was not in accord with proper standards of care, as well as being contrary to the New York State Construction Code. On cross-examination of one of the defendants' employees, it was brought out that there were about 5,000 "people days" of use a year of these stairs. The employee testified that all accidents were eventually reported to him. However, he admitted he had not consulted any of the hotel accident records, only the hotel's lawyers. It is only necessary to note that every hotel has records of accidents—accidents are commonplace occurrences in hotels, and insurance companies insist on records. The record also contains testimony that the steps were in the same structural condition when first constructed in the fall of 1961.

The main question in the case is whether the charge to the jury concerning the use of the stairway was erroneous. The majority of the appellate division . . . believed that the charge was proper and in accord with that given in the case of De Salvo v. Stanley-Mark-Strand Corp., 281 N.Y. 333, 338, 23 N.E.2d 457, 458. The dissenters were of the opinion that a portion of the charge to the jury constituted reversible error. That portion of the charge reads as follows: "If you find that this stairway had been in daily use for years, and its condition during such use was substantially the same as on the day of the accident, and that during such use there was no other accident, if you find that, such proof *negates* the possibility that the condition of this stairway was a dangerous one" (emphasis added). An exception was taken.

We agree with the dissenters. A new trial should be granted. In *De Salvo v. Stanley-Mark-Strand Corp.* . . . the plaintiffs contended that a balustrade in a theatre around the opening on a floor was not high enough to protect people from falling over. The theatre had been operating for *twenty-three years* at the time of the accident, during the course of which hundreds of thousands of people had passed by the rail without mishap. This is quite different from a situation where there were only four years' experience. In this case, the plaintiff, Sarah Orlick, testified that the area was inadequately lighted and the stairway in question was not properly constructed by reason of the absence of a handrail, and that the carpeting in the foyer, on the stairway, and in the corridor leading to her room were all of the same design and color and created an illusion of one level plane. Under these circumstances, *De Salvo* does not apply.

The defendant in that case produced evidence to establish that the theatre of the defendant was designed by a well-known architect, that it was constructed similar to like classes of structures when the theatre was built, and that it had been in constant use for many years without incident. It was for these reasons that this court reversed and dismissed the plaintiffs' complaint. In the instant case, the language is strong. It in effect charged a directed verdict in favor of the defendants. In *De Salvo* this court simply said that its use for a great many years safely warrants its continued use without the imputation of imprudence or carelessness.

It seems to us, then, that the language in the charge "negates the possibility that the condition of this stairway was a dangerous one" was a serious error.

We have concluded that in some inexplicable way, the *De Salvo* case is believed to support a proposition of law that applies to all buildings that "continued use for a long period of time in substantially the same condition, without incident, *negates* negligence" (emphasis added). We find nothing in *De Salvo* which supports this interpretation of the language, and certainly nothing which would support any language as strong as the charge given under the facts of this case.

The majority, we think, erred when they enunciated a rule of law that holds that where a defendant points to scanty evidence of no accidents in a condition claimed to be dangerous or defectively constructed and that had existed for a period of only four years, then, as a matter of law, such defendant is immune from a claim that the condition complained of was negligent, defective, or dangerous. In our opinion, the trial court should have charged that the evidence of no prior accidents (as scanty as it was) would merely be a *factor* for consideration and not in any way be conclusive on the issue of the nature of the condition of the stairway. In conclusion, we would again state that the theory that continued usage without incident "negates" negligence is inapplicable to the circumstances of this case. When the justice presiding at the trial in the case at bar so charged, it constituted reversible error, as it must have misled the jury.

Ruling of the Court: Accordingly, the order appealed from should be reversed and a new trial granted.

How much wear and tear resulting from regular use will be tolerated before a hotel becomes liable in "slip-and-fall" cases? A verdict of $100,000 for the plaintiff, of which she was 25 percent negligent, can be costly for the hotelier. The plaintiff, Janet Hopf, a seventeen-year-old guest of the defendant's hotel, was severely injured when she slipped on a wet spot on a wooden walkway at the rear of the lobby. The defendant had claimed the right to a directed verdict on the grounds that there was insufficient evidence that it had actual or constructive notice of the existence of the moisture on the floor. The court said that the correctness of this position is essentially irrelevant because the record shows evidence that the surface upon which the fall occurred had become dangerously worn, smooth, and therefore slippery, and also that the entire area was insufficiently lighted. This, according to the court, was ample evidence that the defendant had negligently maintained its premises so as to have required that the liability issue be submitted to the jury (194th St. Hotel Corp. v. Hopf, 383 So.2d 739 [Fla., 1980]). The jury may well have based its liability finding upon these areas, rather than that of the moisture on the walkway.

Duty Owed Guests in Dining Rooms, Bars, and Similar Places

Because the dining room and bar of a hotel are open to the public at large, they are of special concern to hotelkeepers who can be held liable for accidents that at first glance seem to fall outside this responsibility. In a bar or in any other place where liquor is served, innkeepers have an added responsibility since they can be held liable for the actions of an intoxicated guest. They need not even be on the premises since an employee can act, or not act, for the employer.

Slippery Floors

Almost any accident can happen in a dining room, banquet hall, or bar, including accidents caused by slippery floors. In Cline v. Texas Hotel, 392 S.W.2d 594 (Texas, 1965), the plaintiff attended a luncheon along with several hundred other persons. When she left her table, she slipped and fell heavily on the floor, sustaining severe and permanent injuries. She claimed that the floor was exceedingly slippery and therefore unsafe. However, she admitted that in the past she had experienced the slipperiness of the floor and for this reason was not allowed to recover. The holding of the court was that a plaintiff-invitee cannot recover if he or she knew of the condition and realized and appreciated the danger.

Highly polished and waxed floors are the cause of most floor cases. For example, in Mitchell v. Baker Hotel of Dallas, Inc., 523 S.W.2d 316 (Texas, 1975), the plaintiff slipped while walking on a polished floor at a banquet. The question was not whether there was a duty owed to the plaintiff, but whether that duty was breached by the defendant in having a highly polished floor. The court held that the plaintiff had to show negligence on the part of the defendant in his waxing or maintenance of the floor. The plaintiff failed to do so; therefore, the defendant was not held responsible for the injuries of the plaintiff.

Closeness of Chairs and Tables

The case of LaPlante v. Radisson Hotel Company could influence restaurateurs or hoteliers serving a banquet. This case revolves around one question: How close may one place tables, chairs, and people at a banquet? The court said it was a jury question whether thirty-six inches between tables was adequate spacing. The defendant knew that during a three-hour banquet, many guests would have to use the restrooms, and that it was foreseeable that because of this close proximity, one might fall and sustain serious injuries.

Case Example	LaPlante v. Radisson Hotel Company
	292 F.Supp. 705 (Mich., 1968)
	(NEVILLE, District Judge)

This case involves what appears to be a novel question concerning which there is a paucity of authority. It is presently before the court on the defendant's motion for judgment notwithstanding the jury verdict for plaintiff or, in the alternative, for a new trial. Simply stated, the question is whether a jury may find a hotel negligent and an injured plaintiff free from contributory negligence where the hotel, in hiring itself out to stage a banquet for 1,200 paying guests in one of its banquet rooms, allegedly set the banquet tables so close to each other as to leave inadequate aisles and room between seated guests, causing the plaintiff to trip over a chair when attempting to leave the room and thereby injuring herself.

On this motion, the evidence must be viewed in the light most favorable to the verdict. The jury could find that the plaintiff, a semiretired school teacher from Kalamazoo, Michigan, sixty-seven years of age, was a guest at the defendant's hotel for the purpose of attending the national convention of a professional education sorority of which she was a member. The convention meetings and related banquets were all held at the defendant hotel.

On August 10, 1967, the convention staged its final banquet, and the plaintiff was in attendance. The banquet arrangements had been made some months earlier, with the accession and prior approval of a seating sketch or chart by at least some of the sorority's national officers, though the chart had not been seen by the plaintiff. The room in which the banquet was held is claimed by the defendant to have a maximum seating capacity of 2,000, though only 1,200 were in attendance that evening.

Long tables, seating twelve to eighteen persons each, were placed at preset distances apart, which the defendant claims was forty-two inches, though the jury could find from evidence the plaintiff introduced that the actual distance between tables was somewhat less. Further, there was evidence that at least at some of the tables, the chairs were back to back to those at the next table. The testimony of at least one witness other than the plaintiff indicated a crowded condition.

There was testimony that near the entrance to the banquet hall, there was ten feet of vacant space, more or less, from which the inference could be drawn that if used, such would have permitted the spacing of all the tables farther apart. Also, in a certain area were a number of circular tables, seating a lesser number of persons per square foot than the long banquet tables and which, if replaced by long banquet tables, the jury could find would have allowed more space for all tables. The room was set up with a series of three head tables in stages and, nearby, a large simulated birthday cake commemorating an anniversary of the sorority.

There was testimony that waitresses were unable to move down the aisles between the long tables, and at the table at which the plaintiff was seated, the plates of food were passed down by the waitresses from person to person from the end of the table. The hotel manager testified this was not a good practice, and he did not permit it, if discovered. The plaintiff testified she had determined by later experimentation that, seated at a table in normal manner, there were eighteen inches between the edge of the table and the back of her chair; that on this night her chair touched that of the person at the next table backing into her; that if his or her similar distance was no more than eighteen inches, this left but six inches between the backs of chairs even if, as the hotel manager stated, the edges of the tables were placed forty-two inches apart.

The banquet began at 8:00 P.M., and the plaintiff came to the hall and selected a seat about in the middle of one of the long tables.

Several hours later, at approximately 11:15 P.M., before the banquet program was over and while the lights were dimmed, with a spotlight on the head table and/or the birthday cake, the plaintiff decided to leave the banquet hall to meet her son-in-law as prearranged. Moving sideways, she negotiated a path between chairs as the various people moved in toward the table to accommodate her. The jury could find that not realizing the position of the final chair, and believing she had negotiated herself to the main aisle, plaintiff caught her foot on the leg of that last chair and tripped and fell, injuring herself. Based on this evidence and the medical testimony as to the extent of her injuries, the jury awarded plaintiff the sum of $3,500.

The defendant's first challenge is that the evidence as a matter of law is insufficient to allow a finding of negligence on the part of defendant to stand. The court believes to the contrary, and that the evidence above recited is sufficient to permit the jury to come to the factual conclusion that they did: that the plaintiff's injuries were the proximate result of the defendant's negligence in crowding the tables too closely.

The defendant contends that since there was no violation of any statute or ordinance pleaded nor proved, the burden was on the plaintiff to show by expert testimony or otherwise the standard of care to which the defendant's conduct should have conformed. Put another way, the defendant claims that there was insufficient proof of a violation of any duty since there was no evidence of what reasonably prudent hotel management would do under the same or similar circumstances, and thus it was error to permit the jury to speculate as to the standard of care against which the defendant's conduct should be measured.

The issue becomes one of whether a jury should be permitted, without expert testimony, to draw upon their own knowledge, background, and common experience to determine what the standard of care should be and, hence, whether any departure therefrom occurred.

Certainly the nature of the case is not scientifically complicated nor technical. While some training and experience in catering and hotel management may be a necessary prerequisite to the handling of a banquet for 1,200 people, the court is of the view that such training or background is not a *sine qua non* to the ability to determine what is unreasonable crowding and what is not. The lay juror, knowing no more than the next person about catering procedures, could determine from the evidence in this case whether or not the tables were too close for safety. Though the evidence on the point is not conclusive one way or the other, the court is of the opinion that this was a fair question for the jury and not insufficient as a matter of law. The rule of evidence applied in determining the appropriateness of opinion "expert testimony" is whether the subject involved is so distinctively related to some science, profession, business, or occupation as to be beyond the ken of the average layman. Here the court is not convinced that expert testimony was required or would necessarily have been helpful to the jury. . . .

The plaintiff argues, perhaps with some merit, that if a standard is required to be established by evidence from a caterer or other expert person engaged in the industry, the defendant's catering manager himself testified forty-two inches to be the standard, and there was evidence from the plaintiff herself and from another witness that the tables were less than that distance apart and perhaps no more than thirty-six inches. The court, while retaining some doubt as to the accuracy of the measurement observations of these witnesses, cannot say as a matter of law that the jury could not believe and be convinced by their testimony.

The defendant's next claim is that the court erred in refusing to direct a verdict in the defendant's favor on the issue of the plaintiff's contributory negligence and assumption of risk. While there is evidence to support a favorable jury finding on either or both of those theories, and the court did instruct liberally on both of them, in no way can it be said that reasonable minds could not differ on these issues; hence, a directed verdict would have been inappropriate. At the time of the plaintiff's fall, the room was nearly dark, though the plaintiff did testify she could see her feet. The spotlight was on the head table and the birthday cake. The jury could find that the hotel reasonably could foresee that during a banquet commencing at 8:00 P.M. and lasting until after 11:00 P.M., a number of people would leave the hall to go to the restrooms or for other purposes; that with a program in progress, the lights might well be dimmed and vision made more difficult; and that with the crowded or overcrowded conditions, such a fall as occurred might be anticipated. The question of plaintiff's contributory negligence was a fair fact question for the jury, and this court does not feel it can substitute its judgment for the jury's where there is substantial evidence upon which a finding could be based.

The defendant's next claim of error is that the amount of $3,500 awarded by the jury is so excessive as not to be justified by the evidence and constitutes a verdict motivated by passion and prejudice. The medical evidence clearly was ample to sustain such a verdict, and it is not excessive so as to require a new trial.

The defendant's final ground for its new trial motion asserts alleged prejudicial closing argument by the plaintiff's counsel. The court found nothing so prejudicial as to require a mistrial then nor a new trial now. Assuming, *arguendo* [to assume something as true for the sake of argument], that some prejudicial remarks were made, they may be considered *de minimis* [insignificant, minute, or frivolous]. In one instance, a particular statement by the plaintiff's counsel concerning the plaintiff's use of her savings was promptly and properly cured by appropriate admonition and cautionary instruction to the jury. . . .

Ruling of the Court: A separate order has been entered denying the defendant's motion for judgment notwithstanding the verdict or in the alternative for a new trial. Judgment for plaintiff.

Foreign Substances on the Floor

Most accidents in a dining room, restaurant, or snack bar come in cases in which a foreign substance on the floor causes a guest to slip and fall. Who is liable? The general rule holds that when a business invitee is injured by slipping on a foreign substance on the defendant's premises, and the evidence implies the defendant's or his servants' negligence, the case should go to the jury. It is not easy to predict the outcome of such cases. However, if the substance was on the floor through the act of a third person or it is not known how it got there, there must be evidence that the defendant was made aware of the substance and was negligent in not removing it.

When these rules were applied in the *Kauffmann v. Royal Orleans, Inc.,* case, the restaurant was not liable when the plaintiff hurt herself by falling on an orange peel while being escorted to her table. The *Kauffmann* case is the general rule and not the exception; customers are anxious to sue someone even if they fall and are hurt by their own negligence.

Case	**Kauffmann v. Royal Orleans, Inc.**
Example	*216 So.2d 394 (La., 1968)*
	(JOHNSON, Judge)

This plaintiff fell to the floor of the restaurant called the Rib Room operated by defendant, The Royal Orleans, Inc. She filed this suit against the hotel and its public liability insurer for alleged personal injury damages. After trial the Civil District Court for the Parish of Orleans rendered judgment for the defendants and the plaintiff has appealed.

On December 30, 1964, the plaintiff took her cousin, Mrs. Pearla Schwartz, and Mrs. Schwartz's two young grandsons to The Royal Orleans Hotel to have lunch in the Rib Room. All tables were occupied when they arrived. After they had waited some thirty minutes, the headwaiter, Hans Mueller, went to the cocktail lounge to tell Mrs. Kauffmann that a table was available, and he led Mrs. Kauffmann to the table. With Mr. Mueller in the lead, followed closely by Mrs. Kauffmann, they were walking between the other tables occupied by other patrons toward the table where Mrs. Kauffmann and her guests were to sit. When Mr. Mueller reached the table, he turned to pull out a chair to seat Mrs. Kauffmann. Right at that instant, Mrs. Kauffmann fell to the floor alongside her table. Mrs. Kauffmann described her fall by saying that the waiter was leading her to the table and she stepped on a piece of orange or lemon peel and "my legs just slipped from under me and I fell, and I was in a sitting position when I realized that I was down." She did not see the peel until after she fell. She said it was on the floor close to her right side. She was given assistance to get up, after which she sat at the table and had lunch with her guests. After lunch, she took her guests to the Steamer President on the Mississippi River for a boat ride in the afternoon. Mrs. Kauffmann said she and Mr. Mueller were walking between other tables and she thinks she could have touched the other tables as she walked along. She would not exactly describe the space where they walked as an aisle. At first she testified that she slipped on the peel, but when asked how she could be certain about it she answered: "Because I slid on it and it was there and it was the only thing." When she saw the peel, it was by her side and not at her feet.

Mr. Mueller testified that the lunch hour started at 11:30 A.M., when the floors were cleaned and then inspected by him and the housekeeper, at which time the peel was not on the floor. He said the peel could not have been on the floor for any period of time because he walked back and forth over that area many times and if it had been there he would have picked it up; that all the waiters are instructed to watch out for foreign material on the floor; that if anything is found they must pick it up; that a busboy is always assigned to constantly check for such objects and, if any appear, to clean them up during the meal period; that when he was assisting Mrs. Kauffmann to get up, he saw a very small piece of orange or lemon peel close beside her and that it was fresh in appearance. Other employees of the hotel described the system followed to clean and keep the floors clean of foreign objects, and the instructions given the waiters and busboys, who keep close watch on the floor for any object that should not be there; but, on this occasion, none had been found and none reported to them. Some of these witnesses had started employment there after this occasion, but their explanations were the same as those who were working there on that day.

Mrs. Schwartz testified by deposition that she did not see Mrs. Kauffmann fall because she and her grandsons were not following Mr. Mueller and Mrs. Kauffmann to the table, though Mr. Mueller said Mrs. Kauffmann and her whole party were following him to the table.

Counsel for plaintiff wrote in his brief that the captain, meaning the headwaiter, Hans Mueller, testified that Mrs. Kauffmann "slipped and fell on an orange or lemon peel." Mr. Mueller did not say that, but only said that after the fall, he saw the piece of peel in the vicinity of where she fell.

We quite agree with the argument of counsel for plaintiff that Mrs. Kauffmann had every reason to believe that the headwaiter would not conduct her through an aisle that was dangerous or on which there was some foreign object on which she might slip and fall. We will add that this would be true if Mr. Mueller knew of the presence of such an object or had any reason to suspect that the object was on the floor. That argument does not relieve plaintiff of the burden of proving there was negligence on the part of any hotel employee in carelessly dropping the foreign object on the floor, or that the employee had actual knowledge that such an object was on the floor at the time, or, if the employees had no actual knowledge of the object being on the floor, that the object had gotten on the floor by some other means and had been there long enough to constitute constructive notice or knowledge of its presence. We also agree that Mrs. Kauffmann was not required under these circumstances to keep her eyes constantly on the floor when she was following the headwaiter on that occasion.

In many decisions by appellate courts in many slip and fall cases in this state, it has been held that each case must be judged on the facts of that particular case. The issue before this court now is: Do these facts prove that the hotel employees failed to exercise reasonable care in the hotel's floor cleaning and inspection system, and did Mrs. Kauffmann slip on a foreign object, the presence of which on the floor the employees had actual or constructive knowledge?

We find that the testimony in our case is convincing that the hotel employees were instructed to keep the floors free of any foreign objects, and that the system followed in the Rib Room was sufficient to enable the court to find and hold that the premises were kept in a reasonably safe condition. There is no evidence that the waiters, busboys, and porters did not perform the duties assigned them. The time lapse between observations and inspections of the floor make it reasonable to assume that the small piece of peel found on the floor could have been there only a very short time, probably only a very few minutes or few seconds. No one had seen it, and we believe that there was no knowledge or notice of it and there was no negligence proven on the part of these employees. We are not even sure that Mrs. Kauffmann's foot slipped on the peel. It was not near her feet and it still had a fresh appearance. If her foot had slipped on it, it is most likely that it would have been crushed. . . .

Counsel for the defendant has correctly and concisely stated the principles of law that support our findings against the plaintiff in this case, as follows:

"Plaintiff has failed to carry her burden of proof; plaintiff has failed to show that the alleged extraneous substance on the floor of the Rib Room of The Royal Orleans was placed there by the owner or one of his employees, or if placed by someone else, that the owner or his employees had actual knowledge of the presence of the substance or that it had remained in such a position of danger for such a length of time that the owner or his employees should have had knowledge of the presence of the substance."

Counsel has cited a number of decisions that adhere to these principles. Some of the cases he cites contain facts that do not bring those cases in line with the present case.

Of course we have here again, as in many, many cases of all types, that there has been no showing that the trial court committed manifest error in its factual and legal determination. The only decision we can make is to affirm the trial court.

Ruling of the Court: For these reasons, the judgment appealed from is affirmed with costs to be paid by plaintiff.

Hanging Mirrors in Dining Rooms

One would not question the right of a restaurateur to install large plate glass mirrors in the dining room. But when one of these mirrors (measuring 3½ × 7 feet) fell on a guest and severely injured her, it was found that she could collect for the negligence of the restaurateur. She claimed *res ipsa loquitur* in Deming Hotel Company v. Proux, 36 N.E.2d 613 (Ind., 1968). The court said that the negligence (if any) of the contractor in installing the mirror in the dining room was not available as a defense to the dining room proprietor because the mirror was under the exclusive control and management of the defendant and his servants, and that injury would not have taken place if proper care had been exercised.

Food Service

A bizarre case occurred in the dining room of the Caribbean Beach Hotel where Francis Howard Young, aged ten, and his father were eating on New Year's Eve. The son volunteered to pick up a dessert (cherries jubilee) for his father. The waiter, applying rum in a careless way, sprayed not only the chafing dish and sterno heater but also the plaintiff's shirt, which became a flaming torch that severely burned the plaintiff. Both the father and the son sued the hotel in *Young v. Caribbean Associates, Inc.* The son recovered, but the father, who agonized while the son was burning and in excruciating pain, could not recover. This case should prompt restaurateurs to set up rigid controls in the use of inflammable liquids that could severely injure guests.

Case Example	**Young v. Caribbean Associates, Inc.**
	358 F.Supp. 1220 (V.I., 1973)
	(WARREN H. YOUNG, District Judge)

This is a tort and breach of warranty action tried by the court without a jury. A father and his ten-year-old son seek recovery for mental anguish suffered by the father and bodily injuries suffered by the son brought about in unusual circumstances. The son, Francis Howard Young, was staying with his parents at the defendant, Caribbean Beach Hotel. On New Year's Eve, 1969, the family was having dinner in the hotel dining room. At the end of the meal, the son volunteered to go through the dessert serving line to bring a cherries jubilee for his father. As the son reached the head of the serving line, the waiter in charge of flaming and serving the cherries jubilee found it necessary to kindle the flames by adding more rum to the chafing pan. He took a bottle of hundred-and-fifty-one proof rum, which was stoppered with a narrow "slow pour" spout, and proceeded to pour the rum directly into the pan. As he did so, the spout either dropped out or was popped out by an internal combustion in the rum bottle, and a quantity of volatile rum gushed out. An abnormally high flame resulted that reached out to touch the boy, setting his shirt on fire. The boy suffered severe burns and has undergone considerable treatment for skin and flesh grafts and plastic surgery. The several *ad damnum* clauses in the multiple counts of the amended complaint request $200,000 compensatory damages and $100,000 exemplary damages for the son and $19,912 medical specials and $25,000 mental anguish damages for the father. The complaint bottoms recovery principally upon negligence of all defendants, but the breach of warranty and products' liability allegations were aimed primarily at Sears, Roebuck & Company, the vendor of the allegedly highly flammable boy's shirt.

Initially, and regrettably, I must disallow the father's claim of damages for mental anguish. The anguish of seeing one's ten-year-old son in flames must be horrible and nightmarish, and the continuing anguish of seeing, hearing, and sympathetically feeling the child's ensuing pain and suffering must be, to say the least, debilitating and depressing. However, the general rule is that where the defendant is guilty of no more than negligence, a third party may recover only if he had some fear for his own safety. . . . Perhaps the basis for the rule is a belief that the defendant otherwise owed (and breached) no duty to an unthreatened bystander; or, as a secondary but perhaps preferable explanation, a fear that the causal chain to the bystander will grow so attenuated that liability will be out of proportion to the wrong. For these reasons, the rule applies even where the bystander is a parent of the victim and so might be expected to suffer particularly deep and genuine anguish. The restatement has adopted this majority view. . . . Since the law of the Virgin Islands is guided by the restatement, the father has no recovery for what I believe to be an experience of genuine anguish.

The father's right to recover his expenditures for medical specials and the son's right to recover compensatory damages for his bodily injuries are clear. The hotel is, at the very least, accountable for its serving waiter's negligence in using an improperly stoppered bottle, which permitted the "slow pour" spout either to fall out or pop out, thereby discharging a large quantity of volatile rum. Moreover, as the evidence tended to show, the hotel's serving waiter was negligent in the first place in pouring the rum directly from the bottle and not from an intermediary bowl or pitcher. An experienced maitre d'hotel and chef testified that to pour directly from a bottle was to invite the flame to catch onto the stream of rum and leap from the chafing pan to ignite the vaporous gases inside the bottle, blowing out the cork and turning the bottle into a veritable "flame thrower" or "blowtorch," capable of throwing a flame ten to fifteen feet. Although I need not decide that this in fact did happen, I do find that it was negligent to pour directly from the bottle and not from an intervening bowl or wide mouth pitcher. In a sense, the dessert waiter does not seem morally culpable, for he had not been trained in the proper handling of flambès. Nonetheless, he and his employer should be responsible for the injuries caused to the boy, no matter how inadvertently they came about.

I further find that the negligence of the hotel and its serving waiter was the sole and proximate cause of plaintiff's injuries. The hotel for a time relied in part on the theory that the boy's shirt was itself highly flammable as evidenced by the vigor with which it burned, and that this was an important intervening cause of the holocaust that developed. With this theory in mind, as well as the thought of allocation of damages between joint tortfeasors, the hotel impleaded Sears, Roebuck & Company as a third-party defendant. At the trial, however, a written statement of the waiter was produced that indicated that a substantial quantity of the rum had gushed directly onto the boy's shirt. This itself would be more than enough to support the combustion, no matter what the flammability of the shirt fabric might be. The third-party complaint against Sears was therefore dismissed upon the motion of plaintiff and Sears's counsel, with no objection raised by defendants' counsel. The action then proceeded against the serving waiter and the hotel alone. I also find that the boy was not guilty of contributory negligence. Although there was some testimony indicating that he was warned to stand back, the warning would have been, at the very best, an insufficient caution to a normal boy of plaintiff's years.

With the question of liability settled, I must now address myself to the matter of damages. The father's medical expenses, and reasonably related outlays, have totaled some $12,352.08 to date. In addition, some further surgery will be needed in order to minimize the burn scars on the boy's face and body. Although it is difficult for the medical experts to estimate the costs of these future comtemplated operations, the uncontroverted estimate given at trial of $6,000 appears reasonable. The father's total "special" damages would therefore come to approximately $18,352.08.

The most important and troublesome issue of damages is the award of compensable damages that must be granted to the son for his pain, suffering, permanent disfigurement, and the effect thereof upon his psyche and social adjustment. That his pain was considerable is unquestioned. The boy was on fire for more than several seconds before any one of the astonished bystanders came to his rescue. Before falling to the floor, he tried desperately to tear his shirt off. Finally, after perhaps a full half minute of time, one of the waiters came to his rescue with a tablecloth to snuff out the fire. The father actually saw his son on fire, but was unable to rush to his side because of the crowded dining room. When he reached his son, the waiters were already carrying the boy out of the dining room to the hotel office. An ambulance was called and soon the boy and his father were taken to the Knud Hansen Memorial Hospital Emergency Room. Supportive and anti-shock treatment was rendered. The boy was treated by doctors Roy Anduze and Alfred Heath. Much of the treatment consisted of prevention of shock and infection that involved, among other painful manipulations and dressings, debriding of the dead skin tissue, which is a particularly painful process. Doctors are reluctant to give painkillers for fear of causing the patient to become addicted to drugs. The boy was released from the St. Thomas hospital on January 17, 1970, and was flown with a medical attendant to Washington, D.C.

At the Washington Hospital Center, several skin grafts were performed by Dr. Fry. On June 17, the boy was again admitted to the hospital for several injections of steroids into the hypertrophic scarred areas. Hypertrophic scarred areas are scars that are thickened and raised from the healthy, normal skin. There was hospitalization again in October 1970 for further operations to improve the scarred areas.

From my personal observations of the boy's scars, I would say that the scars on his right cheek and beneath his chin are unsightly, as are the scars on his chest and on the backs of both hands. The scar underneath the chin is actually a keloid and is red in color. There are two keloid formations on the chest. There was an attempt to remove one by excision, but the result was a scar worse than the one removed.

The doctor obtained skin for the skin grafts from the boy's left and right thighs. These areas are approximately six inches long and two and-a-half inches wide. These are called "donor sites" that will eventually become less noticeable, but, as indicated, they may always appear as "patches."

The medical testimony was generally that the boy received second and third degree burns over 30 percent of his body's surface. The boy has no injuries to his organs, nor to his eyes. He can make a fist and move his fingers in the normal way. In sum, he has no physical disabilities. The doctors are of the opinion that the scars and keloids on the face and chest areas can be further improved by a combination of excision and injections. One doctor opined that surgery can make noticeable improvements and improve the boy cosmetically. However, there would have to be between three and five hospitalizations to achieve this improvement. The medical consensus is that time alone will show improvement on the scarred areas and that within a few years much of the scars should become less noticeable.

In attempting to reach some appraisal of the amount of dollar damages to compensate the boy for his pain, suffering and cosmetic disfiguration, I am referred to the several cases cited in 22 Am.Jur.2d § 393, pertaining to burns. Whether those annotations help to determine the amount of the damage award is questionable. It is no easy undertaking to make a judicial pronouncement that a certain damage award will fully compensate the boy for his pain, suffering and disfigurement and, at the same time, appear reasonable to the defendants for their negligence. A good judgment will probably be one which satisfies none of the parties. That being said and without more, I award the boy $80,000 and the father $18,352.08. . . .

Ruling of the Court: Since I do not regard the Virgin Islands law pertaining to the award of counsel's fees to the prevailing party as being a call for full and complete reimbursement, I will award $6,000 counsel's fees against defendants in favor of Sears and $12,000 counsel's fees against defendants in favor of plaintiffs.

The court ruled that the father could not recover for mental anguish he suffered seeing his child burning because the general rule is that where the defendant is guilty of no more than negligence, a third party may recover only if that person had some fear for his or her own safety. There is, however, a contrary view that seems to be growing in acceptance in jurisdictions around the country. In D'Ambra v. United States, 518 F.2d 275 (R.I., 1975), a mother who witnessed her four-year-old son being run over and killed by a U.S. mail truck was entitled to recover for shock suffered by her as a result of witnessing the tragedy, even though she suffered no direct physical impact and was not in the zone of danger. The court said that the mother was not negligent and was foreseeably in the vicinity of the child and therefore could recover for that emotional distress resulting from having seen the actual occurrence, rather than having been told about it by another.

Duty Owed Guests Outside and in Special Areas

The first section of this chapter covered the rights of guests inside a hotel or restaurant, but many establishments have additional areas that are its responsibility as well. Loading docks, drive-up areas to unload guests' goods, restaurant valet service, beaches and swimming pools, as well as ski slopes and golf courses are often considered part of the premises. How much care is owed guests in these areas is the subject matter of this section.

Doorman Service and Outside Doors

When guests arrive at a hotel by car or taxi, it is normal to stop in front of the hotel where the doorman takes their luggage and has someone take away their car for storage. A hotel or restaurant need not furnish a doorman or valet service, but when it does, the doorman acts on behalf of the hotel. In *Kurzweg v. Hotel St. Regis Corporation* the hotel was liable for the doorman's negligent conduct.

Case Example	Kurzweg v. Hotel St. Regis Corp.

Case Example

Kurzweg v. Hotel St. Regis Corp.
309 F.2d 746 (N.Y., 1962)
(SMITH, Circuit Judge)

Plaintiff, descending from a cab stopped in the second lane from the sidewalk in front of the Hotel St. Regis, was injured when a car nearer the curb backed up. She sued the owners of both vehicles and the hotel owner, alleging against the latter negligence of the hotel doorman. The hotel owner moved to dismiss under Rule 12(b) R.F. Civ. P. for failure to state a claim on which relief could be granted. The court, Richard H. Levet, J., granted the motion and on reargument reaffirmed his action, both without opinion. Judgment was entered dismissing as to the hotel owner, with certification under Rule 54(b) F.R.C.P. that judgment was final against plaintiff in favor of said defendant and that there was no just reason for delay in the entry of the judgment. This appeal by plaintiff followed. We find that the complaint sufficiently states a claim against the hotel owner upon which relief could be granted, and reverse and remand.

It is the hotel's contention that it was under no duty by New York law to furnish a doorman, and that therefore failure of the doorman to act cannot found an action against it. But New York has held liable a person under no duty to act who voluntarily undertakes to act and causes injury through his negligent act or failure to act. Moreover, even if positive misfeasance were required, the language "did negligently fail to perform its duty" is sufficiently broad to allow proof of such misfeasance. The complaint is sufficient against the motion under 12(b) (6) "if under any reasonable reading, the complaint states a claim upon which relief can be granted."

Ruling of the Court: Reversed and remanded.

Grounds

When guests use the sidewalk of a hotel or restaurant, they must take care where they walk. All cases, however, are not the hotel's or restaurant's fault. But in *Sherman v. Arno* it was the owner's fault; the guest, while walking on the sidewalk on a bright day, did not notice the sidewalk had a drop because a painted stripe showing the drop was nearly worn off. The plaintiff won.

Case Example	Sherman v. Arno *383 P.2d 741 (Ariz., 1963)* *(LOCKWOOD, Justice)*

Plaintiff (appellee) Juanita Marie Arno obtained a judgment against defendants (appellants) Max Sherman, Mortimer M. Levin, and Michael Robinson, doing business as Flamingo Hotel, for injuries sustained by plaintiff in a fall caused by stumbling over a single step down from a sidewalk on defendants' premises while she was there in the capacity of a business invitee. . . .

The facts, stated in the light most favorable to sustaining the judgment and allowing plaintiff every reasonable inference, are as follows: On March 30, 1958, plaintiff and a friend drove to the Flamingo Hotel for the purpose of lunching at the restaurant operated there. It was a bright sunny Sunday afternoon when they emerged from the restaurant at its south exit to go to plaintiff's car, which she had left in the parking lot across from this exit. There was a driveway between the building wall containing the exit and the parking lot, and because there was quite a bit of traffic on the driveway, she decided not to cross the drive until there was an open space between the moving cars and she had a clear view of her car. A paved walkway (hereafter referred to as the "walk") ran parallel to and between the building and the driveway in a westerly direction till it met the public sidewalk about sixty-four feet from the exit.

Plaintiff was familiar with the hotel, but she testified that she had never used this walk before, nor had she previously even known it was there. While waiting for traffic on the driveway to clear, she moved along the walk toward the public sidewalk. About fifteen feet from the west end of the walk there was a single step down which plaintiff testified she did not notice or see as she came out of the restaurant. Because her attention was drawn to the automobiles passing by, she continued walking until, as she related at the trial:

"A. Well, I was walking down the sidewalk and all of a sudden I just, there was no sidewalk there and my—did you want me to demonstrate?

"Q. No. Just tell us, describe it as best you can.

"A. I took a step. All I knew, I was just down and I had fallen and hit the edge of my hip against the cement edge of that step."

That plaintiff was severely injured from her fall is not the issue here.

The walk itself is a terra cotta (reddish) color and was "glaring bright" in the afternoon sun on the day in question, according to plaintiff's testimony. Although the sidewalk is relatively level, there is one step at the south exit from the restaurant and two more steps where the west end of the walk intersects with the public sidewalk, in addition to the step where plaintiff's accident occurred. The step where plaintiff fell is approximately four to five inches in height. The riser is painted white and is visible as one approaches from the west, but not from the east as plaintiff approached it. A single white strip, about an inch and a half wide, is painted along the top or nose of the step across the walk. A witness, Irvin E. Larsen, testified that it was his duty to keep the stripe painted in order to make it visible to persons using the walk. He further testified that if the step was not painted so that it would be plainly visible, then "someone would have fallen down on his duty." Exhibit 4, a photograph of the step, taken some time after the accident, shows that the white stripe on the step is nearly worn off. The plaintiff testified:

"Q. Exhibit 4, Miss Arno, shows a strip of white paint or what has been a strip of white paint along the upper edge of that step. Can you tell us whether or not there was any paint on that step that day as you approached it?

"A. Well, I can almost positively say there wasn't any paint visible at all."

The basis of plaintiff's action was that defendants were negligent in the construction and design of the step in having it placed in such an unusual and unexpected place on the walk; that they had neglected to keep the white paint on the step properly maintained; and that they were negligent in not having some type of warning to users of the walk that a step was located there.

Defendants maintained, however, that they had exercised the entire duty required of them to use due care in making and maintaining the premises reasonably safe for the customers, and that as the step was openly and obviously visible, no warning was required to be given to any users of the walk. They also asserted sole and contributory negligence on the part of the plaintiff.

The issues of sole and contributory negligence of the plaintiff were submitted to the jury and determined adversely to defendants. There was sufficient evidence from which the jury could have reached this decision, and its determination is conclusive.

The questions before us are: Was the trial judge justified in allowing the jury to determine whether the condition was dangerous; and if so, was it due either to negligent construction or design, or improper maintenance, and was the existing condition open and obvious? Defendants claim that allowing these questions to be submitted to a jury would in effect require defendants to be insurers of business invitees, when their duty was merely to exercise the care necessary to make the premises reasonably safe. It is true that defendant is not liable to invitees for injuries resulting from dangers that are obvious, reasonably apparent, or as well known to the person injured as they are to defendant as the owner or occupant of the premises, and defendant is not bound to warn plaintiff of such a peril or risk. Plaintiff readily admits that these principles of law are correct, but disagrees with defendants' application of the law to the facts herein.

Defendants cite a number of cases involving a fall occasioned by a change of elevation that hold for the defendants therein. Many of these cases fall into the category where the court found as a matter of law the plaintiff was contributorily negligent. Others involve falls on entering or leaving buildings or stepping off from the sidewalk to the street.

Here the step upon which plaintiff stumbled was approximately two-thirds of the way down a long walk, and not at the entrance to any building or a mere step down to a parking area or another sidewalk. In refusing to grant defendants' motion for a directed verdict, the trial court said:

"Well, is the evidence not so much on the height of the step, or the fact that between the door and the street there are going to be some steps, but isn't the evidence that should be submitted to the jury whether or not it was negligence to place it in such an unsuspected place?

"I would agree with your argument completely if the fall had been at the door or at the street, but to have a single step in the middle of a sidewalk, I don't know whether it is negligence or not, but I think it creates enough of a question to let it go to the jury."

We agree with the trial court's analysis.

There was further evidence that even though designing and building the step in such a place may not have constituted negligence, the step may have been negligently maintained. The photographic exhibits in evidence show that there were at least some times when the paint on the step was so worn that it could but barely be discerned, and plaintiff testified that it was not visible at the time of her fall, although defendants maintained it was always kept striped. This evidence, combined with the fact that there were no other signs or warnings of a step, might properly have been considered in determining negligence on the part of the defendants.

As to the claim that the condition, if dangerous, was open and obvious, we need only examine the location of the step and its relation with the conditions of its surrounding environment. It is evident that the step would be obvious to one traveling the walk toward the step, with the riser in view, in the opposite direction from that in which the plaintiff was walking. However, moving in the same direction as was the plaintiff, the walk could have a "deceptively level appearance." There was evidence that the walk was the same color on both levels; that the white paint on the top of the step was completely worn; that the red terra cotta walk was bright and glary, especially to one just coming out of a building into the bright sunshine of an afternoon in Tucson, Arizona. The jury might reasonably have inferred a person using this sidewalk might be distracted from the place where he was walking while observing cars passing in the driveway, especially if, as in plaintiff's case, his car was in the parking lot across the drive and he was looking for a place to cross to it, and that defendants could have foreseen this. . . .

A four-inch step in the glaring afternoon sunshine on the walk might present at least as much difficulty to perceive as a ten-foot drop in the gloaming—both could have the appearance of being level.

The jury was adequately instructed on all points concerning the duty of the defendants, as owners of the premises, toward the business invitee. The court explained that a possessor of premises is not an insurer of the safety of business invitees, but is only required to exercise ordinary care to maintain the premises in a reasonably safe condition. The court also stated that the owner is not required to give an invitee notice or warning of an obvious danger existing on the premises, and that if the jury found the condition either obvious or reasonably apparent to an ordinary prudent person in plaintiff's position, then the jury should find for defendants.

Ruling of the Court: We find that the case was properly submitted to the jury and that no error was committed by the trial court in denying defendant's various motions.

However in Pincus v. Kiamesha Concord, Inc., 263 N.Y.S.2d 895 (1965), the court ruled the plaintiff could not recover when he went out of his way to save five or ten feet and stepped on a railroad tie that had rotted away, falling and injuring himself. In the Sherman case, the plaintiff had the right to assume the sidewalk was safe and conformed to normal engineering principles. In the Pincus case, the plaintiff went looking for a problem and found it.

Can a resort hotel be held liable for an injury to a child when the child walks into the side of a motor vehicle while crossing a private way connecting the children's play area with a parking lot where her parents are seated in a car? There is a distinct possibility that it can, according to the case of DiSalvo v. Armae, Inc., 390 N.Y.S.2d 390 (1976). The plaintiff contended that the resort provided an unsafe arrangement for its guests' recreation in that they had encouraged adults to split up from their children by providing a play area for the children separated from the area where the adults would go by a private, little-used dirt road. In the court of original jurisdiction, the judge dismissed the case, claiming that there was no liability under these circumstances, especially inasmuch as the child walked into the side of a pickup truck, and the driver was absolved of any fault for the injury.

The plaintiff appealed to the Supreme Court Appellate Division, which upheld the lower court's ruling. The plaintiff then appealed to the court of appeals, which reversed the findings of the two lower courts. It held that evidence of the great number of activities on the Fourth of July holiday and evidence that the children's play area was separated from the adults was sufficient evidence to permit a finding in favor of the child. The theory put forth was that the arrangements made by the resort on the Fourth of July were such to encourage the separation of adults and children. The fact that the road was used so infrequently increased the peril for children too young to be expected to exercise care and made their parents unalert to any traffic. The court further said that all of the circumstances had to be taken into consideration by the jury: that the accident occurred on a festive holiday early in the summer season; significant entertainment had been arranged to attract the adults and the children; and the danger of lulling the guests into a false sense of security was an arguably foreseeable risk. With all of the circumstances in mind, it would be a jury's job to determine whether under the circumstances, the resort owner should have closed the road to prevent any motor vehicle traffic on it; or that the resort was not negligent at all and the accident was due to the negligence of the parents; or that no one was negligent at all.

Many resorts owe their popularity to the outside activities and sports participation they offer. This creates a question as to the liability of the resort for injuries sustained by a guest while using some of the sporting facilities. Would you say that a hotel can be held liable for the injuries that a guest received while using a toboggan slide provided by the hotel? The federal district court in New York held that under the circumstances presented in the case of Bazydlo v. Placid Marcy Co., Inc., 422 F.2d 842 (N.Y., 1970), it could, and the court of appeals affirmed the position. The court said that the hotel recognized the risk that a toboggan might leave the run and failed to maintain the sidewalls sufficiently to turn the toboggan away from obstructions. In the case, the toboggan jumped from the run and struck a steel pole, causing the plaintiff to suffer injury. The hotel argued that the plaintiff had assumed the risk of injury as a matter of law merely by getting on the toboggan and riding down the run, realizing that there was some danger in so doing. The court disagreed, saying that despite the risk, the plaintiff still had the right to rely on the duty owed to her by the hotel to maintain the run in a reasonably proper condition, and it was this failure on the part of the hotel that created the liability.

A New York state court in the case of Callahan v. Buck Hill Inn and Golf Club, 409 N.Y.S.2d 416 (1978) seems to hold contrary to the Bazydlo case, but it is distinguishable. In the Callahan case, the plaintiff brought suit against the inn for injuries sustained while ice skating at the inn's rink, alleging that the ice in the rink was in a defective and dangerous condition and that the defendant had actual or constructive notice of this and did not remedy it. The case was tried before a jury, and the jury found for Buck Hill Inn. On appeal, the appellate court said that the jury had returned a verdict for the defendant and that there was no reason to disturb it. In short, the court was saying that the jury is the ultimate trier of fact and, on the evidence, apparently found that either the ice was not in a defective condition or else the inn's operators did not know or reasonably could not have been expected to know about it. Therefore there was no liability because the plaintiff had assumed the risk of injury should she fall due to no fault of negligence of the inn.

The rationale that emerges from a comparison of the two cases seems to be as follows: Guests who participate in sports that have an element of risk involved assume the risk of any injury that they may sustain from participation that is reasonably associated with the sport. But if the hotel or inn fails to maintain the sporting facility in the condition that the guest could reasonably expect it to be, then this negligence on the part of the inn gives rise to liability for any injury.

Lighting Required for Guests

The high cost of energy makes it easy to understand why lighting is often kept to a minimum. Yet even when only a few rooms are rented, the motel itself and any area used by the public must be properly lighted. How much is enough light? The case of *Bowling* v. *Lewis* is a good example of a situation where the attempt to save a few dollars on lighting led to a guest's injury and a lawsuit.

The question of whether a guest is contributorily negligent by going to his room in the dark can only be answered by the question of how would he get there otherwise? Generally, contributory negligence is a jury question and depends on the facts of the case.

Case Example	Bowling v. Lewis *261 F.2d 311 (S.C., 1958)* *(BARKSDALE, District Judge)*

This diversity action was instituted by appellant, James L. Bowling, against the appellees, Maggie K. Lewis and Lillian Kulchycke, for the recovery of damages for personal injuries that he alleges he sustained as the result of the negligence of appellees. There was a trial with a jury and, at the conclusion of plaintiff's evidence, the district judge granted defendants' motion for a judgment of involuntary dismissal, and plaintiff has appealed. Taking the evidence and reasonable inferences to be drawn from it, in the light most favorable to the plaintiff, as we must, . . . the facts are substantially as follows:

Having previously made a reservation, James L. Bowling, a Greyhound bus driver of Washington, D.C., arrived at defendants' motel on the ocean front at Myrtle Beach, South Carolina, the afternoon of Sunday, May 15, 1955, intending to spend a week of his vacation there. He was accompanied by his wife and two small children. The room to which he and his family were assigned was located at the righthand corner facing the ocean on the ground floor of one of the two buildings comprising defendants' motel. The car-parking area was to the rear of this building, and the only means of access from the parking area to the ocean-front rooms was a concrete walkway leading around both sides of the building. This walkway was from two to three feet wide, and some two or three feet from the sides of the building. Immediately adjacent to the walkway, on the side toward the building, there was a wall composed of rough, jagged, coral stones piled loosely on top of each other without mortar, which was ten to twelve inches high, approximately ten to twelve inches wide at the bottom, and somewhat pyramidal in shape. It was uneven and irregular, due to the varying sizes of the stones. Between the wall and the side of the building, there was a flower bed. The stone wall was removed by the defendants before the trial.

Tuesday evening, after his arrival on Sunday, Bowling and his family left the motel about 7:15 P.M., and drove to the amusement area some distance away. As the Bowlings left the motel, dusk was coming on, electric lights were on in the motel office and one or more of the other motel rooms. Also, the motel advertising sign was lighted up and a lantern-type electric lamp was lighted that provided sufficient illumination to enable anyone to use the walkway around the building without difficulty. After spending some time at the amusement area, the Bowlings returned to the motel about 9:15 P.M. and parked their car in the place assigned to them in the parking area to the rear of the motel. Although the night was cloudy, foggy, and very dark, there were no lights whatever in or about the entire motel, with the exception of a small, yellow, bug-repellant light at the front of the building that provided no effective illumination to the rear or sides of the building. All the other lights had been turned off while the Bowlings were at the amusement area.

In order to provide light enough for his wife and children to reach their room, Bowling did not extinguish the headlights of his car. These lights did not shine directly on the walkway, but did provide sufficient light for Mrs. Bowling, carrying the smaller child in her arms and leading the older one by the hand, to reach their room safely, proceeding along the concrete walk on the righthand side of the building facing the ocean. After waiting long enough for his wife and children to reach their room, Bowling turned off his headlights, and waited momentarily to give his eyes an opportunity to adjust to the darkness. With eighteen years of experience as a bus driver, he had very good night vision. Although it was then very dark, Bowling thought he could safely find his way along the walkway to his room, as he had used this walkway a number of times since his arrival at the motel on Sunday. He proceeded very cautiously around the right rear corner of the building and along the concrete walkway toward the faint glow of light at the end of the building from the yellow light in front of his room. Just after he had turned the corner and was proceeding along the walkway, his foot struck a stone on or immediately adjacent to the walkway. He turned his ankle and fell to his left into and across the wall of jagged rocks adjacent to the walkway, the fall resulting in the injuries that are the basis of this action.

The Bowlings had no flashlight, but a friend, expecting to go fishing with Bowling, arrived before daylight the next morning and he had a flashlight. Using it, he and Bowling found a stone, from nine to ten inches in diameter, lying in the walkway immediately adjacent to the stone wall where Bowling had stumbled and fallen. Approximately the length of his body farther forward, they found two or three additional stones lying in the walkway. When Bowling reported the accident later in the morning to Mr. Lewis, husband of the appellee Lewis and manager of the motel, Mr. Lewis replaced the stones that had fallen out of the wall and stated that "he did not understand why this year he had had so much trouble with the rocks falling off and that evidently the rocks had fallen off into the sidewalk and it had never happened before, . . . but this year, several times, they had." That evening, appellee, Mrs. Lewis, said that she had not kept the lights burning because the regular summer season had not yet started and it was too expensive to keep the lights on with only one tenant in the building.

In explaining to the jury his reasons for sustaining defendants' motion for an involuntary dismissal, the trial judge stated his conclusion that plaintiff's evidence was insufficient to sustain the charge of negligence, and moreover, the evidence did establish that plaintiff was guilty of contributory negligence as a matter of law. Hence, there are two questions presented to us on this appeal:

1 Was plaintiff's evidence sufficient to go to the jury on the question of negligence; and

2 Did the evidence show that plaintiff was guilty of contributory negligence as a matter of law?

We are of the opinion that the first question must be answered in the affirmative, and the second question in the negative.

Considering first the question of defendants' negligence, the general rule seems to be that innkeepers owe to their guests the duty of exercising ordinary and reasonable care for their safety.

"The law imposes a duty on an innkeeper or similar proprietor to furnish safe premises to his patrons and to provide articles of furniture that may be used by them in the ordinary and reasonable way without danger. . . ."

No South Carolina cases declaring the degree of duty owed by an innkeeper to his guests have been cited to us by counsel, nor do we find any. . . .

Applying this standard to the facts of this case, it seems clear to us that on the issue of defendants' negligence, the evidence was amply sufficient to go to the jury. Bowling was using the walkway provided for his ingress and egress to and from the room assigned to him and his family. It was the duty of the defendants not only to exercise reasonable care to keep this walkway free from stones that might cause one using it to fall, but it was also their duty to provide sufficient light to enable guests to use the walkway in safety. Defendants' failure to sufficiently illuminate the walkway was not excused by the fact that the summer season at Myrtle Beach had not commenced, nor by the fact that the Bowlings were the only guests at that time.

It is true that there is no evidence that defendants knew of the presence of the stone on which Bowling twisted his ankle on the walkway. Therefore, appellants rely on the South Carolina rule that a merchant is "not liable for injuries caused by some defect in the premises, in the absence of any evidence tending to show that he or his agents knew or should have known, by the exercise of reasonable diligence, of the defect."

However, that contention is not sound under the circumstances of this case. Mr. Lewis, husband of one defendant and manager of the motel, admitted that rocks falling off the stone wall and into the sidewalk had been giving trouble that year, and the continued maintenance of the wall of loosely piled, rough, and jagged stones, immediately adjacent to the walk, with knowledge of their propensity for falling onto the sidewalk, was enough to take the case to the jury under the above quoted rule. However, defendants' negligence was predicated, not solely on the presence of the stone on the walkway, but also on the breach of their duty to provide sufficient illumination to enable a guest to use the walkway in safety. We are satisfied that plaintiff's evidence was amply sufficient to go to the jury on the question of defendants' negligence.

Coming to the question of contributory negligence, of course, in numerous instances a plaintiff's contributory negligence as a matter of law appears from his own evidence, but it is well settled that ordinarily the question of contributory negligence is one for the jury. . . .

As was said in 43 C.J.S. Innkeeper, Section 22, pp. 1184, 1185:

"Under some circumstances a guest or lodger is deemed guilty of contributory negligence in using a dark or unlighted stairway or in using a dark or unlighted passageway, as in instances where lighted stairways, or the means of providing light, are available to him. On the other hand, it is held that a guest cannot be charged with contributory negligence or assumption of risk merely because he uses a darkened stairway where the elevator is out of commission and the stairway is the only means available for passing between the room and the ground floor, or where, on instructions from an employee, he uses an insufficiently lighted hallway, but exercises care; and contributory negligence and assumption of risk have been found absent in other circumstances. . . ."

We are satisfied that the evidence in this case does not establish Bowling's contributory negligence as a matter of law. It is true that he testified that when the accident happened, it was very dark, the only light anywhere being the dim glow from the yellow bulb in front of his room. However, he was using the only available means of ingress to his room. There was no one present upon whom he might call for light. He was familiar with the concrete walkway and knew its location. He and his family had used it as a means of ingress and egress several times since their arrival; in fact, he and his family had proceeded from their room to their car along this walkway safely about two hours earlier that same evening. Mrs. Bowling and the children had safely proceeded along this walkway immediately before the accident. Bowling had every reason to believe that he could safely use this walkway, with which he was familiar. The question of his contributory negligence should have been submitted to the jury. It follows that this case must be reversed and remanded for a new trial.

Ruling of the Court: Reversed and remanded.

The case of Rappaport v. Days Inn of America Corporation, 250 S.E.2d 245 (N.C., 1979), seems to indicate that innkeepers must illuminate the parking lots in which guests must park their cars while staying at motels. In the *Rappaport* case, the plaintiff, an eighty-two-year-old woman, fell in the defendant's parking lot as she attempted to go to her room in the darkness. She tripped because she failed to see a six- or seven-inch step up to the walk from the parking lot surface, which was not illuminated in any way. The lower court apparently felt there was no actionable negligence and that the plaintiff was contributorily negligent as a matter of law for having tried to go to her room in the darkness, and it granted the defendant's motion for a directed verdict. The court of appeals upheld the lower court, and the plaintiff appealed to the Supreme Court, which reversed the lower two courts by saying that the case should have gone to the jury. It reasoned that under the factual situation presented, a jury would be permitted, although not required, to find that the plaintiff was a guest at the defendant motel, that had failed to exercise adequate care to provide adequate lighting for the parking lot destined for the use of its invited guests. The evidence tended to show that not only was the parking lot inadequately lighted, but that it was pitch dark. The innkeeper is under the duty to keep that portion of the premises in a reasonably safe condition so as not to expose guests to danger unnecessarily. This duty implies the duty to make reasonable inspections and correct unsafe conditions. A breach of these duties would constitute actionable negligence on the part of the defendant and would support a verdict in the plaintiff's favor. The court went on to say that merely because the plaintiff attempted to go to her room in the darkness does not constitute contributory negligence as a matter of law.

People do fall because of carelessness and/or some other reason not connected to negligence of the landowner. But the case of Withrow v. Woozencraft, 559 P.2d 425 (N.M., 1977), shows another possibility for a lawsuit against a hotel or motel owner. The plaintiffs, guests of the motel, told the desk clerk they would be leaving before 5 A.M. the next morning. There was a concrete pad off the porch extending into the parking area where their car was parked. The lights for the area were on a timer, and they went off at 4:30 A.M. At 5 A.M. it was still dark outside. The plaintiff tried to turn on the porch light that was adjacent to the motel room, but it was connected to the master timer, which lost power at 4:30 A.M. Because it was too dark for the plaintiff to see outside, she opened the door of the room to allow the inside light to shine onto the porch. Nevertheless, she missed her footing on the edge of the cement pad, injuring herself. The defendant argued that the plaintiff was contributorily negligent as a matter of law, and the trial court agreed. This argument is based on the theory of stepping into the dark with knowledge of a dangerous condition. The question of whether this is a "step in the dark" case where the application of contributory negligence doctrine should be applied as a matter of law is most questionable. It would seem that this is a jury question and should not be for the courts to decide.

Duty Owed Guests in Swimming Areas

Countless millions of Americans swim, and the proliferation of hotel, motel, club, private, public, and even restaurant swimming pools has made swimming more than accessible to travelers. Many state statutes require stringent rules to be followed, and the law of torts has demonstrated a remarkable elasticity to accommodate incidents stemming from this widespread recreational activity.

Swimming pool accidents may range from simply slipping on the tile floor, diving, hitting floats or other paraphernalia in the pool to those caused by a swimming pool not having equipment required by law.

The location of many resorts on beaches presents additional problems. For instance, is the resort hotel liable for the frontage that it has on the beach? No one owns the ocean, but many places have *riparian rights* (rights of a person owning land bordering on a body of water) that can create problems.

Anyone owning a swimming pool must adhere to relevant legislative enactments. Supposedly, these statutes are for the protection of all people intending to use a pool. In *Harris v. Laquinta-Redbird Joint Venture*, the court said that not having "life poles" or "shepherd's crooks" as required by statute was a jury question.

When a case goes to a jury on this type of question, the results are often similar to those obtained in malpractice suits, where juries tend to be severely biased against the physicians and for the patients.

Case Example	**Harris v. Laquinta-Redbird Joint Venture**
	522 S.W.2d 232 (Texas, 1975)
	Rehearing Denied March 18, 1975
	(CORNELIUS, Justice)

Appellant filed suit against appellee for damages resulting from the drowning of her son, Ned Harris, in appellee's motel swimming pool. At the close of evidence from both parties, the district court directed a take nothing verdict. The parties will be referred to as in the trial court.

Plaintiff based her case upon the alleged negligence of defendant in failing to provide a lifeguard, failing to warn of the absence of a lifeguard, and failing to have a life pole and a separate throwing line available as required by Dallas City Ordinance No. 8479. We have concluded that plaintiff made a case for the jury on the issues of negligence and proximate cause in failing to provide a life pole as required by the ordinance, and that the directed verdict was therefore improper.

In judging the propriety of the court's action in directing a verdict, we must disregard all adverse evidence and consider only that evidence, together with all reasonable inferences properly drawn therefrom, favorable to plaintiff's case. If there was any probative evidence of negligence and proximate cause, the directed verdict was improper. Since defendant elected to proceed with its evidence after plaintiff closed her case, the issue is to be decided from the evidence on the whole case rather than on plaintiff's case alone. . . .

The evidence, viewed most favorably to plaintiff's case, was as follows:

Ned Harris was in Dallas with his sister and other young people attending Expo '72. They were staying at defendant's motel that had a small swimming pool as part of its facilities. Several of the group, including Ned, had gone swimming there on Wednesday night without incident, and on Thursday night, Ned and others again went swimming. While he was in the pool on that evening, Ned encountered some difficulty and began to call for help. Two of his companions, a boy and a girl, successively got in the water and tried to get hold of him, but were unable to do so. Mr. Albuquerque, who was a guest at the motel, saw Ned struggling in the water and jumped in to attempt a rescue. By the time he got into the water, Ned had submerged and was at or near the bottom of the pool, and Albuquerque could not get to him because of the resistance of his own clothing and shoes. Albuquerque then got out and a friend of his dived in, but he was also unable to reach Ned. These two men then grabbed two aluminum poles that were nearby and used them to reach the victim. As neither pole had a hook, loop, or other pulling facility on it, the men could not get hold of Ned to pull or lift him out of the water, but could only push him in an attempt to move him to shallow water.

After some time and considerable difficulty, they finally succeeded in pushing the boy to the shallow portion of the pool, where he could be reached and was pulled out of the water. Attempts to revive him failed. Albuquerque testified that because the poles had no hook or pulling facility, it was difficult to move the boy and it "took some time, I don't know how much, but it took seconds or minutes to do this because the poles, of course, they are long and aluminum, and we used them to push, not to pull, because there was no way to get ahold." He further testified that if the poles had been equipped with some type of pulling device he could have effected a speedier recovery. One of the poles bent as it was used in an attempt to push Ned to the shallow area.

Ordinance No. 1479 of the city of Dallas regulating the operation of public and semipublic swimming pools, required that one unit of "safety equipment" be available at all such pools at all times the pools were in use. One unit of lifesaving equipment was defined by the ordinance as including "a life pole or shepherd's crook type of pole with minimum length *handle* of twelve feet; . . ."

There was evidence that the poles that were provided at the pool were merely straight aluminum poles without any hook or pulling device. The court was therefore required to decide whether a straight pole without such a hook or pulling device was a "life pole" within the meaning of the ordinance. If it was not, the jury could have found from the evidence that the defendant violated the ordinance in failing to provide a life pole. Such a violation would be negligence per se. . . .

The same general rules of construction that apply to statutes apply also to municipal ordinances. . . . The prime objective in such construction is to determine the intention of the legislative body. . . . To assist in ascertaining the legislative intent, resort may be had to several sources. Among these are (1) the object and purpose of the enactment and the evils sought to be prevented; (2) the meaning of the words actually used . . . ; and (3) the construction placed upon the enactment by the officers or agencies charged with its administration or enforcement. . . . In determining the meaning of the words used, an attempt will be made to harmonize the various provisions of the enactment, and the words will be given their usual and ordinary meaning, except that where technical words or words of a particular art, trade or activity are used, they will be given the meaning recognized by persons engaged in that particular art, trade, or activity. The testimony of persons engaged in or familiar with that art, trade, or activity is admissible to explain the meaning.

Considering first *the object and purpose of the ordinance* and the evils sought to be prevented, it is obvious that the requirements for lifesaving equipment were designed to facilitate the rescue of persons in danger of drowning. With respect to a "life pole," it is common knowledge, and was confirmed by inferences from the testimony, that a pole without a pulling device is reasonably effective to rescue only those persons who are still conscious and able to grasp the pole so that others can pull them to safety; whereas, a pole with a hook or pulling device can be used to retrieve unconscious persons who may still be alive and subject to resuscitation even though they are submerged.

In view of the fact that a comprehensive unit of lifesaving equipment was envisioned by the ordinance [the required equipment also included a ring buoy with rope, a separate throwing line, a guard line separating the shallow and deep portions of the pool, and a telephone with selected list of numbers for ambulance, hospitals and rescue units], it seems unreasonable to suppose that the requirement would be satisfied by a pole that would be effective in the former case but not in the latter case. The phrase "life pole or shepherd's crook type of pole" surely did not mean either a pole *with* a hook or pulling device or one *without* such a device, but rather one of either type or designation *with a pulling device*. This appears to be further illustrated by the additional phrase "with minimum length *handle* of twelve feet." If the ordinance meant a straight pole without anything else, it could have simply said "a life pole at least twelve feet in length." The use of the word "handle" seems to presuppose that there would be something more.

In considering *the meaning of the words used*, we believe the term "life pole" is not one of common parlance or usage, but was used in the ordinance in a technical sense as applied to the particular trade or activity that the ordinance regulated—the operation of a public swimming pool and the lifesaving activities relating to it. As to the meaning of the term when applied to such activity, the only testimony was from defendant's own witness, Dean Gray, who was chief of the Water Quality Surveillance Section of the City of Dallas Health Department. One of his duties was the inspection of swimming pools and the lifesaving equipment required by the city ordinance. He testified that "life pole" and "shepherd's crook" were two names for the *same piece of equipment*, and that a life pole "has a U, looks like a U-shaped end on it, looks like a shepherd's crook." To the question: "When you say life pole or shepherd's crook, you're talking about one and the same thing, is that correct?", he answered, "Yes, sir, ..." The testimony of Gray, who was familiar with the meaning of the words in the trade or business to which they applied and who was also an officer charged with the administration and enforcement of the ordinance, was entitled to weight.

Since all of the aids to construction that were available to the trial court were to the same effect, we believe it was established that a "life pole" as required by the ordinance must be one equipped with a hook or other pulling device. The jury could have found from the evidence that defendant did not have such a life pole available, thus rendering defendant guilty of negligence per se.

It next becomes necessary to determine if, from the evidence and inferences to be drawn therefrom, the negligence in failing to provide a life pole could have been a proximate cause of the death of Ned Harris.

In the context of this case, proximate cause would be an act or omission that caused or failed to prevent the injury. . . . It is ordinarily a fact question for the jury. In the determination of that fact question the jury is allowed broad latitude to infer proximate cause from the evidence and the circumstances surrounding an accident . . . . Hopson v. Gulf Oil Corp., 150 Tex. 1, 237 S.W.2d 352 (Tex., 1951). . . . This is especially so in drowning cases where it is not possible to produce direct proof that a person could have been rescued if a lifeguard or proper lifesaving equipment had been provided.

In this case, the testimony of defendant's own witness, Albuquerque, made it clear that the lack of a pole with a hook or pulling device caused a significant delay in the rescue because the poles could only be used to push the boy to the shallow portion of the pool where he could be retrieved by hand. His testimony also made it clear that the retrieval would have been quicker had the pole been equipped with a hook. The testimony also confirmed that the boy had not been submerged long when Albuquerque and his friend began to use the poles. Albuquerque first observed the boy "bobbing up and down" in the water. When Albuquerque made his unsuccessful attempt at rescue by entering the water, Ned had descended to or near the bottom of the pool. Albuquerque and his friend then got out and used the poles. Reasonable minds could infer from this evidence that had the poles been as required by the ordinance, the boy could have been retrieved quickly enough to prevent his death. Prompt resuscitation efforts are frequently successful, even though the victims have already lost consciousness when such efforts are begun. Many cases have held that circumstances similar to those here were sufficient to make a fact issue on proximate cause. The cases cited are not analogous on the issues of negligence, but are analogous on the issue of proximate cause.

A careful analysis reveals that in the cases of this type that have held evidence of proximate cause to be insufficient, there was no evidence to indicate the circumstances surrounding the death. A body was simply found lying under or floating upon the water, with no indication of how or when death occurred. . . .

For the reasons stated and in view of the liberal rules approved in Hopson v. Gulf Oil Corp. and many other cases, we conclude there was probative evidence of such causal relation and foreseeability as are required for a finding of proximate cause, and that plaintiff was entitled to have such issue submitted to the jury. Points of error 2 and 3 are therefore sustained.

Ruling of the Court: The judgment is reversed and the cause remanded for a new trial. Plaintiff's other point of error is overruled.

On Rehearing   In its motion for rehearing, appellee asserts that Mr. Albuquerque testified only that the pole he used did not have a hook or pulling device, and that therefore there is no evidence that the pole used by his companion did not have such a hook.

Mr. Albuquerque testified in part as follows:

". . . I saw these aluminum poles there, and I picked one up, . . . I picked up another one and gave it to Joe, and *both of us then pushed.* . . . This took some time, I don't know how much, but it took seconds or minutes to do this because *the poles, of course, they are long and aluminum, and we used them to push, not pull, because there was no way to get ahold* (SF224). . . .

"Joe and I, we both used the poles, one on each side of the pool. . . ." (SF225).

"Q. Did that pole you talked about have a hook on it?"

"A. No, sir."

"Q. Had it had a hook on it, could you have placed it down into the water, hooked onto the body and pulled him out?"

"A. The hook on the end of the pole would make a speedier recovery of the boy. . . ."

"Q. *had there been a pole with a hook,* you could have at least made it easier for you?"

"A. I would say it would make a speedier recovery" (SF239).

We believe a reasonable interpretation of Albuquerque's testimony is that neither pole had a hook or pulling device. Of course, there was other testimony about poles. One witness testified that there was no pole at all at the pool except a wooden stick about ten feet long. Another witness testified that there was one pole about five feet long that did not have any hook. The motel manager testified that a "shepherd's crook" was a part of the equipment kept by the motel and that it was in the pool area when Ned Harris drowned. Mr. Nagy testified that the morning after the drowning, he inspected the pool and found "the shepherd's hook" pole, which had been bent, but Mr. Albuquerque testified that the pole he used was the one that was bent in the rescue attempt. These were simply conflicts in the testimony that only the jury could resolve and the adverse portions of which we must disregard in determining the propriety of a directed verdict against appellant.

Ruling of the Court: The motion for rehearing is respectfully overruled.

When beach property is involved in a lawsuit, the question of how much notice of dangerous conditions must be given to guests is paramount. Suppose signs were posted by the hotel warning guests of dangerous surf conditions—does this negate the hotel's duties to a guest who goes swimming and is injured when thrown on the beach by high waves?

The case of Tarshis v. Lahaina Investment Corporation, 480 F.2d 1019 (Hawaii, 1973), is not very encouraging for hotelkeepers. Granted, the case had to be retried by the trial court, but the court did state that summary judgment could not be used to allow the hotel to win without producing evidence of contributory negligence on the part of the plaintiff.

According to the facts of the *Tarshis* case, the plaintiff-appellant had gone swimming in a dangerous surf and had been injured when a huge wave tossed her on the beach. The Lahaina Hotel, where she was a registered guest, had that day set out six red flags on its beach indicating dangerous conditions, along with four warning signs to that effect. The appellant had seen the flags, but not the signs. She contended she had received no verbal warning from the hotel and the water had not looked dangerous to her. The lower court held for the hotel; but the appeals court found the hotel had failed to warn the appellant adequately, and the case was remanded for retrial.

Swimming Accidents

The Hawley family were guests of the Holiday Inn Motel, where their eleven-year-old daughter received instruction from the diving instructor. The father was injured when he dove from the side of the pool, as the instructor had done that afternoon with his daughter. The lower court awarded the plaintiff $150,000 damages (Kalm, Inc., v. Hawley, 406 S.W.2d 394 [Ky., 1966]). On appeal, the court reversed the lower court in view of the following facts. Although the plaintiff was a registered guest for several days and had used the swimming pool, he was considered to be contributorily negligent as a matter of law in executing a "pike dive" from a position on the edge of the swimming pool that was halfway between eight-foot and five-foot depth markers. (In a pike dive the diver enters the water head first, with arms and hands extended above the head in as nearly a vertical position as possible. It is considered a deep water dive.) The court decided that the plaintiff knew that the bottom of the pool sloped and that special facilities were available for diving in the pool. This opinion overruled Louisville Water Company v. Bowers, 64 S.W.2d 444 (Ky., 1933), which proclaimed that "the law did not require the plaintiff to make a critical examination that the depth was sufficient to make the dive."

The rationale of this and similar cases is that the plaintiff assumes the risk of injury by making a deep dive at a point substantially removed from the diving board. The argument that the instructor had dived from the side of the pool and not the springboard was not controlling because the instructor was an experienced diver and could compensate for the depth.

In McKeever v. Phoenix Jewish Community Center, 374 P.2d 875 (Ariz., 1962), the ten-year-old daughter of the plaintiff McKeever was drowned while playing with the other children of the family. The shallow area was roped off, but the children jumped into the deep part and scurried back to the shallow area several times while playing. The deceased (Mary Agnes) had been left by her father for roughly five minutes when the accident occurred. The qualified lifeguard on duty did everything in his power to assist in the rescue of Mary Agnes. Furthermore, all necessary and required safety devices to swimmers were on hand.

The court first stated that the doctrine of res ipsa loquitur was not applicable and, therefore, all elements of negligence had to be proved against the defendant. The reason in this case seems quite obvious. The evidence did not give rise to an inference of responsibility by the motel for the injury. These conjectures had to be eliminated before res ipsa loquitur could be applied to the case. Additionally, the defendant's negligence had not been established as the proximate cause of the drowning. The defendant was expected to keep the pool in a safe condition, to have safety equipment ready and qualified personnel on hand; this he did. He was not an insurer of all guests, which would have been prohibitive in cost and personnel.

The case of Tucker v. Dixon, 355 P.2d 79 (Colo., 1960), had a different ending. The owners-managers permitted pool-cleaning equipment, including large, heavy floats, to remain beside the pool. The evidence showed that the floats were sometimes used as playthings in the pool. The eleven-year-old plaintiff-guest went swimming upon her arrival at the motel. When surfacing from a dive, the plaintiff struck her mouth on a float.

The court on appeal said the motel had at least constructive notice of the floats being in the pool because they could reasonably anticipate that the floats could be detached from other equipment and placed in the water "at any time." It therefore followed that the defendant's activities were the proximate cause of the plaintiff's injuries. The court found for the plaintiff.

The swimming pool presents hoteliers with an unsolvable dilemma. It helps to attract business, but it has high maintenance, energy, and labor costs, and it opens up a new avenue of liability.

Hooks v. Washington Sheraton Corporation, a landmark case in the hotel–swimming pool area, was decided in a federal district court in the District of Columbia in 1977. Hooks was rendered quadriplegic when he struck the bottom of the swimming pool at the Sheraton Hotel in Washington, D.C., after diving from the pool diving board. The case is tragic in its consequences, and the question is whether it could have been prevented. Students should gain an appreciation of how thoroughly all facets must be investigated before a decision is made to change or alter an existing facility or before adding a new one.

Case Example

Hooks v. Washington Sheraton Corporation
578 F.2d 313 (1977)
Rehearing denied January 17, 1978
(ROBB, Circuit Judge)

This diversity case arose out of the injuries suffered by eighteen-year-old Thomas Hooks when he dove from the three-meter diving board at the Sheraton Park Hotel in Washington, D.C., in June 1971. The pool was equipped with a high performance aluminum "Duraflex" board that propelled Hooks, who was not an experienced diver, into shallow water where he struck his head on the bottom. As a result, Hooks is a quadriplegic. Hooks and his parents sued the operator of the pool, the Washington Sheraton Corporation (hereafter Sheraton) and its parent, ITT, alleging negligence in the construction and operation of the pool. Specifically, plaintiffs alleged that the depth of the water in the diving area of the pool did not comply with applicable District of Columbia regulations and that it was too shallow for a three-meter Duraflex diving board.

The district court held a bifurcated trial on the issues of liability and damages. The jury found Sheraton liable to the plaintiffs and awarded $6,000,000 to Thomas Hooks and $1,000,000 to his parents. On motion by Sheraton, the district court ordered a new trial on the issue of damages unless plaintiffs filed remittiturs of the amounts exceeding $4,500,000 and $180,000, respectively. Plaintiffs filed the remittiturs.

In its appeal from the finding of liability, Sheraton contends that the district court improperly instructed the jury on the standard of care owed by hotelkeepers to their guests, and on the issue of negligence per se. Sheraton also contends that the damages awarded to Thomas Hooks are grossly excessive for three reasons: (1) the inclusion of evidence of the effect of inflation on Hooks's future expenses; (2) the exclusion of evidence of the impact of income taxes upon Hooks's future earnings; and (3) the closing argument by plaintiffs' counsel, which Sheraton says was inflammatory.

We conclude that only one of Sheraton's complaints is valid: The evidence concerning income taxes should have been received. Nevertheless, for reasons hereinafter stated, we affirm the judgment.

Liability   Sheraton contends that the district court improperly instructed the jury on a hotelkeeper's duty of care, that contrary to the law of the District of Columbia, the instruction required Sheraton to give what Sheraton calls an "absolute warranty of safety" to its guests. Sheraton cites Bellevue v. Haslup, 80 U.S.App.D.C. 181, 182, 150 F.2d 160, 161 (1945) (per curiam); and Picking v. Carbonaro, 178 A.2d 428, 429 (D.C.C.A., 1962). Appellees argue that the doctrine of implied warranty is now the law of the District of Columbia. Whether the Bellevue decision remains the law of the District of Columbia is an issue we need not reach because, read in context, the instruction here is not a warranty charge.

The district court began its instructions on the issue of negligence by properly instructing the jury that:

"[T]he owner of a hotel is liable for failure to use reasonable care to keep safe such parts of the premises as he may retain under his control either for his own use or for the common use of the guests or tenants of the hotel.

"It is the duty of the tenants or guests to exercise ordinary care for their own safety. In other words, the owner of a hotel is not an insurer of the safety of his guests, but he does owe to them the duty to exercise reasonable care for their safety" [emphasis added].

The court then proceeded to instruct the jury on the general law of negligence, negligence per se, contributory negligence, and assumption of risk. The court's reference to warranty came in the context of the instruction on assumption of risk:

"Before this rule [assumption of risk] is applied to defeat the plaintiff's claim, however, you must be satisfied by a preponderance of the evidence that the danger or hazard that caused the injuries of the plaintiff was open and apparent; that he was aware of it; or that in the exercise of reasonable care, should have been aware of it; and that he voluntarily exposed or subjected himself to whatever hazard or danger might reasonably have been involved.

"You are instructed that the owner or the operator of a hotel warrants to its patrons that the facilities of said hotel are safe for the use by its patrons, free from defects and dangerous designs, and that such facilities can be used in the use and manner for which they were intended without danger or risk of injury and that such facilities are reasonably fit and suitable for their intended use [emphasis added].

"When a patron of such a hotel uses such facilities in the manner and method they were intended to be used, he does not assume the risk of injury and is not chargeable with contributory negligence if he sustains an injury in so doing."

It is apparent from the language before and after the sentence relating to warranty that in this sentence the court was explaining to the jury that when using the defendant's pool in the manner for which it was intended, Thomas Hooks did not assume the risk of injury from defects or dangerous design of which he was not aware, and that he was entitled to rely on the hotel's representation that there were no such hidden perils. We think the jury could not have understood the one sentence, delivered in the course of seven pages dealing with negligence, to mean that the hotel owed an "absolute warranty of safety" to its guests. This we think is plain in light of the clear statement at the outset—that the hotel is not an insurer and that it owes its guests a duty of reasonable care. Accordingly, we reject the argument that the instruction improperly imposed upon Sheraton a duty to give its guests an absolute warranty of safety.

Sheraton also contends that the district court erred in instructing the jury on the issue of negligence per se because Sheraton had explained that any possible violations of the applicable District of Columbia regulations were consistent with due care. At trial Hooks offered evidence from which the jury could conclude that the pool failed to meet District of Columbia regulations concerning the depth of water required to be directly under, as well as extending out from, the end of the three-meter diving board.

Paddock, the third-party defendant, introduced evidence on the dimensions of the pool that showed that there might have been minor violations of the regulations. In an effort to explain any violations, Sheraton called Mr. Brink, the chief of the District of Columbia Bureau of Air and Water Quality, to testify that the plans for the pool had been approved by his bureau.

In H.R.H. Construction Corp. v. Conroy, 134 U.S.App.D.C. 7, 411 F.2d 722 (1969), this court drew a distinction between cases in which the defendant offers no explanation of a violation of a statute or regulation and those in which the defendant introduces evidence tending to show that its failure to comply with the statute or regulation is consistent with the exercise of due care. The instruction on negligence per se is proper only when no explanation is made. "Sheraton urges us to hold that its evidence of the approval of the plans, the custom of inspection during construction, and the issuance of the operating license for the pool was enough to negative the inference of negligence per se. We disagree."

Mr. Brink testified that he personally approved the plans for the pool in 1960. He also testified that it is the custom for inspectors to check compliance during construction, and that a license to operate the pool would not have been issued unless the pool had been built according to the plans. Mr. Brink did not testify from personal knowledge that the pool was so constructed, nor did anyone else. As it turned out, the pool was not so constructed. The approved plans called for a wooden diving board.

In 1968 Sheraton replaced the original board with a high-performance aluminum "Duraflex" board. Several experts, including the 1976 U.S. Olympic diving coach, testified that this type of board at the three-meter height is unsafe for the inexperienced divers likely to use a hotel pool. A college diving coach said that a Duraflex board "has a great deal more of elasticity and projects people higher in the air. . . . [I]f a person's balance is forward at the time [he leaves] that board, it's going to send him a lot farther out."

Moreover, the aluminum board extended five inches farther into the pool than the original wooden board. This seems at first a small modification, but it is of particular importance to the question whether the pool depths violated District of Columbia regulations. The regulations require ten feet of water directly under the board and extending out from it for twelve feet. Thereafter, the bottom may incline toward the surface at a rate of one foot of depth for every three feet of distance from the board. Obviously, as the board extends farther over the water, the distance from the end of the board to the point where the bottom inclines toward the surface is reduced. The area where the bottom slopes up is where the injury occurred. Finally, plaintiffs introduced evidence that on the day of the accident, the pool's water level was several inches low. This, too, would reduce the depth of the water under and out from the diving board. There was no showing that the District of Columbia approved these deviations from the plans approved by Mr. Brink in 1960. We conclude, therefore, that the negligence per se instruction given here was proper under the circumstances.

Damages   On the question of damages Sheraton contends that the jury award was so grossly excessive that it indicates a "runaway" jury motivated by passion and prejudice. The remittiturs, argues Sheraton, were insufficient to remedy the problem. Specifically, Sheraton objects to the admission of evidence of estimated future inflation, to an allegedly inflammatory closing argument, and to the exclusion of evidence of the effect of income taxes upon Thomas Hooks's future earnings.

We note at the outset that the district court has broad discretion to order a remittitur in lieu of a new trial, and we find no abuse of that discretion here. With respect to Sheraton's specific allegations of error, two are not properly before this court. Appellants conceded at oral argument that the issue of inflation had not been raised in the district court; therefore, it will not be considered here. Similarly, the objection to counsel's closing argument is not properly before us. Sheraton first raised this objection in its motion for a new trial, too late to preserve the point. We have reviewed the arguments in question and find no basis for treating them as plain error.

Sheraton's third contention with respect to damages is more troublesome. The district court permitted Sheraton to cross-examine plaintiffs' expert economist and statistician on the effect of income taxes upon Thomas Hooks's lost future earnings. In a subsequent ruling on plaintiffs' objection to this line of questioning, however, the court ordered the testimony stricken and admonished the jury to disregard it. . . .

We conclude that evidence of probable income taxes on lost future earnings should have been admitted.

The question remains whether a new trial on the issue of damages is required by our holding. For the reasons set forth below, we believe that the remittitur already filed by Thomas Hooks in the amount of $1,500,000 more than compensates for any error in excluding evidence of the effect of income taxes. . . .

We have no doubt that we have the power to order a further remittitur as a condition of affirmance, but we are persuaded that the remittitur below is sufficient. It reduced the jury verdict by 25 percent and was more than three times the maximum amount assignable to the trial court's error. The district court arrived at an amount of recovery that it found in conformity with the interests of justice. We are not inclined to upset that conclusion.

Ruling of the Court: The judgment is affirmed.

Innkeepers owe guests' visitors the same duties and obligations that they owe to guests, provided that the visitors remain within the boundaries of the invitation. A Tennessee court dealt with this question in the case of Kandrach v. Chrisman, 473 S.W.2d 193 (Tenn., 1971), that concerned the death by drowning of a young man who was visiting his fiancé while she was a guest at the defendant's motel. The suit was brought by his mother for wrongful death. The young man and his fiancé, neither of whom could swim, had gone to the motel pool together. No one else was in the pool, and as he was either walking or standing in the water, he suddenly started to struggle and sank beneath the surface and drowned.

The case seemed to hinge on the fact of whether the deceased was still a guest of his hostess at the time that he stepped into the swimming pool. Because there was a sign at the end of the pool farthest from where the guests enter the pool area that read "Motel Guests Only," the lower court held that the visitor ceased to be an invitee upon entering the pool and that the motel from that time on owed him only the duty owed to a mere licensee or trespasser. It directed a verdict for the defendants. The plaintiff appealed. The appellate court reversed the lower court, saying that a bona fide guest of a patron of a hotel or motel is in fact an invitee of the hotel or motel so long as that person is within the bounds of the invitation.

Boisterous Conduct and Horseplay at a Pool

When boisterous conduct and horseplay are going on in a pool, accidents may occur. In Gordon v. Hotel Seville, Inc., 105 So.2d 175 (Fla., 1958), the plaintiff, swimming face down, was struck by a body that landed on her. The plaintiff fainted and was taken from the pool in hysteria. The court would not allow summary judgment and further ruled that the defendant, as an operator of a swimming pool in an amusement or recreational area, was under the same duty to invitees who were paying guests as was customarily imposed on the operators of a public amusement area.

However, in Cohen v. Suburban Sidney-Hill, Inc., 178 N.E.2d 19 (Mass., 1961), no inference of negligence could be made at the country club where a twelve-year-old youth climbing the ladder of the diving board fell backward and was injured. Three lifeguards were on duty, though not at that particular spot. The court said that the injuries sustained were not attributable to a breach of duty on the part of the owner and held for the defendant.

The same kind of ruling may be used when a guest falls or is shoved off a diving board. The injuries cannot be anticipated or guarded against by the owner (Burns v. South Shore Country Club, 196 N.E.2d 189 [Mass., 1964]).

Glass in Wading Pool

In Bristol v. Ernst, 27 N.Y.S.2d 119 (1941), the plaintiff's foot was severely cut on a piece of glass at the bottom of the pool. The jury could have found that the glass causing the injury could not have been detected nor its presence prevented in the exercise of ordinary care, even though ordinary care included the duty of reasonable supervision. In essence, to hold to the contrary would bring about an absolute liability concept that would make the hotel an insurer of the guests. This is not the intent of the common law.

Using a Pool without Permission

A hotel without a swimming pool of its own had an arrangement with the owners and operators of a nearby pool to allow its guests to use the pool. Without notifying the pool owners, guests who arrived late one night dived into the deep end of the pool. Because the pool was being drained and cleaned, it had only about two feet of water left at the time of the accident. The plaintiffs were injured and sued the hotel and pool owners for negligence.

The court showed that the plaintiff failed to exercise ordinary care for his own safety by diving at 5 A.M. without giving the slightest heed to existing conditions. This contributed to his injury and made his own negligent act a concurring proximate cause of his injury (Ryan v. Unity, Inc., 55 So.2d 117 [Fla., 1951]).

Lake and Beach Swimming

Swimming pools may be considered more accident-prone than any other type of swimming facility, but lakes are also a source of accidents. In Montes v. Betcher, 480 F.2d 1128 (Neb., 1973), that occurred in a resort located on a large body of water, the plaintiff took a running dive off a short boat dock and was severely injured when he hit a jagged piece of concrete resembling an anchor that had been constructed by the resort owners. In this case, the court also used the doctrine of comparative negligence and allocated blame according to the negligence of each party (see chapter 8).

An accident that occurs all too often involves a guest who is struck by a surfboard while swimming at a hotel's beach. In Landrum Mills Hotel Corporation v. Ferhatovic, 317 F.2d 76 (P.R., 1963), the hotel brought in evidence that it had warning signs to alert guests to the surfboards in the area; however, the jury found that the hotel was negligent in having a surfboard in the water at the time the plaintiff was bathing.

Special Duty Owed Guests

In addition to hotelkeepers' responsibility to provide reasonable care for the safety of guests, they also owe a "special duty" to some. This special duty is the care required for specific groups of people needing special protection. Among such groups are minors, the handicapped, the elderly, and the mentally ill.

Rights of Minors

Like adults, minors are owed care by the occupiers of land. The extent and degree of this care will be considered in this section. With minors, the element of surprise is ever present and, to some extent, the impossible should be expected. Hoteliers and restaurateurs should take into account childish instincts and impulses because children are presumed to have less ability to take care of themselves than adults. *Baker v. Dallas Hotel Company* should alert hoteliers to all possibilities and to avoid them by preventive maintenance. Even if window screens are not required, what is the hotel's liability when it does have screens but they are defective?

Case	**Baker v. Dallas Hotel Co.**
Example	*73 F.(2d) 825 (Tex., 1934)*
	(SIBLEY, Circuit Judge)

Mr. and Mrs. Robert F. Baker sued the Dallas Hotel Company, owners and operators of a hotel in Dallas, Texas, under the Texas death statute, Article 4671 *et seq.*, Rev. Stats. of 1925, for the death of their infant son, Bobby, who fell from a window of the twelfth story of the hotel. On the evidence, the judge held that no actionable negligence appeared on the part of the defendant and that there was contributory negligence on the part of the plaintiffs and directed a verdict for the hotel company. Mr. and Mrs. Baker appeal, and assign as the sole error the refusal to permit the jury to pass upon the issues of negligence.

The evidence shows without substantial conflict that the Bakers, having with them the child two years and five months old, registered as guests of the hotel and were assigned to a room with adjoining bath on Wednesday. At about nine o'clock the next Saturday morning, Mrs. Baker had just bathed the child and left him playing with his blocks on the floor near the center of the room while she was washing something in the adjoining bathroom. Mr. Baker was in bed, awake, but with his back toward the window a few feet away. The sash was raised, but the opening was covered by a wire window screen that they knew was there, but had never examined. The windowsill was about the height of Bobby's face. In front of it was a radiator that did not extend the whole length of the sill, but left a space on each side. The cut-off valve of the radiator was under one of these spaces, and Bobby could have stepped upon this valve and climbed into the window. Neither Mr. nor Mrs. Baker knew he was near the window until, after a short absence, she returned from the bathroom and saw him sitting sidewise on the windowsill with his head pressed against the screen, and before she could reach him the screen opened outwards and he fell below and was killed.

An examination of the screen showed that it was hinged at the top and was intended to be secured from opening outwards by two spring plungers of metal, one on each side near the bottom of the screen frame, that passed through the frame into holes in the wooden window facing. The screen was old, and the springs had become weak, and the window facing had grooves worn by the ends of the plungers from each hole outwards so that the plungers got but little hold in the facing. A slight pushing on the screen was found by experiment sufficient to open it. The hotel company had employees whose duty it was to inspect windows and screens. This screen had not been reported as out of order to the superintendent, but he did not know whether it had been reported to the housekeeper or carpenter. There were heavy iron grills outside of some of the windows of the hotel, but none on this window.

The Texas statute giving a right of action for death by wrongful act in Article 4672 provides: "The wrongful act, negligence, carelessness, unskillfulness, or default mentioned in the preceding article must be of such character as would, if death had not ensued, have entitled the party injured to maintain an action for such injury." The child's right of action, if he had not died, is therefore directly in question. A parent's negligence is not in Texas ordinarily imputable to a child plaintiff, . . . but since the parents here sue for their own use and benefit, they may be defeated by their own contributory negligence. . . . And such is the general rule elsewhere. . . .

The diligence of counsel has produced no case relating to the liability of an innkeeper for an injury to a child guest due to a defective window screen. An innkeeper is not an insurer of the safety of his guests, but owes to them ordinary care to see that the premises assigned to them are reasonably safe for their use and occupancy. . . .

When a child of tender years is accepted as a guest, the inexperience and the natural tendencies of such a child become a part of the situation and must be considered by the innkeeper. We do not mean that the innkeeper becomes the nurse of the child, or assumes its control when accompanied by its parents, but only that he is bound to consider whether his premises, though safe enough for an adult, present any reasonably avoidable dangers to the child guest. The control and general responsibility for the child accompanied by a parent or nurse is with the latter, who are also bound to exercise ordinary care to keep the child from harm. As has been stated, when parents are complaining of the negligence of the innkeeper, their own negligence that contributes to the injury is a good defense to their suit. Negligence is not attributable as such to a child of two and a half years. . . . The conduct of such a child being natural, spontaneous, and instinctive is like that of an animal and is similarly to be anticipated and guarded against by those charged with any duty in respect to the child.

What then should this innkeeper and these parents have anticipated that this child might do, and what have they respectively done or failed to do that was negligent? There is no statutory requirement respecting hotel windows or window screens, obedience to which would be diligence and failure to comply with that would be negligence per se. There is no course of decisions establishing any rule applicable specially to children and hotel windows. The only available standard of care is the conduct of the ideal person of ordinary prudence, to be judged by the jury as a question of fact. A jury should consider whether the defects attributed to this screen were known to the innkeeper or had existed for such time as that he is to be charged with knowledge of them, whether he should in due prudence have anticipated that a child of this age would be attracted towards the window, and would climb to see what was outside, and might be led to lean against the insecure screen and be endangered; and whether another room, or at least a warning about the insecurity of this screen, was due.

On the other hand, the jury ought also to inquire whether the parents should not have anticipated the same danger and kept better watch over the child or have tested the screen, and whether they themselves were contributorily negligent if the innkeeper was negligent. The innkeeper and the parents perhaps ought equally to have anticipated the danger of a child trying to get into the window, but the duty of inspecting the screen is not the same. The responsibility for the premises is primarily on the innkeeper, and the guest may generally assume that they are safe. But it is argued that the screens are there to keep insects out and not to keep children in, and there is no duty on the innkeeper to have them safe for the latter purpose, and parents have no right to rely on them for such purpose. . . . But yet if the screen to all appearances, and as screens are usually found, would serve to protect the child, the false appearance of an insecurely fastened screen might easily mislead the parent or even inspire confidence in a child to lean against it. . . . Though there was no original duty to have any screen in the window for the purpose of keeping the child in, the jury might conclude that prudence would as respects this child have required that it be as securely fastened as screens customarily are, lest it prove a deception and a trap.

We agree with the trial judge that the failure to have protecting grills at the windows is not negligence. Their absence was apparent, and no law and no custom requires them. But on the issues of negligence in the innkeeper touching the condition of the screen, and in the parents touching their conduct, we are of opinion that jury questions exist. Children have often fallen through insecurely fastened window sashes and screens so that the jury might conclude that such a thing is reasonably to be anticipated by those under duty to guard against danger. . . . The duty of parents to watch over their infant child is to be viewed in the light of all the demands made at the time upon them, and the circumstances usually make negligence on their part a question for the jury.

Ruling of the Court: The judgment is reversed, and the cause is remanded for further proceedings not inconsistent with this opinion.

A child's walking into a glass door or panel has not led to uniform court decisions. In Waugh v. Duke Corporation, 248 F.Supp. 626 (N.C., 1966), a child less than seven years old walked into a glass panel leading to a courtyard and was severely hurt. Similar accidents had involved other guests in the motel. The court ruled for the child. On appeal, it stated that the duty of an innkeeper to an infant guest is greater than that owed to an adult and that the innkeeper is bound to consider whether the premises, although safe enough for an adult, present any reasonably avoidable dangers for a child. In this case, even though the glass was properly installed and of normal thickness, the negligence lay in the failure of the motelkeeper to warn the plaintiff of the potential danger of the glass panels.

It has already been established that those who have not arrived at the age of discretion require a relatively higher degree of care for their safety than do adults. That degree of care is commensurate with the attending facts and circumstances of each case. In cases holding to the contrary, the plaintiffs were either sixteen or older (A. C. Burton Co. v. Stasny, 223 S.W.2d 310 [Texas, 1949]), had entered the building by the same door or door adjoining the glass panel (Crawford v. Given Bros., 318 S.W.2d 123 [Texas, 1958]), or were considered social visitors (Bua v. Fernandez, 251 N.Y.S.2d 773 [1964]).

Reasonable Accommodations for Children

The jury in Seelbach, Inc., v. Cadick, 405 S.W.2d 745 (Ky., 1966), awarded $56,000 to an eight-month-old infant who fell from an adult bed against hot radiator pipes in a hotel room where no baby crib was furnished. The hotel had at least one crib available when the family arrived at this hotel, but the hotel clerk did not offer or give the plaintiffs a crib. The court of appeals held that a jury could properly hold a hotel negligent for failure to provide a baby bed while maintaining exposed hot radiator pipes in the hotel room. The court said that a hotel owes its guests a "duty to provide articles of furniture that may be used by them in the ordinary and reasonable way without danger." The court also said that the negligence was not in the exposed pipe in the room; the question rather was whether the hotel was negligent in failing to furnish reasonable accommodations.

But in Rubin v. Olympic Resort, Inc., 198 N.Y.S.2d 408 (1960), when a six-year-old child fell out of the top tier of a double bunk bed at the defendant's resort hotel, the court held that the parents were not entitled to recover since they failed to prove that there was no guardrail on the bed or that no guardrail was available as optional equipment. Furthermore, the parents failed to prove that the child had actually fallen out of bed. The court said it was not prepared to state that a bunk bed without a guardrail was a dangerous instrument in and of itself. Such a bed, even with a guardrail, might be very dangerous to a child six months old. Without a guardrail, such a bed may be entirely safe for a child of fourteen. The parents should have determined what equipment was necessary or suitable. The hotelkeeper could not be presumed to know.

Injuries Caused by Fire

Most states have passed statutes expressly listing the equipment each hotel is required to have for fire protection. At common law, it was the duty of owners of a public house to exercise reasonable care for the safety of guests; they were not considered to be liable as an insurer.

In Pirtle's Administratrix v. Hargis Bank and Trust Company, 44 S.W.2d 541 (Ky., 1931), the deceased was a guest in the Combs Hotel, Hazard, Kentucky, and died when the hotel was destroyed by fire. It was charged that the defendant negligently failed to provide the hotel with an iron stairway on the outside of the building, and with firefighting equipment. The court said that it was a firmly fixed rule that one injured by a violation of a statute may recover from a defendant any damages sustained because of a violation of this rule. However, the court pointed out that such violation must be the direct and proximate cause of the injury. Therefore, in Ford v. Adams, 206 S.W.2d 970 (Ark., 1947), in which there was a violation of the statute requiring ropes in all hotel rooms, the court held that the lack of such ropes was evidence of negligence, but that it was not conclusive the injury was caused by this violation; hence, it was a question for the jury to decide.

A contrary ruling was given in Moore v. Dresden, 298 P. 465 (Wash., 1931), in which the defendant hotelkeeper was convicted of negligence in failing to maintain adequate fire escapes as required by the laws of the state. The court ruled that a hotelkeeper who fails to comply with a statute will be convicted of negligence, irrespective of all questions of the exercise of prudence, diligence, care, or skill. If, therefore, the failure to comply with a statute is the proximate cause of the injury to a guest, and this guest is without contributing fault, the case is decided in his or her favor, and all that remains to be done is to assess damages.

But when a case revolves on the question of whether the proprietor is negligent in not warning the guest, the court holds that the hotelkeeper must exercise ordinary care in warning the guest. And when a statute requires notice, "it is the innkeeper's duty to give a guest such warning as reasonable, prudent persons would give under like circumstances, taking into consideration the extent of the fire, the size of the building, and the equipment of the hotel installed for the safety and protection of his guests (cited in Parker v. Kirkwood, 8 P.2d 340 [Kemas, 1932]).

In Burrows v. Knotts, 482 S.W.2d 358 (Texas, 1972), in which a suit was brought against the defendant hotel owner by the children and heirs of a guest who died in the hotel fire, the jury found the defendant guilty and awarded the heirs $40,000 to compensate the deceased for the conscious physical pain and mental anguish suffered before his death. On review, the court of appeals said that innkeepers are not insurers of the safety of their guests, but innkeepers do owe guests a duty to furnish and maintain a safe place in proper condition. Their responsibility is limited to the exercise of ordinary or reasonable care, and proof must be made of negligence and proximate cause. An innkeeper who discovers a fire on the premises must exercise ordinary prudence and warn the guests. The court said that in this case there was sufficient time to warn the guests; hence, the innkeeper would be liable for lack of notice to the guest. The award was reduced from $40,000 to $10,000 because the jury failed to distinguish between the periods of consciousness and unconsciousness of the deceased and therefore rendered an excessive verdict of $30,000.

The case of Cloward v. Pappas, 387 P.2d 97 (Nev., 1963), in which the plaintiffs lost personal property and were injured during a motel fire, presents elements of law and fact that are unique. (See the case on page 442.)

1   The state of Nevada has a statute allowing recovery for loss by fire only if the defendants are grossly negligent. Were they?

2   What care is required by the hotelkeeper at common law against fire in a hotel?

3   The furnace that caused the fire had just been repaired. Was the independent contractor liable?

4   The manager, who had recently suffered from a heart attack, gave no warning to his guests. Must a hotelkeeper warn guests?

5   In addition to the personal property lost in their room, the plaintiffs lost their car parked outside. What care is owed guests who park their car in a carport furnished for their convenience?

6   Is the common law as interpreted by the court constitutional?

Independent Contractors

The question of whether a hotel is responsible for independent contractors such as physicians, lawyers, and others who come on their premises for any reason is somewhat dependent on the facts of each case. In the case of *Stahlin v. Hilton Hotels Corporation* the hotel was held liable for negligence in sending the doctor's employee, who was not licensed as a nurse, to take care of a guest when help was requested.

Case Example	**Stahlin v. Hilton Hotels Corporation** *484 F.2d 580 (Ill., 1973)* *(ESCHBACH, District Judge)*

This diversity action resulted in a jury verdict against defendants Andersen and Hilton and a directed verdict in favor of defendant Addenbrooke. The jury fixed damages in the amount of $150,000 in favor of Aloysius Stahlin and $60,000 in favor of his wife, Louise, on her loss of consortium claim. Andersen and Hilton appeal from the verdict and judgment. Plaintiffs cross-appeal from the directed verdict in favor of Dr. Addenbrooke. We affirm as to Andersen and Hilton, but we reverse as to Addenbrooke and accordingly remand for a new trial of the issues relating to his liability.

The primary questions raised on appeal by Andersen and Hilton relate to the sufficiency of the evidence to support the verdict against them, the propriety of the trial court's action in relieving plaintiffs of a certain pretrial stipulation, and the correctness of certain instructions given the jury.

Plaintiff Al Stahlin checked into the Conrad Hilton Hotel in Chicago, Illinois, on May 24, 1966, for the purpose of attending a sales convention. After an afternoon at the race track, he and Mr. Ken Bishop returned to their room at the hotel and began to get dressed for a company dinner that evening. As Stahlin was hurriedly dressing, he got his foot tangled in his shorts, fell backward, and struck his head against the wall about two and a half feet above the floor. Stahlin had to be helped to his bed by Bishop, and the two men stayed in the room rather than attend the company dinner. Stahlin complained of a headache, and Bishop observed a bruise or blood coming to the surface at the back of Stahlin's head. A short time later that evening, Stahlin became nauseous and vomited. Bishop then decided to call the management of the hotel for a doctor. Bishop spoke to the assistant manager, described what had happened to Stahlin and was told that "some help" or a doctor would be sent. Fredarica Andersen came to the room about half an hour later and identified herself as a nurse. After learning the facts of the occurrence from Bishop, she examined and felt the back of Stahlin's head and took his temperature, blood pressure, and pulse. She observed a bottle of pills on the table next to the bed and learned that Stahlin had a prior heart condition. Bishop testified that she and Stahlin discussed the fact that the pills were a blood thinner or anticoagulant he was taking for the heart condition. Stahlin complained to her of a terrific headache, and she further learned that he had vomited earlier. Before she left, Mrs. Andersen told Stahlin to stay in bed for twelve hours.

Mrs. Andersen died prior to trial. The following record that she made of her visit was received in evidence:

"Pt was putting on his trousers and fell against the wall in his room, bumping back of head. Before this happened, he had been to the race track, had several drinks, ate a beef sandwich, and vomited contents of food and liquor. Pt took a codeine derivative tablet—also has a coronary condition, refused to go to hospital, will stay in bed for 12 hours. 13/p—15⅝—tem. 98.6 F.A."

Bishop testified that Mrs. Andersen said nothing to Stahlin about seeing a doctor or about going to a hospital. Stahlin did not testify.

Stahlin slept uneasily that night and was up several times. He vomited four or five times. Stahlin remained in the room the next morning when Bishop left to attend the 9 A.M. meeting of the convention. When he returned to the room between 12:00 and 12:30, he found Stahlin in a semicomatose state. An ambulance was called and Stahlin was taken to the hospital. He was diagnosed as having a subdural hematoma. Surgery was immediately performed to relieve the pressure on the plaintiff's brain caused by the large blood clot or hematoma. Plaintiff suffered residual brain damage.

In addition to the foregoing sequence of events, the evidence at trial established that Mrs. Andersen, although commonly referred to at the hotel as a nurse, was not in fact licensed in the state of Illinois either as a registered nurse or a licensed practical nurse. She had been employed for many years by Dr. Addenbrooke in the medical department of the hotel, which department was under his supervision during its entire period of existence from 1948 through 1968. For some time prior to and including the month of May 1966, the medical department was without the services of a physician during the nighttime hours. Dr. Addenbrooke left Mrs. Andersen in charge of the medical department at night with the full knowledge and consent of the hotel management. During these hours it was the practice of the hotel to refer guests in need of medical assistance to Mrs. Andersen.

She charged a standard rate of $15.00, the same amount charged for a doctor's night room call. This amount was added to the guest's bill, collected by the hotel, and remitted to Dr. Addenbrooke in accordance with their long-standing practice. Dr. Addenbrooke let Mrs. Andersen use her own judgment in making room calls and merely provided her with a list of specialists to whom she could refer guests. Mrs. Andersen did not consult with Dr. Addenbrooke concerning her room calls and her findings were not reviewed by him.

We believe the evidence was sufficient to support a finding that Hilton was negligent in sending Fredarica Andersen to Stahlin's room in response to Bishop's request for help. Whether Bishop specifically requested a doctor and whether the assistant manager represented that a doctor would be sent are not determinative of this question. Bishop related the circumstances of Stahlin's problem, and Hilton undertook to render assistance. As the trial court correctly charged the jury, "The operator of a hotel owes no duty to provide any service for a guest who may be ill or injured. If, however, it undertakes to provide such service for any person, it must exercise ordinary care to provide such services that it has undertaken to give." . . . We agree with plaintiffs that the duty undertaken by Hilton was more than merely "sending someone up" to Stahlin's room. Reasonable care under the circumstances required that the hotel send a doctor, or at the very least a licensed nurse, to provide the medical assistance requested on behalf of Stahlin. Moreover, while Hilton denied that it had knowledge of Mrs. Andersen's lack of a license, there is ample evidence in the record from which the jury could find that the failure to inquire as to her qualifications constituted negligence on the part of Hilton. Hilton knew she was making room calls on sick and injured guests and charging the same amount as a doctor. It was the established practice of the hotel to send her to a guest's room in response to a request for a doctor. Under these circumstances, since Hilton knew she was not a doctor, the jury could reasonably find the hotel chargeable with such further knowledge that a reasonable investigation would have revealed—that is, that Mrs. Andersen was not a licensed nurse. Hilton relies on Tansey v. Robinson, 24 Ill.App.2d 227, 164 N.E.2d 272 (1960), in support of its position that plaintiffs were required to show that the hotel had actual knowledge of Mrs. Andersen's lack of qualifications. However, the court in *Tansey* held that liability for the negligent acts of an independent contractor may be predicated upon a failure to exercise reasonable care in selecting a careful and competent contractor. . . . Hilton states in its brief that both Dr. Addenbrooke and Mrs. Andersen were independent contractors. Thus, under the rule stated in *Tansey*, Mrs. Andersen's lack of a nursing license in Illinois was a matter that could have been determined by Hilton upon inquiry, and it was a matter that the jury could properly take into consideration in determining whether Hilton was negligent in carrying out its voluntary undertaking to provide medical assistance for Stahlin.

With respect to Mrs. Andersen, the evidence and the reasonable inferences therefrom support the jury's verdict against her estate. The evidence established that although she was not a licensed nurse, she went to Stahlin's room, identified herself as a nurse, and proceeded to examine Stahlin. She learned about the fall and the blow to plaintiff's head and was told that he had a severe headache and had vomited earlier. There was also evidence that she knew not only of Stahlin's heart condition, but also that he was taking a blood thinner–type pill called Dicumarol therefor. Plaintiffs produced expert testimony that a reasonably well-qualified registered nurse, apprised of the facts known to Mrs. Andersen after her examination of Stahlin, would have referred him to a hospital where neurosurgical services could have been sought on the night of May 24, 1966. Bishop testified that Mrs. Andersen said nothing about Stahlin seeing a doctor or going to a hospital that night and merely told him to stay in bed for twelve hours. There was further expert testimony that Stahlin exhibited the classic symptoms of a developing subdural hematoma at the time he was examined by Mrs. Andersen. Since the jury could reasonably conclude from the foregoing evidence that Mrs. Andersen failed to exercise the degree of care required of a reasonably well-qualified nurse, the verdict would be sustainable even if she had been licensed as required by the Illinois Nursing Act, 91 S.H.A., Sections 35.33 and 35.54. In addition, however, the expert testimony at trial established a sufficient causal connection between her violation of the Nursing Act and the plaintiff's injury to constitute *prima facie* evidence of negligence.

Finally, we are persuaded by a review of the evidence as it relates to the alleged negligence of Dr. Addenbrooke in authorizing Mrs. Andersen to engage in extensive diagnosis and treatment activities that the trial court erred in directing a verdict in his favor. The evidence showed that Mrs. Andersen, although not even a licensed nurse, was permitted to make room calls on sick and injured hotel guests, and was permitted to use her own judgment without benefit of instructions from Addenbrooke other than a list of medical consultants, and without subsequent review of her findings by Addenbrooke. She charged the same amount for a room call as a doctor, which amount was collected by the Hilton and remitted to Addenbrooke. Thus, there was evidence in the record from which the jury could find that Addenbrooke permitted and authorized Mrs. Andersen, as a general practice and on the particular night in question, to perform duties performed under Illinois law only by licensed physicians. The acts performed by Mrs. Andersen with respect to Stahlin could reasonably be found to constitute medical diagnosis, prescription, and treatment so as to fall within the foregoing statutory prohibitions. Given this state of the record, the jury should have been permitted to consider whether the delegation of such duties by Addenbrooke to Mrs. Andersen constituted negligence and whether such negligence was a proximate cause of Stahlin's disability.

Accordingly, the judgment is affirmed as to the defendants Hilton and Andersen. As to the defendant Addenbrooke, the judgment is reversed and remanded for a new trial as to his liability.

Ruling of the Court: Affirmed in part and reversed in part.

In an entirely different type of independent contractor suit, a window washer was injured when a bolt to which his safety belt was attached broke (Afienko v. Harvard Club of Boston, 312 N.E.2d 196 [Mass., 1974]). The Harvard Club tried to claim indemnity from the claim by saying the window washer's employer and contractor were liable. The Supreme Judicial Court held that the evidence sustained the finding that the club was negligent in maintaining the bolts for window washing and therefore was not entitled to indemnity. In its lengthy opinion, the court said that a club owed the employee of an independent contractor working on the club's premises the duty to disclose hidden or concealed defects of which it was aware or should have been aware as an exercise of reasonable care. The jury award of $200,000 was allowed to stand.

Can a hotel delegate its duties toward a guest and thereby avoid liability in the event that the party to whom the duty was delegated to negligently performs the duty? No. In the case of Bardwell Motor Inn v. Accavallo, 381 A.2d 1061 (1977), the hotel operator contracted with the defendant to replace a glass panel in the front entrance door. The contractor removed the glass panel and the push bar from the door and left the premises without advising the plaintiff, the hotel operator, that the doorway had been left in a dangerous condition, without posting any warnings, and without leaving anyone behind to warn people of the danger. A business patron of the hotel fell and sustained personal injuries when trying to open the door. The hotel settled the claim brought against it by the injured man and then sought to recover from the contractor the sum they paid the patron.

The court held that the innkeeper had a nondelegable duty to keep the premises reasonably safe for guests and patrons. But the independent contractor owed both the innkeeper and guests the duty of carrying out the job with reasonable care and attention. Because the contractor acted negligently on the job, he was liable not only to guests for any injuries sustained as a result of his failure, but also to the innkeeper for any loss he sustained.

Security

Rooms and Public Areas

How much security is owed to guests in their hotel room? A dining room? A public area of a hotel? In Phillips Petroleum Company of Bartlesville, Oklahoma v. Dorn, 292 So.2d 249 (Fla., 1974), a husband and wife who were registered guests of the hotel were assaulted by three men who had gained entrance to their room. Mrs. Dorn resisted and was beaten. Jewelry and cash were taken and the plaintiffs were bound and gagged. The court agreed that registered guests in a hotel are business invitees to whom the hotel owes a duty of reasonable care. The question the court had about the lower court's verdict for the husband was that the instructions to the jury set a standard of care greater than that required in public areas. In Florida the hotelkeeper owes only a duty of reasonable care, whereas other states require a high degree or very high degree of care.

The court of appeals also said the plaintiff-guests had a right to rely on the innkeeper to do "all in his power" to avoid or prevent an assault by a stranger. Does this mean the jury could find that a large corporation like Phillips Petroleum Company should employ a guard for every room in the hotel? In this case, the plaintiff won in the lower courts, but the judgment was reversed in the Supreme Court and remanded for a new trial.

Occasionally, facts do vary and what is looked upon as reasonable care may not come out that way when all the facts are in. In *Nordmann v. National Hotel Company*, the jury and the court agreed that the protection the guests received was not reasonable care. The court appeared to extend the doctrine of foreseeability set forth in *Schubert v. Hotel Astor*, discussed earlier in this chapter, that maintained that hotelkeepers and their employees must foresee certain situations that could become dangerous to guests. In the *Nordmann* case, the failure of the hotelkeeper to anticipate that a large crowd at a banquet could bring about a robbery and assault in a guest room was grounds for the guest's recovery.

Case Example	Nordmann v. National Hotel Company
	425 F.2d 1103 (La., 1970)
	(RIVES, Circuit Judge)

Mr. and Mrs. Nordmann sued the National Hotel Company for damages that resulted from a robbery and assault committed upon them in a Jung Hotel room in New Orleans between 12:10 A.M. and 1:10 A.M. on October 18, 1965. The Nordmanns, accompanied by a friend and business associate, William Mixon, registered into the hotel as paying guests the previous afternoon. That evening, with several other friends, they attended a ball in the hotel ballroom. The hotel contains some twelve hundred guest rooms, and there were some twelve to fourteen hundred people at the ball. Shortly after midnight, when the Nordmanns left the ball and started up to their room, they entered a self-serving, automatic-type elevator. They were followed by the man who later robbed and assaulted them. When they left the elevator, they did not notice that this man followed until Mr. Nordmann put the key in the door. At that time, the man thrust a gun in Nordmann's back and pushed them into the room and on the bed. He took such money as Nordmann had in his wallet, fifty dollars, forced him to lie face down on the bed, had Mrs. Nordmann get a razor blade from the bathroom and cut a section of a venetian blind cord with which he tied Nordmann's hands behind his back. He announced that "It's not just the money I want, that's not all I want." He proceeded to make indecent advances to Mrs. Nordmann, repeatedly slapping and hitting her, and forced her to mix him two drinks. Finally, on her plea to let her mix him another drink or get water for her husband, Mrs. Nordmann was permitted to go back into the bathroom. She described the conclusion of the assault thus: "So, when I got into the bathroom I turned my head, and as I turned my head I could see that he walked over to my husband and pulled his collar loose, and when he did, I don't know what came over me, but the bathroom door was close enough to the knob of the main door, that I said, 'Dear God, don't let that chain be on that door,' because I reached out and I turned that knob and I opened that door and I ran screaming down the hall. That's all that I remember as far as that episode was concerned." The assailant fled down an inside fire escape and has never been captured.

This appeal is from a judgment entered on a jury's verdict for $16,000 in favor of Mrs. Nordmann and for $5,000 in favor of Mr. Nordmann.

The appellants argue that "the verdict of the jury is contrary to the law and the evidence." This contention is almost frivolous. The law imposes upon innkeepers at least ordinary or reasonable care to protect their guests against injury by third persons, and some cases call for the exercise of a higher degree of care. In this case the court, by its instructions, held the defendants to a standard of ordinary or reasonable care to protect the hotel's guests from injury by third persons.

The complaint charged the defendants with negligence in the following particulars:

1 Permitting criminals, sex deviates, and vagrants to wander indiscriminately about the hotel;

2 Failure to maintain a competent staff of employees;

3 Failure to maintain adequate security personnel;

4 Failure to summon the police immediately; and

5 Failure to have the hotel security officer investigate the incident as soon as it was reported to a hotel employee.

The evidence was ample to support the jury's verdict. For its twelve hundred rooms, and with a large ball in progress, the hotel had on duty at the time of the robbery and assault only one security officer, one room clerk, and one bellboy. The jury could, with reason, determine that the defendants had failed to perform their general duty to protect their guests. The evidence of the defendant's negligence after the incident was reported is much stronger.

The occupant of the adjoining room was David DuCharme, an insurance adjustor, who happened to be working on some of his papers when his attention was distracted by the happenings. He heard in a male voice the demand for a knife, for a razor blade, and a woman's voice in response, then "the man who had directed the demand for the knife told the woman to cut down the venetian blind cord."

Mr. DuCharme continued to describe in detail just what he had been able to hear of what was happening in the next room. He became convinced that a robbery and assault were taking place. Taking the telephone, he got under the bed covers to prevent his own report from being heard, and got the telephone operator to whom he stated in substance: "I said, 'This is Dave DuCharme in room 1048. There is a holdup or there is a robbery and attempted rape'—I believe were very near the words I used—'going on in the room next to mine.' . . . I said, 'This is an emergency. Call the police immediately. This is an emergency.' And I repeated myself, 'There is a robbery and attempted rape going on in the room next to me. It is an emergency. Call the police immediately.' " Instead of taking action herself, the operator responded that, "I will connect you with the room clerk." When the room clerk answered, DuCharme repeated substantially the same report: "I said, 'I have just told the operator, and I am telling you.' I said, 'This is an emergency. I want you to call the police immediately.' And I identified myself again. I said, 'This is Dave DuCharme in room 1048. There is a robbery and attempted rape going on in the room next to mine.' And I repeated myself two or three times again and stated, 'This is an emergency. Call the police immediately.' " The room clerk's response was "Well, you know, it takes the police fifteen or twenty minutes to get here," and DuCharme replied, "I didn't ask you any questions about time. I told you this was an emergency and to call the police immediately." DuCharme estimated it took approximately five minutes in which even to report the robbery and assault.

That was only the beginning of the delay. The room clerk admitted that he did not immediately call the police. There were policemen on duty in the ballroom, but they were never summoned. Instead, the room clerk started looking for the security officer or house detective. The jury could have found from the evidence that the police were not actually called until more than forty minutes after Mr. DuCharme notified the telephone operator and the room clerk of the "emergency" and "robbery and attempted rape." When the police finally were called at 1:11 A.M., according to the time precisely stamped by time clock, patrolmen arrived at the hotel within four minutes, but long after the assailant's escape. Indeed, Mr. DuCharme confronted the room clerk with a demand for the reason the police were not notified earlier and met only the desultory response, "We were real busy at the time and we can't be calling the police for everybody that calls down here." There was ample evidence to support the jury's verdict.

In the light of the evidence as to the suffering, mental anguish, shock, and injury to the nervous systems of Mr. and Mrs. Nordmann, we cannot hold the district court in error for failing to grant a motion for new trial or to require a remittitur of damages. Indeed, we agree with the appellees' counsel that the damages were modest.

Ruling of the Court: The judgment is affirmed.

Undoubtedly, the primary area of concern to hoteliers, restaurateurs, and travelers alike today is that of security. An examination of the various cases and media accounts dealing with attacks, robberies, and rapes of guests in their rooms or on hotel premises accentuates the reason for this concern. Fires, too, are a security problem. The loss of property and personal injury suffered as the result of criminal activity, coupled with the loss of life, property, and human suffering resulting from fires, has cost the hotel industry millions of dollars in damage payments and has caused guests additional millions for uninsured and unreimbursed losses. The concern of prospective guests about security is a threat to the hospitality industry in general, and especially to resort facilities. Business travelers must travel in order to do business, but vacationers need not travel to experience fear and concern over their personal safety and the loss or damage of their possessions. The challenge is clear: Guests will flock to those hoteliers who can convince them that they shall be secure and sheltered from harm as a guest.

In the majority of states, innkeepers have a duty to use ordinary care to provide for the safety of their guests. In a significant minority of states, the innkeeper's duty is raised to that of a high degree of care. Both types of care, however, may not be too different from each other. Ordinary care is not a static, clearly defined concept. One definition will not fit all properties in all locations at all times. The security that would constitute ordinary care in a relatively quiet and tranquil location with a low crime rate might be considered to be grossly negligent if employed in a high-crime-rate area with a history of attacks, rapes, and muggings and a history of entries into guests' rooms. Security thus becomes a relative concept that must be determined for each individual property.

The case of *Peters v. Holiday Inns, Inc.*, provides a good illustration. In reading the case, students should pay particular attention to the court's reasoning process in arriving at what one should consider in trying to determine what would be necessary to constitute ordinary care in this circumstance.

Case	**Peters v. Holiday Inns, Inc.**
Example	*278 N.W.2d 208 (Wis., 1979)*
	(COFFEY, Justice)

Appeal is taken from a summary judgment entered in favor of the defendant-respondent Holiday Inns, Inc., a Tennessee corporation. The defendant wholly owns the stock of M.H.I., Inc., a Wisconsin corporation that operates a motel known as the Holiday Inn West located at 201 North Mayfair Rd., Wauwatosa, Wisconsin. In the early morning hours of December 31, 1975, the plaintiff-appellant Francis J. Peters, a motel guest, was assaulted and robbed in his room. Peters commenced this action, alleging the motel was negligent in permitting two intruders access to his room that resulted in his being beaten and robbed. The plaintiff and defendant concede the facts leading up to and culminating in the assault on Peters, although the plaintiff presented additional facts to the court at a summary judgment hearing.

Shortly before 3:00 A.M. on December 31, 1975, a car containing four males parked in front of the motel's entrance. The four men sat in the car for a short time before one of the car's occupants entered the motel lobby. The lobby is in the motel's main building, while the plaintiff's room, no. 185, is located in a separate but adjacent structure. The assailant, a former employee of the motel, was known as Elvis to the employees on duty. Upon entering the motel, he asked whether "Uncle George" was working that night and after being told he was not scheduled to work, "Elvis" left the lobby. Rather than exiting the building, the assailant entered the motel's kitchen area, where he stole one of the bellboy shirts.

The activities of the four men were observed by a Wauwatosa policeman who was routinely patrolling the defendant's premises in an unmarked squad car. The officer became suspicious after seeing the man who departed earlier from the car return and then observed the auto proceed to the rear of the parking lot near the adjacent motel rooms. The patrolman then entered the motel and questioned the two employees on duty concerning their conversation with "Elvis." The employees informed him that a short time ago, the patrons of room 143 had phoned the desk to report that a man knocked on their door claiming their room phone was out of order and that he had a message for them from the desk. The patrolman, upon receipt of this information, alertly suspecting something unusual, called headquarters and requested the aid of additional squads that arrived at the scene shortly thereafter.

The imposter "messenger," after being denied entrance to room 143, apparently proceeded to Peters's room, no. 185. The man knocked on the door and repeated the same *modus operandi*, informing Peters his phone wasn't working and that he had a message for him from the desk. The plaintiff-appellant explains that he looked through the door's one-way viewer and saw a man in the hallway wearing a bellboy's white shirt, the type worn by Holiday Inn personnel. Peters opened the door, believing the message was the 6:30 A.M. "wake-up call" he had requested. Two men pushed their way into the room and held the plaintiff at gunpoint while one of the assailants searched Peters's pants and room. They found approximately $700 in cash and a set of keys to the plaintiff's bowling alley. The intruders forced Peters to accompany them, apparently intending further criminal activity. The plaintiff was pushed into his own car and, at this time, the police converged upon the vehicle and the four men were apprehended at the scene.

At the time of the assault, the outside entrance to the separate structure housing rooms 143 and 185 was neither locked, monitored by closed circuit television, nor manned by motel staff or security personnel. Further, it is not necessary to pass through the lobby before entering the building. The only security provided by the motel was a dead bolt lock on each room, as well as a chain lock and a one-way viewer. It is pointed out that the hallway outside rooms 143 and 185 was well lighted at the time of the assault. It was established by affidavit that the inn did not employ security guards as, in the past five years, there had been few incidents requiring calls to the police for help and the police routinely patrol the motel entrance and parking lot.

On December 13, 1976, following a hearing on the defendant's motion for summary judgment, the trial court granted the motion based upon the affidavits submitted by the parties and additional evidentiary facts presented to the court at the hearing. The trial court expressed its reasoning for the decision in the following language:

"Now, plaintiff argues that he has a right to present this evidence to the trier of the fact. That is true only if the evidence, if presented to the trier of the fact, drawing all reasonable inferences in favor of it, would sustain a verdict in favor of the plaintiff. I cannot find that it would. I find to the contrary, that it would not, and that under the circumstances present at the time and place, no more diligent or effective circumstances could have existed for the preservation, care, and protection of the plaintiff than in fact existed on the occasion in question. Had the police department not been fortuitously on the premises, I could view the plaintiff's complaints with a different point of view. I think unquestionably, absent the presence of the police officers on the occasion in question and the report of the phone call by the desk clerk to the police department, there would be presented to the jury a question of reasonable diligence."

The presence of the police is described as "fortuitous" as they were on the scene during a routine patrol of the premises. Further, their investigation was not initiated by a report from the motel personnel, but rather because of the suspicious circumstances personally observed by the Wauwatosa patrolman in the parking lot area.

Throughout this opinion we will refer to the residents of the Holiday Inn as guests of a motel or hotel interchangeably.

Issues:

1   What degree of care is required of a hotel or innkeeper in providing security measures to protect the personal safety of its guests?

2   Did the trial court err in granting summary judgment for the defendant based upon the conceded and additional facts presented, as well as the parties' affidavits and briefs presented?

In this case, the court is called upon to establish the standard of care to be imposed upon an innkeeper to provide adequate security measures for the safety of his guests. Prior to this decision, the court considered a restaurateur's duty to protect his customers from bodily injury as a result of a third party's assaultive conduct. In Weihert v. Piccione, 273 Wis. 448, 78 N.W.2d 757 (1956), a restaurant patron was injured when an altercation broke out between other customers. *Weihert* held that a restaurant owner owes his customers the following duty of care in protecting them against bodily injury:

". . . the proprietor of a place of business who holds it out to the public for entry for his business purposes (including a restaurant) is subject to liability to members of the public while upon the premises for such a purpose for bodily harm caused to them by the accidental, negligent, or intentionally harmful acts of third persons, if the proprietor by the exercise of reasonable care could have discovered that such acts were being done or were about to be done, and could have protected the members of the public by controlling the conduct of the third persons, or by giving a warning adequate to enable them to avoid harm" (*Weihert* at 456, 78 N.W.2d at 761).

In our mobile society, travelers carry sums of money because of necessity and the problems caused by the lack of adequate identification for cashing checks in areas away from home. Thus, innkeepers should foresee that necessarily large amounts of monies and credit cards are carried by their guests and, consequently, increased security is required in these days of rapidly increasing assaultive crimes. Certainly hotel patrons can expect that reasonable security will be provided, combined with the friendliness, hospitality, and graciousness so widely advertised by modern hotels.

In Osborne v. Montgomery, 203 Wis. 223, 242–43, 234 N.W. 372 (1971), it was noted that once a legal duty has been imposed, the standard of care to be exercised is defined in the following language:

". . . the degree of care that the great mass of mankind ordinarily exercises under the same or similar circumstances. A person fails to exercise ordinary care when, without intending to do any wrong, he does an act or omits a precaution under circumstances in which a person of ordinary intelligence and prudence ought reasonably to foresee that such act or omission will subject him or his property, or the person or property of another to an unreasonable risk of injury or damage."

Thus, the conduct of hotel innkeepers in providing security must conform to the standard of ordinary care. In the context of the hotel-guest relationship, it is foreseeable that an innkeeper's failure to maintain adequate security measures not only permits but may even encourage intruders to rob or assault hotel patrons. Therefore, we hold that a hotel has a duty to exercise ordinary care to provide adequate protection for its guests and their property from assaultive and other types of criminal activity.

In A.E. Investment v. Link Builders, Inc., 62 Wis.2d 479, 214 N.W.2d 764 (1974), the court stated that a duty of care arises under the following circumstances:

"A defendant's duty is established when it can be said that it was foreseeable that his act or omission to act may cause harm to someone. A party is negligent when he commits an act when some harm to someone is foreseeable. Once negligence is established, the defendant is liable for unforeseeable consequences as well as foreseeable ones. In addition, he is liable to unforeseeable plaintiffs" (*A.E. Investment* at 484, 214 N.W.2d at 766).

Thus, in meeting its standard of ordinary care, a hotel must provide security commensurate with the facts and circumstances that are or should be apparent to the ordinarily prudent person. In other words, an innkeeper's standard of care in providing security will vary according to the particular circumstances and location of the hotel.

Accordingly, as the degree of care that an innkeeper must exercise will vary in relation to the attendant circumstances, relevant factors in deciding whether a hotel has exercised ordinary care in providing adequate security are: industry standards, the community's crime rate, the extent of assaultive or criminal activity in the area or in similar business enterprises, the presence of suspicious persons, and the peculiar security problems posed by the hotel's design. A hotel's liability depends upon the danger to be apprehended and the presence or absence of security measures designed to meet the danger. The particular circumstances may require one or more of the following safety measures: a security force, closed-circuit television surveillance, dead bolts and chain locks on the individual rooms, as well as security doors on hotel entranceways removed from the lobby area.

Consequently, we apply the ordinary care standard to the facts of this case in determining whether the defendant motel was entitled to summary judgment. The plaintiff's primary contentions are that the motel was negligent in: (1) allowing suspicious persons to roam about the premises unsupervised during the early morning hours; (2) permitting the suspicious person to gain access to the Holiday Inn uniforms, thus enabling the man to pose as a hotel employee; and (3), as it is not necessary to pass by the motel lobby, the motel failed to provide security personnel, television monitoring equipment, or other security devices, including locks on the outside doors leading to the hallways in the separated motel building where room nos. 143 and 185 were located so as to prevent ingress to all but motel patrons. The trial court described these contentions as "potentially valid," but nonetheless concluded the evidentiary facts did not raise competing inferences that would sustain a verdict in favor of the plaintiff. The trial court's rationale is stated in the following language:

"The fortuitous presence of the police department, however, establishes the fact that the plaintiff in fact was protected by the most effective means that could have prevailed; that if in fact the defendants were less than diligent with regard to the security installation, such as the stolen indicia, the security force, and the building locks, in fact then, that was not causal of the plaintiff's loss because it was supplanted by the effectiveness of the fortuitous presence of the police department, and the motion for summary judgment in favor of the defendant is granted."

We hold, based upon the applicability of the established duty of ordinary care imposed on a hotel to provide security and the facts and circumstances presented by the parties, that reasonable persons could draw competing inferences as to whether the defendant motel provided adequate security. The present case raises a jury question as to whether or not the presence of the assailant in the motel lobby, not for purposes of renting a room, but looking for a certain motel employee at 3:00 A.M., was a suspicious circumstance requiring the motel staff to monitor the intruder's whereabouts.

We do not agree with the trial judge that the "fortuitous presence" of the Wauwatosa police, as a matter of law, supplants the causal relation between the absence of other security measures and the plaintiff's assault.

A hotel's duty to provide reasonable security requires that preventative safety measures must be taken under certain circumstances. The police were present before and during the attack, yet this did not prevent the occurrence. This fact necessarily raises a triable issue regarding whether the fortuitous presence of the police in plain clothes and unmarked cars was the most effective security alternative commensurate with the size of the area to be protected. A jury may consider it more persuasive that security personnel in uniform patrolling the motel premises would have discouraged the assailants.

The defendant contends that its affidavits establish *prima facie* proof of the motel's compliance with Section 160.31, Stats. (1973), renumbered Section 50.80, Stats., by ch. 413, Laws of 1975. Section 160.31, Stats., precludes a hotelkeeper's liability for a guest's monetary loss if the hotel provides the following:

". . . (a) have doors on sleeping rooms equipped with locks or bolts; (b) offer, by notice printed in large plain English type and kept conspicuously posted in each such room, to receive valuable articles for safekeeping, and explain in such notice that the hotel is not liable for loss unless articles are tendered for safekeeping; (c) keep a safe or vault suitable for keeping such articles and receive them for safekeeping when tendered by a guest. . . ."

We note that the trial court did not render any factual findings relative to the applicability of this statute to the plaintiff's $700 property loss. Therefore, although the statute may be controlling in the present case, the issue has not been tried and should be considered at the trial on remand of this action, together with the issue of the motel's liability for Peters's personal injuries.

The proof at trial may very well establish that the lower court's decision was correct. The issues in this case were sufficiently complex to raise reasonable doubts of uncertainty and a jury should have been given an opportunity to return a verdict. Hotel liability cases requiring a plaintiff to prove the innkeeper's failure to exercise ordinary care commensurate with the circumstances are difficult cases that will present our trial courts with many matters of complex factual proof that usually cannot be decided on the basis of affidavits in support of summary judgment.

Ruling of the Court: Judgment reversed and cause remanded for proceedings consistent with this opinion.

Juries all over the country are telling hoteliers that they will tolerate neither poor security procedures nor failure to improve and replace inadequate security devices with newer and more protective devices. The changes in crime rate, plus shortcuts utilized in the construction, maintenance, and policing of hotel properties in an effort to economize, are taken into consideration by the juries. In fact they are quite vocal about announcing their displeasure with the "profit-motive" school over the "safety-of-guests-first" school. The volume of their protest is measured in dollars. In the case of *Margreiter* v. *New Hotel Monteleone, Inc.*, the jury was so upset that it awarded the plaintiff $750,000, a sum the judge thought was almost twice the amount that should be awarded.

Case Example	**Margreiter v. New Hotel Monteleone, Inc.** *640 F.2d 508 (La., 1981)* *(REAVLEY, Circuit Judge)*

Douglas Margreiter was severely injured in New Orleans on the night of April 6, 1976. He sued the Monteleone Hotel, saying that he was taken from his room there by two men who had a key to that room, the use of an elevator, and unimpeded access and exit into an alley permitted by the hotel's lack of care to protect its guests. The hotel contended that Margreiter was on an intoxicated venture and met his fate outside the hotel. The jury found in favor of Margreiter. The judgment was reduced from $750,000 to $400,000 by remittitur. We affirm.

Margreiter was chief of the pharmacy section of the Colorado Department of Social Services and was in New Orleans to attend the annual meeting of the American Pharmaceutical Association. On Tuesday evening, April 6, he had dinner at the Royal Sonesta Hotel with two associates from Colorado who were also attending the association meeting, and who had adjacent rooms at the Monteleone Hotel. Margreiter returned to his room between 10:30 and 11:00 P.M. His friend Peebles returned to his adjoining room at the same time. His friend Bogan was to come by Margreiter's room later to discuss what meetings of the association each would attend on the following day.

Skipping what the parties dispute, we know that an unconscious Margreiter was found about three hours later in a parking lot over three blocks from the Monteleone. The police who were summoned recall only that they regarded him as highly intoxicated, but they did get him to Charity Hospital. The next morning his friends learned of his predicament and had him removed to Hotel Dieu. There is no dispute but that Margreiter had been severely beaten, or that he endured great suffering and retains some effects of his injuries.

Margreiter testified that when he entered his room, he turned on the television and began to look at the program of association meetings for the following day. Shortly thereafter, two black men unlocked his door and entered. One went to the television to turn up the volume; the other struck Margreiter on the head before he could complete a telephone call for aid. Except for a few impressions of being taken down the hall into an elevator and finally out of the building into a dark alley, his memory is limited mostly to a recollection of pain. His memory is then blank until after a craniotomy had been performed and he awoke in a Denver hospital two weeks later.

The basis for the hotel's liability is the care it owed to a guest to protect him against injury by third persons. (See Nordmann v. National Hotel Company, 425 F.2d 1103 [5th Cir. 1970].) The finding of the jury that the hotel was negligent in failing to exercise reasonable care to protect the plaintiff against injury by third persons, and that this was a proximate cause of his injury is supported by the evidence that two men with control of an elevator and a key to the room could abduct Margreiter with complete impunity.

The freight elevators, which operate manually and exit in the back of the hotel rather than into the lobby, are supposed to be shut and locked at 11:00 P.M. The hotel has fifteen floors with 597 rooms and on this occasion was entirely full with from 1000 to 1200 guests. The one security officer had gone home ill, and the only security was afforded by an assistant manager at the lobby desk and an employee who was supposed to have been at the back door that exited upon the alley. The hotel had been given notice that there had been a fifteen-room burglary that afternoon at another hotel two blocks away. The hotel had no cameras, heat-sensing devices, or adequate alarms; and the evidence tended to prove that the exits were unguarded and unsupervised.

The hotel does not defend its security devices or the care it exercised to protect Margreiter. It contends that the entire case is a sham and that the whole story of the plaintiff is not worthy of belief. It emphasizes the opinion of the policemen that Margreiter was highly intoxicated. It picks at the usual inconsistencies in testimony and the lack of lucid memory of Margreiter. It emphasizes his ability to fly back to Denver on a commercial flight and his failure to return to New Orleans to describe his assailants particularly and see to their prosecution. It concludes that Margreiter must have gone out of the hotel on his own, become intoxicated, and fallen into the wrong company.

The hotel's contentions are addressed to the wrong arbiter. The jury has already rejected them, and the record easily supports the decision of the jury. There is no evidence that a midnight frolic was the practice or disposition of this plaintiff. His two associates who testified corroborated his activities and plans of the evening. Bogan said that he was to come by the room later. Peebles testified that the television in Margreiter's room was unusually loud. The plaintiff himself testified to the attack in his room and his abduction. The jury was entitled to believe him. We are unable to say that reasonable jurors could not arrive at that verdict, and we must therefore uphold it and the action of the trial court in refusing motions for directed verdict and for judgment notwithstanding the verdict.

The hotel also argues that Margreiter's injuries were not so great and that he has essentially recovered, concluding: "As soon as he gets his money, Mr. Margreiter will have a 'miracle at Lourdes' remission of his symptoms that 'prevent' him from working." The hotel concludes that there is no sound basis in the evidence for the damage award of $400,000. Again, we disagree. The evidence clearly establishes the nightmarish experience of Margreiter in New Orleans and supports a finding that the consequences of those injuries do and will persist. He was severely beaten and left unconscious on the streets of the French Quarter. Three hours later he was taken to Charity Hospital and treated like a drunk. When his friends finally learned of his whereabouts, because the hospital had found his hotel key and inquired of the Monteleone office, he was found tied hand and foot on a hospital cart, showing massive contusions and lacerations about his face, bleeding at the mouth, and passing blood rectally.

When he returned to Denver, surgery was necessary to remove a clot on his brain. He suffered permanent damage to his brain. The consequences were continuing headaches, traumatic neurosis, and epilepsy that is controlled only by a drug that causes side effects. A bone in his ankle was broken and efforts to repair it finally required a bone graft from his hip. His teeth were broken, causing a malocclusion. An eardrum was perforated and he now has a hearing loss and ringing in his ear. His hair suddenly turned white and his friend Bogan, who is seventy-eight years old, declares that he hopes he never looks so old as Margreiter does at fifty-five. There was evidence that his injuries caused a substantial loss of earnings and earning capacity. In addition to consultation with his doctors, his drug bills each month exceed $30.

We do not regard the amount of the judgment as excessive. Margreiter makes no complaint of the trial judge's action in requiring remittitur of $350,000 from the jury's award of $750,000.

The other complaints of the appellant that were directed at matters of evidence and trial procedure were all proper rulings of the trial court and clearly within his discretion.

Ruling of the Court: The judgment is affirmed.

It appears that the Margreiter jury was so angry that it wanted to strike out at the defendant. At least two factors readily present themselves as possible explanations. The first is that the security was nonexistent for a property this size, especially in view of the fact that a large number of burglaries had recently taken place in a neighboring hotel. This disregard for the safety of the guests would be significant in the damage-assessment process. The second would be the defensive posture taken by the hotel. When it was apparent that it could not defend on the issue of adequate security, the hotel turned its aggressiveness on the plaintiff as an individual and tried to mask its shortcomings by alleging that the plaintiff was a fraud.

Security Personnel and Weapons

Should security personnel in a hotel have weapons? In a recent case involving a Holiday Inn—where weapons were allowed until two years before the plaintiff's husband, a security officer, was killed while trying to capture a man who allegedly was trying to break into a guest's room— we were denied an answer to the question because the case was settled as the jury was deliberating. The day after the shooting, the security guards were armed, and Holiday Inn hired an outside security force.

There is no easy answer to the question. A gun is a dangerous instrument in the hands of someone not well trained in its use. Such a person can be a danger to guests and to the hotel. The answer might be not to hire anyone for security who cannot be trusted to handle a gun properly. A hotel that would have a security guard go about rounds unarmed and with no means of protection, especially in a high-crime area, runs the risk not only of putting an employee in an atmosphere of danger, but of being held civilly liable for anything that happens to the guard.

A Problem for the Future?

The case of Tetalman v. Holiday Inn, 500 F.Supp. 217 (Ga., 1980), presented some interesting questions for the court to decide, but issues that were not raised might become even more important in the future. Marc Tetalman had gone to a convention in Atlanta, Georgia, and while there was assaulted and murdered. His widow brought an action against the city of Atlanta as the executor of Marc's estate and in her own behalf, alleging that the city had advertised itself as being safe when in fact it was not. She also argued that the failure of the city to keep its confines safe for travelers violated Marc's constitutionally protected right to travel, a violation, she contends, that amounted to deprivation of his civil rights. Therefore, the city was liable to the plaintiffs.

The court said that such was not the case. The representations by the city that it was safe for conventioneers acted to encourage travel rather than to curtail or restrict it. The court went further and said that the death could not be attributed to the city either because the assailant was unknown and there was no apparent connection between the assailant and the city so as to hold the city responsible. Although the plaintiff did not prevail in the *Tetalman* case, the theory that she sought to invoke was interesting and points out the fact that travelers want protection and will sue if they do not get it.

Another theory could have been explored but was not. That is a suit based upon misrepresentations by the city that Atlanta was a safe place for conventions in an effort to induce potential conventioneers to have their meetings in Atlanta. Even if it should be found that the representations were made by people other than city officials, the city had apparently adopted this as its official position because it did not deny the representations and permitted people to rely on them. The representations were made for the express purpose of inducing people to come to Atlanta to spend money there. This would be profitable to the merchants in the city and to the city itself. Therefore, the city was engaged in a profit-making venture, and as such, it lost the sovereignty's protection as liability for its torts.

Making a representation that something is a true fact when you know, or should have known, that it was not is a misrepresentation. If this misrepresentation is made for the purpose of inducing someone to act, and they do act in reliance on the truth of the representation, this could be an exposure to liability. Therefore, not only would the city face exposure, but suppose that you as a hotelier, in an effort to promote your hotel's convention or other business, advertise that your hotel is located in a city that is safe, knowing well that security and safety are a prime consideration of travelers in general. You and your hotel could be held liable if in fact this is not true, and a guest who relied upon the representation is injured. A positive representation on such a vital question as security would not, in our opinion, amount to "seller's talk," which would not make for actionable misrepresentations, but rather would go right to the heart of the relationship. There are no cases yet, but the position we have set forth is the result of the logical extension of accepted concepts of municipal and tort law.

Management Principles

In most instances, the owners of land have a responsibility to persons coming onto the land, but this responsibility is not the same for all persons. As a general rule, hoteliers should have a standard operating procedure for protecting guests, employees, and other visitors, as the status of a person entering a hotel may change. Some persons come in as invitees and because of their actions become licensees, as in the *Ortner* case. The greatest care required of the hotelier and restaurateur is to the invitee. This duty can range from due care to a high degree of care (as with elevators). They should set up a system whereby thorough inspections of all premises are conducted at all times of the day or night to be certain conditions are adequate.

To fulfill such duties, the hotelkeeper should institute maintenance and inspection procedures for the following:

1 Clean room.

The manager should develop an inspection routine and inspection form. Personnel should be trained to check periodically floors, beds, and furniture. Chairs especially should be checked periodically to tighten bolts; the date of inspection should be noted.

2 Showers and water faucets.

According to court cases, a hot water temperature between 135°F and 145°F is adequate. Mixing valves and faucet handles should be checked periodically. The maids should run the cold and hot water each day and check faucet handles. The supervisor should also check the faucet handles (see *Brown Hotel* v. *Marx*). Instructions to guests on how to use the shower and shower curtains might also be useful.

3 Air conditioners.

Check to see if they are adequately fastened, and check air filters on a regular schedule.

4 Windows, shades, curtains, and screens.

These items should be checked at least monthly (see *Messina* v. *Sheraton*).

5 Lights and lighting fixtures.

There should be a routine check of these items. A faulty switch may have dire results for a person with a weak heart.

6 Animals and insects.

Rodents and especially cockroaches are difficult to control in old buildings. A reliable exterminator and a good sanitation program will help to control this problem (see the *DeLuce* case).

7 Lobby and common areas.

Check for burned-out lights in corridors cluttered with breakfast dishes and other articles such as beds or furniture. When construction is going on in the lobby or other areas, the area should be roped off.

8 Elevators.

An inspection schedule should be followed closely, and emergency procedures should be developed and posted in the elevator to deal with power or mechanical failures and to extricate guests from the elevator. A close watch should be kept for nonleveling elevators. A bull horn, flashlights, and a first aid kit should be available. The notice of inspection must be posted in or close to the elevator. Only hotel personnel should operate freight elevators. The hotelier is responsible for the inspection.

9 Restaurants, bars, and dining facilities.
The same type of care is required as above. For how close tables and chairs may be placed for a banquet, see the *LaPlante* case—here a thirty-six-inch space was a jury question. Where flaming dishes are served in a restaurant (see the case of *Young v. Caribbean Associates*), there should be adequate notice that accidents could occur. A procedure should be developed to deal with foreign substances on the floor. One San Francisco establishment put a collapsible cover over a spill until it could be cleaned up. The cost was insignificant and the results were excellent. Slip-and-fall cases can be bothersome. Again, employee training is important, especially in a very busy place. Most waiters do not want to stop profitable work to do something that is the management's responsibility.

10 Outside lighting and sidewalks.
Because hotels cannot dictate when their guests must return to their rooms and what condition they will be in, adequate lighting and safe walks are necessary. Hotel and motel owners who have parking areas adjacent to their accommodations must be aware of the lighting problem. They should examine at night the lighting situation and be certain there is adequate lighting at all times of the night. They should not wait until someone gets hurt before acting. They should set up a system of inspections to watch for burned-out or broken light bulbs and other potential hazards.

11 Swimming pools.
Swimming pool instructions should be followed to the letter. All statutory enactments on rules and regulations governing safety, life guards, and sanitation must be adhered to. Revival equipment for drowning victims may be purchased. The posting of signs in swimming pool areas may be helpful. Horseplay should be halted before accidents occur. In swimming pool areas, beverages should be served only in plastic containers. No one should be able to use the pool when it is not open; adequate controls should be instituted.

12 Children.
Children should be of particular concern to hotels and restaurants. High chairs and cribs should be provided, and any possible problems should be foreseen. Consultation by experts in this area might be highly beneficial.

13 Fire.
There are over 13,500 fires a year in hotels and motels. The manager should provide adequate equipment and establish emergency procedures for employees to follow in case of fire. Prevention is an essential factor.

The hotel-motel industry is vulnerable in many areas as to its security. Hoteliers should carefully look at a preemployment screening program. Such a program is especially critical for guards and night personnel. In addition, they should pay close attention to room control. Issues to be considered are as follows:

1 A lock and key system.
Because professionals can make or acquire a key at their leisure,this is perhaps the weakest link in the industry.

2 Peepholes.
A hole in the room door allows guests to make visual identification.

3 Adequate surveillance of hallways, elevators, lobbies and other common areas.
Although the use of video equipment is rare, it should be a requirement.

4 Proper identification of persons requesting keys or information about guests or their phone numbers.

5 Adequate fencing, lighting, and surveillance of parking lots, walkways, and area around motels.
In Walkoviak v. Hilton Hotels Corporation, 580 S.W.2d 623 (Tex., 1979), a guest parked his car at the hotel parking area where he was accosted, beaten, stabbed, and robbed. The hotel could not have a summary judgment and was remanded to the trial court with comments about parking and security.

6 Sufficient guards and night personnel for security.
In Yamada v. Hilton Hotel Corporation, 376 N.E.2d 227 (Ill., 1977), where one guest was killed and another badly injured, the question again was whether security was adequate. At the time of the attack, there were only five guards to care for twenty-four floors and 2,144 guest rooms, an arcade, plus all the common areas. The question must be asked whether the happening could have been prevented with more security personnel?

7 Adequate knowledge of the night report.
The night report should be checked carefully to see if the police should be notified of any strange happenings in or around the hotel. An accurate night report is especially important because if force must be used at a later date, justification for such action would not be so difficult to prove.

QUESTIONS FOR DISCUSSION

1 Define licensee, invitee, and trespasser as they pertain to the service industry.

2 Must a hotel provide a crib for a four-year-old child? Or for a five- or six-year-old child?

3 Explain the relevance of the res ipsa loquitur doctrine for a hotel guest. What conditions make it operative?

4 If a rat bites a guest in a hotel, what kinds of arguments may be used by the hotelkeeper to absolve himself from liability?

5 Many injuries occur in bathrooms. What are the general rules as to bathroom appliances, such as porcelain faucets, hot water, bath mats, and falling ceilings?

6 What duty is owed a hotel guest in the lobby, restaurant, elevators, and on the stairs?

7 What is the general rule pertaining to foreign substances on a restaurant floor?

8 Must a hotel employ a doorman? If a doorman is present when an accident occurs, can the defense be used that a doorman is not needed and hence the hotel is not liable for his actions?

9 Is a beach connected to a hotel considered part of the hotel? If a guest drowns, can the hotel be sued? Can the plaintiff win? Why or why not?

10 If a statute requires certain appurtenances to be present when a swimming pool is being used and they are not there, can the owners be held liable if a person drowns? If so, under what conditions?

11 Contents

11 The Hotelkeeper's Responsibility for Guests' Loss of Property

> *"No law can possibly meet the convenience of everyone: We must be satisfied if it be beneficial on the whole and to the majority."*

LIVY

T he common laws that protect a traveler's property are still in existence in most states; however, under certain conditions, travelers receive only a fraction of their property's value when it is lost. This chapter considers the relationship of the guest and the hotelkeeper and the myriad problems associated with the loss of a guest's valuables. Its intent is not to take sides with either the guest or the hotelkeepers, but rather to attempt to clarify the legal concept. Our principal aim is to acquaint hotel personnel with the problems associated with safeguarding guests' and their own property. The experiences of others in this area can be instructive.

Hotel Theft

The *New York Times* on March 2, 1980, reported that there are about 40 thefts a week from hotel rooms in Paris; and New York City reportedly had some 2,800 reported crimes committed in the one hundred hotels located in midtown Manhattan during 1976. Undoubtedly these figures are low because many acts of pilferage are never detected by guests. Perhaps a chambermaid just slips some of the money out of a guest's wallet in a room rather than take the wallet or all of the money. In many instances guests will not notice the loss. Also there are instances when guests notice an item like their camera missing, but cannot remember whether they took it out with them and lost it or whether it disappeared from the room. Nevertheless, the reported cases alone constitute a serious problem in the hotel industry. In fact, the problem is so serious that in 1975 the New York City police department organized a special hotel unit comprised of members of the police force who specialize in hotel cases. The members of the unit and the security forces at the various hotels work together and hold weekly meetings where they share information and alert each other about potential problems. This policy of having security work with the local police on a regular basis is extremely important in keeping a hotel security force well informed about new methods of breaks and when there might be a particular run of robberies and the methods used.

Hotel thefts and crime are an industry problem and should be so handled. Management policy should include a complete exchange of information among the security forces of all area hotels and concerted action with the common goal of reducing the incidents of hotel crimes.

It is difficult to place the responsibility for these crimes on any one group. According to the police, the problem is multifaceted. Yet police reports consistently cite the carelessness of hotel guests. Police reports also cite the reluctance of guests to return from another city or state to testify against the thief, thus adding to a difficult situation for law enforcers.

Hotel thefts are on the rise. New York City hotels have attempted to stem this increase by increasing their security forces, hiring trained professionals for staff positions, warning guests to lock their rooms and put their valuables in the hotel safe, installing closed-circuit television in the hallways, changing locks frequently and installing new locks without passkeys, instituting tighter security checks on employees, installing electronic lobby doors that can be opened only by the desk clerk when he recognizes a guest, and installing new electronic lock devices that are changed for each guest using the room.

Most hotel thefts are the work of professionals seeking money, jewels, and credit cards, according to the New York Times of March 1, 1971. Most professional hotel thieves can make their own master keys. They generally travel first class, often registering as guests in the hotel they plan to rob. The many tricks of the thief include "casing" a hotel; acquiring confidential information from maids, bartenders, or other hotel personnel; and knowing the best time to strike. Professional thieves generally do not carry a weapon because they know that if they are caught with one, the charge is much stiffer; if they are surprised in the act, they often convincingly pretend drunkenness.

Although newspaper accounts of hotel thefts are often exaggerated, the career of a hotel thief can be profitable. In 1966 the Harbour Isle Spa Hotel in Miami Beach reported a theft of $2 million in jewels, along with other belongings. In Fort Worth, pearls worth $1 million were stolen from a guest's room. The 1974 Pierre Hotel robbery in New York, one of the largest ever, had a reported loss of over $4.5 million. In 1977 the Sherry Netherland was robbed of several hundred thousand dollars in a theft quite similar to the Pierre Hotel robbery. Three years previously, $900 thousand had been stolen from the same hotel. Nearly $90 thousand was stolen from the Drake Hotel in Illinois in 1975 and from the Alamo Motel in Iowa in 1978. At the Mayfair Regent in New York in 1979, gunmen looted $100 thousand from nine guests. Also in 1979 a theft of $1.3 million occurred at the Desert Palace Inn in Nevada, and in 1981 thefts severed a chain and stole $50 thousand worth of jewels from a Sonesta Hotel in Louisiana.

According to an article by Carey Winfrey appearing in the *New York Times* on September 7, 1977, one hundred midtown hotels reported 2,800 crimes (up from 2,000 five years ago). The article stated that the better the police get, the better the criminal gets. But not surprisingly, the article claims that 70 percent of hotel employees account for these crimes. One of the more publicized thefts includes the theft of $75 thousand worth of Cheryl Tiegs's jewels taken from a locked metal box at the Carlyle Hotel.

Keys

Anyone given a key to a hotel room can easily have it duplicated. It is equally easy for a guest to leave a hotel and not return the key, permitting it to fall into the wrong hands. In Milner Hotels v. Lyon, 196 S.W.2d 364 (Ky., 1946), the court recognized that carrying away hotel keys is a widespread habit. The hotel in question, with 227 guest rooms, had an average of fifty keys a month carried away, only about one-third of which were eventually returned.

In this particular case, it was revealed that no hotel regards the failure of a guest to turn in the key as an indication that person intends to retain the room. As a matter of common practice, a hotel considers a room as vacant at a certain hour in the late afternoon. Otherwise, there would be a substantial number of rooms left vacant at all times. It was pointed out that a misunderstanding about the occupancy of a room can be costly and embarrassing.

In the *Milner Hotels* case, a couple named the Boscoes arrived at the hotel without substantial baggage and paid for one day's lodging in room 506. The next day they paid for another day and again occupied the room. Under the rules of the hotel, which were displayed in the room, a guest's right of occupancy ceased at 3 PM—the checking out hour. At this time, if the guest had not made known his desire to stay longer, the room was inspected and, if there was no indication of continued occupancy, it was considered to have been vacated. In this instance, the Boscoes had not turned in the key to the room, nor had they been heard from; and after an inspection, the room was considered vacant. Plaintiff Lyon's baggage was transferred to this room about two hours later, and the door was locked by a hotel employee. But the Boscoes did in fact return, appropriated Lyon's property, and had the bellboy take it to a taxi. Obviously, keys can fall into the wrong hands—unscrupulous hands in this case—and thereby jeopardize the guest's property, the hotelkeeper's reputation, and constitute a financial loss as well.

Insurance

Often, many people are not personally insured against the loss of their valuables. A traveler may have a policy covering only certain items, a trip policy covering a specific period of time with a limited amount of coverage, or a homeowner's policy with a specific clause covering property losses. In each instance, the insurance company may sue in either its own name or in the name of the insured traveler. Insurance policies generally carry an additional clause that states that the insuree (traveler) must cooperate with the insurance company if necessary. This can be a burdensome clause, as it may require the traveler to appear as a witness and give testimony if the case goes to trial. A well-known singer who lost an $8,000 fur coat refused to appear in court against the hotel when asked to by the insurance company. She claimed it was not worth the effort, and the insurance company consequently did not pay her for the loss.

Thus, the stage is set for a study of problems pertaining to theft and loss of property by hotel, motel, and restaurant guests. We will discuss the hotel owner's liability for such property and the statutory requirements about posting—giving guests notice of the extent of such liability. The guest's requirement to disclose the value of any property deposited with the hotelkeeper is also examined.

A section dealing with the beginning and end of a hotel's liability for guests' property includes a discussion of property in transit, storage liabilities, and property of sales representatives, as well as the hotel's obligations in forwarding mail and packages. The responsibility of hotels for guests' cars or other checked properties is examined in the context of *infra hospitium* ("within the hotel"), which includes a thorough discussion of bailments.

Finally, the last two sections examine the hotelkeeper's obligations with regard to fire-damaged or mislaid goods. Management principles at the end of the chapter provide a useful summary of key points.

Absolute Liability for Guests' Goods

The general rule of common law provides that a hotelkeeper is held liable for any loss by their guests unless the loss was caused by an act of God, the public enemy (in time of war), or by the fault of the guest. Such liability obviously should not be imposed on anyone in charge of the property of another without strong reason. This rule, originally established as a public policy, was dictated by necessity and contributed in no small measure to increasing safe travel and trade. It has been argued in some cases that the reason for this rule no longer exists. However, guests must rely on the hotelkeeper for protection. Therefore, the courts seem justified in applying the insurer's liability rule in case of the disappearance of a guest's property.

What do *absolute liability* and an *insurer* of the goods of a guest mean? Both terms mean that the hotel is liable for the goods of the guests if lost or stolen under all circumstances (with the exceptions noted earlier). Thus places of public accommodation find themselves in a serious and precarious position. Every hotelier should be familiar with the following important sections on statutory modifications to the absolute liability rule.

Prima Facie Liability Rule—Minority View

Illinois, Indiana, Maryland, Texas, Vermont, and Washington uphold the *prima facie* ("on the face of it") rule. This rule modifies the common law rule by adding the following provision: Hotelkeepers are liable only if the loss occurs through their negligence. Therefore, the rule in these states encompasses the general rule that hotelkeepers are the insurer of the goods of their guests unless the loss is caused by an act of God, the public enemy (in time of war), or the contributory negligence of the guest. Under the *prima facie* rule, hotelkeepers can also exculpate themselves from the loss by proof that the loss did not occur through any neglect on their part and that of their servants, for whom they are responsible. Justification for this rule was stated in Laird v. Eichold, 10 Ind. 212, 215 (1858):

> Innkeepers, on grounds of public policy, are held to a strict accountability for the goods of their guests. The interests of the public, we think, are sufficiently subserved by holding the innkeeper *prima facie* liable for the loss or injury of the goods of this guest; thus throwing the burden of proof upon him, to show that the injury or loss happened without any default whatever on his part, and that he exercised reasonable care and diligence.

This rule, then, has the provision that the hotelkeeper can prove that they or their employees were not liable for the loss of the guest's goods. For example, the goods could have been stolen by robbers with no negligence on the part of the hotel.

Exceptions to the Absolute Liability Rule

Practically every law has exceptions, and the absolute liability rule against the hotelkeeper for guests' goods is tempered by three: a loss attributed to an act of God, an act of the public enemy (in time of war), and the contributory negligence of the guest.

An Act of God

An act of God is a natural or physical event that results in some casualty, thereby exonerating the hotelkeeper from liability for the guest's property. Generally, events such as earthquakes, lightning, rain, snowstorms, tornadoes, and floods are considered acts of God.

An example of this exception is illustrated in Wolf Hotel v. Parker, 158 N.E. 294 (Ind., 1927), in which the guest's goods were stored in the defendant hotel's basement; the goods were subsequently damaged by a heavy rainfall that backed up water into the basement. The plaintiff claimed negligence on the part of the hotelkeeper for failing to provide traps and shutoff valves in the sewer and drain system that would have prevented water from backing up in the basement. Was this an act of God?

In its decision, the court instructed the jury that an act of God that would excuse the hotelkeeper from liability must not only be the proximate cause, but it must also be the sole cause. If the injury was caused by an act of God commingled with the negligence of the hotelkeeper, and if the guest himself was free of contributory negligence, then the hotelkeeper would be liable for the guest's goods.

The court also pointed out that if the hotelkeeper knew, or by reasonable diligence could have known, that the hotel basement could flood after a heavy rainfall and took no steps to prevent it, the exception could not be used as a defense. Whether the plaintiff was a guest of the hotel or a roomer made no difference to the outcome of the case; the negligence of the defendant hotelkeeper or rooming house operator was the crux of the case.

The Public Enemy

The second exception to the hotelkeeper's liability is if the goods are lost or destroyed by an act of the public enemy—that is, the adversary of a government at war.

In Johnston v. Mobile Hotel Company, 167 So. 595 (Ala., 1936), a guest was held at gunpoint by two men who took all his money and valuables. Both parties submitted that the decisive question in the case was whether an innkeeper is liable at common law for his guest's loss of money and valuables when the loss is occasioned by robbery within the inn, without negligence on the part of the innkeeper or his employees.

In this case, the court stated that because the loss was not caused by an act of God or by the guest's own doing (contributory negligence), and since "robber" was not covered by the term *public enemy*, the guest was entitled to recover—if the jury believed his testimony.

Contributory Negligence

If a guest is negligent in taking normal precautions to safeguard his own goods (in the absence of comparative negligence statutes), he is not normally allowed to recover damages. If, for instance, a guest leaves his suitcase in a hotel area that is not customarily used for such purposes, he cannot recover.

The case of Cohen v. Janlee, 92 N.Y.S.2d 852, 95 N.E.2d 410 (see also rev'd. mem.), illustrates another form of negligence on the part of a guest that allowed her no recovery. Her fur coat was stolen from her room while she slept; however, she had left her door open for a female friend who was returning later. Under the disclosed circumstances, the court held that the guest, in not taking the normal precaution of locking the door to her room before she went to bed, knowing full well that she had a valuable coat in her room, facilitated the theft and therefore was to be considered guilty of contributory negligence. The guest's negligence was at least a contributory cause (proximate cause) of the theft.

Statutory and Common Law Modification of the Absolute Liability Rule

Before the 1851 legislation that modified the absolute liability rule, the courts liberally interpreted reasonable rules governing the innkeeper to temper the advantage the guest had over the hotel. Of course, the problem was the interpretation of what constituted a reasonable rule. Since the innkeeper's risk was great, the courts felt that the innkeeper should be allowed to exercise more direct and efficient control over a guest's goods.

Chief Justice Day, in the case of Fuller v. Coats, 18 Ohio St., 343 (1868), stated the case for the innkeeper:

> To enable the innkeeper to discharge his duty, and to secure the property of the traveler from loss while in a house open to the public, it may, in many instances, become necessary for him to provide special means, and to make necessary regulations and requirements to be observed by the guests, to secure the safety of his property. When such means and requirements are reasonable and proper for that purpose, and they are brought to the knowledge of the guest with the information that if not observed by

him, the innkeeper will not be responsible, ordinary prudence, the interest of both parties, and public policy would require of the guest a compliance therewith; and if he should fail to do so, and his goods are lost solely for that reason, he would justly and properly be chargeable with negligence.

The limitations on the hotelkeeper were severe and perhaps the most severe had to do with sufficiency of notice. The notice required was equivalent to *actual* notice. For instance, posting a notice on the door of a guest's chamber was held to be effective only if it was found that the guest did see it or was negligent in overlooking it.

As hotels became larger and travel more frequent, legislation was enacted to codify the "reasonable rule" doctrine. The following concepts have been included in legislation passed in most states:

1   The innkeeper is not liable for losses sustained by guests, except for wearing apparel, personal baggage, or money necessary for traveling expenses and personal use. Jewelry, large sums of money, and other valuable property has to be turned over to the innkeeper for safekeeping. (The problem of what is considered valuable immediately presents itself here.)

2   Many states have passed laws changing the common law about loss of property by fire or overwhelming force from absolute liability to a liability based on ordinary and reasonable care for the guests' goods.

3   In enacting the statutes, most legislatures have substituted constructive notice for actual notice. Actual notice is defined as notice expressly and actually given and brought home to the guest directly. Constructive notice, on the other hand, is information or knowledge of a fact imputed to a person by law, because he could have discovered the fact by proper diligence, or because his situation was such as to put upon him the duty of inquiry. This is very important in understanding the law on posting (giving the guest notice of what the law is).

4   Recovery is usually based on some prescribed amount of money. (See appendix 1 for states' limiting liability statutes.)

5   Because a statute changes or modifies the common law, the courts interpret the statute in a very exacting way. If the statute is not *strictly* complied with, the common law rules prevail. These statutes generally deal with the posting of the statutes, as required by the statute; the requirement of a hotel safe; and the type of valuables that must be stored in the safe or put under the hotelkeeper's control.

There are also additional requirements the hotelkeeper must adhere to before he can use the statute as a defense.

Conspicuous Posting

Posting is the actual calling of the guests' attention to the fact that there is a law controlling their valuables while they are in the hotel. The hotel owner must follow the points of law precisely. If the statute designates five conspicuous places, it means just that. If hotelkeepers are uncertain, they should consult their hotel-motel association or their attorney. For instance, in the case of *Insurance Company of North America, Inc., v. Holiday Inns, Inc.*, the hotelkeeper could not prove that he had posted in all places as required by the statute. This case is important because it involves a great deal of money ($35,000); it is also a relatively recent (1972) case; and, additionally, it involves the largest hotel chain in the world.

Case Example

Insurance Co. of No. America, Inc., v. Holiday Inns, Inc.
337 N.Y.S.2d 68 (1972)
(MEMORANDUM DECISION)

. . . . This appeal involves the liability of an innkeeper for jewelry that was missing from a guest's room. On August 10, 1968, jewelry valued in excess of $35,000 was found to be missing from a guest's room at appellant's motel in Saratoga Springs. After investigation, respondent paid $35,000 pursuant to an insurance policy and became subrogated to any claims the guest had against appellant. Respondent then sued appellant alleging two causes of action, the first based upon an innkeeper's common law liability as insurer of a guest's property and the second grounded on negligence. Appellant's answer set up Section 200 of the General Business Law and the alleged negligence of the guest as defenses to the action.

Respondent moved to dismiss the affirmative defense, asserting that appellant had not fully complied with the posting requirements of Section 200. This statute provides that an innkeeper may limit his liability by providing a place for the safekeeping of designated valuables and by informing the guests thereof "by posting a notice stating the fact that such safe is provided . . . in a public and conspicuous place and manner in the office and public rooms, and in the public parlors of such hotel, motel, or inn." The statute further provides that the innkeeper shall be relieved of liability in the event a guest neglects to deposit his valuables in such safe.

In support of its motion, respondent introduced the transcript of the examination before trial of appellant's general manager. This testimony clearly indicated that appellant had not posted the required notice in all of the public rooms of the motel, although such notices were posted in the guest rooms. In opposition, appellant submitted only the affidavit of its attorney, which was not based on personal knowledge and asserted no evidentiary facts. Special Term properly found that this affidavit was of no probative value. . . .

On this appeal, appellant urges that the defense based on Section 200 should not have been dismissed because there were unresolved questions of fact. This contention is without merit. No facts have been alleged that would tend to establish the existence of the statutory defense. We have examined the remainder of appellant's contentions and find them to be without merit.

Ruling of the Court: Order affirmed, without costs.

What, then, constitutes conspicuous posting? In North River Insurance Company v. Tisch Management, Inc., 166 A.2d 169 (N.J., 1960), the document requiring posting by law was placed under the glass on a dresser top in the hotel room. The document was two and one half inches square and was displayed among many other items describing the hotel and its features. In considering whether this constituted conspicuous notice, the court said that a guest who glanced at the total display of printed material on the dresser could assume that its general import was advertising, and thus would not take time to read the notice that set forth the requirement that a person should deposit his goods. In conclusion, this was not considered conspicuous posting.

The printing of a notice on the registration card is also not considered sufficient posting and cannot operate as a substitute for required posting unless specified by statute. As used in most statutes, the word *post* generally means to nail, attach, affix, or otherwise physically fasten a notice in the places where stipulated by statute, or to record a notice in the places where stipulated by statute, or to record a notice in a book or on a card that is kept on the desk. In Olson v. Crossman, 17 N.W. 375 (1883), the court said that when a statute requires the posting of notice by a hotelkeeper, the statute cannot be complied with by simply printing the notice at the head of the register in which guests sign their names.

Millhiser v. Beau Site Company, 167 N.E. 447 (N.Y., 1929), is a leading case on proper posting that constitutes notice. Though a statute in New York limits the amount recoverable in cases where an object of undisclosed value is lost to $250, the plaintiff in this case recoverd the full amount ($50,000). As the court explained its verdict, to relieve the innkeeper of the heavy burden placed upon him by the common law, the legislature enacted certain statutes that would limit an innkeeper's liability. But when a hotel failed to post the notice as required by statute, the innkeeper's full liability would continue. In this case, the Biltmore Hotel had posted the following notice in its public rooms and guest rooms: "A safe is provided in the office of this hotel for the use of guests in which money, jewels, and other valuables may be deposited for safekeeping." However, the notice neglected to post the limiting qualifications of the statute. The court said that the posting of the statute by the defendant hotel had led the guest to the erroneous conclusion that if valuables were deposited according to the notice, the depositor would be protected to the extent of the liability of the hotel. "It is unquestionably misleading and unfair to require the guest to deposit valuables for safekeeping in a safe and, in case of loss, to permit the hotel to assert a limitation of liability without any notice of such a right to the guest. If, however, Section 200 is printed and posted with the notice, a guest is notified of the true situation and acts with knowledge."

If the *Holiday Inn* case shows an advantage to the plaintiff-guest, then the case of DeBanfield v. Hilton Hotels Corporation, 231 N.Y.S.2d 906 (1962), demonstrates the advantage to hotelkeepers when they do post and follow the statute to the letter. In this case, someone removed all the plaintiff's belongings, valued at $3,500, from his hotel room while he was absent. He contended that keys were accessible to nonguests from the desk and that the hotel room was easily accessible from a nearby balcony. The *DeBanfield* case can be dissected as follows:

1 A guest-innkeeper relationship existed.

2 The hotel guest was not contributorily negligent in his actions leading to the loss of his goods.

3 Neither the hotelkeeper nor his employees were negligent in caring for the goods of the guest.

4 Under common law doctrine, the hotelkeeper was the insurer of his guests' goods.

5 The guest won the case.

6 However, the hotel pleaded its statutory defense under Section 201 of the General Business Law of New York and, therefore, was liable only for the provisions of the statute. (This aspect of the law is discussed in depth later in the chapter.)

7 If contributory negligence could be proved against the plaintiff-guest, the hotel would not have to pay anything.

Although in this case the hotelkeeper lost, his loss was limited to $500. As a point of interest, most hotelkeepers do not carry insurance on this type of loss because the insurance premiums are prohibitively high, especially where the statutes provide for a high limit of loss to the hotelkeeper and, of course, a great many losses are incurred.

Generally, the courts are required to make sure that the requisites in limiting liability statutes are rigidly adhered to because any statute in derogation of a common law right must be strictly construed. Some states, however, have enacted statutes similar to the one in existence in the state of Kentucky. It provides that "all statutes of this state shall be liberally construed with a view to promote their objects and carry out the intent of the legislature, and the rule that statutes in derogation of the common law are to be strictly construed shall not apply to the statutes of this state." Thus, in the case of Roth v. Investment Properties of Lexington, Inc., 560 S.W.2d 831 (Ky., 1978), a Kentucky court found that the limiting liability statute was applicable in a case where the innkeeper had not posted notice in the office and public rooms of the inn. Instead, they were posted on the doors in each of the private rooms, and the posting consisted of an earlier copy of the law, which had since been changed slightly. The court thus held that the legislature intended to exempt innkeepers from liability for the loss of property if they provided a place for safekeeping and gave guests reasonable notice of the availability of the safe place.

The decision in the *Roth* case was possible only because of the peculiar statute permitting such a finding. Such liberal thinking on the part of the court is very limited; the general rule is strict compliance with the statute's requirements. Hoteliers should look to their attorney to ensure that they comply with the requirements in the statute for their state.

A Delaware case, Skyways Motor Lodge Corp. v. General Foods Corporation, 403 A.2d 722 (Del., 1979), had what may seem to be an opposite outcome, holding that a failure to post as required by the statute denied the hotel protection of the limiting liability statute. The statute required that the hotel post the notice in "every lodging room and other conspicuous places." The hotel had posted the notice on the motel room door of each guest room and also had the notice printed on the guest registration card. The court held that Skyways failed to comply with the posting requirements. Although the two cases seem to reach opposite results on substantially the same factual situations, the statute in *Roth* specifically said that carrying out the purpose of the enactment of the statute was the primary concern, whereas Delaware had a statute mandating strict compliance with the statute.

Posting Requirements

Guests of hotels often are unaware that the full amount of any loss they suffer will not be paid to them for personalty stolen from their rooms and that in cases of stolen jewelry, none of their loss will be paid if the state statute requires jewelry to be deposited in the hotel safe. That is why just about every jurisdiction that has limiting liability statutes on its books has included in the statutory language that the hotel must post the statute in a manner calculated to give guests notice of the existence of the limiting liability statute, its terms, and what they have to do to gain the maximum protection. Even though conspicuous posting is required, it is unarguable that all guests will not read these notices, and it may even be assumed that most of them will not. Nevertheless, a hotel that has posted the notice as required is protected. That is why the place and the manner of posting and even type size become important factors in determining whether the statute is applicable.

Terry v. Lincscott, 617 P.2d 56 (Ariz., 1980), is not the best case to demonstrate the exact requisites of notice, but it is interesting in that it presents a good case for the analytical dissection of a case to see how it could have gone either way, depending on which judge heard the case. The notice as recorded in the case is questionable except as to Arizona.

In *Terry* v. *Lincscott*, the plaintiffs, while guests at the Scottsdale Hilton Inn, had jewelry and other items stolen from their room. They alleged a myriad of counts in their complaint, including the hotel's failure to provide adequate security with inadequate use of security guards, improper locking devices on the door, failure to increase security knowing of the high rate of thefts in the Scottsdale Hilton, and failure to warn the plaintiffs of the number of thefts and burglaries committed in the Scottsdale Hilton prior to December 28, 1977. Additionally, the hotel placed in the guests' room the following notice that the plaintiff believes does not conform to the statute: "PLEASE Safety Deposit Boxes for your valuables are available at the Reception Desk. We recommend that you deposit all valuables. We also suggest you double bolt your door when using the patio door to the swimming pool. Arizona Statutes do not hold hotels liable for missing valuables, nor do we have insurance coverage. So, please deposit your valuables.''

The statute required that the innkeeper maintain a fireproof safe and give notice by posting in a conspicuous place in the office or in the room of each guest that the innkeeper is not liable for loss of or injury to any articles, such as money and jewels, not deposited in the safe, *that is not the result of the innkeeper's own act* (emphasis part of the statute).

The plaintiffs' arguments concentrated on the phrase of the statute "that is not the result of his own act" in that this, they contended, preserves a cause of action against the innkeeper for his negligent inaction in failing to provide adequate security and in failing to warn the plaintiff of the number of thefts within the hotel.

One of the questions the court had to resolve was whether depositing the valuables in the innkeeper's fireproof safe was misfeasance or nonfeasance. *Misfeasance* is active misconduct working positive injury to others, and *nonfeasance* is passive inaction, including failure to take steps to protect *them* from harm. The reason for the distinction may lie in the fact that by misfeasance, the defendant has created a new risk of harm to the plaintiff, while by nonfeasance, he has at least made his situation no worse, and has merely failed to benefit by interfering in the affair.

In this case, the court held that before a guest could ask for and recover full liability, the valuables would have to have been placed in the safe. The guest could recover only if a theft from the safe was caused by the innkeeper's negligent act or omission. But in this case, where the guests did not deposit their valuables, the negligence on the part of the defendant had to be active—an act of misfeasance—rather than nonfeasance—an omission or failure to act. The court said that failure to provide adequate security and failure to warn guests about prior thefts were deemed claims of nonfeasance; hence, no claim existed.

Regarding the adequacy of the notice that failed to refer to a *fireproof* safe, the court agreed that the notice posted by an innkeeper must strictly comply with the terms of the statute in order to effectively relieve the innkeeper of common law liability. However, the term *safe* or safety-deposit box adequately conveys to the reader that the valuables are protected from danger, including fire. Therefore, the posted notice did comply with the statutory requirements. It was obvious, the court decided, that the innkeeper made a realistic and forceful attempt, in language that was readily understandable, to convey the most vital information and to encourage their guests to use the safe. The trial court correctly determined that the notice complied with the statutory requirements.

In the *Terry* case, the notice was placed on the dresser in their room, which constituted posting in a conspicuous place. By contrast, see North

River Insurance Co. v. Tisch Management, Inc., 166 A.2d 169 (N.J., 1960), where the court held that it was a question of fact for a jury to decide the adequacy of a notice when the posting was placed under glass on the dresser as a small appendage to a larger general hotel directory. A contrary ruling was upheld in Platt v. New Irvington Hotel of Lakewood, Inc., 204 A.2d 709 (N.J., 1964).

Providing a Safe

Almost invariably, the states that have passed limiting liability statutes relative to the personal property of guests specify that jewelry, money, securities, and other things of "small compass" that have value must be put into the hotel safe if the guest is to get the benefit of even the limited sums available for the loss of such property. Such statutes thus have created reciprocal obligations between the innkeeper and guest if the guest is to recover anything at all and if the innkeeper is to receive any protection. A guest who fails to meet this obligation will receive nothing in the event of a loss, unless the innkeeper had failed to meet this statutory obligation. In that event, the innkeeper would be totally liable to the guest for the full value of the stolen or tortiously damaged property.

Zaldin v. *Concord Hotel* concerns the New York limiting liability statute that requires hotels to provide a safe for guests and imposes on guests the duty of putting their jewelry in it in order to get even the limited payment in the event of theft. The guest in this case had endeavored to do just that, but the safe was closed and the items could not be accepted by the hotel and stored there; thus, the plaintiffs were compelled to take their jewelry back to their room, where two diamond rings were stolen. Was the hotel obligated to keep the safe open twenty-four hours a day? Apparently the New York court thought so. If the safe was not always available, then there was no limitation on the hotel's liability. Because the hotel had failed to comply with the statute, it lost statutory protection. Thus, the common law that was in existence before the statute applied. It held that the hotel is fully liable as an insurer of its guest's property.

Case Example **Zaldin v. Concord Hotel**
421 N.Y.S.2d 858 (1979)
(FUCHSBERG, Judge)

We treat here with Section 200 of the General Business Law, a statute delineating the responsibilities of the hotel industry with regard to the valuables of its millions of patrons.

Plaintiffs, registered guests, bring suit on a theory of absolute liability for the loss of two valuable diamond rings that disappeared from their hotel room. In its answer, the defendant hotel pleaded Section 200 by way of affirmative defense. Asserting that the hotel's vault was not available to guests at the time they attempted to place the jewelry there for safekeeping, plaintiffs moved for summary judgment or, in the alternative, for an order striking the defense. Special Term held, *inter alia,* that the hotel's failure to provide access to its safe at all times did not necessarily preclude it from claiming the protection of Section 200 and, concluding that the "reasonableness of the vault hours should be left to the judgment of the triers of fact," denied the motion. On review, the appellate division in effect ruled that since the statute does not speak of "reasonable hours," a hotel's maintenance of vault facilities, even when available to guests only at limited times, generally entitles the hotel to the statutory benefits; on that basis, the court granted summary judgment to the defendant, dismissing the complaint on the law. (The notices that the hotel posted, stating the fact that a "safe is provided," complied fully with the statute.)

On our review, we hold that a hotel may not claim the limitations on liability afforded it by Section 200 of the General Business Law at times when it fails to make a safe available to its guests. We therefore determine that summary judgment should not have been granted and the complaint, accordingly, should be reinstated. Our reasons follow.

Section 200 of the General Business Law reads: "Whenever the proprietor or manager of any hotel, motel, inn, or steamboat shall provide a safe . . . for the safekeeping of any money, jewels, ornaments, bank notes, bonds, negotiable securities, or precious stones, belonging to the guests . . . and shall notify the guests or travelers thereof by posting a notice stating the fact that such safe is provided . . . in a public and conspicuous place and manner in the office and public rooms . . . and if such guest or traveler shall neglect to deliver such property . . . for deposit in such safe, the proprietor or manager . . . shall not be liable for any loss of such property, sustained by such guest or traveler by theft or otherwise." Beyond this, in the absence of a special agreement in writing, the statute goes on to limit a hotel's liability for property so deposited with it, whether the loss is sustained "by theft or otherwise," to a sum not exceeding $500.

. . . It is agreed that on Friday afternoon, the plaintiffs William and Shelby Modell, accompanied by their daughter and son-in-law, checked into the defendant's large resort hotel. No one disputes but that the hotel provided a safe-deposit vault for the use of its guests and that shortly after the plaintiffs' arrival, the daughter requested and was assigned one of its boxes. Plaintiffs allege that she then placed two diamond rings belonging to her mother in the box and that late the following afternoon, she withdrew them from the box for her mother to wear while attending the Saturday evening festivities sponsored by the hotel.

Sometime after midnight, however, upon the conclusion of the hotel's nightclub performance and before retiring, when the Modells and their daughter attempted to redeposit the jewelry, a hotel desk clerk informed them that the vault was closed and that they would have to retain possession of their valuables until it was opened in the morning. The defendant concedes that it would not allow guests access to the vault between the hours of eleven in the evening and eight in the morning. The Modells claim they thereupon secreted the jewelry in their room only to find, upon arising at about 9:00 A.M. that the chain lock with which they had secured the room had been cut from the outside and the rings were missing. They promptly notified the hotel and police, of what they took to be a theft.

In now applying the statute to this factual framework, we first remark on the obvious: The statute's wording is plain. This is not a new observation. Almost from the time the legislation was enacted, the courts recognized that "there is nothing in the statute itself indicating any intent other or less extensive than the unequivocal language imports." So we by no means tread the quicksand that surrounds a case in which less than definitive statutory language requires a choice among differing interpretations, the resolution of which, in turn, compels a choice among differing canons of construction. Rather, when, as here, a statute is free from ambiguity and its sweep unburdened by qualification or exception, we must do no more and no less than apply the language as it is written.

Thus read, the statute offers the innkeeper an option: "Provide" a safe for your guests and sharply restrict your liability; or, feel free to do absolutely nothing about a safe and continue the risk of exposure to open-ended common law liability. But, whichever choice you make, since the statute is in derogation of the common law rule, to obtain the benefit of the more circumscribed liability that Section 200 affords, you must conform strictly with its conditions.

The statute fixes no time when a safe may or must be provided. Nor does it mandate availability around the clock. *A fortiori*, it does not limit the operation of a safe to a "reasonable time." These matters are left entirely up to the hotel. The statute makes no effort to evaluate cost or convenience. Neither does it distinguish between large and small inns, between those that cater to the large convention and those that cater to the individual patron, between those that come alive at night and those that do so in the day, between those that have a wealthy clientele and those that do not. The legislative formula is uncomplicated. It says, straightforwardly, that "whenever" a safe is provided, the liability limitations shall be applicable. Conversely, at those times when an innkeeper chooses not to provide a safe for the use of its guests, he cannot claim the statutory protection.

In the face of the simplicity that characterizes the statute's structure, the hotel relies on two venerable cases to import into the statute certain unexpressed exceptions. To the contrary, these cases, on close analysis, are in keeping with our interpretation. Thus, in Rosenplaenter v. Roessle, 54 N.Y. 262, where a newly registered procrastinating guest lost his valuables during his delay in delivering them to the safe, the court indeed did suggest that "there must be a brief period after the arrival of a guest at a hotel before he can make the deposit, and during this brief period, the statute affords the hotelkeeper no protection"; however, the unwarranted interpolation of this element of uncertainty turns up only as dictum for, in the end, the result, not inconsistent with today's holding, was to deny recovery. Similarly, Bendetson v. French, 46 N.Y. 266, a case permitting common law recovery against an innkeeper for a loss occurring after a guest had removed his valuables from a safe in preparation for his departure, should not be viewed as creating a permissible deviation from the terms of the statute; rather, as the opinion in that case makes clear, the loss was attributable to negligence on the part of baggage-handling hotel employees and, hence, essentially, the statute was not dispositive.

The defendant, also, would have us read the statute as though the phrase "as soon as" had been substituted for the word "whenever" and, similarly, "equip" for "provide." But neither the express language of the statute nor its avowed purpose permits us to sanction what, in effect, would amount to a substantive change, indeed, a literal rewriting of a carefully conceived and well-weathered statute. Had the legislature meant to incorporate such qualifications, it easily could have done so. To the contrary, in the one hundred twenty-five years of the legislation's long life, no such restriction has ever been essayed, despite periodic legislative tinkering in other respects.

More specifically, nowhere does Section 200 suggest that an innkeeper may provide a safe part of the time and yet gain the benefit of the exemption all the time. Taken to its logical conclusion, this would not only deprive guests of their common law right to seek recovery of their full losses against the innkeeper; but, by curtailing the period during which the surrogate medium of a safe is to be available, it also would leave the guests bereft of a full-time replacement for the innkeeper's former round-the-clock incentive to maintain security. Had a statute as explicit in concept and form as is the one here been intended to give a hotel the advantages of a dramatic limitation on its liability for losses while still retaining the privilege to encroach on the temporal scope of the *quid pro quo*—a safe such as would afford the guests protection—surely it would have said so.

The defendant, therefore, may not have been entitled to base an affirmative defense under Section 200 and certainly was not entitled to receive summary judgment on that account. Nevertheless, on the record before us, it was correct to withhold granting summary judgment to plaintiffs. Especially since the plaintiffs' daughter made no affidavit in support of the motion, the further development of relevant facts may be in order, including *inter alia*, ones relating to the circumstances surrounding the actual disappearance of the rings, to whether the theft occurred at the time when the safe was not available to these guests and, of course, to the value of the rings.

From all this flows our conclusion that the order of the appellate division should be modified by reversing the grant of summary judgment to defendant and by reinstating the complaint and otherwise should be affirmed.

Ruling of the Court: Order modified, with costs to plaintiffs-appellants, in accordance with the opinion herein and, as so modified, affirmed.

Now let us assume that the guest did not attempt to place the jewelry in the safe, but went right to her room, where the rings were stolen. Not until the next morning did the guest discover that even if she had tried to put her rings in the safe, this would not have been possible. Do you believe that the results would be the same as *Zaldin?* We believe so. Our reasoning is that because there must be strict compliance with the limiting liability statute in order to claim statutory protection, the availability of the safe is a condition precedent to invoking the protection. If that condition is not met, then the statute never comes into play and the common law rules apply. The moral is that the safe must be available for guests to deposit their valuables at any time of day or night in order to trigger the protection of the statute.

Total Notice to Guest

What constitutes notice to guests that their recovery will be limited to a fraction of any large loss from a bank-type safety-deposit box in a hotel? In *Depaemelaere v. Davis,* the hotel did post partial notice that "a safe was provided in the office for the use of guests in which money, etc., . . . can be deposited for safekeeping." According to the court, this notice could lead the guest to believe he was protected to the full extent of his deposit.

Several points make this case notable. First, the Belgian guest deposited $18,000, of which $10,000 was lost. The question was, How could he prove he had that amount of money in the safe? (The guest did recover the $10,000 from the hotel.) Second, the notice reproduced only part of the total law required to be posted.

Case	**Depaemelaere v. Davis**
Example	*351 N.Y.S.2d 808 (1973)*
	(HARRY T. NUSBAUM, Judge)

In the case at bar that was transferred from the Supreme Court pursuant to the provisions of CPLR 325(d), the plaintiff, a Belgium national, sues to recover the sum of $10,000 allegedly missing from two envelopes deposited for safekeeping in a safe containing individual safe-deposit box compartments maintained by the hotel for the use and convenience of its guests.

The defendant pleads by way of defense that its liability is limited to $500 by reason of the provisions of Sections 200, 201, and 206 of the General Business Law. It further pleads as a defense the plaintiff's contributory negligence and its own freedom from negligence.

From the testimony adduced during the trial, it would appear that on April 14, 1971, the plaintiff, a guest at the hotel, requested the use of a safe-deposit box in which he placed an envelope containing $18,000 in cash. Again, on April 30, he deposited another envelope in the safe-deposit box containing $8,000 in cash. I am satisfied from the testimony of the plaintiff, his wife, and one of the plaintiff's customers, who paid a part of the sums in question to the plaintiff, that the plaintiff did in fact deposit the sum of $26,000 in the hotel safe-deposit box in the safe maintained by the hotel for that purpose.

On May 12, 1971, the day before the plaintiff was scheduled to return to Belgium, he requested the safe-deposit box in order to remove the money therefrom. Upon opening the box, he noticed that a rubberband placed by him around one of the envelopes was askew. He thereupon immediately sat down with his wife on a bench near the hotel desk, opened up the envelopes and counted the money. He found $5,000 in old bills missing from each envelope for a total of $10,000. The loss was immediately reported to the hotel employees and the police department, whose investigation of the loss proved fruitless.

It is alleged by the hotel that the sole key to the box remained in the possession of the plaintiff during the period from April 14 through May 12, except for the brief periods the key was given to the desk clerk for the removal and locking of the box in the safe on April 14, April 30, and May 12.

The process of removing and locking up the safe-deposit box in question was similar to that employed generally by banks. Two keys are required to do so: the customer's key and the hotel master key. Neither key by itself could effect a removal of the box from the safe. However, unlike bank procedures, the box at the time it is removed from the safe and returned to the safe is hidden from the view of the depositor by the safe door that opens in such a manner as to obstruct any view into the room housing the safe.

These facts virtually undisputed except by implication leave two unanswered questions, the resolution of which will be dispositive of the matter: (1) Were the notices of limitation of liability conspicuously posted as required by law so as to effect notice to the plaintiff that would limit the defendant's liability, and (2) did the defendant as bailee of the plaintiff's property come forward with a suitable explanation of the claimed loss that would free it from the implication of lack of ordinary care?

I am of the opinion that both of these questions must be answered in the negative. The applicable sections of the General Business Law, Sections 200, 201, and 206 must be read together, and those sections when read together require not only that a notice be posted advising the guests of the hotel that a safe is available for the deposit and safekeeping of money, jewels, negotiable securities, and precious stones belonging to the guests, but also that notice be given to the guests of the hotel's limitation of liability imposed by law upon the guests when such facility is used. . . .

The facts with respect to the notices posted by the hotel in the instant case appear to be as follows:

In the guest's room in the hotel, a notice is posted that advises him in legible, clear type: "We have safety-deposit boxes that are available for you without charge. We will appreciate your cooperation."

At the time the guest registered at the hotel, there was printed legibly and clearly on the registration card the following legend: "Money, jewels and other valuables, and packages must be placed in the safe in the office, otherwise, the management will not be responsible for any loss."

It is to be noted that in both of these instances, the guest is not advised of any limitation liability or of the fact that the hotel is not required to take for deposit money, jewels, or other valuables valued in excess of $500.00. The only notices that allegedly notified the guest of this limitation of liability are contained in a notice to guests that is posted at the right-hand side of the registration desk, which notice is not in his direct line of vision and which notice he will see only if he turns to face that wall; and a notice in one other place vaguely described as being in the lobby of the hotel near the elevators.

These notices, which are on a seven-by-nine-inch card, contained in black large type approximately a quarter of an inch tall a legend that reads as follows: "Notice to guests. A safe is provided in the office for the safekeeping of money, jewels, ornaments, bank notes, bonds, negotiable securities, and precious stones belonging to guests." There then follows in clear type a space for the posting of daily rates and charges, and then in letters approximately a sixteenth of an inch high or less, the provisions of the General Business Law that to my mind are illegible and unreadable except from a distance of ten to twelve inches.

Thus, the guests of the defendant's hotel are advised of the existence of the safe, requested to place their valuables in the safe, warned of the consequences if such request is not complied with, but notified of the hotel's limited liability with respect to such property deposited in the safe by notices posted only in technical compliance with the law, which in effect give no notice of the limitations.

In my opinion, it was the intention of the legislature to see to it that real and effective notice of the hotel's limitation of liability was given to its guests. This conclusion is reached and bolstered by the provisions contained in each of the sections dealing with limitations of liability that state that a printed copy of the section be posted "in a public and conspicuous place and manner." In the case at bar, I do not regard the posting of the notice setting forth the hotel's limitation of liability as a posting in a "public and conspicuous place and manner," sufficient to effect a limitation of liability. In fact, it is my belief that the notice and warning on the registration card and the notice in the guest's room would lead a guest to the conclusion that he must deposit his valuables in the hotel safe in order to be safeguarded, . . . and that no limitation of liability exists if he complies with this request.

However muddy and unclear the law may be with respect to what constitutes posting in "a public and conspicuous place and manner," it is clear that the failure to deposit property for safeguarding pursuant to the provisions of Section 200 of the General Business Law will free the hotel of any liability for loss, even if such loss occurred through its own negligence. . . . The corollary must therefore be held to be equally true. A finding that the guest did not receive proper notice of the limitation of the hotel's liability should render it fully liable if the guest's valuables are deposited pursuant to the provisions of Section 200 of the General Business Law. . . .

Under the common law, the liability of an innkeeper was that of an insurer of the property of a guest unless it could be shown that such loss was occasioned by the fault or negligence of the guest. As the sections in question are in derogation of the common law rule relative to the liability of innkeepers, they must be strictly construed.

These facts have been established to my satisfaction. The money was deposited as claimed by the plaintiff in this action. Upon his attempted withdrawal of the monies deposited, $10,000 was found to be missing, and no adequate explanation has been proffered by the hotel for the mysterious disappearance of the money. I am of the opinion, therefore, that the hotel's liability for such loss has been established. . . .

Not having been notified of the necessity of advising the hotel if the property deposited exceeded $500 in value or of the necessity of making a separate agreement with respect to such property if it exceeded $500 in value, the plaintiff cannot be held to have been contributorily negligent with respect to its loss.

Ruling of the Court: Judgment is accordingly awarded to the plaintiff in the sum of $10,000 with interest, as demanded in the complaint.

Special Information on Notice

Innkeepers cannot limit their liability for a guest's property if not covered by statute because a hotel is considered a quasi-public place. However, this does not mean that hotelkeepers cannot contract for protection, but rather that they cannot limit their liability in the absence of a statute. Certainly they can refuse to take certain goods (with a few exceptions) under the reasonable rule doctrine. The underlying theory must be that since the parties are not on an equal footing, public policy requires that the guest be protected from contractual limitations or exemptions.

The right to reasonable rules by a hotel is unquestionable; however, unreasonable rules create a problem. Therefore, hotelkeepers cannot cause unnecessary inconvenience to guests by forcing them to deposit articles of personal or daily use but only such property as is convenient for them to deposit. If reasonable rules are brought to a guest's attention and he does not comply, he will not recover for a loss because it was his own fault.

The following are examples of cases in which the plaintiff has lost:

1 The plaintiff asked a chambermaid where to leave his baggage while visiting someone and was told to leave it with the porter. The guest did not recover when it was stolen from the porter's room (Wilson v. Halprin, 1 Daly 496 [N.Y., 1865]; 30 How. PR 124).

2 The plaintiff left his coat in a public part of the hotel when it was required to leave such articles with the innkeeper (Fuller v. Coats, 18 Ohio St. 343 [1868]).

3 The guest had been in the hotel before. However, before he entered his room this time, his goods were lost. As he had had notice, he could not recover (Widen v. Warren Hotel Co. 159 N.E. 456 [Mass., 1928]).

4 Before going up to his room, the arriving guest removed certain clothing and went into the dining room. He could not recover for valuables stolen from his trunk (Rosenplaenter v. Roessle, 54 N.Y. 262 [1873]).

5 The guest left a large sum of money and a railroad ticket on his bed. The hotel was not held liable for the loss of these items (Griffis v. Buckofzer, 103 S.E. 800 [Ga., 1920]).

Disclosure of Value

Most travelers are reluctant to disclose the value of the property they have with them. Travelers may be afraid of having their property stolen or of inviting questions from the IRS, for example. Regardless, guests must decide whether to disclose the fact that they have valuable jewelry, a large sum of money, or other valuables that must be put into the safe to comply with the statute, as well as for safety.

Over the years, hotel guests have sustained small and large losses of valuables. The guest and hotelkeeper have differing views on who should be liable for the guest's goods. But the final arbiter is the court, with or without a jury.

A case in point demonstrates how a Michigan court handled the disclosure problem. In Oppenheimer v. Morton Hotel Corporation, 210 F.Supp. 609 (Mich., 1962), the guest, a jewelry salesman, deposited a briefcase containing diamonds purportedly valued at $50,000. In Michigan the hotelkeeper is considered as a depository for hire; and his or her liability for a valise and contents is limited to $50. A hotelkeeper can enter into an agreement for property with a value of more than $50, but the agreement *must* be in writing and be signed by both parties. The diamonds disappeared. The safety-deposit envelope said only that the innkeeper "assumed no liability other than that provided for in the Innkeeper's Act of this state, which has limited our liability so that in no event can we be liable for more than the amount specified in said Act. The employee accepting this envelope has no authority to accept same if the contents are valued at more than the amount specified in said Act." In an analysis of the case, the court said:

1   The intent of the statute (Section 18.312) is to have the guest offer his goods to the hotelkeeper. The guest offered a briefcase.

2   The statute expressly states that the hotelkeeper is *not* obliged to receive valuables exceeding $250. No declaration of value was made.

3   The burden of disclosure of valuables rests upon the guest. The guest made no mention of value except to state that he believed any goods put in a safe were valuable; hence, he did make a pseudodisclosure. The court did not accept this.

4   The statute wording relied on by the guest states, "but every innkeeper shall be liable for any loss of the above enumerated articles of a guest in his inn, caused by the theft or negligence of the innkeeper or any of his servants." The court countered that this applied *only* when the guest had offered to deliver his valuables and the hotelkeeper had refused or omitted to take them for deposit into the hotel safe and had refused to give the guest a receipt for those valuables. If, under such circumstances, the valuables were subsequently lost, the burden would then be placed on the hotel to show that the loss was not caused by theft or negligence of the hotelkeeper or his employees.

5   The guest testified that, even if asked, he would not have disclosed the briefcase contents. Admittedly, the guest had offered the hotel a briefcase for safekeeping. Therefore, the court ruled that it was impossible for a bailment contract to be created by the parties in relation to the diamonds, because it was the deliberate, studied, planned intent of the guest to not disclose the briefcase contents.

6   The guest's argument was that the act of depositing something for safekeeping is notice to the hotel that it has value. The court's answer to this was that any deposit constitutes notice only to the extent set forth in the statute, and in the case of a valise and contents the value is $50. Justice Cardozo's opinion in Honig v. Riley, 155 N.E. 65 (N.Y., 1926), involving a similar statute[1] is appropriate here:

> The guest at any inn who delivers goods to the innkeeper for storage or safekeeping in a place other than his own room must state the value of the

1   New York General Business Law, McKinney's Consol. Laws, C. 20, § 201.

goods and procure an appropriate receipt. If he fails to do this, the liability of the innkeeper is limited to $100. In no event, however, is there to be liability in excess of $500 except for fault or negligence. There are similar provisions in respect of liability for merchandise samples or merchandise for sale. From the *beginning of the section to the end, the exemption from liability in excess of the prescribed maximum is absolute where value is concealed. Only where value is stated and a receipt delivered is the exemption made dependent upon freedom from negligence or other fault* [emphasis added].

The judgment was for the plaintiff, who received $50 for the loss of the valise and its contents.

Negligence of the Hotelkeeper and Employees

An important factor in negligence cases is a point of law that makes the hotel liable for proving it was not negligent. The *DeBanfield* v. *Hilton Hotels Corporation* case discussed earlier occurred in a state in which the plaintiff had to prove that the hotel was negligent. It is frequently difficult, if not impossible, for hotel guests to demonstrate that their baggage was removed from the checkroom or their valuables from the hotel safe through the hotel's negligence. Many courts hold that once a *prima facie* case of liability has been established by proof of an innkeeper-guest relationship and by proof of the loss or damage to the guest's property, innkeepers then must exonerate themselves from liability—either by bringing themselves within an exception to or limitation of the rule imposing liability or by showing their freedom from fault.

In Kalpakian v. Oklahoma Sheraton Corp., 398 F.2d 243 (Okla., 1968), the Oklahoma court interpreted the statute as allowing no recovery (in the absence of a written agreement for a value of more than $300), regardless of how the loss was sustained. A similar Rhode Island statute was also thus construed in Hoffman v. Louis D. Miller & Company, 115 A.2d 689 (1955).

State courts do not always agree whether a guest can recover if the hotel management is involved with the loss in some way.[2] Even cases within the same state are inconsistent. In most cases in which guests could not recover, it was because they did not declare the value of the goods deposited in the safe, or they did not get a receipt for the goods.

Value of Goods in Safes

Not all states specify whether hotels should inquire as to the value of goods to be deposited in the safe. Indeed, this ambiguous situation may cause the hotel to lose the case. In *Sagman* v. *Richmond Hotels*, the guest deposited jewelry valued at $100,000. Recovery by the guest rested

---

2   For an enumeration of states that do and do not support the right of a guest to sue for negligence when an innkeeper or employees are involved, see 37 A.L.R.3d 1276.

on whether it was the duty of the guest to notify the hotel of the value or that of the hotel to make inquiry concerning the value.

The assigning of this responsibility presents a dilemma. Because guests know the value of their goods, perhaps they should report. On the other hand, hotelkeepers could refuse to accept items if their value exceeds what they want to have in their safes. And how can hotelkeepers decide whether jewelry and other valuables are, in fact, worth what the depositor claims?

Seemingly, hotels are not banks or depositories for extremely valuable items, but newspaper accounts of hotel robberies and of the value of the stolen goods belie this. The 1974 Pierre Hotel robbery of $4.5 million is not an everyday occurrence, but other hotels catering to the affluent must store valuables of this magnitude. Perhaps new industry standards should provide for hotel storage of extremely valuable items. For example, a special room with highly sophisticated protective equipment might be set aside to protect guests' property. Should there be an additional fee for this special service? Could an insurance policy be purchased for each customer, based on the declared value of the goods? Hotels that offer such specialized protection, in addition to stricter hotel security, could charge guests for such services.

Case Example   **Sagman v. Richmond Hotels**
138 F.Supp. 407 (Va., 1956)
(STERLING HUTCHENSON, Chief Judge)

These are actions brought by H. Sagman, and others, against Richmond Hotels, Incorporated, to recover the value of certain jewelry alleged to be in excess of $100,000. Plaintiffs contend that on or about July 15, 1950, Herman Sagman became a guest at the Hotel King Carter in Richmond; that at the time he had in his possession the jewelry here involved contained in a valise or bag of the type usually used by traveling jewelry salesmen, in which occupation he was employed at the time; that when he checked into the hotel and registered with the desk clerk he announced his desire to place the valise in the vault maintained by the hotel in its office for the purpose of safekeeping valuables. The clerk directed him to give the valise to a bellboy who, with the assistance of the clerk, placed it in the vault. Sagman had been a guest at the hotel on a prior occasion during that year and on numerous occasions previously. He informed the clerk that the contents of the valise were valuable, but he did not indicate the amount of value nor was an inquiry made of him upon that point. On previous visits he had had jewelry placed in the vault without any statement concerning its value. He was given a check or receipt for the valise.

The hotel had posted proper notice in compliance with the provisions of Section 35–10 of the Code of Virginia. Sagman was aware of this fact.

Upon requesting his valise on July 17, 1950, which was Monday following his registration, Sagman was offered a valise that he declined to accept, stating that it was not his. Upon being opened by the hotel manager, it was found to contain bricks wrapped in out-of-town Sunday newspapers.

This action was instituted to recover the alleged value of the jewelry.

The defendant has filed a motion for summary judgment fixing its maximum liability at $500 under the provisions of the Virginia statute that the defendant contends limits its liability to that amount under the facts above recited.

The question presented does not appear to have been passed upon by the Virginia court. Counsel cite and quote from a number of cases of other states involving statutes limiting the liability of innkeepers. The statutes involved differ from the Virginia statute and, for that reason, the cases are not particularly helpful.

It will be seen from reading the Virginia statute that it places upon the keepers of hotels, inns, and ordinaries the duty to exercise due care and diligence in providing honest servants and employees and to take every reasonable precaution to protect the person and property of guests and boarders. This statute then provides that no keeper shall be held liable in an amount greater than $300 for loss of property of a guest when such loss takes place from the room occupied by the guest. It then recites that the keeper shall not be held liable for any loss by a guest of jewelry, money, or other valuables of like nature if the keeper shall have posted in the room occupied by the guest in a conspicuous place and in the office a notice stating that jewelry, money and other valuables of like nature must be deposited in the office, unless such loss shall take place from the office after such deposit is made. The concluding sentence is as follows: "The keeper of any such hotel, inn, or ordinary shall not be obliged to receive from any one guest for deposit, in such office, any property hereinbefore described exceeding a total value of $500."

It is upon the sentence last quoted that the defendant bases the motion now before the court. It contends that the guest should have notified the clerk that the value of the jewelry was in excess of $500 and thereby afforded the hotel an opportunity of either assuming responsibility for its full value or declining to accept such responsibility in excess of $500.

As I view the situation, it boils down to one question that may be stated as follows: Is the duty upon the guest to inform the hotel of value or upon the hotel to make inquiry concerning value?

In seeking the answer, there is to be considered the common law duty of the innkeeper to his guest and the reasons therefore. In early days when travel was hazardous by danger from outlaws, inns and hotels were places of refuge for the traveler. They were usually placed at convenient distances, operated by local people of integrity who were familiar with local conditions and prepared to protect the inmates by force if necessary. Many references to these conditions both in this country and abroad may be found in historical writings of fact and fiction. To encourage commerce and trade, it was found expedient to safeguard those engaged in traveling; whether for business or social reasons, the law placed upon the innkeeper duties of an insurer. With the change brought about by more efficient law enforcement and the improvement of facilities for the accommodation of guests, the severity of the common law requirement on the part of innkeepers is no longer necessary. As a consequence, statutes have been enacted limiting their liability. Ordinarily, such a limitation is conditioned upon some affirmative action by the innkeeper. In the instant case, it is conditioned upon posting the signs referred to. Compliance with the statutory requirement results in protection of the innkeeper against liability beyond the statutory provisions.

It must be borne in mind that such statutes are enacted for the benefit of the innkeeper, and in order to bring himself within the limitation of liability, he must comply with the statute. The defendant in this case has complied with the statutory requirement. However, the last sentence of the statute requires interpretation. In some states, the statute provides that the liability is limited unless the innkeeper consents in writing to assume a greater liability. There is nothing in the Virginia statute relating to an agreement. It merely says that the innkeeper shall not be obliged to receive property exceeding the total value of $500. Nowhere does the statute nor the required notice bring to the knowledge of the guest that he must declare the value of his property to be protected nor does it place upon him the duty to do so. By reason of the nature of the business of an innkeeper, judicial notice will be taken of the fact that many guests are not residents of the state, but are strangers from elsewhere. Judicial notice may also be taken of the fact that an overwhelming majority of guests are not lawyers nor acquainted with the duties imposed by law upon the innkeeper. The innkeeper, upon the other hand, obviously is familiar with the requirements of the statute. He has complied with the requirements by posting notice. He is chargeable with both constructive and actual notice of the law enacted for his benefit. So, we come to the question of determining where should lie the duty of disclosing or making inquiry concerning the value of the jewelry placed with the innkeeper for safekeeping.

It is my view that the duty is upon the innkeeper to make inquiry concerning the value. He may at his option decline to accept responsibility under the statute, or he may require as a condition permission to examine it and satisfy himself as to value. In the case of money, he probably would desire to have it counted before accepting liability. Should he fail to make such inquiry, he does so at his own risk and is liable for resulting loss, depending upon proper proof.

Ruling of the Court: Accordingly, the motion for summary judgment limiting the amount of liability will be overruled.

Valuables Versus Personal Goods

Obviously, a rule stating that a guest must deposit all personal goods with the hotelkeeper for safety would not be reasonable. But which goods must be put in the safe? Most state statutes provide that money, jewels, ornaments, bank notes, bonds, negotiable securities, and precious stones must be turned over to the hotelkeeper for safekeeping. But ambiguities still exist. For instance, are cufflinks ornaments? How much money may guests keep in their room? Can they keep a watch in their room? A fur coat? A $10,000 fur coat?

This problem is illustrated in the case of Federal Insurance Company v. Waldorf Astoria Hotel, 303 N.Y.S.2d 297 (1969), in which the court ruled that cufflinks valued at $175 were not an ornament that had to be put in a safe. This case also considered whether a watch need be deposited in the safe. The court stated that a watch is neither a jewel nor an ornament as these words are used and understood either in common parlance or by lexicographers. A watch is not used or carried as a jewel or ornament but as a timepiece, an article of ordinary wear and daily use by most travelers of every social class.

However, in a similar case in the state of Washington, the results were quite contrary. In Walls v. Cosmopolitan Hotels, Inc., 534 P.2d 1373 (Wash., 1975), the guest left his $3,685 watch on a nightstand and went down to dinner. When he returned, the watch was gone. The door was damaged and the lock was in questionable repair. The guest pleaded the poor condition of the door, but he was met with the argument that he should have deposited the valuable watch in the safe. The court ruled that the watch was a "valuable property of small compass," and therefore the hotel was relieved of all liability. This, then, was a condition precedent (the guest had to meet certain conditions before he could attempt to collect) whereby the guest had the responsibility of depositing his valuables. If the court had not decided that the watch was valuable property of small compass, the guest could have won the case.

In Brewer v. Roosevelt Motor Lodge, 295 A.2d 647 (Me., 1972), the plaintiff guest was raped and robbed of her $400 watch. The question of her recovery for the total value of the watch was clouded by Maine Statute 2904. Under this law, if the guest had deposited the watch (if categorized as jewelry or personal ornament) with the hotelkeeper, her recovery could have been as high as $300. However, under Section 2904, the hotelkeeper-guest relationship was that of a depository for hire, and without an agreement in writing for a greater amount, the limit for all innkeepers was set at $50. A depository for hire is liable only for failure to exercise ordinary care—that is, care such as people of ordinary prudence usually exercise over their own property.

In this case, the lower court ruled as a matter of law that there was no obligation on the part of the defendant hotelkeeper to anticipate the unforeseeable intrusion of the plaintiff's assailant, and thus there was no breach of due care for which the defendant was responsible, either in damages for injuries to her person or for the theft of her property.

There is a further important aspect to the Maine statutes. The court stipulated that the innkeeper's liability was limited to $300, regardless of whether he had complied with conditions in reference to a safe, vault, the locking of doors, windows, and transoms, or the posting of laws. This is, by far, the most inclusive of such statutes and it greatly favors the innkeeper.

Hotel Liability for Guests' Valuables: The Nevada Cases

The Nevada limiting liability statute is quite different from that found in many other states because it does away with the innkeeper's common law liability toward the property of guests left in the guest's room. The only exception is instances when the innkeeper or owner of the hotel has committed acts of gross negligence. The statute seems to indicate that the innkeeper's liability is dispensed with only as to property that is left in the room. Therefore, if property is left at the hotel desk or in the safe, it seems that a bailment situation would be created.

The Nevada statute was applied in the case of Levitt v. Desert Palace Inn, 601 F.2d 684 (N.Y., 1979), that involved the loss of jewelry valued by the plaintiffs at $1 million, which they claimed was stolen from their room while they were sleeping.

The plaintiffs were nonpaying guests at the defendant hotel, where they were attending the Alan King Tennis Tournament. Upon arrival they deposited all of their jewelry in the hotel safe, where it remained until Mrs. Levitt needed some of it for a grand ball. She selected several pieces and returned the jewelry case with the remaining jewelry to the safe-deposit box. After the ball, Mrs. Levitt placed the jewelry on top of the dresser near the bed, Mr. Levitt engaged the dead bolt, and they went to bed. The next morning Mrs. Levitt instructed Mr. Levitt to return the jewelry to the safe-deposit box. He placed the jewelry into a handkerchief and brought it to the box. Later that afternoon, when Mrs. Levitt was packing in order to leave and the box had been sent for, she examined the contents and realized that five pieces were missing. Mr. Levitt had failed to notice that the five major pieces were missing when he had taken the jewelry back earlier.

From the evidence introduced, a jury would be warranted in finding that someone had entered the Levitt room while it was unoccupied and removed the dead bolt, replacing it with another bolt that appeared to be functioning properly, but was not. While the Levitts slept, someone picked the cylinder lock and easily gained access to the room.

There was evidence that there had been two incidents of dead-bolt tampering about a year before the plaintiffs' visit and another just a few weeks before. The hotel had started to make the dead bolts tamperproof, but the one in the plaintiffs' room had not been fixed yet. The housekeeping staff had been given instructions to check the dead bolts daily to ensure that they were functioning properly.

The plaintiff argued that the statute is applicable only as to personalty "left alone in the room," and because they remained in the room with the jewelry, it had not been left alone there. Therefore, the statute was inapplicable, and the common law liability applied, with the hotel liable to them for the full amount of their loss, $1 million. The defendant hotel countered with the argument that the statute was applicable whether the parties were in the room or not, just so long as the property was in the room when the loss occurred. The hotel would be liable only if it had been guilty of gross negligence, which, it asserted, was not the case.

The lower court jury found for the plaintiffs and awarded damages of $548,599. The defendant appealed to the circuit court of appeals, where the judge reversed the findings of the jury, holding that as a matter of law the defendant could not be found liable in view of the statute. The court agreed with the defendant that the presence of the sleeping plaintiffs in the room did not alter the effect of the statute and that liability could be imposed only if the defendant was guilty of gross negligence, which it was not.

The next time the issue was reported was in September 1980, about fourteen months after the *Levitt* case. The case was Owens v. Summa Corporation, 625 F.2d 600 (1980), and the facts were very similar to those in the *Levitt* case. The dead lock bolt had been replaced by a dummy, and a thief entered the room at night when both of the plaintiffs were sleeping and stole jewelry. Although similar thefts had occurred previously, the Sands Hotel did not endeavor to replace the dead bolts. The district court judge entered judgment for the defendant, and the plaintiffs appealed. It is undisputed that the hotel had a safe for guests to use and that the plaintiffs knew about it, but the plaintiffs denied knowing of a courier service whereby hotel personnel would come and get the jewelry and take it to the vault. The plaintiffs raised the question of the standard of care that the innkeeper owes to guests. The court said that the defendant violated the standard of care to which the plaintiffs would have been entitled to at common law; however, the common law was no longer applicable because the statute had replaced it. The hotel had not been grossly negligent and, therefore, the statute was applicable.

These two Nevada cases could be the signs of a modification of the limiting liability statute; enactments that started in 1851 in Massachusetts and New York in 1853. In effect, these statutes take away the innkeeper's limiting liability provision that they are liable only for a fraction of the guests' loss, even when the valuables are placed in the hotel's safe.

Hotel's Liability from Beginning to End

Initial Responsibility

The hotelkeeper becomes responsible for the goods of a prospective client as soon as the mutual intent of the two parties is to become guest and hotelkeeper. This relationship does not necessarily depend on the guest's signing a registration card (unless required by statute), but on the deliverance of the guest's goods. The hotelkeeper-guest relationship can begin at the airport when the hotel van picks up the guest. The decisive factor is the intent of the parties. If the guest has a confirmed reservation, there is very little doubt about when the relationship begins. On the other hand, if the client hopes to get a room and there is indeed a room available, the hotelkeeper-guest relationship could begin when the guest arrives at the hotel.

The case of Swanner v. Conner Hotel Company, 224 S.W. 123 (Mo., 1920), treats the question of when a person becomes a guest. The plaintiff came to the hotel with the intent of acquiring a room; however, there was no room available at that time. Because he was familiar with the hotel, the plaintiff left his luggage where he had seen the bellboys put it on previous visits, although a checkroom was available. At 10 P.M. the plaintiff returned and was assigned a room, but his luggage was gone. The verdict was for the plaintiff in the lower court and in the court of appeals because, the courts reasoned, there was indeed a hotelkeeper-guest relationship. The guest had delivered his bags to the hotelkeeper; they were placed where such bags were usually deposited; but they were not returned to the guest.

Property in Transit

When a guest gives a luggage check to a bellhop so that he can pick up the luggage at the airport or a similar place, who is responsible for the luggage if it is lost? Recent cases treating this question are quite rare, but the pertinent legal principles may be demonstrated by the following Colorado and New York cases.

In Keith v. Atkinson, 111 P. 55 (Colo., 1910), a bellboy was given a guest's baggage check issued by the railroad station; however, he did not bring the trunk or return the check. On appeal, the plaintiff won the case. The court reasoned that the presentation of the baggage check (which represented the luggage) made the hotelkeeper liable for the goods, even though the luggage was not within the walls of the hotel. Adhering to this doctrine, the courts claimed there was an innkeeper-guest relationship: there was a delivery of the goods (symbolically, through the delivery of the check); however, the goods were not conveyed to the guest.

The facts of the New York case, Davidson v. Madison Corporation, 177 N.E. 393 (N.Y., 1931), are quite similar, except that an expressman (an independent contractor) was sent to get the trunk. The expressman's truck and the trunk (valued at $10,000) were lost, and the guest sued the hotel. Again, the plaintiff won, but the legal principle involved was different. The court stated that it did not support the reasoning in the Keith case (that the delivery of a railroad check represented a symbolic delivery of the baggage). Rather, while the baggage was in the custody of the railroad or the expressman, liability for it lay with whomever was in custody—either the railroad or the independent contractor. It then followed that the liability, if any, lay in negligence for the nonperformance of a contracted duty. Although this logic differs from that in the Keith case, the court still arrived at the same result: The plaintiff won. Here, the legal point was that the contract to transport the luggage was negligently performed and there was no negligence on the part of the plaintiff.

In 1937 the New York state legislature passed a statute limiting the liability for property in transit to or from a hotel to the sum of $250, unless the guest states on a written receipt that the value exceeds $250.[3] In that case, "the keeper shall not be liable beyond five hundred dollars

---

3 New York General Business Law §§ 203(a), 203(b).

unless it shall appear that such loss or damage occurred through his fault or negligence."

Assume that a hotel guest's bags were lost by the airline. The guest checked into the hotel, and the next day, when the airline located her luggage, they delivered it to her hotel and it was placed on the bellhop stand. By the time the bellhop was ready to deliver the baggage to the guest's room, it had disappeared. Furthermore, assume that there was a limiting liability statute in operation in the state where the hotel was located. Would the limiting liability statute apply under these circumstances? It would if the incident occurred in New Mexico, according to the case of Albuquerque Hilton Inn v. Haley, 565 P.2d 1027 (N.M., 1977).

The plaintiff argued that the statute was inapplicable because its wording provided that the limitation was applicable only to property "brought by . . . guests into the hotel." Because the property was not brought into the hotel by the guest but by an airline agent, the rule that requires strict construction of any statute in derogation of a common law right would bar the application of the statute, and the old common law insurer's liability would be applicable. Supposedly the guest was entitled to recover the full value of her luggage and its contents instead of the $1,000 limit provided by statute. The trial court found for the hotel; the court of appeals found for the guest; and the State Supreme Court reversed the court of appeals and reinstated the trial court's finding. It agreed that generally statutes in derogation of common law rights must be strictly construed. But the statute also sought to eliminate the harsh common law rule as to absolute liability for a guest's property. Therefore, the statute was considered to be remedial in nature. The purpose of this type of law is to correct the existing law that is not working, or that has caused harm instead of good. The rule as to remedial statutes in this state is that they are to be liberally applied so as not to defeat the purpose of their enactment. Therefore, when a statute is both in derogation of a common law right and is remedial in nature as well, the statute should be strictly construed to determine whether it does modify the common law, and if it is remedial, its application should be liberally construed. Therefore, applying the liberal construction in this case, it extends the statute to cover luggage delivered by someone else to the hotel.

The case of *Salisbury v. St. Regis* is not typical of what can happen when one leaves a hotel. Here the plaintiff and wife, after surrendering their room key, made arrangements to have the hotel hold their luggage while they spent the day in town. Their luggage was lost, as was its content, valued at $60,000.

Case Example	Salisbury v. St. Regis-Sheraton Hotel
	490 F.Supp. 449 (1980)
	(LASKER, District Judge)

On the morning of November 22, 1978, Mr. and Mrs. Roger Salisbury concluded a three-day stay at the St. Regis–Sheraton Hotel in New York.

While Mr. Salisbury paid the bill and surrendered their room key, Mrs. Salisbury checked their luggage with a bellhop in the lobby. The couple was to spend the day in town and return for the luggage that afternoon. Mrs. Salisbury did not inform the hotel when she checked the luggage that one of their pieces, a cosmetic case, contained jewelry and cosmetics worth over $60,000 and did not ask that the case be kept in the hotel's safe. Nor did she inform the hotel that the value of the case and its contents exceeded $100.

When the Salisburys returned to the hotel to retrieve their luggage at about 4:30 that afternoon, the cosmetic case containing the jewelry was missing. Mrs. Salisbury sues to recover the value of the case and its contents.

It is undisputed that posted conspicuously in the public areas of the hotel was a notice informing guests that the hotel provided a safe for the safekeeping of their valuables, and notifying them of the provisions of Sections 200 and 201 of the New York General Business Law.

Relying on these provisions, the hotel moves for summary judgment on the grounds that the undisputed facts establish that its liability cannot exceed $100, and therefore federal subject matter jurisdiction is lacking. Mrs. Salisbury cross-moves for summary judgment, asserting that Sections 200 and 201 are inapplicable here because she was no longer a "guest" of the hotel at the time the loss occurred.

The question, then, is whether Mrs. Salisbury ceased to be a "guest" within the meaning of Sections 200 and 201 when she checked out of the hotel, even though she arranged to have the hotel hold her luggage for the day. The two cases on which Mrs. Salisbury relies are clearly distinguishable. In one, Crosby v. Fifth Ave. Hotel Co., 20 N.Y.S.2d 227 (1939), *modified*, 17 N.Y.S.2d 498 (1940), a departing guest stored two trunks with the defendant hotel and returned to reclaim them several years later, only to discover that the hotel had sold them. The court concluded that the relationship involved was not that of innkeeper and guest, but rather that of bailee and bailor. Here, however, the lost luggage was not stored with the hotel for a lengthy period, but simply held for the day as an accommodation to departing guests. In the other case relied on by Mrs. Salisbury, Ticehurst v. Beinbrink, 129 N.Y.S. 838 (App.T.1911), the plaintiff arranged to leave his horse at an inn while he continued his journey by train. The court held that the plaintiff, who simply sought to board his horse, was not a "guest,"— "a transient person who resorts to or is received at an inn for the purpose of obtaining the accommodations that it purports to offer." This definition, however, applies quite well to the Salisburys.

It is not uncommon for a hotel to hold luggage for a few hours after guests check out as an accommodation to them. This would appear to be one of the services that a hotel performs for its guests in the normal course of its business, and there is no reason why it should be deemed to alter the otherwise existing legal relationship between them. Accordingly, we conclude that Sections 200 and 201 are fully applicable in the circumstances of this case and precludes any recovery against the hotel for the loss of Mrs. Salisbury's jewelry and limits any recovery for the loss of the case and its other contents to $100 (Adler v. Savoy Plaza, Inc., 108 N.Y.S.2d 80).

While we thus conclude that the hotel has an absolute defense to Mrs. Salisbury's suit for the value of her jewelry, we note that even if the relationship involved here were deemed a gratuitous bailment, as Mrs.

Salisbury contends it should be, the hotel's liability would be limited to the value of articles ordinarily found in a cosmetics case, even if Mrs. Salisbury could establish that the hotel was grossly negligent in caring for her case (Stephens v. Katz Parking System, 348 N.Y.S.2d 492, 495 1973). Even under her own view of the law, Mrs. Salisbury could not recover the value of her lost jewelry.

Ruling of the Court: Since the most that could be recovered in this action is $100, it is evident that the amount in controversy does not exceed $10,000, and therefore federal subject matter jurisdiction is lacking. Accordingly, the defendant's motion for summary judgment dismissing the complaint is granted, and the plaintiff's cross-motion for summary judgment is denied.

It is so ordered.

Property of Guests Left for Storage

Guests sometimes do not take along all their property when they leave the hotel. In Dajkovich v. Hotel Waldorf Astoria Corporation, 137 N.Y.S.2d 764 (1955), the guests left their goods (at least fifteen suitcases) and did not return for seven years because of World War II. In the interim, the hotel sold the goods under the assumption that the sale of the property after six months was covered under Section 207 of the General Business Law. The hotel subsequently claimed the limiting liability statute for $100 under Section 201 of the General Business Law. The majority of the court did not accept this, and the hotel had to reimburse the total value of the sold property.

A dissenting opinion in the case held that because the plaintiff had not returned to claim her luggage for some seven years, the hotel could legally sell the baggage as allowed by Section 207 of the General Business Law. Nevertheless, there was evidence that when the plaintiff's friends had offered to remove her baggage a year prior to its sale, the hotel clerk had assured them it would be safe in the hotel. Although a dissenting opinion has no merit as to the holding of the court, it is significant here to show that the hotel had been notified one year prior to the action taken.

Property of Sales Representatives

Even in the common law days, the law concerning an innkeeper's duties and liability relative to a traveler's personal property recognized a distinction between personal property brought into a hotel for personal use by the traveler and the personal property brought into the hotel for commercial purposes. The common law insurer's liability imposed on the innkeeper ran only to articles brought into the hotel for the guest's personal use and convenience as a traveler and not to merchandise brought into the hotel for the purpose of doing commerce. The reasoning behind this position is that the degree of the exposure to liability that innkeepers are held to assume should be applicable only to that which they can reasonably assume travelers would have in their possession as travelers and not for what they might have in their possession for the purposes of setting up a commercial business in their room.

Mr. Justice Harlan wrote the majority opinion in the case of Fisher v. Kelsey, 121 U.S. 383 (1887). He put the status of the salesman for recovery and theft of his samples in this way:

> Although Fisher was received by the defendants into their hotel as a guest, with knowledge that his trunks contained articles having no connection with his comfort or convenience as a mere traveler or wayfarer, but which, at his request, were to be placed on exhibition or for sale in a room assigned to him for that purpose, they would not, under the doctrines at common law, be held to the same degree of care and responsibility, in respect to the safety of such articles, as is required in reference to baggage or other personal property carried by travelers. He was entitled, as a traveler, to room for lodging, but he could not of right demand to be supplied with apartments in which to conduct his business as salesman or merchant. The defendants, being owners or managers of the hotel, were at liberty to permit the use of one of the rooms by Fisher for such business purposes, but they would not, for that reason and without other circumstances, be held to have the goods in their custody, or to have undertaken to hold and safely keep them as constituting part of the property that he had with him in his capacity as a guest. Kent says that, "if a guest applies for a room in an inn for a purpose of business distinct from his accommodation as a guest, the particular responsibility does not extend to goods lost or stolen from that room."

This reasoning was carried into most limiting liability statutes. With this in mind, let us analyze some of the cases dealing with sales representatives' samples and the innkeeper's liability toward the guest whose commercial personalty is stolen. The first case is Hanover Insurance Company v. Alamo Motel, 264 N.W.2d 774 (Iowa, 1978), in which a person insured by the plaintiff had been a guest at the defendant hotel and had been robbed there of jewelry valued at $89,628. The guest was a jewelry company salesman. The company filed a claim with the plaintiff and was paid $50,000. The plaintiff became subrogated—that is, whereby one person is substituted for another in claiming a lawful right or debt—to any rights that the jewelry company may have had against the defendant hotel as the result of the loss and brought action against the hotel seeking to recover the value of the jewelry.

Iowa had a limiting liability statute in effect at the time of the loss, which the plaintiff claimed was inapplicable to this case. The lower court found for the defendant, and the plaintiff appealed. The appellate court concluded the opposite: that the limiting liability statute was indeed applicable. However, it reversed the lower court's decision and remanded the case back, holding that the limiting liability statute was an affirmative defense and must be pleaded as such. An affirmative defense introduces new matters that even if the plaintiff's contentions are true, constitute a defense to the complaint. An affirmative defense goes beyond the mere denial of the plaintiff. The limiting liability statute imposes upon the defendant the burden of affirmatively pleading the statute as a defense and further pleading that he had complied with all of the requisite conditions imposed upon an innkeeper before the statute would become effective. Failure to so plead the statute and compliance with it denied the innkeeper the protections the statute was calculated to give.

This case shows that the mere existence of the statute on the books does not give hoteliers protection. Hoteliers must comply with it in order to give rise to its benefits. Furthermore, a hotelier who plans a defense based on the statute must raise this defense in the pleadings and set forth that they have complied with the obligations it imposes.

Another significant question was raised in the opinion. The judge avoided deciding it, and properly so because it was not before him for determination. That question was: If the statute, which treats guests of various kinds differently, were held to be operative, would hoteliers run afoul of certain constitutional doctrines because it denied the guest equal protection of the law?

Another case, Associated Mills, Inc., v. Drake Hotel, Inc., 334 N.E.2d 746 (Ill., 1975), shows that the limiting liability statute will be rigidly applied. A guest can avoid its limitations only by strict adherence to any prerequisites that would create an exception. The plaintiff sought to recover $87,000 in damages from the hotel as a result of the disappearance of a prototype working model that had been manufactured by the plaintiff and was being used by it in a sales program to demonstrate the benefits offered by the finished product. The plaintiffs also claimed that because the model was the only one in existence, they lost sales, to their financial detriment. The plaintiffs alleged that the hotel, through its agents, had orally agreed to plug and seal the room where the model was being displayed and thereby prevent overnight entry into the room and removal of the model. The hotel had also agreed that they would order the hotel personnel not to enter and clean the room during the night. The next morning, the plaintiff discovered that the room had not been plugged and sealed or locked, that it had been cleaned, and that the model was missing.

A limiting liability statute in effect in Illinois at the time said:

No hotel or the proprietor or manager thereof is liable for the loss of or the damage to any merchandise samples or other merchandise for sale brought into a hotel by a guest or other owner thereof, regardless of whether such loss or damage is occasioned by theft, the fault or negligence of such proprietor or manager or his agents or employees, or otherwise unless the guest or other owner had given written notice of the bringing of such merchandise into the hotel and of the value thereof, and the receipt of such notice has been acknowledged in writing by the proprietor or manager prior to or at the time such merchandise is brought into the hotel by such guest or other owner. Where such notice is given and acknowledged as provided in this section, neither the proprietor or manager thereof is liable for loss or damage to any such merchandise samples or merchandise for sale in any sum exceeding $250, regardless of whether such loss or damage is occasioned by theft, the fault or negligence of such proprietor or manager or his agents or employees, or otherwise, unless the manager or proprietor of such hotel has contracted by separate agreement in writing to assume a greater liability.

The plaintiff claimed that the defendant was liable because he had breached the agreement he had made with him. The defendant said that the plaintiff's claim must fail because the working model constituted a merchandise sample within the meaning of the statute and that the plaintiff had not met the notice and acknowledgement requirements. Even if he had, the recovery would be limited to $250. The defendants admitted making an oral agreement with the plaintiff, but the only way the hotel could be held liable for a sum greater than the $250 is if there had been a separate written contract with the hotel in which it assumed a greater liability than that imposed by the statute. The court agreed with the defendant.

Pacific Diamond Co., Inc., v. Hilton Hotels Corporation, 149 Cal.Rptr., 813 (1978), deals with the theft of a salesman's samples. The salesman, a guest of the hotel, was beaten and robbed of $150,000 worth of diamonds a few minutes before leaving the hotel. He had just arrived from business meetings, went up to his room to pack, and kept the diamonds with him during this time.

The question raised in this case involved the concept of a "coming and going" exception to the limiting liability statutes. Should there be a period of time during which guests are checking in and out of the hotel that the statute does not apply, during which the guests would have an opportunity to avail themselves of the safe and to pack valuables at the end of their stay?

The court recognized that there was a case that by implication seemed to hold that there is such an exception. However, the facts warranting the application of such an exception are absent here in that the salesman had plenty of time to deposit the diamonds in the safe before he went up to his room to pack and to retrieve the jewels as he was leaving.

Waiver of Limiting Liability

When a hotel management allows its employees to substitute their own reasonable rules for provisions of state statutes, many ambiguities result. Such substitutions in states that allow them must be done with legal advice, as the following section shows.

The case of Fuchs v. Harbor Island Spa, Inc., could probably have been dealt with by proving lack of notice to the guest, as required by statute; but the court chose an alternative course. Because the hotel had instituted its own requirements (reasonable rules) that were at odds with the state requirements, it could not claim as a defense the fact that this procedure had been in effect for some time.

As demonstrated previously in Brewer v. Roosevelt Motor Lodge, 295 A.2d 647 (Me., 1972), Maine is one of the few states that allows recovery for missing property, even if the hotel does not give notice as required by law. Carried to its logical conclusion, this could make hotelkeepers and their employees careless in their protection of a guest's property. A more sensible rule is enunciated in Judge Tuttle's decision in the *Fuchs* case that states that if the hotel does not follow the procedure of the statute, it waives its right to avoid liability on the basis of noncompliance.

Case Example   **Fuchs v. Harbor Island Spa, Inc.**
420 F.2d 1100 (Fla., 1970)
(TUTTLE, Circuit Judge)

This is an appeal from a judgment in a jury-waived suit for recovery of the value of jewelry that was stolen from the safety-deposit boxes of the defendant hotel. At issue is the question whether a guest who complies strictly with the procedures set up by the hotel itself is denied recovery because neither the hotel nor the guest made an effort to comply strictly with the provisions of Florida Statute 509.111, F.S.A. ["The proprietor . . . of a hotel . . . *shall in no event, be liable* or responsible for any loss of any monies, securities, jewelry or precious stones of any kind whatever . . . *unless the owner thereof shall make a special deposit of said property and take a receipt in writing therefor* from the proprietor . . . which receipt shall set forth the value of said property. . . ." (emphasis added)] The question is complicated in this case by reason of the fact that the hotel management, without regard to the provisions of the statute offered the use of the safety-deposit boxes to the guests and by the further fact that upon registering, the guest was presented with a registration card that read: "Money, jewels, and other valuable packages must be deposited at the office to be kept in the safe, *otherwise, the management will not be responsible for any loss.*"

The plaintiff below also contended that the hotel company could not rely upon the protection afforded by the statute because the required notice was not posted within view from the registration desk or anywhere else in the office, hall, or lobby, despite a requirement to that effect as contained in Section 509.101, Florida Statutes, F.S.A.

There is ample evidence to support the following statement of the factual situation that brought about the judgment of the trial court.

The plaintiffs were paying guests at defendant's hotel on or about March 31, 1966. The registration card presented to each plaintiff and used by them for registration purposes bore a prominent notation, to wit: "Money, jewels and other valuable packages must be checked at the office to be kept in the safe, otherwise the management will not be responsible for any loss." The safe-deposit boxes were built and maintained by the hotel in an alcove off the main lobby for the use of paying guests. A guest who desired the use of a safe-deposit box was given a card at the registration desk by defendant's employee. The card form had space allotted only for (1) guest's name and address; (2) the dates; (3) the guest's room number; (4) signature specimens of those authorized access to the safe-deposit box and the safe-deposit box number. The guests, either at the registration desk or in the "safe-deposit box room" would deposit items in the safe-deposit box and return it to the hotel employee for safekeeping. Two keys were required to open the box. The guest kept one key, the hotel kept the other. Thereafter, when the guest desired access to the box, he entered the "safe-deposit box room" that was adjacent to the registration desk, produced his key and requested the box from the attendant. Each plaintiff requested the use of a safe-deposit box and each received one in the described manner.

The defendant did not give actual notice to any plaintiff of the requirements of the Florida statute as contained in Section 509.111, . . . nor that its procedure for depositing valuables was different than that prescribed by the statute in order to make the defendant liable for a loss of deposited property occasioned other than by the hotel's own negligence. At no time did the defendant ever advise any plaintiff of any procedure for depositing money or jewelry other than the use of safe-deposit boxes, nor was any other procedure routinely used. Upon handing the safe-deposit box and its contents to the defendant for safekeeping, no receipt was offered by the defendant to the guest for his signature, and the defendant did not inquire about the value of the contents. Upon handing the safe-deposit box and its contents to the hotel personnel for safekeeping, no plaintiff either asked for a receipt or advised defendant of the value of the contents. Under its safekeeping procedure, defendant had no knowledge of the nature or value of property deposited or withdrawn by plaintiffs. Defendant made no attempt to ascertain the nature of the value of the property at any time.

The posted notice of the provisions of the Florida statute, Section 509.111, F.S.A., was a form furnished by the Florida Hotel and Restaurant Commission. The notice set out Section 509.111 in abridged form. A copy was posted *inside a closet* in each guest room, and on one wall of the "safe-deposit box room." This was a separate room from the lobby of the hotel.

A robbery occurred at the hotel during early morning hours of March 31, 1966, during which the safe-deposit boxes broken into included those safe-deposit boxes that the plaintiffs were using. The contents of the plaintiffs' safe-deposit boxes were taken by the thieves and have not been recovered or returned.

There was not, as there could not be, of course, under the circumstances, much dispute as to the contents of the boxes. Judgment was entered for various amounts in favor of the several plaintiffs. The trial court entered judgments in the amounts of $65,257 and $151,261.72, respectively, in favor of the plaintiff Fuchs and the Federal Insurance Company as subrogee of other guests from whom it had received assignments of their claims upon settling the claims with the insureds.

The recitation of facts, all of which were stipulated, presents such a clear case crying out for affirmance of the judgment of the trial court on the equities that we are not surprised to learn that the highest Florida court to which we can look to determine "the way [in which] the Erie winds blow," Delduca v. United States Fidelity & Guaranty Co., 357 F.2d 204, 206 (5 Cir., 1966), supports this appealing method of disposition of the case. Just as did the trial court, we place our judgment of affirmance on the case of Safety Harbour Spa, Inc. v. High, 137 So.2d 248 (Fla.App.,1962), for, as all know, in this diversity action we must seek to determine the Florida law with respect to the interpretation and application of this Florida statute. . . .

The equitable principles which are here so appealing both to the trial court and to us were equally appealing to the Florida Court of Appeals when it made it plain (*Safety Harbour, Inc.*) that where a hotel adopted a procedure in dealing with the valuables of its guests different from that provided for in the Florida statute, designed to protect innkeepers from the claims if they followed the procedures set out in the statute, the innkeepers' law was not such a matter of public policy that the court should hold that it could not be waived by the innkeeper, the person for whose benefit the protection was afforded by statute.

Here, if it had been the purpose of the hotel to lull a guest into a sense of false security with respect to protecting his valuables, no better means to that end can be devised than that adopted at the registration desk. As we have pointed out above, when he registered, the guest had presented to him a registration card that had the legend: "Money, jewels, and other valuable packages must be deposited at the office to be kept in the safe, otherwise the management will not be responsible for any loss." By clearest implication this said, "If money, jewels, and other valuable packages are deposited at the office to be kept in the safe, management *will* be responsible for any loss." This is precisely what the plaintiffs here did. They requested a safe-deposit box at the desk, obtained a key, and deposited their valuables in the box. Neither the clerk at the desk, nor anything handed to the guests, nor any sign within view of the desk warned the guest that he had the obligation to request from the clerk a receipt on which he would indicate the value of the jewelry or other valuables and make a "special deposit," whatever that means, of the valuables in order to be able to hold the hotel responsible if the valuables were stolen or otherwise lost. To be sure, there was an abbreviated notice of the provisions of Florida statute posted in the "safe-deposit box room," and inside the closet in the bedrooms there was also posted this excerpt. The trial court found it unnecessary to determine whether this was a compliance with the requirements of the statute itself, although the court did hold that this provision must be read as a part of the exculpatory provisions contained in Section 509.111. . . .

Now, turning to the critical Florida decision, we find that the interpretation placed on it by the appellant is totally incorrect. It takes the position that the only issue passed upon by the Florida courts was the amount of the loss. This, in spite of the fact that the court described a procedure for the handling of valuables of guests that was inconsistent with the requirements of the statute, and in spite of the fact that the court concluded its opinion, brief though it was, by saying, "the testimony below showed the method that the hotel had been using for several years in accepting the deposits of its guests for safekeeping. We are of the opinion that since the hotel *did not require a strict compliance with the statute*, they cannot avoid liability on this ground" (emphasis supplied).

This is precisely the basis upon which the trial court found that the hotel could not prevail on its defense. The court said:

"Defendant may not avoid liability under Section 509.111, Florida Statutes, since it instituted a procedure for depositing valuables that did not require strict compliance with the statute. . . .

"The hotel registration form warns guests that valuables must be placed in hotel safe-deposit boxes, "otherwise the management will not be responsible for any loss." Guests must follow the hotel's procedure to store valuables in a hotel safe-deposit [300] box, and are never given actual notice that the hotel does not intend to insure safekeeping. A guest making a deposit might reasonably conclude that the hotel had assumed responsibility for safekeeping for property notwithstanding Section 509.111. When both hotel and guest are charged with knowledge of the statute, the court will not speculate whether the hotel purposely circumvented compliance with Section 509.111, or the guest knowingly forewent the protection that accompanies compliance. Here, as in *Safety Harbour, Inc.*, the hotel instituted a deposit procedure that when followed, failed to produce a Section 509.111 deposit. The hotel thereby waived its right to avoid liability on the basis of noncompliance."

With this reasoning we concur completely and find it to be entirely consistent with the Florida law.

Ruling of the Court: The judgments are affirmed for plaintiff.

Hotels can voluntarily waive the limitations provided by the statute. Most statutes expressly state that the hotel and the guest can enter into a written agreement that will impose liability on the hotel for the full value or any portion thereof that the parties agree upon. If according to a statutory requirement, such an agreement must be in writing, an oral agreement is ineffective, and the statutory limitation will be imposed.

The limitation can be held inoperable in other ways. Hoteliers or their agents may do something that results in the imposition of a legal prohibition against their being able to take advantage of the statute's limitations. This is known as the *doctrine of equitable estoppel*. Equitable estoppel is a principle whereby a person whose conduct has induced someone to act in reliance on it cannot later take a position that is inconsistent with the conduct. Let us say that I induce you to do something, and acting in reliance on my inducement, you do that, and you are harmed as a result. Thereafter, I am estopped (prohibited) from asserting that I should not be liable to you for your damages.

The necessity for written waivers and what constitutes equitable estoppel are discussed in the case of Mitsuya v. Croydon Management Company, 448 F.Supp. 811 (N.Y., 1978). In that case, the desk clerk at the defendant hotel approached the plaintiff, a guest at the hotel, and commented upon her jewelry. He told her that the hotel maintained safe-deposit boxes that she could use free of charge to keep her valuables for safekeeping, and he further informed her of the limiting liability statute. Before this, the plaintiff had been unaware either of the existence of safe-deposit boxes in the hotel or of the limiting liability statutes. As a direct result of the desk clerk's intervention, the plaintiff delivered her jewelry to the hotel for deposit in the boxes. While in the possession of the hotel, the jewelry disappeared, and the plaintiff brought an action to recover for its full value.

Mitsuya claimed that the desk clerk had orally modified the terms of the statute and that she had incurred the loss because she had put the jewelry into the safe-deposit boxes, relying on the desk clerk's representation. She claimed that her loss was the result of such reliance, which was suggested by the hotel's agent; therefore, the hotel in equity must be estopped from asserting the statutory liability limitation. In effect the plaintiff was saying, "You can't use the statute against me if I did what you told me to do."

The court refused to accept either of the plaintiff's arguments and held that the limiting liability statute was applicable. It reasoned that the statute by its terms mandated that any modification, waiver, or alteration of the limitations of liability provided for in the statute had to be in writing. As to the plaintiff's allegations that the desk clerk had orally induced her to deposit the jewelry, the court said that under the proper factual conditions, the defendant hotel could be equitably estopped from pleading and availing itself of the limiting liability statute. However, this was not such a case. The clerk in this instance merely told the plaintiff exactly what the law was. He told her about depositing the jewelry and that it was subject to a limitation. This constituted no more than informing her of what she would have read on the posted notices. The court did say that the circumstances would have been different if the desk clerk had told the plaintiff that there was no limit on liability if the jewels were deposited.

Liability for a Guest's Automobile

The automobile, in which over 85 percent of travelers arrive at a hotel, is not considered a "valuable" or "personal property" of the guest. That is not to say that cars are not valuable, but a car is treated differently from other types of goods.

The courts of the various states do not agree on the type of relationship that exists when a car is parked in a hotel parking lot or in the building itself. Problems arise when a guest's parked car is damaged or stolen while the guest is in the hotel or restaurant. A further complication has to do with valuables left in the car.

Perhaps the best way to approach the problem is to determine who has the title—that is, control over the car or property. To simplify the law, the real titleholder is the *bailor*, and the person having control over the automobile for a finite length of time is the *bailee*.

Who, then, is liable when a guest's car parked at a hotel is damaged or stolen, or property is stolen from the car? Determining liability is clouded by the question of what the law considers as part of a hotel or restaurant. The doctrine of *infra hospitium*, a legal concept that originated in the early days of innkeeping mainly for the protection of the guest, deals with this question.

Doctrine of *Infra Hospitium*

Infra hospitium ("within the walls of the inn") is a legal concept that holds hotels answerable for the loss of guests' goods when the guests are not within the hotel proper. This doctrine, however, does allow some leeway for hoteliers. They have the power to (1) select the area they intend to use as an extension of their place of business; (2) control the area; (3) charge a fee for the service commensurate with the degree of care and security required; and (4) make arrangements with other businesses or subcontractors about which the guest need know nothing.

The basic question is whether a hotel should be liable for a guest's property when the loss occurs somewhere outside the hotel proper—in such varied locales as a parking lot, skiing area, lake, tennis court, golf course, or stables—that is, where guests are under the impression they are still in part of the hotel. The problem is similar when a guest has an accident in such a place (see chapter 10).

In large cities where space is at a premium, many hotels must park the guest's car at some distance from the hotel. Is the car considered to be within the hotel (*infra hospitium*) when in reality it is ten blocks away from the hotel?

Infra hospitium is a general doctrine, but familiarity with it can lead to management principles that prevent damage to or loss of a guest's car. State differences and the nature of the guest-innkeeper relationship can materially affect the results of a case.

Guest, Hotel, and Car Relationships

Three possible relationships can occur when a guest's car is left at a hotel: (1) innkeeper-guest; (2) bailor-bailee; and (3) lessor-lessee. Each of these relationships creates different liabilities. But, as a general rule, the hotelkeeper can be held responsible for the loss of the guest's automobile if either the first or second relationship exists. Of course, the monetary consequences may vary. In the third relationship, the hotel will generally have no liability in the absence of certain conditions (discussed later).

Innkeeper-Guest Relationship

Under the innkeeper-guest relationship, the court subscribes to the doctrine of *infra hospitium*. Under this doctrine, the goods of a guest need not always be within the walls of the inn to render the innkeeper liable. It is sufficient if the goods are placed by the hotel or by its agents in a certain place.

In the case of Merchants Fire Assurance Corporation v. Zion's Securities Corporation, 163 P.2d 319 (Utah, 1945), the court found that when a guest, upon the instructions of the hotel clerk, left his car on the "loading platform" in front of the hotel, it was tantamount to the innkeeper's placing it there himself.

Joseph Beale, in *The Law of Innkeepers and Hotels*, states the rule as follows: "If the innkeeper, himself, without the direction of the guest puts property of the guest that has been given to him, in a place outside the inn, or even entirely separate from it, the innkeeper is liable for it."[4] Again, in *Merchants Fire Assurance Corporation,* the defendant hotelkeeper argued that the keys were never delivered to the room clerk by the guest. The court stated that the plaintiff told the bellboy where the keys were and that this was the same as if she had handed the keys to the clerk or the employee of the hotel who was authorized to take care of the car. "We therefore hold that when the keys to the car came into possession of the bellboy, the car was in the care and under the charge of the hotel, and it became liable for its loss or damage while it was thus in its custody."

When the court holds that there is an innkeeper-guest relationship, the hotel is the *insurer* of the guest's car and contents. The case of Governor House v. Schmidt, 284 A.2d 660 (D.C., 1971), deals with this situation. Here, the guest's car was considered as being *infra hospitium* (in the hotel's basement garage, which was accessible only through the hotel lobby or by way of a ramp). The hotel absorbed all costs of parking in the garage, even though the garage was managed by a separate entity and was itemized as such on the hotel bill. Regardless, the hotel was the insurer of the guest's car and contents. Unless there is a specific statute limiting reimbursement for loss of the guest's goods, the hotel will have to pay the entire cost of a car and its contents.

The court in the *Governor House* case made note that where the doctrine of *infra hospitium* was properly applied, it was irrelevant that the hotel was not on notice as to the contents of the automobile left in its custody.

Bailment

A bailment is a contract by which one transfers the possession of one's personal property to another, with the understanding that it is to be held for a certain lawful purpose and that it will be returned to the owner after that purpose has been accomplished. The person holding title to the property is the *bailor*, and the person receiving possession or custody of the personal property (chattel) is the *bailee*. During the bailee's possession of and control over the bailed goods, he can exclude possession by other persons, including the bailor in some cases.

Not all transactions dealing with title and possession are bailments. The elements essential to a bailment are: (1) the title to the property, or a superior right of possession must be with the bailor; (2) the bailee must have lawful possession without title; and (3) the bailee must owe a duty to return the property to the bailor or disperse of it as directed by him. Bailment is a common transaction that exists even if the parties to the transaction are not aware of it.

---

4 Joseph Beale, *The Law of Innkeepers and Hotels* (Boston: William Nagle Book Co., 1906), Section 154.

Lending a lawn mower to a neighbor is a bailment. Rentals of personal property and the pledging of personal property as security for a loan involve bailments. When people find a lost article and take it into their possession, a bailment is implied. (This important aspect of bailment will be discussed later in this chapter under the topic of lost, mislaid, and abandoned property.)

Bailments may be classified as (1) gratuitous, in which one of the parties to the bailment receives no compensation or consideration for the promise; (2) mutual-benefit, in which both parties receive benefits from the relationship, and (3) exceptional or extraordinary, in which special rights are granted to one of the parties (see Table 11–1).

Gratuitous Bailment

Many bailments come about with very little thought of their consequences. Gratuitous bailments are of two kinds: those for the sole benefit of the bailor and those for the sole benefit of the bailee. In gratuitous bailments, a person is not required to accept goods in bailment, even though he promised to do so, since there is no consideration for his promise.

A bailment for the sole benefit of the bailor exists when the bailee agrees to keep, repair, or transport without charge the personal property delivered to him. The following examples of a bailment for the benefit of the bailor will clarify the duties and liabilities of the bailee.

Mary, who worked for John in the kitchen as a cook, asked John to keep her watch until her shift was over. John had to leave unexpectedly and put Mary's watch in his locker, forgetting to lock it. The watch was missing when John returned. Is John liable for the watch? Even though this was a gratuitous bailment (John received no pay for his service), he should have exercised at least some care over the watch. In fact, John was grossly negligent concerning his accepted trust.

In another sample bailment, Henry, who was in a hurry to get to work, asked his friend John if he could leave his car with him. John

Table 11–1.   Duties and Liabilities in a Bailment

	If Bailment for	Must Exercise	Liable for
Gratuitous bailments	Sole benefit of bailor	Slight diligence	Gross negligence
Gratuitous bailments	Sole benefit of bailee	High diligence	Slight negligence
Mutual-benefit bailments	Benefit of both bailor and bailee	Ordinary diligence	Ordinary negligence
Exceptional or extraordinary bailments	Benefit of bailee	High diligence	Slight negligence

consented and parked the car in his driveway. While John was shopping, Henry's car was stolen. Is John again liable to his friend? In this case John was not liable because bringing the car from the street to the yard constituted a reasonable amount of care for the bailment.

A further important point in a bailment for the sole benefit of the bailor is that if the bailee incurs expenses while caring for the personal property, the bailor must reimburse the bailee.

If the bailor lends property to the bailee and receives no consideration for its use, the result is a gratuitous bailment solely for the benefit of the bailee. Examples are borrowing a book, camera, or a friend's car. In this type of bailment, the bailee is required to take great care of the property lent to him because the bailment is solely for his own benefit. The bailed property must be used only for the stipulated purposes set forth by the bailor, and the bailee must pay for all ordinary expenses of upkeep and protection of the property and must return the property to the bailor when the bailment is at an end.

In an example of such a bailment, John borrowed the hotel's truck and trailer to haul his boat to a launching ramp. While on the road, John became involved in an accident resulting from his own carelessness. Because the bailment was for the sole benefit of John (the bailee), he owed great and extraordinary care in the use of the truck and trailer and would be liable for negligence. The care referred to here is a higher degree of care than a prudent person ordinarily exercises in connection with his or her own property.

Mutual-Benefit Bailments

A bailment is for the mutual benefit of both parties when each party receives some benefit or consideration from the agreement. An example of a mutual-benefit bailment is when one person rents personal property from another, as in the case of a car rental.

In a mutual-benefit bailment, each party to the contract agrees to certain duties. The bailor agrees not to interfere with the bailee's possession or use of the article during the agreed length of time. The bailor must also warn the bailee of any defects in the bailed property that might result in injury to the bailee or might interfere with the use of the article.

For example, Jerry rented an automobile for one day. While he was driving the car, the steering gear broke, causing an accident in which he was injured. Jerry had not been warned by the bailor that the steering gear was defective, and he sued for injuries. The bailor answered that he did not know of the defect when Jerry rented the car. In this type of case, the bailor is responsible for any loss or injury suffered by the bailee. The bailor's claim that he did not know of the defect does not affect his liability for the bailee's injuries.

On the other hand, the bailee is required to take ordinary care of the property. He is not liable for loss or damages caused by an act of God or the willful act of a third party. Under a mutual-benefit bailment, the bailee agrees to use the bailed property as set forth by the contract or only for the purposes permitted by the bailor.

In this type of bailment, the bailee may place a lien on the goods in his possession until he is paid for his services. This lien on the bailed property is only for services rendered and only for as long as the bailee retains possession of the property. This is usually referred to as a *possessory lien*. When the bailee gives up the goods, his right to the lien terminates and subsequent service does not reestablish the original lien. One further important point is that if the bailment provides for credit rather than cash payment, the bailor must have his goods returned to him on demand as the bailee then has no right of a lien.

Exceptional Bailments

Exceptional bailment belongs to a *nongratuitous class*—that is, with payment and consideration. Because of its exceptional character, the law requires more than ordinary duties of the bailee and a much greater degree of diligence. Bailees in this class of bailment include postmasters, innkeepers, and common carriers.

Innkeepers are classified as exceptional because of their relation to the public and their guests. They depend on the public for support and, in turn, guarantee their guests care and protection. Because of this submission of guests to their care and the placement of baggage and personal effects in their control, the law has determined that their liability should be more than that of an ordinary bailee; it should be in the nature of an insurer.

The case of *Kula v. Karat, Inc.*, which occurred in a hotel with a gambling casino, shows that an innkeeper's bailment for a guest's goods is an exceptional bailment. Here, the guest deposited $18,000 in the hotel safe; his partner subsequently withdrew and gambled away the entire amount. The fraud statute in this case is relevant as there must be an agreement in writing that a guest will be responsible for the gambling debts of another. Therefore, a supposed oral permission did not relieve the hotel of its responsibility. The guest received his $17,000, and the casino had to return $17,000 to the hotel.

Case	Kula v. Karat, Inc.
Example	*531 P.2d 1353 (Nev., 1975)*
	(BATJER, Justice)

The appellant (the plaintiff-guest) and his companion, referred to in the record only as Goldfinger, were guests in the respondent's Stardust Hotel in Las Vegas, Nevada (the defendant-hotelkeeper). Appellant availed himself of the hotel's service for the safekeeping of valuables and money and deposited $18,300 with a cashier in the casino. This deposit was made solely in appellant's name; he was given a receipt for the amount of the deposit and advised that he might withdraw funds from the cashier by signing for them, and that the money could be withdrawn only upon his signature.

During the next two days, appellant and Goldfinger gambled in the respondent's casino. There was testimony that they gambled from the same funds and freely exchanged chips to make bets. During that period, appellant made withdrawal as well as deposit transactions with the cashier.

On the evening of June 7, 1969, there was $18,000 on deposit with the cashier before Goldfinger lost $500 and was without funds to cover the loss. He asked Philip Ponto, respondent's shift boss, to telephone appellant for a guarantee of the loss. Ponto called appellant. The text of that telephone conversation is in dispute. Appellant testified that he authorized Ponto to give Goldfinger credit to the extent of $1,000, but no more. Ponto's testimony confirms the $1,000 authorization and relates that he specifically asked appellant if Goldfinger could gamble against the entire safekeeping deposit and received an affirmative response.

In any event, Goldfinger was permitted to gamble with chips procured by signing "markers" totaling $18,000. When Goldfinger stopped gambling, the shift boss requested the safekeeping receipt that he needed to send to the cashier's cage with the "markers." It is alleged that Goldfinger agreed to go to the room and get it, but instead he disappeared.

That morning appellant went to the cashier's cage and made a demand for the $18,000. When informed of the actual credit extended to Goldfinger, he acknowledged the $1,000 authorization and demanded $17,000, which is the amount prayed for in his complaint.

The trial court properly found a bailment had been created by the deposit of the money with respondent. A bailment of money is as well recognized as the bailment of any other personal property.

Appellant and a witness for respondent both testified that the money could only be withdrawn upon appellant's signature. Appellant steadfastly maintained that the money in safekeeping belonged only to him. Respondent accepted deposits and authorized withdrawals from the safekeeping fund only upon appellant's initials. It recognized ownership in him and refused to allow Goldfinger credit against the fund until approval was obtained from appellant. This evidence of ownership in appellant is not overcome by the testimony from one witness for the respondent that "[H]e [Kula] said he only owned half of it," nor by the fact that appellant and Goldfinger had both made bets from money previously withdrawn from the deposit in safekeeping. Appellant's sharing of chips with Goldfinger is not sufficient to show joint ownership over a deposit of money held by the respondent under a bailment contract made only in appellant's name and subject to withdrawals only upon his signature.

Here the $18,000 was never delivered to Goldfinger, but retained by respondent as its own upon the ground that appellant had orally authorized respondent, through its employees, to permit Goldfinger to gamble against the deposit.

Although the district court, in its oral decision, indicated a possible joint ownership of the money in safekeeping by appellant and Goldfinger, in its findings, it simply concluded that respondent was the bailee of the money placed in safekeeping and that respondent was obligated to use ordinary and reasonable care in its handling. No further conclusion was reached. Nevertheless the district judge found in favor of respondent, and this appeal followed.

The respondent is estopped to claim that Goldfinger had any right, title, or interest in the money on deposit, and it would have been error for the trial court to find any. There is authority for the broad rule that as long as the relationship exists, a bailee may not, in any case, dispute or deny the title of the bailor, or his ultimate right to possession, either by claiming title in himself, or as a justification for his refusal to return the property, or by asserting title in a third person.

Where a bailee, either for hire or gratuitously, is entrusted with care and custody of goods, it becomes his duty at the end of the bailment to return the goods or show that their loss occurred without negligence on his part. Failing in this, there arises a presumption that the goods have been converted by him, or lost as a result of his negligence, and he is accountable to the owner for them.

It is difficult to discern from the record whether or not the trial court, in reaching its decision, relied upon the disputed evidence purporting to show an oral commitment by appellant to be financially responsible for the gambling losses of Goldfinger to the extent of the amount of money in safekeeping. However, if it did, such reliance was in error because NRS 111.220 renders void an agreement to answer for the debts of another that is not in writing.

Since the making of the alleged oral agreement by appellant to be responsible for the gambling debt of Goldfinger has been put into issue through denials in respondent's answer, to which no responsive pleading was required, appellant could avail himself of the benefit of NRS 111.220 without pleading the same. . . .

Although appellant is bound by the admission contained in his pleadings that $1,000 be retained by respondent, . . . he is entitled to recover the $17,000 that was converted.

Ruling of the Court: This matter is reversed and remanded with instructions to enter a judgment in favor of appellant not inconsistent with this opinion.

The Hotelkeeper as a Bailee

A hotelkeeper or anyone else who takes care of another's car assumes a great responsibility. The value of an automobile can range from as low as a few hundred dollars to over $25,000. The hotelkeeper is included as part of the group legally considered as professional bailees. Because of the quasi-public nature of the accommodations industry, hoteliers are not allowed to exculpate (limit by contract their liability) themselves from liability for loss or damage to bailed property as a result of their own negligence.

The case of *Ellerman v. Atlanta American Motor Hotel Corporation* depicts the general rule as it pertains to the hotelkeeper-guest relationship when a bailment is in force. If a statute stipulates what guests can recover for damages or loss of their car, it is controlling, and a hotelkeeper cannot limit liability to an amount less than authorized by that statute.

Case	**Ellerman v. Atlanta American Motor Hotel Corp.**
Example	*191 S.E.2d 295 (Ga., 1972)*
	(BELL, Chief Judge)

Plaintiff, a guest at a motor hotel operated by the defendant, placed his automobile in the defendant's parking facility. He was required by the defendant to leave the ignition key with the defendant's employee, and the latter parked the vehicle in an area unknown to plaintiff. At the time, plaintiff was given a claim check that was admitted in evidence at trial and in which plaintiff in his testimony admitted reading. It provided in part as follows: "Liability. Cars parked at owner's risk. Articles left in car at owner's risk. We reserve privilege of moving car to other section of lot. No attendant after regular closing hours." Prior to delivering the ignition key and the car to the attendant, the plaintiff removed a raincoat from the interior, placed it in the trunk of the car, and kept the trunk key. When plaintiff checked out of the motel, his car was found missing. The car and its contents have never been recovered. The plaintiff's suit sought to recover the value of the items of personalty contained in the trunk that he alleged were allowed to be stolen through the defendant's negligence. Plaintiff had been paid by his insurance company for the loss of the automobile. The trial judge directed a verdict for the defendant.

The fact that plaintiff has settled with his insurance company for the loss of the automobile will not operate to bar the plaintiff from bringing this suit to recover for the items of personalty contained within the trunk on the theory of splitting of the claim. . . .

The rule prohibiting splitting causes of action is for the benefit of the defendant tortfeasor, to protect him from a multiplicity of suits. There is no evidence here showing a judgment, settlement, or pending action against the defendant for the loss of the automobile.

The defendant contends that the depositing of the automobile with the defendant's attendant under these circumstances does not give rise to a bailment relationship because of the disclaimer of liability printed on the claim check given to plaintiff. He relies upon our decision in Brown v. Five Points Parking Center, 121 Ga. App. 819, 175 S.E.2d 901, as controlling. As we view this issue, *Brown* is not in point. *Brown* dealt with an ordinary parking lot. There is no special statute governing that operation. This case involves a parking facility operated by a motel as a part of its service, and this creates the relationship of innkeeper and guest. . . .

It is recognized that an ordinary bailee by contract may limit or completely exculpate himself from any liability for loss or damage to the bailed property as a result of his own simple negligence.

However, an innkeeper is not an "ordinary" bailee. Many courts and texts have described an innkeeper as a "professional" bailee. . . . Unlike an "ordinary" bailee, the "professional" bailee is often precluded from limiting by contract liability for his own negligence as violative of public policy. The reasoning utilized is that the public, in dealing with innkeepers, lacks a practical equality of bargaining power and may be coerced to accede to the contractual conditions sought by the innkeeper or else be denied the needed services. We think that both the principle precluding the limitation of liability and the reasoning underlying it are sound. The general assembly, by Code Section 52-111, authorizing a limitation of liability, has preempted the field on that subject. We are therefore constrained to hold that the legislative preemption cannot be avoided by a special contract and that any such contract purporting to further exculpate the innkeeper is contrary to the public interest and policy and cannot be enforced.

Ruling of the Court: Judgment reversed.

In Dispeker v. The New Southern Hotel Company, 373 S.W.2d 904 (Tenn., 1963), the plaintiff turned his car over to a hotel bellboy to park in the hotel parking lot. After the bellboy went off duty, he returned to the lot and, without authorization, took it out for a joyride, smashing it. Is the hotel liable for the damage he caused? The court held that it was. It said that even though there was no showing of affirmative negligence on the part of the hotel, the hotel was liable just the same. When the car was delivered to the bellboy, a bailment for hire was created between the plaintiff and the hotel. Under the legal obligations that arise as the result of the creation of the relationship of a bailment for hire is an implied promise on the part of the bailee (hotel) to return the property to the bailor (plaintiff) when he requests it and that he will deliver it to no one else. In this instance, the hotel delivered the car to its off-duty employee rather than to the bailor, which the court found an act of misdelivery. The bailee's liability for misdelivery is absolute, regardless of the presence or absence of negligence on the part of the bailee. Therefore, the hotel must reimburse the plaintiff for his loss.

Another aspect of possible liability on the part of the hotel in a situation similar to that presented by the Dispeker case would be whether there had been any negligence on the part of the hotel in hiring the bellboy. If he had had a rather extensive police record and had shown propensities toward the commission of larcenous acts, especially concerning motor vehicles, then there may be liability imposed even in an ordinary bailment claim. The negligence defeating the hotel's claim of no negligence is the failure to redeliver and the hiring of the bellboy.

Goods of Guests Left in Automobiles

Whether the hotel is liable for a guest's personal property that was stolen from the guest's automobile while it was parked in the hotel's parking facility depends upon the factual circumstances in the case. In Brown v. Christopher Inn Co., 344 N.E.2d 140 (Ohio, 1975), the plaintiff, Ms. Brown, had checked into the defendant hotel and had signed the register indicating her occupation to be "antiques." She had driven up in a van filled with antiques that she was going to display in an antique show. The desk clerk gave her a key and directed her to meet a certain porter on the upper level of a parking garage owned by the hotel, which provided parking for hotel guests at no extra charge. The plaintiff did not tell the desk clerk or anyone else in a management position what was in the van. She met the porter and was directed to a place in the garage, but refused to park there, saying that she preferred a space under a light so that the van, which had valuable antiques in it, would be clearly visible. The porter told her not to worry because security guards were on duty. About 11:00 P.M. the plaintiff checked the van to make sure that it was secure. When she checked it the following morning, it had been broken into, and the entire contents were gone.

Brown conceded that there was no evidence of negligence on the part of the defendant, but held that it was liable because the defendant had guaranteed the safety of her valuables and thus became an insurer of them as the result of the statements of the porter. At the conclusion of the evidence, the defendant filed a motion for a directed verdict, saying that the plaintiff had failed to introduce enough evidence to meet the minimal burden of proof required for her to establish a case. The court apparently agreed with the defendant, directing the jury to find for the defendant as a matter of law.

The case of Dumlao v. Atlantic Garage Inc., 259 A.2d 360 (D.C., 1969), involved a situation where the plaintiff checked into a hotel, removed clothing from the back seat of the car, and then delivered the car to an employee of the hotel for parking. He left a few articles of clothing in the back seat and a cigarette lighter in the glove compartment. The plaintiff also said that there was a $1,000 set of drums in the trunk. He had opened the trunk when he was unloading the clothing. The bell captain had observed him removing a cosmetic case, but could not see if there was anything else in the trunk. The bell captain asked if there was any more personal property in the car, but he received no response from the plaintiff. An employee of the defendant garage picked the car up shortly thereafter and took it to the garage for parking, according to an agreement that it had with the hotel. A few days later, when the plaintiff checked out of the hotel, the hotel was unable to deliver his car or its contents, nor could it account for its disappearance. Before the plaintiff had left his car at the hotel, the garage had informed the hotel that it would not be liable for property of guests left in the cars delivered to it that might be stolen or lost. The car was located some time later, but all of the personalty was gone. The plaintiff sued both the hotel and the garage for the loss he sustained, claiming that both were liable to him as bailees.

The jury awarded the plaintiff $143, representing the value of the clothing in the back seat and the cigarette lighter. Those were the only personalties of damage to the plaintiff because the court had directed the jury to bring in a verdict in favor of the hotel as to the items in the trunk. The court also ordered the jury to bring back verdicts in favor of the garage and a verdict in favor of the garage in the cross-claim filed against it by the hotel.

The plaintiff appealed. The appellate court sustained the finding of the lower court. It agreed there had been a bailment between the plaintiff and the hotel as to the car and the contents, which the hotel or its agents were aware of. But the court said that in order to have a bailment, there must be a delivery by the bailor and an acceptance by the bailee of the subject matter of the bailment. Where the subject matter of the bailment is the contents of a car, acceptance of the contents must be based upon either express or imputed knowledge, such as when items are in plain view. Here, there was no evidence to show knowledge of what was in the trunk, and, therefore, there could be no bailment.

As to the hotel's appeal of the two directed verdicts in favor of the defendant garage, the court disposed of them simply. It said that the plaintiff could not establish a claim against the garage because there was no privity (connection between parties as to some particular transactions) between them either by bailment or authorized subbailment. As to the directed verdict in the claim of the hotel against the garage, the court did not have to determine the question of whether there was a bailment because it held that the ordinary terms of a contract for bailment can be altered to limit the liability of the bailee if the bailor had actual notice of those altered terms prior to the delivery of the property. In this case, the hotel had been informed that the garage would not be liable for items left in the cars so that even if there was a bailment in existence between them, the disclaimer was effective, and the jury would have to find for the garage.

The case presents the question of whether an automobile and its contents that were lost or stolen while in the custody of a motel in which the plaintiff was a guest, as well as any personal property left in the car, were subject to the limiting liability statute. The court in the case of Kushner v. President of Atlantic City, Inc., 251 A.2d 480 (N.J., 1969), held that it did. The court said that at common law a traveler's horse and wagon would be covered under the common law absolute liability rule as property that the traveler had brought *infra hospitium causa hospitandi* (such property as the guest has with him for the purposes of his journey and is necessarily incident to travel). The court reasoned that inasmuch as it was the legislature's intention to abolish the common law absolute liability by the enactment of limiting liability statutes, it followed that the limitation was intended to be applicable to anything that was covered by the absolute liability rule. Therefore, the horse and wagon—now transformed into an automobile—that was covered by the common law rule is now subject to the statutory limitation. The New Jersey statute, however, excepts from the operation of the limitations of the statute property whose loss was the result, or the fault, or the negligence of the hotelier. Therefore, although the automobile was subject to the limiting liability statute, its limitation would not be applicable if the loss was due to the defendant's negligence. The court held that its loss was due to the negligence of the hotel. When the car was delivered to the hotel's care, a bailment was created. Bailment law provides that upon showing a delivery of the bailed property to the bailee and a failure on the part of the bailee to redeliver the bailed property, or upon the redelivery of the property in a damaged condition, there arises a presumption of negligence on the part of the bailee for the failure to redeliver or for the damaged condition of the bailed property. This presumption requires the bailee to prove that the loss or damage occurred from a cause other than through its negligence. If it cannot prove that the loss did not result from its negligence, then it should at least prove that it exercised reasonable care in protecting the property. The court held that the defendant failed to rebut the presumption and was liable to the plaintiff.

Other Parking Lot Cases

Numerous cases arise where a car that has been placed in a parking lot is stolen or damaged. What is the responsibility of the parking lot proprietor? This depends on whether there is a bailment, and the test is whether the proprietor takes possession and control of the car or merely rents the space occupied by the car. Applying this test, the Georgia Court of Appeals in Goodyear Clearwater Mills v. Wheeler, 77 Ga. App. 570, 49 S.E.2d 184 (1948), classified parking lot cases into the following three classes:

> In the first class of parking lot cases, where there is a clear delivery of possession to the parking lot proprietor or his agents by virtue of a claim check, and where the parking lot agent retains the keys, drives the car into the lot, parks it, and redelivers it to the customer at the entrance or exit of the lot only upon the presentation of the claim check, the courts have uniformly held the transaction to be a bailment, and the rights and liabilities of the parties have been governed accordingly.

> In the second class of cases, where although a fee is paid, a claim check may be given, and the parking lot may be enclosed, the customer drives his own car into the lot, parks it, locks it or not as he chooses, retains the key, and returns to claim the car himself and drive it away without consulting the parking lot proprietor or attendants. In this group, it is generally held that there is no bailment because the essential elements of delivery and possession are absent.

> In the third class of cases, the manner of conducting the parking lot business is much the same as in the second class with the lot proprietor assuming no possession of the automobiles parked on his lot with the difference that he assumes responsibility by reason of his conduct toward the customer or by virtue of an express agreement. In these cases, although the elements of bailment are absent because of lack of actual physical control and possession of the car itself, the rights, liabilities, and remedies of the parties are much the same as they are in the case of a bailment.

Lessor-Lessee

The great majority of cases in which car owners attempt to recover for damages to or for the loss of their car when left in a parking lot or garage are concerned with whether the car owner's evidence is sufficient to show a contract of bailment between the parties and the legal consequences of that contract, if it exists.

When car owners receive permission to park their car in a lot or garage without assumption of control of the vehicle by the lot operator, the relationship between the parties is that of licensor and licensee. However, if the parking arrangements call for the car owner's exclusive use of a designated space, without any control of the vehicle by the lot operator, the relationship is that of lessor-lessee. This was the situation in the case of *Weinberg v. Wayco Petroleum Company.*

Case Example	Weinberg v. Wayco Petroleum Co.
	402 S.W.2d 597 (Ct. App. Mo. 1966)
	(BRADY, Commissioner)

This was an action by Weinberg (plaintiff) against Wayco Petroleum Company (defendant) for the theft of personal property that occurred while Weinberg's car was parked in Wayco's parking garage. The circuit court awarded Weinberg a $500 judgment. Reversed on appeal.

Weinberg was the holder of a "Parkard" issued by Wayco, for which he paid $10.50 per month, and which entitled him to park his automobile at Wayco's garage located in St. Louis. This garage had five stories and entrance was gained by inserting the "Parkard" into a slot, causing the entrance gate to open. This was a so-called self-park garage and there were no attendants on duty at the time Weinberg parked his automobile at about 11:30 P.M. on September 25, 1962. After securing admission to the garage with the Parkard, Weinberg parked his own car, locked it, and took the keys with him. When he returned to his automobile in the evening of September 27, he found it had been broken into and certain personal property stolen from it. The automobile had not been moved.

The "Parkard" stated: "This card licenses the holder to park one automobile in this area at holder's risk. Lock your car. Licensor hereby declares himself not responsible for fire, theft, or damage to or loss of such automobile or any article left therein. Only a license is granted hereby, and no bailment is created." Weinberg testified that prior to this occurrence he had read this language on the card and knew what it said.

With respect to cases involving automobiles and the contents thereof, when loss occurs after the automobile is left in a parking lot, the relationship between the parties is usually one of bailment or license, and whether it is one or the other depends upon the circumstances of the particular case and especially upon the manner in which the parking lot in question is being operated and with whom control of the allegedly bailed article or articles is vested.

A "bailment" in its ordinary legal sense imports the delivery of personal property by the bailor to the bailee, who keeps the property in trust for a specific purpose, with a contract, express or implied, that the trust shall be faithfully executed, and the property returned or duly accounted for when the special purpose is accomplished or that the property shall be kept until the bailor reclaims it. This court has said that "the term 'bailment' . . . signifies a contract resulting from the delivery of goods by bailor to bailee on condition that they be restored to the bailor, according to his directions, so soon as the purposes for which they were bailed are answered."

It is obvious from the facts in the instant case that there was no delivery to Wayco sufficient to create the relationship of bailee and bailor between the parties here involved. Cases of the nature here involved are to be distinguished from those where the parking operation is such that the attendants collect a fee and assume authority or control of the automobile by parking it and/or retaining the keys so that the car can be moved about to permit the entrance or exit of other automobiles, and where the tickets that are given to the owner of the automobile are issued for the purpose of identifying the automobile for redelivery. In such instances, a bailment relationship is almost invariably held to exist. In the instant case, Wayco never secured control or authority over Weinberg's automobile. No agent or employee of Wayco parked it, or kept the keys to it, or issued any ticket whereby the automobile could be identified by comparison of a portion of the ticket left with the automobile when it was parked. Weinberg parked his own automobile, locked it, and took the keys with him. Certainly Wayco, the alleged bailee, did not have the right under these circumstances to exclude the purposes of the owner or even of anyone else who might have had the keys. In the instant case, Weinberg never made a delivery, actual or constructive, of the automobile to Wayco under circumstances leading to the creation of a bailee-bailor relationship between them.

Ruling of the Court: Judgment reversed on appeal.

Clearly, the states are not guided by any uniform principle concerning parking lot cases; but it is an important area of concern that should have some uniformity. In 1980 Judge Michael L. McCarthy pronounced what we believe are the most logical criteria to judge the liability of a parking lot owner or operator to a person who parks in the lot. In the case of Garlock v. Multiple Parking Services, Inc., 427 N.Y.S.2d 670 (Buffalo City Court, 1980). (It should be noted that this is a city court opinion and is not binding on any other court.)

The plaintiff entered a parking lot operated by the defendant one evening at about 7:30 P.M. He paid the attendant the nominal flat rate of fifty cents and was directed by the attendant to park his car and take his keys with him. The plaintiff returned at about 11:30 and found his car had been burglarized and vandalized. A tape deck and eight tapes had been stolen, and the upholstery had been slashed. The agreed-upon total loss and damage combined was $506. The plaintiff further stated that the attendant appeared to be in an intoxicated condition when he returned, although he did not appear to be so when he arrived. The plaintiff brought suit against the parking lot owner, as well as the parking lot operator, for the damages. The plaintiff filed a motion for summary judgment, as did the defendant. The defendant had filed an answer denying the plaintiff's allegations and further alleged that it did not own the property, merely operated the parking lot, and had a sign posted showing that the lot closed at 9:00 P.M. The lot was not fenced; the attendant did not take possession of the automobiles or their keys; the attendant did not customarily remain after the 9:00 P.M. closing time; and the defendant did not know whether the attendant had remained there until 11:30 the night of the damage and theft. The court noted that the lot was located in a high-crime area. There was no evidence as to when the alleged vandalism occurred.

Judge McCarthy started his written opinion with the observation that the legal history of recovery in this type of a case hinged on the resolution of the question as to whether a bailment has been created. The essence of the *Garlock* case is that Judge McCarthy rejected the no bailment—no liability theory as against public policy in Buffalo. Furthermore, the statute in Buffalo required each commercial parking lot operator to obtain insurance coverage not exceeding $20,000 for fire, theft, and vandalism covering vehicles parked or stored on the licensed premises. He said it was clear from the ordinance that the city fathers intended that those who profit from the storage of vehicles should include risks of loss or damage to the vehicles as a cost of doing business. Thus, parking lot operators would then have to make a decision as to what security to provide based on the rates charged. Judge McCarthy concluded that if the present judicial trend continued, insurance companies would be receiving premiums but not paying out claims.

Thus, the bailment theory as a basis of recovery in parking lot cases is no longer appropriate. Then citing a series of cases that had abolished the distinction between trespasser, licensee, and invitee; abolished the attractive nuisance doctrine; and abolished the invitee doctrine, the judge stated that these cases were seeking to establish a new standard, of "reasonable care under the circumstances whereby foreseeability shall be a measure of liability" (Basso v. Miller, 386 N.Y.S.2d 564 [1976]). Then Judge McCarthy said the same reasoning should apply in the cases where automobiles are left with others. Therefore, it was no longer necessary to dwell on the common law subtleties that had been utilized in determining whether a bailment existed because that kind of reasoning no longer was applicable to determine liability. The question of liability no longer hinged on whether a bailment existed, gratuitous or otherwise. The only question now is whether the defendant exercised reasonable care under the circumstances whereby foreseeability sets the standard of care to be met.

The *Garlock* case presents what can properly be categorized as good law and is an excellent example of judicial reasoning in applying the flexible common law that grows and becomes applicable to the times, the changing circumstances, and the needs of the public.

Liability for a Guest's Property in a Restaurant, Bar, and Cloakroom

Kuchinsky v. Empire Lounge, Inc., illustrates the general rule on loss of coats and similar property—the plaintiff-guest must show failure on the part of the defendant-restaurateur to exercise ordinary care. The same is true in a hotel when a guest leaves her mink jacket in an unattended cloakroom.

Case	**Kuchinsky v. Empire Lounge, Inc.**
Example	*134 N.W.2d 436 (Sup. Ct. Wis., 1965)*
	(CURRIE, Circuit Judge)

This was an action by Kuchinsky (plaintiff) against Empire Lounge (defendant) to recover for the loss of Kuchinsky's coat. The trial court dismissed the complaint and Kuchinsky appealed. Affirmed.

Kuchinsky entered the Empire Lounge as a customer and hung his coat on a clothes tree near his table. His coat was stolen while he ate.

A case very much in point is *Montgomery v. Ladjing.* There the plaintiff entered the restaurant kept by the defendant with a party of friends; he removed his overcoat and hung it on a hook affixed to a post near the table at which he seated himself; the attention of neither the defendant nor of any of his employees was called to the coat in any way; and fifteen minutes later, the coat was missing. The court held that the plaintiff had wholly failed to show failure on the part of the defendant to exercise ordinary care and declared:

"The rule to be deduced from all these cases therefore is that before a restaurant keeper will be held liable for the loss of an overcoat of a customer while such customer takes a meal or refreshments, it must appear either that the overcoat was placed in the physical custody of the keeper of the restaurant or his servants, in which cases there is an actual bailment, or that the overcoat was necessarily laid aside under circumstances showing, at least, notice of the fact and of such necessity to the keeper of the restaurant, or his servants, in which case there is an implied bailment or constructive custody, that the loss occurred by reason of the insufficiency of the general supervision exercised by the keeper of the restaurant for the protection of customers temporarily laid aside."

In *National Fire Insurance Co. v. Commodore Hotel*, the plaintiff was a guest at a luncheon held at the defendant's hotel. She hung her mink jacket in an unattended cloakroom on the main floor across from the lobby desk. After the luncheon and ensuing party, the plaintiff went to the cloakroom to retrieve her jacket and discovered it was gone. The court held that no negligence had been established against the defendant and stated:

". . . In any event, we do not feel that it is incumbent upon a hotel or restaurant owner to keep an attendant in charge of a free cloakroom for luncheon or dinner guests or otherwise face liability for loss of articles placed therein. The maintenance of such rooms without attendants is a common practice, and where the proprietor had not accepted control and custody of articles placed therein, no duty rests upon him to exercise any special degree of care with respect thereto.

"Likewise, failure to post a warning disclaiming responsibility would not seem to constitute negligence when, as here, a guest is aware that a cloakroom is unattended, adjacent to the lobby, and accessible to anyone and has used it under similar circumstances on many prior occasions. The absence of such warning signs does not appear to have been material in a number of decisions absolving proprietors from liability, although when posted they appear to be regarded as an added factor in establishing such nonliability."

Ruling of the Court: Affirmed.

Whether a restaurant is liable to one of its patrons whose coat is stolen from an unattended free cloakroom where the patron had been directed by a waitress to hang his coat after it had fallen off a chair was addressed in the case of Black Beret Lounge and Restaurant v. Meisnere, 336 A.2d 532 (D.C., 1975). Originally, the lower court had found the restaurant liable, even though a notice posted in the cloakroom disclaimed liability. The lower court evidently felt that because the patron had put his coat in the cloakroom at the request of the waitress, there was liability. The appellate court reversed and said there was no liability because there never had been any delivery of the coat into the possession and control of the restaurant so a bailment never was created. The court also said that there must be a change of possession and control in order for a bailment to come into existence. (One wonders whether the result would have been different if the patron, instead of bringing his coat into the cloakroom, had handed it to the waitress to take there. Such action would have constituted change of possession and control.) If a restaurant has a cloakroom attendant on duty to whom the patron's garment is delivered and issues an identifying check as proof of receipt of the garment, a bailment is created, and there would be liability on the part of the restaurant for any garment that is stolen, lost, or damaged. The relationship created would be that of bailor and bailee, and the law concerning that relationship would apply.

Many states have statutes that limit the degree of financial exposure that a restaurant has to the patron. In New York, for example, the restaurateur's maximum liability for a checked item, unless a fee is paid for the service, is $75. Until June 1981, the New York courts had held that the customary tip of thirty-five cents per garment that patrons in a restaurant paid was not a fee for checking the garment, but a gratuity left by the patron on a voluntary basis. In June 1981, the appellate division of the New York State Supreme Court reversed a lower court decision that had awarded a woman $9,578 for a sable coat that had vanished after being checked in a restaurant cloakroom and reduced the damage award to $75, the maximum under the statute. The court said that unless the restaurant exacted a fee and not simply accepted a voluntary tip for the checking service, the statutory limitation would apply (Weinberg v. D–M Restaurant Corporation, 442 N.Y.S.2d 965 [June, 1981]).

The court further held that there was no requirement in the statute that there be notice of the limiting liability law posted. Consequently, the failure of the restaurant to post notice or advise the patron of the existence of the limitation did not prevent the limitation from being applicable.

A different type of case is presented in Shamrock Hilton Hotel v.

Caranas, in which a guest left a purse containing jewelry valued at $13,062 in the restaurant. The purse was later lost through the hotel's negligence. In this case, constructive bailment came about by operation of law. A busboy took the purse to the cashier, and it was later misdelivered, thus placing the restaurant-hotel in a position of being a bailee (mutual bailment) liable for the contents of the purse, even though the restaurant did not know and had no way of knowing the value of the contents. Leaving the purse in the restaurant was not the proximate cause of the loss, but the misdelivery was. The plaintiff-guest won and recovered the total value of her loss.

Case	**Shamrock Hilton Hotel v. Caranas**
Example	*488 S.W.2d 151 (Texas, 1972)*
	(BARRON, Justice)

This is an appeal in an alleged bailment case from a judgment *non obstante veredicto* in favor of plaintiffs below.

Plaintiffs, husband and wife, were lodging as paying guests at the Shamrock Hilton Hotel in Houston on the evening of September 4, 1966, when they took their dinner in the hotel restaurant. After completing the meal, Mr. and Mrs. Caranas, plaintiffs, departed the dining area leaving her purse behind. The purse was found by the hotel busboy who, pursuant to the instructions of the hotel, dutifully delivered the forgotten item to the restaurant cashier, a Mrs. Luster. The testimony indicates that some short time thereafter, the cashier gave the purse to a man other than Mr. Caranas who came to claim it. There is no testimony on the question of whether identification was sought by the cashier. The purse allegedly contained $5.00 in cash, some credit cards, and ten pieces of jewelry said to be worth $13,062. The misplacement of the purse was realized the following morning, at which time plaintiffs notified the hotel authorities of the loss.

Plaintiffs filed suit, alleging negligent delivery of the purse to an unknown person and seeking a recovery for the value of the purse and its contents.

The trial was to a jury that found that the cashier was negligent in delivering the purse to someone other than plaintiffs, and that this negligence was a proximate cause of the loss of the purse. The jury further found that plaintiffs were negligent in leaving the purse containing the jewelry in the hotel dining room, and that this negligence was a proximate cause of the loss.

A motion for judgment *non obstante veredicto* and to disregard findings with respect to the findings that plaintiffs' negligence was a proximate cause of the loss of the purse and its contents was granted, and judgment was entered by the trial court for plaintiffs in the amount of $11,252 plus interest and costs. Shamrock Hilton Hotel and Hilton Hotels Corporation have perfected this appeal.

We find after a full review of the record that there is sufficient evidence to warrant the submission of appellees' issues complained of and to support the jury findings on the special issues to the effect that the misdelivery was negligence and a proximate cause of the loss to appellees.

Article 4592, Vernon's Tex.Rev.Civ.Stat.Ann. (1960), does not apply to limit the hotel's liability to $50 since its proviso declares that the loss must not occur through the negligence of the hotel, and such limiting statute is not applicable under the circumstances of this case.

Contrary to appellants' contention, we find that there was indeed a constructive bailment of the purse. The delivery and acceptance were evidenced in the acts of Mrs. Caranas's unintentionally leaving her purse behind in the hotel restaurant and the busboy, a hotel employee, picking it up and taking it to the cashier, who accepted the purse as a lost or misplaced item. The delivery need not be a knowingly intended act on the part of Mrs. Caranas if it is apparent that were she, the quasi or constructive bailor, aware of the circumstances (here the chattel's being misplaced), she would have desired the person finding the article to have kept it safely for its subsequent return to her.

As stated above, the evidence conclusively showed facts from which there was established a bailment with the Caranases as bailors and the hotel as bailee. The evidence also showed that the hotel, as bailee, had received Mrs. Caranas's purse and had not returned it on demand. Such evidence raised a presumption that the hotel had failed to exercise ordinary care in protecting the appellees' property. When the hotel failed to come forward with any evidence to the effect that it had exercised ordinary care, that the property had been stolen, or that the property had been lost, damaged, or destroyed by fire or by an act of God, the appellees' proof ripened into proof by which the hotel's primary liability was established as a matter of law.

Further, this bailment was one for the mutual benefit of both parties. Appellees were paying guests in the hotel and in its dining room. Appellant hotel's practice of keeping patrons' lost personal items until they could be returned to their rightful owners, as reflected in the testimony, is certainly evidence of its being incidental to its business, as we would think it would be for almost any commercial enterprise that caters to the general public. Though no direct charge is made for this service, there is indirect benefit to be had in the continued patronage of the hotel by customers who have lost chattels and who have been able to claim them from the management.

Having found this to have been a bailment for the mutual benefit of the parties, we hold that the appellants owed the appellees the duty of reasonable care in the return of the purse and jewelry, and the hotel is therefore liable for its ordinary negligence. . . .

Appellants urge that if a bailment is found, it existed only as to "the purse and the usual petty cash or credit cards found therein" and not to the jewelry of which the hotel had no actual notice. This exact question so far as we can determine has never been squarely put before the Texas courts, but as appellants concede, the general rule in other jurisdictions is that a bailee is liable not only for lost property of which he has actual knowledge, but also the property he could reasonably expect to find contained within the bailed property.

We believe appellants' contention raises the question of whether or not it was foreseeable that such jewelry might be found in a woman's purse in a restaurant of a hotel such as the Shamrock Hilton under these circumstances.

Although the burden may rest with the appellees to prove that the jewelry was a part of the total bailment and the issue of whether it was reasonably foreseeable that such jewelry might be contained within the lost purse ordinarily should have been submitted by appellees, it remains for the hotel to object to the omission of the issue if it wishes to avoid the possibility of deemed findings by the court. . . . We cannot say as a matter of law that there is no evidence upon which a jury could reasonably find that it was foreseeable that such jewelry might be found in a purse under such circumstances as here presented. It is known that people who are guests in hotels such as the Shamrock Hilton, a well-known Houston hotel, not infrequently bring such expensive jewelry with them, and it does not impress us as unreasonable under the circumstances that one person might have her jewelry in her purse either awaiting a present occasion to wear it or following reclaiming it from the hotel safe in anticipation of leaving the hotel.

We find that the question of whether it is reasonably foreseeable that a woman, under the circumstances of this case, might keep jewelry in a purse, which is determinative of whether there was a bailment of jewelry and whether the negligence in losing the purse was a proximate cause of losing the jewelry, is an omitted issue in the grounds of recovery to which the submitted issues are reasonably or necessarily referable. Appellants were on notice that recovery was sought primarily for the value of the jewelry and that the only ground for recovery was the hotel's negligence with respect to the bailment, purse and contents. This is reflected in appellants' second amended original answer where they allege that there was no bailment as to the jewelry within the purse.

The record reflects no timely objection to the issues submitted or to the omitting of a special issue, and therefore in support of the judgment and in accord with Tex.R.Civ.P. 279, we deem it to be found that one might reasonably expect to find valuable jewelry within a purse under the circumstances of this case in support of the judgment below. It follows that the findings of negligence and proximate cause of the loss of the purse apply to the jewelry as well, which is deemed to be a part of the bailment. There was no error in the judgment insofar as it was complained that there was no bailment of the jewelry and that there was no connection between the findings of negligence and proximate cause as regards the purse and the jewelry.

Appellant's final point of error complains of the trial court's granting of appellees' motion for judgment notwithstanding the verdict and disregarding the jury's findings on special issues that appellees' leaving the purse was negligence and a proximate cause of the loss of the jewelry.

We find Vollmer v. Stoneleigh-Maple Terrace, 226 S.W.2d 926 (Tex.Civ.App.–Dallas, 1950, writ ref'd), cited by appellees, to be in point. There the plaintiff was a guest in the Stoneleigh Hotel and paid monthly to park his automobile in the hotel's adjacent garage. On the evening in question he drove his car to the hotel entrance and turned it over to an employee of the defendant, who parked it in its usual spot. While the employee was parking another car, he heard the noise of the starting motor and arrived just in time to see plaintiff's car being driven away. The jury found that the defendant was guilty of several acts of negligence, each of which was a proximate cause of the loss of the vehicle. It also found that the plaintiff, Vollmer, was negligent in accepting the garage facilities as furnished by the defendant; in failing to keep a proper lookout for his own automobile; in failing to remove the keys from the automobile; and in failing to see that there was a sufficient number of attendants to guard his automobile. Each of these acts was found to be a proximate cause. The court of civil appeals reversed the judgment of the trial court in favor of defendant and rendered judgment for plaintiff, holding that the plaintiff's contributory negligence was not a proximate cause as a matter of law. The court stated:

"As appellant (plaintiff) aptly points out, while the car was in the possession of defendant, the duty of care as between the parties rested solely upon it, plaintiff being relieved of further duties in connection with a proper lookout, safeguarding of keys, etc."

The busboy and cashier assumed possession and control of the purse per instructions of the hotel with respect to articles misplaced or lost by customers. This assumption of possession was as complete as that of defendant's employee in *Vollmer v. Stoneleigh-Maple Terrace*. In each instance, once the bailee assumed possession, he alone had the duty to safeguard the bailed article. We find therefore under these facts that the negligence of Mrs. Caranas was not a cause ". . . that in a natural and continuous sequence produces an event . . ." of this nature.

The trial court's action in disregarding special issue number eight pertaining to proximate cause is therefore authorized and is proper under the circumstances. . . . The active cause that produced the loss was wholly independent of the negligence of Mrs. Caranas, and the hotel's primary duty of ordinary care to its paying guest was clear.

Ruling of the Court: The judgment of the trial court is affirmed for plaintiff.

The case of Summer v. Hyatt Corporation, 266 S.E.2d 333 (Ga., 1980), also involved hotel guests who had dinner in the hotel restaurant and lost property. The only difference—and it apparently is a substantial one—is that in the *Summer* case, the plaintiff was seated on a portion of the dining room that revolved. When she was seated, she placed her handbag on a stationary portion of the dining room next to her table. As the portion she was sitting on revolved, she was taken away from her handbag, which contained valuable items, and when the section had returned to the point where she had left her handbag, it was gone. There was no evidence that the handbag had come into the possession of any hotel or restaurant employee so as to create a bailment. The purse was recovered, but the valuable items were gone.

The plaintiff sued the hotel to recover the full value of the items lost, claiming that the loss was the result of the defendant's negligence or of the maintenance of a nuisance by the defendant. Maintenance of a nuisance involves knowingly doing something that interferes with someone else's enjoyment of their own property. The defendant asserted that the items that were lost were of the type that required her to store them in the safety-deposit boxes at the hotel in accordance with the posted rules governing limitations of liability toward guests for the theft or damage of their property. In order for the defense to be applicable, it would be necessary for the court to find that the plaintiff, who was a registered guest in the hotel and was eating dinner in the hotel dining room, still had the status of a guest insofar as her relationship with the hotel was concerned. The court said that indeed this was so, holding that the restaurant patrons could be governed by different rules. Therefore, the plaintiff's status while in the dining room was still that of a guest of the hotel. Because the plaintiff retained her status as a guest and therefore was bound by the statutory provisions concerning a hotel's liability for damage or theft of a guest's property, the hotel had no liability with regard to loss or damage.

Checkrooms

Many hotels, restaurants, clubs, concert halls, museums, and other public businesses have checkrooms available to safeguard guests' valuables. What is the responsibility of a checkroom to guests who check their possessions?

In Hackney v. Southwest Hotels, Inc., 195 S.W.2d 55 (Ark., 1946), the guest left a camera valued at $300 in the hotel baggage room and was given a receipt for it. On the check was printed a notice that limited the liability of the innkeeper to $25. Nevertheless, the court held that the innkeeper was acting in the role of bailee for hire, and it ordered the hotel to pay in full because the item was not taken from the guest's room. The court stressed the fact that the statute did not list a checkroom as a place that was relieved from the absolute liability of the common law and added, "We would be reading into the statute something that is not there if we permitted the hotelkeeper by language on the claim check to limit the extent of his liability concerning property especially entrusted to his care, and concerning which property, he would be an absolute insurer but for the statute, and concerning which property, the legislature did not provide for the limiting of the extent of the liability of the hotelkeeper."

Unless a statute or court interpretation states that a checkroom is part of a hotel, a checkroom where personal property is checked enters into a bailment. A question that could arise about a checkroom bailment is whether the fact that there is no fee for checking goods creates a gratuitous bailment and therefore only slight care is owed to the guest.

In *Aldrich v. Waldorf Astoria Hotel, Inc.*, several additional questions are raised and answered. First, what rights does a concessionaire have if he runs the checkrooms for the hotel and the hotel comes under a limited liability statute? Second, what is the position when the checkroom requires no fee but a tip is expected and customary? And does the acceptance of one check for two or more coats by the guest constitute contributory negligence on the part of the guest in not requiring two checks?

Case Example	**Aldrich v. Waldorf Astoria Hotel, Inc.**
	343 N.Y.S.2d 830 (1973)
	(RICHARD S. LANE, Judge)

When Mr. and Mrs. Aldrich presented themselves at the Waldorf's checkroom at the conclusion of the Vienese Opera Ball, Mrs. Aldrich's mink jacket was missing. The checkroom was operated for the Waldorf by Harry Cantor, but this fact was not revealed in any way to the guests.

The Waldorf and Mr. Cantor seek to avoid the ordinary consequences of the law of bailments by relying on the limitation of liability contained in Section 201 of the General Business Law. Such limitation is not available to Mr. Cantor because he is not a hotel, motel, or restaurant. The statute is in derogation of common law liability and must be strictly construed . . . . Nor can the Waldorf hide behind the statute because it is applicable only where no fee or charge is exacted for checking. Here the thirty-five cents per garment familiar to those who participate in New York's social whirl was paid. Whether called a gratuity or otherwise, one need only try to check a coat without paying it to realize that it is indeed a fee.

The above determinations render it unnecessary for the court to reach the issue of whether there has been sufficient posting to comply with the statute. The Waldorf uses the standard card approved by the New York State Hotel Association that bears a legend at the top "Notice to guests" in large black type. The legend is followed in equally large black type by a message concerning the availability of a safe in the office, and then in slightly smaller, lighter, but still eminently readable type comes information concerning rates. Finally, and occupying two-thirds of the card in legible but very tiny type, are printed the provisions of several sections of the General Business Law, including Section 201. Such a card in a frame was hung on the wall between the elevators on the ballroom floor where departing guests would have ample opportunity to see it, but arriving guests would have their backs to it. There was also evidence that such cards were at either end of the forty- to forty-five foot checking counter at the Waldorf, which is divided by pillars into four or five checking stations. The court is highly dubious as to whether this constitutes the posting "in a conspicuous place and manner" as required by the statute. It is clear that without a showing of such posting, no limitation is available. . . . But what constitutes "conspicuous" posting has not been delineated in any recorded decision to the court's knowledge.

The Waldorf and Mr. Cantor also defend by alleging contributory negligence on the part of Mr. and Mrs. Aldrich in accepting only one check for two garments. This is not an uncommon practice in checkrooms across the city. It was initiated here and generally by and for the convenience of the checkroom, and plaintiffs will not be held contributorily negligent for merely failing to protest it.

Finally, the Waldorf defends on the grounds that it was not responsible for the checkroom, having franchised it to Mr. Cantor. Under the circumstances, this position flies in the face of the ordinary principles of agency. So far as Mr. and Mrs. Aldrich and the other guests were concerned, they were entrusting their coats to the safekeeping of the Waldorf.

Ruling of the Court: Plaintiff may have judgment against defendants for $1,400, together with the cost and disbursements of this action. The Waldorf has cross-claimed against Mr. Cantor based upon an indemnity agreement. No evidence thereon was adduced, however. Accordingly, the cross-claim will not be adjudged and this determination is specifically without prejudice to its renewal.

In Jacobson v. Belplaza Corporation, 80 F.Supp. 917 (N.Y., 1949), a dining room waiter suggested to a guest that he put her mink in the checkroom. A proper check was issued to the waiter, but when he returned to the checkroom for the coat, it had been surrendered to an unknown person who did not have the check but had described the coat. The checkroom was managed by a concessionaire for profit. The guest sued the hotel and won because the concessionaire could not plead a statute that was passed only for the benefit of the hotelkeeper. A guest need not inquire who owns the checkroom, but has the right to assume that the hotel does.

A classical case of checkroom loss occurred in Fidelman-Danziger, Inc., v. Statler Management, 136 A.2d 119 (Pa., 1957). The plaintiff was not a guest of the hotel, but needed a place to keep his briefcase (containing jewelry valued at $7,000) during his stay in Pittsburgh. His receipt contained an exculpatory clause stating that the hotel was not liable beyond a stipulated sum. The goods were stolen during a brief period of time when the attendant was absent. The plaintiff sued the hotel for negligence, although the checkroom was run by a concessionaire who had "the exclusive privilege to render checking and washroom services in the William Penn Hotel in the city of Pittsburgh, Pennsylvania, for a consideration of $12,000" (to be paid the hotel) and other stipulations. There were no provisions about checkroom service fees, but the concessionaire could keep the "gratuities."

The court ruled on the following facts:

1   The checkroom patron was not a hotel guest.
2   The patron did not intend to be a hotel guest.
3   There was a bailment between the patron and the checkroom operator.
4   The fact that the first day of bailment was free for the patron did not affect the relationship, as it was expected that everyone using the checkroom would be considerate and tip the attendant.
5   A prima facie case came about when the patron proved delivery, requested the bag's return, and it was not returned.
6   It was up to the defendant to prove a loss consistent with due care.
7   The plaintiff's case rested entirely on negligence of the hotel and on his own contributory negligence (failure of plaintiff to warn the defendant of the value of the bailed property).
8   The fact that no instructions were given on the liability of a checkroom operator was an error that could warrant a new trial.
9   The hotel rather than the concessionaire was sued. The court supported this, based on the theory that a possessor of land is liable for bodily harm occurring on land leased to concessionaires.

10   In this case, the owners and management (Statler Management, Inc.) of the hotel permitted the concessionaire to conduct business activities on the hotel premises in the name of the hotel, and they exerted supervision over the concessionaire. People using the checkroom could logically assume they were dealing with the William Penn Hotel. The question of the concessionaire as an independent contractor was moot.

Fire and the Hotelkeeper's Liability

The legislatures in most states, whether wisely or unwisely, clearly exempt a hotel proprietor from liability for loss of personal property that is kept in a guest's room and is destroyed by an "unintentional" fire. Where there is no statute, the courts are not agreed as to whether the so-called common law insurer's liability rule should be applied. Other courts have adopted the so-called *prima facie* liability rule, making innkeepers presumptively liable unless they can show that the loss was caused without fault or negligence on their part or that of their agents and servants.

The case of *Cloward* v. *Pappas* raises several questions. First, is a hotelkeeper liable when a fire destroys the guest's property and no negligence is shown on the part of the hotel? Second, when a car is parked in a space that is a part of the hotel, is the hotel liable for the car's destruction? Third, is the hotel liable for injuries to a guest during a fire? And, fourth, how much of an alarm must a hotelkeeper give when there is a fire in the hotel? Although the *Cloward* case did not hold the motelkeeper liable for not warning his guests, the general rule is that a hotelkeeper must make every effort to warn all guests.

Case	Cloward v. Pappas
Example	387 P.2d 97 (Nev., 1963)
	(THOMPSON, Justice)

This litigation arose from the fire of March 14, 1961, that destroyed the Pony Express Motel on South Virginia Street in Reno, Nevada. Mr. and Mrs. Cloward and Mr. and Mrs. Rodgers, invited guests of the motel, joined as plaintiffs in an action against the owners. They sought to recover damages for the loss of personal property left in their rented motel rooms, for the loss of Mr. Cloward's car that was parked in a carport adjoining his room, and for personal injuries and incidental medical expenses incurred by each. As to the chattels that were "left in their rooms," the plaintiffs charge the owners with gross negligence (N.R.S. 651.010). The claim of Mr. Cloward for the loss of his car is based on a common law concept that an innkeeper is liable as an insurer for the loss of his guests' personal property from fire. For the personal injury claims and kindred expenses, a third standard for recovery is urged—that the owners breached their duty of ordinary care to invitees.

The case was presented to the court without a jury. Only the issue of liability was tried. If liability was found, then the claims for damages were to be litigated later. The court found that the owners were not liable to the plaintiffs. We are asked to review this ruling.

The Pony Express Motel was composed of two strings of units separated by an inner courtyard. One string ran along the southern boundary of its property and the other along the northern boundary. The office was to the east and adjoined the manager's living quarters. Extending west from the office and the manager's unit was the southerly series of motel rooms. They adjoined each other in pairs, each pair being separated by double carports. There were oil-burning, forced-air furnaces in the rear of the carports for units 3 and 10. Mr. and Mrs. Cloward occupied unit 6, and Mr. and Mrs. Rodgers unit 7 of the southerly series of units. The Cloward car was in the carport adjoining his motel room.

The fire probably started near 10 P.M. The exact time of its inception is not known. The point of origin was believed to be the furnace room adjacent to unit 3. The sole evidence as to the cause of the conflagration was the opinion offered by an investigator of the Reno Fire Department. He believed that a strong wind caused a downdraft in the flue, forcing the fire out of the furnace firebox and igniting nearby material. He supposed that but for the strong wind, the fire would not have occurred. One or two days before, the furnace had been repaired. Whether it was in good working order on the day of the fire was a controverted issue of fact that the court resolved in favor of the owners.

A guest in unit 3 notified the motel manager of the fire, who in turn telephoned the fire department. After doing so, the manager and her husband gathered a few personal belongings (the dog, a bird cage, some medicines, etc.), got into their car, and left. She was concerned for her husband's welfare as he was afflicted with a heart disease. The first fire unit was on the scene by 10:21 P.M. (within four minutes after receiving notice) and radioed for additional help. The motel manager did not notify any of the motel guests that a fire was in progress. Her husband had requested an unknown volunteer to do so. The record is silent as to what, if anything, the unknown helper did. None of the plaintiffs were notified. They learned of the fire themselves and evacuated in haste, leaving behind the chattels for which they now seek a recovery in money damages. We do not know whether a prompt warning by the motel manager would have enabled the plaintiffs to avoid damage, nor indeed whether a warning could have been given under the circumstances. Both the time available to warn the motel guests and the speed with which the fire spread from unit to unit is not made clear. Reasonable, but opposing, inferences could be drawn from the evidence introduced.

From these facts and from the inferences to be drawn therefrom, the trial judge concluded: "There was no negligence on the part of defendants or their agent that caused the fire, and there was no negligence by defendants or their agent that caused damage to or loss of the property of plaintiffs or bodily injury to them. Mrs. Taylow (the manager) and her husband acted as reasonably prudent persons under all the circumstances. There was no credible evidence as to time of the fire, its spread, or the acquisition of knowledge of its existence. A determination in favor of the defendants necessarily results." It seems to us that each of the trial court's conclusions could properly be made from the facts as we have related them. The issues of negligence and proximate cause were fact issues about which reasonable minds could differ. Therefore, we affirm the judgment denying plaintiffs a recovery for their personal injuries and related expenses, as their claims were premised upon the charge of ordinary negligence. We must also affirm the judgment denying plaintiffs relief for the loss of property left in their motel rooms, for if the defendants were not negligent, *a fortiori*, they were not grossly negligent so as to impose a liability under N.R.S. 651.010.

There remains for determination the issue posed by the claim of Mr. Cloward for the loss of his car that was parked in the carport adjoining his motel room. As to this claim, it is urged that the motel owners have the liability of an insurer. The trial court did not deal specifically with this proposition. We must assume from the conclusions made by that court (hereinbefore quoted) that a liability for the property of guests not left in their rooms would exist only if the owners were found to be negligent. That court apparently rejected the so-called common law insurer's liability rule. We must decide whether it was correct in doing so.

N.R.S. 1.030 provides that the common law is the rule of decision in Nevada unless repugnant to or in conflict with the laws or constitution of this state or of the United States. What is the common law rule that the plaintiffs ask us to apply? In general terms, it is that an innkeeper is practically an insurer of the safety of property entrusted to his care by a guest and, in the event of loss, he may exonerate himself from liability only by showing that such loss or injury resulted from an act of God, or of the public enemy, or from the fault of the guest himself. . . . We do not think that this rule has application to the case before us. Mr. Cloward's car was not entrusted to the care of the motel operator. The possession and control of the car remained with Mr. Cloward. He kept the key. The lower court did not err in failing to apply the common law insurer's liability rule.

Ruling of the Court: Affirmed.

Fire codes set the minimal standards of fire safety that a hotel or motel must comply with in order to avoid invoking some sort of punitive action on the part of the state, municipality, township, or their administrative agencies. In some instances, buildings constructed before the enactment of the code or regulation are exempted from compliance with it. There are various types of these so-called grandfather clauses; some totally exempt the owners of a building from ever complying with the code, while others merely postpone the time by which there must be compliance. The latter take into consideration the fact that capital may have to be raised to finance the payment for the necessary work and equipment and also that the work must be done while the building is occupied and, therefore, will be more time-consuming. Still others provide for exemption from compliance if certain prerequisite factors or conditions were in existence, as the following case demonstrates.

The case of Northern Lights Motel, Inc., v. Sweaney, 561 P.2d 1176 (Alaska, 1977), concerns a fire in the defendant's hotel resulting in the death of Stumbaugh, a guest. The plaintiff (executor of Stumbaugh's estate) argued that the hotel construction violated the building code and that this constituted negligence per se so the defendant must pay damages. The defendant argued that the grandfather clause exempted it from compliance with the code.

The Alaska regulations said strict compliance was not necessary when it did not "constitute a distinct hazard to life and property in the opinion of the state fire marshal." The code also permitted the continued use of existing property so long as the "use or occupancy was legal at the time of the passage of this code, provided that such continued use is not dangerous to life." The building code was passed in 1959, and the defendant's building and its addition were constructed in 1964 and 1966. Therefore, the grandfather clause had no application.

However, the Alaskan regulations posed a different problem because they were amended in 1972, years after the construction. The question that it raises has to do with the meaning of the term *existing conditions*. Does it refer to the conditions existing at the time of the inspection, or those existing at the time of the adoption of the code? The court held that these words were an attempt to give the fire marshal some discretion in dealing with code violations in structures not currently under construction. Its purpose was to give the fire marshal the ability to negotiate with the building owner as to the best way to remedy minor defects without being required to close the building to the public every time that defects are discovered. This construction required that the state authorities must have expressly or implicitly accepted the condition of the building. There was no evidence of any inspection by any state officials, nor had any officials said or implied that the conditions were unduly hazardous. The only evidence about the condition of the building was contained in a borough report that gave the building a clean bill of health, but that the preparer of the report admitted was based upon faulty information. In any event, there was no proof that the borough inspector had been authorized by the state to make the inspection and report, and by law the state was the only one who could give the exemption. Therefore, the court held that there were no exemptions under the law running to the defendant, and, therefore, the defendant was bound to comply with the code requirements. The court went on to say additionally that the violation of the code constituted negligence per se.

An interesting question concerning compliance with building codes is whether compliance with the code is all that is needed. Codes establish the minimum requirements that must be met to avoid criminal penalties and punishment for violation of regulations or laws in a manner other than by imposition of civil liability. Although it is true that if hoteliers have complied with the building codes and ordinances, they will escape the imposition of the negligence per se doctrine, can they nevertheless be held negligent? We believe that they can. It is essential for hoteliers not to stop at meeting the minimum code requirements or at resting secure within the exemption of a grandfather clause. Compliance of that sort protects one only from criminal prosecution, but not from civil liability.

Hoteliers should accept the codes as only a starting point and work up from there. The MGM hotel in Nevada suffered a terrible fire in 1980. After that, the hotel modified the building with a sprinkler system, a computerized alarm system, and a series of televisions costing more than $5 million—changes not required by the statute.

The vast majority of the courts throughout the United States hold that in order to impose liability on a defendant for the violation of a building or safety code, an injured plaintiff must prove that the violation was the proximate cause of the injuries. In Hendricks v. Nyberg, Inc., 353 N.E.2d 273 (Ill., 1976), the plaintiffs sustained injuries as the result of smoke inhalation during a fire at the defendant's hotel while they were guests. The plaintiffs admitted that the defendants were not responsible for the fire's origin, but the defendant was in violation of several sections of the Chicago Municipal Code. Evidence of these violations was introduced into evidence by the plaintiff despite the defendant's objections as to the relevancy. The lower court found for the plaintiffs and awarded Mr. Hendricks $40,000 and Mrs. Hendricks $5,000.

On appeal, the upper court reversed the jury finding and sent the matter back to the lower court for a new trial. It stated that the violation of a statute creates no liability unless the violation is the proximate or legal cause of the claimed injuries. The court said that there was a dispute as to whether the clerk on duty that night was certified—one of the code requirements—and that the absence of a certified clerk may have had some bearing on the injuries sustained by the plaintiffs. But as to the hotel's lack of compliance with the code concerning fire extinguishers and an alarm system, the court held that these violations in no way contributed to the injuries of the plaintiffs and that by letting this information into evidence, the court could have very easily prejudiced the jury. Therefore, the case should be retried.

The case of Herberg v. Swartz, 578 P.2d 17 (Wash., 1978), is quite different. The defendants had purchased a hotel, and, at the time of sale, it was inspected for compliance to the state's minimum fire and life safety standards. Approximately twenty-three violations were discovered, but the inspectors permitted the hotel to continue operating as long as the violations were corrected within five and a half months. About two months later and the defects virtually untouched, an arsonous fire was started, and it was determined that at least five of the violations contributed substantially to the rapid spread of the fire. The fire spread so rapidly that the building was virtually reduced to a shell before the firefighters arrived. The defendant hired a demolition company to knock down a remaining wall that presented a threat to others. As the demolition employees were tearing down one section of the building, another section collapsed and came down on the plaintiff's building, causing the damage being sued for.

The court found that because at least five of the violations contributed to the rapid spread of the fire and thus, ultimately, damage to the plaintiff's property, the defendant was liable to the plaintiff. The court held that the fire codes and safety regulations had been enacted to protect persons situated such as the plaintiff, as well as tenants or guests. That, coupled with the fact that the violations had contributed significantly to the cause of the damages sustained, was sufficient to make the violations of the statutes constitute negligence per se, permitting the court to instruct the jury that the defendant was negligent as a matter of law.

Although the violations of the codes were being continued with the apparent consent of the municipality and its agents, such consent did not act as a bar to the liability of the defendants. It merely allowed the hotel to remain open and operate without the imposition of sanctions by the state on the criminal side of the court. It did nothing to protect the hotel against civil liability for negligence in continuing the violation. Another interesting question this case raises is whether there is any civil liability on the part of the city and its agents for permitting the hotel to open before correcting the large number of violations detected.

A guest can be sued by the hotel if the guest negligently causes damage to the hotel property. The case of Fireman's Fund American Insurance Companies v. Knobbe, 562 P.2d 825 (Nev., 1977), concerns a suit brought by an insurance company against four guests whose negligent smoking damaged a hotel insured by the plaintiff. The hotel filed a claim for damages with the plaintiff, which had insured it, and the plaintiff paid the hotel the amount of its damages. After it paid the hotel's claim, the insurance company became subrogated to the hotel's rights against those whose negligence had caused the fire and its resulting loss.

In the case, two married couples were sharing a room in the hotel. All four smoked, and it was determined that a cigarette of one of them caused the fire. Firemen's Fund brought suit against all four, alleging both standard negligence theory and the doctrine of res ipsa loquitur. The defendants moved for summary judgment, which was denied by the court because it felt that there was a conflict of material evidence under the negligence theory; but the court did grant the motion insofar as the application of the res ipsa loquitur doctrine was concerned. The insurance company stipulated that in the absence of the application of the res ipsa doctrine, it would be unable to meet the necessary burden of proof to establish negligence so as to impose liability.

As you will recall, an essential element in invoking the doctrine is that all the requisites to bring it into play must be met. Included among these requisites is that the plaintiff must show that the instrumentality that caused the damage or injury was under the exclusive control of the defendant. The general rule is that where any of several defendants, wholly independent of each other, may be responsible for the plaintiff's injury, the doctrine of res ipsa loquitur cannot be applied.

In the Firemen's Fund case, neither the particular defendant nor the particular instrumentality (which cigarette) was known, so the doctrine could not be applied. The court went on to say, "Cases must occasionally happen where the person really responsible for a personal injury cannot be identified or pointed out by proof, as in this case; and then it is far better and more consistent with reason and law that the injury should go without redress than that innocent persons should be held responsible upon some strained construction of the law developed for the occasion."

Robbery and the Hotelkeeper's Liability

Will a robbery negate a hotelkeeper's responsibility for a guest's goods? Under common law, robbery was not an exception to the general rule; hence, a guest could collect for such a loss. With the introduction of limited liability statutes, however, this question comes up routinely as hotel robberies increase.

In *de Saric v. Miami Caribe Investments, Inc.*, the court stated that the Florida statute did cover robbery because it limited a hotel's liability for "any loss" of a guest's property. However, the case was returned for retrial because of other factors.

In this case the plaintiff was also suing for the negligent infliction of mental distress. As in some other states, the Florida view is that there must be "physical impact" for the plaintiff to be able to recover for mental distress.

A third concern in the *de Saric* case deals with the question of posting. The case was remanded for further trial on several points that are very important to the traveler and to the hotel industry. Florida is one of the states that require a hotel to accept at least $1,000 worth of valuables, making posting a relevant factor.

Case	**de Saric v. Miami Caribe Investments, Inc.**
Example	*512 F.2d 1013 (Fla., 1975)*
	(COLEMAN, Circuit Judge)

Appellants, Peruvian citizens, filed suit, in diversity of citizenship, against the corporate owner of a Miami hotel and against its Pennsylvania insurer. Recovery was sought for "negligent infliction of mental distress" [appellant's terminology] and for the value of property robbed of appellants while they were guests in the hotel on January 21, 1971.

After discovery and depositions, the district court granted a defense motion for summary judgment. We affirm in part and, in part, vacate and remand.

Dalila Pardo de Saric and her daughter, Luz-Maria Saric, registered at the McAllister. They were assigned room 1049, were escorted to that room immediately after checking in, remained in the room for some forty-five minutes to an hour, and upon opening the door to leave for the first time since registering, were met by two masked robbers, one of whom was armed with a handgun.

By the menace of the gun the robbers forced their way into the room. There is no evidence that either of the victims were ever struck or jostled with the weapon. One of the intruders forced Luz-Maria Saric into the bathroom, where she fainted and fell to the floor. Upon regaining consciousness, she was examined by one of the robbers for hidden jewelry. Dalila Pardo de Saric was required to lie on the floor, with gun to her head, while jewelry, money, and traveler's checks were taken from her purse. . . .

Luz-Maria testified in her deposition that neither robber struck, hit, or abused her, that she received no physical injury as a result of the robbery, but she alleges that she suffered a traumatic neurosis accompanied by physical manifestations such as dyspepsia, trembling, hyperventilation, flatulence, and difficulty in swallowing.

Appellants have framed the appellate issues in the following language:

1 Whether mere impact, without signs or marks of physical injury, is sufficient to maintain an action for the negligent infliction of mental distress under the law of Florida;

2 Whether Florida statute, Section 509.111, applies to the facts of this case;

3 Whether the statute violates the Florida Constitution;

4 Whether the statute violates the equal protection clause of the Fourteenth Amendment.

The above-mentioned Florida statute limits a hotel's liability for the loss of money or valuables by its guests to those items deposited with the hotel management in exchange for a written receipt stating the value of the property deposited. The hotel is mandatorily required to accept for safekeeping valuables aggregating no more than $1,000 in value. Liability for loss is limited to $1,000 unless the hotel voluntarily accepts a greater amount (Florida statutes § 509.111 [1972]).

Florida law further requires a hotel to post notice of this limitation of its liability (Florida statutes § 509.101).

We shall discuss the issues in the order presented.

After the district court decided this case, the Supreme Court of Florida decided Gilliam v. Stewart, 291 So.2d 593 (1974).

That decision, it seems to us, clearly reaffirmed the "physical impact" rule theretofore prevailing in Florida, pursuant to which the summary judgment denying recovery for "mental distress" was correct.

At common law, innkeepers were insurers of the property of their guests, and their liability was like that of a bailee. Since the innkeeper was being compensated for his services, he was a *bailee for hire* and thus subject to the standard of ordinary care. . . . Many jurisdictions, including Florida, have limited an innkeeper's liability by statute. Enacted, as they were, in derogation of the common law, these statutes have been strictly construed.

In its decision, the district court apparently relied on Ely v. Charellen Corporation, 5 Cir., 1941, 120 F.2d 984. As it develops, this case is the last word in this court or from the Florida courts dealing with the issue that thirty-four years later now makes its second appearance.

In *Ely*, the plaintiff registered at a Florida hotel. Jewelry was stolen from her room. At that time, as today, Florida law provided that a hotel was not liable for the loss of valuables unless deposited with the hotel management [Chapter 16042 Florida Acts § 40 (1933), the forerunner of the present Section 509.111]. Also in effect at that time, as today, was a requirement that the hotel post notice of this and other rules (Chapter 16042 Florida Act § 38 [1933]). In *Ely*, as in the case *sub judice*, neither party complied with the statutes in that the plaintiff left valuables in her room and the hotel had failed to post notice of its liability limitations.

The plaintiff argued that the hotel's obligation to post notice of the act had to be met before the hotel could claim its benefits. This court, in a one-page opinion, held that because Section 40 listed no exceptions, no liability would attach to the hotel proprietor for the loss of jewelry unless it was deposited with the hotel. We noted that Section 40 provided that *in no event* would a hotel be liable for loss of goods not deposited with the hotel (emphasis ours). This same "in no event" language appears in the present statute. The statutes have been amended by the Florida legislature three times since *Ely*, always retaining the "in no event" phraseology that *Ely* held to be decisive regardless of whether the statutory notice had, or had not been, posted.

The outstanding, unreversed decision in *Ely* is binding on us.

In their brief, appellants state their position on this point as follows:

"As the plaintiffs had not yet deposited their valuables with the management at the time of the robbery, we have stipulated that if the statute applies to the facts of this case, and is constitutional, then the plaintiffs are barred from recovering for their loss of personal property. If, on the other hand, the statute does not apply, or is unconstitutional, then the defendants are strictly liable for plaintiffs' loss of personal property."

We are of the opinion that the statute does apply because it refers to *any loss*, which could apply to losses by robbery, as well as from any other source. Accordingly, we cannot accept the argument that the statute applies only to items that guests have carelessly left in their rooms, subject to the possibility of theft.

This leaves only the constitutional argument.

Neither the pleadings nor the remainder of the appellate record explicitly indicate whether the Section 509.101 notice, in the form required in 1971, was posted or not posted by the hotel. The summary judgment, as would ordinarily be true in such instances, made no finding on this point. Summary judgments depend on the absence of any genuine issue of material fact.

The appellants say that a failure to post the notices would render Section 509.111 violative of both the federal and Florida Constitutions and further argue that posting the notice was an affirmative defense; hence, a failure to post must be assumed on summary judgment because the posting was not pleaded or shown.

It is a fact, however, that the answer filed on behalf of the hotel stated "that the hotel has no responsibility at all for the personal property of the plaintiffs in accordance with Florida statute, Section 509.111, which provides for the only conditions under which this defendant can be liable for personal property."

The plaintiffs did not counter this defense by motion to strike it for failure to post notices nor did it offer any proof by deposition or otherwise that the Section 509.101 notices had not been posted.

In a picture of the lobby, facing the elevators, we note the following: "HOTEL RULES   Between 11 P.M. and 7 A.M. registered guests only will be allowed to go up to the rooms." This is followed by a statement of the rule in Spanish. So, at least some notices were posted.

In this state of the record, we do not believe that the ends of justice would be served by our indulging in a factual assumption as to whether the statutory notice was or was not posted. Moreover, the constitutional issues now raised were not submitted to (and thus not decided by) the district court.

We vacate the judgment of the district court insofar as it involved the alleged property loss. In that respect, we remand the case for its consideration of and judgment on the following points:

1 Were the statutory notices posted?

2 If not posted, does the interpretation rendered in *Ely* v. *Charellen Corporation* render the statute invalid under either the state or federal constitutions?

3 For such further proceedings as the resolution of these questions may make appropriate.

Ruling of the Court: The judgment of the district court denying recovery for personal injuries allegedly caused by mental distress is affirmed.

The judgment as to property losses is vacated and the cause is, in that respect, remanded for further proceedings not inconsistent herewith.

Responsibility for Lost or Mislaid Goods

Guests often forget such items as umbrellas, coats, hats, clothing, and handbags. Some are left behind in large quantities—one large hotel accumulated over two hundred umbrellas in one year. Valuables like jewelry, money, and fur coats are also forgotten in surprising numbers. Who owns the property left behind either voluntarily or involuntarily at a hotel or restaurant? Under certain conditions, the old adage of "finders, keepers" applies. Under others, the owner of the property has superior rights to the goods. The final arbiter on such matters is the court, which interprets the intent of the true owner—whether the property was lost, mislaid, or abandoned.

Many states have enacted so-called finder statutes, explicitly spelling out the procedure to follow when property is found before the finder can acquire rights, if any, to the property. Finders can also be guilty of larceny if they do not turn over found property to the person accountable for it while a search is made for the true owner.

The following case demonstrates the problems associated with lost, mislaid, and abandoned property. In *Jackson* v. *Steinberg* $800 found by a hotel maid was kept by the hotel while an unsuccessful search was made for the true owner. The case also defines various types of mislaid goods.

<table>
<tr><td>Case
Example</td><td>**Jackson v. Steinberg**
200 P.2d 376 (Or., 1948)
(HAY, Justice)</td></tr>
</table>

The plaintiff in this case is Mrs. Laura I. Jackson. The defendant is Karl Steinberg, who is engaged in the hotel business in Portland under the assumed business name of Arthur Hotel. Mrs. Jackson was employed by defendant as a chambermaid in his hotel.

The facts of the controversy are not disputed. Plaintiff entered defendant's employ on October 13, 1946. In describing her duties, she testified: "Well, where a guest checks out we are supposed to change the linen and dust and clean up the room, leave clean towels, and arrange the furniture like it should be, and take out anything that doesn't belong in there. Q. What do you do with what you take out? A. If it is of any value we take it to the desk clerk; if it isn't of any value we put it in the garbage." On December 30, 1946, while cleaning one of the guest rooms, she found eight one-hundred-dollar bills, U.S. currency, concealed under the paper lining of a dresser drawer. The bills were stacked neatly, and her attention was drawn to them only by reason of their bulk having made a slight bulge in the lining. She removed the bills and delivered them immediately to the manager of the hotel in order that they might be restored to the true owner, if he could be found, and subject to her claims as finder. When she entered defendant's employ, she had installed new paper linings in all dresser drawers in the guest rooms under her care, and the bills were not in this particular drawer at that time.

The hotel, during the period in question, was much patronized by seamen, some of whom, after being paid off in the port of Portland, brought considerable sums of money with them into the hotel, usually in bills of large denominations. Defendant made an unsuccessful effort to discover the owner of the bills by communicating, or attempting to communicate, by mail with each of the persons who had occupied this particular room from mid-October through December 31, 1946. Plaintiff then demanded of defendant that he return the money to her as finder, but he refused. She then, on July 10, 1947, filed this action in the District Court of Multnomah County to recover the sum of $800 of defendant as money had and received. Defendant's affirmative defense was that as an innkeeper, he is required, both at common law and by the Oregon statute, to hold the bills as bailee for the rightful owner.

Plaintiff had judgment in the district court. On appeal to the circuit court, the case was, by stipulation, tried by the court without a jury. Defendant appeals from an adverse judgment.

Defendant's theory, and the basis of his assignments of error, is that the bills constitute mislaid property, presumed to have been left in the room by a former guest of the hotel, and that as innkeeper, he is entitled to custody of the bills and bound to hold them as bailee for the true owner. Plaintiff, on the other hand, claims the right to the possession of the bills as treasure trove, as against all persons but the true owner.

Lost property is defined as that with the possession of which the owner has involuntarily parted, through neglect, carelessness, or inadvertence. It is property that the owner has unwittingly suffered to pass out of his possession, and of the whereabouts of which he has no knowledge.

Mislaid property is that which the owner has voluntarily and intentionally laid down in a place where he can again resort to it and then has forgotten where he laid it.

Abandoned property is that of which the owner has relinquished all right, title, claim, and possession, with the intention of not reclaiming it or resuming its ownership, possession, or enjoyment.

"Treasure trove consists essentially of articles of gold and silver, intentionally hidden for safety in the earth or in some secret place, the owner being unknown." The foregoing is a modern definition, sufficient for the purposes of the present discussion. Another is: "Money or coin, gold, silver, plate, or bullion found hidden in the earth or other private place, the owner thereof being unknown."

From the manner in which the bills in the instant case were carefully concealed beneath the paper lining of the drawer, it must be presumed that the concealment was effected intentionally and deliberately. The bills, therefore, cannot be regarded as abandoned property.

With regard to plaintiff's contention that the bills constituted treasure trove, it has been held that the law of treasure trove has been merged with that of lost goods generally, at least so far as respects the rights of the finder. Treasure trove, it is said, may, in our commercial age, include the paper representatives of gold and silver.

The natural assumption is that the person who concealed the bills in the case at bar was a guest of the hotel. Their considerable value and the manner of their concealment indicate that the person who concealed them did so for purposes of security and with the intention of reclaiming them. They were, therefore, to be classified not as lost, but as misplaced or forgotten property, and the defendant, as occupier of the premises where they were found, had the right and duty to take them into his possession and to hold them as a gratuitous bailee for the true owner.

The decisive feature of the present case is the fact that plaintiff was an employee or servant of the owner or occupant of the premises and that in discovering the bills and turning them over to her employer, she was simply performing the duties of her employment. She was allowed to enter the guest room solely in order to do her work as chambermaid, and she was expressly instructed to take to the desk clerk any mislaid or forgotten property that she might discover. It is true that in the United States, the courts have tended to accede to the claims of servants to the custody of articles found by them during the course of their employment, where the articles are, in a legal sense, lost property. In Hamaker v. Blanchard, 90 La. 377, 35 Am.Rep. 664, a servant in a hotel found a roll of bank notes in the public parlor. It was held that as the money was found on the floor of a room common to all classes of persons, there was no presumption that it was the property of a guest, and that when the true owner was not found, the plaintiff was entitled to recover it from the innkeeper to whom she had delivered it. In the case at bar, however, the bills were not lost property. . . .

On this branch of the case, the terse comment of a distinguished textwriter will suffice to express our own view: "In those cases where servants are hired to clean up premises, it seems that it might well be held that in finding things in the course of such cleaning, the found property should belong to the master on this ground alone.''

The position of the defendant in the case at bar is fortified by the fact that as an innkeeper, he is under common law and statutory obligations in respect of the found bills.

"When a guest gives up his room, pays his bills, and leaves an inn without an intention of returning, the innkeeper's liability as such for the effects of the former guest left in his charge ceases, and he is liable thereafter merely as an ordinary bailee, either gratuitous or for hire, depending upon the circumstances.''

Our statute, Section 55–203 O.C.L.A., in effect when the facts of this case transpired, provides that when baggage or property of a guest is suffered to remain in an inn or hotel after the relation of guest and innkeeper has ended, the innkeeper may, at his option, hold such property at the risk of such former guest.

Where money is found in an inn on the floor of a room common to the public, there being no circumstances pointing to its loss by a guest, the finder, even if an employee of the innkeeper, is entitled to hold the money as bailee for the true owner. It would seem that as to articles voluntarily concealed by a guest, the very act of concealment would indicate that such articles have not been placed "in the protection of the house" . . . and so, while the articles remain concealed, the innkeeper ordinarily would not have the responsibility of a bailee therefor. Upon their discovery by the innkeeper or his servant, however, the innkeeper's responsibility and duty as bailee for the owner becomes fixed.

Ruling of the Court: The plaintiff in the present case is to be commended for her honesty and fair dealing throughout the transaction. Under our view of the law, however, we have no alternative other than to reverse the judgment of the lower court. It will be reversed accordingly.

Not satisfied with the ruling in *Jackson* v. *Steinberg*, the plaintiff-maid brought the case up again in the Supreme Court of Oregon. Again the court ruled that the defendant had the right to the money and this time went further in stating that he could not relieve himself of the duty to keep the money until the true owner (if found) claimed it. If the money was not claimed, it would belong to the defendant-hotelkeeper.

The principle of lost or abandoned property is best illustrated in the case of Paset v. Old Orchard Bank and Trust, 378 N.E.2d, 1264 (Ill., 1978). The plaintiff, who had a safety-deposit box in the bank, found over $6,000 on a chair. She delivered the money to the bank for its rightful owner, who never showed up. The bank tried to find the owner but was unsuccessful in doing so. By court sanction the plaintiff was made rightful owner of the money after the appropriate time. This decision prevailed despite the fact that the money was found in a place from which the general public was excluded. The court ruled that the property was "lost property" and a finder is entitled to possession to the exclusion of all others except the true owner.

Management Principles

Hotelkeepers are often as responsible for the safety of the guest's property as they are for the safety of the guest. Both robbery and mislaid or forgotten possessions often create serious legal situations in the service industry. As a general rule, a hotel is responsible for its guests' goods if there is no statute to the contrary. Over the years, most state legislatures have passed laws that protect the hotelkeeper from the rigors of the common law rule of absolute liability—if the hotelkeeper meets certain conditions. These rules are mainly obligatory on the hotelkeeper and are considered condition precedents—that is, hotelkeepers must prove that they followed the letter of the law. There are some exceptions to this. Generally, such rules deal with the following matters:

1 Every hotelkeeper must post as many notices in as many places as required by law. The *Holiday Inn* case demonstrated the necessity for strict compliance, as did the *Depaemelaere* case where posting only part of the notice cost the hotel $10,000. Because notice of the limitation on recovery by a guest is constructive notice to the guest, posting is essential and the statute must be strictly construed. Even where posting in a room is required and the notice is placed with other notices under glass on a bureau top, this could be interpreted as not complying with the statute.

2 If a hotel safe is prescribed (most statutes so state), a safe must be on hand. Usually, the type of safe is not precisely described. The types of goods that a guest must place in the safe are generally jewelry and any other valuables. But because such personal items as watches and reasonable sums of money need not be placed in a safe, they are covered under common law (see *Federal Insurance Company* v. *Waldorf Astoria Hotel*).

3 Unless a state court has decreed that it is the responsibility of the hotel to ask the value of the goods being put into the safe, the hotel need not ask the value. There is an assumption that the limit is that of the statutory provisions.

4 Most states adhere to the rule that if the hotelkeeper or manager steals the goods, then the guest may recover as if the statute did not exist. This is not true of an employee. The law of each state should be reviewed on this problem.

5 The hotel manager should exercise care as to the goods of a guest on both arrival and departure. The guest becomes a bona fide guest as soon as there is a mutuality of intent; the guest also has a reasonable time in which to depart from the hotel (see *Spiller* v. *Barclay Hotel*).

6 In general, a salesman's goods do not come under the common law rights of guests. However, salesmen and similar people are an important economic group and must be protected.

7   Based on custom and usage, a hotel can be held liable for the mail and packages of guests, especially if guests ask that packages be forwarded (see *Baehr* v. *Downey*, Chapter 9).

8   Giving a stub to guests for their valuables does not constitute notice as set forth in statutes. A stub that is part of an identification check is not considered generally as anything more than identification for that particular parcel. It does not constitute a special writing (which is included in most statutes and increases the value of the goods) to modify the statutory provisions. The hotel should give complete instructions on when and with whom such procedures should be followed (see *Kalpakian* v. *Oklahoma Sheraton*). The hotel need not accept valuables exceeding the statutory provision. In any case, reasonable rules should be set forth and be made known to all personnel. Although safety-deposit boxes are treated differently, the *Hotel Pierre* case and similar cases create serious questions on what a hotel's responsibility is.

9   Some states do not have protective statutes covering goods in rooms. Care should be taken to hire trustworthy personnel to clean guest rooms.

10   When goods are left with a hotel for safekeeping over a long period, they cannot be sold like goods that are taken by rights of a lien, or like lost or mislaid property (see the *Dajkovich* case).

11   It is important that all employees be trained not to waive the hotel's rights by changing the provisions of a statute in order to accommodate a guest's wishes.

12   In general, cars and valuables are not covered under the limiting liability statutes; rather, a bailment exists between the hotel (or its contractee) and the guests. Even when a car is sent to an outside garage for storage, the hotel is still liable under the doctrine of *infra hospitium*. Granted, the hotel will implead the garage, but again a legal case is costly and unnecessary (see *Governor House* v. *Schmidt*). There is a minority view to the contrary.

13   A coatroom in a hotel may be, but not always is, a legitimate extension of the statutory provisions protecting a hotel. Because a concessionaire does not come under this provision, a hotel should have the concessionaire take out insurance and post a bond for any possible losses (see *Aldrich* v. *Waldorf Astoria Hotel, Inc.*).

14   The rights of a bailee are concisely set forth in *Kula* v. *Karat*. These rights are practically inviolate. The goods entrusted to the bailee must be returned.

QUESTIONS FOR DISCUSSION

1   What is the general rule concerning a hotelkeeper's liability if a guest loses luggage or valuables?

2   In what way may a hotelkeeper be considered an insurer?

3 Hotels are not always liable for guests' goods. Name the exceptions and give examples. What is an exculpatory clause? Is it legal in a hotelkeeper-guest relationship with regard to guests' goods?

4 Many states have modified the common law absolute liability of a hotelkeeper by statute. What common features do most of these statutes possess?

5 What types of goods must a guest deposit in a hotel safe for protection? Under what conditions is such deposit nullified?

6 Should guests disclose the value of their valuables? Why or why not? If their value is disclosed, must the hotelkeeper accept them for deposit if their value exceeds the statutory limiting liability?

7 Can guests contract for a greater coverage for their valuables than allowed by statute? If so, what is necessary to make this contract legal?

8 If the hotelkeeper steals valuables left for safekeeping with the hotel, will this negate the hotelkeeper's limiting liability statute? What is the situation if a hotel employee steals such goods?

9 What constitutes posting of the limiting liability statutes? What is not considered posting?

10 When does the hotelkeeper's duty to protect guests' goods begin and end? Are there any special provisions to this beginning and end of the hotelkeeper-guest relationship?

11 What precautions must a hotelkeeper take when a guest leaves luggage in storage with the hotelkeeper? Can the hotelkeeper sell the luggage if it is left for a long period of time? How is the lien law applicable here?

12 What precautions for the safety of products must salesmen be afforded when they are hotel guests?

13 Under what conditions can a hotel employee waive the hotel's limiting liability statute? What is the effect of such a waiver, if allowed?

14 Can a hotel lien for nonpayment of a hotel bill include the hotel guest's automobile? Why or why not?

15 What is the doctrine of *infra hospitium*? How does it function? What is its effect?

16 What is a bailment? Define a gratuitous bailment and a mutual bailment. Which relationship would a hotelkeeper rather have with guests—a hotelkeeper-guest relationship or a bailment for the guest's goods?

17 If a guest leaves behind goods in a restaurant, what precautions should the restaurateur take for these goods? Why?

18 Concessionaires (for example, cloakroom operators) are said to be at a disadvantage when they run their business in a hotel. Why? What precautions should the hotelkeepers take to protect themselves?

19 What are the relative rights of a guest versus those of the hotelkeeper when a fire destroys a guest's goods, or when a guest's goods are stolen?

20 If someone finds lost goods in a hotel room, who gets to keep such goods? What is the situation with mislaid goods?

12 Contents

12 Rights of the Hotelkeeper and Restaurateur

> *"A person who becomes a hotel guest or lodger voluntarily agrees to all of the consequences that by law flow from such a relationship to the owner."*
>
> McPHERSON v. UNIVERSITY MOTORS, INC.,
> 193 N.W.2d 616 (Minn., 1972)

Hotel and restaurant operators have the right to conduct their business as they see fit—subject, of course, to the prohibitions built into either legislation or the common law. The fact that the law forbids discrimination in hotels and restaurants should not interfere with the efficient operation of a hotel or restaurant because all hotels and restaurants are equal before the law. In the preceding chapters we investigated the rights of guests; in this chapter we explore the rights of the service industry management.

Every hotelkeeper and restaurateur needs protection. For example, in 1980 Florida hotel and motel owners conservatively estimated their loss from defrauding guests at considerably over $1.5 million. Every state recognizes the need for criminal legislation to protect the service industry against fraudulent guests.

The Civil Rights Act cannot be interpreted as a blanket order requiring hotels and restaurants to admit everyone. Rather, it prohibits a certain type of discrimination that is considered unacceptable under the Constitution. Keeping this in mind, we will now investigate under what conditions a hotelkeeper or restaurateur may refuse a guest accommodations or a meal. In addition, we will also consider under what conditions guests can be evicted.

Although a hotel lien has been part of the hotelier's basic right since time immemorial, some state courts have now found the hotel lien unconstitutional because it deprives a guest of due process of law. Where the lien is permitted, the hotelier must know what property comes under this lien and when the lien may or may not be used. When a guest tries to slip out without paying his bill, the hotelier has little time to determine what the guest's rights are. Hotelkeepers should already be familiar with the intricacies of this law; otherwise, they will have to pay the consequences. A wrong move could lead to a lawsuit accusing the hotelier of false arrest, slander, humiliation, or false imprisonment. (Liens are discussed in more detail later in this chapter.)

We will also investigate current statutory provisions for protecting hotelkeepers and their possible limitations, as well as the rights of the hotelkeepers to protect their property. Under common law, unless statutes provide otherwise, people can use whatever force is necessary to protect the sanctity of their property, up to and including killing an intruder. Can a hotelkeeper or an employee go so far as to take an intruder's life if he believes his guests' lives are in jeopardy? Under certain conditions the answer to this serious question is yes.

To clarify hotelkeepers' rights, the rights of the states should be compared with those of the federal government. If the federal government has not spoken on a given subject, the right under the Tenth Amendment is considered that of the state. The same is true of hotels and restaurants. Whatever aspect of the management of hotels, restaurants, and similar places that is not under the control of statutes or the common law is within the legal province of the entrepreneur—provided that the rules are not arbitrary, capricious, or against human decency (the so-called reasonable rules).

Setting Reasonable Rules

A discussion of reasonable rules should be of great practical interest to future hoteliers. As mentioned in previous chapters, the hotel has an inherent right to make and enforce reasonable rules. Such rules may be designed to prevent immorality, drunkenness, or any form of misconduct that may offend other guests, bring the hotel into disrepute, or be radically inconsistent with the generally recognized proprieties of the community.

A 1975 District of Columbia case could have profound legal as well as management implications for hoteliers and restaurateurs. The case of *Kelly* v. *United States* allows a hotel to make a reasonable rule "barring" an undesirable from the premises, such as a known prostitute or a known criminal. In this case, the hotel had a reasonable rule that allowed it to bar a person from the premises for cause. The defendant (the person barred by the hotel) returned after being barred and was arrested and convicted of unlawful entry. The *Kelly* case shows that, first, the hotel or restaurant should post its reasonable rule about barred guests, and second, there must be a statute allowing a person to be arrested because of an unlawful entry.

Case   **Kelly v. United States**
Example   *348 A.2d 884 (D.C., 1975)*
               (YEAGLEY, Associate Judge)

Appellant was convicted in a nonjury trial of unlawful entry, a violation of D.C. Code 1973, Section 22–3102. This appeal followed.

Between the months of January and March 1974, appellant was seen by the chief of security at the Statler Hilton Hotel on approximately five occasions. He first noticed her in the hotel bar speaking with a guest with whom she later went upstairs. On one occasion when she was in the lobby all night, a police officer assigned to the vice squad told the hotel's security officer that appellant was a prostitute and showed him a copy of her criminal record and her mug shot.

On March 18, hotel security officers again noticed appellant in the hotel. At that time she was once more observed going upstairs with a guest. After about an hour in the guest's room, she came out of the room alone. She was stopped by the hotel security officers and informed of the hotel policy of not allowing any unregistered guests above the lobby. She was also told of the conversation with the police vice squad officer and was read a "barring notice." [The notice said: You are hereby notified that you are not permitted entry in the Statler Hilton Hotel, 1001 Sixteenth Street, Northwest. In the future, if you return to the Statler Hilton Hotel and gain entry, you may be subject to criminal prosecution for unauthorized entry.] Furthermore, she was told that if she returned to the hotel, she would be arrested and charged with unlawful entry.

On August 19, security officers were called to the fifth floor of the hotel. They waited outside one of the rooms until appellant emerged with two male companions. She was then placed under arrest.

Appellant was tried without jury, and on her motion for judgment of acquittal, counsel argued that the statute was not applicable to a hotel and accordingly a hotel could not issue a valid barring notice. . . .

The proffered evidence that appellant was visiting a legally registered guest at the hotel was properly excluded as inadmissible hearsay. Even if we were to assume *arguendo*, however, that the person she was visiting was legally registered at the hotel, we could still not agree with appellant's contention. It is a general rule that:

". . . 'an innkeeper gives a general license to all persons to enter his house. Consequently, it is not a trespass to enter an inn without a previous actual invitation,' but, 'where persons enter a hotel or inn, not as guests, but intent on pleasure or profit to be derived from intercourse with its inmates, they are there, not of right, but under an implied license that the landlord may revoke at any time.' The respondent did not enter the hotel as a guest nor with the intention of becoming one, and it was his duty to leave peaceably when ordered by the landlord to do so, and in case of his refusal to leave on request, appellant was entitled to use such force as was reasonably necessary to remove him."

The court in State v. Steele, 106 N.C. 766, 11 S.E. 478 (1890), expressed the rule this way:

"The duty and legal obligation resting upon the landlord is to admit only such guests as demand accommodation. . . . The right to demand admission to the hotel is confined to persons who sustain the relation of guests, and does not extend to every individual who invades the premises. . . . The landlord is not only under no obligation to admit, but he has the power to prohibit the entrance of any person or class of persons into his house for the purpose of plying his guests with solicitations for patronage in their business."

It necessarily follows that if a hotel has the right to exclude someone, and he or she receives appropriate notice of his exclusion, that person's subsequent presence in the hotel is without lawful authority. Thus he or she is subject to arrest for the crime of unlawful entry. The unlawful entry statute, D.C.Code 1973, Section 22–3102, provides:

"Any person who . . . being (in or on any public or private buildings) without lawful authority to remain therein or thereon shall refuse to quit the same on the demand of . . . the person lawfully in charge thereof, shall be deemed guilty of a misdemeanor."

In the instant case, appellant concedes that she was warned not to return to the hotel. She also admits that she was in the hotel on the evening of August 19, 1974. Consequently, under the authorities cited above, with which we agree, her entrance into the hotel was unlawful being in violation of D.C.Code 1973, Section 22–3102.

Appellant seems to imply that she was barred from the hotel solely on the basis of the conversation between the hotel security officer and the police officer. This fails to take into account that the security officer also observed appellant sitting in the lobby all night and that he had observed her previously on several other occasions meeting guests in the bar or lobby with whom she later went upstairs. There was thus an independent basis for the barring of appellant, and the barring notice was issued by the hotel. The policy is solely within the hotel's discretion and to be invoked by it when the hotel manager or security officer concludes the person is undesirable. The police lack authority to bar persons from the hotel, and evidence is absent that the police officer requested or even suggested that the hotel advise appellant she was prohibited from further entry.

Appellant's other grounds for reversal, namely that the hotel policy was unreasonably and discriminatorily applied and that the government's evidence was insufficient, are without substance.

Ruling of the Court: Accordingly, the judgment appealed from below is affirmed for the defendant.

Generally innkeepers extend an invitation to all, including nonguests, to enter their facility. Their presence upon the premises, even though not as the result of a direct invitation, does not constitute a trespass. They are considered implied invitees or licensees. This implied license can be revoked by the innkeeper at any time. Therefore, persons who enter a hotel where they are not, and do not intend to be, guests, are required to leave the premises if asked. If they refuse or fail to leave, the hotel operator is justified in using as much force as is reasonably necessary to remove them (Hopp v. Thompson, 38 N.W.2d 133 [S.D., 1949]). A person who has been asked to leave and does not becomes a trespasser, and the force of any trespass statute in existence in the state where the property is located comes into effect. This permits the operator to use reasonable force to evict the trespasser, as well as the right to prosecute the person as a criminal trespasser.

In DeWolf v. Ford, 86 N.W.2d 616 (Minn., 1972), the court said, "To these reserved rights of the innkeeper [to make reasonable rules], the guest must submit." There are, of course, certain conditions to be observed. In evicting any guest who willfully violates reasonable rules, the hotelkeeper must ascertain that the person is indeed a "guest" and not a "tenant." A tenant has a legally recognized interest and must therefore be proceeded against through legal channels. Obviously, an eviction must be carried out in a reasonable manner. Only after a guest refuses to leave a hotel after he has been requested to leave and has been given a reasonable opportunity to do so may the hotel forcibly evict him from the premises, and only such force as is reasonably necessary may be used.

What types of rules may a hotel or restaurant put into effect? How can one judge whether the rules are reasonable? Obviously, excessive rules would result in the loss of guests.

In *People v. Thorpe*, the freedom of religion was pitted against a hotel rule that prevented Jehovah's Witnesses, whose doctrine dictates preaching the word of God from door to door, from entering the hotel. The court ruled that a hotel rule created for the good of hotel guests took priority over the right of freedom of religion. A hotel, unlike a community, in which such practices are allowed, must take more stringent care to safeguard its guests. Although the argument in this case was made for religious freedom, a similar argument can be made for freedom of speech. The Supreme Court has decided that the right of free speech has certain restrictions—for instance, a person cannot shout "Fire!" in a crowded theater when there is actually no fire. Our basic freedoms are not unbridled.

Case	People v. Thorpe
Example	*101 N.Y.S.2d 986 (1950)*
	(BUSHEL, City Magistrate)

Defendants are charged with the offense of disorderly conduct in violation of No. 722 of the Penal Law. They are members of a religious group known as Jehovah's Witnesses. Each of these defendants asserts that he is a minister of the gospel and preaches from door to door under the direction of the Watchtower Bible and Tract Society, Inc., a corporation established by law for religious purposes.

Defendants entered the Endicott Hotel located at 81st Street and Columbus Avenue, New York City, at 10:30 A.M. on Saturday morning, February 4, 1950. The defendant Thorpe proceeded to the second floor and the defendant Van Dyk to the top floor of the hotel. Each went from door to door down the hotel corridors, knocking to gain the attention of the hotel guests, and, upon the door being opened, sought to impart to each person thus approached the religious doctrines advocated by the Jehovah's Witnesses. Literature was tendered by the defendants consisting of a book, booklet, and magazine. Contributions, if not actively solicited, were certainly encouraged and, in any event, were admittedly accepted.

The defendants continued their mission until halted by the hotel manager. They conducted their activities as quietly as possible and seemingly without undue annoyance of the hotel residents. When the hotel manager learned of their presence, he asked the defendants summarily to desist. The defendant Thorpe explained that he considered it his constitutional right to preach from door to door, which was, he claimed, established as an appropriate method of preaching in accordance with the tenets of his faith. The defendants refused to leave the hotel, whereupon a police officer was summoned who, upon arrival, informed to defendant Thorpe that the hotel management had a right to insist that the defendants' activities stop and that they forthwith leave the hotel. Defendant replied that he had a right to stay there and, admittedly, told the officer then in uniform, "If I was to leave, he would have to put me under arrest."

In the meantime, the hotel manager located the defendant Van Dyk pursuing his activities on one of the upper floors. He was requested to leave the hotel. Defendant Van Dyk thereupon went down to the hotel lobby with the manager, the police officer, and defendant Thorpe, who had been escorted by the policeman to the street. The hotel manager admonished the defendants that they could not return to the hotel. The defendants accompanied the officer to a police telephone call box. The officer, after speaking to his sergeant on the telephone, advised the defendants that they had no right to return to the hotel. Defendants insisted that it was their right to preach in the hotel and, admittedly, "returned shortly to the hotel with the intention of resuming their preaching activity." Indeed, defendant Van Dyk, prior to the arrest made a telephone call from the lobby to secure legal advice as to the right to preach in the hotel.

As the able brief submitted by defendants' counsel indicates, this case presents another facet of the legal problems presented by the activities of the Jehovah's Witnesses that have reached our highest courts. It is urged that a conviction will result in abridgement of the liberties of press and worship guaranteed by the First and Fourteenth Amendments of the United States Constitution and by the Constitution of the State of New York.

It was long ago held that "from the very nature of the business, it is inevitable" that a hotel owner "must, at all reasonable times and for all proper purposes" have "control over every part" of the hotel, "even though separate parts thereof may be occupied by guests for hire." . . . The hotel management rightfully may exercise control designed to serve the convenience, comfort, or safety of guests and their property. A person who is not a guest "has in general no legal right to enter or remain" in the hotel against the will of the management.

The hotel management may guard against the possible dangers and annoyances of trespassers or unsolicited visits, and to that end it may, and it is common knowledge that it usually does, exclude all uninvited visitors from the private hotel corridors and from gaining access to the private accommodations of the hotel guests, regardless of whether the one excluded is actually engaged in an otherwise lawful mission, be it commercial, political, or religious.

It was entirely proper for the hotel management to enforce that policy here. That some or even many of the hotel guests may not have found the preaching activities of the defendants objectionable did not deprive the hotel manager of the right to compel observance of such policy. . . .

There is no need to disagree with the contention in defendants' brief that a hotel "is a private place and the fact that invitees of guests may come and go out of the hotel by the hundreds and thousands each day does not change the legal status of the property." It is likewise therein acknowledged that the term "public place" is relative; indeed "what is a public place for one purpose is not for another."

The hotel manager, in stopping defendants' preaching activities and in requesting them to leave the hotel, infringed no rights of the defendants "since the Constitution does not guarantee them any right to go freely onto private property for such purposes." . . . More recently the Court of Appeals stated unanimously that, "no case we know of extends the reach of the Bill of Rights so far as to prescribe the reasonable regulation by an owner of conduct inside his multiple dwelling." The court held that, "A narrow inner hallway on an upper floor of an apartment house is hardly an appropriate place at which to demand the free exercise of those ancient rights." . . .

Greater vigilance is normally demanded and expected of a hotel in the adoption of measures designed to serve the comfort, convenience, and especially the privacy of its guests, as well as their safety and the safety of their property.

The hotel manager, hence, rightfully halted the defendants' preaching activities and justifiably summoned police aid in ejecting them from the hotel. After they were ejected, and notwithstanding that they were admonished not to return to the hotel by the police officer, the defendants, nonetheless, did return for the express purpose of proceeding with their activities, announcing that they proposed to do so unless arrested. In that situation the hotel manager and the police officer were faced with the necessity of offering physical resistance on the street to re-entry of the defendants. Defendants' course, therefore, was calculated to occasion a breach of the peace. It is not prerequisite to arrest on a charge of disorderly conduct that a breach of the peace shall have actually occurred. The defendants' conduct, "at the very least, was such that it tended to disturb the public peace and quiet and to occasion a breach of the peace. That, under our cases, is sufficient."

The police officer's admonition to the defendants that they do not return to the hotel to continue their preaching activities was under the circumstances here present "a useful precaution to avoid possible disturbance." The defendants' refusal to accede to the request of the police officer and their defiance and disregard of his instructions were calculated "to annoy, disturb, interfere with, obstruct, or be offensive to others" within the purview of Subdivision 2 of No. 722 of the Penal Law. The police officer was, therefore, justified in arresting the defendants at their invitation. The evidence establishes their guilt of disorderly conduct.

Ruling of the Court: The defendants are found guilty. Sentence suspended.

Effective hotel management calls for rules of behavior, deportment, and safety. Nevertheless, not all rules are obeyed. What should hotelkeepers or restaurateurs do about infractions? Primarily, of course, they should try to keep out those persons whom they believe are or will become undesirable. In the *Thorpe* case, the hotelkeeper used the police to evict the defendant, who was charged with disorderly conduct. In a similar case discussed in chapter 7, a restaurant owner evicted a patron who had violated the rule that did not permit barefoot restaurant patrons. He called in the police, who arrested the patron (Feldt v. Marriott Corp., 322 A.2d 913 (D.C., 1974).

Since the *Thorpe* case was decided, much has happened. New legislation and new case law make the holdings subject to intellectual debate. Let us examine here possible future considerations.

Our first considerations will be directed to the right of people engaged in religious pursuits to enter a hotel, take an elevator to a floor where guests are accommodated, and then go from door to door endeavoring to engage in religious conversation with the guests. They politely withdraw if the guest does not wish to discuss the matter. If the guest is receptive, they will endeavor, in a peaceful manner, to convince the guest to follow their way of worship.

For our discussion we must first assume an absence of any statute or ordinance that forbids such room-to-room religious activity. Since the decision in the *Thorpe* case in 1950, the U.S. Congress has enacted the Civil Rights Act of 1964 that has two significant provisions for our example. First, it legislatively proclaims that hotels have the status of a place of public accommodation. Second, as places of public accommodation, they cannot discriminate against persons because of race, color, religion, or national origin. Section 2000a of the act states: "Equal access. All persons shall be entitled to the full and equal enjoyment of the goods, services, facilities, privileges, advantages, and accommodations of any place of public accommodation, as defined in this section without discrimination or segregation on the ground of race, color, religion, or national origin."

Thorpe was a "person" within the act who was entitled to "equal access," which included "full and equal enjoyment of the . . . facilities, privileges, advantages . . . of any place of public accommodation." It could be reasonably argued that he was denied equal access because of religion, in violation of the Civil Rights Act.

Another argument is that the Civil Rights Act, in making hotels places of public accommodation, legislatively declared them to be, minimally, places dedicated to the public use. As a place dedicated to the public use, was it sufficiently so dedicated to have created a right to practice First Amendment rights in it, even over the objections of the owners? Arguments could be made either way. If so, then a person such as Thorpe would be entitled as a matter of right to enter the hotel and carry the gospel according to his beliefs.

What about a hotel that has rooms for transients and also provides long-term accommodations for persons who have the legal designation of tenants, which invokes a different body of law? Tenants have total possession of their premises; the space they occupy is their home. Thus, a person such as Thorpe in such a hotel is using the common hallways of the hotel as a means of ingress to the tenant's door. He does not intend to, nor does he, speak of religion at any time until he knocks upon the tenant's door and asks if he can come in and speak of his religious beliefs. Whatever discussion takes place thereafter is in the tenant's premises. Can the hotel bar such a person merely because he is walking down the common hallways on the way to try to speak with a tenant under the circumstances set forth? Bear in mind the fact that these persons are well dressed, well mannered, and well behaved; they are not creating a disturbance nor are they "undesirables." What do you think?[1]

Refusing a Guest Lodging

A hotelkeeper can legitimately refuse a guest lodging for many reasons. It has been the rule that if a hotel has no accommodations, it may refuse persons desiring accommodations. Such a denial is an affirmative defense; that is, the hotelkeeper must prove that no rooms were available (Jackson v. Virginia Hot Springs Co., 209 F. 979 [W.Va., 1914]; Browne v. Brandt, 1 K.B. 696 [1902]). The question of what a "full house" is will be determined by the facts, both actual and circumstantial, in each case. If a hotelkeeper accepts a later guest after refusing a prior request for accommodations, this action could become evidence for a jury. With proper proof, a full house can include "out-of-order" rooms that are being painted or refurbished, as well as all rooms being held for reservations.

In a pertinent New York case, the court ruled that the hotel was too full. In People v. McCarthy, 119 N.Y.S.2d 435 (1953), the manager was charged with operating a house of ill repute. The state attempted to prove that for the twenty-two rooms in the hotel, there were thirty-three separate rentals in one night, making it obvious that some of the rooms were used by more than one patron during the same night. This practice was not an isolated occurrence.

However, the defendant's defense was based on Section 513 of the penal law of New York that makes it a misdemeanor for an innkeeper to refuse to receive guests "without just cause or excuse." The court said that it would not be without just cause or excuse to make a fair inquiry to ascertain whether the couple that desired accommodations was in fact married; nor would it violate Section 40 of the civil rights law to make such an inquiry. Hotels or motels with a nightly 150 percent occupancy rate are described as being in the "hot pillow trade."

The hotelkeeper can also refuse persons who are intoxicated, disorderly, unclean, or suffering from a contagious disease (Markham v. Brown, 8 N.H. 523 [1837]; State v. Steele, 106 N.C. 766 [1890]; Goodenow v. Travis, 3 Johns 423 [N.Y., 1808]). The courts have also allowed ho-

---

1   See Heffron v. International Society for Krishna Consciousness, U.S. Supreme Court, No. 80–795 (Minn.).

telkeepers to refuse known criminals or persons of bad reputation because of the effect such guests have on the reputation of the hotel. The courts permit hotels to protect the reputations of present and future guests, using the maxim, "You are known by the company you keep."

Unquestionably, a prospective guest who is not able or willing to pay a reasonable price for accommodations may be refused accommodations. In states where price control is in force, a hotel cannot charge more than the legal price. But one can do indirectly what one cannot do directly—that is, one can discriminate against certain people by charging a high price for a room. It is dubious whether the courts will permit this type of discrimination, although price discrimination as such is not illegal, except where the state has established a price ceiling. However, if a high room price is charged uniformly to all customers, this is not discrimination. If the guest refuses to pay in advance as required, it can be used as grounds for refusal.

In cases where a guest has unusual property (such as firearms or explosives) that the hotel manager does not customarily receive, the hotel also has grounds for refusal. The question of pets has been complicated recently by statutory inhibitions in all states that forbid the refusal of a person with a seeing eye dog; on the other hand, local laws may prohibit animals in hotels or restaurants. Accepting some but not all pets can lead to possible lawsuits (see 28 Am. Jur. 569).

The fact that hotelkeepers close up at night does not permit them to refuse a guest. A hotel is presumed to be open for the reception of travelers at all hours (Rex v. Ivens, 7 Car. & P. [Eng.] 213, 219 [1835]).

The Consequences of Refusal

What are the consequences of wrongfully refusing a guest? The guest can sue the hotel for general damages, which may include the expenses of going to stay elsewhere and personal injuries because of the refusal. If the refusal is because of race, color, or creed, most state and federal statutes have penalty clauses. The hotel guest may sue for "severe physical and mental strain and nervous shock." Under laws other than hotel law (unless a specific state statute permits this action), one cannot sue and recover (Boyce v. Greeley Square Hotel Co., 168 N.Y.S. 191 [1917]). Today, it is not impossible to have criminal charges brought against a hotelkeeper under certain circumstances.

The right to refuse a guest for limited reasons cannot be considered a blanket reason to refuse all persons. Age is not proper grounds for refusal, and if a hotel refuses service because of age, the proprietor may be subject to both criminal and civil proceedings.

Arbitrary, unreasonable hotel rules could be comparable to refusing a person lodging or food—for example, requiring a three- to five-day stay of a transient guest who desires a hotel room. (Chapter 3 includes a complete discussion of this kind of rule.)

Changing and Entering a Guest's Accommodations

Only two cases have been reported on the hotelkeeper's right to change a guest's accommodations, and both cases agree on the innkeeper's right. In Doyle v. Walker, 26 U.C.Q.B. 502 (1867), the plaintiff-guest sued the defendant hotel for trespassing and for allegedly taking his goods from his room. The court said that whatever the guest's rights are to be reasonably entertained and accommodated, the hotelkeeper has the sole right to select the room or apartment for his guest, and, if he finds it expedient, to change it. The hotelkeeper does not become a trespasser while transferring the guest's belongings.

This finding was followed in Hervey v. Hart, 42 So. 1013 (1906), where the court added that the defendant innkeeper was not liable if he offered the plaintiff proper accommodation in lieu of the room previously assigned to him. Although this may be true, it is questionable whether this is a good policy and, indeed, whether the two cited cases would stand on appeal today because more attention is given to individual rights in contemporary cases.

A better approach would be to ask the guest to move, or at least to offer comparable accommodations. Many hotelkeepers believe that because they own the hotel, they can do whatever they want in the hotel. However, guests can and will take steps to safeguard their status in the hotel.

To manage the hotel effectively, a hotelier undeniably has the right to select a guest's accommodations in the absence of a contract to the contrary. But removing a guest from an assigned room is a questionable practice, unless there are compelling reasons. The argument could be made that this act constitutes a breach of contract, and the tort of trespass may be possible against the hotelkeeper. It is better to discuss such a situation in advance with the hotel's attorney.

The second proposition, the right to enter a guest's room, has been settled in favor of the innkeeper, with certain exceptions. Most courts hold that when guests are assigned a room, they have an express or implied understanding that they are to be the sole occupants during the time that it is set apart for their use. The innkeeper retains the right of access only when necessary for the general conduct of the inn or to attend to the needs of a particular guest.

Under certain circumstances, a hotelkeeper can be considered negligent in not entering a guest's room. For example, in Gore v. Whitmore Hotel Company, 83 S.W.2d 114 (Mo., 1935), the plaintiff was severely injured when bags thrown from the hotel's windows caused him to be violently pushed by other persons off the sidewalk and against the side of a moving taxicab. There was no evidence identifying the room from which the bags had been thrown because all rooms were filled with conventioneers. The court said that the defendant, as a matter of law, was obliged to exercise reasonable care to identify the offenders and the rooms used by them in the perpetration of the wrong. Because the defendant had the right to send his employees into several rooms each day to service them, the jury found that the defendant had the means to ascertain from which rooms the pillows, laundry bags, and telephone books were absent. The defendant was not liable unless he could, by the exercise of ordinary care, have abated the condition in time to prevent injury to the plaintiff.

Selecting Accommodations for a Guest

Though furnished identically and of the same size, all hotel rooms are, in fact, different. In many instances the room location is important—its height, view, or other factors determine the best room. Whatever the situation, the hotelkeeper has the right to select the guest's room.

The 1971 case of *Nixon v. Royal Coach Inn of Houston* treats this point. A lone woman was given a room in a "remote" part of the hotel where she was subsequently assaulted. In this case, the plaintiff could not recover from the hotel on negligence because she was assigned a remote room. The selection of a guest's room has always been the hotelkeeper's prerogative.

Case Example	**Nixon v. Royal Coach Inn of Houston** *464 S.W.2d 900 (Texas, 1971)* (SAM D. JOHNSON, Justice)

Summary judgment case.

Appellant Virginia Key Nixon brought suit against appellee Royal Coach Inn for injuries received when she was assaulted by an unknown assailant inside the Royal Coach Inn motel. Defendant's motion for summary judgment was granted. From the judgment rendered against her, appellant perfects this appeal. . . .

On December 4, 1968, Virginia Key Nixon was twenty-eight years of age, married, and in the employ of General Electric Company of Dallas as a systems analyst. On this particular day her work required her to come to Houston. She drove her automobile from Dallas to Houston and, arriving after it was dark, checked in the Royal Coach Inn alone at approximately 8:30 P.M. A motel employee directed her to the room to which she was assigned, which was some distance away from the main desk. After depositing her luggage in her room, she left the hotel to eat outside the motel area. Approximately one hour later, she returned to the motel, parked her car in the parking lot in the rear of the motel, and entered the building. She ascended the stairs and, while in the process of unlocking the door to her room, was attacked by an unknown assailant. She testified that though she did not lose consciousness, everything went black, and then she started screaming. It was at this time that she saw an unidentified man running down the hall in the direction of the main desk. Her screams brought no assistance, but she was able to reach the office switchboard through the phone in her room. Individuals came to her assistance in response to her phone call.

In her original petition, appellant alleged that appellee was negligent in only two particulars: "(1) billeting a single woman in a remote room in a desolate area of the motel and (2) failing to furnish adequate guards for the protection of its guests as a reasonable prudent innkeeper would have done under the same or similar circumstances."

Appellant brings two points of error: that "the trial court erred in summarily rendering judgment against appellant when there was a fact issue presented" and that "the trial court erred in summarily rendering judgment against appellant and thereby holding that there was no duty owing to appellant, a guest, on the part of the appellee innkeeper." These points of error will be overruled and the judgment of the trial court will be affirmed.

An innkeeper is not an insurer of the safety of its guests. An innkeeper's responsibility to his guests is limited to the exercise of ordinary or reasonable care. We are cited to no authority that requires an innkeeper to assign any guest to a particular room or to any particular part of a hotel or motel. Nor has our attention been directed to any part of the record that would indicate that the appellant was in fact billeted in a remote or desolate area of the motel. Aside from the foregoing, which we consider fatal, an assault by an unknown assailant under the instant record permits no other conclusion except that it was a new and intervening cause altogether disassociated with any act of omission or commission on the part of the appellee. . . . "In order to charge the innkeeper with liability for injury to the person of his guest, negligence on the part of the innkeeper must be shown in connection with the very circumstances that produced the injury." . . . The instant allegation of negligence is most tenuous and its support is wholly lacking.

Ruling of the Court: The judgment of the trial court is affirmed for the defendant.

But other (lower court) decisions have questioned the hotel's prerogative to select a guest's room. In Garzelli v. Howard Johnson's Motor Lodges, Inc., 419 F.Supp. 1210 (N.Y., 1976), singer Connie Francis was raped at knifepoint in a Long Island Howard Johnson's Motor Lodge. She recovered $2.5 million in damages for her inability to continue her lucrative career, and her husband was awarded $150,000 for the profound change in his wife's sexual habits. The rationale of the court was that the motel failed to put the singer in a "safe and secure room," as the intruder gained access to the room through an improperly locked sliding glass door. A September 1976 ruling by Brooklyn federal court Judge Thomas C. Platt upheld the jury award to Francis, but the award to her husband was ruled excessive; his compensation was reduced to $25,000.

Many similar cases hold to the well-established principle that American juries penalize slack security in cases of rape attacks and are likely to make those they find negligent pay large damages.

If this trend continues, hotelkeepers will be forced to protect their guests by hiring their personnel more carefully and using technological devices to forestall such occurrences. The *Nordmann* case (see chapter 10) is a very good example of a hotelkeeper who was negligent in his security measures and in training his personnel. In the *Brewer* case (see chapter 10), the hotel was not found liable for the rape of a guest because the defendant was able to show that his security was adequate and that the entry of a rapist-burglar was unforeseeable.

Evicting a Guest

The right to evict a guest is one of the hotelkeeper's basic rights. In McBride v. Hosey, 197 S.W.2d 372 (Texas, 1946), the court said that a guest had the right to leave the hotel at any time, and the defendant had the right to withdraw hotel privileges at any time. The court reasoned that public inns are conducted for travelers and transient persons, and it is not the duty of the innkeeper to keep a guest who has lost that status—that a person is not entitled to stay indefinitely and on reasonable notice may be ejected without any other reasons. If the right of possession (dominion and control over property) exists in the hotel, the hotelkeeper has the right to evict a guest, provided no more force than necessary is used.

Failure to Pay Hotel Bill

Eviction for failing to pay a hotel bill is ordinarily carried out by asking the guest for the amount due and requesting him to leave by a certain hour if the bill is not paid. If the guest fails to pay after such a demand, the hotel may evict him—usually by locking the room after removing the guest's baggage. In certain states the hotel has the right to hold such baggage under common law lien or by a statutory lien for the unpaid bill. If the guest fails to pay after such a demand, the hotel has the right to evict him physically, but it should not use any more force than necessary.

In Sawyer v. Congress Square Hotel Company, 170 A.2d 645 (Me., 1961), the plaintiff-guest was evicted because of nonpayment of charges. It was the court's opinion that:

> [I]f a room is rented for a definite period under such circumstances that the occupant assumes full control over it and does not receive the ordinary services that the hotel offers to guests, the relationship of hotelkeeper and guest does not exist. There are of course borderline cases. But where, as here, a person occupies a room in a hotel, registers as others do, receives maid service, and has the benefit of other incidental services that the hotel gives, she is a guest, and this is true in spite of the fact that the stay may be a long one and that she pays on a weekly or a monthly basis.

The appeal of the plaintiff-guest was denied, and the defendant hotel won the case.

Overstaying

Occupying a room beyond the agreed time can also become a reason for eviction. The contract for a room is for a definite time, be it one day or one year. When this period is over, the contract has been satisfied and the guest must leave. If they do not leave, their contract is breached, and the hotel can do one of two things. Either it can assume that a new contract exists on a day-to-day basis and the guest is subject to the cost of the room; or, if the hotel has made other commitments for the room, it can evict the guest. A good practice that most innkeepers have adopted is to print or stamp the date of departure on the registration card and on a copy given to the guest with an oral comment of the departure date.

Even at common law, the innkeeper can remove a stay-over who refuses to leave, using as much force as is reasonably necessary. A stay-over in this position is wrongfully upon the premises and has the status of a trespasser.

Hawaii, Louisiana, and North Carolina, as well as Puerto Rico, have passed statutes that codify the common law position. For example, Hawaii's statute, Hawaii Rec. Statute 468K–8 (Supp. 1978), specifies: "Any guest who intentionally continues to occupy an assigned bedroom beyond the scheduled departure without the prior written approval of the keeper shall be deemed a trespasser." This modifies the common law slightly in that there is no requirement on the part of the innkeeper to request that the overstaying guest leave.

Louisiana's statute specifies the criteria that innkeepers must meet in order to avail themselves of the statute. Additionally, this statute makes it a crime for a guest to stay over if the innkeeper has complied with the statute.

North Carolina's statute requires the innkeeper to issue a written statement specifying the time period during which the guest may occupy an assigned room and have the guest initial it so that a valid contract comes into existence. At the end of the period specified in the contract, the innkeeper automatically has the right to lock the former guest out of the room. The statute even denies the former guest the right to enter to reclaim any personal property and permits the innkeeper to remove it without liability, except for loss or damage resulting from the removal. The terminology of the statute permits the use of reasonable force in preventing the lodger from reentering the room.

Puerto Rico requires the hotelier to call the police to physically remove a holdover (P.P. Laws Ann. It. 10 #719, 720 [1976]). In the absence of statutes specifically covering the rights of innkeepers with regard to overstays, innkeepers should proceed with caution in effecting their eviction so as to avoid the possibility of lawsuits.

Persons of Ill Repute

In Raider v. Dixie Inn, 248 S.W. 229 (Ky., 1923), the hotelkeeper evicted the plaintiff-guest when he found out that she was a prostitute. Although this is a 1923 case and mores have changed, the courts still use this case as an adequate reason for eviction.

When the plaintiff returned on the day of eviction, her baggage had been put in the lobby and she was informed of the reasons for her eviction. The defendant had the good sense not to make a scene; otherwise, the case could have had a different ending. The plaintiff, however, said she had been humiliated. In its opinion, the court stated, "It appears, therefore, fully settled that an innkeeper may lawfully refuse to entertain objectionable characters, if to do so is calculated to injure his business or to place himself, business, or guest in a hazardous, uncomfortable, or dangerous situation. The innkeeper need not accept anyone as a guest who is calculated to and will injure his business. A prizefighter who has been guilty of law breaking may be excluded. Neither is an innkeeper required to entertain a card shark; persons of bad reputation or those who are under suspicion; drunken and disorderly persons; one who commits a trespass by breaking in the door; one who is filthy or who subjects the guests to annoyance."

The decision in *Raider* v. *Dixie Inn* probably could not stand up today unless it could be proved that the plaintiff was practicing her illegal trade. What constitutes an objectionable character is a debatable question, and the hotelier choosing this route of eviction should proceed carefully.

Intoxication and Disorderly Conduct

A hotel has the right to evict a person who is intoxicated and disturbs other guests. Intoxication alone is not adequate reason in most states for eviction. There must be a disturbance of the peace, disorderly conduct, threatening of other guests, damage to the room, or the like. And if the guest became drunk in the hotel bar, the hotelier must take care of the guest as much as possible and must attempt to sober him up before he can cause any damage. (Chapter 13 deals further with this situation.)

Seriously or Contagiously Ill Guests

Hotel operators have the right to evict a guest who contracts a contagious disease. They must use extreme care, however, not to bring about a worsening of the guest's condition, which generally means that the public health authority, a doctor, and, of course, an ambulance should be called if the condition necessitates (see discussion of *Boyce* v. *Greeley Square Hotel Company* in chapter 3).

Breaking House Rules

House rules should be posted in conspicuous places, preferably in guest rooms. The rules should be kept to a minimum, and they should indicate serious breaches of house policy. If the hotel has a swimming pool, a house rule that bars guests from walking in wet swimsuits through the lobby is reasonable, but alternative directions should be provided. All regulations concerning the pool should be at poolside, as well as in rooms. Of course, rules on pets must be supported by the removal of pets that are sneaked into guests' rooms. Allowing exceptions could make the hotel liable to discrimination lawsuits.

Persons Not Registered

When a person is not or has never been a guest of the hotel, the hotelkeeper can evict the person without cause. Unfortunately, that person can still bring action against the hotelkeeper, even though the probability of the plaintiff's winning is practically nonexistent.

In Hennig v. Goldberg, 68 N.Y.S.2d 698 (1947), the court held that a nonregistered guest had no standing as a guest, even though in this case the plaintiff had permission from a registered guest to use the room. The rights of a guest are not assignable or transferable; therefore, a guest cannot give another person the status of guest when it is not in his or her power to do so. A much cited case illustrating this same principle is Warren v. Penn Harris Hotel, 91 Pa. Sup. Ct. 195 (1927) (see the discussion in chapter 4).

Persons without Baggage

Unquestionably, persons coming to a hotel for immoral purposes can be refused a room. But how does one determine the identity of such persons? In certain states where adultery, fornication, and unnatural acts are not considered illegal, persons who are not man and wife can register, unless hotel rules bar such persons (see chapter 6).

In Coquelet v. Union Hotel Company, 115 A. 813 (Md., 1921), a married couple was refused accommodations because they had no baggage. The hotel had a rule that stated that couples without baggage would not be accepted. The couple had spent an afternoon in Baltimore, had seen a movie, and had had dinner at the Caswell Hotel (operated by the defendant). The plaintiff, who had been shell-shocked by the war, became ill, and the couple decided to stay overnight in Baltimore. They were not allowed to register, however, because they had no luggage. When he was later asked why the plaintiff had been refused a room, the desk clerk gave no reasons. The plaintiff and his wife found accommodations elsewhere, but they brought an action of slander against the hotel.

The defendant hotel had an established house rule stating that persons without baggage could not be assigned a room in the absence of proper identification, which the court held was entirely reasonable. On appeal, no evidence was presented that the plaintiff had credentials showing he was married. (It is debatable whether most married people can actually prove that they are married.)

The so-called slanderous words allegedly uttered by the desk clerk were something Mrs. Coquelet had assumed from his tone of voice; the altercation had not been overheard by any other persons. However, if the discussion had been malicious on the part of the desk clerk and had been overheard by others, the court would have held for the plaintiff—accusing any woman of unchastity, whether married or not, is slanderous.

The hotel rule requiring luggage (although weak) provides that guests be truly travelers. Furthermore, the bags serve as security for the extension of credit. Therefore, it is reasonable for a hotelkeeper to make inquiries as to the identity of couples coming to the hotel without bags. Such inquiries should be made tactfully, with proper regard for the rights of the persons involved. The mere absence of luggage does not in itself indicate an immoral or illegal intent.

Business Competitors

If a business competitor comes to stay in one's hotel or eat in one's restaurant, but not to act as a competitor trying to solicit customers, he cannot be refused. But when a business competitor comes onto one's property to attempt to solicit customers, he can unquestionably be enjoined from such an unlawful practice.

In Champie v. Castle Hot Springs Company, 233 P. 1107 (Ariz., 1925), the court held that an innkeeper could refuse a competitor access to his inn when the competitor came to solicit the innkeeper's trade. Such an action, however, is not comparable to granting a monopoly to the innkeeper, or to depriving a guest of his freedom.

Can a business competitor who comes to the hotel to deliver food and liquor ordered by a guest (assuming the hotel offers such services) be kept out of the hotel? The answer seems to be yes, because such services will lower the hotelkeeper's total volume of business and therefore constitute outright competition. If permission is granted to the competitor, however, to carry on his business, he can become subject to a special fee (such as a "corkage charge").

Although such a case has never been tested, the argument could be made that a rule barring competitors is in violation of states that have antimonopoly statutes, such as New York's General Business Law, Section 340 (known as the Donnelly Act). Among other things, this act provides that "every contract agreement, arrangement, or combination whereby . . . competition or the free exercise of any activity in the conduct of any business, trade, or commerce or in the furnishing of any service in this state is or may be restrained . . . is hereby declared to be against public policy, illegal, and void."

The only such case on record, Eagle Spring Water Company v. Webb & Knapp, Inc., 236 N.Y.S.2d 266 (1962), concerns a commercial building owner who refused tenants the right to select their own vendor for bottled drinking water. Here, the court ruled that the arbitrary choice by the landlord of tradespeople for various services was unrelated to the protection of any legitimate interest in the property by the landlord; therefore, the tenant was able to obtain injunctive relief from such an arbitrary decision.

The *Eagle* case has several relevant points for the hotel industry. The atmosphere of a hotel can be one of its most important attributes, and a hotel must protect itself against incompetent independent contractors (who could jeopardize the hotel's business) by refusing them the right to carry on business in the hotel. Thus, business competitors can be barred from the hotel, or the hotel may select exclusive concessionaires to cater to guests.

Illegal Eviction or Detention

The eviction of a person from a room for cause is proper. It should be carried out considerately; no harsh words or force should be used unless absolutely necessary.

In Milner Hotels, Inc., v. Brent, 43 So.2d 654 (Miss., 1949), an eviction for cause was handled very badly. In brief, the plaintiff-guest paid the room rent for her husband, daughter, and herself weekly. The rent was paid up for one more day when the plaintiff tried to pay for an additional week while her husband was out of town. At this time she was not permitted to do so and was told to vacate her room by the manager, who said in a loud and angry voice, "We do not want you here." This exchange took place in the hotel lobby where it was overheard by numerous persons. The woman was also locked out of her room, and her clothes were kept from her and the child. Both mother and daughter suffered from the lack of clothing and were humiliated, embarrassed, and mentally distressed because of the damage to the plaintiff's reputation. Her clothes were returned five days later, along with an additional bill that she refused to pay.

The plaintiff had been a witness in a prior case against the Milner Corporation. The manager of the Earle Hotel (owned by the Milner Corporation) later admitted to Mrs. Brent that he had been ordered to get rid of all persons connected to the previous case—in which he had been a codefendant.

The plaintiff won in the lower court, but the defendant appealed the decision, arguing that only nominal damages and not a punitive award should go to the plaintiff. The defendant also argued that the manager's evidence (as a party in the first case) should not have been allowed as evidence. The defendant's first point as to damages was rejected by the court because it is a well-established law that punitive damages are due when there is (1) a wrongful act, (2) intentionally performed, (3) with a gross disregard of rights, and (4) willfulness.

All four elements were present in this case. Certainly, slanderous words uttered before many people constitutes a wrongful act. The manager spoke these words with intentional malice and in gross disregard of the plaintiff's rights. In this case, the judge also believed that the words were willful and that punitive damages should be awarded.

Punitive Damages for Illegal Eviction

The hotelkeeper's right to evict creates certain responsibilities. An illegal eviction can be costly for the hotel or for those doing the evicting. In the case of Lopez v. City of New York, 357 N.Y.S.2d 659 (1974), the plaintiff hotel guest brought suit for illegal eviction, as well as for damages and mental suffering. A New York City agent carried out the illegal eviction, thus allowing the court to award the plaintiff damages for both lost goods and mental suffering. The fact that the defendant was the City of New York had no effect on the outcome of the case; the same results and rationale would have ensued if the hotel itself had been the defendant.

How to Evict

It has been consistently held that when the right to evict is employed against a guest who is obviously obnoxious or for some other reason, the hotelkeeper may forcibly remove the guest without resort to legal process—provided that no more force is used than is necessary. Of course, the question is what is the right amount of force. Obviously, if the guest is obstreperous, one must counter force with force, making sure there are witnesses (preferably not of the hotel staff) to prove the force used by the guest. This rule follows in any eviction by a hotelkeeper or restaurateur—that only reasonable force may be used, or whatever force is necessary to counter force on the part of the guest.

One very important consideration in an eviction proceeding is that the person being evicted must be a guest and not a tenant; also, the eviction must be for one of the previously stipulated reasons. If an eviction is prompted by personal reasons, or because of race, color, or creed, without provocation, the hotel can be held liable.

A house officer should be carefully instructed on how to evict a guest. His actions are imputed to the hotelkeeper. In extreme situations, the police should be asked to help. At no time should slanderous words be used. A properly executed eviction for cause is not actionable, but lawful eviction accompanied by slanderous words can lead to an action for slander by the guest. In all situations eviction should be a last resort remedy.

Refusing a Diner

Under common law a restaurant, unless it was part of an inn, had the right to select its guests and to refuse any person. The Civil Rights Act's antidiscrimination clause prohibits the refusal of a person because of race, color, or creed.

In Harder v. Auberge Des Fougeres, 338 N.Y.S.2d 356 (1972), the plaintiffs had confirmed dinner reservations, but when they arrived they were refused service. This case supports the proposition that refusal of service by a restaurant is an intentional tort and therefore is actionable. Of course, if the restaurant can show grounds for refusal that could alter the outcome of the case—such as drunkenness, improper dress, or unwillingness to pay the bill—it will not be held liable.

The *Harder* case raises the question of when a guest may be refused service. Must an 8 P.M. dinner reservation be honored at 10 P.M.? What rights do guests with reservations have? Accepting a reservation constitutes a contract—an offer, an acceptance, and valid consideration. The damages recoverable if the guest wins depend on a number of factors. Restaurateurs can damage their case by arguing with the guest and inadvertently slandering him. Slander allows the jury to award a guest a high judgment.

Force and Care Required to Protect Guests

To a certain degree, guests are under the protection of their host—whether it is a hotel, motel, or restaurant. The hotel is the guest's home away from home, and his or her ensuing rights in such a relationship have been discussed in previous chapters. In what ways should hotelkeepers protect their guests? How much force can they use? When must they call in the police or hire in-house guards? The next two cases deal with these questions.

The first case, *Edwards v. Great American Insurance Company* (see chapter 10), pertains to the type of force hotelkeepers may use to protect their guests. The hotelkeeper shot at some prowlers late in the evening, hitting one of them. The amount of force was extreme, but it was justified in this case because of the time of day (night), the neighborhood, past occurrences, and the fact that prior thefts had been reported to the police. Obviously, reporting thefts and suspicious people on or near the premises is advisable if extreme force (use of a gun) is a future possibility.

Using a weapon that can maim or kill an intruder should be the last resort of a hotelkeeper protecting guests or employees. As demonstrated in the *Edwards* case, however, it is the general rule that innkeepers or restaurateurs must, if it is in their power to do so, protect guests while they are on the premises. To justify the use of a deadly weapon, the hotelkeeper must have reasonable fear of loss of life or serious bodily injury to himself or his guests.

In cases in which the hotelkeeper did not protect his guests, juries found that he owed at least ordinary and reasonable care to protect his guests against injury. Therefore, in the *Nordmann* case (see chapter 10), in which the plaintiffs were assaulted in their room after attending a banquet for 1,200 guests, it was found that the hotel did not notify the police soon enough, nor did it have enough personnel on duty to protect the guests. The plaintiff's wife was awarded $16,000 and he himself received $5,000.

Detaining Employees

An employer of a hotel or restaurant can require as a condition of employment that employees submit to a reasonable examination when they enter the place of business.

In Greenbaum v. Brooks, 139 S.E.2d 432 (Ga., 1964), an employer who experienced shortages in merchandise hired a "personnel analyst" to investigate. The plaintiff, who was interrogated in the employer's office, brought charges of false imprisonment against the employer, although the personnel analyst hired by the employer did the actual "interviewing."

Was the employee unlawfully detained and deprived of his personal liberty? The charge of false imprisonment is a difficult action to refute. All an employee or guest must demonstrate is that the restraint was effected through words, acts, or gestures that induce reasonable apprehension that force will be used if the person does not submit. In essence, the plaintiff must believe that he is in reasonable fear of personal injury or difficulty.

In this case the independent contractor (personnel analyst) was considered the agent of the employer, and the employee won the case.

Statutory Provisions to Protect the Hotelkeeper

The Hotel Lien

The area of the innkeeper's law that concerns the innkeeper's lien has been the subject of much litigation. Although a pattern has emerged as to what can be expected from the U.S. Supreme Court on questions of compliance with federal constitutional guarantees, the matter is in fact relegated to the states for decision on a state-by-state basis as to the legality of the old common law innkeeper's lien.

The early common law placed many duties and liabilities on innkeepers, but it also protected them from dishonest guests who would leave with their accounts unpaid. The medium selected for that protection was the innkeeper's lien that extended to all personalty that the guest brought into the inn and was for the full amount of all expenses incurred as a guest.

The lien was a possessory lien; that is, the innkeeper had to retain the possession of the goods and chattel upon which the lien applied. Once possession was given up, the lien was lost, and the innkeeper would have no further rights to it, even if the goods came into his possession legally later.

Over time all of the states enacted legislation reestablishing the lien, and its application continued, until 1970 when the judicial revolt against the statutes that codified the lien began. This revolt encompassed not only innkeepers' liens, but all possessory-type liens that could result in deprivation of an individual's property without due process of law.

The attack was launched in the state of California in the case of Klim v. Jones, 27 315 F.Supp. 109 (Cal., 1970), in which the court ruled that the California innkeeper's lien statute was unconstitutional because it allowed hoteliers to take property of guests without due process of law, thereby violating the Fourteenth Amendment. Similar cases followed in other states, and eventually the U.S. Supreme Court pronounced on the matter.

In Sharrock v. Dell Buick-Cadillac, Inc., 379 N.E.2d 1169 (N.Y., 1978), the plaintiff and defendant disagreed over a bill concerning work done on a car, and she refused to pay. The defendant imposed a lien and turned the car over to an auctioneer for sale. The court found that the acts of the defendant in selling the plaintiff's car in that manner did violate her due process rights under the Fourteenth Amendment because it permitted her to be deprived of property without a hearing. Furthermore, the statute permitted a private citizen to exercise a traditionally public function; hence the function becomes the act of the state and, therefore, state action prohibited by the Fourteenth Amendment.

The Supreme Court spoke on the matter in Flagg Bros. v. Brooks, 436 U.S. 149 (1978). Brooks and her family had been evicted from their apartment, and their belongings had been stored at the Flagg Bros. storage company warehouse. Brooks had not paid her storage charges, and Flagg threatened her with the sale of her stored belongings pursuant to New York's Uniform Commercial Code unless she paid her storage account. She brought a class action against Flagg, seeking damages and injunctive relief and a declaration that such a sale would violate her due process and equal protection rights.

The Supreme Court held that the pertinent section of the Uniform Commercial Code did not violate the due process clause of the Fourteenth Amendment because there was no state involvement to bring it into play, and most rights secured by the Constitution are protected only against infringement by governments. The burden was on Brooks to establish not only that Flagg acted under color of the challenged statute, but also that its actions were properly attributable to the state of New York. This she could not do because there was no overt official involvement by the state of New York. Furthermore, the court did not believe that there was any action permitted the Flagg Bros. by the statute that may be fairly attributed to the state of New York. In order for it to be said that the state of New York delegated powers to Flagg Bros. that would meet the state action requirements of the Fourteenth Amendment, Brooks must show that there was a delegation by the state of a power "traditionally *exclusively* reserved to the State." Although many powers traditionally have been performed by the state, very few have been exclusively reserved to it. The Court said that basically this was a controversy between a creditor and a debtor, and the settlement of such disputes is not traditionally an exclusive public function. This was essentially a private matter that in no way involved the state so as to create a constitutional question under the Fourteenth Amendment.

The third case that will help establish the present status of the lien law is the *Sharrock* case again. This time we are looking at how the Court of Appeals for the State of New York disposed of it (Sharrock v. Dell Buick-Cadillac, 408 N.Y.S.2d 39 [1978]). The *Brooks* case had been decided by the U.S. Supreme Court just two months before. But clearly the New York courts were looking for a way to strike the present laws down so that there could be a guarantee of due process to anyone who was going to be irrevocably denied of their property. The New York court found such an instrumentality within the framework of the constitution of the state of New York. As the highest court of the state, its dictates on the constitutionality of a state law would be binding on all courts, for this was a state question and not a federal one.

The New York court was bound to accept the ruling of the Supreme Court and held that there was no basis for finding the code section violative of the Fourteenth Amendment. However, the court went on to say that the mere fact that the activity might not constitute state action for purposes of the federal Constitution does not mean that the same result must be reached when the claim is made that it is violative of the state constitution. The court said that there was no requirement in the New York Constitution for state action, but that did not mean that the state constitution eliminates the necessity of any state involvement at all. Rather the absence of state action language merely provides the basis for applying a more flexible state involvement requirement than that currently being imposed federally.

Common law afforded the defendant only the right to possession;

it was the state that authorized the enforcement of the lien by means of an *ex parte* sale of the vehicle without first affording its owner an opportunity to be heard. By so doing the state did not merely give its seal of approval to the common law lien; instead it entwined itself into the debtor-creditor relationship arising out of otherwise regular consumer transactions. By the passage of the statute, the state not only authorized the creditor to bypass the courts and adopt the sale procedure, which is less likely to afford the debtor due process, but encouraged him to do so by making it easier, faster, and less cumbersome. It thus encouraged the creditor to adopt this patently unfair procedure, insulated him from any criminal or civil liability arising out of the sale, and further required a state agency, the Department of Motor Vehicles, to recognize and record the sale, thus enabling a garageman to transfer title to that which he would not otherwise be deemed to own.

The court determined that the enforcement of the garageman's lien constituted meaningful state participation. It then went on to say that fundamental notions of due process require that before a state may deprive a person of a significant property interest in aid of a creditor, that person must be given notice and an opportunity to be heard prior to deprivation of that interest. The court then said that the statute at issue fell far short of due process, and it made it clear that the garageman's right to maintain his possessory lien was unaffected by its decision in the *Sharrock* case; it is merely that he cannot sell the vehicle until a method has been devised that will satisfy the due process requirements of the state constitution.

So where are we now in this matter of innkeeper's liens? The reasoning applied to others who are beneficiaries of some sort of a possessory lien is equally applicable to the innkeeper. The U.S. Supreme Court has clearly indicated that the possessory lien does not arouse the protection of the Fourteenth Amendment. Furthermore there is no state action in the enactment of the statutes determining the rights of those who become possessors of a lien as the result of a creditor-debtor relationship. Therefore, the states are now free to make their own determinations regarding the problem. Liens are as valid today as they ever were under the common law, except when modified by statute.

Rights under the Lien

The hotelkeeper's lien differs from other types in that it attaches to the property even though hotelkeepers may not have the property physically in their possession. They may prevent the guest from removing property from the premises and take possession of it themselves until the hotel charges have been paid. The lien of the hotelkeeper attaches as soon as the guest is received, and if the property is later sold by the guest, the lien is not affected (Smith v. Colcord, 115 Mass. 70 [1874]).

The hotelkeeper must determine to what property the lien applies.

The court has held in general that most property that a guest brings into the hotel is under the lien—except for goods the hotelkeeper or employees know do not belong to the guest (Lurch v. Brown, 65 Misc. 190, 119 N.Y.S. 637 [1909]); or for property that belongs to an accompanying guest with whom the hotel has no direct contract (McIlvaine v. Hilton, 7 Hun 594 [N.Y., 1876]); or when two people using the same room keep separate accounts.

This lien is so powerful that it has few exceptions. When goods are stolen, the general rule is that no person has a better title to them than the true owner. There are a few minor exceptions to this rule in the Law of Negotiable Instruments, or when the legislature has decreed in statutes who should be the true owner. But when hotel owners, unaware they are dealing with stolen property, attach a lien to such goods, they have a better title to these goods than their original owner (the true owner). These bizarre results can and have happened.

Liens have been held valid on such diverse objects as pianos; goods with chattel mortgages against them (provided the hotel had no actual notice of this); valuables in a safety-deposit box; stolen property (as long as the hotel had no notice of the theft) (Walters v. Gerard, 189 N.Y. 302; Lurch v. Wilson, 62 Misc. 259); and automobiles (Chesham Auto Supply v. Beresford Hotel, 29 Times L.R. 584). It is not limited to articles necessary for travel. Goods of traveling sales representatives can be subject to a lien; however, in Massachusetts, New York, and several other states, an innkeeper has no lien upon the property of seamen who have shipped for a voyage. Nor does it extend to a person's necessary wearing apparel and certain personal jewelry, such as wedding rings.

Although the lien is considered general, it cannot be used on debts incurred during a previous visit by a guest. A temporary removal of the goods by the guest during which the relation of guest and innkeeper continues will not prevent the hotelkeeper from holding the goods to cover the whole debt.

Items on a guest's bill that can be included in a lien are service charges for delivery of a guest's baggage to and from the hotel, valet service, C.O.D. charges, and money advanced (a reasonable amount). However, no lien will hold when the services were rendered by a doctor or an independent contractor, even if this contractor is the owner of one of the shops in the building.

Generally, a hotelkeeper is under no duty to investigate the ownership of the baggage that a guest brings in with him. The hotelkeeper's lien extends, therefore, to chattels (personal property or animals) brought on the premises, irrespective of ownership. Certain exceptions exist. Within reasonable limits, and with due regard to their own business and the convenience of other guests, hotelkeepers allow guests to bring or to have sent chattels of a guest's own selection. Since the guest expects the hotelkeeper to receive chattels as if they were part of his luggage, neither the guest nor a third person has any cause to object to the hotelkeeper's having a lien on such chattels.

In the case of Hickman v. Thomas, 16 Ala. 666 (1849), the court said that because the government had a privileged position, no lien could be placed against the guest's goods. Hotelkeepers cannot place a lien on property brought to their hotel by a guest if they are aware that a third party owns it or if they are aware that the property is stolen. However, the lien on such goods is valid if the hotelkeeper was unaware of such third-party ownership. The lien is terminated when the bill is paid. The hotelkeeper must then return the guest's property.

The lien has been held to be valid against a guest who is incapable of making a contract. This is justified because the innkeeper's lien is created by law and not by contract. In an early case, Watson v. Cross, 63 Ky. 148 (1865), the court said that even though the indebtedness was incurred by a minor, the hotelkeeper was obliged to accept minors as guests. Therefore, it would be legally absurd to compel a person to make a contract and allow the other party to avoid the obligations of that contract.

American courts enforce the rule that the goods of the wife may not be held under the hotelkeeper's lien when it appears the indebtedness was contracted by her husband (Geobel v. United Rys. Co. of St. Louis, 181 S.W. 1151 [Mo., 1915]). The same is true if a third person contracts to pay the bill of a guest (Baker v. Stratton, 19A 661 [N.J., 1890]). When hotelkeepers have a lien on the personal baggage of their guest, and the guest attempts to take it away, they can be held for theft (Regina v. Hollingsworth, 4 Terr. L.R. 168 [Canada, 1899]).

Defrauding the Hotelkeeper and Restaurateur

All states plus the District of Columbia have passed statutes that seek to protect the innkeeper and hotelier from fraudulent guests. (Appendix 3 lists the citation for each state's statutes dealing with defrauding an innkeeper.) Much of the legislation in this area has been recently enacted or recently revised, and many of the statutes provide different classifications of the crime and the penalties to be imposed depending upon the amount and value of the goods or services received as a result of the fraud.

The classification of crimes into misdemeanor or felony categories, depending on the sums involved, and the punishments imposed for violations tend to show the seriousness with which the states approach this type of crime. Perhaps because of the transitory status of the perpetrator of such crimes or perhaps because once the services have been rendered, there can be no repossession of the product, the legislatures decided to impose heavy penalties on the violators. For example, in Alabama if the amount involved is $25 or less, it will constitute a misdemeanor punishable by a fine up to $1,000 and imprisonment at hard labor up to twelve months; if the sum exceeds $25, it is considered to be grand larceny, a felony, and the punishment accordingly is much more severe.

Hoteliers should familiarize themselves with the statutes in their respective states. If *any* of the elements required are missing, then there is no case and the guest cannot be found guilty of violating the statute. The case of Cottonreeder v. State, 389 So.2d 1169 (Ala., 1980), points up the consequences of failing to meet these requisites.

In the *Cottonreeder* case, the defendant had taken lodgings in an Alabama hotel. When he was first registered, he was told that he would have to pay his rent daily before 2:00 P.M. He complied with this request for about ten days and then started paying every other day, which the hotel went along with. Then he started skipping to every few days and then weekly. He asked the manager if he could pay the bill weekly because other methods were interfering with his meetings. The manager agreed so long as the bill was under $200 weekly. The defendant later skipped a period over two weeks and then paid. When he made that payment, he said that he would still make weekly payments. The payment that he made at that time was the last he was to make. The manager continued to ask for the payment, and the defendant said he would pay. When the bill reached $1,033.99, the manager locked him out and sought the complaint. After the charges were filed and before trial, the defendant paid the full amount of the bill. The manager said that about ten days or so before she locked the guest out of his room and brought the charges, she stopped believing him. She further testified that the defendant had never refused to pay her; he just did not pay.

The lower court convicted the defendant, and he appealed. The Court of Criminal Appeals for the state of Alabama reversed the conviction, stating that before a jury can be permitted to convict a defendant of this crime, which requires a fraudulent intent, there must be attending circumstances in connection with the act done that bespeak fraud. The court said that in order for the misrepresentation to constitute fraud, it must be a false statement of a material fact intentionally made to induce another party to act in reliance on the truth of the statement.

In the case of State v. Croy, 145 N.Y.2d 118 (Wis., 1966), the court reached a different result. The defendant had clandestinely left the hotel without informing the management of his departure. He left his luggage behind. When he left he owed the hotel bills that had accumulated for room, board, long-distance telephone calls, and other items. The statute in Wisconsin provides that it is fraud on a hotel or restaurant keeper if a person who "had obtained food, lodgings or accommodations at any hotel, motel, . . . intentionally absconds without paying for it." The defendant argued that he could not be found guilty because he had left his luggage behind and that the statute was violated only if he had surreptitiously removed his luggage and thereby denied the hotel their innkeeper's lien. The court disagreed, holding that a reading of the statute called for a different conclusion. The statute used the term *intentionally absconds*, which the court interpreted to mean *clandestinely leaves*, such as the defendant did here, and that is all that was necessary.

The *Wagoner* case presents us with another instance where the courts said that there must be proof of the intent to defraud before a defendant can be found guilty of defrauding an innkeeper. Even in the presence of statutory language authorizing the finding of sufficient intent to defraud, the courts are reluctant to jump to that conclusion if other reasonable conclusions are possible.

Case Example	Wagoner v. State
	617 P.2d 895 (Okla., 1980)
	(BUSSEY, Judge)

The appellant, Carlton Lee Wagoner, was charged in the District Court of Canadian County with a violation of 21 O.S.1971, Section 1503, Defrauding an Innkeeper. The jury found the appellant guilty of the above charge after former conviction of a felony and assessed a sentence of one-and-one-half years' imprisonment, in conformance with 21 O.S.1971, Section 51. The defendant was sentenced accordingly.

The pertinent facts reveal that on June 18, 1978, the appellant and his common-law wife, Lucinda Sherman Wagoner, rented a room at the Phillips Motel in El Reno from the complaining witness, Virgil Hendricksen. The two lived in the room, along with Ms. Wagoner's two children, until early August when the children left, and the appellant and his wife moved to a smaller room in the motel. In late September, Hendricksen observed that the appellant's car had been gone from the parking lot for three or four days. He testified that he entered the room, not knowing whether the appellant had departed permanently or intended to return, and found numerous articles of clothing. On the fifth day of the appellant's absence, Hendricksen removed the appellant's belongings from the room. Hendricksen further testified that the appellant had established credit with him during his occupancy and had made periodic payments, although the balance was never completely paid. He testified that at the time the appellant departed, a balance of $419.98 remained unpaid. Hendricksen's testimony revealed that Ms. Wagoner telephoned him in late September and advised him that she and the appellant planned to return. He testified he could not remember the exact date of this call or the length of time the appellant had been gone at the time of the call. His record showed, however, that on October 2, 1978, a $50.00 payment was made by Ms. Wagoner on the balance of the account. This payment was made approximately one week after he had sought out the appellant at a local bowling alley where the appellant had promised to pay the entire balance as soon as he could raise the money.

The appellant's first assignment of error is that the trial court erred in overruling his demurrer to the evidence since, he argues, the state failed to make a *prima facie* case against him. More specifically, his contention is that the evidence presented by the state in its case in chief was insufficient to show the requisite intent to defraud, necessary for a conviction under the statute.

The statute under which the appellant was convicted, 21 O.S.1971, Section 1503, reads in pertinent part:

"Any person who shall obtain food, lodging, services, or other accommodations at any hotel, inn, restaurant, boarding house, rooming house, motel, or auto camp, with intent to defraud the owner or keeper thereof, . . . if the value of such food, lodging, services, or other accommodations be more than twenty dollars ($20.00), any person convicted hereunder shall be deemed guilty of a felony and shall be punished by imprisonment in the state penitentiary for a term not exceeding five (5) years. . . . Proof that such lodging, food, services, or other accommodations were obtained by false pretense or by false or fictitious show or pretense of any baggage or other property, or that he gave a check on which payment was refused, or that he left the hotel, inn, restaurant, boarding house, rooming house, motel, apartment house, apartment, rental unit or rental house, trailer camp, or auto camp without payment or offering to pay for such food, lodging, services, or other accommodations, or that he surreptitiously removed or attempted to remove his baggage, or that he registered under a fictitious name, shall be *prima facie* proof of the intent to defraud mentioned in this section; but this act shall not apply where there has been an agreement in writing for delay in payment."

In its brief, the state argues that the evidence that the appellant left the motel without paying or offering to pay is sufficient to establish a *prima facie* showing of intent to defraud. While a plain reading of the statute could support such an interpretation, this court in the case of McLemore v. State, 55 Okl.Cr. 155, 27 P.2d 172 (1933), construed the statute (then O.S.1931, Section 2097) in a different light. This court stated:

"The statute, while general in its terms, is particularly directed against those who make direct false pretenses or constructive false pretenses as by a fictitious show of property, or who give worthless checks or other negotiable paper or makes other false pretense, or who register under a fictitious name, or who surreptitiously leave with intent to defraud. Under a fair construction it cannot apply in a case as made by the prosecution here, where defendant is not a transient, but resides at the place where he obtains lodging, where he obtains for a long period of time credit on a promise to pay, although he does not carry out such promise. A mere failure to pay is not a crime."

The facts in *McLemore* are similar in many respects to the facts in the instant case. As construed there, the fact that the appellant left the motel for a few days is insufficient alone to show an intent to defraud. Furthermore, the testimony of Hendricksen revealed that the appellant, through his wife, contacted him before their return to El Reno, and after their return made a partial payment on the balance owing the motel, as well as a promise to satisfy the obligation. This testimony further negates any inference of an intent on the appellant's part to defraud the complaining witness.

In Oglesby v. State, Okl.Cr., 411 P.2d 974 (1966), this court stated that while specific intent can be inferred from circumstantial evidence, there must be sufficient evidence present to support the inference. Furthermore, where the evidence brought forth by the state affords no reasonable ground for an inference of specific intent, the question should not be submitted to the jury.

In the instant case, the state's evidence was insufficient on the issue of intent to defraud to warrant presenting the question to the jury. The appellant's demurrer should have been sustained.

Ruling of the Court: The judgment is, accordingly, reversed.

Management Principles

Restaurants and hotels have the right to make reasonable rules to protect their property and business; however, they must apply such rules equally to all. Among the usual reasonable rules are those prohibiting pets, requiring coats and ties in dining rooms, prohibiting solicitation in rooms or dining rooms (see *People* v. *Thorpe*), and prohibiting bare feet (see *Feldt* v. *Marriott Corporation* discussed in chapter 7). Hotelkeepers and restaurateurs should not take advantage of their guests by putting unreasonable rules into effect. More and more guests will question such rules.

Nor does a hotel have to accept all persons who apply for rooms. The reasons can be:

1 No accommodations (a positive defense on the part of the hotelkeeper).
2 The person is intoxicated.
3 The person has a contagious disease.
4 The person is a known criminal.
5 The person is unclean or disorderly.
6 The person is not willing to pay the price (of course, the hotel can demand payment in advance).
7 The person has a pet.
8 The person has dangerous property (firearms).
9 The person is a business competitor who will try to solicit your guests.

A hotelkeeper may change a guest's room under certain conditions. However, this procedure is rather questionable because the room belongs to the guest during the contracted stay. The room change could be regarded as a trespass. Granted, the hotelkeeper has the right (with caution) based on custom and usage to make up the room. It is possible for a guest to inform the management that this service is not desired; then the question of a room change may become serious.

It would seem reasonable that a hotel has the right to select a room for the guest unless a specific room has been previously contracted for (see *Nixon* v. *Royal Coach Inn*). The court in the Connie Francis case, however, stated that the motel failed to put the plaintiff in a "safe and secure room."

Along with the right to select one's guests (with certain prohibitions) goes the right to evict guests. Guests may be evicted for the following reasons:

1 Failure to pay a bill when due;
2 Overstaying the contracted time, which amounts to a breach of contract;
3 Although some court cases state that hoteliers may remove a guest who has a bad reputation, they should consult their attorney before taking this step;
4 Intoxication or disorderly conduct;
5 Refusal to adhere to house rules;
6 A person suffering from a contagious disease may be removed (consult the text for limitations);
7 A person who is not registered may be removed.

People without bags cannot be refused a room simply because of the lack of baggage, but because the hotel would not be able to enforce a lien against the guests' goods in case they did not pay, payment should be demanded in advance. If a hotel does refuse such a guest, it should be done graciously to avoid an action of slander. A reasonable rule on this matter may not hold up in court.

Only certain personnel should be allowed to evict a guest, as approved by management. Because an eviction may lead to a suit against the hotel, a very polite method should be used, avoiding all discussion. Usually guests will be outraged and their language less than polite, and the words of the hotelier or employees may be used against the hotel later. An illegal eviction can result in a large damage award because a hotel guest can sue for mental suffering and humiliation (see *Lopez v. City of New York*).

Restaurants not honoring confirmed dinner reservations have been found liable, as this is an actionable tort (see *Harder v. Auberge Des Fougeres*). But there can be valid reasons for refusing a person with a dinner reservation, as explained earlier in the chapter.

Hotels owe guests a duty to protect them from burglars, rapists, prostitutes, and similar people. It may employ at least reasonable force and, under certain conditions, a great deal of force. However, firearms should be used only as a last resort (see *Edwards v. Great American Insurance Company* in chapter 10). The failure to protect guests may be costly, as in the Connie Francis case award of $2.5 million and the Nordmann case award of $21,000.

To limit employee stealing, a hotelkeeper may stop employees to check them and any parcels they are carrying. However, it is better if all personnel agree to this as a part of their contract. When employees are unionized, this stipulation depends to a great extent on the bargained rights between the union and management. Stealing is a crime, but misdirected suspicion could lead to an action by the employee for false arrest, trespass, slander, or another cause.

In light of the questionable status of the hotel lien, it is suggested that this remedy be used only when all other methods have failed. In certain states, the lien is prohibited as violating the Fourteenth Amendment due process of law clause. Other states have recently upheld the hotel lien, and in most states today the lien is legal.

Many states afford hoteliers protection against the "skipper," the con man, and others who prey on guests. The Colorado statute on this matter is progressive, making the defrauding of a hotelkeeper a felony and not a misdemeanor.

Caution should be used when discussing the guest's delinquent account and what you intend to do about it. Hoteliers should never approach guests with the threat that if they do not pay their bill, they will be prosecuted for defrauding an innkeeper. Criminal statutes are the means by which the state punishes those who choose to violate its laws; they are not the instrumentalities to be used by creditors to intimidate their debtors into paying their accounts. Statements like, "Pay your account or else I'll have you prosecuted under the statutes for defrauding an innkeeper," could get innkeepers in trouble. If an innkeeper made such a statement and prosecuted, and the defendant was found innocent, the latter could file a civil suit for malicious prosecution and even for extortion, especially if the innkeeper used threats of prosecution to get guests to pay a bill that they dispute. You should be cautious in what you say or do. If your guests commit an act that you believe may subject them to criminal prosecution, ask your attorney what to do.

QUESTIONS FOR DISCUSSION

1 Why is a lien a questionable method for a hotelkeeper to use for protection against nonpayment by a guest?

2 What type of protection is afforded hotelkeepers against persons attempting to defraud them?

3 What kinds of reasonable rules may hotelkeepers or restaurateurs impose on their place of business? What defense can be invoked by a patron against reasonable rules?

4 What grounds are available to hotelkeepers or restaurateurs allowing them to refuse service or accommodations to certain customers?

5 Can a hotel select the accommodations for its guests? Is there any special duty owed the guests?

6 Once a hotel has received a person as a guest, what grounds can be used to eject the guest? If the guest is evicted illegally, what are the consequences?

7 Hotelkeepers are required to protect guests against intruders. How far can they go in protecting them?

8 Does a hotelkeeper have to accept all persons who apply for a room? Why or why not?

9 Must a hotelkeeper who wants to search employees because of thefts in the hotel have a search warrant? Can the hotelkeeper search guests? Explain in each situation.

10 If a hotel or restaurant is entertaining a full house, what precautions should it take and why?

11 When would a hotelier use a lien against a guest? Are there any precautions? Does every state have a lien law?

13 Contents

13 Liabilities and Rights of Restaurateurs and Bar and Tavern Operators

"Whatever one may say in praise of Our Lady of the Common Law (to whom I do bow), clarity and precise outline of her rules of law are not the chief jewel in her crown."

LLEWELLYN, The Common Law Tradition

Today's restaurateur provides a vital service to the general public while operating under state inspection and control. "Eating out" is no longer a luxury reserved for the wealthy or special occasions.

This chapter will examine the duties and rights of restaurateurs and similar operators. We will deal with the following questions: Is there an implied warranty that restaurant food is fit to eat? To win a case must a patron who breaks a tooth or is poisoned prove negligence? What effect does the Uniform Commercial Code have on the selling of food in a restaurant? What safety measures can customers expect in a restaurant or place serving alcoholic beverages? Does the fact that liquor is served have an effect on the patron-restaurateur relationship? What effect does a Dram Shop Law have on the serving of alcoholic beverages or the law of negligence? In addition, we will cover the ever-present problem of discrimination. In this chapter the word *restaurant* will denote any place that serves food or alcoholic beverages to the public.

Food Service in Restaurants

Is serving food in a restaurant a sale of food in the conventional sense, or is the food incidental to other services? In a sample case, a customer orders chicken sandwiches for her family; one sandwich contains a small but lethal chicken bone. The Law of Sales, which took precedence until the Uniform Commercial Code was adopted by all states, deals with this problem, which is representative of any situation in which a restaurant patron or a purchaser of food from a grocer is injured by poisonous food or a foreign substance contained in it. Liability cases resulting from unsafe food products and involving wholesalers, manufacturers, retailers, restaurateurs, customers, and ultimate consumers have become increasingly complicated by the interplay of tort and contract principles, medieval superstitions, and modern public policy concepts.

Under the theory of negligence, recovery in our hypothetical case is highly improbable because the burden of proof of negligence rests on the plaintiff. Moreover, in cases where the original manufacturer of the food product, and not the middleman (the wholesaler, jobber, or retailer), is negligent, the plaintiff may find that the defendant is beyond his jurisdiction.

What then is the general rule applying to the purchase of a meal or take-out food in a restaurant? Perhaps the best analysis of this problem was written by Justice Carrico in Levy v. Paul, 147 S.E.2d 722 (Va., 1965). In this case, the plaintiff (a three-year-old child) consumed food and became ill with food poisoning. The defendant won up to the Court of Appeals. The only question at this point was whether the food was wholesome and whether there was an implied warranty of wholesomeness attached to the transaction between a restaurant-keeper and a patron.

Judge Carrico answered in the affirmative after a review of the authorities on this point and concluded that the decided weight was in favor of holding that an implied warranty of wholesomeness does attach to the restaurateur-patron relationship.

Judge Carrico also discussed the sanitation laws that could hold the restaurant guilty of a criminal offense for selling unfit food prepared under unsanitary conditions. However, the defendant could escape civil liability for serving such food through the legal fiction that the transaction did not, after all, constitute a sale. The same argument was applied to the licensing of the restaurant to sell wine and beer. According to Judge Carrico, it would take a specious bit of logic to

> . . . conclude that when a customer orders a ham sandwich and a glass of beer in a restaurant that the beer is sold to him but that the sandwich, served and paid for at the same time, is not so sold.
>
> The holding that the transaction between a restaurantkeeper and his patron is a sale, carrying an implied warranty of wholesomeness of the food served, is required to maintain consistency with our other decisions relating to foodstuffs. . . . We have consistently held that there is an implied warranty of wholesomeness imposed upon those who manufacture or sell foodstuffs.
>
> The purpose of such a warranty . . . is "to require a person who sells or purveys articles of food to insure their being wholesome and fit for human consumption."

Such a purpose arises out of an even greater necessity in the case of food served in a restaurant. As was said in Cushing v. Rodman, 65 App.D.C. 258, 82 F.2d 864, 868–869, 104 A.L.R. 1023:

". . . The customer does in fact rely upon a dispenser of food for more than the use of due care. He depends upon the experience and trade wisdom of the dispenser in selecting the articles or ingredients of the food, and upon his skill in the preparation and service thereof. The customer has no effective opportunity to inspect or select so far as wholesomeness is concerned. . . ."

To hold that no implied warranty is applicable here would create a strange inconsistency in the law. In such a situation, a customer who is made ill from eating an unwholesome ham could recover from the corner supermarket where he purchased the ham. But if, instead, that same person becomes ill from eating a sandwich prepared with the same ham at the next-door restaurant, he would be denied recovery against the restaurateur.

The reasoning that would arrive at such a conclusion smacks of a lack of a sense of reality. Such reasoning stems from the old-fashioned notion that the patron acquired no title to or property in the food placed before him in an eating place. When a patron orders and pays for a meal in a restaurant, whose food is it if not his? Does it still belong to the restaurateur, who is free to retrieve it at will if not yet eaten?

These questions answer themselves. As was said in Betehia v. Cape Cod Corporation, 10 Wis.2d 323, 103 N.W.2d 64, 66, "Today if one takes home from a restaurant part of his steak for his dog, he could hardly be accused of larceny."

Sound considerations of public policy demand that we avoid the inconsistencies that would naturally arise from a holding that the restaurateur-patron relationship does not involve a sale carrying an implied warranty. We answer that demand by holding that the furnishing of food by a restaurant-keeper to a patron is a sale and does carry an implied warranty that the food is wholesome and fit for human consumption, for the breach of which the restaurant-keeper is liable for consequential damages.

Uniform Commercial Code

All the states and the District of Columbia, as well as other areas under United States law, have adopted the Uniform Commercial Code (UCC). In essence, the UCC is a set of uniform rules designed to simplify, clarify, and modernize the law governing commercial transactions.

Not all states, however, need treat the sale of food as an implied warranty under the Code. In Ray v. Deas, 144 S.E.2d 466 (1965), the Georgia court said that although it had previously followed the Connecticut–New Jersey rule, in which the serving of food in a restaurant was considered a service, it now overruled that doctrine and considered the transaction a sale. In this case the patron bit into an "unyielding" substance while eating a hamburger and broke his tooth.

The court held that the food was not wholesome under the implied warranty of the UCC, which provides: "Unless excluded or modified . . . a warranty that goods shall be merchantable is implied in a contract for their sale if the seller is a merchant with respect to goods of that kind. Under this section the serving for value of food or drink to be consumed either on the premises or elsewhere is a sale" (UCC, § 2-314). In its analysis the court stated that the legislature had evidenced its intention of abrogating and repealing the substantive rule of law expressed in previous cases; therefore, the UCC should be followed.

What Is Wholesome Food?

Defining any food that can be eaten as wholesome is pure fiction. One of the problems that plagues the industry deals with "foreign" materials found in food, such as bones, stones, glass, or rodent parts. How pure the food should be is another question the courts have to contend with, particularly since certain illness- and death-causing organisms have a twenty-four-hour incubation period, whereas others have a several-day incubation period.

A restaurant guest who becomes sick after a meal or finds a foreign substance in food is quick to blame the restaurateur. The case of *Webster v. Blue Ship Tea Room* is instructive on food law. Judge Reardon of the Supreme Court of Massachusetts treated the question of breach of implied warranty apart from and under the UCC (and, additionally, offered an acceptable fish chowder recipe).

Case Example	Webster v. Blue Ship Tea Room, Inc.

Case Example

Webster v. Blue Ship Tea Room, Inc.
198 N.E.2d 309 (Mass., 1964)
(REARDON, Justice)

This is a case that by its nature evokes earnest study not only of the law but also of the culinary traditions of the Commonwealth that bear so heavily upon its outcome. It is an action to recover damages for personal injuries sustained by reason of a breach of implied warranty of food served by the defendant in its restaurant. An auditor, whose findings of fact were not to be final, found for the plaintiff. On a retrial in the Superior Court before a judge and jury, in which the plaintiff testified, the jury returned a verdict for her. The defendant is here on exceptions to the refusal of the judge (1) to strike certain portions of the auditor's report, (2) to direct a verdict for the defendant, and (3) to allow the defendant's motion for the entry of a verdict in its favor under leave reserved.

The jury could have found the following facts: On Saturday, April 25, 1959, about 1 P.M., the plaintiff, accompanied by her sister and her aunt, entered the Blue Ship Tea Room operated by the defendant. The group was seated at a table and supplied with menus.

This restaurant, which the plaintiff characterized as "quaint," was located in Boston "on the third floor of an old building on T Wharf, which overlooks the ocean."

The plaintiff, who had been born and brought up in New England (a fact of some consequence), ordered clam chowder and crabmeat salad. Within a few minutes she received tidings to the effect that "there was no more clam chowder," whereupon she ordered a cup of fish chowder. Presently, there was set before her "a small bowl of fish chowder." She had previously enjoyed a breakfast about 9 A.M. that had given her no difficulty. "The fish chowder contained haddock, potatoes, milk, water, and seasoning. The chowder was milky in color and not clear. The haddock and potatoes were in chunks" (also a fact of consequence). "She agitated it a little with the spoon and observed that it was a fairly full bowl. . . . It was hot when she got it, but she did not tip it with her spoon because it was hot . . . but stirred it in an up and under motion. She denied that she did this because she was looking for something, but it was rather because she wanted an even distribution of fish and potatoes." "She started to eat it, alternating between the chowder and crackers which were on the table with . . . [some] rolls. She ate about 3 or 4 spoonfuls then stopped. She looked at the spoonfuls as she was eating. She saw equal parts of liquid, potato, and fish as she spooned it into her mouth. She did not see anything unusual about it. After 3 or 4 spoonfuls she was aware that something had lodged in her throat because she couldn't swallow and couldn't clear her throat by gulping and she could feel it." This misadventure led to two esophagoscopies at the Massachusetts General Hospital, in the second of which, on April 27, 1959, a fish bone was found and removed. The sequence of events produced injury to the plaintiff that was not insubstantial.

We must decide whether a fish bone lurking in a fish chowder, about the ingredients of which there is no other complaint, constitutes a breach of implied warranty under applicable provisions of the Uniform Commercial Code, the annotations to which are not helpful on this point. As the judge put it in his charge, "Was the fish chowder fit to be eaten and wholesome? . . . [N]obody is claiming that the fish itself wasn't wholesome. . . . But the bone of contention here—I don't mean that for a pun—but was this fish bone a foreign substance that made the fish chowder unwholesome or not fit to be eaten?"

The plaintiff has vigorously reminded us of the high standards imposed by this court where the sale of food is involved . . . and has made reference to cases involving stones in beans, . . . trichinae in pork, . . . and to certain other cases, here and elsewhere, serving to bolster her contention of breach of warranty.

The defendant asserts that here was a native New Englander eating fish chowder in a "quaint" Boston dining place where she had been before; that "[f]ish chowder, as it is served and enjoyed by New Englanders, is a hearty dish, originally designed to satisfy the appetites of our seamen and fishermen"; that "[t]his court knows well that we are not talking of some insipid broth as is customarily served to convalescents." We are asked to rule in such fashion that no chef is forced "to reduce the pieces of fish in the chowder to miniscule size in an effort to ascertain if they contained any pieces of bone." "In so ruling," we are told (in the defendant's brief), "the court will not only uphold its reputation for legal knowledge and acumen, but will, as loyal sons of Massachusetts, save our world-renowned fish chowder from degenerating into an insipid broth containing the mere essence of its former stature as a culinary masterpiece." Notwithstanding these passionate entreaties we are bound to examine with detachment the nature of fish chowder and what might happen to it under varying interpretations of the Uniform Commercial Code.

Chowder is an ancient dish preexisting even "the appetites of our seamen and fishermen." . . . The word "chowder" comes from the French *chaudière*, meaning a "cauldron" or "pot." "In the fishing villages of Brittany . . . *faire la chaudière* means to supply a cauldron in which is cooked a mess of fish and biscuit with some savoury condiments, a hodge-podge contributed by the fishermen themselves, each of whom in return receives his share of the prepared dish. The Breton fishermen probably carried the custom to Newfoundland, long famous for its chowder, whence it has spread to Nova Scotia, New Brunswick, and New England." . . . Our literature over the years abounds in references not only to the delights of chowder but also to its manufacture. A namesake of the plaintiff, Daniel Webster, had a recipe for fish chowder that has survived into a number of modern cookbooks and in which the removal of fish bones is not mentioned at all. One old time recipe recited in the New English Dictionary study defines chowder as "A dish made of fresh fish (esp. cod) or clams, stewed with slices of pork or bacon, onions, and biscuit. 'Cider and champagne are sometimes added.' " Hawthorne speaks of ". . . [a] codfish of sixty pounds, caught in the bay, [which] had been dissolved into the rich liquid of a chowder."[1] A chowder variant, cod "Muddle," was made in Plymouth in the 1890s by taking "a three or four pound codfish, head added. Season with salt and pepper and boil in just enough water to keep from burning. When cooked, add milk and piece of butter." The recitation of these ancient formulae suffices to indicate that in the construction of chowders in these parts in other years, worries about fish bones played no role whatsoever. This broad outlook on chowders has persisted in more modern cookbooks. "The chowder of today is much the same as the old chowder. . . ." The all embracing Fannie Farmer states in a portion of her recipe, fish chowder is made with a "fish skinned, but head and tail left on. Cut off head and tail and remove fish from backbone. Cut fish in 2-inch pieces and set aside. Put head, tail, and backbone broken in pieces, in stewpan; add 2 cups cold water and bring slowly to boiling point. . . ." The liquor thus produced from the bones is added to the balance of the chowder. . . .

Thus, we consider a dish that for many long years, if well made, has been made generally as outlined above. It is not too much to say that a person sitting down in New England to consume a good New England fish chowder embarks on a gustatory adventure which may entail the removal of some fish bones from his bowl as he proceeds. We are not inclined to tamper with age-old recipes by any amendment reflecting the plaintiff's view of the effect of the Uniform Commercial Code upon them. We are aware of the heavy body of case law involving foreign substances in food, but we sense a strong distinction between them and those relative to unwholesomeness of the food itself, e.g., tainted mackerel . . . and a fish bone in a fish chowder. Certain Massachusetts cooks might cavil at the ingredients contained in the chowder in this case in that it lacked the heartening lift of salt pork. In any event, we consider that the joys of life in New England include the ready availability of fresh fish chowder. We should be prepared to cope with the hazards of fish bones, the occasional presence of which in chowders is, it seems to us, to be anticipated, and which, in the light of a hallowed tradition, do not impair their fitness or merchantability. While we are bouyed up in this conclusion by Shapiro v. Hotel Statler Corp., 132 F.Supp. 891 (S.D.Cal.), in which the bone that afflicted the plaintiff appeared in "Hot Barquette of Seafood Mornay," we know that the United States District Court of Southern California, situated as are we upon a coast, might be expected to share our views. We are most

---

1 Nathaniel Hawthorne, *The House of Seven Gables* (Boston: Allyn & Bacon, 1957), p. 8.

impressed, however, by Allen v. Grafton, 170 Ohio St. 249, 164 N.E.2d 167, where in Ohio, the Midwest, in a case where the plaintiff was injured by a piece of oyster shell in an order of fried oysters, Mr. Justice Taft (now Chief Justice) in a majority opinion held that "the possible presence of a piece of oyster shell in or attached to an oyster is so well known to anyone who eats oysters that we can say as a matter of law that one who eats oysters can reasonably anticipate and guard against eating such a piece of shell . . ." (P. 259 of 170 Ohio St., p. 174 of 164 N.E.2d).

Thus, while we sympathize with the plaintiff who has suffered a peculiarly New England injury, the order must be

Exceptions sustained.

Ruling of the Court: Judgment for the defendant.

The outcome was different in Deris v. Finest Foods, Inc., 198 So.2d 412 (La., 1967). While eating a banana split at an establishment operated by Finest Foods, the plaintiff bit into something hard, which she discovered to be pieces of glass. She called it to the attention of the waitress and the manager. With the manager, she called her doctor from the defendant's place of business and told him that she believed that she had swallowed some glass. He gave her instructions, and she was so emotionally upset with the fear that she would be injured by the ingested glass that she took nerve pills and ate some bread as the doctor instructed. She saw the doctor the next day and suffered no effects other than those emotional in nature.

The court held that there was sufficient evidence to establish that the plaintiff had actually swallowed some glass that had been present in the banana split and that a lower court finding for the plaintiff was proper and therefore sustained. The court said that in cases of this type, both manufacturers and vendors of foodstuffs designed for human consumption are virtually insurers that such merchandise is wholesome and free from foreign materials and deleterious substances. The court ended by saying, "Under Louisiana law, the proprietor of a public eating place who serves a food fabricated by him and containing a foreign substance to a paying guest for immediate consumption on the premises is under an absolute liability for damages proximately resulting from the impurity, under the theory of an implied warranty of fitness."

There are indeed tests for the wholesomeness of food under the UCC. Some jurisdictions use the "reasonable expectation" test, while others employ the "foreign natural" test.

Reasonable Expectation Test

Which test of wholesomeness is used depends to a great degree on the jurisdiction in which the case takes place. In Zabner v. Howard Johnson's Inc., 201 So.2d 824 (Fla., 1967), the court applied the reasonable expectation test. While eating maple walnut ice cream, a patron suffered punctured gums and fractured teeth from the presence of a walnut shell. As applied to an action for breach of the implied warranty, the reasonable expectation test is keyed to what is "reasonably" fit. If it is found that a walnut shell ought to be anticipated in walnut ice cream and guarded against by the consumer plaintiff, then the ice cream is reasonably fit under the implied warranty. As applied to the action for common-law negligence, the test is related to the foreseeability of harm on the part of the defendant. The defendant is not an insurer but has the duty of ordinary care to eliminate or remove any harmful substances that the consumer would not ordinarily anticipate and guard against. Hence, the question of what is reasonably expected by the consumer becomes a jury question in most cases.

Foreign Natural Test

Not all states ascribe to the reasonable expectation test. Some jurisdictions hold that a harmful substance present in food to which it is *natural* cannot be a legal defect or a breach of the implied warranty of reasonable fitness of such food.

The leading case in point is Mix v. Ingersoll Candy Company, 59 P.2d 144 (Cal., 1936), which was brought both on the theory of implied warranty and of common law negligence. The plaintiff was injured by a chicken bone in a chicken pot pie. The court held the defendant was not liable under either theory since chicken bones were natural to the meat served and were not a foreign substance; it was common knowledge that chicken pies occasionally contained chicken bones. Therefore, their presence ought to be anticipated and guarded against by the consumer.

The reasonable expectation advocates believe the reasoning of the foreign natural believers is fallacious because it assumes that all substances that are natural to the food in one stage or another of preparation are anticipated by the average consumer in the final product served. It does not logically follow that chicken bone slivers are to be expected in chicken soup or nutshell pieces in nut breads. Those substances are indeed natural to those foods, but they may cause as much injury as pieces of glass or pebbles. The foreign natural doctrine, of course, has some relevance in determining the relative negligence of a food processor. But in practical usage, the naturalness test must be qualified by the particular type of dish in which the substance is found—chicken bones are entirely to be expected in a roast chicken but not in a chicken salad sandwich. This is the reasonable expectation test.

Privity of Contract

Under common law, only the persons directly involved in a purchase and sale could bring about a cause of action against the person who breached the implied warranty. In contract law privity denotes a mutual legal relationship.

In the service industry, the principle of privity applies in the case of Conklin v. Hotel Waldorf Astoria, 161 N.Y.S.2d 205 (1957), in which a guest of the hotel invited a guest to lunch. The guest's guest was subsequently injured by a piece of glass in a luncheon roll. The check was paid by the hotel guest. The defendant hotel claimed there was no privity of contract between the guest's guest and the hotel because the bill was paid by the hotel guest. Not agreeing with the defense, the court held that when the food orders of the plaintiff and her friend were accepted, it was implied that the defendant agreed to serve each of them (not just the bill payer) food fit for human consumption. In another state that adhered to the privity principle, the plaintiff-guest would have lost.

Unwholesome Food—Proof

When a person eats in a restaurant or buys take-out food and becomes sick later, is that adequate proof that the food eaten at or from the restaurant caused the sickness? In the case of Renna v. Bishop's Cafeteria Company of Omaha, 218 N.W.2d 246 (Neb., 1974), the plaintiff felt ill after having breakfast. His doctor diagnosed the problem as acute pancreatitis caused by the food purchased at the defendant's cafeteria. Under examination the doctor admitted that fasting followed by a hearty meal (which was the situation) could cause the same symptoms, whether the food was wholesome or not. The doctor could not with reasonable certainty say that the food consumed was infected or poisoned.

The gist of the case is that the restaurateur who serves food to paying guests for immediate consumption on the premises impliedly warrants the food is wholesome and fit for human consumption and is liable for injuries to a customer. Before this rule becomes applicable, there must be proof that the food sold is unwholesome and not fit for human consumption.

According to the doctor under cross-examination, the plaintiff's symptoms could have been caused by wholesome food as well. Therefore, all the plaintiff could prove was that he became ill following the ingestion of his breakfast at Bishop's. But he could not prove that the food was unwholesome, and therefore the court did not allow the case to go to the jury.

From a practical point of view it is quite reasonable that some protection should be afforded restaurateurs, since without such protection anyone could say he had been poisoned when, in fact, his symptoms could have been caused by some unrelated factor.

Exceptions to the Uniform Commercial Code

The general rule under the UCC seems to be absolute, imposing a strict liability upon the restaurateur and food-serving establishment. Food served to patrons must be wholesome and contain no deleterious substances, and it must be fit for human consumption.

But is there an exception? Can a case be made for the patron who assumes the risk of eating food that could be poisonous? In Bronson v. Club Comanche, Inc., 266 F. Supp. 21 (V.I., 1968), the plaintiff knew that occasional cases of ciguatera fish poisoning occurred in the Virgin Islands. (Certain fish in the Caribbean and Pacific contain the toxin causing ciguatera fish poisoning. The disease is characterized by nausea, vomiting, diarrhea, cramps, muscle weakness, sweating, chills, and fever. In severe cases, loss of speech, respiratory and body paralysis, coma, and death may result. Neither care in the handling or selection of the fish reveals the presence of the toxin, nor does cooking destroy it.) After eating a fish dinner, the plaintiff became sick and brought a cause of action against the Club Comanche restaurant.

Granted, contributory negligence is not available as a defense to the defendant when such negligence consists merely of the failure on his part to discover the defect in the product. On the other hand, the court said that when contributory negligence consists of a voluntary and unreasonable proceeding to encounter a known danger, the defense of assumption of risk may be a defense in such cases. Of course, the patron who is fully aware of the danger and nevertheless proceeds voluntarily to make use of the product and is injured by it is barred from recovery. This has sometimes, perhaps more accurately, been described as ceasing to place any reliance on the implied warranty, rather than assuming the risk. The plaintiff in the Bronson case was denied a new trial and the defendant was found not guilty of serving fish containing ciguatera poison.

Should the restaurateur or patron be liable in such a situation? In this case, the court thought the patron knew as much as the restaurateur. This is a novel approach. During a red tide infection off the New England coast who would be responsible for the effect on a patron who eats the seafood knowing the probability exists that such seafood could be contaminated and dangerous if eaten? Would newspaper reports be adequate to notify the public?

Travel Guide Rating and Reviews

All high-quality restaurants would like excellent or outstanding ratings in travel guides. The ratings in the Guide Michelin can greatly reduce or increase the volume of a European restaurant's business. Similar guides are consulted by millions of American travelers in selecting restaurants and hotels.

Do restaurateurs who believe they have received an unjustifiably low rating have any legal recourse? In 1970, two restaurants were assigned one- and two-star ratings out of a possible maximum of five. They asked the court for an injuction to prevent Socony Mobil Oil Company from selling or otherwise distributing the *Mobil Travel Guide* containing the ratings that were below their expectations.

The restaurants complained that they were rated too low and that the ratings were unwarranted, unjustified, and detrimental to the corporations and their respective businesses. The defendant stated that it made its rating decisions based on five opinions as to the quality of food, excellence of kitchen management, elegance of decor, excellence of service, attitude of management, and other criteria. Hence, the ratings were reached with great care and with cross-checks.

The court held for Mobil, refusing the injunction to prevent the sale or distribution of the *Guide*. In the court's opinion, the differences between the parties were basically differences of judgment or opinion, and in such a situation, the court should not try to find either party right or wrong. Restaurant proprietors expose themselves to public criticism that may come from those who write professionally about eating places, or from ordinary persons who merely talk to their friends. In the absence of fraud, malicious misrepresentation, willful disregard, or indifference to the facts—in short, considerably more than a difference of opinion—the court could not conceive that such criticism (a low star rating) would be actionable.

The *Mobil Travel Guide* in fact recommended all the establishments listed in it, although some more highly than others. Mobil had also argued that praise (that is, a recommendation) could not under any circumstances be actionable. The court was not as sure on this point, expressing some doubt about the universality of that proposition. Damning with faint praise can be an effective way of damning.

Related to the question of ratings is the question of the amount and kind of public comment that can be made about a restaurant and its food by one engaged in the broadcasting or publication media. The case of Shylock, Inc., v. Covenant Broadcasting Corporation of Louisiana, 352 So.2d 379 (La., 1978), grew out of a statement that a radio commentator made during a broadcast: "On the menu is a mixed grill, which is good veal, steak, lamb, and liver, all served together and which unfortunately bears the same name as a kind of cat food that you can find at your neighborhood supermarket." The restaurant sued the broadcaster and the radio station alleging that the statement was defamatory in nature and resulted in damage to the restaurant's business in the amount of $100,000. The plaintiff did not allege that the statements were maliciously made. The defendants filed a motion for summary judgment, which was granted by the lower court; the plaintiff appealed. The Louisiana Court of Appeal sustained the lower court's action reasoning as follows. The United States Supreme Court has held that states may define for themselves the appropriate standard of liability for a publisher or broadcaster of defamatory falsehoods injurious to a private individual so long as they do not impose liability without fault.

In Louisiana, as well as most other states, the essential elements for such liability are: 1) defamatory words; 2) publication—that is, communication to some person other than the one defamed; 3) falsity; 4) malice, actual or implied; and 5) resulting injury. If words are considered defamatory per se, malice is inferred from the mere fact of their publication. Words that are defamatory per se impute to the person the commission of a crime or subject him to public ridicule, ignominy or disgrace, and are susceptible only of one meaning. Words not actionable per se fall short of these requirements and are actionable only in consequence of extrinsic facts where the surrounding circumstances and conditions are taken into account to determine whether the statements published unjustifiably tend to injure the reputation of a person or reflect shame and disgrace upon him. The test is the effect that the article is fairly calculated to produce, the impression that it would naturally engender, in the minds of the average persons among whom it is intended to circulate.

Certain liberties are permitted when a comment is about a public figure, but merely because a person owns and manages a restaurant does not make him a public figure. When restaurateurs advertise their restaurants publicly in an effort to promote business, neither they nor their restaurants are transformed into public figure status for purposes of the application of the libel law.

Although protection under the First Amendment is strong in the matter of free speech and publication, the privilege is not absolute and will yield to a publication wherein it is shown that actual or implied malice existed towards a private individual.

Kosher Foods

The sale of kosher foods by a restaurant, hotel, or commercial market may be subject to statutes or ordinances prohibiting misrepresentation of such food. Such statutes have consistently been regarded as valid; the courts have rejected a variety of constitutional challenges. In Sossin Systems, Inc., v. Miami Beach, 262 So.2d 28, 52 ALR3d 955 (1972), the court upheld a statute prohibiting the sale of so-called kosher food, when in fact the food was not kosher. The Orthodox Jew who travels has a right to expect that a restaurant advertising "kosher" foods will serve foods prepared in accordance with Jewish religious requirements. Usually a symbol (a *plumba*) is affixed to kosher food by a person authorized by the rabbinate.

Defrauding of guests can be assumed if nonkosher foods are found in an establishment advertising kosher foods. Generally, the courts tend to hold that one who enters the field of kosher trade assumes certain obligations not usual in other areas, and the supervision of kosher food preparation by a rabbi is a prerequisite. This has been firmly established in New York and Florida, where penal codes prohibit misrepresentation in the sale of kosher foods.

Alcoholic Beverages in the Service Industry

Under common law an inn was required to take care of travelers' needs for food, shelter, and entertainment. Food included libation as well as nourishment for the body. Over the years the sale of alcoholic beverages has been a subject of concern, both as to its legal and illegal serving and the consequences.

Common Law Liability

Until quite recently, it was uniformly held that under common law an action could not be maintained against the vendor of alcoholic beverages for furnishing such beverages to customers who, as a result of being intoxicated, injured themselves or another person (Vesely v. Sager, 95 Cal. Rptr. 623 [1971]). According to the common law rule, the consumption and not the sale of liquor was the proximate cause of injuries sustained as a result of intoxication. Proximate cause can be defined here as a natural and continuous sequence, unbroken by any new, independent cause, producing an injury, and without which the injury would not have occurred. This is the "but for" test. In other words, the defendant's conduct is the cause of the event if the event could not have occurred without it.

Many intoxicated persons who have caused injury have had little or no money. Yet, over time, social justice came to demand retribution, resulting in legislation against the person or persons who sold or gave the individual too much to drink. Prior to this legislation, if an intoxicated customer injured or killed an innocent person while driving, the family of the injured or deceased party would have cause of action only against the drunk driver and not against the person who sold the driver the alcoholic beverage.

Not all states have passed statutes to rectify this injustice; most still follow the common law; and others allow recovery on the common law tort of negligence. The common law dealing with alcohol consumption was influenced by the "able-bodied man" concept—that people who drank alcohol could hold their liquor and therefore were responsible for their actions.

Civil Damage Acts or Dram Shop Acts

In recent years, a growing number of state legislatures and courts have carved out exceptions to the common law rule. In particular, while recognizing the common law's application to the "able-bodied man" concept, an exception has been made in cases where liquor is served to minors or obviously intoxicated persons in violation of a statute.

The large number of motor vehicle accidents caused by drunk drivers have prompted the legislatures of many states into enacting statutes to protect innocent third parties. Additionally, the courts of many states are reevaluating the old common law thinking on the problem. For example, in 1980 about half of the 51,900 fatalities in motor vehicle accidents were alcohol related. In many of these cases, those killed or injured were innocent third parties whose estates were denied adequate damages because the person who caused the accident lacked insurance or means to pay the legitimate awards of damages being made by juries. The answer the legislatures turned to was to impose liability on those who served liquor in violation of the law because they were in fact as responsible for the injuries and fatalities as the one who actually caused the accident. The statutes imposing the liability upon the vendor of alcoholic beverages took the form of Dram Shop Acts or Civil Damage Acts.

About fifteen states have passed legislation that allows general third party recovery of a vendor making an illegal sale of an intoxicating beverage in violation of the law. Six other states have statutes that allow recovery to certain third parties providing conditions imposed by statute have been met. Other states have found recovery possible under the common law as read and applied to current times. Appendix 2 presents a state-by-state analysis of such legislation.

Those who sell alcoholic beverages have a duty, not only to the patrons they serve and the public at large to be careful not to serve beverages in contravention of the law, but also to their employer not to perform acts that could result in damage awards that could force the business to be sold or destroyed in order to meet the judgments returned against them. Some of these illegal sales have resulted in verdicts that have ruined both the party who served the alcoholic beverage and the employer.

According to the Associated Press of May 6, 1976, a Beverly Hills bar poured the shot that may be heard round the nation. In this case, which was settled out of court, alcohol led to the loss of Claire Cox's life, of actor James Stacy's left arm and leg, and earned motorist Carter Gordon a term in the state prison for manslaughter and drunken driving. Cox was a passenger on Stacy's motorcycle when it was rammed in 1973 by Gordon's car. In addition, the Beverly Hills bar ("The Chopping Block") that served Gordon lost a $1.9 million suit under a state law that makes taverns liable for the actions of their patrons. Stacy won an additional $175,000 settlement from the city of Los Angeles on his claim that the road where the accident occurred was poorly maintained. This case is not unique in the size of the awards. Indeed, many such cases throughout the United States have been won, and the situation may worsen. Since the Stacy case, California has repealed its Dram Shop Act.

In reviewing the cases that follow the new view, the best rendition can be found in Rappaport v. Nichols, 156 A.2d 1 (N.J., 1959), in which the court said, in part:

> Where a tavern keeper sells alcoholic beverages to a person who is visibly intoxicated or to a person he knows or should know from the circumstances to be a minor, he ought to recognize and foresee the unreasonable risk of harm to others through action of the intoxicated person or the minor. The Legislature has in explicit terms prohibited sales to minors as a class because it recognizes their very special susceptibilities and the intensification of the otherwise inherent dangers when persons lacking in maturity and responsibility partake of alcoholic beverages.

> When alcoholic beverages are sold by a tavern keeper to a minor or to an intoxicated person, the unreasonable risk of harm not only to the minor or the intoxicated person but also to members of the traveling public may readily be recognized and foreseen; this is particularly evident in current times when traveling by car to and from the tavern is so commonplace and accidents resulting from drinking are so frequent. . . . If the patron is a minor or is intoxicated when served, the tavern keeper's sale to him is unlawful; and if the circumstances are such that the tavern keeper knows or should know that the patron is a minor or is intoxicated, his service to him may also constitute common law negligence.

> Today, the hazards of travel by automobiles on modern highways has become a national problem. The drunken driver is a threat to the safety of many. The responsibility of a tavern keeper for contributing to the intoxication of a patron has long been regulated by statute (Alcoholic Beverage Control Law). It is understandable that early cases did not recognize any duty of an innkeeper to the traveling public because a serious hazard did not exist. Through lack of necessity, this phase of negligence liability did not develop. However, there did exist General Common Law Rules of negligence liability based on foreseeability and proximate cause. It is a well established, sound principle of legal philosophy that the common law is not static. Under the skillful interpretation of our courts, it has been adapted to changing times and conditions of our civilization.

> The crucial issue in all of the cases involving liability of a seller of alcoholic beverages seems to be the matter of proximate cause. Many of the cases constantly cited have arbitrarily held that the selling of the intoxicating liquor is too remote in time to be a proximate cause of resulting injury.

> However, it is well settled that for a negligent act or omission to be a proximate cause of injury, the injury need be only a natural and probable result thereof; and the consequence be one which in the light of the circumstances should reasonably have been foreseen or anticipated.

> The increasing frequency of serious accidents caused by drivers who

are intoxicated is a fact which must be well known to those who sell and dispense liquor. This lends support to those cases which have found the automobile accident to be "the reasonably foreseeable" result of furnishing liquor to the intoxicated driver, at least where the person furnishing the liquor knew that the intoxicated person would be driving on a public highway.

Many Dram Shop Acts or Civil Damage Acts afford remedies unknown to the common law, and in many instances are quite radical. An example of such extremism may be found in Williams v. Klemesrud, 197 N.W.2d 614 (Iowa, 1972), in which the defendant purchased a bottle of liquor for a friend for purely social reasons from a state liquor store and became liable in damages for injuries caused by this friend when he subsequently drove an automobile while intoxicated. Under the statute, a right of action was afforded "against any person who shall, by selling or giving to another . . . intoxicating liquors." It was also held that this Dram Shop statute imposed strict liability, rendering inapplicable a contributory negligence defense.

The statutes of the various states are often similar in scope but differ in their interpretations. A study of the numerous relevant cases does, however, reveal a common factor: where a jury is involved, the innocent plaintiff is favored in awards.

In the 1967 New York case of *Mitchell v. Shoals, Inc.*, the plaintiff was able to recover, even though she had been drinking with her escort-defendant, who later drunkenly drove into the side of a building, causing her injury. The New York court apparently felt that the plaintiff did not procure or cause the intoxication of the other person. At least two states, Illinois and Michigan, do not allow recovery when the injured person has participated in the drinking party.

Mitchell v. Shoals is important because it alerts a bartender-owner to the consequences of allowing a customer to become inebriated and then drive a car.

Case Example	**Mitchell v. Shoals, Inc.**
	280 N.Y.S.2d 113 (1967)
	(FULD, Chief Judge)

On February 2, 1960, after having dinner together, the plaintiff, Yvonne Mitchell, her escort, Robert Taylor, and another couple drove to The Shoals, a restaurant on Staten Island, at about 9:00 P.M. for "a few drinks" and some dancing. Between dances, they had their drinks. Miss Mitchell, after consuming several, passed out and remained asleep for the rest of the evening. Taylor, who was on a diet of "double" bourbons "straight," became drunk and noisy. At one point, after he had fallen to the floor, the bartender was told not to let him have anything more to drink. Despite this admonition and Taylor's obviously intoxicated condition, the bartender—responding with "don't bother me; he is having a good time . . . let him enjoy himself"—served him three or four more double straight bourbons. The two couples left the restaurant at about 1 o'clock in the morning. The plaintiff, still asleep, was assisted to the car and placed in the front seat and Taylor, not to be dissuaded from driving, got behind the wheel and drove off. He apparently lost control of the car some nine miles from the restaurant; it left the roadway and crashed into a building. He was killed and the plaintiff was seriously injured. She brought this action for damages, under New York's version of the Dram Shop Act (Civil Rights Law, § 16, now General Obligations Law, Consol.Laws, c. 24–A, § 11–101), against the defendant restaurant. The jury returned a verdict in her favor, and a divided Appellate Division affirmed the resulting judgment. (The verdict was for $30,000; however, since the plaintiff had settled her claim against Taylor's estate for $6,000, the judgment was reduced, by that amount, to $24,000.)

The Alcoholic Beverage Control Law renders it a crime for any person to sell or deliver any alcoholic beverage to one who is intoxicated or under the influence of liquor (§§ 65, 130, subd. 3).

Although the statute—its forerunner goes as far back as 1873 (L.1873, ch. 646; see Note, 8 Syracuse L.Rev. 252)—does not give the inebriated person a cause of action if he is himself injured (see Moyer v. Lo Jim Cafe, . . . 240 N.Y.S.2d 277, affd. . . . 251 N.Y.S.2d 30), it does entitle any one else injured "by reason of the intoxication" of such person to recover damages from the party dispensing the liquor. There is no justification, either in the language of the legislation or in its history, for exonerating the latter simply because he had also served, and brought about the inebriety of, the third person who was hurt. As long as the latter does not himself cause or procure the intoxication of the other, there is no basis, under the statute, for denying him a recovery from the party unlawfully purveying the liquor.

In the case before us, the plaintiff had herself become drunk while drinking with Taylor but she had not, in any sense, caused or procured his intoxication. She had neither purchased the drinks nor encouraged him to take more than he could weather. The plaintiff had simply had a few drinks and passed out before her escort's inebriacy became really serious. This did not amount to a guilty participation in his intoxication. To deny her a remedy because her own alcoholic capacity was limited would impair, if not go a long way toward defeating, the purpose of the statute.

In two or three states, the courts have held that the plaintiff's mere participation in drinking with the person whose drunkenness caused the injury may be sufficient to prevent recovery under the Dram Shop Acts of those states. . . . We need not, and do not, go that far. It is our view that the injured person must play a much more affirmative role than that of drinking companion to the one who injures him before he may be denied recovery against the bartender or tavern keeper who served them. The plaintiff before us comes within the coverage of the statute and the defendant was properly held accountable.

It is only necessary to add that, although the trial court was in error in casting its charge in terms of contributory negligence on the part of the plaintiff, it is apparent from what has already been written that the error was harmless and may be disregarded.

Ruling of the Court: The order appealed from should be affirmed, with costs.

In the 1970 New York case of McNally v. Addis, 317 N.Y.S.2d 157, a somewhat different situation caused difficulty as to the interpretation of the Dram Shop Act. The facts are straightforward—a minor was killed in an automobile accident while intoxicated. (There was 0.28 percent ethanol in the decedent's blood; in general, 0.1 percent is considered intoxication.) The parent sued the defendant bar owner under General Obligation Law Section 11–101, which gives any person so aggrieved this cause of action. The defendant bar owner was absolved, because four elements are necessary for recovery in such a case: (1) the unlawful sale, (2) of liquor, (3) to an intoxicated person, (4) which caused injury.

The plaintiff's son was seventeen years old; eighteen is the legal drinking age in New York. Point two was questionable because the minor drank beer. After a detailed description of what constitutes alcohol, 3.2 beer was found to fall in this category. Point three, the most difficult to prove, could not be proved in this case. The court stated that under the Dram Shop Act, a consumer's purchases of intoxicating beverages from other establishments did not absolve a defendant from full liability if his violation of the statute was established. In this case, the problem was one of proof. Because the autopsy was done ten hours after the automobile accident that occurred after the decedent left the defendant's premises, there was no proof that the alcohol had been consumed in the defendant's establishment. Therefore, the plaintiff-father could not recover.

A further important point is the fact that the defendant's violation of the Alcoholic Beverage Control Law, which prohibits sale to minors, did not create an independent cause of action, nor was it negligence under the Dram Shop Act. Consequently, a person (in this case, the father) standing in the shoes of a minor, sober when served, does not have a cause of action under the Dram Act.

The last point concerning damages, although moot, was discussed and it was found that if the plaintiff could recover, he could recover only for injury to his person, property, means of support, or otherwise; "otherwise" may permit recovery for mental distress.

The *McNally* case deals with other very important principles that are not necessarily present in all Dram Shop Acts, but they may serve as a guide.

1   The Dram Shop Act attaches responsibility upon sellers of intoxicating beverages, although their acts may only remotely contribute to an accident.

2   Violation of the Dram Shop Act is negligence as such, and the contributory negligence of the injured person is no defense.

3   The plaintiff has the burden of proof and must establish that there was an unlawful sale of liquor (to a minor or intoxicated person) that caused the injury.

4   Under the Dram Shop Act, the fact that a consumer purchases intoxicating beverages from other establishments does not absolve defendants from full liability if *their* violation of statute is established.

5   Generally, beer is considered liquor in regulatory legislation.

6 "Legal intoxication" is the impairment of the capacity to think and act correctly, coupled with partial loss of the control of physical and mental facilities.

7 The Dram Shop Act was not intended to impose absolute liability without some notice accorded the seller regarding dangers attendant to a prohibited sale. In other words, the seller must have notice of a consumer's near-intoxicated condition by means of objective outward appearances.

8 Action for damages under the Dram Shop Act is separate and distinct from usual wrongful actions or death actions.

9 In the absence of a statute to the contrary, an action of negligence on account of sale of liquor will hold despite violation of the Dram Shop Act and may generally be asserted where the Dram Shop Act does not apply.

10 Though in New York the Alcoholic Beverage Law provision prohibits sales to minors, as in all other states this is not an absolute liability provision, but its violation is some evidence of negligence in a common law negligence action.

11 It follows that a parent's action for loss of a child's services is derivative; parents may recover only if the minor could have recovered. This is true in any case.

12 In the *McNally* case, the plaintiff could not recover for the death of his minor son because proof of intoxication could not be supported. However, the common law negligence action was also dismissed because, among other things, it would at least be contributory negligence on the part of the minor to have offered false identification. A minor must exercise the care which an ordinarily prudent person of his age, capacity, and experience would exercise under similar circumstances.

13 A minor may assume the risk of injury, and this can be done by the voluntary consumption of alcoholic beverages.

The *McNally* case is important because it lays down certain basic principles pertaining to the Dram Shop Act. It should not be read as an abolition of the act, however; rather, certain stipulated facts must be proved. In this case no proof was admitted to show that the defendant knew or had any way of determining that the plaintiff's son was intoxicated, a key element for recovery under the Dram Shop Act.

Hotels may rent out a portion of their premises for private parties over which they have little or no control. The question then arises as to what duties or obligations this gives rise to with regard to injuries suffered by third parties that are not on the hotel's premises. There is no question that hoteliers must keep their premises reasonably safe for those who are lawfully on them, but does any duty extend beyond the actual bounds of the property? The court in the case of Upthegrove v. Myers et al., 229 N.W.2d 29 (Mich., 1980), addressed this problem. The case involved the administrator of the estate of a man killed in an automobile accident.

The administrator brought suit against Myers, the operator of the motor vehicle, as well as the Troy Hilton Operating Company, the owners of the hotel where a group had rented a private room for a party that Myers had attended and at which he became intoxicated. Those who were invited to the party were expected to bring their own liquor. Employees of the hotel delivered only ice and glasses. The hotel had had problems with young people renting rooms for parties before, and they tried to discourage the practice. However, if they did have a party and the guests got loud, the security guards would break it up. In this case, the hotel employees asked most of the participants in the party to leave. Myers left, got into his car, drove approximately four miles, and plowed into the rear of the deceased's car, killing him almost instantly.

Clearly, a dram shop situation is not presented here because that would have required a sale of an alcoholic beverage by the hotel to Myers. The plaintiff was proceeding on a theory that liability should be imposed on the hotel for failing to supervise the party. The court held that there was no such duty owed to the deceased by the hotel. The court said, however, than an innkeeper does have a duty to protect guests of guests from injury and must exercise ordinary care and prudence to keep the premises reasonably safe for them. Although there is no law on the subject in Michigan, cases from Missouri and Minnesota were cited for the proposition that the duty to keep the premises reasonably safe extended to passersby in the immediate vicinity of the hotel. These cases recognized a duty to protect a passerby after a relationship has arisen between the hotel and the passerby due to the proximity of the passerby to the hotel. The proximity gives the passerby the right to rely on the hotel's reasonably safe condition. The court said that this theory was not applicable in the present case because the accident took place four miles from the hotel, beyond the scope of the extension of duties to passersby.

The important thought that hoteliers should take from the *Upthegrove* case is that they should exercise some degree of control over activities which go on in their facility that may create liability for them for events that may occur outside of the premises. That is, if there is a heavy drinking party going on in one of their hotel rooms, it is reasonably foreseeable that someone might throw something out of a window and hit a passerby; therefore, hoteliers should take steps to control the activity in the room.

Liability of Restaurateurs and Tavern Keepers

Guests of a restaurant or tavern sometimes suffer injury at the hands of some third person or an employee while on the premises. Who is liable? This depends, to a great extent, on the circumstances of the case and the state in which it occurs. Are employers liable for the actions of their employees? Needless to say, an employer cannot personally be present in the business establishment at all times.

In *Schell* v. *Vergo*, the court set forth the general rule and its exceptions. Here a lawyer complaining about a pinball machine was assaulted by a bartender and subsequently received $100 for pain, suffering, and humiliation caused by the blow on his jaw.

Case **Example**	**Schell v. Vergo** *4 N.Y.S.2d 644 (1938)* *(TOMPKINS, Judge)*

This is an action for assault committed by the defendant McGillicuddy while in the employ of the defendant Vergo. McGillicuddy has not answered. The plaintiff alleges that the defendant Vergo was, on December 10, 1937, the owner of a barroom and restaurant known as Vergo's Grill, located at 244 Monroe Avenue in the City of Rochester, N.Y. The defendant Vergo's answer admits this allegation. The plaintiff further alleges that while a patron of defendant Vergo's place of business, on December 10th, he was assaulted by the defendant McGillicuddy, an employee of Vergo's. He seeks a recovery herein against both defendants.

At the conclusion of plaintiff's case, the defendant Vergo moved to dismiss the complaint upon the ground that this Court did not have jurisdiction of actions for assault.

The evidence shows that about 1:00 A.M. on the morning of December 10th, the plaintiff, homeward bound, stopped at the defendant Vergo's place of business; entered that part where the defendant has a bar. The plaintiff purchased a glass of beer, paid for it, and then proceeded to experiment with a machine sometimes termed a "pin ball" machine. Not satisfied that the machine correctly reported the results of his skill or luck, he complained to McGillicuddy who had served him the beer in question. McGillicuddy failed to show interest. Shortly after, plaintiff again complained to McGillicuddy and asked for return of the nickel or nickels he had fed into the machine. The bartender was still unsympathetic. The plaintiff then turned from where he had been talking to the bartender, with the intention of leaving. Before, however, he had taken more than a step or two, he felt the impact either of McGillicuddy's fist or of something wielded by him, upon the left side of his face and jaw. The plaintiff's knees wobbled, but he saved himself from completely falling to the floor. He then left defendant's place of business and proceeded homeward to find solace in such applications as his unprofessional efforts might suggest. That he must have suffered pain, is evident from his photograph taken next day, which showed an oversized cheek, unbeautiful to the eye. Not only did the plaintiff suffer acute pain, but he was also, being a lawyer, subjected to humiliation on appearing in public and among sympathetic but curious friends, with a cheek swollen most noticeably beyond its natural regular proportions. This condition continued for several days. At the time of the trial, the plaintiff's appearance had entirely regained its usual dignified expression.

May the owner of a saloon or barroom, where malt liquors are sold, be held liable for his servant's willful assault upon a guest? Plaintiff was a guest. McGillicuddy, who served plaintiff with beer, was Vergo's servant.

The general rule is that a master is not responsible for the torts of his servant unless committed in the conduct of his business. . . . There are exceptions to this rule. They grow out of the duty owing by the master to the person injured. Among the oldest of these exceptions are common carriers and innkeepers. . . .

In 15 Ruling Case Law, under the topic of "Intoxicating Liquors," it is said, in paragraph 197, page 428, referring to the duty and liability of a saloon keeper to patrons on the premises "the greater number of decisions and the better reason, appear to favor placing on the proprietor the duty of seeing to it that the patron is not injured either by those in his employ or by drunken or vicious men whom he may choose to harbor . . . and where such an act was done by the defendant's servant left in charge of the saloon, such was held to present even a stronger case against the defendant. . . ." The case seems to me to be a salutary application of the extension of the obligations of an innkeeper to safeguard his guests, to the proprietor of a saloon, which is now, by provisions of Section 40 of the Civil Rights Law, a place of "public accommodation."

Ruling of the Court: Judgment in favor of the plaintiff, against each defendant, in the sum of one hundred dollars, as damages for his pain, suffering and humiliation.

Many injuries are related to the serving of alcoholic beverages, because a normally peaceful person may turn violent under the influence of alcohol. How much force may a restaurant owner or employee use against a drunk and obstreperous guest or against someone they know habitually overindulges with violent consequences? Training employees to handle such situations can do much to avoid legal complications.

In Sweenor v. 162 State Street, Inc., 281 N.E.2d 280 (Mass., 1972), a patron attempted to prevent another inebriated patron from falling off his bar stool. This good deed cost the plaintiff a broken thigh bone, a hospital stay, ten months of disability, and a permanently crooked leg.

Here the court set forth the duty that a Massachusetts bar operator owes patrons. According to the court, the defendant owed a duty to a paying patron to use reasonable care to prevent injury to him by a third person, whether the act be *accidental, negligent,* or *intentional.* The jury had to determine whether the defendant failed to conform to this duty by continuing to serve the boisterous patron liquor and by failing to restrain or remove him from the premises. Furthermore, the jury had to consider whether the injury to the plaintiff was foreseeable. Liquor given to one already drunk may well make that individual unreasonable and aggressive and may enhance the possibility of irrational acts. Also, liquor impairs an individual's sense of balance. The jury would have been warranted in finding that the patron's fall from the bar stool was predictable and that the instinctive reaction of one nearby would be to try to catch the falling person.

Another point made by the court was that the good samaritan act of the plaintiff in trying to catch the falling patron did not, as a matter of law, constitute contributory negligence or assumption of risk. A jury's verdict is not easily predictable in such cases; however, juries are composed of more restaurant patrons than owners.

Most states have no Dram Shop or Civil Damage Acts imposing civil liability. Therefore, the cause of action in such states must be under the common law action of negligence. Granted, under common law no action for damages could ordinarily be maintained against the vendor of intoxicating liquors; however, in some states the common law has been modified to allow a patron to bring such a cause of action.

The case of Pierce v. Lopez, 490 P.2d 1182 (Ariz., 1972), occurred in such a jurisdiction. The patron sustained a blow on the head from a pool cue wielded by another patron. The evidence in the case was insufficient to support a case of negligence against the defendant—alleging he knew of the patron's propensity for violence and failed to take action to protect the plaintiff. For the plaintiff to win such a case, it must be proved the defendant knew of the other patron's propensity for violence.

Patrons Injured by Other Patrons

What is the law as to injury of patrons by other patrons? The general rule seems to be that the duty of a tavern keeper to protect a patron from injury by another patron arises only when one or more of the following circumstances exist:

1 A tavern keeper allows a person who has a known propensity for fighting or acting quarrelsome on the premises. For example, in McFadden v. Bancroft Hotel Corporation, 46 N.E.2d 573 (Mass., 1943), a military organization held its annual convention in the hotel operated by the defendant. The plaintiff-conventioneer's assailant had arrived two days previously and had been holding drinking parties in his rooms. The intoxicated assailant struck the plaintiff in the face, knocking him to the floor, with no provocation as the plaintiff and his wife sat in the hotel grill room. Several hotel detectives and city police officers were in the room at the time. According to the court, it was the defendant's duty to exercise reasonable and ordinary care for the safety of the plaintiff in the circumstances, although the hotel was not an insurer of the plaintiff's safety. Because the hotel's agents had witnessed the behavior of the assailant prior to the attack, the jury could find that the assailant should have been removed from the room before the assault. The defendant's duty was not limited to an obligation to warn the plaintiff. The court also held that there was no contributory negligence on the plaintiff's part, as the assault was unpredictable and completely unprovoked.

2 The tavern keeper allows someone who is aggressive to such a degree that the tavern keeper knows or ought to know he endangers others to remain on the premises. In the case of Coca v. Arceo, 376 P.2d 970 (N.M., 1962), summary judgment was not granted to the owners because the plaintiff had an altercation with another woman in the presence of the bartender before the other woman struck the plaintiff with a beer bottle. The plaintiff alleged that the bar owners failed to exercise reasonable care to protect her from injury at the hands of the other patron, because they knew or should have known of the earlier altercation.

3   The tavern keeper has been warned of danger from an obstreperous patron and fails to take suitable measures for the protection of other patrons. In Kane v. Fields Corner Grille, Inc., 171 N.E.2d 287 (Mass., 1961), the plaintiff-customer in the defendant's bar was assaulted by another customer who had previously been disorderly and boisterous in the bartender's presence. The facts of the case warranted a finding that the defendant was negligent and therefore liable.

4   The tavern keeper fails to stop a fight as soon as possible after it starts. In Shank v. Riker Restaurant Associates, Inc., 216 N.Y.S.2d 118, affd. 222 N.Y.S.2d 683, an unidentified "hoodlum" using abusive language had been creating a disturbance in the restaurant for over twenty minutes before the plaintiff's entry. The manager was found negligent and the defendant-owner was liable for the assault upon the plaintiff by the hoodlum and his companions.

5   The tavern keeper fails to provide a staff adequate to police the premises (see Martin v. Barclay Distributing Company, 91 Cal.Rptr. 817 [1970]).

6   The tavern keeper tolerates disorderly conditions. According to the evidence in Kimple v. Foster, 469 P.2d 281 (Kan., 1970), the owner-manager should have been alerted to the probability of violence when an unruly gang invaded the tavern for about four hours. When a patron is hurt in such a case, the courts have held that the owner or manager should have taken affirmative action to maintain order, either by demanding the offending persons leave, by calling the police to enforce such a demand, or by other reasonable means.

Case Example	Kimple v. Foster
	469 P.2d 281 (Kan., 1970)
	(FONTRON, Justice)

This action was commenced by the three plaintiffs, John Stanley Kimple, Ernest I. Stahly, and Larry A. Morris, to recover for personal injuries sustained while guests at The Roaring Sixties, a Wichita nightspot. The case was tried to a jury which awarded damages to each plaintiff in the sum of $6500. The defendant, Bill G. Foster, owner of the offending tavern, has appealed.

For the three victims, the evening of July 7, 1966, began innocently enough. The men met in the afternoon for a business conference, following which they had dinner together. About 9:00 PM they dropped into The Roaring Sixties, where they ordered a pitcher of beer. Soon thereafter the tavern exploded with a frenetic violence which more than matched the picturesque character of its name.

The record reflects that when the plaintiffs entered the tavern, a group of males was gathered around a table some distance away. These characters had been patronizing the tavern since afternoon, drinking beer, pyramiding empty beer cans on their table, harassing patrons, brawling and behaving generally in a fashion that may be termed, at best, as obnoxious.

Shortly after they had taken their seats, the plaintiffs, none of whom were in anywise boisterous or unruly, were approached by one of the aforesaid male characters who bummed a light for his cigarette. After being accommodated, he returned to his peer group across the room. In a matter of minutes, several members of the graceless group surrounded the table at which the plaintiffs were seated, all seemingly itching for trouble. One of their number accused the plaintiffs of making uncomplimentary remarks about his girl friend (one of the go-go dancers who also served as waitresses) and invited them outside for a fight. When this gracious invitation was firmly declined, the gang began its vicious attack by kicking the chair out from under Mr. Kimple. The ultimate result of the ensuing affray was that all three plaintiffs were injured amidst an unrelenting rain of blows, kicks and missiles. Further details of the gory assault will be related when and as required.

The basis of the plaintiffs' claims against Mr. Foster, the proprietor of The Roaring Sixties, was his failure to provide them with the protection to which they were entitled as his guests. There is actually little dispute between plaintiffs and defendant with respect to the general proposition that a tavern operator owes his patrons the duty to exercise reasonable care for their personal safety. In this jurisdiction the general rule has been phrased in Huddleston v. Clark, 186 Kan. 209, 349 P.2d 888, in these words:

"While the owner and operator of a public tavern and grill is held to a stricter accountability for injuries to patrons than is the owner of private premises generally, the rule is that he is not an insurer of the patrons, but owes them only what, under the particular circumstances, is ordinary and reasonable care."

We find this rule to be in substantial accord with the prevailing doctrine which is expressed in 40 Am.Jur.2d, Hotels, Motels, Etc., Section 112, p. 987:

"A proprietor of an inn, hotel, restaurant, or similar establishment is liable for an assault upon a guest or patron by another guest, patron, or third person where he has reason to anticipate such assault, and fails to exercise reasonable care under the circumstances to prevent the assault or interfere with its execution. . . ."

To similar effect is Reilly v. 180 Club, Inc., 14 N.J.Super. 420, 82 A.2d 210, wherein the court said:

"It is in the law the duty of a tavernkeeper to exercise reasonable care, vigilance, and prudence to protect his guests from injury from the disorderly acts of other guests. . . ."

Although, as we have said, the defendant does not seriously question this legal maxim, he calls our attention to its qualification in the following particular: That the proprietor's duty to protect his patrons does not arise under the rule until the impending danger becomes apparent to the tavern keeper, or the circumstances are such that an alert and prudent person would be placed on notice of the probability of danger.

Pursuing this theme, the defendant asserts that the record is entirely bereft of evidence which would tend to place him on notice of impending danger. In making this assertion, we believe the defendant is mistaken. As we view this record, there is ample evidence to have alerted both the defendant himself and his go-go girl manager to the probability of violence erupting from the rowdy and unruly gang which had infested the tavern since afternoon.

We shall make no attempt to set out the evidence in detail. It is sufficient to say that "the guys" around the beer can pyramid, who ranged in number as high as eight or ten, were high and belligerent at 4:30 that afternoon and "maybe wanted to start a fight"; that about 5:15 or so the male manager (Mr. Foster) was in the tavern and set the boys up for a free beer; about 5:30 or 6:00 a fight broke out in which one of the fellows from the "pyramid" table hit and ran another guy out of the tavern; that the group was loud and boisterous and "would have gotten thrown out [of any other bar], because of the noise they were creating and the belligerence or sarcasm toward other people."

There is further evidence from a member of the gang that Foster's employees knew of this prior fight because they turned on the lights to stop it; and that there was another incident at the tavern over a hat involving some farm boys and one of the gang took the hat and everyone got to joking about it.

Mr. Foster himself testified that he was in the tavern from 5:00 to 6:00 that afternoon; that the boys were then building the pyramid of beer cans; and that he bought the boys a round of free beer.

We think the foregoing evidence was clearly sufficient, if believed by the jury, to warrant the jury in concluding that the defendant Foster, himself, had knowledge of facts which should reasonably have placed him on notice that trouble might well be expected from the unruly, belligerent group, and that an explosion might erupt which would endanger the safety of his patrons. True, Mr. Foster denied that any disturbance took place in the tavern while he was there, but there is evidence from which a contrary inference could well be drawn. Moreover, the defendant was aware of the gang's presence when he left his place of business and had helped to assuage its members' thirst by providing free beers all around.

Not only may notice be imparted to the defendant himself, but his go-go manager, whose duty it was to maintain order in the absence of her employer, was on the scene as the storm clouds gathered, and she took no steps to forestall the approaching tempest. The evidence is to the effect that before the physical attack commenced, the plaintiffs and other patrons repeatedly told the girls to summon the police, but to no effect. In fact, it may fairly be concluded from the evidence that the police were not called until the battle had raged for some ten minutes or so, during which time at least two of the go-go girls joined in the fray and belted the plaintiffs.

A case with similar overtones arose in our sister state of Minnesota (Priewe v. Bartz, 249 Minn. 488, 83 N.W.2d 116, 70 A.L.R.2d 621). There, a barmaid was in charge of her employer's place of business when an inebriated customer challenged another intoxicated customer to a fight. The barmaid did no more than to tell both inebriates to step outside if they wanted to fight. The police were not called although there was ample time for doing so. In upholding a verdict against the tavern owner in favor of an innocent third party who sustained injuries as a result of the fight, the Minnesota court said:

". . . [T]here can be no doubt that Mogen, the operator of a 3.2 beer establishment, owed a duty to those coming upon his premises to exercise reasonable care to protect them from injury at the hands of other patrons. . . .

". . . The duty of the proprietor was not met by the admonition of the barmaid that the parties should go outside if they wanted to fight. . . .

There must be some affirmative action to maintain order on the premises by demanding that such a person leave or by calling the authorities to enforce such demand. . . ."

In Peck v. Gerber, 154 Or. 126, 59 P.2d 675, 106 A.L.R. 996, the plaintiff was a guest in a restaurant at which alcoholic drinks were served. He was injured when two young men had an altercation, one of whom was knocked over and against him. The Oregon court upheld a verdict in the plaintiff's favor and in the course of its opinion stated:

"A guest or patron of such an establishment has a right to rely on the belief that he is in an orderly house and that the operator, personally or by his delegated representative, is exercising reasonable care to the end that the doings in the house shall be orderly. . . ."

In our opinion, there is ample evidence to establish that both the defendant and his designated manager had notice of sufficient facts to have alerted them to the potentiality of danger to the guests of The Roaring Sixties. A case in point is Coca v. Arceo, 71 N.M. 186, 376 P.2d 970, wherein the court said:

"The rule [of notice] does not require a long and continued course of conduct to find that the proprietor had knowledge of the violent disposition of the other patron—all that is necessary is that there be a sequence of conduct sufficiently long to enable the proprietor to act for the patron's safety. It is not necessary that the proprietor know of a history of a series of offenses against the peace. . . ."

The defendant complains of instructions given the jury to the effect that none of the plaintiffs were guilty of contributory negligence. Under the circumstances shown by the record we find no error in this respect. There is no evidence to indicate that plaintiffs were misbehaving or rowdy in any particular; the evidence, indeed, is quite to the contrary. They consistently sought to evade trouble until it was forced upon them.

Although the chief instigator of the attack accused one of the men of making a derogatory remark about his girl, this was rank hearsay on his part. Patrons sitting near the plaintiffs' table heard no remarks of an objectionable nature. The plaintiffs denied any disparaging utterances on their part, and the go-go girl herself, who may or may not have inflamed her boy friend's ire to fighting pitch, did not appear at the trial to favor the court with her version of the affair. . . .

Mr. Kimple, at the time of the fight, was wearing a steel plate in the front part of his skull, the aftermath of a former head injury resulting from an accident. Over the defendant's objection, Kimple testified to the fact and as to its possible consequences. We think no error resulted, if for no other reason than that Mr. Kimple also testified the plate was now loose.

Exception is taken to the court's instruction as to damages. The objection is focused on references to future pain and suffering and future disability, the basis of the objection being there was no evidence of future disability, pain or suffering. In all candor it must be acknowledged that as to Stahly and Morris there was no testimony going to the effects which might be expected from the beatings in the future, even though both men sustained severe injuries incapacitating them for considerable periods of time. In the case of Kimple, there was evidence, as already pointed out, from which it might be inferred that the plate in his skull was loosened in the affray, thus affording some basis for future disability as to him.

It must be said that the trial court did qualify its references as to future effects with the limiting expressions "any" and "if any." Moreover, the jury did not separate the amounts awarded into individual items and it is impossible to determine whether any allowance whatever was made for future pain, suffering and disability. Accordingly, we cannot say that prejudice resulted from the instruction on damages, even though the trial court might well have observed the admonition found in PIK 9.01, at page 255, that where evidence of future damage is lacking, all reference thereto should be deleted from the instructions.

Ruling of the Court: Prejudicial error has not been made to appear, and the judgments are affirmed as to each plaintiff.

Tavern keepers cannot foresee each and every possible danger to their patrons. The fundamental principle of tort law involved is analogous to the body of law set forth in the various "business invitee slip-and-fall" cases discussed in chapter 8. There is no negligence unless: (1) the dangerous or injury-causing condition was created by the proprietor; (2) the proprietor had knowledge of the dangerous or injury-causing condition; or (3) the dangerous or injury-causing condition was of such nature and duration that the proprietor was charged with constructive notice thereof. In other words, the question is whether the tavern keeper had knowledge of the problem or could have been charged with constructive notice of the coming event.

The case of Slawinski v. Mocettini, 31 Cal.Rptr. 613 (1963), deals with aspects of these principles. Slawinski had a scuffle with one Wilson in Mocettini's bar, after which Slawinski remained in the bar and Wilson left. About thirty minutes later, Wilson returned with a gun and killed Slawinski. This case resulted in a jury verdict for Slawinski's survivors; however, the trial court subsequently granted the bar owner's motion for a new trial. The appellate court affirmed the new trial, stating in part:

> While the standard of care is that of an ordinarily prudent person, yet it must be realized that reasonable care is a relative term in that the amount of care must be commensurate with the risks and dangers attending the activity being pursued. . . . *The test of whether the duty of reasonable care is discharged is the probability or foreseeability of injury to a plaintiff.*
>
> In the instant case, although there was conflicting evidence as to whether Wilson had a reputation as a hot-tempered person, it was uncontroverted that the respondents and their employees were not aware of this fact and had never experienced any trouble with Wilson. . . . *There is no evidence that the [bar owner's employees] had any way of knowing that Wilson would return* (emphasis added).

Intoxication as Nullifying Consent

Who is liable when an intoxicated patron consents to Indian wrestle, resulting in injury to himself? In Hollerud v. Malamis, 174 N.W.2d 626 (Mich., 1970), precisely such a situation arose, and the plaintiff-patron sued for assault and battery. The court had to decide whether the patron was so intoxicated that he was unable to express a rational will and whether the bartender (who wrestled the patron) had knowledge of his state.

The judgment that the patron had knowingly and willingly participated in the wrestling match had to be vacated. Furthermore, the court said that the assault and battery case did not depend on the fact that the defendant made unlawful sales of liquor to the plaintiff. Rather, if the plaintiff was in fact intoxicated when he consented to engage in the wrestling contest, his consent was ineffective no matter where he became intoxicated.

The management should always keep in mind that alcoholic beverages can make a person deviate from reasonable behavior. Rules prohibiting Indian wrestling, arm wrestling, and similar sports should be put into effect.

Intoxicated Drivers

Whether to prevent intoxicated people from driving perplexes many tavern operators. The 1974 case of *Vale v. Yawarski* deals with this question, as well as the question of the tavern operator's insurance policy, which had an exclusionary provision. This provision became operative if the operator: (1) sold, served, or gave liquor to someone in violation of any statute, ordinance, or regulation; (2) sold, served, or gave liquor to a minor; (3) sold, served, or gave liquor to a person under the influence of alcohol; or (4) caused or contributed to the intoxication of any person (see the section on insurance later in this chapter).

Case   **Vale v. Yawarski**
Example   *357 N.Y.S.2d 791 (1974)*
                  (STEWART F. HANCOCK, Jr., Justice)

These two interrelated motions for decision arise in separate lawsuits stemming from an automobile accident on June 9, 1973. In the first action plaintiff Vale seeks to recover for injuries suffered when struck by a car driven by the defendant Helmer. It is claimed that Helmer prior to the accident had left Mac's Restaurant or Tavern (owned and operated by the defendant, Marjorie Jay) in a condition which made him unfit to operate a motor vehicle. The second action is by the restaurant owner Jay against the Aetna Casualty and Surety Company to determine the question of coverage and other rights under the Aetna liability policy insuring the restaurant. The Aetna has disclaimed responsibility for the accident under a clause in the policy excluding coverage for liability arising from the wrongful or illegal sale, service or gift of alcoholic beverages. The second cause of action in Vale's complaint against Jay alleges a sale of liquor in violation of the Dram Shop Act (General Obligations Law, Section 11–101) and, thus, is squarely within the exclusion clause of the Aetna policy.

In its first-pleaded cause of action, however, the Vale complaint pointedly omits any reference to a sale of liquor or other activity by Jay which would come within the policy exclusion. Instead, liability is based solely on Jay's failure to fulfill her alleged responsibility as a restaurant operator to "prohibit or attempt to prohibit" Helmer from driving when she "knew or should have known" that he was not in a condition to do so safely. A motion to dismiss this cause of action has been made on behalf of defendant Jay pursuant to CPLR 3211(a)(7) for failure to state a cause of action.

The dismissal motion presents the novel question of whether an operator or owner of a restaurant or bar, aside from common law or statutory liability arising from illegal or improper sale or serving of liquor, can be held responsible to members of the public for failure to keep patrons from driving on the highway when they are apparently not in condition to do so safely. Clearly, the answer to this question will also influence, if not conclusively determine, the resolution of the coverage question and other issues in the declaratory judgment action against the insurance carrier, since the personal injury complaint, absent the first cause of action, would lie entirely within the policy exclusion clause.

We turn then to the question of whether the first cause of action states a valid claim for relief. The courts of New York impose upon hotels, innkeepers, and others in control of premises open to the public, a common law duty to exercise reasonable care for the protection of guests and patrons *on the premises*. . . . This includes the duty to police the premises where necessary to control the conduct of those present and prevent them from injuring others. . . . Under appropriate circumstances, the obligation may extend to persons on the adjacent highway or property, who are injured by the conduct of those on the premises. . . .

The instant complaint, however, does not fall under these well-recognized rules. Instead, it is claimed plaintiff was injured on the public highway beyond the premises because of defendant's failure to fulfill her duty of restraining or prohibiting Helmer, an apparently intoxicated patron, from driving away from the premises. In none of the decisions reviewed has such a duty been recognized either in New York or other jurisdictions. In this Court's opinion, there is in the common law no such duty incumbent on the tavern keeper—a conclusion, it is submitted, which is supported by practical policy considerations. The impossibility of stating with some degree of precision any useful standards of reasonable conduct for tavern keepers charged with the duty of deciding under what circumstances and how to restrain their customers from driving seems obvious. One can envision the variety of problems of the tavern keeper faced with the delicate task of restraining an unruly or determined patron (assuming he is physically capable of doing so) without incurring civil or criminal liability for invasion of the customer's rights.

The plaintiff relies on Berkeley v. Park, 47 Misc.2d 381, 262 N.Y.S.2d 290, which held that a person killed or injured on the highway by an intoxicated driver who was served liquor in a tavern has a valid common law action for negligence against the tavern keeper, in addition to a statutory claim under the Dram Shop Act. . . . In any event, nothing in *Berkeley* suggests that a tavern keeper—in addition to the duties of not supplying liquor to an intoxicated patron and protecting the guests on the premises— must also determine whether each departing guest is an automobile driver and fit or unfit to drive safely and then, if need be, take proper and lawful steps to prevent him from driving.

Ruling of the Court: This court, as stated, finds no basis in the law of New York or elsewhere for the imposition of such duty. The first cause of action must, therefore, be dismissed. . . .

Two similar Massachusetts cases resulted in different verdicts. In each case intoxicated barroom patrons who chose to drive when they left were involved in accidents that caused injuries and death to innocent parties. In Adamian v. Three Sons, Inc., 233 N.E.2d 18, decided on January 5, 1968, the court held that because the defendant provided a large parking facility for the convenience of his guests, he knew that a person leaving the establishment would probably be driving. The court held for the plaintiff Adamian.

In the case of Dimond v. Sacilotto, 233 N.E.2d 20, decided on the same date, an intoxicated minor drove his automobile into a tree, killing his companion. The administrators of his estate could not recover because there was a question of whether the bar owner-operator knew or should have known that the minor's group had arrived by automobile or that the minor would drive away in one, because a town parking lot was available. The difference between the two cases is subtle, but both question whether tavern keepers should make any attempt to learn how their guests arrive and leave. In both cases, the statute providing that no alcoholic beverage shall be sold or delivered on licensed premises to a person known to be a drunkard, or to any intoxicated person was in force.

Limiting Liability Statutes

Under the common law, there were no limiting liability statutes to limit the value that a patron could recover if his goods were lost or stolen while he was a guest of the innkeeper. Beginning with Massachusetts in 1851, limiting liability statutes were passed to protect the innkeeper from such losses.

The case of Davidson v. Ramsby et al., 210 S.E.2d 245, states the general rule to be followed for restaurateurs who provide valet parking service to the restaurant's patrons. In the absence of a statute to the contrary, a restaurateur does not enjoy the same protection as an innkeeper and could be liable for the loss of guests' personal property, which includes not only the automobile but items contained in it at the time that the vehicle is surrendered to the restaurant's attendant. The critical question as to the vehicle's contents is settled by the application of simple bailment law: Did the restaurant have actual or implied knowledge or notice as to the contents of the car at the time which it was left by the patron? Could the restaurateur reasonably have expected the items to have been in the automobile? Obviously this presents a jury question in most instances, although on some occasions it could be ruled upon as a matter of law.

Case Example	Davidson v. Ramsby
	210 S.E.2d 245 (Ga., 1974)
	(EVANS, Judge)

On the evening of December 30, 1971, Gilbert Davidson drove his automobile to the Ambassador Restaurant in Atlanta, Georgia. Upon arrival at the restaurant, he stopped at the entrance, locked the glove compartment, but left the key and several other keys, including the ignition key, in the car. He then gave possession of the car to an attendant so the car might be parked. The attendant, representing Charles Ramsby, who operated the parking lot for Ambassador Restaurants, Inc., gave Davidson a parking check and parked the automobile.

For the mutual purposes of inducing the restaurant trade to use its facilities, Ambassador Restaurants, Inc., had contracted with a private person to furnish the parking facilities to its guests who mutually enjoy the use of the facilities. The cost of same is presumably within the price of the food and drink, and there is no extra charge except for the "gratuitous" tip which is the usual and customary charge for services.

Davidson did not read the language on the parking check. After the attendant parked the automobile, the keys were placed on a peg board in the restaurant, which was numbered according to the parking spaces in which the vehicles were parked. The parking checks used by Ramsby have large numbers thereon, with the words "Ambassador Restaurant and Embassy Lounge," and "Not Responsible for Items Left in Car."

Several hours later, after he had dined, Davidson returned for his car. The automobile was missing from the lot, presumably stolen. It was recovered the following day with numerous articles of personalty missing from the interior, the glove compartment and the trunk. The keys to the automobile were found in the rear seat.

Davidson sued Ambassador Restaurants, Inc., as principal, and Ramsby, as agent, for negligence in allowing the automobile to be removed from the parking lot, which resulted in the loss of the personal items for which he seeks $1,113.07 in damages. The personalty that plaintiff alleges was missing from the car upon its return to him included camera equipment, binoculars, briefcases, sporting equipment, and a tool box and tools. It was not contended by Davidson that defendants had knowledge that such personalty was contained within the car at the time of delivery to defendant.

Defendants answered and denied liability. After discovery, defendants moved for summary judgment, the principal grounds urged in support thereof being first that the exculpatory language on the parking checks absolved defendants, and second, that no bailment was created as to the items of personalty because defendants had no knowledge that same were contained within the automobile.

The trial court granted summary judgment for defendants. The questions to be determined here are as to whether the exculpatory language on the parking ticket absolved defendants from liability, and as to whether a bailment for hire was created as to the items of personalty in the absence of defendants' knowledge of same being contained in the car. A finding in defendants' favor on either of these questions would be sufficient to support the finding in favor of summary judgment for defendants.

Held: A mere disclaimer of responsibility on a receipt is insufficient to absolve one of responsibility where negligence is alleged in the handling of plaintiff's automobile while defendants had it in their possession so as to allow the keys to be used in removing it. Further, there was no evidence that plaintiff was aware of the disclaimer written on the receipt.

Agency may be established by circumstances, apparent relations and conduct of the parties. The parking checks or receipts for automobiles containing the alleged waiver of responsibility had the names of the two establishments owned by the defendant Ambassador Restaurants, Inc., and not Ramsby.

In view of all of the foregoing, we hold that defendants could not escape liability because of the exculpatory language printed on the parking ticket.

We now come to the critical question in this case, to wit, are the circumstances here sufficient to create a bailment for hire *as to the contents of the automobile?*

To create a bailment, express or implied, there must be an actual or constructive delivery of the goods with actual or constructive possession in the bailee, exclusive and independent of the bailor and all other persons. The relationship of the owner of an automobile and the owner of a garage for the storage of such automobile is that of bailor and bailee. Where the object of the bailment is beneficial to both bailor and bailee, the degree of diligence required of the bailee is ordinary care.

In all cases of bailment after proof of loss, the burden is on the bailee to show proper diligence. But as to the *contents of an automobile*, admitting that the automobile is properly shown to be a bailment for hire, when and under what circumstances does a bailment for hire arise as to such contents of which the bailee has no actual knowledge? How far does his liability extend as to contents, of which he has no knowledge or notice? Does the law impose upon the bailee strict liability for the safekeeping of articles stored inside the car, even though he has no notice or knowledge as to such contents? Can the law regard him as a bailee of items entrusted to him, when he has no knowledge or notice that he has been entrusted with such items? In this case, all of the keys to the car were surrendered to the bailee, and presumably he could have made a thorough search of the car to determine for himself what it contained. Does the law contemplate such search, and if so, must each car be thoroughly searched and checked out at time of its delivery to the bailee, and in the presence of the bailor? How many cars of other customers will be backed-up while waiting for this exhaustive search by the person who takes charge of your car at a restaurant or hotel?

If the law is as contended by plaintiff, and if the bailee is responsible for all contents of the car whether he had any knowledge of such contents or not, suppose the car contained an expensive diamond ring of the value of $100,000 (or $100,000 in currency for that matter), must the bailee come up with $100,000 when the car is stolen? What position is bailee in to dispute the car owner's declaration that the automobile did contain such an expensive ring, or $100,000 in currency?

This is a case of first impression in Georgia, so we reluctantly look to authorities from other jurisdictions. The New Hampshire case of Campbell v. Portsmouth Hotel Co., 91 N.H. 390, 20 A.2d 644, discusses this question as to a hotel, and holds that such hotel, though having no knowledge of the contents of the car of its guest, "it might be found that the agreement to take care of the car implied a promise to take care *of what might be expected to be in it.*" (Emphasis supplied.) Under this authority, before the plaintiff could recover, he would first have to introduce evidence to show that the bailee should have expected such items as cameras, binoculars, sporting equipment, etc., to be contained in the car.

Continuing our search into other jurisdictions, in 27 A.L.R.2d 796

Annot. (liability of Bailee for Hire of Automobile for loss of contents) at p. 799, it is stated: "In most of the cases the liability of a bailee for hire of an automobile for loss of, or damage to the contents of the automobile is made to depend on the *absence or presence of notice or knowledge of the contents*" (emphasis supplied). And in 27 A.L.R.2d 796, 811, it is stated: "The rule of *non-liability for loss* of, or damage to, contents of an automobile, *where there is no notice or knowledge of the contents* has been applied to parking lot operators" (emphasis supplied).

Our Georgia courts have decided cases that involve similar facts, but without ever deciding the question here involved. For instance, in Diplomat Restaurant v. Townsend, 118 Ga.App. 694, 165 S.E.2d 317, the only question decided was whether Code Section 52–111 limiting an *innkeeper's* liability to $100 applied to restaurants, and it was held that same did not apply to restaurants. In Ellerman v. Atlanta American Motor Hotel Corporation, 126 Ga.App. 194, 191 S.E.2d 295, the question decided was whether an innkeeper could limit his liability by exculpatory language printed on a check delivered to the car-owner at time of bailment. In Traylor v. Hyatt Corporation, 122 Ga.App. 633, 178 S.E.2d 289, and at 636(7), this court made it plain that it would not decide whether the bailee must have notice as to the contents of the car before being held liable.

In Humphrey v. Merchants & Miners' Trans. Co., 38 Ga.App. 578, 144 S.E. 354, loss of articles from a passenger's room in a steamship were sued for and this court said: "Whether the defendant be treated as an innkeeper or as a common carrier of goods, it would at least be *responsible to the plaintiff for the loss of such articles as the passenger might be reasonably expected to carry on his person*, where the loss occurred as a result of the defendant's negligence" (emphasis supplied). The articles involved were a watch, watchchain, and a small amount of money. In Blosser Co. v. Doonan, 8 Ga.App. 285(2), 68 S.E. 1074, it is held that before the bailee is charged with the duty of safekeeping property, "he must assent to the bailment, either expressly or impliedly." In the case sub judice, the bailees assented as to the car, but it was not conclusively shown that they assented as to the *contents.*

We hold that a bailee for hire as to an automobile is not liable for the contents thereof unless he has actual or implied knowledge or notice as to such contents. If the articles are such as the bailee might "reasonably expect" to be therein, this would be sufficient notice.

But a jury question is made in this case as to whether the articles of personalty sued for, camera, binoculars, etc., were such as the bailees should have "reasonably expected" to be contained in the car.

The judgment of the trial court in granting summary judgment for defendants is reversed, and it is ordered that the case be submitted to a jury for determination as to whether the defendants had notice or knowledge of the contents of the car, and as to whether the articles were such that the defendants should have reasonably expected to be contained therein.

Ruling of the Court: Judgment reversed.

Insurance—Is It Always Valid?

Most restaurants and bars have some type of liability insurance. What types of situations do policies cover and not cover? A policy must be read carefully to determine its limitations.

Many insurance cases deal with intoxicated restaurant patrons who drive away and kill innocent people in the resulting automobile accidents. In the case of Benevolent Protective Order of Elks Lodge #97 v. Hanover Insurance Company, 266 A.2d 846 (N.H., 1970), the Elks' insurance policy agreed to pay on behalf of its insured "all sums which the insured shall become legally obligated to pay as damages," subject to the following exclusion: "Under coverages A and C [Bodily Injury and Property Liability], to liability imposed on the insured . . . as a person or organization engaged in the business of manufacturing, selling or distributing alcoholic beverages, or an owner or lessor of premises used for such purposes, by reason of any statute or ordinance pertaining to the sale, gift, distribution or use of any alcoholic beverage."

The court's decision in the Elks case noted that the policy excluded the strict liability imposed by statutes such as Dram Shop Acts or Civil Damage Acts, but not the liability resulting from the negligence of the insured, as set forth by the plaintiff in the original suit against the Elks Lodge. The court decided that the Hanover Insurance Company policy did not exclude coverage and that the company was required to defend and pay any judgment recovered in the first case.

Insurance law holds that a policy holder cannot recover if the death of the insured was the result of suicide, murder by the beneficiary, or serious criminal conduct by the insured. However, in the Three Sons case the extension of that principle would mean that an insurance company could avoid its contractual obligation whenever the insured violated a criminal statute. The court rejected the argument as fallacious because if the principle were literally applied, the slightest negligence would bar recovery. According to the court, such a result would be generally recognized as impractical and unjust; therefore, the defendant insurance company was obligated to defend the plaintiff in his action without reservation of right as long as it insisted on retaining control of the defense, and legal expenses (totaling $4,350) and any award were to be paid to the plaintiff.

The case of Vale v. Yawarski, discussed earlier in this chapter, also dealt with an exclusionary clause in an insurance policy. The plaintiff (injured by a patron of Mac's Restaurant) sued the intoxicated driver of the car and the restaurant owner. Mac's Restaurant made a motion for a decision to determine whether the restaurant's insurance policy covered this particular case. The insurance company disclaimed responsibility for the accident under a clause in the policy excluding coverage for liability arising from the wrongful or illegal sale, serving, or gift of alcoholic beverages. The restaurant patron had imbibed too much liquor, but the injured plaintiff was not suing under the Dram Shop Act but rather on the alleged duty of nonperformance—that is, the failure to restrain the patron from leaving the restaurant in a drunken condition. There seems to be no obligation on the part of a restaurant owner to prevent a drunken guest from driving a car away from the establishment.

This means that under the Dram Shop Act, restaurateurs cannot seek relief from an exclusionary clause in their insurance policy; they must pay the entire judgment themselves if found guilty. Obviously, the solution to this dilemma is to bar exclusionary clauses, but this is not viable. Tavern keepers can prevent litigation in this area by refusing to serve drunk patrons and minors and by not breaking any laws of the Alcoholic Beverage Control Commission or criminal statutes.

In Trail v. Christian, 213 N.W.2d 618 (Minn., 1973), the court ruled that when a state adopts the Dram Shop Act, the legislature in effect preempts the subject of remedies available for wrongs arising from the improper sale of intoxicating beverages. The court also stated that the Dram Shop Act was confined to injuries resulting from the illegal sale or gift of intoxicating liquors. In another interesting point, the court said that if a restaurateur sold liquor to a minor or already intoxicated individual, the action constituted negligence per se, precluding the restaurateur in a common law negligence action from raising defenses of comparative negligence, contributory negligence, and assumption of risk. In the *Trail* case, 3.2 beer was considered an alcoholic beverage and hence was covered under the Dram Shop Act.

Alcoholic Beverage Laws

Obviously, the Alcoholic Beverage Control Commission makes the laws governing the duties of a liquor licensee, but what are the powers of the municipality where the licensee is permitted to do business? The answer was given in Boston Licensing Board v. Alcoholic Beverage Control Commission, 328 N.E.2d 848 (Mass., 1975), and approved by the United States Supreme Court in Craig v. Boren, 97 S.Ct. 451 (1976).

In this case, the city licensing board had made a rule regulating sexually explicit conduct in licensed establishments. The question was not whether the ABCC could pass such a law, but whether a town could. When the commission passes or amends regulations, it must ordinarily give notice, hold hearings, and allow interested parties to present their views. But a local licensing board can formulate its own requirements, even if the regulations are not as strict as those of the state commission. In other words, a municipality may make laws to control any business activity carried on within its borders. Thus, restaurant operators must be aware of municipal laws as well as state regulations that apply to their businesses.

Master-Servant Relationship

Whether employees act as agents of their employers is a difficult question. The most serious injuries to patrons by employees generally involve detectives, bouncers, and bartenders. In the case of Sixty-Six, Inc., v. Finley, 224 So.2d 381 (Fla., 1969), a guard seriously injured a guest. The jury found that the guard was acting as an employee when he shot the guest. The judgment cost the hotel over $377,000.

The employer, however, is not always liable for the actions of employees. In Fisher v. Hering, 97 N.E.2d 553 (Ohio, 1948), the court held that when a restaurant waitress struck a patron in the face after he accused her of shortchanging other customers it was not within the scope of her employment and that the restaurant owner was not liable for her assault, which arose out of a personal quarrel. Even the continued employment of the waitress did not constitute the employer's ratification of the assault.

As expressed in the *Fisher* case, the rule generally followed is that

> . . . a master is not responsible for the wrongful act of his servant, unless that act be done in execution of the authority, express or implied, given by the master. Beyond the scope of his employment, the servant is as much a stranger to his master as any third person, and the act of the servant not done in the execution of the service for which he was engaged cannot be regarded as the act of the master.

In Kent v. Bradley, 480 S.W.2d 55 (Texas, 1972), the court ruled that a restaurant employee was acting within the scope of his employment when an argument with a customer over the amount of the check resulted in a verbal assault on the guest. Here, because the employee would presumably be the person responsible for adjudicating any discrepancy in a check, the employee was acting for his employer within the scope of his employment. The patron recovered.

Ejecting Unruly Patrons with Force

No one will deny the right of a restaurant or bar owner to eject unruly guests. Indeed, legal action can be taken against owners who do not eject unruly guests before they can cause harm to the other guests. How much force may a bartender or bouncer use to eject such a guest? According to the general rule, *only such force as is reasonably necessary for that purpose.* The use of unnecessary force would render the proprietor liable for any injury. For example, the employer in Steward v. Napuche, 53 N.E.2d 676 (Mich., 1952), was held liable for the actions of his bartender, who used more force than necessary to eject an intoxicated patron who threatened to create a disturbance. The rationale of the court was that the employee, who was in a position of trust and responsibility, acted within the scope of his employment and in the furtherance of his employer's business in attempting to maintain law and order on the premises. The employer was held responsible even though the assault arose from the employee's lack of judgment when he exceeded his authority and duty by inflicting an unjustifiable injury upon the patron.

What constitutes an unruly person? Does complaining about the food served in a restaurant make such a customer an unruly person? And assuming that the person is unruly, how much force can be used in ejecting him? In the case of Vancherie v. Siperly, 221 A.2d 356 (Md.,

1966), the court faced both questions. The plaintiff, a sailor, had entered the defendant's restaurant and ordered scrambled eggs, toast, and a glass of milk. After eating a portion of the eggs, he complained to the waitress, "They just don't taste right," and said he thought "there may be a rotten one in there." The waitress went to the rear of the restaurant and got the defendant. The plaintiff repeated his complaint, and the defendant told the plaintiff that neither he nor his money was wanted. The defendant left and went home. After the defendant left, the plaintiff finished his milk and then went to the register to pay. The waitress said she would not accept payment, and the plaintiff insisted, whereupon the waitress called the defendant. When the defendant arrived, he was carrying a nightstick, which he used to hit the plaintiff.

The lower court awarded the plaintiff $1,000 compensatory damages and $4,000 exemplary damages. The defendant appealed claiming that his motion for a directed verdict should have been granted because he argued that in view of the physical differences between himself and the plaintiff, the force he used was not unreasonable as a matter of law. (The plaintiff was a six-foot-tall, young, and healthy sailor; the defendant was sixty-five years old and partially disabled.) The defendant further claimed that the law governing the case mandated a finding in his favor as a matter of law.

The court agreed that the following law governed the case but said that an interpretation of it did not support the defendant's contention: "An actor is privileged to use reasonable force, not intended or likely to cause death or serious bodily harm, to prevent or terminate another's intrusion upon the actor's lands or chattels, if (a) the intrusion is not privileged or the other intentionally or negligently causes the actor to believe that it is not privileged, and (b) the actor reasonably believes that the intrusion can be prevented or terminated only by the force used, and (c) the actor has first requested the other to desist, and the other has disregarded the request, or the actor reasonably believes that a request will be useless or that substantial harm will be done before it can be made." The law, however, continued: "If the actor applies a force to . . . another which is in excess of that which is privileged, (a) the actor is liable for so much of the force . . . as is excessive."

The court said that even if it was assumed that the plaintiff had become a trespasser by virtue of the fact that he refused to leave after being so ordered, the jury could have found that the force that the defendant applied was in "excess of that which is privileged" and that therefore the defendant was liable. The issue of excessive force was clearly one for the jury, which found against the defendant; there was no error that would justify overturning their finding.

With regard to the question as to whether there was error in awarding exemplary damages, the court said that there was sufficient evidence to support a finding that the defendant in acting was "influenced by hatred and spite and that he had willfully and deliberately inflicted injury to injure the plaintiff." It is clear that in instances where a defendant inflicts malicious and wanton injury, a jury is permitted to award exemplary damages.

Do owners of a restaurant or bar have any duties toward an intoxicated customer whom they seek to evict from the restaurant? The reason the restaurateur evicts a person is to carry out duties toward the other patrons, protecting them from any harmful acts of the inebriated patron while they are on the premises. According to the court, a double duty could be imposed on the restaurateurs or tavern keepers. The first is that they must protect patrons from the acts of the inebriated patron. This is the duty under the requirement that a restaurateur or tavern keeper must keep the premises reasonably safe for patrons. The only way that this duty can be achieved is to remove the inebriated person from the premises. The second half of the double duty now comes into play: the restaurateur or tavern keeper has a duty to avoid committing any affirmative acts that will increase the peril to an intoxicated person. Although there is no duty to take care of a person who is ill or intoxicated and unable to look out for oneself, it is still another thing to eject such a person into a position of danger. If one does and an injury results, there will be liability. The reasoning was developed in the case of Thrasher v. Leggett, 373 So.2d 494 (La., 1979), although it was inapplicable in that case because the injury suffered by the ejected inebriate was the result of his own threatening and disruptive behavior (he swung his fist at the bouncer, missed, and lost his balance, causing him to fall over a railing). The court said that the proper standard to be applied is to determine whether restaurateurs breach their duty to an inebriate when ejecting such a person. The test is whether the restaurateur's conduct is consistent with that which is generally required of a reasonable person under like circumstances.

The Federal Civil Rights Act

Sex discrimination in employment has been declared unlawful by the federal Civil Rights Act of 1964.

Women Bartenders

The states always set the laws that regulate the sale of alcoholic beverages. Indeed, selling liquor is considered a privilege that the state may grant to some and deny to others, or may take away altogether, and which is subject to control under police powers. Under this police power certain states and cities have enacted statutes governing the employment of women in places where intoxicating liquors are sold. Generally, these statutes are divided into four categories:

1   Statutes forbidding the owner or licensee of a liquor establishment to hire females;

2 Statutes forbidding females from accepting employment in places where intoxicating liquors are sold;

3 Statutes limiting the licensing of bartenders to males;

4 Statutes placing certain restrictions on establishments that employ females.

For a long time, such statutes were held as a valid exercise of the police powers of the state and were considered "protective" and "morally beneficial" to the general public. However, in Sail'er Inn, Inc., v. Kirby, 95 Cal.Rptr. 329 (1971), the court ruled that a statute prohibiting women from tending bar violated a section of the California Constitution forbidding sex discrimination in employment. The court noted that such laws, which when applied to women are often characterized as protective and beneficial, would readily be recognized as invidious and impermissible when applied to racial or ethnic minorities. According to the court, the "pedestal upon which women have been placed has all too often, upon closer inspection, been revealed as a cage."

Since 1968, court decisions have viewed older precedents as an obsolete product of a different social and moral climate. Although there have been successful constitutional attacks on the validity of legislative prohibition against female bartenders, *the older decisions are still the rule in many jurisdictions where they have not recently been challenged.*

Recent civil rights legislation will undoubtedly have a profound effect on laws forbidding the employment of women in places where liquor is sold, although several courts have pointed out that tavern owners often do not employ a sufficient number of people to bring the federal act into play. The federal act applies only to an employer engaged in an industry affecting interstate commerce and employing twenty-five or more employees.

Paterson Tavern and Grill Owners Association v. Hawthorne, 207 A.2d 628 (N.J., 1970), dealt with the relevance of the civil rights statute. The court declared the challenged ordinance an invalid exercise of police power, but also pointed out that both the federal and the state Civil Rights Act were inapplicable. As the court noted, the tavern keepers did not have enough employees to be covered.

Sex as a Valid Occupational Qualification

According to the guidelines of the Equal Employment Opportunity Commission, "assumptions of the corporative employment characteristics" of laymen in general and "stereotyped characterizations" of the sexes do not warrant the application of the bona fide qualification exception to the Civil Rights Act. Are there occupations that may be validly limited as to sex? It would be pointless to discuss them here because a number of factors enter into making a specific occupation a one-sex situation.

In McCrimmon v. Daley, 418 F.2d 366 (C.A. 7, Ill., 1969), a Chicago court declared that sex was not a valid occupational qualification for tending bar. In *Paterson Tavern and Grill Owners Association* v. *Hawthorne* the validity of an ordinance prohibiting female bartenders was disproven on grounds other than that of a "bona fide occupational qualification reasonably necessary to the normal operation of that particular business or enterprise."

Management Principles

As a quasi-public establishment, a restaurant has a responsibility to its patrons for their health and safety. Although a restaurant is private and belongs to the owners, this ownership is no longer restricted as it was under common law.

With the advent of the 1964 Civil Rights Act, certain types of discrimination can no longer be practiced. The Uniform Commercial Code (UCC) also has had a far-reaching influence on the operation of a restaurant. Yet neither will burden restaurants if they follow certain basic procedures of good business practice. These include good sanitation, proper employee training, and an adherence to the rule that no one gets something for nothing.

Most states now follow what was once known as the Massachusetts or New York rule—that a place serving food must serve wholesome food, and by law this impliedly warranties its wholesomeness. All states have now accepted most of the UCC. In *Levy* v. *Paul*, Judge Carrico summarized the management's duty when he said the restaurant owner has the experience and skill in the care of food, whereas the customer has no effective opportunity to inspect or select the wholesomeness of the food he will eat. Food service operators have the duty to sell only such food as they would serve to themselves or their families.

Good management techniques and well-trained personnel will probably prevent many pitfalls that face the careless operator. In one case, parts of a rat were sold as fried chicken. Such occurrences are not as rare as they should be. Unfortunately, any person who purchases a business and acquires a license can call oneself a restaurateur. Restaurateurs need pass no test to demonstrate their ability.

But the food service operator is not always at fault when something goes wrong. Confidence men often earn their livelihood by "finding" a foreign substance in food, by presenting a piece of a broken tooth, or by feigning illness. The restaurateur is often only too eager to settle, as such accidents are always possible. However, under other circumstances no recovery may be had.

In the *Webster* case, fish chowder containing a fish bone was not considered unwholesome but unpleasant. And it has been considered reasonable to find a chicken bone in a chicken pot pie (see Mix v. Ingersoll Candy Company, 59 P.2d 144 [Cal., 1936]). The same reasoning has been followed when a bone was found in a plate of roast turkey and in many similar cases.

What constitutes an unwholesome or unnatural substance in food is fairly ambiguous. The results of such legal cases depend on the circumstances and the governing rules of the particular state. The two tests usually applied are the reasonable expectation test and the foreign natural test. Relevant cases may be consulted as to recovery (Friends v. Childs Dining Hall Co., 120 N.E. 407 [Mass., 1918]; Smith v. Gerrish, 152 N.E.2d 318; Wood v. Waldorf Systems, 83 A.2d 90 [R.I., 1951]; Betehia v. Cape Cod Corp., 103 N.W.2d 64 [Wis., 1960]; Zabner v. Howard Johnson's, Inc., 201 So.2d 824 [Fla., 1967]).

In Conklin v. Hotel Waldorf Astoria, described in this chapter, the hotel lost the case not because of the argument made about privity of contract, but because the jury did not believe that a piece of glass in a roll was a wholesome substance. Certainly, the privity of contract issue will be raised by an attorney, but from a management point of view, the important point is how the glass got into the dough and was baked in the roll. It was simply the result of an employee's carelessness.

Restaurants must police themselves to prevent such happenings. Glasses and glass equipment break easily and disperse readily. The good manager will warn personnel to report any broken glass and to make a very careful search of the area to ensure that all pieces have been found. Employees should be made aware of how far broken glass can go. Insurance companies offer short films on such occurrences that can help prevent costly lawsuits. Though the Conklin case went to the Court of Appeals, most are settled earlier, and there are many such cases.

In contemporary times the privity rule will be resisted by anyone caught in its meshes. With the current use of credit cards and charge accounts, it is not always clear or pertinent who is actually paying a bill.

Spoiled food is another serious problem. The following management procedures will help to prevent trouble. If necessary, food should be kept under proper refrigeration (38° to 40°F). Because bacteria grow at room temperature, food should not be left outside the refrigerator longer than necessary. Large containers should be cooled quickly in a water bath; otherwise the center of the container will remain warm for a long time— a dangerous situation.

The following experiment should be helpful in informing employees about good sanitation. Run sterilized (boiled in water) swabs over employees' hands and then set them over petri dishes containing agar agar (a gelatin food on which bacteria thrive and which can be purchased in most drug stores). Incubate the petri dishes at 70°F for 24 to 36 hours. The results should convince employees of the necessity for clean and uninfected hands. Restroom signs can also encourage clean hands.

The case of Sossin Systems, Inc., v. Miami Beach dealt with the serving of kosher food. Many restaurateurs seek to widen their market by advertising kosher food but do not conform to the absolute rules governing it. In the future the states and probably even the federal government will subject the food service industry to a much closer scrutiny. States like New York already systematically regulate food service establishments. The industry may be able to avoid rigid control by policing itself.

Alcoholic Beverages

The basic management principle governing alcoholic beverages is to allow no one to drink more than his or her capacity. However, how much can an individual drink? Does physical size affect capacity? How long can a person continue drinking? It is not a crime to get a person drunk, but he may commit a crime while in this condition. The following basic information about alcohol and drinking may aid management in planning its policies.

The alcohol content of different alcoholic beverages varies. Wine contains 10 to 12 percent of alcohol by volume; beer, 4 to 5 percent; ale, 6 to 8 percent; whiskey, brandy, rum, gin, and vodka, 40 to 55 percent.

Studies on the social pattern of drinking in the United States indicate that 65 percent of the total population drinks alcoholic beverages; 16 percent do not discriminate between wine, liquor, and beer; 15 percent are strictly beer drinkers, while only 4 percent drink wine exclusively, and 7 percent prefer liquor only.[2]

The type and degree of effect depends obviously on the amount of ingested alcohol. The behavioral changes tend to reflect the personality of the individual (happy drunks, sad drunks, fighting drunks, etc.).

There is no constant correlation between blood alcohol level and the manifestations of acute alcoholism. However, the arbitrary levels established by the National Safety Council mainly for use in cases of traffic violations and accidents are generally accepted as a useful guide. At levels of 0.00 to 0.05 percent (one to two bottles of beer or one to two ounces of whiskey) the individual is considered "not under the influence." Levels between 0.05 percent and 0.15 percent (three to eight bottles of beer or three to eight ounces of whiskey) may be called a "preintoxication stage." At 0.05 to 0.10 percent the individual is possibly intoxicated and at 0.10 to 0.15 percent probably intoxicated. Levels over 0.15 percent indicate that the individual is "under the influence"; over 0.20 percent, definitely intoxicated; over 0.30 percent, seriously intoxicated. It should be pointed out that to reach the borderline of intoxication (0.15 percent blood alcohol), an individual of average weight must have consumed at least seven ounces of whiskey in one hour or two or a larger

2   George G. Katsas, "Alcohol, Accidents, and Crime," unpublished manuscript (Massachusetts Department of Public Health).

amount over a longer period of time. Levels over 0.40 percent are considered fatal, although deaths occur at lower blood concentrations.

With the increasing strictness of drinking laws (Dram Shop Acts and Civil Damage Acts), the high amounts of jury awards, the rigid interpretation by courts of negligence law, and the great number of cases being brought to trial, anyone serving liquor should weigh most carefully the advantages (more business) and the disadvantages (less business, more chance of being sued, and more fights). It is difficult to turn away a steady customer who wants another drink. One way to handle a patron who has had enough to drink might be to refuse courteously with the promise of a free drink the next time.

The following procedures should be followed:

1 Do not serve a minor or someone you believe is a minor, even with identification proving age. You are responsible if an accident occurs, and your liquor license could be jeopardized.

2 Refuse someone who, in your own or your employee's judgment, has had enough to drink.

3 Train your bartenders to recognize troublemakers and how they should be handled. Teach bouncers (or so-called social attendants) how to deal with all sorts of situations, when to ask for help, and when to call the police.

4 If a patron becomes obnoxious, call someone for help or ask the person to leave before someone gets hurt. Train your employees how to cope with such situations.

5 Foreseeing potential problems is the duty of the bartender and other employees. Often a person hurt or injured physically or psychologically will threaten to sue the establishment, but 98 percent never follow up. At worst you may lose their business. Try to observe your customers' behavior and take steps to counter obstreperous patrons before it is too late.

Under the *Mitchell* case, discussed in this chapter, even a drinker's companion may be able to recover if injured in an accident. Although a few states, such as Michigan and Illinois, are currently exempt from this rule, future cases will probably end such exemptions—especially in view of the *Todd* v. *Bigelow* case, in which the plaintiff-wife came along merely to be sociable and was therefore able to recover. The *McNally* case is also important in this respect.

Because a restaurant generally cannot limit liability as a hotel can, it should set aside a place to store coats and valuables. Normally, a restaurant is not responsible for a customer's coat or other belongings if they are hung close to the table. However, when a cloakroom is available and the guest does not use it, the usual interpretation is that the restaurant is not liable. States vary on this, so an attorney should be consulted. Even though small claims court judgments may not be high, restaurateurs must appear; otherwise they will have a judgment brought against them, and this judgment, if not appealed, can be used to collect whatever is owed.

Insurance offers essential protection to restaurateurs in this and other areas. The policy should be explained in detail by the insurance agent.

The travel guide is an increasingly popular, and to some even invaluable, reference source on restaurants and hotels. To be recommended by a travel guide, the good restaurant manager serves good food. The usually unannounced, anonymous travel-guide critic not only eats the food but also checks out the atmosphere of the establishment, as well as whether the kitchen is clean and orderly. Ambitious managers will be constantly on their toes.

Restaurateurs must take heed of the liability when their employees or an independent valet service parks guests' cars. The general rule is that they are not exempt from loss of the guests' cars and possibly of personal items left in the cars. Naturally, insurance coverage is mandated, but careful selection of employees is important, and a very rigid control of keys and the system is warranted.

Just as restaurants and bars are governed by special legal principles and management functions, so are components of a new area of the travel industry—campgrounds, mobile homes, and tourist camps—which we will discuss in the next chapter.

QUESTIONS FOR DISCUSSION

1 On what grounds can a person who is served unwholesome food in a restaurant recover?

2 Explain the Uniform Commercial Code as it pertains to the serving of food.

3 Explain the reasonable expectation test and the foreign natural test as they pertain to the serving of food.

4 What effect does privity of contract have on the purchase of food in a restaurant?

5 Explain the exceptions to the Uniform Commercial Code as it pertains to the serving of wholesome food.

6 What rules govern the serving of kosher foods? Must all kosher foods be so marked?

7 What is the Dram Shop Act? What are its general provisions?

8 What is the law in most states pertaining to a drunkard who, after leaving a bar, kills an innocent person on the road?

9 What responsibility is owed a bar patron in a fight? For equipment? Against other patrons or ruffians?

10 When an employee uses too much force in maintaining order, is the employee or the employer liable? Why?

11 Is sex discrimination legal? What kinds of jobs may women be prohibited from doing? Why and how?

14 Contents

14 Campgrounds, Mobile Homes, and Tourist Courts

"Knowledge is more than equivalent to force."

SAMUEL JOHNSON

Camping has become a big business for the service industry. Over a billion dollars is spent each year on trailers, camping equipment, transportation to and from campgrounds, overnight fees, and other related expenses. The cost of a customized trailer alone may run over $30,000, not including its furnishings.

There are over 13,000 private campgrounds in the United States, as well as over 7,500 public facilities. All offer at least a level place to park a car or trailer or to set up a tent. They also provide running water and sanitary facilities. More elaborate campgrounds have electrical hookups, hot showers, swimming pools, recreation halls, playgrounds, volley ball courts, miniature golf courses, fishing ponds, and grocery stores. Now that Holiday Inn, Howard Johnson's, and other large chains have entered the field, camping is becoming big business.

This chapter considers the legal principles necessary for managers of this newest segment of the travel industry. It discusses the obligations, responsibilities, and liabilities such operators have to their guests, as well as regulations and statutes that control their behavior. To begin, the chapter includes a discussion of the special applications of the 1964 Civil Rights Act to campgrounds and trailer parks.

Federal Civil Rights Act of 1964

Widely scattered throughout the country, campgrounds and mobile home parks serve, at least in part, transient or short-term tenants who rent space on the premises. Are such parks and campgrounds public accommodations within the meaning of state and federal civil rights statutes prohibiting discrimination?

The portion of 1964 Civil Rights Act pertaining to accommodations does not mention trailer parks or campgrounds; they are not even discussed in the act's legislative history. According to the public accommodations statute (42 U.S.C. 200a[b][1]), however trailer parks and campgrounds cannot discriminate if they provide space for rental to transient guests. In the act, trailer parks in general fall under the category of "other establishments which provide lodging to transient guests."

In Dean v. Ashling, 409 F.2d 754 (Fla., 1969), a group of black trailer owners was refused accommodation in a trailer park. The district court held that the plaintiffs had failed to prove that space was available in the park at the time of application, but the appellate court said that this decision was excessively burdensome on the plaintiffs. Because a trailer park is an establishment that provides lodgings to transient guests, the test, the court reasoned, should be the same as in a rejection at a motel or hotel, which is a positive defense when accommodations are filled.

State Civil Rights Act

Few appellate-level civil rights cases deal with trailer parks and campgrounds. Whenever these cases do come up, however, the courts generally hold that they do violate the state civil rights acts against racial discrimination or discrimination on other grounds. In the case of Ohio Civil Rights Commission v. Lysyi, 313 N.E.2d 3, cert. den. 419 U.S. 1108 (Ohio, 1974), the trailer park in question rented trailer space without formal agreements, provided water, sewage, and garbage disposal services on an individual basis to each guest, maintained the park on a long-term basis, and sold trailers, cameras, and camera equipment. The Ohio Commission held that the trailer park was a place of public accommodation within the meaning of a state civil rights statute that prohibited racial discrimination in places of public accommodation. The court stated that a "place of public accommodation" referred to any place where accommodations, facilities, or privileges were available to the public. The court also noted that the trailer park offered accommodations to a substantial public on a nonsocial, sporadic, impersonal, and nongratuitous basis in the same manner as an inn, restaurant, or eating place specifically referred to in the statute.

In the Lysyi case, the plaintiff was evicted from the trailer park after she associated with a black person in her trailer. The defendant argued that the state civil rights statute extended only to direct discrimination on the basis of race or color and that the statute had no application to indirect discrimination against a person on the basis of the race or color of his associates. But the court answered that this would result in an overly restrictive interpretation of the statute. The protection afforded by the statute could not be held to extend only to persons of a single or minority race.

In Gregory v. Madison Mobile Homes Park, Inc., 128 N.W.2d 462 (Wis., 1964), the court did not expressly hold that a trailer park was a place of public accommodation, but it recognized that under appropriate facts, the particular trailer park involved in the case could be considered a place of public accommodation within the meaning of the particular statute.

Zoning Regulations

Dangers to public health in trailer and tourist camps have led to the legislation of standards for such enterprises. Fire hazards, improper sanitation, parking, overstaying a limited period of time, morals, safety, and general welfare are the predominant areas treated by such legislation. When first passed, these statutes included a grandfather clause that allowed the present owner to go on as before, but on change of ownership the park became subject to the new regulations. As a general rule, the courts seem to recognize such regulations as valid.

Formerly, trailers, mobile homes, and camping equipment were used mainly by itinerant workers for temporary residences. Such units were seldom fixed to any one spot for long-term occupancy, but were "mobile" in the true sense of the word. Such transience resulted in various legal devices to "protect" communities from campgrounds, trailer parks, and mobile home areas, including restrictions on their use and location.

Zoning regulations expressly dealing with such occupancy of land appear to fall within four general classifications: (1) exclusion of trailer parks and campgrounds from the municipality; (2) exclusion from particular districts; (3) requirements of approval from the municipal authorities or from neighboring property owners; and (4) limits on use and occupancy—for example, restricting the length of time particular trailers or persons may stay in an area.

Total Exclusion

The regulations that exclude trailer parks from a municipality have perhaps aroused the most controversy. They have been challenged on the grounds that the regulations are unreasonable, that they involve an abuse of zoning power, and that they conflict with state regulations that give approval to trailer parks within the state. The courts do not agree on the validity of such regulations.

Motorcycle gangs or party-loving groups may literally take over a camp area, to the consternation of the owner and other users. Among the problems in attempting to bar undesirable persons and groups are the restrictions in the discrimination clause of civil rights acts. (Possible ways of dealing with this are discussed in the section on management principles.)

Regulations that exclude trailer parks from residential, commercial or business, industrial, and agricultural areas have generally been upheld, as well as regulations limiting the time a trailer camp may be occupied by particular persons or trailers, even though such regulations obviously bar the use of trailer parks as sites for permanent residences. Statutes designed to promote health, safety, morals, and general welfare are difficult to attack in a court of law. However, the constitutionality of arbitrary and capricious laws can be challenged in court.[1]

In the case of *Town of Southport* v. *Ross* a private individual kept a house trailer on his premises longer than the "four weeks in every twelve months" as allowed by statute. This case was found to be a valid exercise of the police power designed to promote the health, safety, morals, and general welfare of the town. College towns, where students sometimes purchase trailers as an alternative to dormitory residence, may find the *Southport* case useful in barring such long-term trailer residence.

Case Example	**Town of Southport v. Ross**
	132 N.Y.S.2d 390 (1954)
	(PER CURIAM)

The issue in this case is the validity of Section 15 of the "House Trailer and Tourist Camp Ordinance of the Town of Southport," Chemung County, New York, which reads, "(Duration of Stay) No such house trailer shall be permitted to remain upon any premises other than in a camp for a longer period than four (4) weeks in every twelve (12) months except the time may be extended by action of the Town Board." The material facts are not in dispute.

Before the enactment of the ordinance, defendant permitted one Martha Smith to place her house trailer on land owned by him and his wife and to occupy the trailer as a residence. After the lapse of four weeks after the adoption of the ordinance, application was made to the town board for an extension of the time of occupancy, but no action was taken thereon either to grant or refuse the extension. Instead, this action was brought to recover a civil penalty for the violation of the ordinance. No violation of the ordinance was alleged or claimed other than defendant's failure to limit the stay of the trailer to four weeks. Trial was had before the court without a jury and judgment rendered dismissing the complaint on the merits, from which judgment this appeal has been taken.

The ordinance also contains detailed provisions for the licensing, planning, inspecting and regulating of trailer camps, including provision for sanitary safeguards and proper water supply. Subdivision 21 of Section

---

1 For an excellent review (with updates) on which statutes have been upheld as constitutional and those that have been declared unconstitutional, see 41 A.L.R.3d 546.

130 of the Town Law is specific in authorizing these provisions as well as in authorizing a time limit on the duration of stay of house trailers in portions of the town outside established trailer camps.

It is not questioned that the trailer here under consideration was equipped with sanitary facilities and had an accessible and adequate water supply. But "the fact that no injury has occurred" in the particular case is not determinative as to the validity of the regulation.

In our opinion the ordinance is valid. The judgment should be reversed, on the law and the facts, and judgment granted for plaintiff, with costs in both courts. Settle order on notice.

Ruling of the Court: Judgment reversed, on the law and facts, and judgment granted for plaintiff, with costs in both courts.

In attacking an ordinance, the burden of showing that the regulation is not justified under the state's police power rests upon the party that is trying to overcome the ordinance. If the validity of the legislature's classification for zoning purposes is fairly debatable, the legislative judgment must be allowed to control (Stevens v. Smolka, 202 N.Y.S.2d 783 [1960]).

In the case of City of Cobly v. Hurtt, 509 P.2d 1142 (Kan., 1973), mobile homes were allowed on private property before a new ordinance prohibited them within the city outside of mobile home communities. The court held that this regulation bore a substantial relationship to public health, safety, and general welfare and was not arbitrary or unreasonable.

Liabilities of Campground, Trailer Park, and Mobile Park Owners

Do campgrounds, trailer courts, and mobile home parks owe a different duty to their clients than other businesses? A landlord-tenant or campground-guest relationship can be disputed. The injured party's status is likely to be of great importance, as are questions relating to the area in which the injury occurred and who had control of that area.

Control of the area is illustrated in Sunde v. Tollett, 469 P.2d 212 (Wash., 1970). An oil company employee, after filling a fuel tank supplied by a mobile home park tenant, was injured when the stand supporting the tank collapsed. The park's owners and operators were not held liable for the injury. The court emphasized that the stand and tank were under the tenant's control; the defendant-owner did not dictate the type of tank or support. Furthermore, the rental agreement gave the tenant the exclusive possession right to the lot on which his mobile home was placed. The rationale was simply that when a landlord-tenant relationship exists, the landlord's tort liability is not governed by theories applying to an occupier of land. Landlords were liable to third persons (oil deliverers and the like), the court said, only if they would be liable to tenants for the same injury. The court concluded that the owners owed no duty to their tenants to protect them from an injury caused by their own appliances; neither did they owe such duty to the oil company employee.

Generally, operators must exercise reasonable care to keep trailer parks in a reasonably safe and suitable condition and must also warn invitees or business visitors of dangers.

The case of Hart v. Western Investment and Development Company, 417 F.2d 1296 (Utah, 1969), deals with the question of the duty owed different groups of guests. Here a seven-year-old guest was injured when he fell from a playground device in the trailer park. The area under the playground equipment had been asphalted. The equipment manufacturer had not recommended such installation; therefore, the operator was charged with knowledge of an unreasonable risk. The court held for the minor for hospital costs of $219, as well as for $15,000 in general damages. What the verdict would have been if the trailer park owner had had grass or sand under the playground equipment is debatable. The use of asphalt, however, made the answer quite clear.

A trailer park is not always found negligent or guilty when a minor is injured. In Snider v. Jennings, 161 N.W.2d 594 (Mich., 1968), the court affirmed a judgment entered on a jury verdict against a mother and her two-year-old son, who were occupants of the defendant's trailer camp. The plaintiff had brought an action for the injury sustained by her son when he caught his hand in a service door in a laundry room provided for the use of the tenants. The defendant had testified that in his opinion the door could not have been opened by a two-year-old; indeed, there was no testimony indicating how the door was opened. The court said that since the jury had been properly instructed that a two-year-old child could not be contributorily negligent, the no-cause-of-action verdict could only mean that the defendant was free of negligence.

Admittedly, this verdict is not what one would expect, given the facts. This case is fairly unusual and does not represent the general rule of duty owed to invitees, especially young children. Nevertheless, a jury may render a decision for the defendant.

Another negligence case dealing with the common areas open to all invitees of trailer parks is Shinn v. Johnson, 189 P.2d 322 (Cal., 1948). The defendant maintained washrooms for the benefit and common use of his patrons. The plaintiff was injured when her clothing caught fire from a gas heater flame in the washroom. In a jury trial, the court stated that findings of fact were required to determine whether the gas heater was defective; whether the defendant was negligent in maintaining it with no screen or barrier in front of the flame; whether he was negligent in having failed to repair a broken window over the washbowl to prevent a draft when the outside door directly opposite the window was open; whether such a draft would or did cause the flame to extend beyond the front of the heater; and whether, when the flame under the water heater was automatically shut off, the increased gas pressure would cause the flame in the gas stove, which was connected with the main gas line of the water heater, to increase in volume.

The court, indicating that it was also necessary to determine whether the plaintiff was contributorily negligent, reversed a nonsuit against the plaintiff trailer park occupant and held that the issues of the defendant's liability and the plaintiff's contributory negligence were jury questions.

Cabin v. Skyline Cabana Club, 258 A.2d 6 (N.J., 1969), deals with another aspect of camp liability. During an annual charity carnival held at the defendant's camp, a thirteen-year-old camper lost the tip of a finger when he attempted to unjam the blades of an electric ice-crushing machine being used to make snow cones. The machine was under the supervision of a young counselor. The boy and his parents brought suit against the camp, charging violation of the New Jersey Child Labor Law, which provides that "no minor under 16 years of age shall be employed, permitted, or suffered to work in, about, or in connection with power-driven machinery."

The trial court dismissed the case after introduction of the plaintiffs' evidence on the ground that such facts, even if true, were insufficient to hold the camp liable. The Supreme Court of New Jersey, however, was of the opinion that the information presented was sufficient to allow a jury to find the camp careless in its supervision.

The court reasoned that the statute forbidding a person under sixteen to be "permitted or suffered to work in, about, or in connection with power-driven machinery" could include the camper, even though he was not a paid employee of the camp. A reason behind the Child Labor Law is the protection of children from the dangers of power equipment. Consequently, the camp would not be saved from liability, even though the camper had voluntarily undertaken to fix the ice crusher.

Although it made no difference in this case, the counselor operating the ice-crusher was only fourteen years old. In other instances, he could have subjected the camp to severe penalties. The camp operator should have known the main points of his state's child labor law.

But not all charitable work is fraught with legal liability. In Davis v. Shelton, 304 N.Y.S.2d 722 (1969), plaintiff Michael Davis was a fourteen-year-old member of a Boy Scout troop that was on an overnight camping trip. After setting up camp, both the scoutmaster and his assistant—the only adults in the party—left the site to get a forty-quart can of milk. During their absence, the scouts began to play hide-and-seek. Young Davis was seriously injured when the limb of a tree he was climbing broke under his weight, hurling him to the ground.

The scout sued the local Boy Scout council, the scoutmaster, the assistant scoutmaster, the sponsoring church, and the landowner on whose property the accident occurred. The county court dismissed outright the suit against the council, the church, and the landowner. It believed, however, that there was sufficient evidence to allow a jury to find the scoutmaster and his assistant liable. The plaintiff appealed this decision.

The appellate court agreed that there were no grounds upon which to find the first three defendants liable: the council exercised no supervision over the troop's activities, and the church had nothing to do with the troop's operations. Since control is a prerequisite to the imposition of liability, neither organization could be held responsible for any carelessness by the scoutmaster and his assistant in failing to supervise the scouts. Since the landowner was not aware of the dangerous condition of the tree he, too, could not be held liable.

Even though the scoutmaster and his assistant were not involved in the plaintiff's appeal, the appellate court, in an unusual action, took it upon itself to decide that the leaders also were not liable. The court gave no specific reasons for this finding, although it stated that both were trained and experienced scouters, well qualified to lead the campers.

Although the court's action was unusual, the result itself was not. An analysis of other cases involving injuries to campers shows that unless the camp and its staff is extremely careless, it will not be held liable for the accidents and injuries that naturally accompany the activities of spirited youngsters. Even harm sustained during unsupervised and unauthorized horseplay may not impose liability upon a camp, since it is recognized that children cannot and, indeed, should not be supervised at every moment.

In Roeland v. Geratic Enterprises, Inc., 9 Cal. Rptr. 538 (1961), the plaintiff fell and injured herself while entering the shower connected to a swimming pool provided for trailer park tenants. The passageway to the shower had a smooth floor and was open to the sky. It was an error to grant a nonsuit, the court said, because the jury could have found that the floor was a dangerous condition—such cement is slippery, especially when wet—and that the use of such a floor in a shower area where water is always present created a hazardous condition. The defendant should have had notice of this condition by the very nature of the installation. Furthermore, whether the slippery floor was a dangerous condition, the court stated, was a question of fact and therefore a jury question. A final important point, according to the court, was that direct evidence was not necessary to establish that the defendant had notice of the dangerous condition; such notice could have been established by inference. This is true when a defective condition exists long enough that a reasonable man exercising reasonable care will discover it.

The case of Hersch v. Anderson Acres, 146 N.E.2d 648 (Ohio, 1957), dealing with a poison ivy infection, bordered on being a nuisance suit. After touching the ivy, the plaintiff sustained a severe infection, incapacitating her from work. As a result, she brought an action against Anderson Acres for negligence in not removing the ivy. Even though the defendant won, the case cost time and attorney's fees. Consequently, it might be advisable for camp operators to warn customers about noxious weeds, snakes, and insects.

Acts of God

Any number of unusual accidents may befall a trailer park or camp owner. In the case of Rector v. Hartford Accident and Indemnity Company of Hartford, Connecticut, 120 So.2d 511 (La., 1960), rehearing denied, the plaintiff rented space to park her trailer in Twin Cedar Trailer Park. During a storm, an elm tree about two or three feet wide fell across her trailer, causing her certain alleged injuries. A jury awarded the plaintiff a total of $10,400 for injuries and damages. On appeal the plaintiff asked for $41,000, including attorney's fees.

The main defense in this case consisted of the contention that the accident and resulting damage were the result of an act of God, for which the defendant was not liable. Indeed, the defendant's insurance policy had an exclusionary provision to this effect. In reversing for the defendant, the court offered an enlightening definition of an act of God:

> An act of God is an unusual, extraordinary, sudden, and unexpected manifestation of the forces of nature which man cannot resist. The fact that no human agency can resist an act of God renders misfortune occasioned solely thereby a loss by inevitable accident which must be borne by the one upon whom it falls. On the other hand, when an act of God combines or concurs with the negligence of the defendant to produce an injury, the defendant is liable if the injury would not have resulted but for his own negligent conduct of omission.

> No one is liable for an injury proximately caused by an act of God, which is an injury due directly and exclusively to natural causes, without human intervention, which could not have been prevented by the exercise of reasonable care and foresight. The application of this rule may preclude any recovery for injuries caused by extreme weather conditions, . . . or extraordinary and unprecedented . . . winds. . . .

> An act which may be prevented by the exercise of ordinary care is not an act of God.

In summation of this particularly long case, the court said that the only way the plaintiff could have avoided the effect of this act of God (winds over fifty-four miles per hour) would have been to prove that there were reasons for the defendant to remove this tree prior to the date of the storm. But there was no reason to believe this tree was other than sound and healthy in every respect; therefore, there was no failure to exercise reasonable prudence, diligence, or care, or a necessity to have the tree removed. The judgment was reversed and the suit was dismissed at the plaintiff's cost.

Illegal Search and Seizure

Guests of campgrounds and trailer parks have the same right to be free of illegal searches as home owners. Operators of such areas cannot allow searches without warrants. The section in chapter 9 relating to hotels and inns applies also to trailers and camps.

A search warrant must describe with particularity the place to be searched and the things to be seized (Trupiano v. United States, 334 U.S. 699 [1948]). Moreover, a limited search incident to a valid arrest is permissible, although the proper scope of such a search has presented much difficulty. In *Trupiano*, federal agents raided a farm to look for illicit distilling operations. The arrest of one of the petitioners without an arrest warrant was held as valid, but the seizure of the apparatus without a warrant was held unconstitutional.

However, in United States v. Rabinowitz, 339 U.S. 56 (1950), officers obtained a warrant for the arrest of a dealer of forged postage stamps, but they searched the desk, safe, and file cabinets in his one-room place of business without a search warrant. The appeals court reversed the conviction, relying on the *Trupiano* case. Nevertheless, the Supreme Court again reversed: "to the extent that Trupiano . . . requires a search warrant solely on the basis of the practicability of procuring it rather than upon the reasonableness of the search after a lawful arrest, the case is overruled."

Probable cause can also support a search without a warrant. In Draper v. United States, 358 U.S. 307 (1959), the court sustained a conviction on narcotics taken from the defendant's person by the arresting officer. The court found the search and seizure valid as incident to a lawful arrest. The arrest without a warrant was valid because the officer "had probable cause and reasonable grounds to believe" that the defendant "was committing a violation" of the federal narcotics laws. Probable cause exists where "the facts and circumstances within [the arresting officers'] knowledge and of which they have had reasonably trustworthy information [are] sufficient in themselves to warrant a man of reasonable caution to believe that an offense has been or is being committed." The court emphasized "the difference between what is required to prove guilt . . . and what is required to show probable cause for arrest or search." According to the court, the arresting officer may consider hearsay evidence in deciding whether there is probable cause for arrest.

The above information is relevant because trailers and camping equipment are pulled by cars, making the automobile and, in some cases, the trailer subject to a search without a warrant. Allowing a search without a valid warrant by police could bring a lawsuit against the owner of a trailer park or camp for trespass.

Liens

Placing a lien on a trailer or camping equipment by the campground or trailer park owner is subject to the same limitations as the innkeeper and others entitled to a possessory liens as discussed in chapter 12.

Utility Rates

A public utility company is empowered to charge an equal tariff for any one group. If no provisions are made for reselling the utility by statute, it is illegal to sell such a product at a profit.

The case of Land v. City of Grandville, 141 N.W.2d 370 (Mich., 1966), involved the sewer rates charged to a 150-unit mobile park and a 15-unit motel. The plaintiff sought a declaratory judgment holding the sewer ordinance invalid. The case was dismissed as unreasonable and arbitrary. The court had to decide whether the following statute was constitutional and not confiscatory, or whether it was arbitrary against trailer parks and others similarly situated.

> In the event two or more lots, parcels of real estate, residences, dwelling units, or buildings discharging sanitary sewage, water or other liquids into the sanitary sewage system of the city either directly or indirectly, are users of water and the quantity of water is measured by a single water meter, then, in each case for billing purposes, the minimum charge for sewer rates and charges shall be *multiplied* by the number of lots, parcels of real estate, residences, dwelling units, or buildings served through the single water meter (emphasis added).

In its analysis, the court said that:

1 Municipal regulations for using water must be reasonable but are not required to be uniform or to be based on the value of property where the water is used.

2 The "reasonableness" of utility rates such as those for sewage service depends on a comprehensive examination of all the factors involved.

3 Modern trailer parks should be classified as dwellings or residences for sewer rental purposes.

4 The minimum charge for sewer rates should be multiplied by the number of parcels, residences, dwelling units, or buildings served through a single water meter. This also holds true for motels or trailer parks having single water meters.

In the case of *La Nasa v. New Orleans Public Service, Inc.*, the trailer park had charged its occupants higher rates than the stipulated tariff for electricity. The plaintiff sought injunctive relief prohibiting the utility company from cutting off the electric current at their trailer park. The court said that although each trailer could be metered, the electricity used would have to be billed at the tariff rate to the customer. The fact that the trailer park operator installed 174 meters at a substantial cost did not dissuade the court from ruling against the plaintiff, who wanted to continue charging a certain rate for parking the trailer, plus an additional charge for electricity consumed by the trailer occupant. The court did not feel that the plaintiff was entitled to having the injunction lifted so that he would have electricity.

Case Example	**LaNasa v. New Orleans Public Service**
	66 So.2d 332 (La., 1953)
	(FOURNET, Chief Justice)

   The plaintiff, Dr. Joseph A. LaNasa, the operator of an automobile house-trailer park in the city of New Orleans known as the Beacon Trailer Park, is appealing from a judgment of the District Court recalling and dismissing at his cost the rule nisi for a preliminary writ of injunction, previously issued against the defendant, New Orleans Public Service, Inc., prohibiting its agents from cutting off the electric current at the trailer park and from in any manner interfering with plaintiff's use thereof at the said park.

   The plaintiff, in the business of furnishing space and utilities for the parking of trailers, secures his electricity from the defendant under a contract that specifically provides: "Customer agrees not to resell or share with others service supplied hereunder." The service is rendered in accordance with defendant's Schedule LP-3, duly filed with and approved by the City of New Orleans, the regulatory authority, and contains the provision: "This schedule is applicable to the total alternating current electrical requirements of any customer at one location except an individual family residence or an individual family apartment. . . . *Service hereunder shall be taken from a single service through one meter, is for the exclusive use of the Customer, and shall not be resold or shared with others.*" Under this schedule the energy charge is based on a graduated descending scale of 3¢ per kwh for the first 500 kwh used, to ⁷/₁₀¢ per kwh for all additional over 22,500 kwh (emphasis ours).

   This trailer park, established in 1944, is equipped with an electrical distribution system that transmits electricity from the defendant's meter (located within the grounds) to fuse and switch boxes placed in receptacles on poles at the spaces reserved for the parking of each trailer, with provision for connection with the trailer, and it was customary to charge a fixed rate for ground rent plus an added charge for electricity, varying from $1 to $3 per week, based on the size of fuses in excess of 10 amperes used by each trailer—100 kwh being allowed at no additional charge to each trailer operating on a 10 ampere fuse. During the summer of 1951, plaintiff installed some 20 private meters, spotted at various locations, in an effort to learn if certain families were consuming an extravagant amount of electricity and thus account for his reduced profit in spite of increased business. As a result of this check, he purchased and installed 154 recording meters during the months of August, September, and October, 1951, and began charging the tenants on the basis of the electricity consumed by each trailer instead of the flat fee previously charged according to the size of fuse, calculated at 4¢ per kwh for consumption in excess of 100 kwh—there being no charge for the first hundred hours. When a representative of the defendant called at the Park in early November, he noticed that the submeters had been installed; the plaintiff was promptly notified that a rate violation existed or was possible, and that the submeters must be removed or electricity would be cut off. Plaintiff then brought this suit to enjoin the defendant's threatened action.

Both in oral argument and in brief counsel for plaintiff contends that plaintiff was not reselling electricity, since he made no profit therefrom, but was merely checkmetering to arrive at a fair charge with respect to each tenant. He urges the significance of noting the "vast difference" in meaning between the term checkmetering, and the term submetering, which is said to mean remetering *and reselling*—it being one of plaintiff's principal contentions that if any practice is prohibited by the contract and Schedule (which must be construed against the defendant), it is only the practice of remetering and reselling at specific charges.

Counsel also urges a plea of estoppel, based on his contention that the plaintiff has been "sharing" electricity with his tenants since 1944 with no attempt at concealment; that the elaborate distribution system by which the trailers received electricity was visible to everyone entering the park, including defendant's meter readers, and that, relying on defendant's acquiescence over a period of seven years, plaintiff expended $3,280 for the meters, the use of which at specific charges is merely a more equitable method of calculating the share of each trailer; so that the defendant, by its laches and silence, is now estopped from asserting that the plaintiff may not share electricity without breaching the contract.

It is clear under the facts here presented that the plaintiff was reselling the electricity he received under a contract prohibiting such practices; he first made a charge of $1 to $3 per week, based on the size of the fuses in excess of ten amperes used by each trailer; after installation of the private meters, his charges were based on his own rate schedule in proportion to consumption exceeding 100 kwh; and the absence of intention on his part to make a profit or to compete in the public utilities business (as he insists) avails him nothing.

His plea of estoppel is equally without foundation. The fact that the defendant knew of the distribution system fails to signify acquiescence on its part in plaintiff's practices, since the furnishing of electricity received from the defendant to the several trailers parked within the grounds was neither a sharing nor a reselling of the electricity with others within the meaning of the contract, but was merely the use of the electricity in conducting the plaintiff's business, as contemplated by the contract and schedule. The record clearly shows that as soon as the defendant's agent discovered that meters had been installed within the receptacles housing the fuses and switch boxes, the plaintiff was immediately notified of the contractual violation and was requested to remove the submeters, the defendant offering to install as many meters as would be requested and to open separate accounts for each customer.

The plaintiff's original complaint that he was being singled out for unwarranted treatment since other trailer park operators in New Orleans were charging for electric current under the same type of installation as plaintiff's without objection from the defendant—naming Pelican Trailer Park and Avalon Trailer Park—was not mentioned in oral argument and, according to the tenor of his brief, is no longer being urged. In any event, the record shows that inspections were made by the defendant at these locations, disclosing that the meter installations at one were the property of defendant, each covered by a separate account; and that at the other, where submeters were found to have been installed, it was agreed that these would be promptly removed.

Counsel for plaintiff has also argued that in any event he has the right to retain and use his meters for "remetering or checkmetering or for any other purpose so long as no specific charge based on consumption is made," so that plaintiff is entitled to the injunction "subject only to the modification that no specific charge based upon consumption shall be made." In supplemental brief counsel recognizes that a question has been raised as to whether or not this issue is properly before the court, and contends that "even if the *plaintiff*-appellant *did not specifically pray for this right*, nevertheless under the prayer for general relief, the court has the right to render such judgment as the pleadings and the evidence may justify and/or as would be given in a new suit, to avoid circuity of action."

A mere reading of the petition affirmatively discloses that the plaintiff is seeking one thing only, and that is to enjoin the defendant from cutting off his electrical service so he may be permitted to continue business under his present set-up of using the individual meter system and charging for the amount of electricity consumed. The entire evidence, including plaintiff's affidavit, clearly shows that the sole purpose and use of the meters is to gauge the amount of electricity each trailer uses so that plaintiff can charge the customers accordingly. In other words, according to the record the plaintiff wants to continue his method of doing business—charging a certain rate for the parking of the trailer, plus an additional charge for and in accordance with the amount of electricity consumed while so parked. Under these circumstances we do not feel that the plaintiff is entitled to the relief sought.

Ruling of the Court: For the reasons assigned, the judgment appealed from is affirmed. [The plaintiff, Beacon Trailer Park, cannot continue charging for electricity.]

Also pertinent is a 1972 decision by the California Court of Appeals in Boynton v. Lakeport Municipal Sewer Department, 104 Cal.Rptr. 409 (1972). The appellate court agreed with the trial court that the sewer rate plan was not discriminatory and was valid. It found a water rate resolution invalid only insofar as it charged owners of apartment houses, motels, trailer parks and similar places $.25 for each additional unit over two in number for the first 1,000 cubic feet or a fraction thereof of water used. The court concluded that the water rate resolution was invalid to the extent that it charged higher minimum rates to commercial users. The judgment was reversed in that respect and the matter was remanded for amendment in accordance with the decision.

Limiting Liability Statutes

Under common law an innkeeper was liable for the loss of a guest's goods while in the inn. Subsequent legislative enactments have limited certain types of accommodations for loss of property to a prescribed amount. Trailer park and campground owners should familiarize themselves with the law as it relates to them.

In the 1959 Florida case of *Cole v. Carmell*, the defendant received instructions from the plaintiff to release his trailer to the plaintiff's brother, who was due to arrive within a few days. A person falsely representing himself to be the brother obtained possession of the trailer. When the damaged trailer was returned, personal items were missing, for which the plaintiff sued the trailer park owner. The Florida limiting liability statute that protects hotels, apartment houses, and the like also protects trailer court operators under certain conditions.

This case, the court believed, was not covered because it was not the legislative intent to limit the liability of a trailer court operator for his negligent act in releasing control of a trailer, the value of which was self-evident. The case against the trailer park owner was affirmed for $700. (The management principles section in this chapter has a further discussion on the liabilities of trailer park and camp operators.)

Case Example

Cole v. Carmell
112 So.2d 278 (Fla., 1959)
(HORTON, Judge)

The appellee owned a house trailer which was located on space in the Ollie Trout Trailer Park. Before departing the Miami area, appellee gave instructions to Sidney Olsen, manager of the trailer park, to release the trailer to his brother, Donald, who was due to arrive from the north within the next few days. Approximately a week later, one Louis Levensque appeared at the trailer park, falsely representing himself to be Donald Carmell, and obtained possession of the trailer from Olsen. Levensque was subsequently apprehended and convicted of the theft. The trailer was returned to appellee, though damaged to some extent.

This suit was brought against the trailer park and Olsen to recover damages for the personal items removed from the trailer, damages to the trailer and transportation costs occasioned by Olsen's negligently releasing the trailer to the thief. Upon a jury trial, the court refused to instruct the jury, at the request of the appellant, to the effect that damages, if found, should be limited to $100, pursuant to Section 509.111(2), Fla.Stat., F.S.A. "The proprietor or manager of a hotel, apartment house, rooming house, motor court, trailer court or boarding house in this state, shall, in no event, be liable or responsible to any lodger, boarder, guest, tenant or occupant for the loss of wearing apparel, goods or other property, except as provided in subsection (1) hereof, unless it shall be made to appear by proof that such loss occurred as the proximate result of fault or negligence of such proprietor or manager or an employee thereof, and in case of fault or negligence he shall not be liable for a greater sum than one hundred dollars unless, the lodger, boarder, guest, tenant or occupant, shall, prior to the loss or damage, file with the proprietor, manager or clerk of said establishment an inventory of his effects and the true value thereof, and such proprietor, manager or clerk is given the opportunity to inspect such effects and check them with such inventory; provided however, that the proprietor, manager or clerk of a hotel, apartment house, rooming house, motor court, trailer court, or boarding house in this state, shall, in no event, be liable or responsible to any guest, lodger, boarder, tenant or occupant for the loss of wearing apparel, goods or other property or chattels, scheduled in such inventory in a total amount exceeding five hundred dollars." Subsequently, the jury returned a verdict for the appellee in the amount of $700. Judgment was entered on the verdict and the defendants appealed.

The sole issue presented is the trial court's failure to instruct the jury pursuant to Section 509.111(2). It immediately becomes apparent that house trailers were not under consideration by the legislature when the act was originally passed in 1874 (§ 4, Ch. 1999). It was not until 1947 that motor courts and trailer courts were included along with hotels, apartment houses, rooming houses and boarding houses. However, we feel the intent of the statute was to limit the liability of hotels, etc., for goods deposited for safekeeping when their value could not be ascertained without some disclosure from the tenant. . . . If such disclosures were not required, the hotel, motel, boarding house, apartment, etc., managements would have no way to ascertain the value of goods deposited with them that were subsequently lost or stolen.

Conversely, we do not feel the legislature intended to limit the liability of a trailer court operator for his negligent act in releasing to another control over a trailer located on the premises, the value of which is self-evident. In such cases, the trailer owner pays for the space on which the trailer or lodging facility rests, but not for the actual facilities afforded by the trailer itself. In such circumstances the trailer court operator would have no control over the interior of a trailer such as would the manager of a hotel, motel or boarding house over the interior of their lodging facilities. The facts presented we conclude rendered inapplicable the limited liability provisions of the statute.

Ruling of the Court: Accordingly, the judgment is affirmed.

Eviction

Like hotelkeepers, trailer park owners can evict transients for many reasons without a formal procedure. Trailer park owners are subject to all statutory provisions of the state and, of course, of the federal Civil Rights Act. However, although they cannot refuse individuals because of race, color, creed, or national origin, they need not accept a drunk or a group that shows signs of being a disturbing influence. Trailer park operators may also formulate and post reasonable rules to keep out undesirables (see chapters 6 and 12).

In the case of Ratel v. Tremblay, 114 N.Y.S.2d 283 (1952), the landlord tried to evict a tenant who rented by the month. However, the eviction could not be carried out because Tremblay was a tenant and therefore a set procedure had to be followed to evict him from the trailer space. This case is important because it delineates that very narrow line between tenant (permanent, by the month) and transient (temporary). If Tremblay had been a transient, the plaintiff-owner could have evicted him without cause after a short term had been overstayed.

Donovan v. Environs Palm Beach, 309 So.2d 561 (Fla., 1975), was a similar case. Here the defendant did not renew her lease in the mobile home park—leading to eviction proceedings against her. Because the plaintiff did not allege one of the grounds contained in Section 83.271, F.S., Chapters 73–182 and 73–330, Laws of Florida, the court said that it was an error to have entered a judgment for possession against the plaintiff. Even under the new 1975 statute, the eviction would not be possible. The statute reads:

> In the event a tenant does not enter into a written lease or upon the expiration of a written lease the tenancy may be terminated in accordance with the provisions of section 83.69, which section is cumulative of all other sections in this part and shall be deemed to supercede any provisions in conflict therewith.

Obviously, various states wish to protect such tenancies and make it very difficult to remove any *tenant* (not a transient) without following the law strictly.

When dealing with mobile homes, one must remember that the relationship is that of landlord and tenant. A trailer home is no less a home because it is mobile—it is as much a home or residence as one which is stationary. Modern trailer parks afford living accommodations for many American families today and should not be classified as other than dwellings or residences (Artman v. College Heights Mobile Park, Inc., 173 N.W.2d 833 [Mich., 1969]).

Management Principles

The camping, mobile home, and tourist court sector of the service industry is still in its infancy. Many large corporations are now joining the thousands of small campground owners, and as the camping industry grows in complexity, so do its problems—legal and otherwise.

Campgrounds and related accommodations come under the 1964 Civil Rights Act and as such are quite similar to hotels, motels, and inns. Therefore, refusing a would-be campground guest is legal only if there is a valid reason for doing so; otherwise discrimination charges may follow. The hotel sections in chapters 6, 7, and 8 should be reviewed, as much of the information in them applies also to campgrounds. Many states have also passed specific statutes regulating campgrounds. In essence, such state statutes cannot be less antidiscriminatory in nature than the federal law, but can be more antidiscriminatory, as the *Ohio Civil Rights Commission* v. *Lysyi* case shows.

The campground owner also has the right to make reasonable rules to safeguard its property and to protect guests and their property. If the state statute does not explicitly prohibit against certain groups (such as motorcycle gangs or large, rowdy groups), the Civil Rights Act, which prohibits discrimination on account of race, color, creed, or national origin, may allow barring any undesirable groups. However, any refusal to provide accommodations could still be interpreted as a discriminatory practice and an action could be brought against the campground. Owners should consult their attorneys on this. They should keep rules posted and should treat all persons alike.

The duty owed to guests by campground and trailer park owners is that of reasonable care. Even a playground that is part of a mobile home park, trailer park, or campground falls under that duty. Hence, all playground equipment should be checked periodically, as should the other common areas. A standard operating procedure should be instituted for checking all areas that guests frequent. Special attention should be given to children's equipment and to the places they frequent.

A campground or trailer court owner owes guests the same rights as a hotelier in that no search will be made of a guest's premises without a search warrant. (Chapter 9, which deals with search and seizure, should be reviewed for the correct theory and practice.)

The question of a lien as it applies to a campground or trailer park is rather ambiguous. Although in *Diamond Trailer Sales Company* v. *Munoz*, 382 P.2d 185 (N.H., 1963) the court said that a recorded chattel mortgage was superior to a trailer court owner's lien, it did not say that the lien was invalid and that it could not be used. (The law of liens is discussed in chapter 12.) It is well to remember that New York, California, and some other states do not allow such liens.

Absent a statute, the campground or trailer park owner cannot make a profit from utilities such as electricity or other controlled products that are supplied to guests. To allow this would permit the unscrupulous to take advantage of travelers when they most need the service.

If there is no statute, a trailer park, campground, or mobile home park is not covered by a limiting liability statute—that is, the owner cannot formulate a rule in that respect. The Florida case of *Cole* v. *Carmell*, discussed in this chapter, gives a trailer park owner a limiting liability statute (but not against his own negligence).

A trailer park owner can evict a transient guest who breaks any of the reasonable rules of the park or campground. Again, this is a good reason to formulate reasonable rules and to post them. Bans on pets or motorcycles must be put in writing and posted. All people should be treated equally under such regulations.

This chapter has considered the rights and liabilities of managers in one of the newest segments of the travel industry—campgrounds, trailer parks, and tourist camps. The next chapter of this book examines the legal rights and liabilities of the travel agent, who is becoming increasingly important to all areas of hospitality management.

QUESTIONS FOR DISCUSSION

1   What area of the Civil Rights Act do campgrounds and trailer parks come under? Are guests in these types of accommodations treated differently from hotel guests? Why or why not?

2   Can a trailer (costing approximately $25,000) be placed and used on any lot if the landowner will accept it? Why or why not?

3   Some gypsies want to stay in a campground. The campground operator refuses them accommodations because of their appearance. Is this legal? Why or why not?

4   A guest attempts to fix a broken appliance in a trailer park and is injured. Does she have a cause of action against the park operator? Why or why not?

5   If a trailer park shower (common to all guests) gushes out 190°F water and a guest is badly burned, does he have a cause of action against the park operator? Is the plumber who installed the shower liable? Or is anyone responsible? Discuss.

6   If during a storm an already questionable tree falls on a camper's tent killing two guests, can the campground be sued? Discuss.

7   Does the law afford a trailer or mobile home owner the same rights as the homeowner in that the dwelling cannot be searched without a warrant? Explain.

8   If a guest does not pay rental fees, can the trailer park owner place a lien against the guest's personal property or car?

9   The charge for a space at a certain tourist court is $15.00 per night, plus a fee for electric and sewer connections. Discuss.

10   On what grounds can a tourist court or campground owner evict guests?

15 Contents

15 The Travel Agent— Problems, Rights, and Liabilities

"The price of justice is eternal publicity."

ENOCH ARNOLD BENNETT

Because U.S. citizens have one of the highest per capita incomes in the world, travel in the United States as well as in foreign countries is no longer limited to the wealthy, business persons, and government officials. As the travel industry has grown in complexity and importance, however, so have its inherent problems.

A number of factors have brought about an increased concern about travelers and their problems. According to the U.S. Travel Data Center, the 1980 National Travel Survey showed over 935 million person-trips, an increase of 63 percent over 1974, and over 4.3 billion person-nights, a 56 percent increase over 1974. Additionally, Americans took 90.6 million airplane trips, up 68 percent over 1974, accounting for 142.5 million air person-trips—impressive totals.

Another important factor that has surfaced is the consumer rights movement. Travelers are entitled to satisfaction when their travel plans go awry for reasons other than an act of God, the public enemy (war), or their own contributory negligence. Disappointed travelers will often seek litigation against the negligence of the travel agent or one of the many third-party suppliers that make up the travel industry.

The travel agent has come of age as a dispenser of travel information, data, and the do's and don't's of the industry. Travel agents do not only sell tickets. They are purveyors of information about any place a traveler wants to go, including how best to get there and what to anticipate en route as well as at the destination.

Enlightened travel agents know the pitfalls of the industry. Unless exposed to a case like *Varig*, how would anyone know that travelers have the right to have their baggage on the same plane? How much can one expect to collect if it is not on the plane? A myriad of happenings tell travel agents what they must tell their clients.

This chapter discusses the rights and liabilities of the travel agent, as well as those of the traveler. Because agents deal with other suppliers of travel services, cases illustrating problems with bus companies and hotels illustrate the consumer's right to bring action when plans go awry. The travel agent's various liabilities to clients—including liability for his or her own action, breach of contract, and third-party suppliers—are set out.

Options for Travelers

In an Alka Seltzer television commercial, a vacationing couple is seen sitting beside a swimming pool in a state of great agony. As the camera retreats, it becomes obvious that extensive construction and earth removal are taking place around them. The man shouts over the roar: "I asked the travel agent, where can we go for a little peace and quiet? He says, 'Mr. Fields, I've got just the place! A peaceful little cottage in the heart of the Mellow Mountains.' " The sounds of construction commotion increase. "My head . . . my stomach . . . I need some Alka Seltzer." The travel industry felt so maligned by the ad that they pressured Alka Seltzer's advertising agency to alter the commercial. But the picture it presented was not entirely false.

Many options are open to travelers to obtain the necessary services they require. They may call a hotel or resort directly—many hotel chains have their own reservation systems. Calling an airline, bus company, or railroad for transportation makes travelers independent contractors, and if anything should go wrong, their cause of action lies with the contracted company.

Many travelers, however, have limited knowledge of hotels and other accommodations in distant places. They often turn to a local travel agent for recommendations and reservations. Travel agencies are corporate entities that have no facilities of their own, but they use many independent suppliers to take care of their clients' needs. The travel industry is composed of roughly four groups:

1   Suppliers of travel services, such as hotels, resorts, and airlines or other types of transportation;
2   Travel wholesalers that combine the services offered by suppliers into "package tours";
3   Travel agents who sell either one or two of the above;
4   Travelers themselves, who usually deal with the travel agent, but who sometimes buy services directly from either the supplier of travel services or, far less often, the travel wholesaler.

The Rights of the Traveler

Whom should legal action be brought against when travel plans turn out to be not as presented and purchased? This question is difficult because the disputes often involve relatively small amounts of money and the claims are either settled out of court or are not pursued at all. Sometimes the dispute may occur in a different state or even foreign jurisdiction, making it difficult for the traveler to carry on litigation personally.

Baggage Claims—Domestic

When travelers deliver baggage to an airline for the purpose of having it transported to their destination with them, in effect they are entering a contract with the airline. This contract binds the airline to deliver the baggage to their destination and deliver it to the traveler on his or her arrival. If the airline fails to deliver it at the destination, then it has breached its contract with the traveler. The measure of damages that the traveler would normally be entitled to would be the value of the lost baggage and its contents. However, it has been legislatively decided that the imposition of such a financial burden on the airlines would cripple their ability to operate because of the frequency of loss or delayed delivery.

Each year approximately five million pieces of baggage are lost, mishandled, damaged, stolen, pilfered, delayed in delivery, and so forth. However, the airlines claim that 75 percent of the lost bags are reunited with their owners within twelve hours and 20 percent of the remaining 25 percent are delivered within five days. The remaining 5 percent still amounts to a very impressive number, and payment for such a loss on a dollar for dollar basis could indeed either force the prices of air travel so high that it would be a prohibitive way of travel for most people or would force the airlines into financial ruin. Thus, there are limitations on the amount of recovery permissible in instances of ordinary loss similar to those imposed by the limiting liability statutes relative to innkeepers. Because air travel is both domestic and international in scope, it was not possible to devise one set of regulations to cover both domestic and international flights. Domestic flights are covered by tariffs filed by the airlines with the Civil Aeronautics Board (CAB). The liability for loss is $1,000 as of 1983.

International flights are governed by the Warsaw Convention, an international treaty among the subscribing nations that sets the limits of liability for lost, stolen, damaged, or misdelivered baggage on such flights. Under the convention, the limitation on liability for checked luggage is $9.07 per pound up to forty-four pounds, or just about $400; the limit for carry-on baggage is $400.

The case of *Mao v. Eastern Airlines, Inc.*, demonstrates the effect of the limiting liability tariffs regardless of the amount of the loss. The damages were $1,000, which was awarded because there were two plaintiffs and each was entitled to $500 (observe the date of case). The limitation applies to each passenger and not to each party. Therefore, even if spouses were listed together on one ticket, and even though they may have mixed their belongings together in the same suitcases, each is entitled to recover up to the full amount of the limitation.

Case Example	Mao v. Eastern Airlines, Inc.
	310 F.Supp. 844 (N.Y., 1970)
	(CROAKE, District Judge)

The same degree of enforcement will be given to international flights under the Warsaw Convention. However, unless we come to the conclusion that in all instances the presence of the convention will impose the limitation of liability, therefore allowing airlines to do what they well please, we want to recall to your attention the rule that any legislative act that seeks to restrict or limit an aggrieved party's right to a full remedy for the damage he sustained, shall be strictly construed as to its application and requirements.

Plaintiffs K.H. Mao and Diana Mao instituted the above-entitled action against defendant Eastern Air Lines Incorporated [Eastern] by filing a complaint in this court on July 20, 1967. The complaint alleged that on or about November 5, 1966, Eastern negligently lost baggage containing jewelry owned by plaintiffs worth approximately $29,000.

Plaintiffs moved pursuant to rule 56 of the Federal Rules of Civil Procedure for summary judgment in their favor, holding Eastern liable without limitation and reserving for trial the question of damages. Eastern cross-moved for summary judgment in its favor, seeking a limitation of plaintiffs' recovery to $1,000, the maximum liability allowable under its tariff rules.

On November 5, 1966, plaintiffs purchased two regular passenger tickets from Eastern at New Orleans, Louisiana, for transportation to Washington, D.C. They reported at the Eastern ticket counter before the scheduled departure of their flight and turned over to the Eastern ticket agent three pieces of luggage. This baggage was duly checked by the defendant, and claim tags issued and delivered to the plaintiffs that stated on the back:

"Baggage checked subject to tariffs: including limitations of liability therein contained."

Among plaintiffs' baggage was a "three-suiter" suitcase that allegedly contained twenty-three items of jewelry given to plaintiffs on the occasion of their wedding in New York City on October 29, 1966, and worth approximately $29,000. The value ascribed to the jewelry, which had been passed from generation to generation in plaintiffs' families, represented the opinion of Mr. Mao, who was not in the jewelry business.

In its answer, Eastern admitted that when plaintiffs submitted their baggage claim tags at their destination in Washington, D.C., the suitcase containing the jewelry could not be located and, as a consequence, the property could not be redelivered to plaintiffs.

The only affirmative defense interposed in behalf of Eastern was a partial one, predicated upon rule 71 of the tariff, the pertinent parts of which read as follows:

"The liability, if any, of all participating carriers for the loss of, damage to, or delay in the delivery of any personal property, including baggage (whether or not such property has been checked or otherwise delivered into the custody of the carrier) shall be limited to an amount equal to the value of such property, which shall not exceed the following amounts for each ticket: $500.00 when . . . EA . . . is responsible for the loss, damage, or delay, or when the transportation is entirely over the lines of two or more such carriers and it cannot be determined which carrier is responsible for the loss, damage, or delay . . . unless the passenger, at the time of presenting such property for transportation, when checking in for a flight, has declared a higher value and paid for each carrier via which such property is to be transported an additional transportation charge, at the rate of 10 cents for each $100.00 or fraction thereof, by which such higher declared value exceeds the applicable amount set forth above, in which event carrier's liability shall not exceed such higher declared value. . . . No participating carrier will accept for transportation or for storage personal property, including baggage, the declared value of which exceeds . . . for . . . EA . . . $5,000.00."

Exception 3 of the rule stated that: "EA . . . will accept a declaration of value of money, jewelry, silverware, negotiable papers, securities, business documents, samples, paintings, antiques, artifacts, manuscripts, irreplaceable books or publications, or other similar valuables in excess of $500.00 (U.S. currency) only when such valuable articles are not included in checked baggage."

Conceding that the lost baggage had a value of $1,000, Eastern took the position that its total liability for the loss of the suitcase with the jewelry cannot exceed $1,000 under rule 71(A). This was Eastern's maximum liability under the tariff rules since there was no declaration of higher valuation under rule 71(C).[1]

Plaintiffs raised the issue, however, as to whether the words "sold subject to tariff" printed on the contract of carriage was sufficient to bind an otherwise unnotified traveler.

It is well established that tariffs filed with the Civil Aeronautics Board [CAB] constitute the contract of carriage between airlines and their passengers and, if valid, conclusively and exclusively govern the rights and liabilities between the parties (Tishman & Lipp, Inc., v. Delta Air Lines, 413 F.2d 1401 [2d Cir. 1969]). Moreover, limitations of liability in tariffs required to be filed by air carriers with the CAB are binding on passengers and shippers whether or not the limitations are embodied in the transportation documents. It follows then that plaintiffs in this case, as passengers on a domestic flight, were conclusively deemed to have had notice of the contents of Eastern's tariff and were consequently bound by its limitation as a matter of law.

[1] It will be noted that no less than eighteen carriers, including Eastern, will not accept a declaration of value in excess of $500 on jewelry and other items "included in checked baggage." The reasons for the above were succinctly stated by the hearing examiner at p. 24 of his opinion and quoted by Judge Milton Pollack of this court in *Tishman & Lipp.*

This court noted that plaintiffs did not avail themselves of protection afforded by the use of alternative means of carriage. Apparently, it would have been a simple matter for plaintiffs to have carried the "little" jewelry box aboard the plane and kept it on their person. Plaintiffs also did not choose to ship their valuables as air freight, although they could have easily done so prior to their flight. Had they chosen to ship by air freight, as did the passenger carrying jewelry in the *Tishman* case, plaintiffs would simply be required to deliver the baggage in question to Eastern as freight, have the fact that it contained jewelry noted on the air bill, and pay the applicable charge predicated upon the valuation declared. The above would have been in compliance with those provisions of the air freight tariff.

Plaintiffs chose not to exercise these options and had their luggage, including their jewelry, transported as checked baggage. Having made such a decision, plaintiffs' rights were determined by Eastern's tariff, and their recovery was limited to $500 per passenger, or $1,000, pursuant to rule 71(A). This result was not inequitable for, as the court pointed out in the *Tishman* case:

"[Plaintiff], by failing to put the air carrier on notice of the nature of the baggage contents not only took advantage of the lower air freight rate . . . but deprived the carrier of the opportunity to take the extra precautions the safety of such valuable cargo required. . . . It is only just that the loss should fall on the one who, with knowledge of the value involved, chose to take the chance."

Ruling of the Court: Accordingly, plaintiffs' motion for summary judgment in its favor is denied and Eastern's cross-motion for summary judgment in favor of plaintiffs in the amount of $1,000 is granted.

So ordered.

Baggage Claims—Foreign

Obviously, not all cases against airlines, hotels, or other suppliers of travel services that do not perform as contracted are lost. In *Cohen v. Varig Airlines, S.A. Empresa, etc.,* the airline that had control of the plaintiffs' baggage breached its contract to deliver the bags when the travelers arrived in Rio de Janeiro. It refused to take the bags off the plane in Rio because it would have been too costly. Because of this willful tort by the defendant (Varig), the plaintiffs were subjected to physical inconvenience (eighteen days with no clothing except for what they were wearing and what they could purchase), as well as mental distress. Their travel costs were greatly increased by repeated trips to the airport and the necessary purchase of replacements in a foreign country.

Although the appellate court did not allow the Cohens damages for mental and emotional suffering, physical discomfort, and inconvenience resulting from the loss of their luggage, Justice Sandler, in a dissenting opinion, thought the court should have followed the New York controlling case of Battalla v. State of New York, 219 N.Y.S.2d 34 (1961) allowing recovery.

Though the *Cohen* case is lengthy and detailed, it is of interest to both travelers and the travel industry. Among the important points it discussed are:

1   The Warsaw Convention as a sovereign treaty and how it preempts local law in the areas where it applies;

2   How this case escapes the provisions of the Warsaw Convention;

3   The accepted rule that travelers have the right to expect their baggage to be on the same plane they travel on;

4   The traveler's right to receive baggage at his or her destination;

5   Whether a carrier may limit its liability for a traveler's baggage;

6   Which city had jurisdiction over the loss of baggage: Rio de Janeiro or the travelers' final destination of New York;

7   How one estimates the value of lost clothing and valuables;

8   Whether mental suffering can be compensated for, as it may be in a hotel case;

9   Whether an employee's acts may be attributed to the employer, thereby causing punitive damages to be levied against the carrier.

The verdict in the *Cohen* case should protect all travelers against the arbitrary and capricious actions of airline carriers.

Case Example	Cohen v. Varig Airlines, S.A. Empresa, etc.
	405 N.Y.S.2d 44 (1978)
	(SULLIVAN, Justice)

The only issue presented on this appeal is the amount of damages to which plaintiffs are entitled. Plaintiffs, airline passengers, sued for and recovered the full value of luggage checked with and subsequently lost by the defendant, Varig Airlines, as well as consequential damages for the mental and emotional suffering, physical discomfort, and inconvenience resulting therefrom. Both parties concede that inasmuch as an international flight was involved, the Warsaw Convention is applicable. Varig asserts the limitation of liability provisions of the convention, which, if applicable, would limit plaintiffs' recovery to $700. Plaintiffs contend that the limitation of liability provisions of the convention are inapplicable because of Varig's willful misconduct in the handling of their luggage.

In July of 1974, plaintiffs, Charles and Hermaine Cohen, husband and wife, were on a twenty-eight-day tour of South America. They had departed from New York on their itinerary that included Bogota, Lima, Asuncion, Iguassu Falls, Rio de Janeiro, Manaus, Belem, Paramaribo, Georgetown, and the return flight to New York. On July 18, they boarded Varig flight #601 at Iguassu Falls, bound for Galeao Airport in Rio de Janeiro. Later, after takeoff, they learned that their flight would terminate in Sao Paulo, Brazil, and that they would be transferred to another flight that was scheduled to land at Dumont Airport in Rio de Janeiro.

Upon their arrival at Sao Paulo, plaintiffs spoke to a Varig sales representative about the possibility of obtaining passage on a flight to Galeao Airport in Rio de Janeiro since they were scheduled to depart from Galeao Airport early the next morning for Manaus, Brazil. The sales representative, a Mr. Bernsmuller, was able to accommodate plaintiffs and had them transferred to flight #854 on an Electra, scheduled to land at Galeao Airport in

Rio de Janeiro. While they were still at the airport at Sao Paulo, plaintiffs expressed concern that their luggage might not be loaded on flight #854. To assure plaintiffs that matters were being properly taken care of, Bernsmuller had their luggage brought to them and issued two new baggage tickets for flight #854. He further assured plaintiffs that he would personally see that their luggage was placed aboard flight #854. This conversation took place in an area known as "the shed." There was no other baggage in the immediate vicinity. As further assurance, Bernsmuller went out to the airfield to check on the luggage. On his return he stated that he "had personally seen to it that plaintiffs' luggage was actually placed on flight #854." He further stated that he "saw (the luggage) on the plane."

When flight #854 was called, plaintiffs realized that the flight was bound for New York, with a stopover at Rio de Janeiro. They boarded with about thirty other passengers. On the arrival of flight #854 at Galeao Airport on the evening of July 18, an announcement was made that the passengers were to disembark since the flight was continuing its journey to New York on another aircraft, a Boeing 707. It was nighttime. The passengers boarded a waiting bus that drove them to the 707. When it came time to get off the bus to board the 707, plaintiffs protested to the Varig representative in charge that they were not continuing on the flight to New York. They were told to stay on the bus. Plaintiffs were then driven to the terminal building. When they inquired about their luggage, they were directed to the baggage receiving area. After a time, when it became apparent that their luggage was not being delivered, plaintiffs complained to various Varig personnel, including Celestino Pazinatto, Varig's lost and found agent, who twice checked with the ramp supervisor in charge of unloading the Electra and loading the 707. Efforts to locate plaintiffs' luggage were unavailing.

By this time Mr. Cohen was becoming indignant. He kept insisting to Varig's personnel that he had gotten off flight #854, that he had not received his luggage, and that it was being taken to New York on the Boeing 707. When the announcement was made for the passengers of flight #854 to board, Mr. Cohen demanded that his luggage be removed from the New York–bound plane. Varig's personnel refused and told him that they "would not go to the expense of unloading the plane" for him. Pazinatto told plaintiffs that the flight would be returning from New York City in two days and that they could get their luggage back at that time. Mr. Cohen explained that they were leaving the next morning for Manaus, Brazil. He showed Pazinatto his flight tickets and informed him that he and his wife had no clothes other than what was on their backs, that they had eighteen days left on their tour that was taking them to the Amazon jungle and to Georgetown, Guyana, where they had friends and expected to be entertained. When Pazinatto was asked again to go out to the plane to get the luggage he refused, stating: "We will not do it. You will get it back on Saturday morning." When the loading of the 707 was completed, the plane departed.

The interval of time between plaintiffs' arrival at Galeao Airport and the departure of flight #854 for New York was estimated at one-half hour. During this time Varig's personnel steadfastly refused to look for plaintiffs' luggage on the Boeing 707. Testimony adduced at trial reveals that it would have taken one hour to unload the Boeing 707, check the baggage, and reload. After the flight's departure, plaintiffs were given $60 by a Varig representative to tide them over until the luggage came back on Saturday, July 20.

Varig sent tracers to every destination to which its airplanes flew from

Galaeo Airport and radiogrammed New York City prior to the arrival time of flight #854. None of these attempts to locate plaintiffs' luggage was successful.

The next morning, July 19, according to schedule, plaintiffs flew to Manaus. There they made several visits to the Varig office, as instructed, to inquire about their luggage, but without any success. They were unable to purchase ready-made clothes in Manaus, and after two days they left, again in accordance with their itinerary, for the journey by ship down the Amazon River and the completion of their tour.

At trial, plaintiffs testified to the physical discomfort of being without their clothing and personal effects. They also claimed mental distress in the nature of humiliation and embarrassment from being inappropriately attired, either in the same clothing or in ill-fitting, hastily purchased apparel, at social affairs that had been prearranged with dignitaries and friends of high social levels in the countries being visited. For instance, in Georgetown, a dinner at which the chief justice and other state officials were guests was given in honor of Mr. Cohen. He was compelled to wear the same dishevelled suit that he had been travelling in. His wife's predicament was no better. For eighteen days of their tour, plaintiffs were without their water purification implements. They spent needless hours shopping, without success, for suitable clothing. In a humid, tropical climate they had no second set of clothing into which to change. As a consequence, plaintiffs contend that their trip was ruined.

On their return to New York, Varig's regional general manager offered plaintiffs an additional $640 in reimbursement for their lost luggage. When Mr. Cohen remonstrated with him, the general manager stated: "Do you expect us to unload a whole plane just for the two of you? We don't do that."

Thereafter, plaintiffs commenced this action in the civil court for damages for Varig's willful failure to deliver their luggage. Varig interposed a general denial and asserted, *inter alia*, the affirmative defenses of its tariff provisions and the Warsaw Convention.

After a trial without jury, the court held that the Warsaw Convention controlled, inasmuch as plaintiffs were travelling on an international flight. The court found that the provisions of the convention limiting claims for lost baggage to $20 per kilogram, or $700 in the present case, were not applicable since Varig's refusal to unload plaintiffs' luggage constituted "willful misconduct" within the meaning of Article 25(1) of the convention (49 U.S. Stat. 3014, 3020). Plaintiffs were awarded $6,440.65, including $3,250 for their physical inconvenience, discomfort, and mental suffering. The court rejected Varig's contention that the terms of its tariff barred a recovery for consequential damages.

On appeal, Appellate Term, by a divided court, modified the judgment by decreasing the award of damages to $700, holding that there was "insufficient evidence in the record to support the trial court's finding that the act of defendant . . . constituted 'willful conduct' within the purview of Article 25(1) of the Warsaw Convention." Appellate Term granted leave to appeal to this court.

Article 22(2) of the Warsaw Convention (1934 U.S.Av.R. 245 *et seq.*), which generally applies to international air transportation, limits a carrier's liability to $20 per kilogram (i.e., $700 in the instant case) of checked baggage. Article 25(1) of the convention, however, eliminates the limitation of liability where there is willful misconduct by the carrier. Article 25(1) provides as follows: "The carrier shall not be entitled to avail himself of the provisions of this convention that exclude or limit his liability, if the damage is caused by his willful misconduct or by such default on his part as, in accordance with the law of the court to which the case is submitted, is considered to be equivalent to willful misconduct."

In Grey v. American Airlines, Inc., 227 F.2d 282, 285, cert. den. 350 U.S. 989, 76 S.Ct. 476, 100 L.Ed. 855, the court of appeals for the 2nd circuit spoke of "willful misconduct" as "a conscious intent to do or omit doing an act from which harm results to another, or an intentional omission of a manifest duty. There must be a realization of the probability of injury from the conduct, and a disregard of the probable consequences of such conduct."

In Goepp v. American Overseas Airlines, Inc., 117 N.Y.S.2d 276, 281, 114 N.E.2d 37, cert. den. 346 U.S. 874, 74 S.Ct. 124, 98 L.Ed. 382, this court construed "[w]illful misconduct," as it applies to the Warsaw Convention, as follows: "Willful misconduct, . . . depends upon the facts of a particular case, but in order that an act may be characterized as willful, there must be on the part of the person or persons sought to be charged, a conscious intent to do or to omit doing the act from which harm results to another. . . . The burden of establishing willful misconduct rests upon plaintiff. . . ."

In Berner v. British Commonwealth Pacific Airlines, Ltd., 346 F.2d 532, 536–537, the court of appeals (2nd circuit) restated the accepted charge on "willful misconduct," as it applies to the Warsaw Convention, in the following language: "Willful misconduct is the intentional performance of an act with knowledge that the performance of that act will probably result in injury or damage, or it may be the intentional performance of an act in such a manner as to imply reckless disregard of the probable consequences . . . [or] the intentional omission of some act, with knowledge that such omission will probably result in damage or injury, or the intentional omission of some act in a manner from which could be implied reckless disregard of the probable consequences of the omission. . . ."

In our view, the facts support the trial court's finding of willful misconduct. As flight #854 readied for departure, plaintiffs' luggage had to be at Galeao Airport in one of three locations—that is, in either the baggage receiving area, where it was not to be found, in the Electra, or in the Boeing 707. On the evidence it is not a fair inference to conclude that plaintiffs' luggage had not been placed on the Electra at Sao Paulo. However, even were we so to conclude, then Bernsmuller's actions in assuring plaintiffs that he had seen their luggage on the Electra would constitute willful misconduct.

The Electra had been unloaded in the darkness of the runway. When plaintiffs' luggage was not delivered to the receiving area, it should have been obvious that it had to have been loaded on the 707 along with all the other passengers' baggage. Pazinatto's advice to wait for the return flight confirms the fact that he full well realized that the luggage had to be on the 707. Although the ramp supervisor was asked to check the baggage being transferred from the Electra to the Boeing 707, it is not clear from the record whether the supervisor even made such a check. He did not testify at trial. The only witness to testify for Varig was Pazinatto. He testified that he personally inspected the Electra, but only after the departure of the Boeing 707. No luggage was found.

While, concededly, this is not the case of ordinary negligence, we must not lose sight of the fact that the standard of proof imposed on a plaintiff who claims willful misconduct by a carrier is to prove his contentions by a fair preponderance of the credible evidence, and no more. In our view, that burden has been met. We are not persuaded otherwise by the fact that plaintiffs' luggage was never recovered in New York, a circumstance as innocuous as the fact that their luggage was never located at Galeao Airport or any of the other airports to which tracers were sent.

The decision not to unload the 707 was motivated by a desire to avoid the expense of unloading and not by any doubt as to the whereabouts of the luggage. The options available to Varig were either to satisfy its contractual obligations to plaintiffs, thereby incurring expense and perhaps delaying the flight, or insisting that plaintiffs take the loss. It chose the latter. The determination was purely a business one.

Furthermore, Varig had a full appreciation of what its decision meant to plaintiffs. Pazinatto had been told that plaintiffs had eighteen more days remaining in their tour of South America. He knew that they could not await the flight's return from New York, that they were leaving for Manaus the next morning. He knew that all of their clothing and necessaries for the trip were inside the missing luggage.

In these circumstances, we conclude that plaintiffs have shown an intentional omission on Varig's part to perform a manifest duty that it owed plaintiffs under the terms of the contract of carriage, with a realization and disregard of the probable consequences of its conduct. Consequently, and in accordance with Article 25(1) of the Warsaw Convention, defendant's liability for the loss of the luggage is not limited by the provisions of Article 22(2) to $20 per kilogram. Hence, the trial court's award of $2,679 for the actual value of the lost luggage and their contents should be reinstated.

Varig claims that the portion of the baggage loss award that compensates plaintiffs for loss of jewelry[2] cannot stand because its own tariff bars recovery for jewelry loss. Varig's tariff cannot limit any recovery for jewelry loss since rule 2(a)(1) of the tariff and Article 23 of the Warsaw Convention both provide that any provision of the tariff attempting to fix a lower limit for the liability of the carrier that is inconsistent with the terms of the convention is invalid. There is no limitation on jewelry loss in the provisions of the convention other than the limitation contained in Article 22(2), which, for reasons already stated, we hold to be inapplicable.

This leaves one final element of the damage award for our consideration. The trial court awarded the sum of $3,250 for both plaintiffs for physical inconvenience, discomfort, and mental suffering. Varig asserts that even if the Warsaw Convention does not limit its liability, rule 16(c)(15) of its own tariff bars recovery for consequential damages. Rule 16(c)(15) provides as follows: "Carrier shall not be liable in any event for any consequential or special damage arising from carriage subject to this tariff, whether or not carrier had knowledge that such damages might be incurred."

This court has upheld tariff provisions similar to the case at bar. In Glen, Inc., v. Emery Air Freight Corp., 264 N.Y.S.2d 876, we upheld a provision limiting a carrier's liability to the value declared on the air bill. However, rule 2(a)(1) of Varig's tariff, which has already been alluded to,

---

2 Approximately $750 was awarded for the loss of jewelry in the wife's luggage.

is, by its terms, subordinate to the provisions of the convention. Rule 2(a)(1) of the tariff provides: "Such carriage shall be subject to the provisions of such convention and to this tariff to the extent that this tariff is not inconsistent with the provisions of the convention."

In this connection, Article 19 of the Warsaw Convention provides that "[t]he carrier shall be liable for damage occasioned by delay in the transportation by air of passengers, baggage, or goods." The trial court properly held that rule 16(c)(15) of the tariff barring the recovery of consequential damages was inconsistent with Article 19 of the convention. Damage caused by delay, quite obviously, contemplates consequential loss. Neither law nor logic suggests any reason why plaintiffs' damages should be any the less because their luggage was lost rather than delayed. We do, however, conclude that this is not the appropriate case for the award of special damages for physical inconvenience, discomfort, and mental anguish.

Damages here should be awarded in accordance with the laws of New York. Whether liability is fastened on a theory of contract or tort, New York is the jurisdiction with the greatest or dominant interest in the matter, and its law ought to apply. Plaintiffs are New York residents. They purchased their tickets from Varig at its New York office. Their trip began in New York. New York was the destination of the flight on which their luggage was lost.

The law has been traditionally reluctant to extend its protection against the infliction of mental distress, even for intentionally inflicted wrongs. This has been equally true in New York. Until it was overruled in 1961, Mitchell v. Rochester Ry. Co., 45 N.E. 354 (1896), which barred a recovery for injuries occasioned by fright where there was no impact or immediate personal injury, represented the law of this state. In that case, the plaintiff claimed fright and excitement and a resultant miscarriage caused by the approach of a team of horses that just managed to stop without striking her.

Courts, however, have been willing to allow damages where the mental anguish accompanies a slight physical injury or some impact upon the person of the plaintiff attends the wrong. In New York, the impact requirement in a cause of action based on negligence was eliminated when the Court of Appeals in Battalla v. State of New York, 219 N.Y.S.2d 34, 176 N.E.2d 729, overruled *Mitchell v. Rochester Ry. Co.* The impact rule was stripped of any vestige of vitality in negligence cases by the Court of Appeals' decision in Johnson v. State of New York, 372 N.Y.S.2d 638, 334 N.E.2d 590, which extended the *Battalla* rationale to a situation where there was not even an apprehension of actual physical harm or threat. In that case, the daughter of a hospital patient was erroneously notified of her mother's death when in fact her mother was alive and well. Damages for emotional harm and mental distress were allowed.

In cases other than negligence, the rule always was that if some independent traditional tort could be asserted, then that cause of action could serve as the vehicle to allege mental damages and a recovery therefor was allowed. Thus, a recovery for mental damages was allowed by our courts in such traditional actions as those for assault, false imprisonment, willful conversion, and malicious prosecution. It has also been allowed in cases of extreme outrage where the tortfeasor's conduct exceeds all bounds of decency usually tolerated by society and is calculated to and does cause mental distress of a serious nature. The following are examples of the type of wrong where recovery has been allowed: threats of harm racially motivated against plaintiffs and their children to prevent them from moving into a certain neighborhood; hounding a plaintiff on the streets and in public places; an invitation, prolonged or repeated, to a woman to sexual intercourse accompanied by the forwarding to her of indecent pictures; the case of a former suitor who, having jilted a woman, wrote her jeering verses and taunting letters; and, finally, those cases involving the mishandling of dead bodies where recovery is allowed on the theory of a "property right" to the body, usually in the next of kin.

One area where New York courts have long recognized a separate cause of action for the intentional infliction of mental suffering, even though the mental disturbance was not attended by any illness or physical injury, is in those cases holding a common carrier liable for insulting a passenger, and the innkeeper or hotelkeeper liable for the insult to his guest.

Although courts are, at long last, moving in the direction of recognizing one's interest to mental and emotional tranquility as an area entitled to legal protection, we know of no authority that sanctions a recovery against a carrier for mental distress and physical inconvenience where the gravamen of the wrongdoing is either the loss or mishandling of luggage. Although Varig's callous disregard for plaintiffs' plight and willful renunciation of its contractual obligation to its passengers was motivated by selfish economic interest and justifies a finding of willful misconduct under the provisions of the Warsaw Convention, we are reluctant to extend the rationale of the insult cases to the circumstances presented here and allow damages for mental suffering. Moreover, in Rosman v. Trans World Airlines, 358 N.Y.S.2d 97, 314 N.E.2d 848, the Court of Appeals, in construing the term "bodily injury" as it appears in Article 17 of the Warsaw Convention, held that psychic trauma alone or even psychic trauma causing bodily injury is not compensable. In our view, plaintiffs are adequately compensated for their loss to the extent the law allows by the recovery of the actual value of their lost luggage and its contents.

Ruling of the Court: Accordingly, the order of Appellate Term, entered November 26, 1976, that modified a judgment, Civil Court of the City of New York, New York County, entered December 15, 1975, should be modified on the law and on the facts, without costs, to the extent of reinstating the damage award of $2,679 and otherwise affirmed.

As in all other cases where legislation seeks to limit the rights of recovery for damages that one has sustained, the one seeking the benefits of the limitation must first establish that compliance has been made with any conditions that the law imposes. Despite the fact that the Warsaw Convention is afforded the status of an international treaty, the requirement is no less rigid, as was demonstrated in Hill v. Eastern Airlines, Inc., 425 N.Y.S.2d 715 (1980). The plaintiff had boarded one of the defendant airline flights to Acapulco, Mexico. The airline lost three pieces of her luggage, and when she filed claim for her loss, she was informed by the defendant that according to the Warsaw Convention as set forth in 49 U.S. Stat. 3014, 49 U.S.C.A. 1502, her loss was limited to $9.07 per pound of luggage. Because she was allowed to carry only forty-four pounds of luggage, this would amount to approximately $400. The plaintiff refused to accept this sum and sued the defendant in small claims court.

Again the defendant relied upon the convention to limit its liability, but the court disagreed.

The ticket issued to the plaintiff was a combination ticket and baggage check and provided a space for the recording of the weight and number of pieces of luggage that the passenger checked, but the space was blank; it never had been filled in by the defendant's employees. Article 18 of the convention imposes liability on the airline for the loss of the luggage, and Article 22 imposes the limitations argued by the defendant; however, the defendant airline completely ignored subdivision 3 of Article 4. The court said that the key to the resolution of the claim was contained in Section f, that reads: "The number and weight of the packages [in combination with the further provision of Article 4, to the effect that the consequence of failing to conform to f is that] the carrier shall not be entitled to avail himself of those provisions . . . that . . . limit his liability." Even though local tariffs may seek to set a limitation on liability apart from the convention, inasmuch as the convention is a United States treaty, it is the supreme law of the land, and the tariffs and CAB regulations are subordinate. Therefore, the convention made the defendant liable to the plaintiff for the full value of what was lost, which was $1,102.50. However, the action was brought in small claims court, and the maximum recovery in such courts in New York at the time was $1,000.

The fact that the action was brought in small claims court makes for an interesting observation. This plaintiff elected to go into a forum that encourages people to act as their own advocate, and it dispenses with the formal rules that govern a trial or hearing in other courts. She did this despite the fact that the court was incapable of giving her the full amount of her damages. There are many reasons that would have motivated her to follow this course of actions. Perhaps the entire amount was so small she could not interest an attorney in handling the case. If she had, she would have had to pay most of the amount recovered to an attorney as a legal fee if she went to a regular court. In small claims court, she got a speedier hearing and decision on the controversy with a minimum investment of money and time. Also, she might have known that small claims courts are more sympathetic to consumers than they are to those who control the situation that gave rise to the controversy.

The lesson to be learned from the *Hill* case, then, is not merely what is contained in the decision about the Warsaw Convention, but also that through the medium of the small claims court, those engaged in the various facets of the hospitality industry have a much greater exposure to the probability of litigation for their shortcomings than they ever had before.

Another instance where actions of the airline personnel were held to have constituted willful misconduct, negating the provisions of the Warsaw Convention relative to the limitation of liability for an airline's delay in delivering baggage, can be found in the case of Compania De

Aviacion Faucett v. Mulford, 386 So.2d 300 (Fla., 1980). The Mulfords, who had boarded a flight on the defendant airline in Cuzco with a destination of Lima, Peru, had been informed by the defendant's employees that their luggage was on board their flight when in fact it had been removed. The luggage was not returned until after they returned home.

The lower court held that the misinformation, which was either "deliberately or recklessly given," constituted "willful misconduct" so as to render the limiting liability provisions of the Warsaw Convention inapplicable. On appeal the lower court was affirmed, and their award of damages in excess of the convention limitations was upheld.

The Warsaw Convention was also held inapplicable so as to limit the losses of an air carrier in the case of Schedlmayer v. Trans International Airlines, Inc., 416 N.Y.S.2d 461 (1979). In the *Schedlmayer* case, the plaintiff, upon request, gave her hand luggage to an attendant for storing in the front of the plane during a charter flight from Austria to New York. After they were in flight, the plaintiff remembered that she had left a camera and $1,300 in currency in the baggage and asked that it be returned to her when they made a stopover. She was told that she could not get it until the aircraft landed at its final destination in New York. When they landed in New York, the plaintiff immediately retrieved her baggage and upon opening it discovered that although the camera was still there, the currency was gone. The defendant refused to reimburse her for the loss so the plaintiff brought an action in small claims court.

The court held that the flight, though a charter, was still subject to the Warsaw Convention. When the stewardess took the bag from the passenger and she was denied access to it at will during the flight, the airline assumed control over the bag, and it assumed the status of checked baggage. This status was not altered by the fact that the stewardess did not issue a claim check. The court held also that there was no evidence that the carrier had taken any precautions to prevent the loss or that the plaintiff was guilty of any contributory negligence. It also held that $1,300 was a reasonable amount for a person planning a two-month trip to the United States. Therefore, the resolution of the problem concerned whether CAB-accepted tariffs denying any recovery for lost money would control, and, if not, what effect the Warsaw Convention as applied to this factual situation would have on the plaintiff's claim.

Regarding the first question, the court stated that the Warsaw Convention was the supreme law of the land. That being the case, Article 4 of the convention provides: "If the carrier accepts baggage without a baggage check having been delivered, or if the baggage check does not contain [certain required information], the carrier shall not be entitled to avail himself of those provisions of the convention that exclude or limit his liability." Therefore, because the baggage when taken by the stewardess was found to have the status of checked baggage and the plaintiff was not issued a baggage check as required by the convention, the defendant could not avail itself of the limitations of the convention and was liable to the plaintiff for the full amount of her loss—in this case, limited to $1,000 because she sued in small claims court.

Traveling with Pets

The airlines make special provisions relative to the transportation of pets. What is the airline's liability, if any, in the event of the death of the animal? The case of Young v. Delta Airlines, Inc., 432 N.Y.S.2d 390 (1980), was presented with this problem when the plaintiff's pet dog died while in the custody of the defendant airline. The plaintiff sued for the value of the dog—it was a valuable breed—and also asked for compensation for the emotional disturbance she suffered as a result. It was also her position that for negligence that resulted in the death of a living pet, the airline should be subjected to punitive damages.

The defendant filed motions for summary judgment on all counts. The court allowed summary judgment on the claim for mental suffering and punitive damages and held that where damages were not for insult to the passenger, but were for negligence in the transportation of the dog, then the recovery is limited to $500 by the applicable tariffs filed with the CAB. The dog was classified by law as the plaintiff's personal property and, despite the sentimental and personal attachment one may feel toward a pet, in the eyes of the law, the dog stood in the same position as an inanimate piece of luggage.

The court in allowing the summary judgment as to the claim for the damages for emotional disturbance cited Cohen v. Varig and said that loss of personal property did not give rise to a right to such damages. It quickly dismissed the claim for punitive or exemplary damages, stating that such were not recoverable in this type of a case under New York law.

The Young case gives rise to some interesting questions. Should the plaintiff have taken out excess value insurance with the airline when she boarded so as to increase the amount of her recovery in the event of the animal's death? In effect, this would have been taking out life insurance on the dog. Does the airline have to sell life insurance on the dog? It seems so. If the Young case, holding that the dog has the same status as luggage, is correct, then it would follow that the airline would have to sell the insurance to the plaintiff. The other question is whether the result would have been any different if the passenger was blind and the dog was a highly trained seeing-eye dog. A logical extension of the Young case would seem to indicate that it would not make any difference. If the dog is personal property in the Young case, it is personal property in our assumption. The fact that there was more dependence and a closer relationship between the dog and the blind passenger would make no difference.

Refunds on Tickets

Another difficult problem facing travelers and travel agents is that of refunds on unused portions of airline tickets. In the case of Levine v. British Overseas Airways Corporation, 322 N.Y.S.2d 119 (1971), the plaintiffs purchased round trip tickets from the Comet Travel Agency for the itinerary of New York-London-Amsterdam-Copenhagen-Stockholm-London-New York. The Stockholm leg of the trip was cancelled, and a refund of $86 was due from BOAC, which the airline did not deny.

The question in this case concerned a practice adopted by many airlines of making refund payments directly to the travel agent (Comet), less the travel agent's commission. The court held that this unilateral agreement between the airline and the travel agent did not bind the plaintiffs or exonerate BOAC from their liability to the plaintiffs on the grounds of this being the usual procedure. The plaintiffs returned their tickets directly to BOAC, not through their travel agent. *They* were not in the travel business, and thus *no custom* existed between them and BOAC or any other airline.

Once the travel agent has paid the fare to the carrier, the traveler has a valid claim for restitution against the carrier. The court further stated that once the plaintiffs' initial purchase of tickets from Comet had been satisfactorily completed, any possible agency relationship that may have existed between them was thereupon terminated. The convenience and accounting purposes (to avoid the extra step of having to collect the commission from Comet) were not allowable. The plaintiff won the case.

The case of Antar v. Trans World Airlines, Inc., 320 N.Y.S.2d 355 (1970), is often cited as a limitation on airlines to reimburse consumers for airline tickets issued on the airline's ticket blanks by a travel agent. Here, Peters (the travel agent) had sold and delivered to the plaintiff a complete tour of Israel, which included ground accommodations in the price of the airline ticket. However, the airline (TWA) refused to honor the ticket. This case differs from the *Levine* case in that the travel agent was treated as a travel broker for the purpose of arranging a trip to Israel, thereby making Peters his own agent and not the agent of TWA. In any case, TWA was an undisclosed principal, and in such a situation, no liability could attach to the principal when the acts of the agent had not been confirmed or ratified by the principal. No proof of this confirmation was shown, nor was it shown that TWA was a party to the fraud perpetrated on the plaintiff.

Suppliers of Travel Services

Bus Companies

In the case of Garza v. Greyhound Lines, Inc., 418 S.W.2d 595 (Texas, 1967), the plaintiff's bowling league contracted with Greyhound to transport the group from San Antonio to Monterrey, Mexico, and back. On June 20, 1965, the plaintiff was injured in the Republic of Mexico as a result of the bus driver's negligence.

Suing in Texas, the plaintiff attempted to have the court apply Texas substantive law. The defendant did not introduce the laws of Mexico as being different from those of Texas; therefore, the trial court was reversed and remanded with instructions that the case be retried on proceedings not inconsistent with the court's opinion. In essence, this means that if a defendant or plaintiff wishes to use the substantive law of a foreign country, the law pertaining to that case must be thoroughly documented by an official copy of the foreign country's law. The defendant did bring in a Mexican attorney who testified concerning Mexican law and also offered to translate the civil code of Mexico—but from a book that was not printed by authority of the Mexican government.

In Hudson v. Continental Bus System, Inc., 317 S.W.2d 584 (Texas, 1958), the plaintiff sued the bus company, a Trailway subsidiary, for injuries she received in Mexico. There was an exclusionary provision on the back of the bus ticket rendering the bus line not liable for any delays, loss, or injury to any person or property. The plaintiff had been informed about the connecting carrier in Mexico; therefore, the court ruled that the issues warranted a jury trial. If the bus line had failed to reveal the connecting carrier's name, then it would have been liable for the damages sustained by the plaintiff.

One important point, the court said, had to do with the ticket contract that did not stipulate which law would apply. Because of this, the parties were bound by the contract under the state of Texas. The general rule on such contracts is as follows:

> Unless a contract otherwise provides, the law applicable thereto at the time of its making, including the law of the place where it is entered into, and the law of the place where it is to be performed, as the case may be, is as much a part of the contract as though it were expressed or referred to therein, for it is presumed that the parties had such law in contemplation when the contract was made. So, when a statute prescribes a duty and a contract is made involving performance of that duty, such statute becomes a part of the contract; or, where the law authorizes the regulation of service rendered the public, such law becomes a part of and controls contracts providing for the public service. Likewise, where a contract is made in contemplation of state law, or of a particular statute, such law forms a part of the contract, whether or not incorporated therein, and the contract will be construed in the light thereof. Similarly, the parties to a contract made with reference to the laws of a jurisdiction other than that of the place of contracting are deemed to have incorporated into the contract the law of such jurisdiction. *However, it has been held that a contract cannot be construed with reference to a foreign law, unless the intent of the parties to be governed by such law is evidence from the instrument itself without the aid of extrinsic evidence* (emphasis added).

One further point was made about the illusive question of the validity of exclusionary provisions printed on the back of a contract. According to the court:

> It is settled law that a carrier may issue tickets and passes containing

binding conditions and limitations, especially where reduced compensation is paid for transportation. However, conditions and limitations are binding upon a traveler only in case he assented thereto. While unobjectionable provisions contained in the body of the writing are ordinarily binding, even though it was not signed by the traveler, *he is not bound by words printed upon the back of the ticket, which were not incorporated in the contract and to which his attention was not directed* (emphasis added).

A rehearing was denied.

Hotels

Another kind of problem may arise when a travel agent books hotel reservations. After a hotel has accepted a traveler, and he or she is mistreated or does not get the services paid for, what remedy is available? In *Sacks v. Loew's Theatres, Inc.,* the plaintiffs were locked out of their rooms, their baggage was removed to the lobby, and they were assaulted. The court said that the travel agent was not liable for tortious acts or a breach of contract by the hotel. It would have been unreasonable to hold that the travel agent had the duty to forewarn the plaintiffs of the possibility that the hotel would commit such acts.

Case Example	Sacks v. Loew's Theatres, Inc.
	263 N.Y.S.2d 253 (1965)
	(NICHOLAS M. PETTE, Justice)

Defendant Cavalcade Tours, Inc. (hereinafter: Cavalcade), moved for judgment dismissing the amended complaint and the causes of action alleged therein as against it, pursuant to CPLR 3211(a)7, upon the alleged ground that said amended complaint failed to state a cause of action on the face thereof as against said defendant Cavalcade.

Loew's Theatres, Inc. (hereinafter: Loew's), Maurer Tours, Inc. (hereinafter: Maurer), Cavalcade and Hotel Americana of Puerto Rico, Inc. (hereinafter: Americana) are all corporations. The amended complaint contains several alleged causes of action against each of said defendants.

Since the causes of action alleged against Cavalcade incorporated the first nineteen paragraphs of the amended complaint, which constitute the first cause of action by plaintiffs Mack Sacks and Veda Sacks, his wife, against defendants Loew's and Americana, reference thereto is necessary. In that cause of action, it was alleged that defendants Loew's and Americana owned, operated, and controlled a hotel in Puerto Rico known as the Americana of San Juan (hereinafter: the hotel); that on October 21, 1964, said plaintiffs, through defendants Maurer and Cavalcade in New York, booked hotel reservations at the hotel for a period commencing November 6, 1964, to November 16, 1964, and that they paid for said reservations; that Loew's and Americana did not make the accommodations available at the time of said plaintiffs' arrival, but that ultimately on that same day, they were accepted as guests; that on November 14, 1964 (two days before the departure date scheduled), without just cause, they were locked out of their room accommodations and assaulted by agents or employees of defendants, and their personal belongings were removed from the room accommodations and placed in the lobby. It is further alleged that by reason of such exclusion and assault, said plaintiffs sustained personal injuries, mental anguish, pain, and suffering, and recovery is sought as to each in the sum of $250,000, plus punitive damages of $750,000.

The plaintiffs Chester Schwimmer, Florence Schwimmer, Rodney Ball, and Silvya Ball make similar allegations against defendants Loew's and Americana, except that the demands for damages on behalf of these plaintiffs are lesser in amount.

In paragraphs 32 to 43, both inclusive, of the amended complaint, each of the plaintiffs sought to recover various sums from defendant Cavalcade, as compensatory damages only, upon the alleged premise that defendants Maurer and Cavalcade acted as tourist booking agents and held themselves out to be "enabled to book and obtain hotel room accommodations" at the hotel, and that prior to October 21, 1964, plaintiffs had entered into an agreement with Maurer whereby, for a consideration to be paid to it, Maurer agreed to obtain and reserve hotel accommodations at the hotel for the period from November 6 to November 16 and that defendant Maurer secured such accommodations through defendant Cavalcade.

Plaintiffs further alleged that defendants Maurer and Cavalcade breached their agreement with plaintiffs in that they knew, or should have known, from their previous business experience with defendants Loew's and Americana that the "activities" (lockout and assault) had taken place before; that the hotel was not reliable with respect to reservations; and that defendants Maurer and Cavalcade should have advised them of such unreliability; and that by reason thereof, defendants Maurer and Cavalcade were liable to them for compensatory damages.

Defendant Cavalcade's instant motion, therefore, posed the issue whether a hotel guest has a cause of action against a tourist agency for a breach of a contract (reservation ordered, confirmed, and paid for) and for the tortious conduct by the hotel and its employees against a guest.

Defendant Cavalcade contended that a booking agent who secures accommodations at a hotel for a guest is not liable to the guest for damages sustained by him as a result of the tortious conduct of the hotel.

This court is of the opinion that an agent is not liable for the tortious conduct of a principal. Regardless of the relationship between plaintiffs and Cavalcade, and even assuming, *arguendo* (without conceding such to be the fact), that Cavalcade was plaintiffs' agent or subagent, Cavalcade would still not be liable as such agent for the tortious acts or the breach of contract of the hotel.

To seek to hold Cavalcade liable on such a tenuous claim that Cavalcade should have known and anticipated that the hotel was unreliable and should have so advised plaintiffs is rather grasping at straws to support an illusory claim that has no basis in law. That Cavalcade, concededly a middleman in the transaction, owed no duty or obligation to plaintiffs to forewarn them of such a farfetched possibility that the hotel would commit the tortious acts complained of is as absurd as it is without merit.

In this court's opinion, any responsibility that Cavalcade had in the subject transaction terminated when it obtained confirmed and paid for reservations at the hotel specifically requested by plaintiffs through the defendant Maurer.

The court has not been referred to any case, nor has it, after independent research, been able to find any case holding a middleman or, as here, a booking agent liable for the tortious acts or breach of contract of the eventual dispenser of the services purchased.

Ruling of the Court: Accordingly, the motion by defendant Cavalcade to dismiss the amended complaint as against it for failure to state a cause of action on the face thereof as against Cavalcade is granted, with leave to plaintiffs, if so advised, to serve an amended complaint within twenty days from the service of a copy of the order to be entered herein with notice of entry thereof.

Liabilities of the Travel Agent

A customer who does not receive the travel services contracted for may take legal action against the travel agent. This section will attempt to set the parameters of the retail travel agent's liability in day-to-day business conduct. These liabilities include the travel agent's own actions and those of employees within the scope of their employment. Under certain conditions travel agents are also liable for the actions of third-party suppliers of travel services.

Liability for Own Actions

Like any other business person, the travel agent will certainly be held liable to the client for intentionally wrongful actions, including such tort actions as fraud, deceit, and trespass. A travel agent will also be held responsible for negligent conduct. Travel agents who intentionally mislead a client are just as liable as if they failed to exercise "reasonable care" in making a client's travel arrangements. Certainly, the travel agent must exercise at least "due care" to avoid liability based on negligence— and very probably a higher standard of care based on what a "reasonably prudent" travel agent would do. (See discussion of reasonable prudence in chapter 8.)

Indisputably, travel agents represent themselves as possessing expertise in making travel arrangements. Accordingly, it should not be unduly burdensome to hold them accountable for their actions, especially when, for instance, they know a booking procedure did not result in a confirmed reservation and do not inform the client of this fact.

A client should be able to rely on the travel information given by the agent. If travelers suffer injuries as a result of an agent's failure to reasonably inform them, the agent will probably be held liable for negligent misrepresentation. Less clear, however, is whether a travel agent should be required to make affirmative representations about the safety or fitness of the service purchased—even in the absence of an agency relationship or the traveler's request.

According to Professor Wohlmuth, the travel agent has "some obligation" to disclose any "significant risks" that attend particular reservations.[3] Although the question of interpretation is ambiguous, most travel agents are aware that many hotels and airlines overbook.

Agency Relationship

Under established principles of agency law, "agents" are not a party to the contracts they negotiate on behalf of their principal; consequently, they are immune from liability if the principal breaches the agreement.

Under the agency concept, the travel agent is a sales representative for the principal, and his liability ends once the travel plans are made final and money has changed hands. Wasserman states that the question of a travel agent's liability to a client has had little review by the courts, and there has been an assumption that travel agents are agents of the suppliers of travel services. He states, however, that a strong argument can be made to the contrary.[4]

Four basic elements comprise an agency relationship: (1) a consensual agreement, (2) a fiduciary relationship between the parties, (3) the principal's right to control the agent, and (4) the agent's power to act for and to bind the principal. When these criteria are applied to the relationship between the travel agent and the suppliers of travel services, it is doubtful that the criteria are satisfied.

First, the relationship between travel agents and carriers is "involuntary" and therefore not consensual. A travel agent seeking to book airline or ship passage for a client usually must have an "agency agreement" with the appropriate carrier conference (an association or group of carriers). Conference agency agreements often specifically prohibit travel agents from representing themselves as general agents for a carrier or in any way implying that they are an office of a particular carrier. Because all major carriers belong to one of the conferences, the travel agent who wishes to book particular forms of transportation must seek conference recognition and agree to abide by the conference's terms.

In contrast, tour wholesalers, hotels, foreign railroads, and sightseeing companies usually accept bookings from any persons who call themselves travel agents. The relationship between these organizations and travel agents is apparently more voluntary than that between carriers and travel agents, and its very open-endedness makes it difficult to hold that any agreement has been reached between the parties.

More important, because travel agents usually represent many suppliers and wholesalers and because suppliers often compete directly with travel agents in offering bookings to the public, the relationship existing between them can hardly be characterized as fiduciary. Indeed, if travel agents owed these parties the duty of loyalty traditionally associated with agency relationships, it would seem that once a travel agent booked with

---

3   Wohlmuth, "The Liability of Travel Agents: A Study in the Selection of Appropriate Legal Principles," 40 Temp. L.Q., 29, 31 (1966).

4   Richard Wasserman, "Recent Developments, Travel Agency Liable to Travelers When Its Failure to Confirm Reservations Ruins Vacations," Columbia L.R. 74: 981–995.

one supplier, competing suppliers supposedly represented by that agent could demand damages for the agent's failure to represent their best interests.

The travel agent can legally bind suppliers and wholesalers only to a limited degree. For example, unless a travel agent is expressly authorized to act as an airline's agent, the airline may not be required to honor or to reimburse a consumer for airline tickets issued by the travel agent when it has not received the money paid for the tickets.

Thus, it seems clear that a court analyzing the supplier–travel agent relationship could reasonably conclude that there was no agreement expressed or implied between the two. Even if a court finds that an agency exists, however, it need not always deny recovery to the consumer against the travel agent.

An agent has a duty to disclose the identity of this principal so that the client can investigate the reputation or credit of the principal. If the agent fails to make proper disclosure, agency law permits the client to assume that the agent is acting on his or her own behalf. Agents themselves therefore become liable as principals.

This rationale has permitted consumer recoveries against travel agents in a growing number of cases. It was also the basis of decision in a recent case that allowed damages for traveler inconvenience. In Siegel v. Council of Long Island Educators, Inc., 348 N.Y.S.2d 816 (1973), a travel agency was held accountable to ten travelers for poorly planning their tour to Israel and for failing to make necessary reservations, despite the fact that all the arrangements were actually made by a tour wholesaler. Apparently deeming the travel agency the agent of the wholesaler, the court held that the agency had represented itself as an agent of an undisclosed principal and, accordingly, allowed damages based on the inconvenience suffered.

A case that summarizes most of the principles presented so far was decided by the New York courts in *Rappa v. American Airlines, Inc.* In that case, the court ordered the defendant airline to pay to the plaintiff the sum of $1,449 that the plaintiff had paid to a travel agent who issued tickets on the airline. The travel agent went out of business before forwarding the money collected for the tickets to the airline, and the airline sought to impose the loss on the traveler. The case presents an insight into the reasoning that a court follows in determining whether there is an agency relationship and, if there is, what the liability consequences are. Read the case carefully for it presents examples of the everyday application of agency law.

Case	**Rappa v. American Airlines, Inc.**
Example	*386 N.Y.S.2d 612 (1976)*
	(NAT H. HENTEL, Judge)

Defendant airlines moves for summary judgment on the ground that no master-servant relationship existed between defendant and Dallys Travel, Inc., a travel agent. Plaintiff arranged for two full-fare and one half-fare round trips from New York City to Honolulu with Dallys Travel Bureau.

The latter issued the requested tickets, after plaintiff paid $1,449 for same, by taking a standard airline ticket blank and imprinting thereon the carrier's identification plate logo, which in this case was American Airlines. The ticket then read: "Passenger ticket and baggage check—issued by American Airlines." Further, the said ticket bears the legend: "It is unlawful to purchase or resell this ticket from/to any entity other than the issuing carrier or its authorized agents." On the face of the ticket, it is also stated that the same is "issued subject to conditions of contract on passenger's coupon." On the reverse side of the ticket there is imprinted: "Issued by carrier whose name is in the 'issued by' section on the face of the passenger ticket and baggage check." The ticket was issued on December 27, 1974, for a flight to Honolulu scheduled for an open date.

In or about January 1975, Dallys apparently went out of business and, thereafter, none of its principals or employees apparently could be located. Prior to this, Dallys had entered into a sales agency agreement with the Air Traffic Conference of America (known as ATC) as late as May 20, 1974, to which agreement the defendant was a participant. Dallys, pursuant to this agreement, did not transmit any of plaintiff's air fare money received to the defendant. In March 1975, plaintiff, having been unsuccessful in seeking a refund of the fare paid from Dallys, went directly to defendant and sought the refund from that quarter. On March 18, 1975, defendant picked up plaintiff's tickets and issued to him a ticket redemption certificate. Now, defendant refuses to make refund on the theory that Dallys was an independent broker and not its agent, but rather plaintiff's agent in the transaction, and thus plaintiff is suing the wrong party. Defendant cites in support of these affirmative defenses Bucholtz v. Sirotkin Travel Ltd., 74 Misc.2d 180, 343 N.Y.Sd.2d 438, aff'd. 80 Misc.2d 333, 363 N.Y.S.2d 415 (App.T., 1974); Siegel v. Council of Long Island Educators, Inc., 75 Misc.2d 750, 348 N.Y.S.2d 816 (App.T., 2nd Dept. 1973); Levine v. British Overseas Airways Corp., 66 Misc.2d 766, 322 N.Y.S.2d 119; Simpson v. Compagnie Nationale Air France, 42 Ill.2d 496, 248 N.E.2d 117; Antar v. Trans World Airlines, Inc., 66 Misc.2d 93, 320 N.Y.S.2d 355 (App.T., 2nd Dept., 1970), all of which are distinguishable from this case because of the Air Traffic Conference Sales Agency Agreement annexed to defendant's moving papers.

The said agreement provides, among other things, the following, which the court places specific emphasis upon:

1 "The agent (Dallys) shall exercise the authority granted by this agreement and present itself as an agent of the carrier. . . ."

2 The carrier (American Airlines) as a member of the Air Traffic Conference is bound by the agreement.

3 As authorized by the carrier, agent may use the identification plate (logo) of the carrier as issued by the carrier, but said plate shall remain the property of the carrier.

4 "The agent may represent himself on letterheads, advertising, telephone listings, and office signs, and otherwise as an 'agent' or 'travel agent' representing the carrier. . . ."

5 "The agent shall report and remit three times each month for all transportation services sold under the agreement to a bank designated by the ATC."

6 All moneys, less applicable commissions to which agent is entitled and collected by agent *"shall be the property of the carrier and shall be held in trust by the agent until satisfactorily accounted for to the carrier"* (emphasis added).

7 The agent shall maintain a bond for the joint and several benefit of the members of the ATC in a minimum amount of $10,000.

With respect to this latter provision, during oral argument of this motion before the court, defendant's attorney admitted that Dallys's abdication of its business responsibilities had caused its bond to be completely depleted and thus there was none available for plaintiff's case. Further, defendant's attorney admitted that in prior cases of this type, defendant had, nevertheless, paid back the customer out of its own funds as a matter of good customer relations, but had decided to draw the line in this case as an issue of some importance to defendant in order to establish a limit to any alleged liability.

Under these circumstances, the court finds ample grounds to distinguish defendant's cited legal authorities in the following ways: In the *Bucholtz* and *Siegel* cases, both cases originated in small claims court, and plaintiffs recovered from defendant travel agents who had sold package travel and tour arrangements and had employed subagent wholesalers. The Appellate Term, in affirming the lower court judgments, held that a travel agent is liable for his acts, even though the other party knows he is acting as agent, if the identity of the principal is not disclosed *(Siegel)*, nor can the travel agent escape liability by imputing knowledge of industry's practice of employing wholesalers to make ground tours and accommodations for the customer *(Bucholtz)*. In both cases, finding in favor of plaintiff-customers, the court relied upon the principles laid down in Unger v. Travel Arrangements, 25 A.D.2d 40, 266 N.Y.S.2d 715. An agent is liable as a principal if the fact of the agency is not known to the customer. If the customer had such knowledge, he cannot recover from the travel agent on the ground of undisclosed principal. The court denied the granting of the motion for summary judgment in favor of plaintiff on the ground of existing triable issues of fact as to whether the principal was known to plaintiff-customer.

In *Levine,* the court dismissed defendant's argument that the travel agent was an agent of plaintiff-customer and permitted recovery, even though defendant mailed refund to the agent. In the *Simpson* and *Antar* cases, the court had found that the carrier had terminated its authority to the travel agents and that plaintiff-customer treated travel agent as his own agent for purposes of arranging the tour. In the instant case, however, plaintiff knew of the agency and demanded a refund of the money paid to the travel agent directly from American Airlines, who, in turn, issued a ticket redemption certificate. The record of the cases relied upon by defendant is not clear as to whether the court in these cases was aware of the existence of the Air Traffic Conference Sales Agency Agreement, which had been signed by ATC, as a representative of the carrier and the travel agent (Dallys).

A recent decision by Mr. Justice Greenfield, Supreme Court, New York County, Air Traffic Conference v. Downtown Travel Center, Inc., 87 Misc.2d 151, 383 N.Y.S.2d 805, upheld the validity of the ATC sales agency agreement and held that under its terms, the travel agent is regarded as a trustee of the proceeds of its ticket sales and, thus, as having no beneficial or equitable interest therein. This court concurs with the reasoning stated and, consequently, concludes that in issuing the ticket redemption certificate to plaintiff, American Airlines had ratified its agency with Dallys. Thus, defendant treated the monies paid by plaintiff to Dallys as its property and is liable for restitution.

In view of the provisions of the ATC Sales Agency Agreement, the court distinctly feels that defendant was most willing to accept all of the benefits under the agreement, including the promotion and sale of its transportation facilities, but was unwilling to accept any possible disadvantages that might arise. It called the travel agent under the agreement its agent; it clothed the agent with authority to issue tickets on its behalf and made the agent its depository for the proceeds of ticket sales. It held itself out, for all intents and purposes, as the principal with whom the unwary customer was actually dealing. It cannot now retire behind a curtain of limited liability on the theory that one, such as Dallys, was its own independent contractor and broker serving the interests only of itself and its customers when, in fact, such agent was serving the primary interests of the carrier involved.

Ruling of the Court: Accordingly, motion for summary judgment dismissing the complaint is denied and, on its own motion pursuant to CPLR 3212(b), the court directs summary judgment in the sum of $1,449, plus interest from date of demand of refund, plus the costs of this motion, to be rendered in favor of plaintiff.

Liability for Breach of Contract

In the case of a breach of contract between a client and travel agent, either aggrieved party can sue. A contract may be in writing—when the client accepts the terms of a Foreign Independent Travel (FIT) contract set forth in an itinerary—or it may be an express or implied oral promise by the travel agent to arrange a particular service. The breach of either type of contract would result, of course, in liability.

In the 1974 case of *Odysseys Unlimited, Inc., v. Astral Travel Service*, the travel agent and the tour wholesaler were found liable for a breach of contract with their clients. The tour wholesaler sued the travel agent, who had stopped payment on two checks to pay for a trip he planned for his client with the tour wholesaler. The travel agent impleaded (brought in) his clients, who had demanded refunds because of the wholesaler's failure to deliver promised reservations. The impleaded travelers then counterclaimed against both the tour wholesaler and the travel agent. They recovered against the travel agent, who, in turn, was indemnified by the tour wholesaler.

On another counterclaim by the travel agent against the tour wholesaler, in which the group that had planned the trip wanted to cancel the "nonrefundable" deposit, the court said that because the tour operator could not show a loss, the deposit had to be returned. In such cases clients suing for breach of contract or negligence may also seek damages for inconvenience, discomfort, humiliation, and annoyance.

Case	**Odysseys Unlimited, Inc., v. Astral Travel Service**
Example	*354 N.Y.S.2d 88 (1974)*
	(JOSEPH LIFF, Justice)

Following an earlier practice, in the summer of 1972, the Paterson and Majewski families began to plan a joint vacation over the Christmas holiday. In doing so, they relied upon Astral Travel Service (Astral), an agency with which they had previously dealt. They looked forward to spending a few days with their five children in the Canary Islands, of course not anticipating the discomfort, inconvenience, and disappointment they would suffer.

In this action, plaintiff Odysseys Unlimited, Inc. (Odysseys), sues to recover on Astral's two checks in the amounts of $676.80 and $875.90 on which Astral had stopped payment. Astral in one counterclaim alleges that its clients, the interpleaded defendants Majewski and Paterson, demanded a refund because of the breach of the agreement for the trip. In a second counterclaim, Astral seeks to recover from Odysseys the sum of $1,345.00 (unrelated to the Majewski-Paterson claim) that represents an advance by Astral for a group tour to the Canary Islands via Iberia Airlines that would have included accommodations at the San Felipe Hotel. Astral, confronted with claims against it by Odysseys, Majewski, and Paterson, interpleaded Majewski and Paterson. Majewski and Paterson counterclaimed, alleging that both Odysseys and Astral breached agreements with them and demanded the return to them of $1,375.90 and $1,076.80, the total cost of their trips. In a second counterclaim, they seek $10,000.00 as damages for having "suffered great inconvenience, humiliation, and pain and for having been compelled to spend their vacation in inferior accommodations" (paragraph 15 of interpleaded defendants' answer). Astral's reply and cross-claim allege that if the interpleaded defendants suffered any damages, it was plaintiff Odysseys' fault and asks that Odysseys be compelled to indemnify it against any judgment that may be recovered by the interpleaded defendants.

Astral (a retail travel agent) suggested to Dr. Paterson and Mr. Majewski a package tour prepared by Odysseys (a wholesale agency). The tour, entitled "Xmas Jet Set Sun Fun/Canary Isle," was scheduled to depart December 26, 1972, by jet for Tenerife, Canary Isles, Puerto de la Cruz, staying at the "delux Semiramis Hotel" and returning on January 1, 1973, by jet. Majewski and Paterson accepted this trip costing $1,375.90 and $1,076.80, respectively, and made their downpayments to Astral. Astral withheld its commission and forwarded the balance along with the reservations to Odysseys, who in turn confirmed the reservations to Astral's Mr. Howard Pollack. Exhibit B is a handsome colored brochure illustrating the Hotel Semiramis, its location, accommodations, etc., designed to excite the eye of anyone contemplating a trip abroad. An information sheet (exhibit A) furnished details of the trip and referred to the accommodations at the "five-star Hotel Semiramis."

On December 26, 1972, the group flew off to the Canary Islands. They arrived at the airport in Tenerife at about dawn and waited about two hours (one-half hour was spent in a bus) before they were taken to the Hotel Semiramis. At this point the passengers had been en route some thirty hours. While at the airport, they saw Mr. Newton, President of Odysseys, who accompanied the group tour. (The inference may reasonably be drawn that he went along because he anticipated the difficulties that were shortly to be encountered.) Two hundred fifty weary but expectant guests arrived at the Semiramis and were presented with a letter from the hotel (exhibit C) advising them that there were no accommodations available to their group. Dr. Paterson confronted Mr. Newton with this letter and the latter acknowledged that there was no space available and that he was looking for others. For about four hours, two hundred fifty people (including bag and baggage except for what was strayed) were in the lobby of the Semiramis until they were divided into groups and directed to other hostelries. The Paterson and Majewski families were brought to the Porto Playa Hotel, that was not fully ready for occupancy because it was under construction and without the recreational facilities and conveniences available at the Hotel Semiramis. Portions of the Porto Playa Hotel were enclosed in scaffolding. Paterson and Majewski testified that work was done in their rooms, water supply was uncertain, electric connections were incomplete, etc., throughout their stay.

The court is convinced that prior to the group's departure, Mr. Newton was aware that there were no reservations at the Semiramis Hotel for his charges. He testified that on either December 18 or 19, 1972, he knew of the overbooking at the hotel. Paterson and Majewski stated that Newton told them at the hotel that the reservations were in jeopardy and would not be honored, but he did not share his knowledge. In his letter of January 12, 1973, addressed to tour members, Mr. Newton confirms the fact that he had been aware of some "problem with overbooking by that hotel" (Semiramis Hotel) and states that his agent (Viajes Aliados, S. A.) "had the foresight to have arranged for alternate accommodations" (exhibit 5). He is at the least disingenuous in asserting that he had assurance from the Spanish National Tourist Office that the Semiramis Hotel would have accommodations for the group because that office informed him that the Hotel Semiramis was "instructed to receive all the members of your group for whom reservations were made." However, the reservations for the tour were not confirmed and, therefore, the hotel was not obligated to accommodate the members of the group (exhibit 3).

Odysseys has not demonstrated that it performed the agreement as required and "[a] party who seeks to recover damages from the other party to a contract for its breach must show that he himself is free from fault in respect to performance."

One of the elements in a breach of contract action is the "performance by plaintiff," and because Odysseys did not produce reservations for Paterson and Majewski at the Semiramis Hotel, recovery on the two checks is denied and the complaint is dismissed.

Majewski and Paterson sue in contract and negligence seeking recovery of their payments for their trip and for their ordeal. Their claims spring from a breach of contract by Astral for its failure to furnish the hotel accommodations agreed upon. Majewski and Paterson are entitled to recover from Astral for the breach of contract. Damages in the usual breach of contract action should indemnify a party "for the gains prevented and losses sustained by the breach; to leave him in no worse, but put him in no better, position than he would have been had the breach not occurred." However, when a passenger sues a carrier for a breach of their agreement concerning accommodations, the "[i]nconveniences and discomforts that a passenger suffers . . . are to be considered in the assessment of the damages. . . . [D]amages arising from a breach of the contract to carry that results in inconvenience and indignity to the passenger while in transit are not limited to the price of passage". . . . and "the discomfort and inconvenience to which" a passenger was put by the breach of the carrier's contract "was within the contemplation of the parties and a proper element of damage." Although these cases concerned accommodations with common carriers, the principle should be applied to the relationship between travel agent and clients. The agent should be "held responsible to: (a) verify or confirm the reservations and (b) use reasonable diligence in ascertaining the responsibility of any intervening 'wholesaler' or tour organizer." Because the contract was violated and the accommodations contracted for not furnished, a more realistic view for awarding damages to Majewski and Paterson would include not only the difference in the cost of the accommodations, but also compensation for their inconvenience, discomfort, humiliation, and annoyance.

Odysseys attempted to mitigate the damages to Majewski and Paterson by offering proof as to the difference in value between what they received (at a four-star hotel) and what was agreed upon (a five-star ménage). However, this evidence is without force because the hotel at which they stayed was under construction, its recreational facilities were nonexistent, and its location was not nearly as desirable as that of the Semiramis. The proverbial expression about a picture being worth a thousand words has particular application to exhibits B, D–1 and 2, and I–1, 2, 3, and 4 to reveal what Majewski and Paterson expected and what they found. Paterson and Majewski are entitled to the return of the total sum each paid for the trip as damages to them and their family for the inconvenience and discomfort they endured.

The tour included a period from December 26 to January 1. The party landed on its easterly journey on December 27. When the Majewskis and Patersons became aware of their predicament, they made heroic efforts to return immediately, but heavy bookings in the holiday season made that impossible. They were constrained to remain and to suffer the results of Mr. Newton's callousness. Had their dealings been directly with the plaintiff, we would have considered the imposition of additional damages. However, their negotiations and dealings were with Astral, who might have exerted greater efforts to see that arrangements were properly made.

Ruling of the Court: In all of the circumstances, we think that it would be appropriate to make the Patersons and Majewskis whole in pocket. Accordingly, they are awarded judgment against Astral in the amounts of $1,076.80 to Paterson and $1,375.90 to Majewski.

On Astral's cross-claim against Odysseys for breach of contract, concerning the Majewski and Paterson claims if successful, Astral is entitled to a judgment against Odysseys in the amount of $2,452.70, less $308.30, which Astral retained as its commission because Odysseys failed to perform its contract and it was Odysseys that was responsible for the fate that befell Majewski and Paterson.

Liability for Actions of Third-Party Suppliers

In frequent cases affecting third-party suppliers, clients seek relief for alleged failures of tour operators to supply the type of hotel accommodations or other services contracted for. One elderly couple had planned for years to visit Madrid, only to find on their arrival that they had no rooms as called for in their reservation. After a costly, fruitless search for accommodations, they had to leave without ever having visited the city. Who was to blame, and whom should the couple sue, if anyone? The *Dold* v. *Outrigger* case discussed in chapter 9 is a good illustration of the problems involved here.

When they are stranded without accommodations in this or a foreign country, people may go to court when they return home. After Mr. and Mrs. Bucholtz had engaged Sirotkin Travel, Ltd., to arrange for a three-day holiday in Las Vegas, they found it necessary to sue the travel agent. The travel agency had booked both the flight and lodgings through a tour wholesaler, rather than by communicating directly with the airlines and hotel. Upon arriving, the Bucholtzs found that no hotel reservations had been made for them. After some difficulty they found out-of-town accommodations, but later sued in small claims court for damages.

On the other hand, the defendant felt the case was sufficiently important to be represented by counsel. The case was duly appealed by the travel agency, and again the court held for the plaintiff in *Bucholtz* v. *Sirotkin Travel, Ltd.*

Case Example

Bucholtz v. Sirotkin Travel, Ltd.
363 N.Y.S.2d 415 (1974)
(PER CURIAM)

In this small claims action, plaintiff seeks to cast defendant travel agency into damages for reservations that went awry. Since it is undisputed that the travel agency had utilized the services of a wholesaler who had put together a "package tour," defendant contends on this appeal that the wholesaler alone is liable for any default in performance.

Allocation of responsibility in the case before us should proceed upon the principles of agency law. In our opinion, where, as here, there is no proof of an independent relationship between the retail travel agent and the wholesaler, the travel agent should be considered the agent of the customer. If, in using a wholesaler to make the travel arrangements, the travel agent acts with the consent, express or implied, of the principal-customer, then, if reasonable diligence has been used in its selection, the travel agent will not be responsible for any dereliction of duty on the part of the wholesaler. If, on the other hand, the travel agent acts without such consent, he will be responsible to the customer for any damage sustained as a result of the acts of the wholesaler.

The court below, in applying these principles, found that the plaintiff did not consent to the employment of the wholesaler. Although its opinion did not so state, the record indicates that the court also declined to hold that knowledge of the practice of employing wholesalers should be imputed to the plaintiff. We see no reason to disturb this determination. The record supports a finding that plaintiff was not informed of the existence of the wholesaler until after the reservations were agreed upon, and it cannot be said that knowledge of this practice is so pervasive among the public as to compel a finding of implied consent.

Ruling of the Court: We find no merit in defendant's remaining contention. All concur. Judgment affirmed without costs.

The *Bucholtz* case may be one of the most significant cases handed down for a mere hundred dollars in damages. In reconstructing the case, it would appear that if travel agents negligently fail to exercise reasonable care in confirming reservations without making the client aware that they were making the reservations through a tour wholesaler, then agents can be held liable on a theory of breach of implied warranty—that is, an implied guarantee to the client that the travel services will be delivered as ordered. Justice would be best served if the travel agent represented the individual consumer rather than the travel services supplier.

The travel agent is not left without remedy. On the contrary, travel agents can recover the damages from the wholesaler. By allowing travelers to recover from the travel agent, the courts are simply granting them an additional avenue of recovery on the theory that the agent breached his duty to exercise reasonable diligence in representing the traveler.

Two years after the decision in the *Bucholtz* case, the New York courts adjudicated a case involving a travel agent and his liability to his client for failure of a third party to perform a service for the traveler that had been arranged for by the travel agent. At first this case may seem to contradict *Bucholtz*, but a close reading indicates that it does not because the liability was founded on breach of contract theory rather than agency theory. This case, *Ostrander v. Billie Holm's Village Travel*, should be read very carefully because it sets forth the various theories of liability that could be utilized in proceeding against a travel agent when clients do not get what they paid for on a trip.

These cases show how careful travel agents should be when contracting to do business on behalf of clients. They should check into the reliability of those whom they select to engage to perform services on behalf of clients. The sympathy of the courts is definitely with travelers. The judgment in the *Ostrander* case was only $45, a small sum financially, but the impact of the decision could result in the future payment of millions.

Case	**Ostrander v. Billie Holm's Village Travel**
Example	*386 N.Y.S.2d 597 (1976)*
	(LAWRENCE NEWMARK, Judge)

In this action, plaintiff arranged for return limousine service from the airport in connection with airline tickets that she purchased from the defendant. In evidence is the receipt or voucher issued by the defendant for the services. The plaintiff's plane arrived approximately three hours late and, in accordance with the instructions given to the plaintiff by the defendant, she telephoned the limousine service, but was unable to make contact for she received no answer. After several further attempts to reach the limousine service, plaintiff attempted to make comparable arrangements, but found that there was no limousine service functioning at that hour and was compelled to take a taxi at a charge of $45.

Defendant disclaims responsibility and explained that it sold the services, issued the voucher, and notified the limousine service that the transaction had been made and would subsequently be billed for the service.

Keeping in mind defendant's acknowledgement that it is not unusual for aircraft to be three hours late, the obvious question is whether the travel agent should be held liable for the failure to furnish limousine service. That ultimate answer must, in turn, be premised on the nature of the relationship between a travel agency and its clients.

What little attention that relationship has received in reported decisions highlights the uncertainty of courts in dealing with this area. For example, in Dorkin v. American Express Co., 74 Misc.2d 673, 345 N.Y.S.2d 891, affd. 43 A.D.2d 877, 351 N.Y.S.2d 190, the court concluded that the true status of a travel agent is that of a disclosed principal. Another court has taken a different view: "Obviously the travel agent is an agent, but the question comes, whose agent?"

The possible bases for the liability of the travel agent to a traveler have been summarized as follows: "The legal responsibility of travel agents to the clients whom they service may be based on one or more of three bodies of legal principles: negligence, agency, or contract. The law of negligence will supply the minimum legal duty of the travel agent no matter what his legal status is said to be. The remainder will hinge on a determination of his legal status vis-à-vis the other participants in the scheme of travel distribution" (Wohlmuth, "The Liability of Travel Agents: A Study in the Selection of Appropriate Legal Principles," 40 Temp.L.Q. 29, 33 [1966], hereinafter cited as Wohlmuth). Since active negligence on the part of the defendant has been neither alleged nor proved, it is not necessary to discuss standard of care demanded of a travel agent.

"An agent is a person authorized by another to act on his account or under his control. An agent is one who acts for or in the place of another by authority from him. He is one who, by the authority of another, undertakes to transact some business or manage some affairs on account of such other." Although the client of the travel agent seldom exercises control over the specifics of the arrangements necessary to accomplish his travel goals, he has the right as part of the relationship to be specific as to the most minute elements of the travel arrangements should he choose to do so. Also, "there is not the slightest indication that an express agreement-creating agency is ever entered into between travel agent and client. They do not generally address themselves to the matter . . . and whatever relationship exists between them appears to be either assumed by the parties to exist or never enters their minds at all" (Wohlmuth). Nevertheless, this court is constrained to follow the holding of Bucholtz that a travel agency is the agent of the traveler.

The determination that the defendant acted as plaintiff's agent is not inconsistent with the view expressed in Dorkin that the travel agent is a disclosed principal vis-à-vis the hotels and carriers he deals with and that the latter should be considered independent contractors in relation to the former. The limousine service cannot be considered a subagent of defendant since no delegation of the responsibility assumed by the travel agent took place.

An independent contractor is "one who, exercising an independent employment, contracts to do a piece of work according to his own methods and without being subject to the control of his employer except as to the result of his work. . . ."

Such was the relationship between this defendant and the limousine service retained by it to transport the plaintiff from the airport to her residence upon the latter's return. The travel agent was only interested in accomplishing this result and presumably had no control over the manner of its accomplishment by the limousine service.

In general, an employer or principal is not liable for damages caused by an independent contractor. There exist, however, at least six recognized exceptions to this exemption: "Thus, it can be said, the hirer or principal remains liable (1) where the thing contracted to be done is unlawful, (2) where the acts performed create a public nuisance, (3) where a duty is imposed by statute or ordinance, (4) where the hirer is under a nondelegable duty to perform the services promised, (5) where the work to be performed is inherently dangerous, and (6) where the principal or hirer assumes a specific duty by contract" (Dorkin).

Exception (6) is applicable to the case at bar. "[W]hen the client asks the travel agent to secure reservations for him, he is making an offer for a bilateral contract to the travel agent that is accepted by the latter when he agrees to try to secure the reservations requested" (Wohlmuth). Here the defendant arranged for the transportation of the plaintiff and issued a confirmation form that was represented to entitle plaintiff to the transportation she desired.

Ruling of the Court: The court finds the defendant liable for the failure of the promised performance. Judgment in favor of plaintiff in the amount of $45.

Disclaimers by the Travel Agent

In the 1974 case of Dorkin v. American Express Company, 351 N.Y.S.2d 190, a husband and wife brought negligence and breach of contract action against the travel service that had supplied them with a planned European tour on which the wife subsequently sustained injuries. The crucial issue, according to the court, was the relationship between the defendant and the foreign bus company on whose bus the plaintiff was injured. Although the plaintiffs' allegations, if proved, were sufficient to hold the defendant liable, the tour bus was owned and operated by an independent contractor. Such a relationship, therefore, precluded any liability on the part of the defendant, either for negligence or breach of contract.

The defendant had agreed to supply the plaintiffs with a European tour, including meals, lodgings, and transportation. American Express Company did not, however, insure the safety of the plaintiff. A disclaimer in the tour contract negated any intent of the defendant to assume a contractual obligation for such safety. The plaintiffs' proof consisted merely of the allegation as set forth in the complaint and bill of particulars. This, according to the court, was insufficient to establish any triable issue. The summary judgment of the defendant was affirmed.

Travel agents frequently insert *responsibility clauses* in their written materials, usually in the form of disclaimer clauses, conditional receipts, or settlement clauses. This type of disclaimer will deter nuisance suits in many instances, but its actual effectiveness in limiting the liability of the travel agent is questionable. In the absence of a statute, the courts have not looked favorably on disclaimers and, when in question, have usually strictly construed the disclaimers. As a result, such clauses are generally invalidated under various legal theories, including insufficient notice to the customer, lack of specificity in the language used, inequality of bargaining power, and, perhaps most important, offensiveness to public policy.

The courts' reluctance to enforce exclusionary clauses stems from the fact that these statements often attempt to avoid all liability on the travel agent's part, thus seriously burdening the court in determining the legal issues involved—that is, the actual relationship and obligations of the travel agent to his customers in a given set of circumstances—and thereby making it difficult, if not impossible, to properly fix liability.

A travel agent might be better advised to use an explanatory clause that defines the relationship between all the parties involved and properly illustrates to the client what liabilities attach to each party. In this clause travel agents can make clear to the client that they are simply agents for a supplier of travel services, but they have no control over them. This kind of clause could work to the travel agent's advantage since it aids the court in an area of the law that is unclear and often unfamiliar in factual situations. Such an approach is consistent with the modern judicial trend of lessening the traditional *caveat emptor* ("let the buyer beware") doctrine, while penalizing those responsible for taking improper advantage of a client. Thus, the court may look more favorably upon an explanatory clause than a general disclaimer clause.

However, an explanatory clause will not relieve travel agents from their own or their employees' negligence or wrongful conduct. If an explanatory clause is used, actual notice must be given to the client. This is a management function and will be covered in the appropriate section.

Insurance

Mistakes and poor judgment can occur in any business. The objective of insurance, of course, is to minimize the errors and omissions of travel agents and their staffs, along with those of third-party suppliers of travel services. Insurance is an extremely important method of protecting the agency against liability. Many types of coverage are available, but to minimize costs a deductible of from $200 to $300 is suggested.

Generally, suit coverage covers the cost of legal defense and of any adverse judgment, both in instances where the travel agent is at fault and where the claim concerns the conduct of third-party travel service suppliers. Insurance, however, should not be a crutch for poor management techniques.

Class Action Suits

Not all disappointed travelers are able or willing to pursue litigation because of high legal costs and the relatively small amounts of damages involved. A traveler may, of course, sue in small claims court as in the *Bucholtz* case discussed earlier. Usually damages allowed there are not very high—ranging from $200 to $1,000. A *class action*—a legal device that permits an individual to sue on behalf of other persons similarly situated—is one solution to this problem. The class action is also a more attractive financial alternative for plaintiffs and their lawyers. If the plaintiffs win the case, their lawyers can claim their fees from the defendants and the fees are proportional to the size of the judgment. An individual who brings suit usually has to pay his or her own legal fees.

In the recent case of Guadagno et al. v. Diamond Tours and Travel et al., 392 N.Y.S.2d 783 (1976), Judge Tierney of the New York Supreme Court granted permission to the five plaintiffs to represent about three hundred complainants in a class action. In this case, the plaintiffs claimed that the defendants—Club Islandia, two Long Island travel agencies, a Long Island tour organizer, and a New York tour wholesaler—misrepresented the nature and quality of accommodations at a Jamaican resort and the availability of sports and other facilities. The judge's ruling in this $1.5 million lawsuit may have a significant impact on future litigation concerning the travel industry. This is probably the first time a class action against a travel agent has been permitted in the United States.

Regardless of the outcome, the significance of this and similar cases lies in the court's decision to allow a class action, rather than limiting the case to the one package tour the five plaintiffs participated in. The judge's decision was that the members of all three charter groups that went to the resort (Club Islandia) in December and January shared a common grievance and should be allowed to join the class action.

Management Principles

Any industry must safeguard the consumer's rights. Only a relatively few travel agents, airlines, other passenger carriers, places of accommodation, and restaurants do not conduct their business professionally or respect travelers' rights.

In a survey conducted to determine the most frequent abuses by travel agents, travelers cited the following complaints:

1   Describing top-of-the-line hotel rooms not available to tour members;

2   Describing rooms in such terms as "deluxe" or "first class" when in fact no such rating system exists in the United States, and such a system varies widely from country to country abroad;

3   Including days spent in transit as part of the promised vacation time, a practice especially flagrant in trips to the Far East and South Pacific, which involve long flights over several time zones (see chapter 3);

4   Substituting advertised facilities with other accommodations at the last minute, leaving the traveler no option but to accept them or stay home (perhaps the most common complaint).

The publicity that mismanaged companies receive reflects on the entire travel industry, although travelers are not entirely blameless in such matters—multiple hotel and airline reservations are the major cause of overbooking. Airlines and hotels could match up home addresses and telephone numbers to discover multiple reservers, but the use of different names and telephone numbers makes this difficult. Customers who are not charged for their reservations simply do not show up, while other valid customers are put on a waiting list. Some travel agents also reserve blocks of seats for planned tours that often do not materialize, leaving seats unused and hotel rooms unfilled. And some airlines may hold seats for VIPs or corporate personnel.

Informing travelers of their rights may be beneficial to the travel industry. Indeed, if the travel industry is permitted to continue certain abuses unchecked, the legislature may have to step in and institute rigorous controls, as they have in the airline industry.

Many travel industry problems can be alleviated by better training of personnel and higher wages. After all, the essential ingredient of the service industry is people—both guests and employees. The guests pay for certain services and the employees supply those services. Thus, the success of a business depends on the quality of its employees.

Travel agents are only one of the parties serving the traveler. Their success depends on straightforward dealings with their customers; hence, the following suggestions are in order:

1   Travel agents should not make wild promises.

2   They should thoroughly familiarize themselves with as many travel destinations as possible through literature, films, discussion with other travel personnel, and personal experience.

3   They should maintain comprehensive files on all travel destinations.

4   They should work in association with other travel agents to sanc-

tion poor travel service suppliers (such as hotels with poor service and substandard food or those that continually overbook). Such an association of travel agents could implement a rating system for travel service suppliers. Thus, the agent would be able to advise customers accurately.

5 Travel agents should also ascertain the employee quality and training of the hotels and resorts they recommend. Good management is the key, and graciousness is an essential characteristic of a good employee.

Often many travel service suppliers are large, impersonal corporations with little regard for an individual traveler's needs. The judgment for the plaintiff-travelers in the *Varig* case is a sign that the courts can and will protect consumers by allowing them to recover even for mental suffering.

Travel agents may become liable in various circumstances, although they do have some protection. When a hotel employee assaults a traveler sent to the hotel by a travel agent, it is not grounds to recover from the travel agent, as shown in the *Sacks v. Loew's Theatres* case. Although the travel agent will win such a case, it can cost considerable amounts in attorney fees and time.

In the *Odysseys* case, the travel agent was held liable for a failure to provide reservations; the travelers were awarded the total cost of their payment for tickets and hotel accommodations, even though the travel agent had made the arrangements through a travel wholesaler. Thus, travel agents should know their wholesaler, and they should ask their customer if they want their reservations confirmed by calling the hotel directly (of course, the phone call is part of the cost of the trip to the traveler).

The *Bucholtz* case is significant because it allowed the plaintiffs to sue in small claims court. All too often travelers have been left stranded in a strange area or country, sometimes without enough funds to return home. They then bring a cause of action against the travel agent because he or she is the expert on travel and should be trusted to make proper arrangements. In such cases disclaimer and explanatory clause forms can protect the travel agent. However, agents have the duty to tell the traveler what they know of the travel destination and should not misrepresent the facts. Also, travel agents should acquire insurance to cover the chance of error or omission. On the other hand, the *Bucholtz* case does set up standards for the industry.

Guadagno v. Diamond Tours and Travel may also have far-reaching implications. A class action can result in an astronomical award to great numbers of similarly treated travelers.

In view of the possibility of such large court awards and the increasing discontent and power of consumers, the travel industry should try to regulate itself more lest it come under the rigid control of the legislators and courts.

QUESTIONS FOR DISCUSSION

1 What components comprise the travel industry?

2 What is the Warsaw Convention Pact, and what effect does it have on the traveling public?

3 What basis have travelers for compensation if their bags are willfully not delivered by the airline when they land at their destination?

4 Under travel law, can humiliation and mental suffering be compensated for?

5 If travelers do not use their tickets for one portion of their trip, from whom can they collect? Why?

6 If a travel agent makes foreign transportation arrangements for a traveler and that transportation is negligently performed, whom can the traveler sue? Why? Which nation's law applies?

7 A hotel company has contracted to take care of a travel agency's customers. Because of overbooking, however, the hotel cannot take care of some of the agency's customers, who must seek other accommodations. Can those customers take action, and if so, against whom? What would the results be? Why?

8 For whom is a travel agent the agent when he or she makes arrangements with: (a) a customer and an airline carrier; (b) a customer and a travel wholesaler; (c) a customer and a foreign hotel; and (d) a customer and a bus company? Who is liable in each case if something goes wrong?

9 The traveler deals directly with the travel agent. Can the travel agent be sued if customers do not receive what they contracted for from an airline, hotel, or bus company?

10 What is the legal validity of a disclaimer provision that a travel agent includes along with a travel package and that is signed by the customer?

11 Two hundred and twenty people are stranded in Hawaii without hotel rooms because the hotel overbooked. Is there any way for these people (who had no place to stay and who had to return home) to recover? If so, from whom can they recover? How should they proceed?

16 Contents

16 Emerging Areas of Concern for the Hospitality Industry

"The older order changeth,
Yielding place to new;
And God fulfills himself in many ways,
Lest one good custom should corrupt the
world."

ALFRED, LORD TENNYSON, *line 408*
Morte D'Arthur

One of the first steps toward solving a problem is recognizing that one exists. Those who are fortunate enough to have the vision to anticipate what new problems may be arising will be able to eliminate such problems completely or at least mitigate their effects on, and costs to, one's operation. This chapter explores certain areas of concern that seem to have emerged as full-blown problems within the past few years.

Consider the status of service charges in a restaurant. Is such a charge that is added to a customer's check part of the restaurant's gross sales, even though the owner distributes the money to service employees? Under the sales and meals tax laws in several states, it could. An awareness of this law could help restaurateurs avoid large legal and accounting fees, not to mention the payment of tax assessments with interest and penalties added to them.

How about a restaurant that advertises selling maple syrup with pancakes when the syrup actually contains no maple syrup at all? This ruling cost McDonald's thousands of dollars in fines plus legal fees. What are the consequences of printing "sixteen-ounce sirloin" on the menu and then using fourteen-ounce sirloins to fill orders?

These are only some of the areas that have come to the forefront in recent years, and we will explore them in this chapter, along with the liability exposure of a facility concerning sexual harassment of employees, requirements of the Equal Employment Opportunity Act, and the need for sophisticated life safety procedures and equipment. Just as the law is constantly changing, the areas that it focuses on are constantly changing.

Tips or Service Charges as Taxable Sales

Restaurateurs, hoteliers, and caterers who collect tips or service charges on behalf of their employees may have to include their value in the gross sales reported for meals or sales tax, even though the money is distributed to employees. How does it happen that the money that employees receive and upon which they pay personal income taxes is included in the employer's income for meals and sales tax purposes? Two factors weigh heavily in this determination. The first is the language and terms of the ordinance or statute that creates the tax; the second is the manner in which the money is collected and disbursed. Although various courts have arrived at different results when dealing with what appears to be the same factual situation, depending on the legislative language used in the statute or ordinance, a definite pattern seems to be emerging that should at least assist us in recognizing the pitfalls.

The Illinois courts in the case of Fontana D'Or, Inc., v. Department of Revenue, 358 N.E.2d 1283 (1976) held that a caterer's automatic inclusion in the billing to customers of a 15 percent service charge was part of the gross sales price of the meals and therefore was subject to the tax imposed upon sales of food and beverages. In interpreting the relevant law, the court said that the statute defined "gross receipts" from the sales of tangible personal property at retail as the total selling price or amount of such sales, and that would be what was subject to the tax. The court interpreted "selling price" and "amount of sale" as the consideration for a sale valued in money, including both cash and services as "determined without any deduction on account of the cost of the property sold, the cost of the materials used, labor or services cost, or any other expense whatsoever," but excluding state or local taxes. Because the service charge was mandatory, it was part of the selling price of the dinners and not a tip or gratuity. Also, the court found no correlation between the amount of the gratuities paid by the customers and the salaries of the caterer's employees, and, therefore, it could not accept the argument that the employer was a mere conduit for the collection and transmission of the gratuities. Nothing in the employer's payroll records or the W-2 slips given to the employees indicated payment of tips or gratuities to them; rather, the sum collected was used by the employer to defray payroll expenses.

The court in the *Fontana D'Or* case disposed of a Wisconsin case, Big Foot Country Club v. Wisconsin Department of Revenue, 235 N.W.2d

696 (1975) that the caterer had cited in support of its position that the service charge or gratuity was in fact a tip collected for employees and not part of the selling price of the meal by stating that they were distinguishable. In the *Big Foot* case, the country club membership had adopted a rule that a service charge would be added to the bills for purchases of food and beverages at the club. The service charges collected by the club were distributed directly to waitresses, busboys, and other service help, excluding cooks, as year-end bonuses. The *Big Foot* court held that the mandatory add-on service charge was merely the codification of the social custom of tipping; that inasmuch as the membership had voted on the rule, the charge was voluntary; and because the members at any time could revoke or modify the rule, it remained voluntary.

An Alabama court in 1977 seemed to have had a situation somewhat like these cases in *State v. International Trade Club, Inc.* The court disposed of the issues quickly and arrived at a well-reasoned opinion. Be attentive to the practicality of the reasoning and the common sense displayed in the result.

Case **Example**	**State v. International Trade Club, Inc.** *351 So.2d 895 (Ala., 1977)* *(HOLMES, Judge)*

This is a tax case. It originated from a final assessment of sales tax entered by the appellant, the State of Alabama, in the amount of $6,381.57. Taxpayer appealed the final assessment to the Circuit Court of Mobile County. That court found the taxpayer was not liable for the tax. Specifically, the trial court found that the 15 percent service charge collected by the taxpayer from its members is not a part of the "gross receipts of sales" under Title 51, Section 786(2)(f), Code of Alabama 1940, and therefore not subject to tax. It is from that decree that the appellant appealed.

The pertinent facts, as set out in a written stipulation of facts, reveal the following:

Taxpayer-appellee is a nonprofit corporation operating a club for the use and benefit of its members. Since its formation in 1966, the appellee has collected a 15 percent service charge from its members in lieu of cash tips left on the table. This charge is a part of the total check that a member signs after completing his meal. Proceeds from this charge go into a gratuity pool for the employees.

The bylaws of appellee require a minimum 15 percent service charge to be added to each check, with no cash tips being allowed. Although this charge is mandatory, there are occasional instances where members have varied the amount because they were pleased or displeased. If a member designates an additional amount, it goes into the pool, unless it is designated to a specific waiter or bartender, in which case it goes to him over and above his regular share of the pool.

The gratuity pool is maintained by appellee and is funded by the service charges received by the waiters, waitresses, bartenders, and busboys. The waiters and waitresses were paid $4 per shift plus their share of the gratuity pool—that is, 85 percent of the service charge, which was 15 percent of the meal cost. The other 15 percent of the service charge was credited on the appellee's payroll against the salary of the busboys who service the dining room. The busboys were paid the federal minimum hourly wage for the period in question.

The two bartenders were paid a guaranteed salary of $182 and $185, respectively, per week. The service charges that were received by the bartenders, on the tickets that they serviced, were credited against their guaranteed salaries. Although the bartenders could not receive less than their guaranteed salary, they could receive more if the service charges with which they were credited exceeded their guaranteed salary. As with the waiters and waitresses, 15 percent of the service charges to be received by the bartenders was paid into the gratuity pool on behalf of the busboys.

The appellee, during the period in litigation, collected and paid the appellant sales tax on all sales, with the exception that appellee did not pay sales tax upon the 15 percent service charge. It is upon that omission that the appellant issued its assessment and upon which this appeal is based.

The appellee contended the service charge was not subject to sales tax because the transaction was simply a substitute for a cash tip given to the waiter or employee and therefore was not subject to tax.

The appellant, however, argued that the service charge was a taxable "labor or service cost" as set out under Title 51, Section 786(2)(f), Code of Alabama 1940, as follows: "The term 'gross proceeds of sales' means the value proceeding or accruing from the sale of tangible personal property (and including the proceeds from the sale of any property handled on consignment by the taxpayer), including merchandise of any kind and character without any deduction on account of the cost of the property sold, the cost of the materials used, *labor or service cost*, interest paid, or any other expenses whatsoever, and without any deductions on account of losses" (emphasis added).

The appellant therefore contended that the service charge was tantamount to a labor or service cost and should be included in the "gross proceeds of sales" and subject to sales tax. The question before this court was one of first impression and we therefore looked to other states for guidance.

The Supreme Court of Wisconsin in Big Foot Country Club v. Wisconsin Department of Revenue, 70 Wis.2d 871, 235 N.W.2d 696 (1975), recognized that a 15 percent add-on service charge was a mere codification by the club's bylaws of the social custom of tipping. The court also said that this would not be subject to the sales tax.

However, the court went further and stated that the result would be different if the service charge was used to bring the wages paid to employees up to a minimum wage level.

In the present case, it is undisputed that 15 percent of the service charge collected was credited against appellee's payroll for minimum wages paid to the busboys. It is clear that the service charge, to the extent of the minimum wages, was a part of the appellee's gross receipts and, therefore, properly subject to the sales tax.

Turning now to the bartenders, we noted above that they have a guaranteed salary that can be increased if the service charges with which they are credited exceed their guaranteed salary. Put another way, they will receive 85 percent of the service charges on their tickets only if such a figure exceeds their guaranteed salary. If such a figure does not exceed the salary, they will receive the guaranteed salary. The question then becomes what happens to the accumulation from the service charges when the bartenders receive the guaranteed salary.

The court in Green v. Surf Club, Inc., Fla.App., 136 So.2d 354, cert. den., 139 So.2d 694 (Fla.1962), aptly stated that: "There may be situations wherein the collection of a fixed service charge is taxable, such as where the assessment and collection thereof has no relationship to the sums received by the service personnel, but is retained by the employer as a portion of the gross proceeds on the sale of food and beverage. *The determinative question in each instance should be whether or not the 'dealer' receives a benefit from the involuntary charge. If he does, he should be taxed. If he does not, no tax should be levied*" (emphasis added).

Clearly, the appellee received a benefit from the service charge concerning the bartenders. If the service charges with which they were credited exceeded their guaranteed salary, the appellee did not have to pay them their guaranteed salary. But if such charges did not exceed the salary, appellee had to pay the salary. However, whatever service charges had been credited to them could be used by the appellee to offset the cost of their guaranteed salary. Therefore, the sums retained by appellee constituted "gross receipts of sales" under Title 51, Section 786(2)(f), Code of Alabama, and were subject to tax.

Lastly, we now turn to the service charge as it relates to the waiters and waitresses. As set out above, they received $4 per shift plus their share of the gratuity pool—that is, 85 percent of the service charge on meals. Appellee argued that the service charge was simply a substitute for a cash tip and was not subject to tax. We agree.

The social custom in this case has been transformed into a club bylaw. This 15 percent is a reasonable amount and corresponds to the usual amount left by the general public in public restaurants. Although this 15 percent is called a service charge, it is more appropriately viewed as a gratuity or tip for the waiters and waitresses. As such, it is not part of the gross receipts of the appellee.

In summary, the service charge as it relates to the busboys and bartenders did not constitute a gratuity or tip and, therefore, fell within the term "gross receipts of sales" as defined in Title 51, Section 786(2)(f), Code of Alabama 1940. The service charge as it related to waiters and waitresses did constitute a gratuity and was without the purview of Title 51, Section 786(2)(f). The trial court is thereby reversed in part and the cause remanded for further proceedings not inconsistent with this opinion.

Ruling of the Court: Affirmed in part; reversed in part; and remanded for entry of a judgment not inconsistent with this opinion.

Some guidelines seem to be emerging that will help hoteliers, restaurateurs, and caterers decide whether to include the gratuity as part of the "selling price" when billing customers and thereby impose the sales or meals tax not only upon the price of the meal but upon the service charge as well. Unquestionably, if the employer is acting merely as a conduit to transmit the gratuity from the customer to the service person, there will be no sales or meals tax due on the service charge if the charge is voluntary and not in a fixed amount. It appears as if some jurisdictions will differ as to whether a mandatory service charge will automatically result in having to include the charge as a portion of the sale for tax purposes.

In addition to the question of whether the service charge is mandatory, it is imperative to determine whether the employer derives any benefit from the receipt of the service charges or tips collected by it, ostensibly on behalf of the service personnel. If, as we saw demonstrated in the *International Trade Club* case, any portion of the sum is used to raise an employee's wage to meet the minimum wage or to meet the level of salaries being paid to persons engaged in similar occupations under similar circumstances, then the sums must be included as part of the sale for taxation purposes. The same would hold true if the service charge or any portion of it was used to meet the guaranteed salary of any employee.

The following questions can be a guide to determining policy with regard to whether to include the service charge or tip collected on behalf of employees.

1   Does the statute governing the taxes on the meals sold specifically require that a service charge be included as part of the sales price for tax purposes?

2   Does the employer derive any benefit from the service charge?

3   Is the service charge voluntary?

4   Is the service charge used in total or in part to meet the minimum wages the employer is obligated by law to pay the employee?

5   Is the service charge used to supplement the wage of the employee in order to raise it to the level of that paid to comparable employees engaged in similar employment?

6   Is the employer merely a conduit for transmitting the service charge from the customer to the service personnel?

An affirmative answer to any of the first five questions means the employer should add the service charge into the customer's bill prior to computing the tax and then remit the tax collected on it to the appropriate tax department. An affirmative answer to the sixth question means that the service charge need not be included in tax computations.

Truth in Menu

A strong consumer movement is underway to compel restaurateurs to be truthful with regard to the representations made in their menus relative to portion size, the grade or quality of what is served, and the origin or source of what is served. Menus attempt to portray the offerings as enticingly as possible, but consumers are becoming more vocal in their protests when they are offered "fresh-picked Maine lobster" but are served langouste, or are offered "sixteen-ounce sirloins" and are served smaller steaks, charging fraud if they do not get what they ordered and paid for.

The consumer's position is finding support in local governing bodies as ordinances and regulations calculated to curb these practices are promulgated. The complaints run not only to the words written on the menu, but to the words spoken by service personnel when they take a customer's order. A waitress who says "fresh orange juice" when in fact it is canned or frozen has misrepresented the product. The same is true of pictorial descriptions of items offered. For example, if a breakfast poster in a restaurant pictorially shows four pancakes in a stack on a plate with four link sausages, it is telling customers that four pancakes and four sausages will be served. If, in fact, fewer are served, customers are not getting what was represented, and that, too, is a fraud or untruthful representation.

The so-called truth-in-menu movement was underway, resulting in regulations and legislation aimed at eliminating these practices—for example, in Washington, D.C., Los Angeles, California, and New Jersey—before various restaurant associations promised they would deal with the problem within their industry without government intervention. They have embarked upon a program entitled Accuracy in Menus (AIM) that began with an informational program designed to advise members of the various items that are commonly misrepresented and the manner in which they are being misrepresented—for example, calling something fresh when in fact it is frozen or canned, or referring to regular chopped meat as chopped sirloin.

The warning to restaurateurs is obvious and direct. It is coming not only from the citizenry and the governments, both state and local, but from the restaurant associations and lobby groups: If they do not cease these practices and police themselves, they will have government supervision and regulations to cope with. The solution is simple: If restaurateurs want to spark up the menu and stimulate the patron's taste buds, they should do so by means other than deception. If menu representations as to weight, grade, quality, place of origin, and product composition cannot be backed up, then the restaurant should serve what was represented or change the wording of the menu or other representation to conform to what is being served.

Sexual Harassment

Sexual harassment is not a new problem to those who seek to operate successful businesses with a high degree of employee morale, but the way it is being dealt with in law is. Because of the development of liability theories that resulted in such conduct being actionable and because of large awards or settlements made as the result of court interpretations of Title VII of the 1964 Civil Rights Act, sexual harassment can no longer be permitted to occur in the employment setting. The Equal Employment Opportunity Commission (EEOC) defines sexual harassment as "unwelcome sexual advances, requests for sexual favors, and other verbal or physical conduct of a sexual nature." Such activity becomes actionable when it adversely affects an individual's terms and conditions of employment.

Studies have indicated that those most susceptible to sexual harassment are usually on the lower strata of the employability pool and have the greatest economic need. The Atlanta Community Relations Commission and the U.S. Labor Department in a combined report concluded that those most vulnerable are recently divorced women with children to support and few, if any, job skills.

In the past, sexual harassment, like many other social ills, was not much talked about. But a series of studies done in the mid-1970s demonstrated the prevalence of the practice. A survey in 1976 by *Redbook* magazine found that 90 percent of its respondents had been subjected to unsolicited and unwanted sexual conduct while on the job. A 1979 article in *Business Week* found that 75 percent of its respondents had been sexually harassed.

Few such problems were reported. The victims were afraid that their credibility would be challenged and that they would ultimately lose their jobs for making their complaints public. Although the tort law of the state was available for them, the state courts were reluctant to find any liability on the part of the employer for any acts of its employees. Moreover, most of the victims were too poor to engage in a lawsuit.

Section 703 of Title VII of the Civil Rights Act of 1964 became the weapon in such cases. It specifically provides that it shall be an unlawful employment practice for an employer (1) "to fail or refuse to hire or to discharge any individual, or otherwise to discriminate against any individual with respect to his compensation, terms, conditions, or privileges of employment, because of such individual's . . . sex" or (2) "to limit, segregate, or classify employees or applicants for employment in any way that would deprive any individual of employment opportunities or otherwise adversely affect his status as an employee, because of such individual's . . . sex." Under the act, the courts could order the employer to reinstate the employee with back pay, and it provided for attorney's fees. Equally, if not more important, is the fact that the employer could not retaliate against the victim for having brought the action, a protection that was not in existence—in the absence of specific legislation—if state court suits were to be pursued.

The first cases brought into court alleging that sexual harassment constituted sex discrimination under Title VII were unsuccessful. The courts refused to accept this conclusion, holding that such sexual harassment was not based upon sex alone; rather it was based on gender plus having sexual relations and, therefore, was not within the purview of the act.

The case of *Heelan v. Johns-Manville*, decided in 1978, is the landmark case in this area. After it, the courts increasingly began to find violations of Title VII and to award damages. The U.S. Supreme Court has not yet ruled on the question, but the majority of inferior federal courts are now on the victim's side. The court in *Heelan* stated that once the plaintiff has established a *prima facie* case, it becomes the defendant's obligation to rebut it by affirmatively establishing the absence of discrimination by the clear weight of the evidence. If the defendant alleges that the plaintiff's termination was for reasons of poor performance, he must establish the same by a clear weight of the evidence.

Case	**Heelan v. Johns-Manville Corp.**
Example	*451 F.Supp. 1382 (1978)*
	(SHERMAN G. FINESILVER, District Judge)

In this action under Title VII of the Civil Rights Act of 1964, as amended, 42 U.S.C. Sections 2000e, *et seq.*, Mary K. Heelan sought damages against her former employer, Defendant Johns-Manville Corporation [JM]. She claimed that her refusal to have sexual relations with her supervisor, Joseph Consigli, resulted in her employment termination.

Defendant denied any impropriety by Consigli or corporate liability. Defendant contended that plaintiff was terminated for insubordination, lack of application, and general inability to perform at the level required of her position.

We find that JM is guilty of sex discrimination under Title VII, and that the retention of plaintiff's job as a JM project director was conditioned on the acceptance of sexual relations with her supervisor, a company executive.

Facts and Conclusions   Much of the testimony is conflicting, not only in pivotal areas but in areas of marginal relevance as well. This case is based largely upon the court's view of the credibility of the witnesses—that is, their worthiness of belief.

We have carefully scrutinized all testimony and the circumstances under which each witness has testified, and every matter in evidence that tends to show whether a witness is worthy of belief. For example, we have taken into account each witness's motive and state of mind, strength of memory, and demeanor and manner while on the witness stand. We have considered factors that affect the witness's recollection and his or her opportunity to observe and accurately relate to the matters discussed. We have considered whether a witness's testimony has been contradicted, and the bias, prejudice, and interest, if any, of each witness. In addition, we have considered any relation each witness may bear to either side of the case; the manner in which each witness might be affected in a decision in the case; and the extent to which, if at all, each witness is either supported or contradicted by other evidence.

With these factors in mind we find the following as facts and enter our conclusions of law.

In 1971, JM, an international corporation, commenced moving its world headquarters from New York to Colorado. The move necessitated temporary offices at Greenwood Plaza near Denver and ultimately complete construction of a $55 million building and amenities at the Ken Caryl Ranch, Jefferson County, Colorado.

Joseph Consigli of the New York home office, as Director of Facilities Planning, was transferred to Colorado to supervise a team to control and oversee the construction of the Colorado headquarters, obtain temporary office space, and assist relocation of one thousand five hundred JM employees and their families to Colorado.

In August 1971, plaintiff was hired by JM as a senior secretary and assigned to Consigli. Her employment with JM continued until May 31, 1974, when she was terminated by Consigli.

The documentary evidence of plaintiff's work performance at JM shows her to be an outstanding employee. All her evaluations rated her consistently excellent. Statements by plaintiff's co-workers also found her to be a good employee and, from their standpoint, no work-related reason existed for her termination. The only person to question plaintiff's competence was her supervisor, and these criticisms did not appear in any of his formal written evaluations, but only in his oral statements and privately maintained notes.

Initially plaintiff's work was typical secretarial work and included assistance in relocation of employees. Her starting salary was $6650 per year. Within a matter of months, plaintiff, under the direction of Consigli, was performing duties best characterized as a facilities planner. Consigli and staff had the responsibility of not only planning the world headquarters, but also the interior design of the Greenwood Plaza office. Thus, a major part of her responsibilities involved coordination with the Space Design Group, a New York design firm responsible for the interior work at Greenwood Plaza. Plaintiff's worth was clearly apparent to Consigli, and in March 1972 he recommended plaintiff for a "two-step" raise, rather than the customary one-step advance. The pay recommendation form noted that the pay raise was a "special merit increase." Consigli rated plaintiff's work as "excellent" in the following five categories: (1) ability, (2) application, (3) job performance, (4) cooperativeness, and (5) capacity for growth. Because of the unusual two-step pay raise, Consigli felt constrained to attach a note to the recommendation form indicating his high regard for Mrs. Heelan's excellent employment record.

In November of 1972, plaintiff was promoted at Consigli's recommendation to the position of "associate facilities planner" and her salary increased from $7,500 to $10,000. Her new position carried with it considerable responsibility and attaining the associate position was a major accomplishment. The job description for the associate position provided that it would be filled by a person with a degree, or its equivalent, in architectural design supplemented by courses in business administration and management. Plaintiff had none of these qualifications. Plaintiff's performance in her more responsible position merited a raise in July 1973. The raise came, in part, as a result of her outstanding annual evaluation that was completed on May 23, 1973. The subjective portion of the evaluation indicated that plaintiff performed her duties as JM's "principal contact with design and planning professions and interior contractors . . . very well and exceeded most objectives." Consigli also noted that Mrs. Heelan's "greatest accomplishment and talent" was "[i]n solving problems and adjusting schedules to meet changing job conditions. Her rapport with the design and planning disciplines is a great asset to the company." In the objective portion of the appraisal, Consigli gave plaintiff the highest grades printed on the form.

Soon after the pay raise recommendation, Consigli recommended plaintiff for a JM "A" award. According to a JM President's Bulletin, the "A" award is given to employees "who, through initiative, ability, and wholehearted interest in the company perform with unusual merit and show extraordinary accomplishments. . . . Administration of "A" awards requires a high degree of managerial judgment. Selection and approval must be exercised with utmost care."

Plaintiff received her "A" award on June 15, 1973, by letter from the president of JM, Dr. William Goodwin, and a monetary award of $1,000. Another raise to $12,100 followed in November. This raise was the result of a company-wide upward adjustment of salary levels and included the following comments: "Mary's application to her work, and often on her own initiative, and job performance has been excellent. She has excellent ability and capacity for growth."

In the spring of 1973, JM began its construction efforts of the world headquarters at the Ken Caryl Ranch. The Architects' Collaborative [TAC] was selected as the architect; Turner Construction Company [Turner] was the construction manager; and Space Design was chosen to do the interior work. To assist him, Consigli hired Eric Dienstbach as project manager to work with the TAC to coordinate its efforts with the requirements of Turner and JM. Plaintiff, as associate of Facilities Planning, had the responsibility of working with Space Design to coordinate its efforts with the requirement of JM and Turner. In the fall, plaintiff told Consigli that she felt that although she was doing the same type of work as the department's single project manager, Eric Dienstbach,[1] she was paid less and held the lower title of "associate." Plaintiff claimed that this was a case of sex discrimination. She requested promotion to project director. Consigli conferred about plaintiff with his immediate supervisor, Francis May, an executive vice president, and Richard Goodwin, then president of JM.

Although Heelan had an excellent performance record, serious reservations were expressed by top management about her attitude, which was, at times, stated to be abrasive and arrogant. After several meetings with top management, Consigli recommended plaintiff's promotion to project manager, which was approved in February 1974.

Mrs. Heelan articulated specific romantic advances made by Consigli beginning in April 1972 and extending through April 23, 1974, when she was informed of her termination. The sexual advances were occasioned as an integral part of her employment. The initial advances were made in April 1972. Consigli explained that the world headquarters duties would involve substantial travel responsibilities and family sacrifices. Plaintiff indicated her willingness to assume the duties and fulfill travel requirements. During the conversation, Consigli put his arm around plaintiff and said that she really did not yet understand the job requirement, but that she would in time. Explicit sexual invitations followed in late 1972 and continued on a regular basis through early 1974. All were refused.

1 Eric is the son of Isabelle Dienstbach, a JM vice president and administrative assistant to the president of JM. Mr. and Mrs. Consigli were personal friends of Mrs. Dienstbach and this relationship certainly assisted Eric's advancement in JM.

In January 1973, Consigli had lunch with Space Design Group's Ronald Phillips. Although they had been discussing business, Consigli began to talk about his affection for Mrs. Heelan. Consigli volunteered that he liked plaintiff very much, but was not sure that he could have an affair with her as he was married. Phillips was surprised by the conversation and did not respond. Later that month Phillips was again brought into the situation, this time by plaintiff. On January 23, plaintiff, who had now worked with Phillips for over a year, told him that she was distressed about her relationship with Consigli. Plaintiff related that he had offered her an apartment if she would leave her husband and consent to an affair. Phillips apparently told no one about his discussions with Consigli and plaintiff.

During the last few months of her employment, Consigli's sexual advances became more frequent, occurring as often as once a week. The final demand came on April 23, 1974. Plaintiff was called into her supervisor's office and told that she was to have an affair or be fired. Plaintiff refused any sexual relations with Consigli and was given notice that May 31, 1974, would be her last day of employment.

The evidence is in conflict as to whether plaintiff was offered another position at JM or extended an offer to return to her former position.

During the months of sexual harassment, plaintiff, for the most part, kept the matter to herself. On occasion, however, she discussed the matter with Eric Dienstbach, Ronald Phillips, Isabelle Dienstbach, and Francis May. On at least one occasion, Consigli mentioned the possibility of an affair to Ronald Phillips.

Although plaintiff repeatedly refused any sexual relationship with Consigli, she did begin an affair with her co-worker, Eric Dienstbach, sometime in September or October. Plaintiff denied the liaison, but the evidence contradicts her position. Both Consigli and Isabelle Dienstbach suspected the affair. Consigli asked Mrs. Dienstbach to question her son about the matter. Eric denied having an affair when questioned by his mother. She testified that she did not believe this denial. Of more importance, however, is the fact that during the discussion Eric told his mother that Consigli was pressuring plaintiff to have an affair with him. Mrs. Dienstbach testified that she did not believe this statement either, but nonetheless questioned Consigli. He denied the charge and Mrs. Dienstbach did not pursue the matter. Just when this discussion occurred is in dispute—Eric saying that it happened in February or March 1974 while Isabelle recalling the incident to have occurred earlier. Whatever the exact date, this discussion provided notice to top JM management that Consigli might have been making sexual advances toward Mrs. Heelan.[2] It also alerted Consigli to the fact that others knew of those advances. At the earliest, the discussion would have taken place in late 1973 since according to Eric Dienstbach, his affair did not begin until September or October. This time period coincides with the time when, according to Consigli, plaintiff's work product seriously declined.

Some time in December 1973 or January 1974, plaintiff made an appointment to speak with Isabelle Dienstbach. Mrs. Dienstbach had for a long period served as a sounding board for many of the female employees at JM who had work-related problems. At the meeting, plaintiff told Mrs. Dienstbach about Consigli's sexual demands, that they were being made

---

2   As noted, Isabelle Dienstbach was an assistant vice president of the corporation and administrative assistant to the then president.

weekly, and that she did not know how to stop the incidents. This meeting was another instance when Isabelle Dienstbach was informed of Consigli's actions. During this period, plaintiff again confided in Ronald Phillips of Space Design Group and Eric Dienstbach.

After plaintiff's notice of termination on April 23, she again sought out Isabelle Dienstbach. Plaintiff discussed the termination with her and was told to schedule a meeting with Francis May. Plaintiff met with May at the end of that month. She informed him, as she had informed Isabelle Dienstbach twice before, that Consigli had fired her not because of her work performance but because of her refusal to submit to her supervisor's sexual demands. May suggested that plaintiff discuss the matter with JM's personnel manager. Mrs. Heelan responded that May was the personnel manager's supervisor and that the personnel manager would in all probability not take action unless May ordered it. May agreed and declined to do anything at that time. After the meeting, May telephoned Consigli and asked him about plaintiff's charges. Consigli denied any wrongdoing and the matter was dropped.

Conclusions of Law   The law in this area is of recent vintage. Few trial courts have published pertinent opinions in the Federal Supplement. In addition, only three courts of appeals have reviewed this issue.

From these opinions a body of law is developing which, first and most importantly, recognizes that sexual harassment of female employees is gender-based discrimination that can violate Title VII. (See also *Note*, Civil Rights, Sexual Advances by Male Supervisory Personnel as Actionable Under Title VII of the Civil Rights Act of 1964, 16 So.Tex.L.J. 409 [1976].)

In order to recover on such a claim, however, the plaintiff must allege and establish that submission to the sexual suggestion constituted a term or condition of employment. A cause of action does not arise from an isolated incident or a mere flirtation. These may be more properly characterized as an attempt to establish personal relationships than an endeavor to tie employment to sexual submission. Title VII should not be interpreted as reaching into sexual relationships that may arise during the course of employment, but that do not have a substantial effect on that employment. In general, we would limit Title VII claims in this area, as suggested by one commentator, to "repeated, unwelcome sexual advances" that impact as a term or condition of employment.

It is not necessary for a plaintiff to prove a policy or practice of the employer endorsing sexual harassment. To demand that a plaintiff prove a company-directed policy of sexual discrimination is merely to extend a claim for relief with one hand and take it away with the other. In no other area of employment discrimination do the courts require such proof. The employer is responsible for the discriminatory acts of its agents.

Thus, to present a *prima facie* case of sex discrimination by way of sexual harassment, a plaintiff must plead and prove that (1) submission to sexual advances of a supervisor was a term or condition of employment, (2) this fact substantially affected plaintiff's employment, and (3) employees of the opposite sex were not affected in the same way by these actions.

This, however, does not end the inquiry. Under certain circumstances the employer may be relieved from liability. As noted by the court in Miller v. Bank of America, 418 F.Supp. 233 (N.D., Cal., 1976), where the employer has no knowledge of the discrimination, liability may be avoided if the employer has a policy or history of discouraging sexual harassment of employees by supervisors, and the employee has failed to present the matter to a publicized grievance board. If the employer is aware of the situation and rectifies it, the employer may not be held liable for the acts of its agent.

This case can be determined on relatively narrow grounds. It is clear that the repeated sexual demands made on Mrs. Heelan by her supervisor over a two-year period developed into a "term or condition" of employment. The facts here do not present a borderline case in which this court must decide whether the acts complained of substantially affected the terms of employment or were nothing more than a personal flirtation unrelated to plaintiff's job. Here we have the paradigm of the repeated, unwelcome sexual advance.

Nor in this case do we have the problem reviewed in *Barnes* v. *Costle* and Munford v. James T. Barnes & Co., 441 F.Supp. 459 (E.D., Mich. 1977), concerning the liability of the employer for the unknown acts of its supervisor-employee. We have considered and reject JM's argument that plaintiff failed to take advantage of JM's internal grievance procedures. First, the evidence fails to establish the existence of any such procedure and second, during her tenure plaintiff advised top management of her allegations. We find that she did everything within her power to bring her charges to the attention of top management. Here, the employer through its highest officers, knew of the charges of sexual harassment. In JM's organizational scheme, Consigli answered to only two people: JM's president, William Goodwin, and its executive vice president, Francis May. May was informed of plaintiff's claims after her termination and did nothing more than call the "accused" for verification or denial. More importantly, the administrative assistant to the president had heard charges of impropriety from two sources prior to plaintiff's termination. Her investigation was no more thorough than May's. The depth and scope of these inquiries can hardly satisfy the corporation's obligation under Title VII.

The effect of the Civil Rights Act of 1964, and particularly of Title VII of that act, has been to impose on employers certain duties that theretofore did not exist. No major employer in this nation can ignore the requirements of equal opportunity in hiring, promotion, and general conditions of employment. What little legislative history that exists in the area of sex discrimination has convinced the courts that "Congress intended to strike at the entire spectrum of disparate treatment of men and women resulting from sex stereotypes." This stereotype of the sexually-accommodating secretary is well documented in popular novels, magazine cartoons, and the theater. As we have indicated, Title VII does not concern itself with sexual liaisons among men and women working for the same employer. Title VII does, however, become involved when acceptance of sexual advances is transformed into a condition of continued employment.

Under the facts of this case, the frequent sexual advances by a supervisor do not form the basis of the Title VII violation that we find to exist. Significantly, termination of plaintiff's employment when the advances were rejected is what makes the conduct legally objectionable. Receptivity of repeated sexual advances by a high-level supervisor was inescapably a condition of the plaintiff's continued employment. The termination of plaintiff's employment as a retaliatory measure when advances were rejected are within the purview of Title VII.

If employers have reason to believe that sexual demands are being made on employees, they are obligated under Title VII to investigate the matter and correct any violations of the law. Moreover, employers must inform employees that management is receptive to such complaints and, if proved true, that management will rectify the situation. If the employer fails to respond to a valid complaint, it effectively condones illegal acts.

Just as the law would not permit an employer to ignore complaints of discrimination based on race, religion, or national origin, Title VII does not permit an employer to ignore complaints that supervisors are imposing as a condition of employment accession to sexual demands.

Although we need not decide the matter, we question whether Consigli himself could not fairly be characterized as the employer, rather than as the supervisor. Here the "supervisor" answers to only two other officers in the entire multinational corporation. When he travels, he is provided with a company hotel suite, a company limousine, and a company chauffeur. "The point on the managerial hierarchy at which supervisors become part of the 'employer' is a question of fact that would have to be determined in each case."

An employer is liable under Title VII when refusal of a supervisor's unsolicited sexual advances is the basis of the employee's termination; acceptance of sexual advances by a supervisor of high-level management cannot be made a condition of job retention, and it constitutes discrimination under Title VII.

Gender-based sexual harassment occasioned on plaintiff is prohibited under Title VII of the Civil Rights Act. Plaintiff was sexually harassed and males were not sexually harassed by plaintiff's supervisor, and a *prima facie* showing of a gender-based application of a practice or policy in violation of Title VII has been proven by plaintiff. JM has failed to rebut plaintiff's *prima facie* case.

Defendant, JM, has failed to affirmatively establish the absence of discrimination by the clear weight of the evidence.

Defendant's allegations that plaintiff's termination was based on poor work performance instead of refusal of a supervisor's sexual advances has not been established. Defendant must establish by clear weight of the evidence that these allegations were not a pretext. This JM has failed to do.

In the context of this case, the employer—JM—is liable for Title VII violations occasioned by discriminatory practices of supervisory personnel.

Ruling of the Court: Plaintiff is entitled to damages in the form of back pay and lost employment benefits. Appropriate considerations include the difference between the salary plaintiff would have made had she remained in the JM organization and that which she has actually made since her departure by way of unemployment compensation, wages, and the like. A determination of the proper amount of damages will be made in a separate order. In addition, plaintiff's attorneys are entitled to an award of reasonable attorneys' fees to be paid by defendant Johns-Manville Corporation.

After the court had awarded the plaintiff judgment that she had been discriminated against and ordered the defendant to pay her back pay and reinstate her, it is reported the plaintiff made an out-of-court settlement with the defendant for a reported $100,000. Why such a large sum? It appears now that there had been an ajudication of actionable sexual harassment under Title VII. The way had been paved for a successful suit in a state court for the damages other than loss of pay that the plaintiff suffered. Once having received the back pay and reinstatement, the plaintiff is almost guaranteed a recovery in the state courts for assault, and, in those jurisdictions where it is allowed, damages for emotional distress, with the possibility of recovering substantial punitive damages as well. The general feeling is that punitive damages would not be recoverable under Title VII.

As the result of cases decided after the *Heelan* case and guidelines promulgated by the EEOC, it is no longer required that any of the supervisors' superiors have knowledge of the acts of harassment. And, under the amended guidelines adopted by EEOC in 1980, the exposure of the employer has been substantially enlarged. (See appendix 4.) Although the guidelines are not law, they do have the effect of law, and it would be advisable for employers to come into conformity with their requirements in order to avoid costly ligitation and damages. The guidelines currently in effect make employers liable for acts of supervisors amounting to sexual harassment, regardless of whether the employer knew about it. The guidelines would seek to hold an employer liable for acts of sexual harassment committed by nonsupervisory employees, if the employer knew or should have known about them and did nothing to stop them. The guidelines go even further by saying that the employer could also be held responsible for acts of nonemployees who commit acts of sexual harassment upon employees in the work place "where the employer (or its agents or supervisory employees) knows or should have known of the conduct and fails to take immediate and appropriate corrective action." The guidelines also recognized what may be termed "discrimination by indirect sexual harassment." This circumstance occurs when one whose sexual favors are solicited by a supervisor or employer grants those favors, and as a result, the grantor is promoted and given pay raises and other better conditions of employment than those to whom these job benefits should have gone on the basis of merit and all other factors normally considered.

Except in cases of sexual harassment by supervisors, the guidelines provide for protection of the employer from being found in violation of Title VII if the employer takes "immediate and appropriate action." The guidelines further stress that prevention is the best method of eliminating sexual harassment and urge employers to take affirmative policies providing for the reporting of incidents and protection of the complaining party and disciplining of violators. If companies implement procedures for the expeditious and confidential handling of complaints of sexual harassment, the occasions of finding violations of Title VII will be eliminated or at least substantially reduced.

What has emerged from the cases and guidelines seems to be heading toward the conclusion that an employer has an implied contractual duty to provide employees with a work environment free of sexual harassment.

If, in fact, such a contractual obligation is implied in the hiring procedure, then it appears that the employee might even have a state cause of action against the employer for breach of contract if, in fact, the employee is subjected to on-the-job sexual harassment.

On-the-job sexual harassment is a problem that requires immediate and thorough action on the part of all employers because of the legal protection afforded its victims. Not only have we seen the expansion through the courts and EEOC of its ramifications in the area of Title VII, but the remedies available in the state courts are starting to result in very high damage awards and fines.[3]

Some states have enacted laws governing the practice of sexual harassment in the work place. For example, California has recently issued regulations covering sexual harassment. Its definition includes but is not limited to: verbal harassment, such as epithets, derogatory comments, or slurs; physical harassment, such as assault, impeding or blocking movement, or any physical interference with normal work or movement; visual forms of harassment, such as derogatory posters, cartoons, or drawings; or sexual favors, such as unwanted sexual advances that condition an employment benefit upon an exchange of favors. The California regulations also specifically provide that punitive damages are recoverable if the violation of the regulations is found to be particularly deliberate, egregious, or inexcusable. And on the federal level, the Reagan administration has committed itself to some form of action on the EEOC guidelines.

The big industries are all taking steps to mitigate the problem and protect themselves against lawsuits. Hundreds of corporations, colleges, hospitals, unions, and government agencies are implementing antisexual harassment policies, complete with a strong statement from management against such harassment, and providing and distributing plans for the reporting of incidents of such harassment, together with a grievance procedure to allow for a rapid and equitable resolution of the problem. The plans also demonstrate the strong sanctions that will be imposed upon the violators. Educational programs that demonstrate what sexual harassment is and the effects it has on the victims should be shown to employees and supervisors alike.

Those engaged in the hospitality industry are perhaps more vulnerable than in most other industries because of the nature of their business, so it is important that hotels and restaurants immediately implement

3   Clark v. World Airways, No. 77–0771, D.D.C. (1980), was awarded $2,500 compensatory damages and $50,000 punitive damages. In a Michigan court, one of the foremen of the Ford Motor Company allegedly promised a female worker easier tasks in exchange for sex. When the Ford Company's motion for a new trial was denied, they indicated that they would not appeal. The total amount of the damages, including interest, was $187,023.

policies. Restaurateurs must be on the alert for maitre d's who expect sexual favors from the waitresses he supervises in return for assigning them the best tables or having them work the most profitable hours. They must be cautious in the uniforms they require waitresses to wear. If the uniforms are too revealing and suggestive and subject the women to abuses and sexual advances by customers, the company could be flirting with a Title VII complaint.

A waitress who was required to wear a "sexy" uniform by her employer described her experience: "I cringe every time I recall that red ruffled minidress uniform that I was required to wear to waitress in the cocktail lounges in Detroit's Metropolitan Airport. The dress—it was actually more of a tutu—was so short it barely covered my rear when I stood upright, let alone when I bent over to serve a drink at one of the low tables at the bar. Its 'V' neckline took such a dramatic plunge that the slightest turn would bare my breasts. When hired, new waitresses were warned that they'd be fired on the spot if they were caught pinning it closed. The finishing touches—sheer nylons and bright red two-inch-high heels—further cheapened the image. My sexpot waitress uniform invited harassment and that's what I got until I took my case to court."[4]

Men had made so many passes at her and had made so many degrading comments to her that she came to regard each customer as a potential enemy. She said one day she realized how the abuses she had suffered over the years had deeply affected her and the other waitresses. She said, "The humiliation had become a way of life; we were no longer shocked when customers placed open pornographic magazines on the table grinning at us and hoping for a response; we began to fear the touching and the grabbing all of the time. We had almost forgotten that we were entitled to respect." She was put in touch with a women's group who brought a class action on behalf of the woman and the other waitresses. The suit, alleging sexual harassment, was brought under Title VII.

The potential for infliction of acts of sexual harassment upon hotel employees is great. Many hotel staff workers are women who are in the most vulnerable classification: low paid, unskilled, easily replaceable job holders who are thrown into an environment that could make them easily exploitable by other hotel employees, guests, or nonemployees who come on the premises for various reasons. The new EEOC guidelines impose upon the employer the duty to provide the employee with a work place free of sexual harassment and intimidation.

Clearly, it is unreasonable for any law or court to require a hotelier to be responsible for every incident of harassment that may arise, especially those involving nonemployees. Therefore the test has become to decide what the manager or employer has done to eliminate as much of this type of intolerable conduct in the work place as is possible.

Employers must provide policy statements on sexual harassment to

---

4 Judith Marentetle, *Glamour*, Oct., 1980, p. 256.

all employees, undertake an educational program designed to inform all employees about sexual harassment, and impose appropriate sanctions on both supervisors and employees for violations.

Equal Employment Opportunity

With the passage of the Equal Employment Opportunity Act in 1972, equal employment opportunity for everyone became the law of the land. As such, implementation and compliance with its provisions and mandates have become an inseparable part of the personnel management function.

The hotel, restaurant, and travel industries have a number of areas within them that they must look to in this regard. In the past, chambermaids were always female and door attendants male. Today any advertisement seeking to hire only females for chambermaid positions and males as door attendants would be in violation of the law. Therefore, management must examine all hiring and employment practices, as well as all company policies and practices relative to work advancement and bestowing of benefits concerning employees. This examination must lead to the elimination of practices that tend to lead toward violations, and if there are violations, to institute remedial procedures—including affirmative action programs—to eliminate them.

The genesis of EEO is the Civil Rights Act of 1964. The provisions of Title VII, Section 703A, read as follows:

> It shall be an unlawful employment practice for an employer (1) to fail or refuse to hire or to discharge any individual or otherwise to discriminate against any individual with respect to his compensation, terms, conditions, or privileges of employment because of such individual's race, color, religion, sex, or national origin; or (2) to limit, segregate or classify his employees in any way that would deprive or tend to deprive any individual of employment opportunities or otherwise inadvertently affect his status as an employee because of such individual's race, color, religion, sex, or national origin.

Section 704B provides that it is unlawful for an employer to "print or cause to be printed or published any notice or advertisement relating to employment by such employer . . . indicating any preference, limitation, specification, or discrimination based on race, color, religion, sex, or national origin." The only exception to this occurs when religion or sex is a bona fide occupational qualification (bfoq)—that is, reasonably necessary to the normal operations of the organization. Only then is it a lawful employment practice to advertise for and hire employees of a particular religion, race, or sex. For example, it may be legal to require a waiter or waitress in an Oriental restaurant to be an Oriental. However, the cook probably would not need to be Oriental because he or she is not seen by the public. It should be noted, however, that the definition of a bfoq has been increasingly narrowed as a result of court rulings over the years.[5]

Title VII as amended by the Equal Employment Opportunity Act of 1972 applies to the following employers:

1   All private employers of fifteen or more persons,
2   All educational institutions, public and private,
3   State and local governments,
4   Public and private employment agencies,
5   Labor unions with fifteen or more members,
6   Joint (labor-management) committees for apprenticeship and training.

Violators of the act are exposed to heavy damage awards as the result of a combination of factors, including the ease with which the law can be unintentionally violated and the ability to bring class action suits for the recovery of damages in Title VII violations. There is one other factor whose importance in the litigation of Title VII actions cannot be minimized: lawyers who intentionally look for areas of violation and then stimulate some of those people affected by the employer's practices that are in violation of the act into bringing lawsuits.

Those in the hospitality industry should be sharply aware of any situations that have even an air of violation about them and then move immediately to eliminate them. Areas in which to be extremely watchful are sex discrimination, equal pay, job assignment, grooming and appearance, seniority, the handicapped, use of conviction and arrest records, height-weight restrictions, age discrimination, and child labor.

Some of the landmark cases in this area are Griggs v. Dukes Power Company, 401 U.S. 424 (1971), involving promotion and transfer policy; United States v. Georgia Power, 474 F.2d 906 (1973), involving the requirement of a high school diploma and aptitude test scores; Albermarle Paper v. Moody, 422 U.S. 405 (1975), dealing with the necessity of any test being administered for the purpose of selecting or promoting employees; Washington v. Davis, 96 S.Ct. 2040 (1976), holding that a test that was job related was legal; and Bakke v. California, 98 S.Ct. 2733 (1978), that involved so-called reverse discrimination (a more qualified individual is denied an opportunity because he or she is not a member of a minority).

All acts of an employer directed toward the curtailment of certain activity that may affect only certain members of a minority does not make such action a violation of Title VII, however. In the case of Garcia v. Gloor, 618 F.2d 264 (1980), courts were faced with just such a problem. The defendant-employer operated a lumber and supply business in Brownsville, Texas. The plaintiff-employee was a native-born American

5   Civil Rights Act of 1964, as amended, 42 U.S.C. §§2000e–2000e (15).

of Mexican ancestry who spoke both English and Spanish. Thirty-one of the defendant's thirty-nine employees were of Hispanic heritage, and a Hispanic sat on the company's board of directors. Most, if not all, of the Hispanic employees spoke English and Spanish, and most spoke Spanish exclusively in their homes. Seventy-five percent of the population in the area where the business facility was located were of Hispanic background, as were most of the customers. The defendant employer had a rule that English was to be spoken at all times except when a customer wanted to speak Spanish, but communications between employees were to be in English at all times.

The plaintiff, admittedly, violated this rule at every opportunity. When the defendant fired him and cited as the reason for the discharge his violation of the rule, the plaintiff filed a complaint with the EEOC, which backed him in his allegation that the rule was violative of the EEO act and the Civil Rights Act of 1964. His claim was that the Spanish language is the most important aspect of ethnic identification for Mexican-Americans.

The court found that although the violation of the rule against speaking Spanish with fellow employees was not the only reason for the plaintiff's discharge, it was a primary one. The court went on to say that the forbidden conduct need not be the sole cause of the discharge in order to have a violation of the act. However, in this instance, the court found that the rule did not violate the statute. The court reasoned that the statute forbids discrimination in employment based on national origin, and that was not involved here. What was forbidden here was the language that a person chose to speak, and that is not national origin. The plaintiff claimed that his national origin determined his language preference; therefore, to deny him his preference and make him speak English discriminated against him because of national origin. The court responded by saying that the plaintiff was bilingual, and he deliberately chose to speak Spanish while at work. There is no authority to the effect that a person has the right to speak any particular language while at work unless they are imposed by statute.

Section 703e of Title VII recognizes that certain jobs must of necessity be performed by one of a particular sex, and to restrict the advertising for someone to fill the position to either males or females alone would not violate the law. An example is a model of clothes for only one sex.

The exceptions afforded under Section 703e were discussed in the case of Dothard v. Rawlinson, 97 S.Ct. 2720 (1977), and the court made it clear that the exception would be sparingly applied when it stated: "We are persuaded—by the restrictive language of Section 703e, the relevant legislative history, and the consistent interpretation of the Equal Employment Opportunity Commission—that the bfoq [bona fide occupational qualification] was in fact meant to be an extremely narrow exception to the general prohibition of discrimination on the basis of sex."

In view of the affirmation of this position by the U.S. Supreme Court, the guidelines of the EEOC establishing this as their guiding rule, and the adherence to this policy by all courts who have considered it, all managers are well advised to seek the counsel of the employer's attorney before making any decision to seek to limit the job availability to a certain sex or person possessed of certain race, color, religion, or national origin.

Life Safety: Emergency Planning

Any fire or threat in a hotel, motel, restaurant, or tavern can be major under certain conditions. To escape what could be a serious situation, every business should have a plan for emergencies. Each business has particular points that should be stressed.

An emergency may be unforeseen, but it calls for immediate trained response. Panic can nullify emergency plans unless one considers how to minimize a panic situation. Well-trained personnel and well-executed plans will do just this.

Bomb Threats

The indiscriminate placing of bombs in premises where people cluster and that are calculated to draw international attention creates a problem that all managers in the hospitality industry should be prepared to handle. The question of a bomb arises as the result of the occurrence of one of the following three events: A call or message is received that a bomb is going to be placed on the premises; a call or message is received that a bomb has already been placed on the premises; or a bomb is discovered on the premises. Actually, management should be alert to the problem all the time. They should alert personnel to observe any suspicious-looking items and check all unusual deliveries to the facility by verifying that the item being delivered was in fact ordered.

Managers never know whether a threat or message concerning a bomb is true, but they cannot afford to take a chance. Immediate and positive action is mandated, with the safety of the guests and employees being the paramount consideration. A bomb detection and procedure policy will instruct all personnel what to do and whom to notify in such a situation.

To demonstrate the seriousness of the situation and the tensions created when a bomb threat is received, let us look at an actual occurrence, which started with what appeared to be an innocent delivery. Purportedly, the delivery was to have been an IBM copy machine. It was 5:50 A.M., Tuesday, August 26, 1980. A white van with the letters IBM painted on it pulled up to Harvey's Resort Hotel Casino in Stateline, Nevada. Two men got out of the van and wheeled an object about four feet long by two feet tall by two feet wide, wrapped in a blanket upon which the letters IBM were also printed, into the casino and left it on the second floor, saying that it was an IBM copying machine that had been ordered. Delivered with the letter was a letter demanding the payment of $3 million for instructions on how to defuse the bomb. The letter advised against attempting to move the bomb or trying to neutralize it with gas or water because the bomb had been constructed so as to explode automatically if any such attempts were made. Efforts were made to deliver the money, but the extortionists failed to make contact as they had indicated they would. Consequently, the money was not delivered.

The authorities were immediately notified and the building was completely evacuated. The letter described the bomb's elaborate and complicated wiring of switches and warned that even the turning of a screw on the instrument would be sufficient to explode it. The letter went on to say that upon payment of the money, the extortionists would deliver instructions to the hotel with information about how to remove the bomb from the hotel and take it to a remote area where it could be detonated with safety.

After all precautions had been taken to preserve human life and safety, and it was apparent that communications had broken down with the extortionists, decisions had to be made as to what to do. Obviously the bomb could not be left where it was forever, for it remained a constant threat. Finally, a remote-control device was attached to the bomb to determine whether it could be safely tampered with. Apparently it could not, because on the afternoon of August 27, the bomb exploded, causing some $3 million worth of damage to Harvey's.

Within forty-eight hours of the blast, customers were coming back to the casino. Despite the damage to the hotel's casino, it appears as if the emergency had been well handled. All efforts were made to preserve the lives and safety of the people first. Then efforts were made to get the information that would minimize the risk of danger to the hotel property, as well as the area. When all else failed, efforts were made to eliminate the threat with the minimum amount of risk to the antibomb personnel and to the property. Whatever loss was incurred was not the result of the failure of the hotel people and the demolition squad to respond to the crisis as they should have.

In order to take precautions against possible disasters resulting from bomb threats, restaurateurs and innkeepers should devise a bomb plan procedure that is best for their particular property, bearing in mind all of the factors that are unique to their operation.

Emergency First Aid

If there is one circumstance that presents a real dilemma to hotel and restaurant owners or managers, it is what to do in a medical emergency. In all probability an attorney would advise them to do nothing but summon medical assistance. The reason is that in the absence of a Good Samaritan statute in the state, action of any type could expose the owner and the facility to a liability that could result in the payment of heavy damage judgments. Generally, the common law rule that applies to such situations is that there is no duty for a hotelier or restaurateur to come to the aid of a stricken person. In the absence of a duty, there can be no liability for failure to respond. However, the general rule has appended to it another rule: Anyone who voluntarily comes to the assistance of the injured or ill person has the duty to act in a nonnegligent manner or else can be held liable for the consequences. This liability does not just attach itself to the employees and managers of places of hospitality, but applies equally to any one who seeks to help the victim. That explains the scarcity of affirmative responses when the call rings out as to whether a doctor is nearby.

A growing movement within the law, however, wants to impose liability for failure to act, and it is starting to receive some support in certain jurisdictions. Those who advocate this theory reason that because of the quasi-public nature of hotels and restaurants, many of the concepts that created an affirmative duty to render assistance in limited cases at common law would be applicable to them. Even at common law, the law imposed an affirmative duty to render assistance because of the public nature of certain businesses, such as in the case of common carriers, which owe an insurer's degree of care. The common law also found affirmative duty to act if the relationship imposed upon the party required one to act. For example, a man has the duty to provide and care for his wife and/or child and see to it that they have the necessaries of life. If he sees his wife or child drowning, he is obliged by law to render them assistance as an extension of his duties to provide and care for them.

We find in the hotel industry and, to a lesser degree, in the restaurant industry that the guest is in a quasi-public place, and that situation could make the relationship somewhat comparable to that of a passenger on a public carrier. Also, the hotelier or the restaurateur similarly is in control of the premises as in the case of public carriers. In addition, the common law duties imposed on innkeepers by their guests demonstrate that the law demanded a great degree of concern for the care and safety of the guest. These greater duties were imposed upon the innkeeper for the express purpose of protecting the guest from harm while traveling. Again, it was the relationship that dictated duties greater than those required to nonguests. Therefore, it appears that there is a parallel between the innkeeper-guest relationship and the husband-wife or father-child relationship. By applying the implications of these analogies, we can readily see a pattern emerging from which a court could find a duty on the part of the innkeeper or restaurateur to render emergency assistance to a guest. Such a finding would not be a radical deviation from the judicial currents, and some courts have indicated a preparedness to so follow.

Therefore, innkeepers and restaurateurs should consult the company attorney to determine the status of the law in their locale and then get a position statement from the owner or party in charge of the property as to the course of conduct to be followed. If it is management's decision that no assistance be offered other than acting with dispatch to get those trained to handle medical emergencies, then there should be a definite procedure outlined and posted in several places so that the response of the employees will be immediate in expediting the summoning of help. Similarly, if the law mandates assistance be rendered or management has made a policy decision to render assistance, a procedural program should be developed and guides written directing the employees what they are to do. This information should be posted in conspicuous places, and copies of the plan should be distributed among the employees. Furthermore, it would be a good idea to arrange with either the American Red Cross or another medical training group to instruct at least some key employees in basic first aid and cardiopulmonary resuscitation. Work schedules should be arranged so that at least one or more of these trained personnel is on the premises at all times and readily available to render assistance.

Elevator Malfunction or Power Failure

Any major or minor power failure or even a simple mechanical problem can cause an elevator to malfunction. Good managers should prepare for the unexpected and have an emergency plan of action available for power failures and elevator malfunctions. Telephone numbers should be readily available of approved elevator mechanics, the police, fire department rescue squad, and hotel employees to be notified.

Because all elevators are not the same, each facility should have a copy of the elevator instruction book and owner's manual available for immediate use. In addition, managers should develop their own operation procedure based on the manufacturer's recommendations, as well as factors unique to their operation.

Security

One of the most volatile segments of the hospitality industry today concerns security. In this day of advanced technology, it is not going to be enough any longer to rely on the age-old lock and key system. Criminals are becoming more sophisticated in their methods; consequently, deterrent and preventive systems must progress accordingly. Crime, both violent and nonviolent, is on the increase, imposing the duty upon hotels to provide the degree of security that is commensurate with the exposure that exists to the guests. No one absolute standard will fit every property in the industry; rather, the security system must be tailor-made for each individual property.

Some may ask whether they can afford to put in the kind of security that would be needed to provide "adequate" protection to guests. The real question is whether they can afford not to. The new plastic cards that open doors to a precoded combination make it possible to change the lock combination after every guest leaves or if a guest loses a key-card. Will a property that does not install them be exposing itself to a liability? How about the dead-bolt lock that can be removed and a dummy put in its place? Would the failure to rivet the lock in place so that it could not be removed render the hotel liable? There are countless situations wherein all could agree that the security could have been a lot better, and if it was, loss or injury could have been prevented.

The hospitality industry presents a unique problem concerning security because so much that it could do to improve security is not compatible with guests' expectations of hospitality. Examples are closed-circuit observation of hallways and even of rooms that are supposed to be vacant and elaborate systems that require guests to disengage a secondary alarm switch with a special key. Guests often do not want to be concerned with their own security, especially if it imposes any effort upon them. They rationalize that they are guests, and it is the hotel's obligation to look out for their safety and protect both them and their property. So in matters of security, innkeepers may not only be concerned with the costs incidental to improving security at the hotel, but must also contend with guests' reluctance to be inconvenienced while being protected.

Every innkeeper should prepare security manuals to be distributed among all employees. These manuals should be tailor-made for the particular property involved, keeping in mind all the matters concerning security that are peculiar to the property.

Innkeepers should also have manuals prepared for all other life safety emergencies. These manuals should cover fires, riots, blackouts, malfunctions in elevators, and swimming pools.

Emergency procedures must be demonstrated not only to the employees but to the guests as well by establishing a practice of periodical drills. Guests may find such practice procedures bothersome, so some public relations work must be done to convince them that it is all for their own good. Perhaps you could relate to them an actual incident reported by two women whose employer had distributed a memorandum to employees concerning how to conduct themselves in the event of a hotel fire. The employer had elected to do this because of concern about his employees' safety while staying at hotels on company business. These two women were guests in a Las Vegas hotel where a fire occurred. Moreover, their room was located right in the heart of the fire. They did exactly what the article had instructed them to do, from opening the hall door to determine whether the fire was in their vicinity, as well as whether the smoke in the hallway made it impassable, to lying on the bathroom floor breathing through wet towels until they finally were rendered unconscious just before fire rescue teams arrived and saved them.

QUESTIONS FOR DISCUSSION

    1 What factors determine whether restaurateurs must report predetermined gratuities or service charges collected on behalf of their employees?

    2 In *Heelan* v. *Johns-Manville*, how might the supervisor's superiors have avoided the sexual harassment lawsuit initiated by Mary Heelan?

    3 When is a manager responsible for the acts of sexual harassment committed by employees? By nonemployees? How can hoteliers or restaurateurs help eliminate sexual harassment in the work place?

    4 Discuss the guidelines of the EEOC and of the U.S. Supreme Court in regard to job availability based on a particular sex, religion, and national origin or language.

    5 What precautions should hoteliers and restaurateurs take in being alert to the possibility of a bomb threat? For what other emergency situations is it critical that managers have predetermined safety procedures?

    6 How is the issue of security in the hospitality industry changing? What legal issues can you foresee as a result of such changes?

Glossary

Ab initio: "From the beginning" (Latin).

Abrogate: The destruction, ending, or annulling of a former law.

Absolute liability: See *strict liability.*

Accessory: A person who had some part in the crime without being present.

> *Accessory before the fact:* A person who, without being present, encourages or helps someone commit a crime.
>
> *Accessory after the fact:* A person who condones a crime by concealing it or the criminal.

Accord and satisfaction: Agreement to settle or compromise a claim and satisfactory payment of the amount agreed upon.

Action: A lawsuit.

Action ex delicto: "Action arising out of a tort" (Latin).

Act of God: A happening not controlled by the power of humans but rather from the direct, immediate, and exclusive operations of the forces of nature.

Actual notice: Notice expressly given to the person directly.

Additur: An increase provided by the courts to an award of damages to the plaintiff.

Adduce: To offer an example or a reason.

Adjudication: The court's formal recording of a judgment for one of the persons in the lawsuit.

Admissible evidence: Evidence that is allowed to be used by the triers of fact in a court proceeding.

Adversary system: Any system similar to that of the United States, Canada, or England where the judge makes the decisions between opposing parties and is not responsible to seek out evidence between the parties.

Adverse: Opposed to or against one's position or interest.

Affidavit: A written statement that has been sworn to before an officer who is permitted by law to administer such an oath.

Affirmative defense: A defense that introduces new matters which, even if the plaintiff's contentions are true, constitutes a defense to the complaint.

A fortiori: With a greater force; said of a conclusion which, as compared with some other, is even more certain or necessary.

Agency: A relationship that exists where one person acts for another.

Agency by estoppel: A situation in which an agent (deputy) of a principal exercises powers that were not actually granted to the agent.

Allegation: In pleading, that which a person will attempt to prove.

Allege: To assert before proving.

Alter ego doctrine: A doctrine that treats the corporation and those owning its stock as identical.

Alternative pleading: Alleges several substantial facts that make it difficult to determine which of the pleadings the person intends to rely on as a basis for recovery.

Amicus curiae: "Friend of the court" (Latin); usually one who is not a party to the lawsuit but is permitted to give to the court information that is in doubt or where the information would not be considered by the court, or when permitted by the court to advise it in respect to some matter of law that directly affects the case in question.

Annul: To cancel a relationship as if it never was.

Anticipatory breach: A breach committed before the arrival of the actual time of required performance.

Appeal: A case that is brought from a lower court to a higher court for rehearing, usually to obtain a review of possible errors by the lower court.

Appearance: The coming into court as a party plaintiff or defendant to a lawsuit.

Appellant: One who appeals from a judicial decision to a higher court.

Appellate court: A court with the authority to review the handling and decisions of a case tried in a lower court.

Appellee: The party in a case against whom an appeal is taken, generally the winner in the lower court.

Appreciation: An increase in value.

Appurtenance: Attached to something else.

Arguendo: Purely for the sake of argument, the parties assume something as true, whether false or true.

Arraigned: Brought before the court to hear and assume the charges and to plead guilty or not guilty.

Arrest: Deprive a person of liberty because of criminal charges or detain a person for some reason that may involve force.

Arrogate: Claim or take something without having any right to it; to usurp or appropriate as one's own.

Assault: Any supposed force that could be marshaled against a person so long as the person could reasonably believe a physical attack was imminent.

Assumpsit: An action of equitable character founded upon contract.

Attachment: A writ to seize (take and hold) by legal procedure.

Attempt to commit: An intent combined with an open act that moves beyond mere preparation.

Attractive nuisance: A doctrine in tort law that holds that one who maintains a condition or instrumentality that is dangerous to young children and that attracts them is under a duty to foresee such danger and protect the children, who are too young to understand and avoid danger.

Aver: To allege, assert, verify or justify as in a formal complaint.

Averment: A statement of the facts.

Baggage: That which a person travels with while on a journey, of short or long duration.

Bail: Valuables, usually money or property, that are put up for release of a person in jail.

Bailee: The person with whom property is entrusted.

Bailment: Property delivered by the owner to another person that must be given up when requested, usually within a short time.

Bailor: Person who gives over property to another.

Battery: The unlawful application of force to the person of another, either willfully or in anger.

Beneficiary: The receiver of some benefit or advantage from a trust.

Best evidence rule: A rule of evidence that requires the most persuasive evidence be used; original documents, not copies must be used.

Bill of exceptions: A written statement submitted to the trial court stating all objections made to the rulings of the trial judge, as well as any instructions given by the trial judge.

Blue laws: The Lord's Day law that forbids certain activities such as selling of certain goods on Sunday.

Boiler plate forms: A preprinted form for a document that is usually sold commercially and that is standardized without tailoring to individual legal problems.

Bona fide: "In good faith" (Latin).

Breach: The failure of performance by a party of some contracted-for or agreed-upon act.

Breach of contract: The nonperformance of an agreement without legal excuse.

Brief: A written statement of a person's case to be submitted to a court of law, usually including a summary of the law involved, a condensed statement of facts, and arguments of how the law applies to the facts.

Burden of proof: In civil cases, the proof must have a preponderance of the evidence; in criminal cases, the proof must be beyond a "reasonable doubt."

Burglary: The breaking and entering into the dwelling house of another at night with the intent to commit a felony therein.

Business judgment rule: The principle that bad results—if made in an honest, careful manner by the corporate powers—will not be interfered with by the courts.

"But for" rule: Primarily refers to the question, Would the accident or happening have occurred "but for" the negligence involved?

Case method or system: The study of actual cases (opinion of the court) and the drawing of a general legal principal based on other similar cases.

Cashier check: A prepaid check issued by a bank that authorizes payment of the stipulated sum of the check on demand to the payee.

Cause of action: The right to bring a suit.

Caveat: "Let him beware" (Latin); usually used with another word such as *emptor* ("buyer") expresses the general idea that the buyer purchased at his or her peril, and no warranties (expressed or implied) are included by the seller.

Certified check: A check containing a certification that funds are available for the amount of the check.

Certiorari: An appeal to a higher court but one that the court need not accept.

Chattels: Any property other than land; includes personal property and animals.

Check: A draft upon a bank and payable on demand, signed by the maker as an unconditional promise to pay a stated amount to the order of the payee.

Citator: A set of books (such as *Shepard's Citator*) that traces the history of a statute or case since it was passed or ruled on.

Civil action: A lawsuit brought by one person on another; action to protect a private remedy; civil right to procure a civil remedy or gain payment for a wrong.

Civil contempt: Usually the failure to do something that the court orders done for the benefit of another party.

Civil law: Law based on a code (such as the famous Code Napoleon) rather than on a combination of laws and judicial opinions.

Civil rights: Rights given to all citizens and defined by positive laws guaranteed by the U.S. Constitution generally defining limitations on governmental action.

Class action: A lawsuit brought by a group of persons who are similarly situated.

Clean hands doctrine: A doctrine that will not allow equitable relief to a person bringing a lawsuit who has been guilty of impropriety in the case.

Code: A compilation of laws such as the motor vehicle laws.

Cognizance: Right of a court to take action.

Cohabitation: Living together; often refers to an unmarried couple living together and having sexual intercourse.

Collusion: Action by two or more persons together for the purpose of committing a fraud.

Color semblance or appearance: Having the apparent authority of law or backed by laws but in fact is not.

Common carrier: One who transports for hire.

Common law: Law emanating from England based on custom and tradition.

Common law marriage: A marriage created by a couple publicly living together as married for a time period sufficient to create a legal marriage.

Common victualler: A keeper of a restaurant.

Comparative negligence: A proportional sharing between plaintiff and defendant of compensation for injuries, based on the relative negligence of each.

Compensatory damages: Award of damages for actual loss suffered by a plaintiff. (Compare with *punitive damages.*)

Complainant: The originator of a lawsuit; the plaintiff.

Complaint: The initial paper filed in court in a civil lawsuit consisting of a statement of the wrong or harm done to the plaintiff by the defendant and a request for specific help from the court.

Conclusion of law: Application of a rule of law to a set of facts.

Condition precedent: A right or obligation created if a certain future event happens.

Condition subsequent: A right or obligation ended if a certain future event happens.

Condominium: A form of separate ownership of individual units in a multiunit development where parts of the development are owned as tenants in common.

Confession judgment: A method of permitting a judgment to be entered against a person in advance of his default on his debt, for a stipulated sum, without the formality, time, or expense of an ordinary legal proceeding.

Conflicts of law: Antagonism that exists between different laws of the same state or sovereignty upon the same subject matter; or when a choice exists between laws of more than one state, in which case the judge makes the decision as to applicable law.

Consanguinity: Blood relationship, kinship.

Consent: To agree.

Consideration: A matter of contract wherein one party agrees to do something in return for something the other party agrees to give them, such as money, goods, property, a promise, and so forth.

Consortium: The right of a married couple to each other's love and services.

Constitutional: Any law decree or court ruling not inconsistent or in conflict with the fundamental law of the state or country.

Constructive: The opposite of actual wherein a law is accepted as a substitute for what is otherwise required.

Constructive notice: Information or knowledge of a fact imputed to a person by law because he or she could have discovered the fact by proper diligence or because the situation was such as to put upon such person the duty of inquiry.

Contempt: Any action by a person or persons to obstruct a court's work or lessen the dignity of the court—for example, disobeying a court order or an official of the court.

Contract: An agreement between two or more persons, legally constituted, for which the court gives a remedy for breach of its provisions.

Conversion: Action that deprives owners of property that legally belongs to them.

Corporate veil: An assumption that all action by the corporation is not that of the owners and therefore not impugned to the corporate officers.

Corporation: An organization that is formed under state or federal law and exists, for legal purposes, as a separate being or an "artificial person."

Corpus delicti: "Body of the crime" (Latin); facts that prove a crime has been committed.

Court: The place where judges work.

The court: refers to action taken by the administrative body of the government to redress a wrong or prevent a wrong or injustice.

Criminal contempt: Acts of disrespect of the courts or its process.

Damages: Money that a court orders paid to a person who has suffered a loss or injury by the person whose fault caused it.

Declaratory relief: Establishes the rights of the parties or expresses the opinion of the court on a question of law without ordering anything to be done.

Decree: A judgment by a court as to its decision on the facts of the case; the power of the court derived from its equity jurisdiction.

Defamation: Injuring a person's character or reputation by false and malicious statements, including libel and slander.

Defendant: One who is sued either in a civil or criminal action; the person against whom the legal action is brought.

Defenestration: Throwing something or someone out of a window.

Defraud: To cheat.

Demeanor: Physical appearance and behavior.

De minimus: Insignificant, minute, or frivolous.

Demise: A term used to describe a conveyance of an estate in real property.

Demurrer: A method of pleading.

Derogation: Partial taking away of the effectiveness of a law; to repeal partially or abolish a law.

Diversity of action or citizenship: Takes place in a federal rather than state court when the plaintiff is a resident of one state and the defendant is a resident of another.

Doctrine of apparent authority: Authority granted by principals to agents to act in their behalf.

Effects: Personal property; in hotel law usually refers to a traveler's baggage.

Enjoin: Require or command; a court's issuing of an injunction directing a person or persons to do, or more likely, to refrain from doing certain acts; to restrain.

Entity: A real being; a separate existence.

Equitable estoppel: Where one of two innocent persons must suffer, the one who made possible the loss must bear the burden.

Equitable relief: Legal action in the court of equity that is just, fair, and right for a particular situation.

Equity court: A court having authority over cases involving various rights or matters of equity rather than matters of the written laws or statutes.

Eschew: To abstain from or shun as something wrong or distasteful.

Escrow: A written instrument deposited with a neutral third party.

Estoppel: A bar to alleging or denying a fact because of one's previous actions or words to the contrary.

Estray: Anything out of its normal place.

Exclusionary rule: A law that prohibits the use in trial of evidence obtained by search and seizure and consequently in violation of a person's Fourth Amendment right.

Ex contractu: "From" or "out of a contract" (Latin).

Exemplary damages: The terms exemplary, punitive, and vindictive damages are synonymous.

Ex parte: "With only one side present" (Latin).

Feasance: Performing a duty; doing an act.

Fee: An inheritance without any limitation placed on it.

Felony: A crime that has a sentence over one year or more; a serious crime.

Forbearance: Refraining from action; not doing something one has a right to do; holding off demanding something one has a right to demand.

Forum: "Court" (Latin).

Forum non conveniens: "Inconvenient court" (Latin).

Franchise: A business arrangement in which a person buys the rights to a name and to sell or rent the products or services of the company.

Full faith and credit: The constitutional requirement that each state must treat as valid, and enforce where appropriate, the laws and court decisions of other states.

Gratuities: Something given voluntarily or beyond obligation.

Gravamen: The essence of a complaint.

Hung jury: A jury that cannot unanimously decide on a verdict, thereby causing a mistrial.

Impute: To assign to a person or other entity the legal responsibility for the act of another, because of the relationship between the person so made liable and the actor, rather than because of actual participation in or knowledge of the act.

In accordance with: In agreement with or following a specific rule or act.

Infra: "Below," "beneath" (Latin); refers to something appearing subsequently in a text.

Infra hospitium: "Within the walls of the inn" (Latin); a legal concept that holds the hotel answerable for the loss of guests' goods when the guests are not within the hotel proper and for accidents and security of guests when in the property of a hotel.

Infra hospitium causa hospitandi: "Such property as the guest has with him for the purposes of his journey and is necessarily incident to his travel" (Latin).

Injunction: A writ commonly used by courts of equity as incident to enforcement of its commands or decrees.

Inter alia: "Among other things" (Latin).

In toto: "In entirety," "in total" (Latin).

Ipso facto: "By the fact itself," "in and of itself" (Latin).

Jurisdiction: Geographical area within which a court has the right and power to operate.

Larceny: Stealing of any kind; petit larceny is usually under $100, grand larceny over $100.

Law court: A court that administers justice according to the rules and practice of the common law but that has no powers dealing with equitable problems.

Lessee: A person who leases or rents something from someone; a tenant.

Lessor: Person who leases or rents land or a building to another person.

Liable: When a person is responsible for something, be it harm to another person or things.

Libel: Written defamation that injures a person's reputation.

Licensee: A person who enters the land with the occupier's permission but only for purposes not connected with the occupier's interests.

Lien: A charge or obligation due or owing against real or personal property for the satisfaction or arising by operation of law.

Long-arm statute: A state law that allows the courts of that state to claim jurisdiction over persons or property outside the state.

Magistrate: A judge with limited power.

Malfeasance: Wrongdoing; sometimes doing an illegal act by a public official.

Minor: A person under the legal age.

Misdemeanor: A criminal offense less than a felony that is usually punishable by a fine or less than a year in jail.

Misfeasance: Doing something wrong.

Mrs. Murphy's boarding house clause: A stipulation that an establishment that has five or fewer rooms for rent and that is actually occupied by the proprietor is excluded from the Civil Rights Act of 1964.

Mutuality of contract: A principle of law that says each side must do something or promise to do something to make a contract binding and valid.

Negligence: The failure to exercise a reasonable or ordinary amount of care in a situation that causes harm to someone or something.

Negligent: Failure to conform to the standard of care imposed by law.

Nonfeasance: Failure to perform a required duty.

Non obstante veredicto: "Notwithstanding the verdict" (Latin); a judge's giving judgment (victory) to one side in a lawsuit even though the jury gave a verdict (victory) to the other side.

Novation: The substitution of another party for one of the original parties to a contract with the consent of the remaining party.

Noxious trades: Harmful or morally corrupting.

Nuisance: Anything that annoys or disturbs unreasonably one's right to enjoy one's property, or violates the public health, safety, or decency of others.

Ordinance: A local or city law; rule or regulation as passed by the officials of a town, city, or other municipality.

Overwhelming force: Force majeur, act of God.

Per diem: "For each day" (Latin).

Per se: "In and of itself," "by itself" (Latin).

Personal service of process: The direct hand-to-hand delivery of a summons to the person being summoned.

Persona non grata: A person not acceptable.

Petitioner: Same as *plaintiff*.

Plaintiff: A person who starts a lawsuit against another person.

Plain view exception: The mere observation of objects in plain view, as opposed to a search to observe that which is open to view, does not constitute an illegal search.

Preamble: Usually introductory comments explaining why a document was written.

Prima facie: Such as will suffice until contradicted and overcome by other evidence.

Privity: Private or inside knowledge or a close, direct financial relationship.

Probable cause: Reasonable grounds for suspicion supported by circumstances sufficient to warrant an ordinarily prudent person reason to believe the accused is guilty of the offense.

Procedural law: Rules of carrying out the lawsuit and the way to enforce rights in court such as laws of pleading, evidence, and jurisdiction.

Promulgate: Publish; to announce officially.

Proximate cause: The real cause of an accident or other injury.

Punitive damages: Awarded in the nature of a punishment, not to enrich the injured party, but for public good.

Pursuant: In accordance with; usually refers to a person's right to do something.

Quantum meruit: As much as one deserved.

Ratification: Confirmation of a previous act done by you or by another person.

Reasonable: Not excessive or extreme.

Rebuttable presumption: A conclusion that will be drawn unless facts or arguments are raised to counter it.

Register: In a hotel, to make oneself known by putting down one's name; book or cards used to keep track of guests.

Reinstate: To put a case back on the calendar.

Remand: To send back; a higher court usually remands a case back to a lower court for action.

Remedial statute: A law, the purpose of which is to correct an existing law that is not working or that has caused harm instead of good.

Remuneration: To pay an equal amount for; to be recompensed.

Replevin: An action in law to get back personal property in the hands of another person.

Reprisal: To take action against.

Res ipsa loquitur: "The thing speaks for itself" (Latin); rebuttable presumption that a person is negligent if the thing causing an accident was in his control only, and that type of accident does not usually happen without negligence.

Res judicata: "A thing decided" (Latin); when a case is decided by the courts, the subject of that case is firmly and finally decided between the persons involved in the suit, therefore no further lawsuit on the same subject may be brought by the persons involved.

Respondent: The party against whom an appeal is brought; the party could have been the plaintiff or defendant in a lower court.

Respondeat superior: "Let the master answer" (Latin); a legal rule that an employer is responsible for the actions of an employee done in the course of employment.

Revocation: To end; to withdraw power or authority.

Riparian rights: Rights of a person owning land bordering on a body of water.

Secular day: A nonreligious day.

Service of process: Formally notifying the defendants of the impending lawsuit by the plaintiff.

Shepardization: A method by which statutes or legal cases are updated to see whether they have been modified or overruled by court decisions or legislature; discovering the present status of a statutory law, court decisions, or administrative decisions.

Slander: An oral defamation injuring one's character or reputation; words falsely spoken.

Stare decisis: When a principle of law has been established by a court of competent jurisdiction, it becomes settled and binding upon the state courts and should be followed in similar cases.

Statute: A law passed by a legislature.

Strict liability: The legal responsibility for damages or injury even if one is not at fault or negligent.

Sub judice: "Under a court" (Latin); before a court or judge for consideration.

Subpoena: An order by a court for a person to appear in court to testify in a case.

Subrogation: The substitution of one person for another in claiming a lawful right or debt.

Sub silentio: "Under silence" (Latin); without any notice being taken.

Substantive law: The basic law of rights and duties as opposed to procedural law; for example, contract law, criminal law, accident law, and laws of wills and real estate.

Subterfuge: Deception; to evade.

Summary judgment: Determination of whether an issue of fact exists.

Supra: "Above" (Latin); in a written work, refers readers to a previous section.

Surety: One who undertakes or guarantees to pay the debt of another in the event the debt is not paid.

Surrogate: A judicial officer of limited jurisdiction in probate and in some adoptions; one who acts for another.

Tavern: A place where alcoholic beverages are sold to be drunk on the premises.

Tenancy: A person's right to possess or hold an estate whether by lease or by title.

Joint tenancy: A single estate in property, real or personal, owned by two or more persons, under one legal paper and having equal rights in everything to share during their lives.

Tenancy at sufferage: A tenancy whereby one is in lawful possession of a lease and subsequently holds over beyond the end of one's expired lease without lawful authority.

Tenancy at will: A right of possession that arises by an express contract or by implication for an indefinite time such as is agreed upon by both parties.

Tenancy by the entirety: Ownership by husband and wife.

Tenancy in common: The possession of property by two or more people wherein each party possesses an undivided interest in the entire property.

Time sharing: A joint ownership of property that unites, combines, or joins together in unity of interest or liability; participated in or used by two or more; held or shared in common.

Tort: A wrong done to another person.

Tortious: Wrongful.

Transient: Passing through with only a brief stay.

Ultra vires: "Beyond," "outside," "in excess or powers" (Latin).

Underseal: A signed document that attests it was made in a most formal manner by a particular sign attached that imports consideration as a necessary part of a valid contract.

Uniform standards: Regular; even; applying generally to all equally.

Unitary rule: A rule that extends coverage to all major and minor aspects of any business enterprise that serves separately identifiable functions.

Variance: A difference between what is alleged in pleading and what is actually proved in trial; official permission to use land or buildings in a way that would otherwise violate the zoning regulations for the area.

Victualler: A keeper of a restaurant.

Violation: Not in accordance with.

Vis major: An irresistible force or a natural disaster.

Vitiate: Cause to fail; destroy the legal effect or binding force of something.

Volenti non fit injuria: "The volunteer suffers no wrong" (Latin); for example, a person who has consented to the activity that caused harm, cannot turn around and sue for damages.

Withhold: To hold back; refrain.

Writ of attachment: The act of taking or seizing property of persons in order to bring them under the control of the court.

Appendixes

APPENDIX 1: Limiting Liability Statutes by States

State	Provide a Safe	Post Notice	Statutory Limitation	Statute
Alabama	yes	yes	$300	§34–15–12
Alaska	yes	yes	$300	08.56.050
Arizona	yes	yes	$500	33–302
Arkansas	yes	yes	$300	71–1107
California	yes	yes	$500	§1859
Colorado	yes	yes	$5,000	12–44–105
Connecticut	yes	yes	$500	44–2
Delaware	yes	yes	Total	24–1502
Florida	yes	yes	$1,000	509.111
Georgia	yes	yes	$100	52–111
Hawaii	yes	yes	$500	507–9; 486 K–4
Idaho	yes	yes	$500	39–1823
Illinois	yes	yes	$500	71–1
Indiana	yes	yes	$600	32–8–17–2
Iowa	yes	yes	$100	105.1
Kansas	yes	yes	$250	36–402
Kentucky	yes	yes	$300	306.020
Louisiana	yes	yes	$100	§2971–2066 et al
Maine	yes	yes	$300	30–2901
Maryland	yes	yes	$300	71–3
Massachusetts	yes	yes	$1,000	140–10
Michigan	yes	yes	$250	427.101, 18–311
Minnesota	yes	yes	$300	327.01
Mississippi	yes	yes	$500	75–73–5
Missouri	yes	yes	none given	419.020
Montana	yes	yes	$500	70–6–501
Nebraska	yes	yes	$300	41–122
Nevada	yes	yes	$750	651.010
New Hampshire	yes	yes	$1,000	Ch.353:1
New Jersey	yes	yes	$500	2A:44–50, 29:2–2
New Mexico	yes	yes	$1,000	49–6–1, 57–6–1
New York	yes	yes	$500	12–200
North Carolina	yes	yes	$500	72–6
North Dakota	yes	yes	$300	60–01–29
Ohio	yes	yes	$500	4721.02
Oklahoma	yes	yes	$300	15–503a
Oregon	yes	yes	$300	699.010
Pennsylvania	yes	yes	none given	37, §61
Rhode Island	yes	yes	$500	5–14–1

APPENDIX 1: Continued

State	Provide a Safe	Post Notice	Statutory Limitation	Statute
South Carolina	yes	yes	$300	45–1–40
South Dakota	yes	yes	$300	43–40–1
Tennessee	yes	yes	$300	62–703
Texas	yes	yes	$50	73–4592
Utah	yes	yes	$250	29–1–2
Vermont	yes	yes	$300	§9–3141
Virginia	yes	yes	$500	35–10
Washington	yes	yes	$1,000	19.48.030
West Virginia	yes	yes	$250	16–6–22
Wisconsin	yes	yes	$300	160.31
Wyoming	yes	yes	none given	33–17–101
Puerto Rico	yes	yes	$500	35–712
Virgin Islands	yes	yes	$200	13–402
Washington, D.C.	yes	yes	$1,000	34–106

APPENDIX 2: State Positions on Third-Party Liability for Sales to Intoxicated Persons or Minors

State, Citation, Statute, Date	Dram Shop States	Limited Dram Shop States	Recovery under Common Law	No Recovery under Common Law
Alabama Maples v. Chinese Palace 389 So.2d 120 (1980) Alabama Code 6, 6–5–71	X			
Alaska Alesna v. LeGrue 614 P.2d 1387 (1980)			X	
Arizona Lewis v. Wolf 596 P.2d 705 (1979)				X
Arkansas Carr v. Turner 385 S.W.2d 656 (1965)				X
California Gonzales v. United States 589 F.2d 465 (1979) Cory v. Shierloh 166 Cal.Rptr. 544 (1980)				X
Colorado Kerby v. Flamingo Club 532 P.2d 975 (1974) Hull v. Rund 374 P.2d 351 (1963) 13–21–103		X	X	
Connecticut Sanders v. Officers Club of Conn. 397 A.2d 122 (1978) Conn. Gen. Stat. Ann. *30–102	X			
Delaware Taylor v. Ruiz 394 A.2d 765 (1978) 4 Del.C. §711		X	X	
District of Columbia Cartwright v. Hyatt Corporation 460 F.Supp. 80 (1978)			X	
Florida Bryant v. Jax Liquors 352 So.2d 542 (1977)			X	

APPENDIX 2: Continued

State, Citation, Statute, Date	Dram Shop States	Limited Dram Shop States	Recovery under Common Law	No Recovery under Common Law
Davis v. Sheappacoosee 155 So.2d 365 (1963) Stanage v. Bilbo 382 So.2d 423 (1980)				
Georgia Keaton v. Kroger Company 237 S.E.2d 443 (1977) Keaton v. Fenton 249 S.E.2d 629 (1978)				X
Hawaii Ono v. Applegate 612 P.2d 533 (1980) HRS §281–78(a) (2)B		X	X	
Idaho Alegria v. Payonk 619 P.2d 135 (1980)			X	
Illinois Parsons v. Veterans of Foreign Wars Post 408 N.E.2d 68 (1980) Illinois Ann Stat Ch.43 * 135	X			
Indiana Parrett v. Lebamoff 408 N.E.2d 1344 (1980) 7.1–5–7–8 & 7.1–5–10–15 (1976)	X		X	
Iowa Ehlinger v. Mardorf 285 N.W.2d 27 (1979) Iowa Code Ann *123.92	X			
Kansas Stringer v. Calmes 205 P.2d 921 (1949)				X
Kentucky Pike v. George 434 S.W.2d 626 (1968)				X
Louisiana Thrasher v. Leggett 373 S.E.2d 494 (1979)				X
Maine Marston v. Merchants Mutual Ins. Co. 319 A.2d 111 (1974) Maine Rev Stat Ann 17*2002	X			

APPENDIX 2: Continued

State, Citation, Statute, Date	Dram Shop States	Limited Dram Shop States	Recovery under Common Law	No Recovery under Common Law
Maryland State v. Hatfield 78 A.2d 754 (1951)				X
Massachusetts Wiska v. St. Stanixlaus 390 N.E.2d 1133 (1979)			X	
Michigan Putney v. Gibson 289 N.W.2d 837 (1980) Michigan Comp Laws Ann *436.22	X			
Minnesota Hannah v. Jensen 298 N.W.2d 52 (1980) Minnesota Stat * 340.95	X			
Mississippi Munford v. Peterson 368 So.2d 213 (1979)				X
Missouri Alsup v. Garvin-Wienke 579 F.2d 461 (1978)				X
Montana Deeds v. United States 306 F.Supp. 348 (1969)			X	
Nebraska Holmes v. Circo 244 N.W.2d 65 (1976)				X
Nevada Davies v. Butler 602 P.2d 605 (1979) Hamm v. Carson City Nugget Inc. 450 P.2d 358 (1969) Nev. Rev Statutes 202.070 (1967)		X		X
New Hampshire Benevolent Protective Order of Elks v. Hanover Ins. Co. 266 A.2d 846 (1970) Ramsey v. Anctil 211 A.2d 900			X	
New Jersey Young v. Gilbert 296 A.2d 87 (1972)			X	

APPENDIX 2: Continued

State, Citation, Statute, Date	Dram Shop States	Limited Dram Shop States	Recovery under Common Law	No Recovery under Common Law
New Mexico Marchiondo v. Roper 563 P.2d 1160 (1977)				X
New York Gabrielle v. Craft 428 N.Y.S.2d 84 (1980) New York Gen Oblig Law*11–101	X			
North Dakota Feuerherm v. Ertelt 286 N.W.2d 509 (1979) North Dakota Cent Code*5–01–06	X			
Ohio Mason v. Roberts 294 N.E.2d 884 (1973) Ohio Rev Code Ann *4399.01	X			
Oregon Miller v. City of Portland 604 P.2d 1261 (1980) Campbell v. Carpenter 566 P.2d 893 (1977) Oregon Rev. Stat 30:730 (1969)		X	X	
Oklahoma Ch.1 37.121	X			
Pennsylvania Couts v. Ghion 421 A.2d 1184 (1980) Majors v. Broodhead Hotel 205 A.2d 873 (1965) Bradshaw v. Rawlings 612 F.2d 135 (1979)			X	
South Dakota Griffin v. Sebek 245 N.W.2d 481 (1976)				X
Tennessee Mitchell v. Ketner 393 S.W.2d 755 (1964)			X	
Vermont Sykas v. Kearns 383 A.2d 621 (1978) Vermont Stat Ann 7 * 501	X			

APPENDIX 2: Continued

State, Citation, Statute, Date	Dram Shop States	Limited Dram Shop States	Recovery under Common Law	No Recovery under Common Law
Washington Shelby v. Keck 541 P.2d 365 (1975) Washington Rev. Code 71.08.080		X	X	
West Virginia Duckworth v. Stalnaker 81 S.@. 989 (1914) West Virginia Code 1142 (60–3–22)	X			
Wisconsin Olsen v. Copeland 280 N.W.2d 178 (1979) Wisconsin Stat Ann 176.35 (1957)		X		X
Wyoming Parsons v. Jow 480 P.2d 396 (1971) Wyoming Stat Ann 12.34 (1957)		X		X

APPENDIX 3: State Statutes Dealing with Defrauding an Innkeeper

Ala. Code 34–15–18, 34–15–19, 34–15–20.
Alaska Stat. § 11.20.480 (1962).
Ariz.Rev.Stat. §§ 13–1801, 13–1802 (1978).
Ark.Stat.Ann. § 41.2204 (Acts 1975).
Cal.Penal Code § 537 (West 1979 amendment).
Colo.Rev.Stat. §§ 12–44–101, 12–44–102 (1973).
Conn.Gen.Stat. § 53a–119(7) (Revised 1979).
Del.Code Ann. tit. 11, §§ 841, 845 (1974).
D.C.Code § 22–1301(b)(1) (1973).
Fla.Stat.Ann. §§ 509.151, 509.161 (West 1972).
Ga.Code Ann. §§ 26–1807, 26–1812 (1977).
Haw.Rev.Stat. §§ 708–830, 708–831 (1976).
Idaho Code §§ 18–3107, 18–3108 (1979).
Ill.Rev.Stat. ch. 71 ¶¶ 4a, 4b (1979).
Ind.Code § 35–17–5–6(1), (3) (1976).
Iowa Code §§ 714.1, 714.2 (1979).
Kan.Stat.Ann. §§ 36–206, 36–207 (1973).
Ky.Rev.Stat.Ann. § 514.060 (Baldwin 1975).
La.Rev.Stat.Ann. § 21.21(1) (West 1979).
Md.Code Ann. Art. 27, §§ 340, 342 (Supp.1979).
Mass.Ann.Laws ch. 140, § 12 (Michie/Law.Co-op 1977).
Mich.Comp.Laws Ann. §§ 750.291, 750.292 (1968).
Minn.Stat. §§ 327.07, 327.08 (1978).
Miss.Code Ann. §§ 75–73–9, 75–73–11 (1972).
Mo.Rev.Stat. §§ 570.010(12), 570.020, 570.030 (1978).
Mont.Code Ann. § 45–6–305 (1979).
Neb.Rev.Stat. §§ 41–127, 41–127.01, 41–128 (1978).
Nev.Rev.Stat. § 205.445 (1957).
N.H.Rev.Stat.Ann. §§ 353:7–353:10 (Supp.1979).
N.J.Stat.Ann. § 2C:20–8 (1979).
N.M.Stat.Ann. § 30–16–16 (1978).
N.Y.Penal Law § 165.15 (McKinney 1975).
N.C.Gen.Stat. § 14–110 (1969).
N.D.Cent.Code §§ 12.1–23–03, 12.1–23–05 (1976).
Ohio Rev.Code Ann. § 2913.41 (1975).
Okla.Stat. tit. 21, § 1503 (1971).
Or.Rev.Stat. § 164.125 (1977).
Pa.Cons.Stat.Ann. tit. 18, § 3926 (Purdon Supp.1978).
R.I.Gen.Laws § 11–18–26 (1956).
S.C.Code §§ 45–1–50, 45–1–60, 45–1–70 (1976).
S.D.Codified Laws §§ 22–1–2(41), 22–30A–8, 22–30A–17 (1979).
Tenn.Code Ann. § 62–707 (1976).
Tex.Penal Code Ann. tit. 7, § 31.04 (Vernon 1974).
Utah Code Ann. § 76–6–409 (Amend. 1973).

APPENDIX 3: Continued

Vt.Stat.Ann. tit. 13, § 2582 (1974).
Va.Code § 18.2–188 (Supp.1980).
Wash.Rev.Code § 19.48.110 (1979).
W.Va.Code § 61–3–40 (1977).
Wis.Stat. § 943.21 (1977).
Wyo.Stat. §§ 6–7–501, 6–7–502 (1977).

APPENDIX 4: Guidelines on Discrimination Because of Sex

(Excerpted from the Federal Register, Vol. 45, No. 219, 29 CFR Chapter XIV Section 1604.11 Sexual Harassment, Promulgated 10 November 1980)

a Harassment on the basis of sex is a violation of Sec. 703 of Title VII. Unwelcome sexual advances, requests for sexual favors, and other verbal or physical conduct of a sexual nature constitute sexual harassment when (1) submission to such conduct is made either explicitly or implicitly a term or condition of an individual's employment, (2) submission to or rejection of such conduct by an individual is used as a basis for employment decision affecting such individual, or (3) such conduct has the purpose or effect of unreasonably interfering with an individual's work performance or creating an intimidating, hostile or offensive working environment.

b In determining whether alleged conduct constitutes sexual harassment, the commission will look at the records as a whole and at the totality of the circumstances, such as the nature of the sexual advances and the context in which the alleged incidents occurred. The determination of the legality of a particular action will be made from the facts, on a case by case basis.

c Applying general Title VII principles, an employer, employment agency, joint apprenticeship committee, or labor organization (hereinafter collectively referred to as "employer") is responsible for its acts and those of its agents and supervisory employees with respect to sexual harassment regardless of whether the specific acts complained of were authorized or even forbidden by the employer and regardless of whether the employer knew or should have known of their occurrence. The commission will examine the circumstances of the particular employment relationship and the job functions performed by the individual in determining whether an individual acts in either a supervisory or agency capacity.

d With respect to conduct between fellow employees, an employer is responsible for acts of sexual harassment in the workplace where the employer (or its agents or supervisory employees) knows or should have known of the conduct, unless it can show that it took immediate and appropriate corrective action.

e An employer may also be responsible for the acts of nonemployees, with respect to sexual harassment of employees in the workplace, where the employer (or its agents or supervisory employees) knows or should have known of the conduct and fails to take immediate and appropriate corrective action. In reviewing these cases the commission will consider the extent of the employer's control and any other legal responsibility which the employer may have with respect to the conduct of such nonemployees.

   f Prevention is the best tool for the elimination of sexual harassment. An employer should take all steps necessary to prevent sexual harassment from occurring, such as affirmatively raising the subject, expressing strong disapproval, developing appropriate sanctions, informing employees of their right to raise and how to raise the issue of harassment under Title VII, and developing methods to sensitize all concerned.

   g Other related practices: Where employment opportunities or benefits are granted because of an individual's submission to the employer's sexual advances or requests for sexual favors, the employer may be held liable for unlawful sex discrimination against other persons who were qualified for but denied employment opportunity or benefit.

Model Program Dealing with Sexual Harassment

(Excerpted from the National Labor Relations Board Policy, Administrative Policy Circular APC 80–2, issued February 21, 1980)

Sexual harassment is a form of employee misconduct that undermines the integrity of the employment relationship. All employees must be allowed to work in an environment free from unsolicited and unwelcome sexual overtures. Sexual harassment does not refer to occasional compliments. It refers to behavior that is not welcome, that is personally offensive, that debilitates morale and that therefore interferes with the work effectiveness of its victims and their co-workers. Sexual harassment may include actions such as: sex-oriented verbal "kidding" or abuse; subtle pressure for sexual activity; physical contact such as patting, pinching or constant brushing against another's body; demands for sexual favors, accompanied by implied or overt promises of preferential treatment or threats concerning an individual's employment status.

Sexual harassment is a prohibited personnel practice when it results in discrimination for or against an employee on the basis of conduct not related to work performance, such as the taking or refusal to take a personnel action, including promotion of employees who submit to sexual advances or refusal to promote employees who resist or protest sexual overtures.

Complaints of sexual harassment involving misuse of one's official position should be made orally or in writing to a higher-level supervisor, to an appropriate personnel official, or to anyone authorized to deal with discrimination complaints (EEO counselor, union official, for example).

Because of differences in employees' values and backgrounds, some individuals may find it difficult to recognize their own behavior as sexual harassment. To create an awareness of office conduct that may be construed as sexual harassment, we will incorporate sexual harassment awareness training in future managerial, supervisory, EEO, employee orientation, and other appropriate training courses. Additionally, a copy of this policy will be placed in each new employee orientation kit.

Index

Unfair competition, 112–24
Uniform Commercial Code (UCC), 496, 497–98, 501, 535
Unitary rule, **162**
United States v. Beach Associates, Inc., 159
United States v. Cantrell, 161
United States v. Carolene Products Company, 91
United States v. Cowan, 275
United States v. Georgia Power, 622
United States v. Gray, 159
United States v. Hilton Hotel Corporation, 105–9
U.S. v. Medical Society of South Carolina, 160–61
United States v. Rabinowitz, 552
United States v. Richberg, 164, 165
United States Code Annotated (U.S.C.A.), 12, 13
United States Code Congressional and Administrative News, 13
United States Constitution. See Constitution, U.S.
United States Reports, 13
United States Supreme Court Digest, 14
Unmarried couples, registration of, 76, 126, 143, 475
Unofficial sources of legal material, 14–16
Unreasonable class legislation, 88–89
Upthegrove v. Meyers et al., 513–14
Uston v. Airport Casino, Inc., 163
Uston v. Grand Resorts, Inc., 163
Uston v. Hilton Casinos, Inc., 163
Uston v. Resorts Int'l. Hotel, Inc., 163
Utility rates, of trailer parks, 553–56, 560

Vale v. Yawarski, 523–24, 529
Valuables, 384; disclosure of value and, 396, 397–99, 399–402; hotel liability for, 403–5; lien and, 484; restaurant liability for, 538–39; in safe, 389, 402–3, 455; stub for, 455–57. See also Baggage; Jewelry.
Vancherie v. Siperly, 531–33
Verdict: judgment notwithstanding the, **27**, 29; of the jury, 27
Vesely v. Sager, 507
Victimless crimes, immoral acts in hotels and, 91–93
Visitors of guests, rights of, 282–84
Vogel v. Eckert, 294
Volenti non fit injuria, 199
Voluntary tort, **187**

Von der Heide v. Zoning Board of Appeals, 109–10

Wading pool, glass in, 348
Wagoner v. State, 487–88
Walk-in, **242**
Wallace v. Shoreham Hotel Corporation, 149–51, 159
Walling v. Potter, 56
Walls v. Cosmopolitan Hotels, Inc., 403
Walters v. Gerard, 484
Walton Playboy Clubs, Inc. v. City of Chicago, 164
Warrant: bypassing for a room search, 272–73; inspection and, 93
Warren v. Penn-Harris Hotel Company, 76, 475
Warsaw Convention, 565–78
Washington v. Davis, 623
Water faucets, injuries to guests and, 371–72
Watson v. Cross, 485
Waugh v. Duke Corporation, 352
Weapons. See Firearms.
Webster v. Blue Ship Tea Room, Inc., 498–501, 535–36
Weinberg v. D-M Restaurant Corporation, 434
Weinberg v. Wayco Petroleum Co., 430–31
Weiser v. Albuquerque Oil and Gasoline Company, 52
Wellsboro Hotel Company's Appeal, 34, 75
Wholesomeness of food, 496–97, 498–503, 535–36
Widen v. Warren Hotel, 397
William Reilly Construction Corp. v. City of New York, 124
Williams v. Klemesrud, 510
Williams v. Milner Hotel Company, 303–4
Wills v. Trans World Airlines, Inc., 251
Wilson v. Benoit, 303
Wilson v. Halprin, 397
Windows, injuries to guests from, 302–3, 372. See also Glass.
Wise v. Roger Givins, Inc., 203
Withrow v. Woozencraft, 336–37
Wolf Hotel v. Parker, 382
Women: as bartenders, 533–34, 535; contracts by, 255; liens on husband and, 485
Wood v. Holiday Inns, Inc., 65–73, 74, 77
Wood v. Waldorf Systems, 536